GOVERNMENT EXPENDITURE BY TYPE AND FUNCTION

FEDERAL EXPENDITURE* (FISCAL YEAR 1993)	AMOUNT (BILLIONS OF DOLLARS)	PERCENTAGE OF TOTAL
National Defense	289.3	19.61
Social Security	304.7	20.66
Income Security	207.4	14.06
Medicare	132.8	9.00
Health	105.0	7.12
Education	52.3	3.55
Veterans Benefits	35.6	2.41
Transportation	36.4	2.47
Commerce and Housing	22.1	1.50
Net Interest	202.8	13.75
All other	86.5	5.87
Total	1474.9	100.00

STATE AND LOCAL GOVERNMENT EXPENDITURE (1992)	AMOUNT (BILLIONS OF DOLLARS)	PERCENTAGE OF TOTAL
Education	306.9	36.95
Civilian Safety	80.7	9.72
Health and Hospitals	28.7	3.46
Income Support, Social Security, and Welfare	193.6	23.31
Transportation	80.1	9.64
Housing and Community Services	15.7	1.89
Recreational and Cultural Activities	12.3	1.48
All other	112.6	13.55
Total Expenditure	830.6	100.00

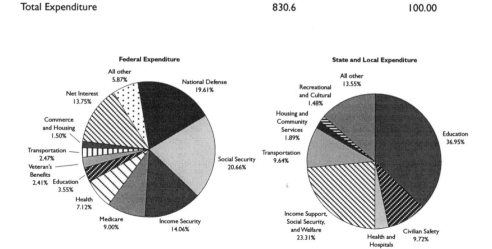

Source: U.S. Office of Management and Budget, Budget of U.S. Government.*Based on unified budget of the Federal government for fiscal year 1993. Amounts differ from data in Table 1.2 which are for calendar year 1993 and are based on NIPA budget data.

Source: U.S. Department of Commerce, Survey of Current Business, September 1993.

Public Finance

A Contemporary Application of Theory to Policy

FIFTH EDITION

Public Finance

A Contemporary Application of Theory to Policy

FIFTH EDITION

DAVID N. HYMAN

North Carolina State University

THE DRYDEN PRESS
Harcourt Brace College Publishers

Fort Worth   Philadelphia   San Diego   New York   Orlando   Austin   San Antonio
Toronto   Montreal   London   Sydney   Tokyo

Acquisitions Editor	Daryl Fox
Executive Editor	Emily Barrosse
Developmental Editor	Jeanie Anirudhan
Project Editor	Michele Tomiak
Production Manager	Carlyn Hauser
Art Director	Melinda Welch
Photo/Permissions Editor	Adele Krause
Product Manager	Craig Johnson

Address for Editorial Correspondence
The Dryden Press, 301 Commerce Street, Suite 3700, Fort Worth, TX 76102

Address for Orders
The Dryden Press, 6277 Sea Harbor Drive, Orlando, FL 32887-6777
1-800-782-4479, or 1-800-433-0001 (in Florida)

ISBN 0-03-011317-2

Library of Congress Catalog Card Number 95-67706

Printed in the United States of America

5 6 7 8 9 0 1 2 3 4 016 9 8 7 6 5 4 3 2 1

The Dryden Press
Harcourt Brace College Publishers

For Linda

THE DRYDEN PRESS SERIES IN ECONOMICS

Baldani, Bradfield, and Turner
Mathematical Economics

Baumol and Blinder
Economics: Principles and Policy
Sixth Edition (Also available in micro and macro paperbacks)

Baumol, Panzar, and Willig
Contestable Markets and the Theory of Industry Structure
Revised Edition

Berch
The Endless Day: The Political Economy of Women and Work

Breit and Elzinga
The Antitrust Casebook: Milestones in Economic Regulation
Third Edition

Brue
The Evolution of Economic Thought
Fifth Edition

Demmert
Economics: Understanding the Market Process

Dolan and Lindsey
Economics
Seventh Edition (Also available in micro and macro paperbacks)

Edgmand, Moomaw, and Olson
Economics and Contemporary Issues
Third Edition

Gardner
Comparative Economic Systems

Glahe
Microeconomics: Theory and Application
Second Edition

Green
Macroeconomics: Analysis and Applications

Gwartney and Stroup
Economics: Private and Public Choice
Seventh Edition (Also available in micro and macro paperbacks)

Gwartney and Stroup
Introduction to Economics: The Wealth and Poverty of Nations

Heilbroner and Singer
The Economic Transformation of America: 1600 to the Present
Second Edition

Hirschey and Pappas
Fundamentals of Managerial Economics
Fifth Edition

Hirschey and Pappas
Managerial Economics
Eighth Edition

Hyman
Public Finance: A Contemporary Application of Theory to Policy
Fifth Edition

Kahn
The Economic Approach to the Environment and Natural Resources

Kaserman and Mayo
Government and Business: The Economics of Antitrust and Regulation

Kaufman
The Economics of Labor Markets
Fourth Edition

Kennett and Lieberman
The Road to Capitalism: The Economic Transformation of Eastern Europe and the Former Soviet Union

Kreinin
International Economics: A Policy Approach
Seventh Edition

Lott and Ray
Applied Econometrics with Data Sets

Marlow
Public Finance: Theory and Practice

Nicholson
Intermediate Microeconomics and Its Application
Sixth Edition

Nicholson
Microeconomic Theory: Basic Principles and Extensions
Sixth Edition

Puth
American Economic History
Third Edition

Ragan and Thomas
Principles of Economics
Second Edition (Also available in micro and macro paperbacks)

Ramanathan
Introductory Econometrics with Applications
Third Edition

Rukstad
Corporate Decision Making in the World Economy: Company Case Studies

Rukstad
Macroeconomic Decision Making in the World Economy: Text and Cases
Third Edition

Samuelson and Marks
Managerial Economics
Second Edition

Scarth
Macroeconomics: An Introduction to Advanced Methods
Third Edition

Stockman
Introduction to Economics
(Also available in micro and macro paperbacks)

Thomas
Economics: Principles and Applications
(Also available in micro and macro paperbacks)

Walton and Rockoff
History of the American Economy
Seventh Edition

Welch and Welch
Economics: Theory and Practice
Fifth Edition

Yarbrough and Yarbrough
The World Economy: Trade and Finance
Third Edition

PREFACE

The fifth edition of *Public Finance: A Contemporary Application of Theory to Policy* has been revised to help focus on emerging fiscal issues of the next century. The textbook continues its comprehensive treatment of economic theory and applications in the field of public finance. Institutional material is integrated with the theory and applied to current issues, emphasizing microeconomic analysis of government functions, expenditures, and finance.

International issues are achieving greater significance in public finance. To provide resources on global issues, each chapter of this textbook has a separate *International View* feature that provides information or analysis on fiscal issues in other nations or explains how increased integration of the U.S. economy into a vast global economy affects economic policy. Each chapter also contains a *Public Policy Perspective* that applies the text analysis to a current issue and provides facts on the U.S. public sector.

This book is adapted easily to a variety of approaches to teaching public finance and incorporates detailed analyses of both expenditure and revenue aspects of public finance. I also provide an abundance of real-world examples and data to provoke students' interest, presenting an unbiased exposition of the field of public finance by discussing opposing views of important issues.

CHANGES IN THIS EDITION

The fifth edition has been extensively updated and revised. Gross domestic product, as opposed to gross national product, is now used to compute ratios showing the share of government in the economy. Many of the *International Views* and *Public Policy Perspectives* have been updated, and several are new, added to highlight current issues.

Changes in public policy regarding government assistance to the poor, Social Security, health benefits, and taxation also are reflected in the revised text. Social Security is now the single most important federal government program, having surpassed national defense in 1993 for the first time. The revision of the book reflects the continued growth of Social Security and other entitlement programs in the United States by providing up-to-date analysis of these programs. The analysis of income support programs now includes a section on the newly expanded Earned Income Tax Credit (EITC) as a means of subsidizing the working poor.

The analysis of Social Security pensions highlights problems associated with aging populations. Chapter 8 has been thoroughly updated to reflect changes in the Social Security and tax law. It includes analysis of the privatization of Social Security systems to deal with problems induced by aging of the population under pay-as-you-go systems. Coverage of intergenerational and distributive effects of Social Security are better highlighted in this new edition. The discussion of the Medicare program has been condensed and much of the more detailed analysis of problems of the Medicare system is now in Chapter 9, integrated with analysis of health care policy.

The chapter on government and health care (Chapter 9) has been revised and reorganized to provide more analysis of the peculiarities of the market for health care services in the United States. Basic supply and demand analysis is used to look at health care policy issues from an economic perspective. Although recent proposals for reform are considered, the goal of the chapter is to discuss issues in health care policy emphasizing the role of government in the financing and provision of health care. The analysis of trends in health care spending in the United States has been updated, and recent projections of future health care spending are presented. A new section on the impact of **asymmetric information** in the market for health care has been added, along with analysis of the effects of such information imperfections on the functioning of the market. The analysis of health insurance has been revised to include more analysis of risk. Supply-and-demand analysis is used to examine factors leading to inefficiency and high cost in health care markets. A new *Public Policy Perspective* examines why growing health care costs are an economic problem for the United States. New sections in this chapter analyze **Medicare** and **Medicaid**, along with recent trends in spending and policy for these existing government health insurance programs. A new section on health care reform has been added to the chapter to discuss issues and policies relating to the role of government in markets for health care and health insurance. Included in this section is analysis of universal coverage and gaps in U.S. health insurance coverage in the 1990s, along with analysis of universal entitlement systems, managed competition, and national health insurance.

The continued openness of the U.S. economy is reflected throughout the book via revision of many of the *International View* features to discuss recent international agreements under GATT and NAFTA. On the tax side, there is more analysis of taxation in foreign nations with particular emphasis on the use of the value-added tax in Europe, Canada, and other nations.

All the tax chapters have been updated to reflect changes in tax law since 1993 and recent empirical research on the economic effects of taxes. Chapter 12 has been revised to reflect changes in deficit reduction laws in the United States and recent trends in both the deficit and economic analysis of its effects. A new section on the effect of deficit finance on political equilibrium has been added. The analysis of the effects of the federal deficit on credit markets and national saving has been updated, and a new section of the incidence of deficit finance has been added. The analysis of the national debt has been updated with the latest available data.

Chapter 14 has been extensively revised to reflect changes in the tax law in 1993. Analysis of taxable income, tax preferences, and tax rate structure has been updated to reflect rules prevailing in 1994. A new *Public Policy Perspective* uses estimates of effective average and marginal tax rates in 1994 to examine the progressivity of the federal income tax. The analysis of excess burden of tax preferences has been revised. Chapter 15 has been revised to reflect changes in the corporate income tax structure and rules enacted in 1993 and effective 1994.

SPECIAL FEATURES OF THIS BOOK

In addition to the boxed features that provide discussion of international issues and public policy, each chapter also has pedagogical features, including learning objectives and concept checks.

To facilitate learning, basic concepts are set in bold type when first introduced, and every chapter concludes with a summary, a list of important concepts, and a short "forward look" that explains the relationship between that chapter and those to follow. Also, each chapter contains ten questions for review. These questions are not problem sets; rather, they are designed to assist students in reviewing the material covered in the chapter by posing questions related to the major points or ideas developed in the text. Four problems are also included after the review questions. Each chapter has an annotated bibliography that offers suggestions for further reading and in-depth study. The bibliography should prove particularly useful in courses with assigned term papers. Liberal use is made of footnotes throughout the book to provide additional source material and to explain and document material. A glossary at the end of the book lists all important concepts in alphabetical order for easy reference.

I have attempted to make this book as self-contained as possible. The book can be used by students who have only minimal backgrounds in economics. Appendices to several chapters facilitate this process. For those weak in basic microeconomic theory, Chapter 1 includes an appendix that provides students with a handy source of reference for basic microeconomic tools, including concise and simple explanations of such concepts as indifference curves, income and substitution effects, consumer surplus, producer surplus, cost, and production theory. This appendix is not designed to provide class material, but it will aid students in understanding the analysis used throughout the book. In classroom testing of this textbook, my own students found the appendix to Chapter 1 a welcome addition to an intermediate-level economics course textbook.

More in-depth analysis of efficiency is provided in an appendix to Chapter 2, which uses Edgeworth-Bowley box diagrams to derive efficiency loci.

The appendix to Chapter 11 derives formulas for the excess burden of taxation and discusses the relevance of compensated demand and supply curves to tax analysis. The appendices to Chapters 2 and 11 are designed to cover more technical material and may easily be skipped without loss of continuity.

POSSIBLE COURSE OUTLINES

This book contains more material than could possibly be covered in a one-semester (or one-quarter) course in public finance. Individual instructors who teach one-semester courses will find enough material in this book to tailor such courses to their own particular needs and interests. Those who teach a two-semester sequence in the microeconomic aspects of public finance could cover Parts One and Two (the expenditure aspects of public finance) in the first semester and Parts Three, Four, and Five (government finance and fiscal federalism) in the second semester. Instructurs who wish to teach the macroeconomic aspects of public finance easily could supplement the material in the text with excerpts from one of the many good macroeconomic books on the market.

I suggest four possible course outlines for a one-semester course, each outline having a particular emphasis. Instructors may adjust these outlines in accordance with their own preferences.

Outline 1: Basic Principles of Public Finance

For intermediate economics courses, with students who have had at least one course in basic microeconomic theory.

1. Chapters 1–5: The economic basis for government activity. Efficiency, market failure, externalities, public goods, public choice, and political equilibrium.
2. Chapters 10–12: Principles of government finance.
3. Chapters 14–17: Application of tax theory to tax policy.
4. Selections chosen from Chapters 6, 7, 8, 9, and 18: Topics in public policy or state and local finance, chosen as time permits and in accordance with the interests of the instructor.

Outline 2: The Functions of Government and Government Expenditure

For courses that specialize in public policy and government expenditure, with students who have had at least one course in economics.

1. Parts One and Two: The economic basis of government activity and application of that theory to selected policy issues.
2. Part Five: State and local government finance.

Outline 3: Tax Theory and Policy

For courses that emphasize taxation, with students who have had at least one course in economics.

1. Chapters 1–2: The functions of government and the concept of efficiency.
2. Chapters 10–17: Government finance, tax theory, and tax policy.

Outline 4: Public Policy

For courses in public affairs or public policy, with students who have had little or no background in economics.

1. Chapters 1–2: Efficiency, markets, and the economic basis for government activity.
2. Selections from Chapters 3–5: Chosen as appropriate to subject emphasis and backgrounds of students. The topics could include externalities, public goods, and political equilibrium.
3. Selections from Chapters 6–9: Issues in public policy. The instructor might wish to omit some of the more difficult sections in these chapters.
4. Chapter 10: Introduction to government finance.
5. Selections from Chapters 11–17: Topics in tax policy, chosen according to the extent to which the instructor wishes to cover the subject.
6. Selections from Chapter 18: Topics in fiscal federalism, chosen according to the objectives of the course. More difficult sections could be omitted.

ANCILLARY MATERIALS

Instructor's Manual/Test Bank

I have prepared a concise *Instructor's Manual/Test Bank* that has been completely revised for this fifth edition. It should be useful to instructors who wish to arrange their lecture notes so that they correspond to the text. The Instructor's Manual summarizes the instructional objectives of each chapter and offers suggestions for supplementing text materials and developing lectures. The Test Bank includes true/false, multiple-choice, and essay questions for each chapter. Answers to end-of-chapter problems appear in the Instructor's Manual.

Study Guide

A *Study Guide*, written by Michael Peddle, Northern Illinois University, includes a list of chapter objectives, problems, chapter summaries, and chapter review questions designed to help your students master topics you cover in class and to prepare for examinations. The "Issue in Brief" section in every chapter presents an application of material in the chapter and includes discussion questions.

The Dryden Press will provide complimentary supplements or supplement packages to those adopters qualified under our adoption policy. Please contact your sales representative to learn how you may qualify. If as an adopter or potential user you receive supplements you do not need, please return them to your sales representative or send them to:

Attn: Returns Department
Troy Warehouse
465 South Lincoln Drive
Troy, MO 63379

Acknowledgments

I am indebted to many friends and colleagues for their criticism and encouragement during the preparation of this book. The manuscripts for the previous editions were reviewed by Dwight Blood, Eric Fredland, Richard McHugh, David Orr, Craig Stubblebine, David Terkla, Donald N. Baum, Temple University; Yuval Cohen, Rutgers University; Randolph M. Lyon, University of Texas at Austin; James P. Marchand, University of California at Los Angeles; Patricia N. Pando, Houston Baptist University; Michael T. Peddle, College of the Holy Cross; John A. Sondey, University of Idaho; John P. Tillman, University of Wisconsin at LaCrosse; Marcus Berliant, University of Rochester; Timothy J. Gronberg, Texas A&M University; Roberto N. Ifill, Williams College; Charles R. Knoeber, North Carolina State University; Stephen E. Lile, Western Kentucky University; James R. White, Hamilton College; Wade L. Thomas, Ithaca College; Gary M. Pecquet, Southwest Texas State University; Joseph J. Cordes, George Washington University; Lori Alden, California State University–Sacramento; Frederic Harris, University of Texas at Arlington; Charles G. Leathers, University of Alabama; Janet Kohlhase, University of Houston; George Zodrow, Rice University; Robert C. McMahon, University of Southern Maine; William E. Even, Miami University; Joseph J. Cordes, The George Washington University; Sherry Wetchler, Ithaca College; Kathleen Segerson, The University of Connecticut; Charles L. Ballard, Michigan State University; Virginia Wilcox-Gök, Rutgers University; J. Fred Giertz, University of Illinois; and Alvin E. Headen, Jr., North Carolina State University. In preparing the fifth edition I have benefited from comments of Lloyd Orr, Indiana University; Davis Taylor, University of Oregon; Samuel H. Baker, College of William and Mary; Mark Showalter, Brigham Young University; and William Kamps, South Dakota State University.

My secretary, Janet Stern, provided expert clerical assistance handling drafts of the manuscript.

Jeanie Anirudhan, Daryl Fox, Michele Tomiak, Melinda Welch, and Carlyn Hauser have been very helpful in guiding the fifth edition through its various phases.

David N. Hyman
Raleigh, North Carolina

About the Author

David N. Hyman, Professor of Economics at North Carolina State University, has taught both undergraduate and graduate courses in public finance there since 1969. Professor Hyman received his Ph.D. in Economics from Princeton University. He has held Woodrow Wilson, Earhart, and Ford Foundation fellowships and was a Fulbright senior research scholar in Italy in 1980. Professor Hyman is a member of the Academy of Outstanding Teachers at North Carolina State University and in 1982 received the Alumni Association Outstanding Teacher Award. He is the author of several widely used textbooks in economics and has published scholarly articles in the *National Tax Journal, Public Choice*, the *Journal of Economic Education*, and other respected academic journals. He is a referee for the *Public Finance Quarterly* and other scholarly publications.

Professor Hyman served the President's Council of Economic Advisers as a consultant under the Reagan administration and as a senior staff economist under the Bush administration. He has also been a guest scholar at the Brookings Institution and has worked as a government budget analyst and as an economist for the Board of Governors of the Federal Reserve System and the U.S. Comptroller of the Currency.

Professor Hyman is also a photographer whose palladium and platinum prints are in the permanent collection of the Corcoran Gallery of Art in Washington, D.C. His photographs have been exhibited by galleries and museums and have been published in art books and on the covers of several novels.

CONTENTS IN BRIEF

CONTENTS

The Economic

Basis for

Government

Activity

I

1

INDIVIDUALS AND GOVERNMENT

LEARNING OBJECTIVES

After reading this chapter you should be able to

1. Use a production-possibility curve to explain the trade-off between private goods and services and government goods and services.
2. Describe how the provision of government goods and services through political institutions differs from market provision of goods and services and how government affects the circular flow of income and expenditure in a mixed economy.
3. Explain the difference between government purchases and transfer payments and discuss the growth of government expenditures in the United States and other nations since 1929.
4. Discuss the various categories of federal, state, and local government expenditures in the United States and the way those expenditures are financed.
5. Determine some of the issues that must be addressed to evaluate the costs and benefits of government activities.

What would it be like to live in a nation without government? There would be no system of courts to administer justice. Provision of national defense would be difficult or disorganized with no central government to maintain and supply the armed forces. You could forget about such programs as Social Security, unemployment insurance, and welfare that provide income support to the elderly, the unemployed, and the poor or disabled. How would police and fire protection to the public be provided? Driving on roads and over bridges that we take for granted could also be a problem because virtually all the highways, streets, and other public transportation facilities we every day are supplied and maintained by governments or their agencies. There would be no public elementary and secondary schools. Higher education, which is heavily subsidized by both the federal and state governments, also would be in trouble. Our system of health care depends on government programs to pay the health care bills of many of the poor, the elderly, and veterans. Institutions ranging from medical schools to public clinics and hospitals would have their operations impaired without government support.

Now that you have finished reflecting on what your life would be like without governments you can better appreciate how much you rely on government services each day. We all benefit from government activities and expenditures. During the past twenty years annual government expenditures in the United States averaged one-third of gross domestic product (GDP).

In economics, we study the ways individuals make choices to use scarce resources to satisfy their desires. If you have taken an introductory economics course, you studied the role of markets as a means of establishing prices that influence individual choices to use resources. In this book you will study the role governments play in allocating resources and how individual choices influence what governments do. You also will study how government policies affect the incentives of workers, investors, and corporations to engage in productive activities.

One lesson you have been taught already, if you have completed an introductory economics course, is that nothing of value can be obtained without some sacrifice. There are costs as well as benefits associated with the activities of governments. The role of government in society is so hotly disputed because we differ in our assessments of the costs and benefits of government programs. Many people think the role of government in the economy needs to be expanded and look to government to help solve their own problems. Others think the role of government in the economy is already excessive and would like to see its scale of influence reduced.

Government expenditures are financed mainly by taxes. U.S. taxpayers give up more of their income each year to support the activities of government than they do to satisfy their desires for such basic items as food, clothing, and shelter. Taxes collected by governments in the United States are nearly three times the annual expenditures on food, nearly eight times the annual expenditures on clothing, and more than three times the annual expenditures on housing. The average U.S. household devotes more than four months of annual earnings to meet its total yearly federal, state, and local government tax obligations. Citizens benefit from the many goods and services made available by governments, but they also pay the costs of these services. We differ in our views about what governments should and should not be doing in part because our valuations of the benefits we get from government differ. We also disagree because of variation in the amount of taxes and other costs each of us pay.

Public finance is the field of economics that studies government activities and the alternative means of financing government expenditures. As you study public finance you will learn about the economic basis for government activities. A crucial objective of the analysis is to understand the impact of government expenditures, regulations, taxes, and borrowing on incentives to work, invest, and spend income. This book develops principles for understanding the role of government in the economy and its impact on resource use and the well-being of citizens.

INDIVIDUALS, SOCIETY, AND GOVERNMENT

Governments are organizations formed to exercise authority over the actions of persons who live together in a society and to provide and finance essential services. Many citizens and resources are employed in the production of government services. Individuals pay taxes and, in many cases, are recipients of income financed by those taxes.

For example, Social Security pensions, unemployment insurance compensation, and subsidies to the poor are financed by taxes.

The extent to which individuals have the right to participate in decisions that determine what governments do varies from society to society. What governments do, how much they spend, and how they obtain the means to finance their functions reflect political interaction of citizens. **Political institutions** constitute the rules and generally accepted procedures that evolve in a community for determining what government does and how government outlays are financed. Through these mediums individual desires are translated into binding decisions concerning the extent and functions of government.

Such democratic institutions as majority rule and representative government offer citizens an opportunity to express their desires through voting and through attempts to influence the voting of others. Under majority rule one alternative (such as a political candidate or a referendum to increase spending for education) is chosen over others if it receives more than half the votes cast in an election. Just as economic theory is usefully applied to analysis of market interaction and individual choice, so can it be applied to political interaction and choices. Modern economics bases the study of government activity on a theory of individual behavior.

The Allocation of Resources Between Government and Private Use

Government provision of goods and services requires labor, equipment, buildings, and land. The real cost of government goods and services is the value of private goods and services that must be sacrificed when resources are transferred to government use. When citizens pay taxes, their capacity to purchase goods and services for their own exclusive use (such as automobiles, clothing, housing, cameras, and dining out) is reduced. The resources that are thereby diverted from private use are purchased or otherwise obtained by government. Taxes also have indirect costs because they distort choices. Taxes affect prices of goods and services and the incentive to work, save, and allocate expenditures among goods and services. Taxes impair the operation of the economy by inducing individuals to make choices based not only on the benefits and costs of their actions but also on the tax advantages or disadvantages of their decisions. The distortion in resource use and loss in output that results from the effect of taxes on incentives is also part of the cost of government activity.

The resources governments obtain are used to provide citizens with goods and services, such as roads, police and fire protection, and national defense. These government goods and services are shared by all; they cannot be used by any one citizen alone exclusively. Other goods and services provided by government are limited in availability to certain groups, such as the aged or children, as with Social Security pensions and public schooling.

The trade-off between government and private goods and services can be illustrated with the familiar production-possibility curve. As shown in Figure 1.1, this

Figure 1.1 ✦ A PRODUCTION-POSSIBILITY CURVE

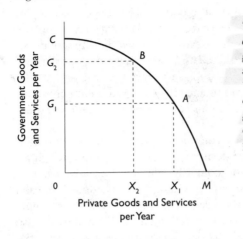

The production-possibility curve shows alternative combinations of government goods and services and private goods and services that can be produced in an economy. The curve assumes that productive resources and technology are given. An increase in government goods from $0G_1$ to $0G_2$ requires a sacrifice of X_1X_2 units of private goods per year.

curve gives the alternative combinations of government goods and services and private goods and services that can be produced in an economy, given its productive resources and technology and assuming that resources are fully employed. **Private goods and services** are those items, such as food and clothing, that are usually made available for sale in markets. **Government goods and services,** such as roads, schooling, and fire protection, usually are not sold in markets. At point A in Figure 1.1, MX_1 units of private goods and services are forgone by individuals so that government can provide $0G_1$ units of goods and services. The resources that would have been employed in producing the private goods and services are used by the government to provide services and exercise its functions.

An increase in the amount of government goods and services provided per year from $0G_1$ to $0G_2$ requires a reduction in the amount of private goods available per year. In Figure 1.1 the annual amount of private goods available declines from $0X_1$ to $0X_2$ as the economy moves from point A to point B on the production-possibility curve. For example, suppose that individuals demand more environmental protection services. To make these services available, governments might raise taxes paid by firms that pollute the air or water or they could enact more stringent regulations that prevent pollution. The new regulations or taxes are likely to increase costs of production for business firms, causing the prices of products produced by these firms to increase and the quantities demanded in the marketplace by consumers to decline. The new policies will result in improved environmental quality, which is a government-supplied good, but also require that households sacrifice consumption of private goods and services to pay for the cleaner environment.

The process also can work in reverse. For example, citizens of the Republics of the former Soviet Union and the United States hope to enjoy a "peace dividend" as we approach the next century, assuming that improved international relationships will allow a reduction in the government provision of military goods and services. The peace dividend is an increase in the amount of resources that can be allocated to private goods and services in both nations as each nation moves from a point like *B* in Figure 1.1 to a point like *A*. The resources diverted from the production of military goods and services also can be used to increase annual production of nonmilitary government goods and services such as education or roads.

How Government Goods and Services Are Distributed

Government goods and services are, by and large, distributed to groups of individuals through the use of **nonmarket rationing.** This means that government goods and services are not made available to persons according to their willingness to pay and their use is not rationed by prices. In some cases the services are available to all, with no direct charge and no eligibility requirements. The provision of national defense services is one strong example of a good that is freely available to all and not rationed by prices. In other cases, such criteria as income, age, family status, residence, or the payment of certain taxes, fees, or charges are used to determine eligibility to receive benefits. For example, to receive Social Security pensions in the United States, individuals must be of a certain age (or be disabled) and have worked for a certain period of time (about ten years) while covered by Social Security and must have paid their share of Social Security taxes during that time. Similarly, a fare must be paid to use the public transportation facilities in cities. If the fares paid do not cover the full cost of operating the system, the deficit is made up by taxes levied by government. To be eligible for elementary schooling in a given school district, children must reside within the boundaries of that district.

In public finance we study how the means of rationing the use of government goods and services and financing their resource costs affect incentives, resource use, and production possibilities.

C H E C K P O I N T

1. What are political institutions?
2. Give four examples of government goods or services and discuss how they are distributed to citizens.
3. Use a production-possibility curve to show the cost of increasing government provision of medical services.

THE MIXED ECONOMY, MARKETS, AND POLITICS

The United States and most other nations today are mixed economies. **A mixed economy** is one in which government supplies a considerable amount of goods and services and regulates private economic activity. In such an economy government expenditures typically amount to between one-quarter and one-half of GDP. Taxes absorb at least one-quarter of national income in the typical mixed economy and governments usually regulate private economic activities and use taxes and subsidies to affect incentives to use resources.

In a **pure market economy** virtually all goods and services would be supplied by private firms for profit and all exchanges of goods and services would take place through markets, with prices determined by free interplay of supply and demand. Individuals would be able to purchase goods and services freely, according to their tastes and economic capacity (their income and wealth), given the market-determined prices. In mixed economies, provision of a significant amount of goods and services takes place through political institutions. This involves interaction among all individuals of the community, rather than just buyers and sellers—as is the case when goods and services are provided by markets.

In a market, buyers are not compelled to purchase something they do not want. Political decisions, however, often compel citizens to finance government services and programs, regardless of their personal preferences.

Circular Flow in the Mixed Economy

In a pure market economy, all productive resources are privately owned by individuals who decide how to use these resources. These individuals, together with others living in their households, make decisions about how to use the resources they own. Their decisions are influenced in part by market prices for goods and services. They offer their resources for sale as inputs in the marketplace.

Private business firms are organized to hire resources in input markets to produce goods and services desired by household members. The products, in turn, are sold by businesses to households in output markets.

In a perfectly competitive market economy no seller can influence prices. Instead, prices are determined by free play of the forces of supply and demand. Given market prices, households decide to sell the resources they own, and firms decide which inputs to buy and what outputs to produce. This process is summarized as a simple circular flow diagram in Figure 1.2. Let's first look at the relationships that would exist in the economy if there were no governments. The lower loop of the diagram represents the input markets, where households sell the resources to firms for market-determined prices. The upper loop is the output market, where an array of outputs is offered for sale to households, which, in turn, pay for them with the dollars earned from the sale of their members' productive resources. The distribution of income depends on the distribution of ownership of productive resources and the prices and other financial returns that resource owners receive from employment of those resources in production. In a pure market economy all goods and services would be produced by businesses.

In the mixed economy government participates in markets as a buyer of goods and services. Figure 1.2 depicts government activities in the central portions of the diagram. Governments purchase inputs from the households and acquire ownership rights of such productive resources as land and capital. Governments use these inputs to provide goods and services that are not sold to households and business firms but are made available through nonmarket rationing. However, governments do

Figure 1.2 ✦ Circular Flow in the Mixed Economy

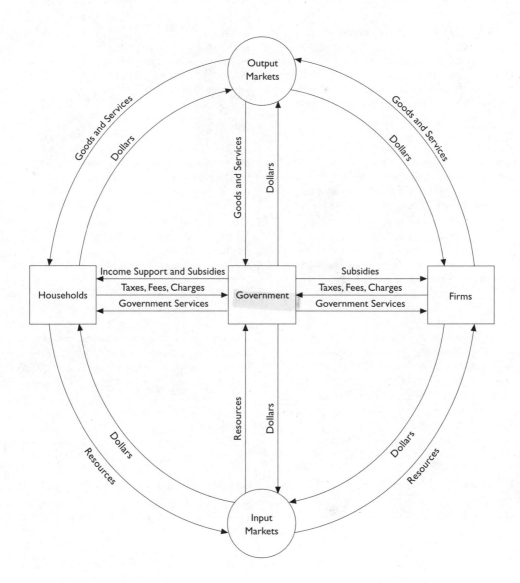

The upper and lower loops represent transactions between households and business firms in markets. Households use the income they earn from the sale of productive services to purchase the outputs of business firms. The inner loops represents transactions between households and government and between business firms and government. Governments purchase productive services from households and outputs of business firms. These purchases are financed with taxes, fees, and charges levied on persons and firms, and the inputs acquired are used to provide government services and transfers.

INTERNATIONAL VIEW

ECONOMIC REFORM AND THE ROLE OF GOVERNMENT IN THE FORMER SOVIET UNION

For more than seventy years the citizens of the Soviet Union lived under an economic system that was drastically different from the mixed economies of the Western world. As a centrally planned economy for most of the twentieth century the Soviet Union was dominated by a ponderous government that controlled much of the means of production and regulated most economic activity. Although the economic situation now changes day by day, it is still useful to examine the extensive role of government in that vast country that led to the economic nightmare Soviet peoples found themselves in during the late 1980s.

As of 1991, there were few free markets in the Soviet Union and almost all the land and capital were owned by the government. Large productive enterprises were government owned and run and the bulk of the labor force was employed either by the government itself or by government-owned enterprises. Government enterprises, although under pressure to earn a profit, still followed orders issued by the central government in 1991. Private enterprise operating for a profit remained on a small scale as of 1991.

Under central planning the political leaders of the Soviet Union dictated what would be produced through a complex economic plan. The prices set by the planners were not determined by the free interplay of supply and demand in the marketplace. Political considerations dominated resource allocation decisions, and the planners favored the production of military goods and services and heavy industry. Consumer goods and services were given low priority by the planners, and consumers often found little merchandise in the government-run stores to purchase. In the late 1980s the economic system in the Soviet Union was creaking. Shortages of food were common in early 1990 and the nation was soliciting the West for foreign aid to help it reform its economy and to feed its citizens!

The Soviet system was inflexible compared to the mixed economies with their large market sectors. Prices in the Soviet economy rarely served as signals that influence profitability and encourage the entry or exit of firms into markets. As a safety valve, there was a vast underground economy in the Soviet Union where many consumer goods could be purchased at very high prices that were beyond the means of the average Soviet citizen. Prices for food and other items in government stores were heavily subsidized by the government.

To move to free markets the governments of Russia and other former Soviet-style economies must sell off government-owned enterprises to private interests. The process of privatizing government enterprises is the first step necessary in the progression toward allowing private ownership of the means of production. This is likely to be a very painful process because inefficient enterprises that cannot turn a profit will have to be shut down. When these enterprises fold, many workers will lose their jobs.

The massive reallocation of resources required to move to a mixed economy implies a long period of transition that is likely to be marked by high unemployment, inflation, and possibly even political instability.

sometimes own and operate enterprises such as the Postal Service, railroads, liquor stores, and state lotteries.

Governments also purchase outputs of business firms, such as paper, cars, bricks, and guns. To pay for them, government requires businesses and households to make various payments such as taxes, charges, and fees and might even require that resources be made available for use by government at rates of compensation below actual market prices (as is the case with compulsory military service). The government uses the productive resources is acquires to produce goods and services including national defense, roads, schooling, police and fire protection, and the many other essential services.

With reference to Figure 1.2, the question of the size of the public sector is one of the allocation of total transactions between the upper and lower loops and the central loops. The central loop transactions are made through political institutions, whereas the upper and lower loop transactions are made through market institutions.

GOVERNMENT EXPENDITURES IN THE UNITED STATES

Let's examine government spending in the United States so that we can get a better idea of the kinds of things governments do in a mixed economy. Government spending can be divided into two basic categories: purchases and transfers. **Government purchases** are those that require productive resources (land, labor, and capital) to be diverted from private use by individuals and corporations so they can be used by the government. For example, to supply national defense services, the government must acquire steel, labor, and other inputs necessary to support the armed forces and maintain aircraft, tanks, ships, and other capital equipment. A municipal government must acquire trucks and hire labor to administer effectively the collection and disposal of garbage.

Government expenditures that redistribute purchasing power among citizens are called **government transfer payments.** These transfer payments constitute a source of income support to recipients who are not required to provide any service in return for the income received. Transfer payments therefore differ from earnings in that they are not payments made in exchange for productive services. You might be surprised to learn that direct transfer payments to individuals constitute more than 40 percent of federal government expenditures in the United States. Included in government transfer payments to individuals are Social Security pension benefits, unemployment insurance benefit payments, and cash payments to low-income persons out of the labor force.

Growth of Government Expenditures

Table 1.1 shows government expenditures in the United States for selected years from 1929 to 1975, and every year from 1980 to 1993. These data reflect outlays each year for federal expenditures, expenditures by state and local governments, and total government expenditures. Ratios of the various categories of government expenditure to GDP in each year provide a rough indication of the relative importance of the government sector in economic activity for each year.

The computed ratios provide only a crude index of government activity in the United States. Ideally, an index of the relative importance of government should measure the proportion of total output produced in the public sector. However, measuring government output is virtually impossible because, in most cases, it is not sold

Table 1.1 ◆ GOVERNMENT EXPENDITURES IN THE UNITED STATES, 1929–1993 (BILLIONS OF DOLLARS)[a]

| | | | | | PERCENTAGE OF GDP | | |
YEAR	GDP	FEDERAL GOVERNMENT	STATE AND LOCAL GOVERNMENTS[b]	TOTAL GOVERNMENT	FEDERAL	STATE AND LOCAL	TOTAL
1929	103.1	2.7	7.7	10.4	2.62	7.47	10.09
1930	90.4	2.8	8.3	11.1	3.10	9.18	12.28
1931	75.8	4.2	8.2	12.4	5.54	10.82	16.36
1934	65.1	6.4	6.5	12.9	9.83	9.98	19.82
1939	90.8	9.0	8.6	17.6	9.91	9.47	19.38
1942	158.5	56.1	7.9	64.0	35.39	4.98	40.38
1945	213.1	84.7	8.1	92.8	39.75	3.80	43.55
1949	259.3	42.0	18.0	60.0	16.20	6.94	23.14
1955	404.3	68.6	29.8	98.4	16.97	7.37	24.34
1960	513.3	93.4	41.8	135.2	18.20	8.14	26.34
1970	1010.7	208.5	102.8	311.3	20.63	10.17	30.80
1975	1585.9	364.2	166.4	530.6	22.96	10.49	33.46
1980	2780.0	613.1	247.9	861.0	22.05	8.92	30.97
1981	3030.6	697.8	274.4	972.2	23.03	9.05	32.08
1982	3149.6	770.9	298.2	1069.1	24.48	9.47	33.94
1983	3405.0	840.0	316.2	1156.2	24.67	9.29	33.96
1984	3777.2	892.7	339.7	1232.4	23.63	8.99	32.63
1985	4038.7	969.9	372.3	1342.2	24.02	9.22	33.23
1986	4268.6	1028.2	409.4	1437.6	24.09	9.59	33.68
1987	4539.9	1065.6	451.4	1517.0	23.47	9.94	33.41
1988	4900.4	1109.0	481.7	1590.7	22.63	9.83	32.46
1989	5250.8	1181.6	518.5	1700.1	22.50	9.87	32.38
1990	5546.1	1273.6	566.9	1840.5	22.96	10.22	33.19
1991	5722.9	1331.2	620.2	1951.4	23.26	10.84	34.10
1992	6038.5	1459.3	659.2	2118.5	24.17	10.92	35.08
1993	6377.9	1495.3	700.1	2195.4	23.45	10.98	34.42

[a]Calendar years based on National Income and Product Accounts (NIPA) and current dollars for each year.
[b]Excludes federal grants-in-aid.
Sources: Council of Economic Advisers, *Economic Report of the President*, various years and U.S. Department of Commerce, *Survey of Current Business*, September 1993 and March 1994.

or easily measurable in units that can be summed. Actual expenditures are an imperfect proxy for government output.[1]

A further problem with the data is that actual expenditures do not measure the full impact of the government on economic activity. Although the regulatory activities

---

[1]See Morris Beck, "Sizing Up the Public Sector: Some Unresolved Issues," in *1983 Proceedings of the Seventy-Sixth Annual Conference on Taxation of the National Tax Association–Tax Institute of America*, ed. Stanley J. Bowers (Columbus, OH, 1983), 10–15, for a discussion of some of the conceptual difficulties in measuring the proportion of government expenditures to GDP.

of the public sector increase the costs of producing private goods and services in order to produce collectively enjoyed benefits (such as cleaner air), these increases are not reflected in the data of Table 1.1.

Despite these limitations, the ratios computed in the table give some rough idea of the extent to which government in the United States has grown since 1929. In 1929, government expenditures accounted for only 10 percent of GDP. Interestingly enough, in 1929, the bulk of government expenditures was undertaken by state and local governing bodies. In that year, federal government expenditures accounted for a mere 2.6 percent of GDP, while state and local government expenditures accounted for the remaining 7.4 percent. By 1960, the federal government accounted for 18.2 percent of GDP, while state and local government expenditures were only 8.14 percent of GDP. The sharp increases in federal expenditures for the years between 1942 and 1945, to more than 40 percent of GDP, reflect the influence of World War II on government activity.

Growth of government spending was rapid after 1960, when total government spending as a percentage of GDP rose from a bit more than one-quarter of GDP to more than one-third of GDP throughout much of the 1970s and 1980s. In the 1980s, government expenditures as a percentage of GDP rose somewhat, to about 34 percent. The share of GDP accounted for by federal government expenditures increased to nearly 25 percent, or one-quarter, of GDP. The proportion of GDP accounted for by state and local expenditures, exclusive of that portion financed by federal grants, was between 9 and 10 percent of GDP throughout most of the 1970s and 1980s. However, in the late 1980s state and local government spending as a share of GDP increased to about 11 percent of GDP.

Federal grants-in-aid are contributions made by the federal government to finance services provided by state and local governments. The importance of these grants increased somewhat in the 1970s, when federal grants rose to more than 3 percent of GDP. In the early 1980s, these grants declined and by 1990 federal grants-in-aid to state and local governments amounted to merely 1 percent of GDP. In drawing up the table, such grants are viewed as expenditures on the federal level, because they are part of a federal program enacted by Congress. But the funds are actually spent by the state and local governments, and their omission from such expenditures tends to underestimate state and local government services relative to federal spending.

The general conclusion that can be reached from the data in the table, given the limitations of the data, is that the importance of the government sector in the United States has grown tremendously since 1929. Since 1929, total government expenditures rose from one-tenth to more than one-third of GDP. Figure 1.3 plots the trend in government spending as a percentage of GDP from 1929 to 1993.

The proportion of GDP accounted for by government expenditures in the United States is low compared with that of other industrial nations. Belgium, the United Kingdom, Canada, France, Italy, and Germany all devote more than 40 percent of the value of their GDP to government expenditures. In Sweden, government expenditures have surpassed 50 percent of GDP.

Current government expenditure is all the more striking when put in historical perspective. Federal government expenditures in the United States from 1870 until the beginning of World War I averaged less than 3 percent of GDP. After the end of

Figure 1.3 ✦ Total Government Expenditures as a Percentage of GDP, 1929–1993

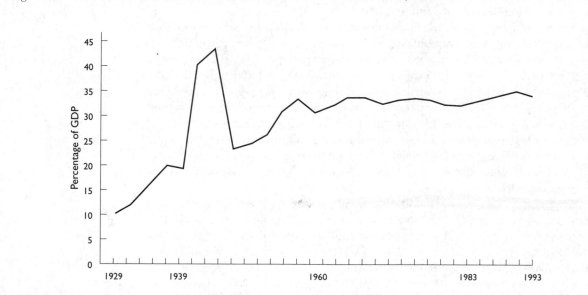

The share of GDP devoted to total government expenditures in the United States has increased dramatically, from about 10 percent to 35 percent, since 1929.

Source: U.S. Department of Commerce.

World War I, federal government expenditures still remained close to 3 percent of GDP until 1930, when federal government expenditures began to grow at a rapid rate. Federal government expenditures increased less than 1 percent per year until 1940. In contrast, federal government expenditures grew at an average of about 8 percent per year from 1948 to 1980.[2]

Similar trends can be observed in other industrial nations. The United Kingdom historically has had a large government sector. Surprisingly, the home of Adam Smith, the champion of the free market economy, was among the nations with the largest government sectors in the world at the beginning of the nineteenth century. In 1801 Great Britain devoted 22 percent of its GDP to government expenditures.[3] In the early 1980s, government expenditures in the United Kingdom accounted for more than 42 percent of GDP.

[2]See U.S. Department of Commerce, Bureau of the Census, *Historical Statistics of the U.S., Colonial Times to 1970* (Washington, D.C., 1975).

[3]Based on statistics in B. R. Mitchell, *Abstract of British Statistics* (Cambridge, England: Cambridge University Press, 1971).

Central government expenditures in Sweden at the beginning of the twentieth century amounted to less than 7 percent of GDP.[4] As the twenty-first century approaches, total government spending in Sweden is nearly 60 percent of GDP!

It probably is not an exaggeration to call the twentieth century the century of government growth throughout the world.

The Structure of Government Expenditure in the United States

Breaking down government expenditures into a few major components will help isolate the kinds of expenditures that are most responsible for the increased importance of the government sector in the economy.

Using the national income and product accounts, federal government expenditures can be divided into four major categories:

1. Purchases of goods and services
2. Transfer payments to persons
3. Grants-in-aid to state and local governments
4. Net interest paid

Table 1.2 presents data on the distribution of these categories of federal government expenditures for 1993. It shows the percent of total federal spending allocated to each category. Figure 1.4 shows how the distribution of federal expenditure has changed since 1966.

During the 1970s a significant shift occurred in the structure of federal government expenditures away from purchases of goods and services and toward transfers. From 1966 to 1983 transfer payments rose from 25 to nearly 44 percent of federal government expenditures. The change observed is of historical importance. It reflects the massive shift toward social welfare programs following the end of the

---

Table 1.2 ✦ FEDERAL EXPENDITURE BY CATEGORY, 1993 CALENDAR YEAR

EXPENDITURE CATEGORY	PERCENTAGE OF TOTAL FEDERAL EXPENDITURE
Transfer Payments	43.58
Purchases of Goods and Services	29.64
Net Interest Paid	12.09
Grants-in-Aid to State and Local Governments	12.45
Other	2.25

Source: U.S. Department of Commerce.

---

[4] See B. R. Mitchell, *European Historical Statistics 1750–1970* (New York: Columbia University Press, 1978).

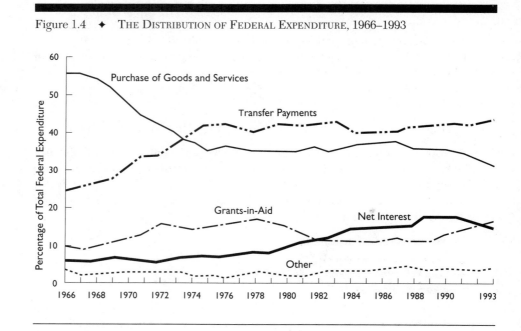

Figure 1.4 ◆ THE DISTRIBUTION OF FEDERAL EXPENDITURE, 1966–1993

Vietnam War and the significant increase in social insurance benefits, such as Social Security pensions, enacted during the 1970s.

Between 1983 and 1985 government purchases began to increase as a percent of total federal government expenditures moving from 33.9 percent in 1982 to 36 percent in 1985. This increase is largely accounted for by increased military spending during the early years of the Reagan administration. During the same period federal transfer payments fell from 41.7 percent to 38.6 percent of total federal expenditures, reversing the trend of the 1970s.

An increased commitment by the federal government to aid state and local governments in the 1970s is reflected in the increase in grants to these governments from 9.9 percent in 1966 to 16.4 percent of total expenditures in 1978. However, from 1979 to 1990, grants to state and local governments declined. These grants currently account for 12.5 percent of federal expenditures.

The increase in federal debt issued to finance the federal deficit is also reflected in Figure 1.4. Between 1966 and 1990, the interest payment on the federal debt increased from 6.3 percent to 14.6 percent of total federal government expenditures. This sharp increase in interest payments by the federal government since 1979 reflects the chronic budget deficits run by the federal government in the 1970s and 1980s. In the early 1990s lower interest rates contributed to declines in net interest paid.

Table 1.3 presents data on the structure of both federal and state and local government expenditures by major type and function. This table is designed to provide some information on the types of services made available by these governments. The figures in the table provide a rough idea of the functions that governments have assumed and how such functions have been distributed in the United States between the central (federal) government and the state and local governments.

Table 1.3 ✦ GOVERNMENT EXPENDITURE BY TYPE AND FUNCTION

FEDERAL EXPENDITURE° (FISCAL YEAR 1993)	AMOUNT (BILLIONS OF DOLLARS)	PERCENTAGE OF TOTAL
National Defense	289.3	19.61
Social Security	304.7	20.66
Income Security	207.4	14.06
Medicare	132.8	9.00
Health	105.0	7.12
Education	52.3	3.55
Veterans Benefits	35.6	2.41
Transportation	36.4	2.47
Commerce and Housing	22.1	1.50
Net Interest	202.8	13.75
All other	86.5	5.87
Total	1474.9	100.00

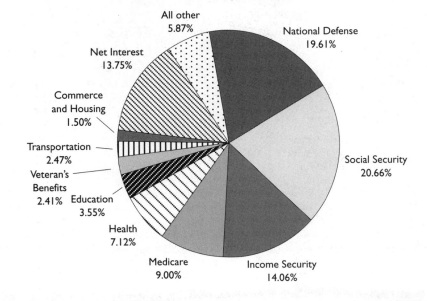

Federal Expenditure

Source: U.S. Office of Management and Budget, *Budget of U.S. Government.*
°Based on unified budget of the Federal government for fiscal year 1993. Amounts differ from data in Table 1.2 which are for calendar year 1993 and are based on NIPA budget data.

(continues)

Table 1.3 ✦ *(continued)*

STATE AND LOCAL GOVERNMENT EXPENDITURE (1992)	AMOUNT (BILLIONS OF DOLLARS)	PERCENTAGE OF TOTAL
Education	306.9	36.95
Civilian Safety	80.7	9.72
Health and Hospitals	28.7	3.46
Income Support, Social Security, and Welfare	193.6	23.31
Transportation	80.1	9.64
Housing and Community Services	15.7	1.89
Recreational and Cultural Activities	12.3	1.48
All other	112.6	13.55
Total Expenditure	830.6	100.00

State and Local Expenditure

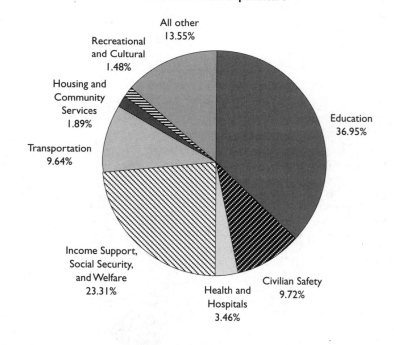

Source: U.S. Department of Commerce, *Survey of Current Business,* September 1993.

As of 1993, the single largest category of federal spending was Social Security, which consists mainly of direct payments to retired and disabled individuals for pensions. With the end of the cold war, Social Security pension payments have surpassed national defense as the largest category of federal spending consisting of nearly 21 percent of federal spending in 1993. In that same year defense spending was a bit more than 19 percent of federal spending.

Income security consists of transfer payments by the federal government mainly to individuals who are poor. These payments accounted for 14 percent of federal spending in 1993. In addition, the federal government provides health insurance for persons older than 65 through the Medicare program and also pays for health services to the poor through the Medicaid program. The sum of payments for health care through Medicare and other federal health programs accounted for more than 16 percent of federal spending in 1993. The sum of federal spending for Social Security, income support for the poor, health insurance for the elderly and other health benefits for eligible persons under federal programs accounts for more than half of all federal spending. Another large chunk of federal spending is interest on the federal debt, which accounted for about 14 percent of the federal budget in fiscal year 1993. Notice that no other category of federal spending accounts for more than 4 percent of the federal budget. Education spending accounts for 3.5 percent of federal spending.

Education, however, accounts for more than one-third of spending by state and local governments, which have the responsibility of providing primary, secondary, and some higher education in the United States. State and local governments, like the federal government, also devote large shares of their budgets to transfer payments that provide income support and other services directly to individuals. As of 1993 nearly one-quarter of the budgets of state and local governments in the United States were devoted to income support, Social Security, and welfare programs. Many of these programs are joint with the federal government and provide income support, medical services, and other assistance to the poor. Other major categories of state and local government expenditure include civilian safety, which includes programs for police, fire protection, and correction institutions. Transportation includes expenditures for roads, bridges, and highways and public transportation facilities. Civilian safety and transportation each account for about 10 percent of state and local government expenditures. Health and hospitals, housing and community services, and recreational and cultural activities are other major expenditures of state and local governments.

FINANCING GOVERNMENT EXPENDITURE IN THE UNITED STATES

Taxes, the principal means of financing government expenditures, are compulsory payments that do not necessarily bear any direct relationship to the benefits from government goods and services received. For example, the right to receive the benefits of national defense services or to use public roads is not contingent on payment of taxes. A citizen who pays $10,000 a year in taxes is defended equally and has no more right to use public roads than the individual who pays little or no taxes.

Determining the means of financing government functions is a public choice that is likely to be based on a number of important considerations. Because taxes are compulsory payments required under the powers of authority of government, many citizens believe that taxes should be distributed fairly. They often, however, differ in their ideas concerning what is a fair distribution of the burden of finance.

Taxes affect economic incentives to produce and consume or to use productive resources in the most gainful way. When part of the gain from a transaction has to be surrendered to the government, the willingness to engage in that activity is naturally reduced. High taxes on interest from savings tend to reduce the incentive to save. Taxes on various consumer goods tend to reduce the amounts of these goods that will be consumed. Taxes on labor earnings can also reduce the incentive to work.

In evaluating alternative means of financing government, desires for fairness in taxation must be balanced with the possible harmful effects of taxes on incentives to produce, consume, and invest. At the extreme, very high taxes on those with high earnings and low taxes on those with low earnings can promote economic equality of income. However, this goal is likely to be achieved at the cost of reduction in incentives for producers to use their resources in activities for which the social returns to production are the highest.

Table 1.4 and the accompanying pie charts provide data on government finances. In 1993 the two major sources of revenue for the federal government were the in-

Table 1.4 ◆ GOVERNMENT RECEIPTS, 1993

RECEIPTS	AMOUNT (BILLIONS OF DOLLARS)	PERCENTAGE OF TOTAL
FEDERAL GOVERNMENT		
Income Taxes	506.7	39.91
Payroll Taxes	517.8	40.78
Corporate Profits Taxes	143.3	11.29
Excise Taxes	50.3	3.96
Customs Duties	19.8	1.56
Estate and Gift Taxes	13.0	1.02
Other	18.8	1.48
Total	1269.7	100.00

Federal

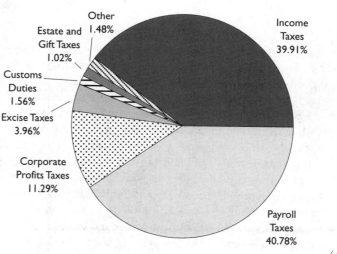

(continues)

Table 1.4 ✦ (continued)

RECEIPTS	AMOUNT (BILLIONS OF DOLLARS)	PERCENTAGE OF TOTAL
STATE AND LOCAL GOVERNMENTS		
Sales Taxes	211.7	23.84
Federal Grants	186.2	20.97
Income Taxes	120.8	13.60
Nontaxes	19.7	2.22
Payroll Taxes	67.4	7.59
Corporate Profits Taxes	31.0	3.49
Property Taxes	186.9	21.04
Other	64.4	7.25
Total	888.1	100.00

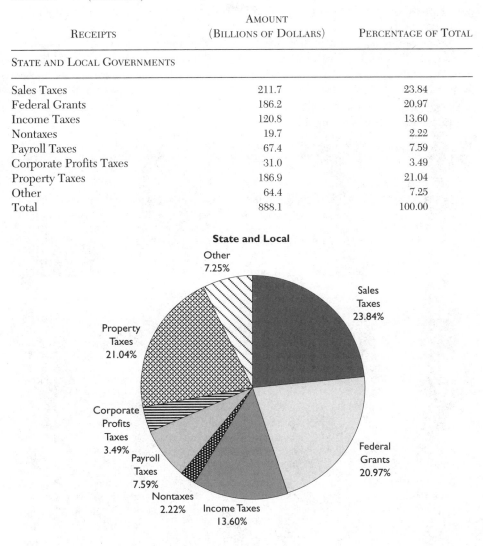

State and Local

Source: U.S. Department of Commerce, *Survey of Current Business,* March 1994.

come and payroll taxes, which together accounted for more than 80 percent of government receipts. The corporate income tax accounted for 11 percent of federal receipts in 1993. Payroll taxes are paid by workers and their employers to finance social insurance programs including Social Security. Payroll taxes now bring in more revenue than income taxes for the federal government. Excise taxes, such as those levied on fuels, telephone service, tires, cigarettes, and alcoholic beverages, accounted for 4 percent of federal revenues in 1993.

Tax and nontax receipts by the federal government have not been sufficient to finance all federal government expenditures in recent years. As a result the federal government budget runs a deficit and must borrow to finance the remaining portion of its expenditures.

State and local governments raised nearly $900 billion in 1993. Table 1.4 shows the sources of revenue for these governments. The most important source of tax revenue for state and local governments is the sales tax, which accounted for 24 percent of revenue in 1993. Personal income taxes accounted for 13.6 percent, and taxes on property for 21 percent of revenue in 1993. Federal grants accounted for 20 percent of state and local revenue in 1993.

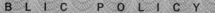

CHECKPOINT

1. What is a mixed economy? How does an increase in government taxation and purchases affect the circular flow of income and expenditures in a mixed economy?
2. What is the difference between government purchases and government transfer payments?
3. List the major categories of federal government expenditure and revenue in the United States.

PUBLIC POLICY PERSPECTIVE

THE PROVISION OF PUBLIC ELEMENTARY AND SECONDARY EDUCATION IN THE UNITED STATES: THE LIMITED ROLE OF THE FEDERAL GOVERNMENT

The quality of public education in the United States is under criticism. Many argue that U.S. students are not up to par with their counterparts in foreign nations. Results of a 1990 National Assessment of Education analysis revealed that one-third of U.S. students in grades 4, 8, and 12 failed to meet the lowest standard in mathematics. Another study by the same organization indicated that 9- and 13-year-old students in the United States do not do as well in science and mathematics as do students in other nations.* Naturally, individuals in the United States look to government to improve the quality of education. George Bush wanted to be known as the "education president" and education was high on the priorities of the Clinton Administration.

However, in the United States public elementary and secondary education is primarily the responsibility of state and local governments. The federal government finances only about 6 percent of the total cost of elementary and secondary education in the United States. In 1993, 70 percent of this federal spending was in the form of programs designed to improve equality of educational opportunity while the remainder went to programs of research and development designed to stimulate educational reform. The federal role in education is constantly being reassessed. Some critics argue that the federal government should simply provide lump-sum grants to states to subsidize education as state governments see fit. Others argue that the federal government should play a much larger role in education by establishing national standards for curricula and testing. However, given the realities of constraints on federal spending and the commitment to reduce the federal budget deficit as we approach the year 2000, it is probably un-

*See Congress of the United States, Congressional Budget Office, *The Federal Role in Improving Elementary and Secondary Education*, Washington, D.C.: U.S. Government Printing Office, May 1993.

realistic to expect a major increase in the commitment of federal expenditures to aid education. The primary responsibility for improving the quality of U.S. public education is therefore likely to remain the responsibility of officials of state and local governments.

The graph on page 24 shows how spending on public elementary and secondary education schools has varied between 1962 and 1990 after adjustment for inflation. State and local government spending on education has more than tripled since 1962, with the state

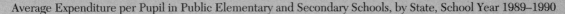

Average Expenditure per Pupil in Public Elementary and Secondary Schools, by State, School Year 1989–1990

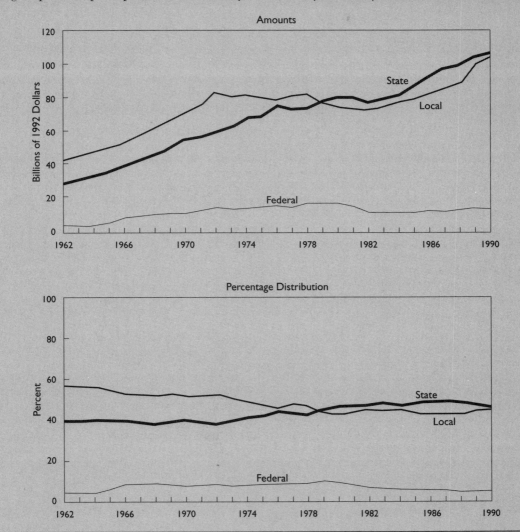

Source: Congressional Budget Office calculations based on data from Department of Education, National Center for Education Statistics, *Digest of Education Statistics, 1992* (1992).
Note: The number of pupils is measured in terms of average daily attendance. Expenditures per pupil are adjusted for differences among the states in the cost of living; see Center for the Study of Educational Finance, "Geographical Cost of Living Differences" (Illinois State University, Normal, IL, April 1991). Expenditures are adjusted to 1992 dollars using the consumer price index for all urban consumers.

SOURCE OF FUNDS FOR PUBLIC ELEMENTARY AND SECONDARY SCHOOLS, SCHOOL YEARS ENDING 1962–1990

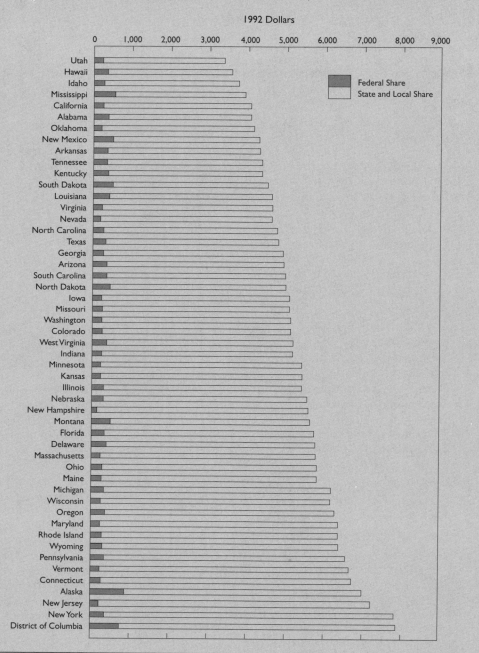

Source: Congressional Budget Office calculations based on data from Department of Education, National Center for Education Statistics, *Digest of Education Statistics, 1992* (1992).

Note: Amounts are adjusted to 1992 dollars using the consumer price index for all urban consumers. Data are interpolated for years with missing values.

government share of the costs increasing relative to local governments. The federal share of the costs of providing public education has hardly increased at all since 1962. Because education is primarily a state and local government responsibility, considerable variation in spending per pupil exists among states and localities. The graph on page 23 shows how expenditure per pupil and the federal share of the expenditure varies in all 50 states and the District of Columbia with states ranked by expenditure per pupil.

MARKET FAILURE AND THE FUNCTIONS OF GOVERNMENT: HOW MUCH GOVERNMENT IS ENOUGH?

Why do we demand government services? How much government is enough? As citizens, each of us has opinions about what governments should or should not be doing. An economic analysis of government seeks to evaluate the costs and benefits of government activities and also to explain the way government spending, regulations, and finance affect resource use and the distribution of well-being in a society.

One reason we demand government services is that in many cases government can provide us with items that we cannot easily make available for ourselves or purchase from others in markets. For example, governments establish property rights to the use of resources and enforce contracts by providing a system of law enforcement and courts. Government power is used through these functions to establish rules that regulate the social interaction among individuals and to settle disputes among citizens. It is almost inconceivable to imagine a society functioning without these rules and therefore without a government.

Political theorists of the nineteenth century called the willing submission of individuals to the authority of government the *social compact.* The existence of government gives rise to further demands for its powers to be used to supply various services to its citizens. Governments also use their power to redistribute income and economic opportunity among citizens. For example, the federal government uses tax revenues to provide income support for the elderly, the unemployed, and the poor. Another function is the stabilization of economic fluctuations to prevent the waste associated with unemployment of productive resources and the undesirable consequences of inflation. Finally, governments regulate production and consumption to achieve such goals as improved health and the elimination of excessive monopolistic control over prices.

The growth in government spending since 1929 reflects increased demands for government services that markets fail to provide. Demands for social insurance such as Social Security old age pensions, unemployment insurance, and government financed health insurance to the aged and the poor is responsible for much of the growth of government spending since 1970. National defense is also a service that we cannot purchase for ourselves in markets and has accounted for many billions of dollars in federal government outlays.

But has government grown too much, too rapidly? Do costs outweigh the benefits of some government functions and services? Could some government services be dispensed with entirely, allowing the resources they absorb to be used elsewhere and allowing a reduction in taxes paid? Should government assets and enterprises such as the Postal Service be sold to private firms to be operated for profit? Have tax-financed Social Security pensions become more generous than initially intended? Should we replace our current system of private health insurance with one that uses government power to guarantee coverage for all citizens?

Have government programs failed to accomplish their goals? For example, does federal assistance to the poor actually improve their well-being or does it instead create a cycle of poverty that extends from one generation to another? Do government programs have unintended effects—for example, do grants to rejuvenate decaying cities decrease the availability of housing to low-income city dwellers? Does waste and mismanagement in government result in unnecessarily high costs for defense projects? Do government regulations prevent useful products from being sold or increase prices of market goods and services?

How much should governments do, and how much should be left to private enterprise and initiative through market sale of goods and services? This is the core question that occupies much of the first part of this textbook. Once we have established the basis for government activity we can examine the impact of government finance on private incentives and resource use.

Summary

Public finance is the field of economics that studies government activities and alternative means of financing government expenditures. Modern public finance emphasizes the relationships between citizens and governments. Government goods and services are supplied through political institutions, which employ rules and procedures that have evolved in different societies for arriving at collective choices. Increases in government goods and services require decreased private use of resources. Government goods and services are usually made available without charge for their use, and they are financed by compulsory payments (mainly taxes) that are levied on citizens and their activities. The distribution of the tax burden itself is determined through the political interaction of citizens.

In modern mixed economies, the size of the government sector ranges between one-quarter and one-half of gross domestic product. A major goal in the study of public finance is to analyze the economic role of government and the costs and benefits of allocating resources to government use as opposed to allowing private enterprise and households to use those resources.

A Forward Look

The following chapter develops a theoretical basis for understanding and evaluating resource allocation. We introduce the concept of efficiency that appears throughout this textbook. Students who wish to review the basic economic theory that serves as a foundation for much of this textbook will find the following appendix useful.

Important Concepts

Political Institutions
Public Finance
Governments
Private Goods and Services
Government Goods and Services
Nonmarket Rationing
The Mixed Economy
Government Purchases
Government Transfer Payments

Questions for Review

1. List four government services and ask yourself how these provide benefits for you and your family. Try

to put a monetary value on these benefits by thinking about what you would be willing to give up to receive them if they were not available.

2. Make a rough estimate of how much you and your family pay in taxes each year. Compare this estimate with the value of services received from the government. Do you think government provides you with benefits that are worth what you give up in taxes?

3. How does the mechanism for distributing and rationing most government services differ from that for distributing goods through markets?

4. List some major political institutions and indicate how they translate desires into collective agreements.

5. What is a production-possibility curve? Show how such a curve can be used to explain how private goods and services must be sacrificed to obtain government goods and services.

6. What is the real cost of government expenditures? Think about your estimate of the taxes you pay and what you could have purchased with that money.

7. Discuss the trends in government expenditures and outlays as a percentage of GDP and use the data to explain why the federal government budget has been in deficit almost every year since 1966.

8. What are the characteristics of the United States economy that make it a "mixed economy" instead of a pure market economy?

9. What is the distinction between government purchases and transfer payments? What is the relative importance of these two types of expenditures in total government expenditures expressed as a percent of GDP? Why are some government purchases necessary to administer transfer payments by government?

10. List the major sources of tax revenue for the federal government. In what ways do the taxes used by state and local governments differ from those used by the federal government? What are other sources of government finance in addition to taxation?

Problems

1. As productive resources and technological know-how increase, a nation's production-possibility curve shifts outward. Use a production-possibility curve to show how resource growth and improvements in technology can allow a nation to increase its production of government goods and services while also increasing its output of private goods and services.

2. Suppose that the federal, state, and local governments in the United States were to engage in a massive campaign to deal with AIDS, drug abuse, and other health problems. The increase in government medical spending would require a massive tax increase. Assuming that resources and technology are fixed, use a production-possibility curve to show the cost of the increased government health services.

3. Suppose that governments increase spending for Social Security pensions. Explain why the increased government spending for pensions will not appreciably increase government purchases of productive resources or the products of business firms.

4. Suppose the federal government were to finally balance its budget. Explain why interest payments by the federal government would still be a large share of federal expenditures even if the federal government did not run a deficit again for several years.

Suggestions for Further Reading

Buchanan, James M. *Public Finance in Democratic Process.* Chapel Hill: University of North Carolina Press, 1967. Provides a classic economic analysis of the processes through which individual choices are related to collective actions and government policy with respect to both expenditures and finance.

Statistical Abstract of the United States. Washington, DC: U.S. Government Printing Office. Published annually. A gold mine of data on U.S. government programs, expenditures, and taxes, as well as facts and figures on just about anything you would care to know about in the United States.

Tax Foundation. *Facts & Figures on Government Finances.* Baltimore, The Johns Hopkins University Press. Published annually. Provides a lot of data and information regarding government spending, revenues, and taxation in the United States.

Wolf, Charles, Jr., *Markets or Governments,* Cambridge, MA: The MIT Press, 1993. An analysis of the role of government in a market economy and the failures of government policy. Also discusses the process of transition in formerly socialist countries.

Appendix
1

Tools of
Microeconomic Analysis

This appendix briefly reviews the tools of microeconomic analysis that are used in this textbook. The uses of these tools are emphasized, and the insights they can provide are indicated. The theories are only briefly described. Students who desire a more intensive review and derivation of relationships can consult a textbook in microeconomic theory.

Indifference Curve Analysis

Indifference curve analysis is a useful tool for understanding choices that persons make regarding purchase and use of goods and services. In this book, indifference curve analysis is also applied to understand choices to give up leisure time to obtain income through work, and to give up consumption today for more consumption in the future.

A combination of various goods and services available for consumption over a certain period, say a month, is called a **market basket.** In this book, the market baskets discussed are combinations of one particular good and the expenditures on *all* other goods. For example, in discussing a person's monthly purchases of gasoline, the market baskets consist of a certain number of gallons per month and a certain amount of money to spend on all other goods and services.

Assumptions About Preferences

The basic assumptions underlying indifference curve analysis are

1. Persons can rank market baskets in terms of most desired and least desired. For any two market baskets, *A* and *B*, the consumer must prefer *A* to *B*, *B* to *A*, or be indifferent between the two.
2. If basket *A* is preferred to basket *B* and basket *B* is preferred to basket *C*, then basket *A* also must be preferred to basket *C*. Similarly, if the person is indifferent between *A* and *B* and also between *B* and *C*, the person also must be indifferent between *A* and *C*. This is called *transitivity*.

3. Persons always prefer more of a good to less of it, other things being equal.
4. The amount of money a person will give up to obtain additional units of a given good per time period, while being made neither worse off nor better off by the exchange, will decrease as more of the good is acquired. This is the *assumption of declining marginal rate of substitution* of a particular good for expenditures on other goods. It is also called the *principle of declining marginal benefit of a good.*

Throughout this book, these assumptions will be assumed to hold.

Indifference Curves and Indifference Maps

An **indifference curve** is a graph of all combinations of market baskets among which a person is indifferent. All points on an indifference curve give the person the same level of satisfaction, or utility, per month. The preceding assumptions assure that the indifference curves between monthly consumption of a particular good, X (such as gasoline), and monthly expenditures on other goods will be downward sloping and convex to the origin. Figure 1A.1 graphs an indifference curve, labeled U_1, for monthly consumption of gasoline and monthly expenditure on all other goods. The market basket corresponding to point B_1 on the graph has 40 gallons of gasoline per month and $60 expenditures on all other goods per month. The point B_2 must correspond to more gasoline but less expenditure on other goods if it is to be a point on the indifference curve U_1. This has to follow from the assumption that persons prefer more to less. If the market basket corresponding to B_2 had more gasoline and

Figure 1A.1 ✦ INDIFFERENCE CURVES

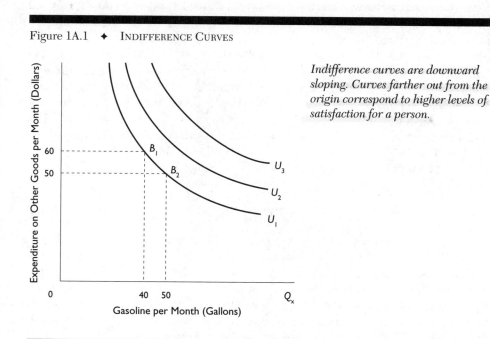

Indifference curves are downward sloping. Curves farther out from the origin correspond to higher levels of satisfaction for a person.

more expenditure on other goods than basket B_1, the person would be better off. This means that B_2 would be on an indifference curve, such as U_2, that corresponds to a higher level of satisfaction. The assumption that persons prefer more of goods and services to less of them implies that indifference curves must slope downward.

The amount of expenditure on goods other than gasoline that a person will give up to obtain another unit of a good X, such as a gallon of gasoline, while not becoming better or worse off is called the **marginal rate of substitution** of good X for expenditure on other goods, or the **marginal benefit** of a good. It is equal to the slope of the indifference curve multiplied by -1. The assumption that the marginal benefit of a good declines implies that indifference curves become flatter as good X (in this case, gasoline) is substituted for expenditure on other goods in the person's market basket each month.

An **indifference map** is a way of describing a person's preferences. It shows a group of indifference curves, as displayed in Figure 1A.1. Because indifference curves farther from the origin include market baskets with more of good X and more expenditures on other goods than those closer to the origin, they correspond to more satisfaction. Persons prefer points on higher curves to those on lower curves. An indifference map describes a person's preferences by indicating how a person would rank alternative market baskets of goods. Market baskets are ranked according to the level of satisfaction or utility that they provide the consumer.

The Budget Constraint

The **budget constraint** indicates the monthly market baskets that the person can afford, given monthly income and the prices of good X and all other goods. Figure 1A.2 shows a person's monthly budget constraint between gasoline and expenditures on other goods. Assume that the price of gasoline is $1 per gallon and that the person's monthly income is $100. A market basket corresponding to 100 gallons of gasoline per month would exhaust the person's monthly income, allowing no expenditures on other goods. This corresponds to point B in Figure 1A.2. Similarly, if the person spent all available monthly income on goods other than gasoline, there would be no gasoline in the monthly market basket. This corresponds to point A on the graph. The budget constraint is a straight line connecting these two points. Market baskets corresponding to points on or below the line are affordable. This above the line, such as C, cannot be purchased with available monthly income. This equation of the budget line is

$$I = P_x Q_x + \Sigma P_i Q_i, \qquad (1A.1)$$

where P_x is the price of good X and Q_x is its monthly consumption. The second term represents the sum of expenditure on goods other than gasoline. The market basket that corresponds to point D in Figure 1A.2 is on the budget line. It represents 40 gallons of gasoline per month and $60 expenditures on other goods. The distance OF on the vertical axis is expenditures on other goods corresponding to point D. The distance AF represents the amount of the person's total income given up to buy gasoline that month. This is $40 when the price of gasoline is $1 per gallon.

Figure 1A.2 ✦ THE BUDGET CONSTRAINT LINE

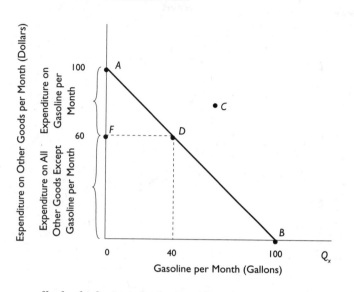

The consumer can afford only those market baskets of gasoline and other goods per month on or below the budget constraint line AB.

Consumer Equilibrium

The consumer is assumed to behave so as to obtain the most satisfaction (or utility) possible, given the budget constraint. This means that the consumer substitutes expenditures on goods other than X for purchases of good X, up to the point at which the highest possible satisfaction is obtained. Because indifference curves are convex, this occurs at a point of tangency between the budget line and an indifference curve. In Figure 1A.3, the consumer equilibrium is represented by point E. The corresponding monthly consumption of gasoline is 60 gallons. The person therefore spends $40 on goods other than X each month when the price of gasoline is $1 per gallon.

The **equilibrium condition** is a tangency between the indifference curve and the budget line, implying that the slopes of these two curves are equal. The slope of the budget line is the extra dollars that must be surrendered to obtain each extra gallon of gasoline, which is the price of gasoline multiplied by -1. The slope of the indifference curve is the marginal rate of substitution of gasoline for expenditures on goods other than gasoline per month multiplied by -1. The marginal rate of substitution can be thought of as the marginal benefit of good X. The equilibrium condition therefore can be written as

$$-P_x = -MB_x$$

or

Figure 1A.3 ◆ CONSUMER EQUILIBRIUM

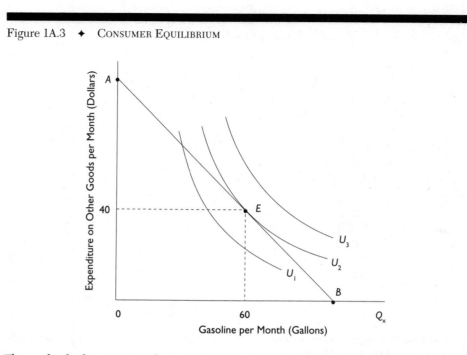

The market basket corresponding to point E is the one that gives the consumer the highest possible level of satisfaction, given the budget constraint.

$$P_x = MB_x. \tag{1A.2}$$

The consumer purchases a good up to the point at which its price equals its marginal benefit.

Changes in Income and Prices

A change in income shifts the budget constraint line in or out parallel to itself without changing its slope. This is illustrated in Figure 1A.4. An increase in income shifts the budget line outward, expanding the number of affordable market baskets. Similarly, a decrease in income diminishes the number of affordable market baskets.

A change in the price of good X changes the slope of the budget line. As illustrated in Figure 1A.5, a decrease in the price of X swivels the budget line outward to a new intercept B', on the X axis. The budget line becomes flatter, reflecting the lower price of X. Similarly, an increase in the price of good X makes the budget line steeper as it rotates to point B''.

Income and Substitution Effects of Price Changes

Useful insights are often obtained by dividing into two separate effects the effect of the price change of a good on the amount purchased per month. The **income effect**

Figure 1A.4 ✦ CHANGES IN INCOME

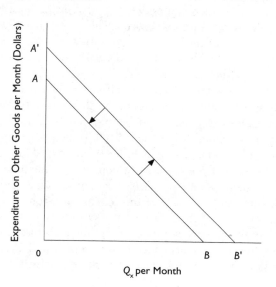

An increase in income shifts the budget constraint line out parallel to itself. A decrease in income shifts it inward.

Figure 1A.5 ✦ CHANGES IN THE PRICE OF GOOD X

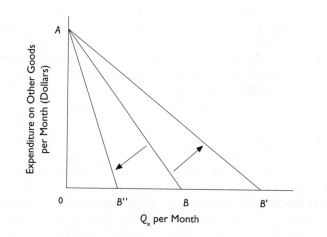

Changes in the price of good X rotate the budget constraint line to a new intercept on the X axis.

is the change in the monthly (or other period) consumption of a good due to the variation in purchasing power of income caused by its price change. The **substitution effect** is the change in the monthly (or other period) consumption of the good due to the change in its price relative to other goods. This is the change that would be observed if the income effect of the price change were removed. Income and substitution effects can only rarely be observed separately. However, it is useful to show how a person's well-being is affected by each of these effects.

Figure 1A.6 shows how the substitution effect can be isolated from the income effect. The person whose indifference curves are shown is initially in equilibrium at E_1. Consuming 60 gallons of gasoline per month and spending $40 per month on other goods, this person's monthly income is $100. If the price of gasoline goes up to $2 per gallon as a result of a tax, the budget line would swivel inward. The consumer is now worse off, in a shift from point E_1 to point E_2. At E_2, monthly gasoline consumption falls to 40 gallons per month. The consumer spends $80 per month on gasoline at the higher price and uses $20 of the remaining income to buy other goods. Suppose the consumer were offered a monthly subsidy (say, by helpful parents) to help buy gasoline after the price increase. If this monthly increase in income were sufficient enough to return the consumer to indifference curve U_2, where the level of satisfaction is the same as before the price increase, the substitution effect could be isolated.

In Figure 1A.6, a $50 monthly increase in income returns the consumer to the level of well-being represented by points on the indifference curve U_2. The consumer's total monthly income would now be $150. The consumer then would be in equilibrium at point E', consuming 45 gallons of gasoline per month at a price of $2 per gallon ($90 per month) and spending the remaining $60 income on other goods. The 15-gallon monthly decrease in gasoline consumption from the initial 60-gallon monthly consumption level is the substitution effect. The remainder of the decrease that would be observed in the absence of the monthly compensating variation in income is an additional 5 gallons per month. This is the income effect. These two effects are labeled separately in Figure 1A.6.

In analyzing taxes, income and substitution effects are often used. For example, taxes that do not affect relative prices but reduce income only have income effects. These taxes are used as benchmarks against which to compare the impact of taxes that have both income effects and substitution effects. The substitution effects stem from the distorting effects taxes (such as the gasoline tax in this example) have on the relative price of goods and services.

The Law of Demand

For most goods, both the income effects and the substitution effects of price increases tend to decrease the consumption of a good. The opposite is true for price decreases. Goods for which the income effect of a price increase acts to decrease consumption (and for which price decreases have the opposite effect) are called **normal goods.** Throughout this text the assumption is that all goods and services discussed are normal goods.

Figure 1A.6 ✦ INCOME AND SUBSTITUTION EFFECTS

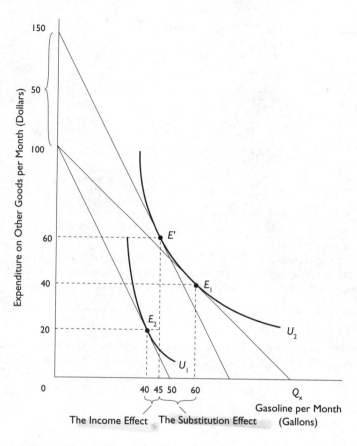

The substitution effect could be observed if the consumer were given an increase in income to offset the decline in satisfaction caused by the price increase of gasoline.

The inverse relationship between price and the quantity of a good purchased per time period is the **law of demand,** which holds that demand curves slope downward, other things being equal. Figure 1A.7 draws a demand curve for a good. Movements along that curve in response to price changes are called **changes in quantity demanded.** A shifting in or out of the curve is called a **change in demand,** which can be caused by changes in income, tastes, or the prices of substitutes or complements for the good.

The demand curve also gives information on the maximum price that a consumer will pay for a good. This maximum price represents the marginal benefit of the good to a consumer. Accordingly, the demand curve in Figure 1A.7 is also labeled *MB.* Points on demand curves throughout this book are interpreted as the marginal benefit (*MB*)

Figure 1A.7 ✦ THE LAW OF DEMAND

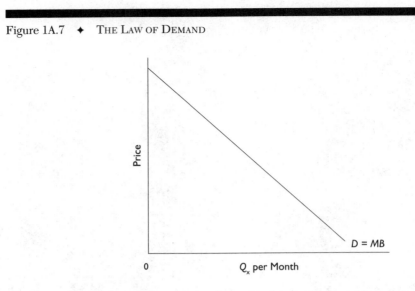

The demand curve depicts the inverse relationship between price and quantity demanded implied by the law of demand. Points on a demand curve also can be interpreted as the marginal benefit of the various amounts of the good available per month.

of the corresponding quantity. Market demand curves are derived from individual demand curves simply by adding the quantities consumed by all purchasers at each possible price.

Price Elasticity of Demand

A useful measure of the responsiveness of quantity demanded to price changes is **price elasticity of demand,** which measures the percentage change in quantity demanded due to a given percentage change in price:

$$E_D = \frac{\% \text{ Change in Quantity Demanded}}{\% \text{ Change in Price}} = \frac{\Delta Q_D/Q_D}{\Delta P/P}. \tag{1A.3}$$

The price elasticity of demand is negative because an inverse relationship exists between price and quantity demanded. The numerator and denominator of Equation 1A.3 always will be of opposite sign. Demand is elastic with respect to price (relatively responsive) when its value is less than -1. Demand is inelastic (relatively unresponsive) when its value is greater (that is, closer to zero) than -1. Demand is said to be of unitary elasticity when its value is just equal to -1.

Consumer Surplus

Demand curves can be used to give an approximation of the benefits that consumers obtain from a good. This is found simply by adding up the marginal benefit of each unit consumed to obtain the total benefit of the total consumption per time period. Assuming that the scale of measurement is compact enough along the quantity axis of the demand curve, this total benefit can be approximated by the area under the demand curve. Throughout this text, areas under demand curves are used as measures of the benefits that consumers receive from a good. In Figure 1A.8, the total benefit of Q_1 units of gasoline consumed per month therefore would be interpreted as the area $0ABQ_1$. This is a dollar approximation of the benefits that consumers obtain from the Q_1 units of monthly consumption.

In most cases, a measure of the *net benefit* that consumers obtain from a good is required. **Consumer surplus** is the total benefit of a given amount of a good less the value of money given up to obtain that monthly quantity. In Figure 1A.8, the amount of money that would have to be given up to purchase Q_1 units of gasoline per month, when its price is P per gallon, is represented by the area $0PBQ_1$. Subtracting this from the total benefit of the gasoline gives the triangular area PAB, which measures the consumer surplus earned on Q_1 gallons per month.

Using Indifference Curves to Explain the Allocation of Time

If leisure is viewed as a good that persons can retain for their own use or supply to others as work, indifference curve analysis can be used to analyze the work-leisure choice. Of the 24 hours available each day, the more leisure hours a person consumes per day, the fewer hours available for paid work. Figure 1A.9 draws a person's indifference curves for leisure hours per day and income per day.

Figure 1A.8 ✦ CONSUMER SURPLUS

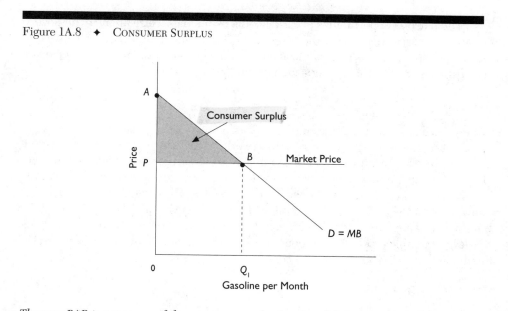

The area PAB is a measure of the consumer surplus (net benefit) that consumers receive from consuming Q_1 gallons of gasoline per month.

Figure 1A.9   ◆   THE WORK-LEISURE CHOICE

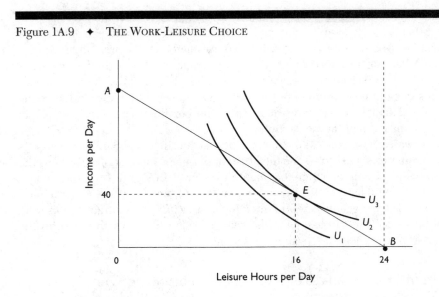

Point E represents the combination of leisure and income from work each day that gives the worker the greatest possible level of daily well-being. In equilibrium, the person whose indifference curves are drawn chooses 16 hours of leisure per day. The person therefore works 8 hours per day.

The person's opportunities to earn income by trading leisure hours to employers in a labor market depend on the wage rate. The income-leisure budget constraint shows the opportunities to earn income by trading leisure in the market. If a person can earn w per hour, then the equation of this budget line is

$$I = w(24 - L), \tag{1A.4}$$

where I is daily money income and L is leisure hours per day. *Leisure* is defined simply as using time for any activity other than work for pay. This equation is represented by the line AB in Figure 1A.9. For example, if the hourly wage is $5, a person who takes 16 hours per day as leisure will work 8 hours and earn a daily income of $40. This person is in equilibrium at point E in Figure 1A.9. The diagram assumes that the only way that the person can earn money income is by giving up leisure. The slope of the indifference curve is the marginal rate of substitution of leisure for income (MRS_{LI}) multiplied by -1. The slope of the budget line in Figure 1A.9 is the wage multiplied by -1. The equilibrium condition at point E is

$$MRS_{LI} = w \tag{1A.5}$$

In the text, applications of this analysis show how the equilibrium is affected by taxes and subsidies that affect wages and provide income independent of work.

ANALYSIS OF PRODUCTION AND COST

The amount of goods or services that can be produced depends on the physical resources employed and technical knowledge available. The **production function** is a way of describing the maximum output obtainable from any given combination of inputs, given technology. *Inputs* are the productive services of land, labor, capital (such as equipment, machines, and structures), and materials. Improvements in technology allow more output to be produced with any given combination of inputs.

Production is usually divided into two periods. The **short run** is that period of production when some inputs cannot be varied. The **long run** is the period when *all* inputs are variable.

The **marginal product** of an input is the change in the total output produced by that input when one more unit of the input is employed while all other inputs are held constant. The theory of production presumes that the marginal product of an input will eventually decline in the short run. This implies a limit to the extra output that can be produced in the short run when at least some inputs are fixed.

Isoquant Analysis

Isoquants are curves that show alternative combinations of variable inputs that can be used to produce a given amount of output. Figure 1A.10 shows an isoquant curve for combinations of capital services (measured in machine hours) and labor services

Figure 1A.10   ✦   ISOQUANT ANALYSIS

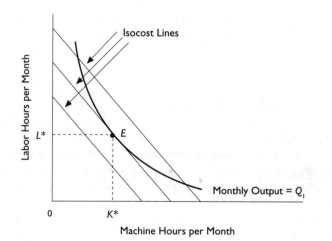

The monthly input combination corresponding to point E represents the minimum cost method of producing a monthly output of Q_1 units.

(measured in labor hours) that can be used to produce Q_1 units of output per month. The curve is downward sloping. This is because reducing the amount of labor used decreases output unless more capital is used, provided that the marginal product of both inputs is positive. It is usually assumed that producers will never employ inputs in amounts for which the marginal products are negative.

The **marginal rate of technical substitution** of one input, capital, for another, labor ($MRTS_{KL}$) is a measure of the amount of labor services that can be substituted for capital services without increasing or decreasing production. $MRTS_{KL}$ is the slope of the isoquant, $\Delta L/\Delta K$ multiplied by -1. The marginal rates of substitution of capital for labor are presumed to decline along a given isoquant, because labor and capital tend to complement one another. Labor can only imperfectly accomplish the tasks of machines and vice versa. As labor is actually substituted for capital, it takes more and more labor hours to make up for each successive reduction in machine hours. The declining $MRTS_{KL}$ give isoquants their convex shape.

It is assumed that producers seek to produce any given output at minimum cost. **Isocost lines** show combinations of variable input services per month that are of equal cost. Figure 1A.10 also shows a family of isocost lines. The equation of any given isocost line is

$$C = P_L L + P_K K, \tag{1A.6}$$

where L is labor hours used per month, K is machine hours used per month, P_L is the price per hour of labor, and P_K is the price per machine hour. C is the cost of the variable inputs, labor and capital. Isocost lines farther from the origin correspond to higher cost. The slope of any isocost line is $-P_K/P_L$.

Figure 1A.10 shows that the minimum cost combination of labor services and capital services (L°, K°) to produce Q_1 units of output per month corresponds to point E. At that point, the isoquant is tangent to an isocost line. Because the slope of the isoquant is $-MRTS_{KL}$ and the slope of the isocost line is $-P_K/P_L$, the condition for minimizing the cost of producing any given output can be written as

$$MRTS_{KL} = P_K/P_L. \tag{1A.7}$$

Cost

Cost is the monetary value of inputs used to produce goods and services. The opportunity cost of using inputs is their value in their next best use. Assuming that all producers generate any given output at the lowest possible cost, it is possible to derive a cost function from isoquants. A **cost function** gives the minimum cost of producing any given output, given current technology. **Cost curves** describe the way this minimum cost varies with the amount of output produced per year (or any other period). Producers are assumed to use the combination of variable inputs for producing any given output that satisfies Equation 1A.7. Cost curves can be derived for both the short run and the long run.

In the short run, the producer can be thought of as being confined to a productive plant or factory of fixed size that cannot easily be altered because of leases and other fixed commitments. In the long run, all inputs can be varied, resulting in more flexibility in production and cost.

Total cost (*TC*) is the value of all inputs used to produce a given output. In the short run, total cost can be divided into two components: **variable cost** (*VC*), which is the cost of variable inputs, such as labor, machines, and materials, and **fixed cost** (*FC*), which is the cost of inputs that do not vary with output. Monthly rent for a one-year lease on a structure is an example of a fixed cost.

Average cost (*AC*) is equal to total cost of production divided by the number of units produced. **Average variable cost** (*AVC*) is variable cost divided by the number of units produced. The difference between average cost and average variable cost is the **average fixed cost** (*AFC*) of output in the short run.

In the short run, average cost curves are assumed to be U-shaped, because the marginal product of variable inputs tends to decline in the short run. After a point, more and more variable inputs are required to produce more output when some inputs are fixed. This increases average variable cost (and therefore average cost) of production after a point. Given input prices, average cost tends to decline at first in the short run and then increase. Short-run average cost curves have the characteristic U-shape drawn in Figure 1A.11.

In deciding how much to produce in the short run, the firm's operators need to estimate the marginal cost of production. This is the extra cost associated with producing one more unit of output. Marginal cost tends to rise at low levels of output and continues to rise as output is increased in the plant. The marginal cost curve always intersects the average cost curve at average cost's minimum level. The marginal cost curve, as well as its relation to average costs, is also drawn in Figure 1A.11.

Figure 1A.11 ✦ SHORT-RUN COST CURVES AND PROFIT MAXIMIZATION UNDER PERFECT COMPETITION

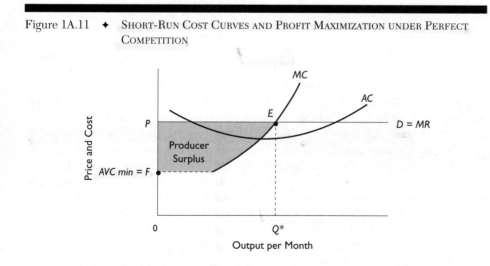

The competitive firm maximizes profits in the short run by adjusting output to Q°, which corresponds to the point at which P = MC. The portion of the marginal cost curve for which MC exceeds minimum possible average variable costs is the short-run supply curve under perfect competition.

In the long run, firms can build additional plants and expand their capability to produce in various ways not available in the short run. Average costs can vary in three ways, depending on the nature of the production function for a particular good in the long run, assuming that input prices are given. **Increasing returns to scale** exist when long-run average cost declines as output is expanded. **Constant returns to scale** occur when long-run average cost remains constant as the industry expands. **Decreasing returns to scale** mean that long-run average costs rise as the firm expands. The actual cost curve in the long run can reflect all three of these possibilities in sequence. In that case, it will be U-shaped like the short-run average cost curve.

PROFIT MAXIMIZATION, COMPETITION, AND SUPPLY

Perfect Competition

Economists usually assume that a firm seeks to maximize profits. The firm's choice of output depends on the extent to which it can influence the price of its product by its own actions. When the firm is only one of many firms producing a small market share of a standardized product, the quality of which does not differ among firms, **perfect competition** is said to exist. A **competitive firm** is one that sells its output in a perfectly competitive market. The distinguishing feature of perfect competition is that no one firm alone in an industry can influence the selling price of its product in any way. The competitive firm is said to be a **price taker** because it takes the price of its product as given.

The competitive firm will maximize profits by producing that output for which price is equal to marginal cost:

$$P = MC. \tag{1A.8}$$

To understand why this is so, think of the firm as sequentially increasing output and asking itself whether each increment in output adds or subtracts from profits. It will continue to expend output until the point at which producing another unit will decrease profits. The extra revenue that the firm gets from each extra unit of output is called the marginal revenue (MR). Because, under perfect competition, the firm cannot influence the price, it follows that the marginal revenue of an extra unit of output is the price at which that output can be sold. This means that the firm can sell any amount of output at the going market price. From its point of view, the demand curve that it faces is a horizontal line, $D = MR$, as shown in Figure 1A.11.

The firm will add to its profits as long as the price at which it sells one more unit exceeds the marginal cost of producing that unit. When price is exactly equal to marginal cost, the last unit produced will bring in as much revenue as the cost involved in producing it, and the net addition to profits will be zero. If the firm produces beyond that point, profits will decline because the marginal cost of producing that extra unit will exceed the marginal revenue it brings in. It follows that firms maximize profits by producing that output for which price is equal to marginal cost of production.

The Short-Run Supply Curve

The marginal cost curve gives a relation between price and the quantity the firm will produce and supply in the short run. It represents the firm's **short-run supply curve** when price exceeds minimum possible average variable costs (*AVCmin*) of production. When price is below average variable costs, the firm shuts down immediately, because when price (*P*) is less than minimum possible *AVC*, the firm will lose more than its fixed costs by continuing to operate in the short run.

The entire market supply curve for a perfectly competitive industry is the sum of the amounts each firm in the industry will produce and offer for sale at all possible output. For any output, points on that supply curve represent the marginal cost to firms of producing that output.

Producer Surplus

Analogous to the concept of consumer surplus is that of **producer surplus,** which is the difference between the market price of an output or input and the minimum price that would be necessary to induce suppliers to make it available for sale on the market. The supply curve tells how much output or input would be offered for sale at alternative prices. In Figure 1A.11, producer surplus is the area *PEF,* where *F* corresponds to minimum possible average variable cost (*AVCmin*). The minimum price at which any producer is willing to supply any given amount of output per month (or year) in a competitive market represents marginal cost. Producer surplus is therefore the difference between price and marginal cost for each quantity. For the total quantity, Q^*, the area represents the sum of producer surplus at each level of output.

Long-Run Supply

Perfect competition also requires free entry and exit into the industry. In the long run, firms can enter or leave an industry. The incentives they have to do so depend on the level of profits realizable in an industry. **Normal profits** represent the opportunity costs of resources of owner-supplied (nonpurchased) inputs invested in a firm. Normal profits are part of a firm's costs. **Economic profits** are those in excess of normal profits. When it is possible to earn economic profits in a competitive industry, new firms will enter. This will increase industry supply and reduce market price. Conversely, when economic profits are negative, firms will leave the industry because they will be unable to cover their opportunity costs (including the normal profit). This will decrease supply and increase the price of the product. The industry is said to be in **long-run competitive equilibrium** when economic profits are zero, so that no incentive exists for firms either to enter or leave.

Under perfect competition, a **long-run industry supply curve** is a relationship between price and quantity supplied for points at which the industry is in equilibrium. Points on such a curve correspond to outputs for which each firm in the industry is maximizing profits. Therefore, price must equal long-run marginal cost (*LRMC*). However, price must also equal long-run average cost (*LRAC*) at the point of equilibrium, because economic profits must be zero in long-run equilibrium. When $P = LRAC$, profit per unit is $P - LRAC = 0$, implying that economic profits, $(P - LRAC)Q$, are zero. Remember that the normal profit is included in costs. If $P > LRAC$, new firms would enter the industry until the price fell to make economic profits zero. If $P < LRAC$, firms would incur losses and leave the industry until economic profits were zero.

Figure 1A.12 shows the equilibrium of a typical firm in a perfectly competitive industry when the industry is also in equilibrium. That firm is maximizing profits in the long run because $P = LRMC$. At the maximum profit output, economic profits are zero because $P = LRAC$. Also notice that at that output, Q^*, $LRAC$ is at its minimum possible level, $LRACmin$. Points on an industry supply curve therefore satisfy the following conditions:

$$P = LRMC = LRACmin. \tag{1A.9}$$

Long-run competitive supply curves can be upward sloping, horizontal, or even downward sloping, depending on how the prices of specialized inputs used by an industry change as a result of the industry's expansion or contraction. If the prices of inputs used by the industry do not change as a direct result of expansion or contraction of the industry, then $LRACmin$ for firms in the industry will be independent of the size of the industry. This is the case of a **constant-costs industry.** In other words, other things being equal, any deviation in price from the original $LRACmin$ can be only temporary. Because input prices are independent of the number of firms in the industry, the $LRAC$ curves will not shift up or down as the industry expands or contracts. Price must always return to the original $LRACmin$ in the long run. This implies that the long-run supply curve is a horizontal line as shown in Figure 1A.13.

Figure 1A.12 ✦ Long-Run Competitive Equilibrium

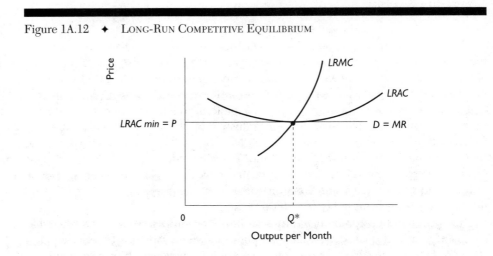

In the long-run competitive equilibrium, $P = LRMC = LRAC$. Points on the long-run supply curve correspond to outputs at which firms in the industry earn zero economic profits

Figure 1A.13 ✦ Long-Run Supply: The Case of a Constant-Costs Competitive Industry

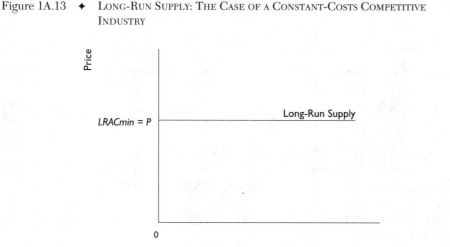

If input prices are independent of the size of an industry, the long-run supply curve is infinitely elastic at a price corresponding to LRACmin, which remains constant as the industry increases or decreases in size in the long run. The supply curve is infinitely elastic at P = LRACmin in the long run.

In an **increasing-costs industry,** the prices of some specialized inputs it uses *increase* as the industry expands and decrease as the industry contracts. This will occur if the firms buy a large portion of the total available supply of these specialized inputs. As the number of firms in the industry increases, the demands for these inputs increase substantially, causing their prices to rise. Consequently, as input prices rise, the *LRAC* curve for all firms in the industry shift up as the industry expands. This is because the height of the *LRAC* curve for any given output depends on input prices and technology. An increase in input prices increases the average cost of producing any given output; therefore, an increase in industry output in the long run results in an increase in *LRACmin*. Price must increase in the long run to result in an increase in quantity supplied. If price did not increase, firms could not cover their opportunity costs of production at the higher input prices and output would not increase. An increasing-costs industry therefore has an upward-sloping supply curve. For example, if the oil-refining industry purchased a large portion of the total available supply of the services of chemical engineers per year, the wages of the engineers would rise when the industry expanded and fall as it contracted. This would imply that the oil-refining industry is one of increasing costs.

A third possibility is a **decreasing costs industry,** in which input prices would decline as a direct result of the industry's expansion. This is an extremely rare case. If it were to prevail, *LRACmin* would actually decline as industry output increased in the long run. This would imply that the long-run supply curve was actually downward sloping!

Price Elasticity of Supply

Price elasticity of supply is the percentage change in quantity supplied in response to any given percentage change in price:

$$E_s = \frac{\% \text{ Change in Quantity Supplied}}{\% \text{ Change in Price}} = \frac{\Delta Q_s / Q_s}{\Delta P / P} \qquad (1A.10)$$

E_S is elastic when greater than one in value and inelastic when less than one.

For an industry of constant costs, for which the long-run supply curve is horizontal, the price elasticity of supply is infinite. If the available amount of an input is fixed, as is the case of land, the price elasticity of supply is zero. A perfectly inelastic supply curve is a vertical line at the available quantity. Figure 1A.14 shows the case of a perfectly inelastic supply of a good.

Figure 1A.14 ✦ A PERFECTLY INELASTIC SUPPLY CURVE

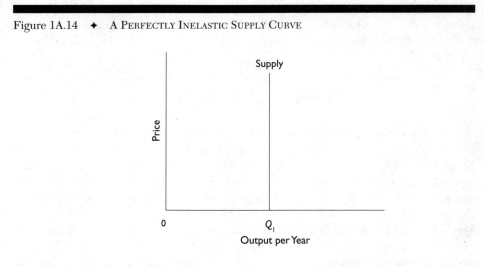

If annual output is fixed and does not vary with market price, supply is perfectly inelastic.

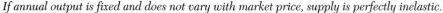

EFFICIENCY, MARKETS, AND GOVERNMENTS

The former Soviet republics and the nations of Eastern Europe formerly dominated by Communist regimes are struggling to transform their old centrally planned economies into mixed economies. This painful process of transition involves privatizing government-owned resources and the introduction of free markets. Decades of central planning in these nations have adversely affected incentives to produce. Living standards in the former Soviet Union and in such Eastern European nations as Czechoslovakia and Romania are on average well below those of industrialized nations in which private ownership of productive resources and free markets have prevailed.

What is it about free and competitive markets that works to squeeze more out of productive resources than has been possible in centrally planned economies? Can markets be relied on to satisfy all the desires of individuals? When do markets fail to supply useful goods and services, and when does the profit motive, which is necessary to keep a market system going, result in undesirable side-effects? To answer such questions we must first develop some norms for evaluating resource use. We must then examine how well markets achieve results that satisfy the criteria we set up to evaluate resource use. After we evaluate free market performance we can then discuss possible defects of markets and examine how these defects give rise to demands for government goods and services.

A useful starting point for analyzing government activities is the study of the role of markets in allocating resources. Markets facilitate exchange of goods and services and inputs. Free exchange between buyers and sellers in unregulated competitive markets often achieves outcomes that rate high in terms of the standards of economic performance used by many economists. However, markets cannot be relied upon to supply all useful goods and services, and sometimes market transactions have undesirable side-effects, such as pollution. In those circumstances, government supply of goods and services through political institutions can result in net gains in well-being to citizens.

In public finance we study both the virtues and defects of the marketplace. In this chapter we begin by defining the concept of efficiency. We then discuss conditions under which markets operate efficiently and examine some instances in which they fail to do so. We also show how government subsidies and taxes can distort resource allocation and cause losses in output and efficiency in markets.

In the next two chapters we show how government programs can result in improvements in resource use and provide additional benefits to individuals that outweigh the additional costs.

Positive and Normative Economics

Positive economics is a scientific approach to analysis that establishes cause and effect relationships among economic variables. Positive theory attempts to be objective, making no presuppositions about what is good or bad or what should be accomplished. It merely formulates hypotheses of the "If . . . then" variety that can be checked against facts.[1] For example, a positive analysis of the impact of a proposal to widen a road can be used to predict how the road will benefit users by reducing the time and money costs involved in getting between two locations. A positive analysis of the impact of a food subsidy to low-income persons can be utilized to estimate the effect of the subsidy on the price of food and the quantity consumed by the recipients. The predictions can then be checked against the facts to determine how well the positive theory has worked.

The normative approach is based on value judgments about what is desirable or what should be done to achieve the desired outcome. Normative theory begins with predetermined criteria and is used to prescribe policies that best achieve those criteria. **Normative economics** therefore is designed to formulate recommendations as to what *should* be accomplished. Because it is based on underlying values, this approach, unlike the positive approach, is not objective. It can evaluate alternative policies and actions only on the basis of the underlying value judgments. If you were to disagree with the values on which a normative theory was based, the resulting prescription would be of little use to you. The normative approach used in public finance theory is based on value judgments embodying an individualistic ethic.[2]

---

[1] For a classic discussion of the positive approach, see James M. Buchanan, "Positive Economics, Welfare Economics, and Political Economy," *Journal of Law and Economics* 2 (October 1959): 124–138.

[2] For an advanced discussion of the normative approach, see Richard W. Tresch, *Public Finance, A Normative Theory* (Plano, TX: Business Publications, 1981), Chaps. 1–2.

Both the positive and the normative approaches are useful, and, in fact, there is a certain dependence between the two approaches. Normative theory cannot make recommendations to achieve certain outcomes without an underlying theory of human behavior. If normative criteria are used to recommend that government authorities undertake a particular policy to increase the incomes of certain individuals, the impact of such actions on incentives to produce and consume must be predicted. Well-intentioned policies can have results opposite to those desired when no account is taken of their effects on economic incentives.

For example, suppose you support government supplied housing with very heavily subsidized rents for poor families because you believe that such policies will enable them to enjoy better and larger apartments. If positive analysis can show that some persons might actually be induced to move into small, publicly provided housing units from larger apartments, you might reconsider your support of the public-housing program. Similarly, you might favor rent-control legislation to keep rents low enough so that the poor can afford to house their families. If, however, positive analysis predicts that such controls result in housing shortages and reductions in the quality of rental units available on the market, some poor families will be made worse off. If these predictions are borne out by the evidence, you might reconsider your support of rent control as a means of aiding the poor.

Positive theory by itself merely embodies techniques of analysis and so can benefit from the work of normative theorists by using normative guidelines to choose which areas of human interaction to analyze. Therefore, the normative approach is useful to the positive approach in that it defines relevant issues.

NORMATIVE EVALUATION OF RESOURCE USE: THE EFFICIENCY CRITERION

Efficiency is a normative criterion for evaluating the effects of resource use on the well-being of individuals. *The **efficiency criterion** is satisfied when resources are used over any given period of time in such a way as to make it impossible to increase the well-being of any one person without reducing the well-being of any other person.* Developed by the Italian economist Vilfredo Pareto (1848–1923), it is often referred to as the criterion of *Pareto optimality.* The criterion represents a precise definition of the concept of efficiency.

The word *efficiency* is part of everyone's vocabulary. To most, efficiency means producing a desired result with a minimum of effort or expense. Synonymous with this is the minimization of wasted effort—that which produces no useful result. The economist's criterion of efficiency is somewhat more precise than the standard dictionary definition. It does, however, embody the same idea.

Let's begin using the efficiency criterion. First, assume that the well-being of any individual increases with the amount of goods and services that he or she consumes per year. It is easy to show how avoiding waste in production will help achieve efficiency. Given available amounts of productive resources and the existing state of technical knowledge in an economy, elimination of wasted effort will allow more production from available resources. The extra production will make it possible for some persons to consume more without reducing the amounts consumed by others. As a result, it would be possible to make some individuals better off without harming anyone else by avoiding waste in production.

Another important aspect of efficiency is freedom to engage in mutually advantageous exchanges. If you are free to engage in transactions for gain, you can obtain more satisfaction out of your income. For example, suppose you have a collection of heavy metal rock compact discs you no longer enjoy. By exchanging those discs for a collection of classic rock and roll tapes that you value more, you can become more content. If you find a person who really wants your heavy metal discs and has a set of classic rock and roll tapes you highly value, then both you and your friend can gain by trading. Freedom to trade is therefore an important aspect of efficiency. Both buyers and sellers can gain in markets when the value a buyer places on an item exceeds the cost the seller incurs by making it available for sale. Constraints that prevent resources being used and traded in such a way as to allow mutual gains will prevent achievement of efficiency. When efficiency is attained, mutual gains from reallocating resources in productive use or through further exchange of goods and services among individuals are no longer possible.

Many citizens argue that not all mutually gainful trades should be allowed. Such individuals demand that the powers of government be used to prevent exchanges they find morally objectionable. They argue that government should exercise paternalistic powers over the choices of its citizens. Thus, it is common to observe laws banning the sale of certain drugs, gambling services, prostitution, and other activities in which some persons might wish to engage but which others find morally objectionable.

The criterion of efficiency is based on an underlying value judgment that individuals should be allowed to pursue their self-interest as they see fit, provided that no one is harmed in the process. Those who wish to intervene to prevent others from pursuing their self-interests disagree with this underlying value judgment. The individualistic ethic underlying the efficiency criterion, therefore, is not acceptable to all persons.

Marginal Conditions for Efficiency

The conditions required for the efficient output of a particular good over a period of time can be derived easily. Analysis of the benefits and costs of making additional amounts of a good available is required to determine whether the existing allocation of resources to its production is efficient. Any given quantity of an economic good available, say per month, will provide a certain amount of satisfaction to those who consume it. This is the **total social benefit** of the monthly quantity. The **marginal social benefit** of a good is the extra benefit obtained by making one more unit of that good available per month (or over any other period). The marginal social benefit can be measured as the maximum amount of money that would be given up by persons to obtain the extra unit of the good. For example, if the marginal social benefit of bread is $2 per loaf, some consumers would give up $2 worth of expenditure on other goods to obtain that loaf and be neither worse off nor better off by doing so. If these consumers could obtain the bread for less than $2 per loaf, they would be made better off. The marginal social benefit of a good is assumed to decline as more of that good is made available each month.

The **total social cost** of a good is the value of all resources necessary to make a given amount of the good available per month. The **marginal social cost** of a good is the minimum sum of money that is required to compensate the owners of inputs used in producing the good for making an extra unit of the good available. In computing marginal social costs, it is assumed that output is produced at minimum possible cost, given available technology. If the marginal social cost of bread is $1 per loaf, this is the minimum dollar amount necessary to compensate input owners for the use of their inputs without making them worse off. If they were to receive more than $1 per loaf, they would be made better off. If they were to receive less than $1 per loaf, they would be made worse off by making that extra unit available. The following analysis assumes that the marginal social cost of making more bread available per month does not decrease as the monthly output of bread is increased.

Figure 2.1A graphs the marginal social benefit (MSB) and marginal social cost (MSC) of making various quantities of bread available per month in a nation. Figure 2.1B shows the total social benefit (TSB) and the total social cost (TSC) of producing the bread. The marginal social benefit is $\Delta TSB/\Delta Q$, where ΔTSB is the change in the social benefit of the good and ΔQ is a one-unit increase in the output of bread per month. The marginal social benefit is therefore measured by the slope of the total social benefit curve at any point. Similarly, the marginal social cost, $\Delta TSC/\Delta Q$, is measured by the slope of the total social cost curve at any point.

The efficient output of bread can be determined by comparing its marginal social benefit and marginal social cost at various levels of monthly output. Look at the output corresponding to Q_1 = 10,000 loaves of bread per month in Figure 2.1A. This monthly output level is inefficient because the marginal social benefit of bread exceeds its marginal social cost. This means that the maximum amount of money consumers would give up to obtain an additional loaf of bread exceeds the minimum amount of money necessary to make input owners, whose resources are used to produce bread, no worse off.

For example, suppose that at Q_1 the MSB = $2 while MSC = $1. The consumer who gives up $2 for the bread is no worse off because marginal benefit is $2. If the input owners making the bread available were to receive $2 from each buyer, they would be made better off because $2 exceeds the minimum amount they require in compensation for the use of their inputs to produce that bread. This demonstrates that the monthly output of 10,000 loaves is inefficient because suppliers of bread can be made better off without harming any consumer by making more bread available.

Similarly, the consumer who obtains the loaf of bread for $1 when 10,000 loaves per month are available is better off because that is less than the maximum amount the consumer would be willing to sacrifice for the bread. If suppliers of bread were to receive $1 for that loaf, they would be no worse off because their marginal costs would be covered. Therefore at least one buyer can be made better off without making the suppliers of bread worse off when the marginal social benefit exceeds the marginal social cost.

Figure 2.1 ◆ EFFICIENT OUTPUT

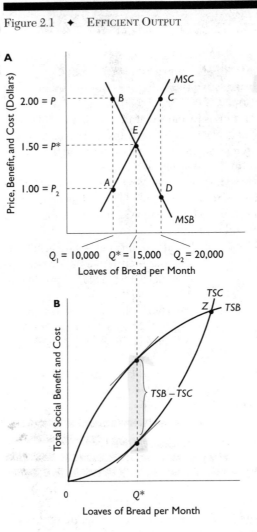

In **A,** *the efficient level of output, Q°, occurs at point E. At that monthly output, MSB = MSC. The monthly output Q° maximizes the difference between TSB and TSC, as shown in* **B.** *Extension of monthly output to the level corresponding to equality of TSB and TSC would involve losses in net benefits. Similarly, output levels Q₁ and Q₂ are inefficient.*

The **marginal net benefit** of a good is the difference between its marginal social benefit and its marginal social cost. When marginal net benefits are positive, additional gains from allocating more resources to the production of a good are possible.

Whenever the marginal social benefit of a good exceeds its marginal social cost, it will therefore be possible to make at least one person better off without harming another by producing more of the good. Net gains from allocating resources to additional production of the good continue just up to the point at which the marginal social benefit of the good falls to equal its marginal social cost. If additional resources were allocated to produce more of the good per month beyond that point, marginal social costs would exceed marginal social benefits. The marginal net benefit of such additional resource use therefore would be negative. In other words, if output were increased beyond the $Q^\circ = 15,000$ loaves of bread per month, consumers would be unwilling to sacrifice enough to compensate input owners for all the costs involved in making the extra units of bread available. The result is that consumers cannot be made better off without harming producers when more than Q° units of output are produced per month.

The **marginal conditions for efficient resource allocation** therefore require that resources be allocated to the production of each good over each period so that

$$MSB = MSC. \tag{2.1}$$

In Figure 2.1A, the efficient output corresponds to the point at which the MSB and MSC curves intersect. This efficient output is $Q^\circ = 15,000$ loaves of bread per month. If $MSB > MSC$, additional net gains from allocating more resources to monthly production of the good will be possible. The extra net gains possible from increasing output from Q_1 to Q° are represented by the area ABE. When $MSC > MSB$, at least one person can be made better off without harming anyone else by reducing monthly output. The output $Q_2 = 20,000$ loaves per month therefore is inefficient. The additional net gains that would be possible by *reducing* output from Q_2 to Q° loaves per month is the area of the triangle CED.

At the monthly output Q° at which $MSB = MSC$, the total net satisfaction (benefits less costs) from using resources to produce the item is maximized. As shown in Figure 2.1B, at monthly output Q° the slope of the TSC curve equals the slope of the TSB curve. At the output Q°, the difference between the two curves in Figure 2.1B is at a maximum. This difference represents $TSB - TSC$ per month; that is the surplus of the total social benefit of the good over its total social cost. This is the net total monthly benefit of the good. Producing more of the good each month until TSB equals TSC (at point Z in Figure 2.1B) would *decrease* the total *net* monthly satisfaction. This is because the monthly difference between total social benefits and total social costs declines as more than Q° units per month are produced. At the point where $TSB = TSC$ the total net benefit of the good is actually zero!

Maximizing the total social benefit of a good would require that monthly production and sales be extended indefinitely. This follows from the assumption that more of a good per month always makes persons better off. The efficiency criterion considers *both* the total social cost and the total social benefit of a good. It strikes a balance between the two by recommending maximization of the difference between total social benefit and total social cost.

C H E C K P O I N T

1. Under what circumstances will a resource allocation be efficient?
2. What are the marginal conditions for efficiency?
3. If the efficient output of mystery books is currently being produced, what is the marginal net benefit of mystery books?

Markets, Prices, and Efficiency Conditions

Now let's examine the workings of a system of perfectly competitive markets. An efficient economic system allocates resources so as to set the marginal social benefit of each good or service equal to its marginal social cost. Markets are, in fact, organized for the purpose of allowing mutually gainful trades between buyers and sellers. A system of perfectly competitive markets can result in efficient resource use in an economy. A *perfectly competitive market system* exists if

1.   All productive resources are privately owned.
2.   All transactions take place in markets and in each separate market many competing sellers offer a standardized product to many competing buyers.
3.   Economic power is dispersed in the sense that no buyers or sellers alone can influence prices.
4.   All relevant information is freely available to buyers and sellers.
5.   Resources are mobile and may be freely employed in any enterprise.

Assume that both buyers and sellers seek to maximize their gains from trading in such a system. Accordingly, buyers maximize the satisfaction they obtain from exchanging their money for goods and services in markets and sellers maximize the profits they earn from making goods and services available to consumers.

The market prices that emerge reflect the free interplay of supply and demand. Neither businesses nor buyers can control prices; they can only react to them. When deciding how much of a good to purchase, buyers consider their own *marginal private benefit (MPB)*, which is the dollar value placed on additional units of the good by individual consumers. When confronted with market prices, consumers trade until they adjust the *marginal private benefit received from consuming a good* per month to what they must forgo to purchase one more unit of the good per month. What they forgo is measured by the price of one more unit, that is, the amount of money they give up which could have been spent on other items. If the value of the money they give up (the price) exceeds the marginal private benefit of that last unit, they would be made worse off by trading those dollars for the good. Therefore, they maximize their gains from trading by adjusting the amount of any good they consume per month (or any other period of time) until the marginal private benefit, *MPB* received is just equal to the price, *P*:

$$P = MPB = MSB. \tag{2.2}$$

The marginal private benefit received by consumers purchasing the good is also equal to the marginal social benefit of the good, provided that no one except the buyer receives any satisfaction when the good is consumed.

Producers maximize their gains from trading each month when they maximize profits. When it is no longer possible to add to them by selling one more unit, profits are maximized. The firm will increase profits whenever the revenue obtained from selling an additional unit exceeds the cost of producing and selling that extra unit. The *marginal private cost (MPC)* of output is the cost incurred by sellers to make an additional unit of output available for sale. The extra revenue obtained from selling one more unit is its price, assuming that the firm can sell as much as it likes at the going market price.

The firm will maximize profits when it adjusts its output sold per month (or any other time period) to the point at which price is equal to the *marginal private cost* of output. If marginal private cost exceeds price, the gains from trade (profit) would decline. It follows that producers maximize gains from trade at the point for which

$$P = MPC = MSC. \tag{2.3}$$

The marginal private cost of output incurred by sellers is the marginal social cost, provided that opportunity cost of all resources used in making the product available is included in the sellers' total costs.

Combining equations 2.2 and 2.3 into one equation gives the following result:

$$P = MPB_i = MPC = MSB = MSC \tag{2.4}$$

where MPB_i is the marginal private benefit received by any given consumer.

A perfectly competitive market, in which both buyers and sellers maximize their net gains from trade, will result in a level of output for which marginal private benefit equals marginal private cost. If consumers are the only recipients of benefits when a good is sold and sellers bear all the cost of making that good available, Equation 2.4 implies that $MSB = MSC$ for the good. The market equilibrium therefore will achieve the efficient output. If this condition is met in all markets and all goods are tradable in markets, the overall allocation of resources in the economy will satisfy the efficiency criterion. When the prices of all goods and services equal the marginal social benefits and marginal social costs of these items, the market system achieves an efficient outcome.

Returning to Figure 2.1A, the MSB curve is the market demand curve. It corresponds to the maximum price that would be offered for various quantities of bread available per month. Under perfect competition, the MSC curve is the market supply curve. It represents the minimum price that sellers will accept to make any given monthly quantity of bread available. The market equilibrium is at point E. At that point, the price of a loaf of bread is $P^* = \$1.50$ and the quantity sold is $Q^* = 15,000$ loaves per month. P^* is the efficient price because it reflects *both* the marginal social benefit and the marginal social cost of the good. This equilibrium output, Q^*, is efficient because at monthly output

$$P^* = \$1.50 = MPB_i = MSB = MSC. \tag{2.5}$$

A system of competitive markets achieves an efficient allocation of resources when Equation 2.4 is satisfied in each market and all goods and services are sold in markets.

When Does Market Interaction Fail to Achieve Efficiency?

It is not surprising that markets operating under conditions of perfect competition produce efficient outcomes. After all, competitive markets are economic institutions that have evolved to allow gains from exchange of goods and services, and that is what efficiency is all about.

In the study of government, it is more interesting to discuss the conditions under which markets and prices will fail to result in the efficient outputs of goods and services. The possibility that political interaction might allow further net benefits to be squeezed from available resources then can be explored. However, political action will not always result in net benefits. Government activity itself can cause inefficiency. For example, the taxes necessary to finance government programs can, as you will soon see, impair the ability of markets to achieve efficiency. The marginal social benefits of a government program must exceed its marginal social costs to result in net benefits.

The basic problem that causes inefficiency in competitive markets is that prices do not always fully reflect the marginal social benefits or marginal social costs of output. This often occurs because of the nature of certain goods, which makes them difficult to package and trade easily in markets. For example, the services of such environmental resources as air and water are often used for disposal of wastes without adequate consideration of the benefits these resources have in alternative uses. This happens because rights to the use of environmental resources are in dispute. Because no one owns these environmental resources, market exchange of the ownership right to use these resources is unlikely. This means that sellers using environmental resources to make goods available do not pay for the right to use those resources. This leads to situations in which the marginal private cost of output incurred falls short of the marginal social cost.

Similarly, for services with collective or shared benefits, it might be difficult to package the benefit flowing from output into units that can be sold to individuals. When packaging into salable units is difficult, so is pricing. A means other than markets therefore must be found to make the social benefits of these goods available. The failure of markets to price and make available certain goods such as national defense and environmental protection gives rise to demands for government production and regulation.

Monopolistic Power

Markets also will fail to result in efficient levels of output when monopolistic power is exercised. A firm exercises monopolistic power when it influences the price of the product it sells by reducing output to a level at which the price it sets exceeds marginal cost of production. A monopolist maximizes profits at a level of output per month (or year) at which marginal revenue (MR) equals his marginal private cost. This is illustrated in Figure 2.2.

The demand curve for the monopolist's product reflects the marginal social benefit of possible levels of output. Assume that the monopolist's marginal private costs reflect the value of all inputs used to produce additional output and therefore reflect marginal social costs. The monopoly firm will produce output Q_M per month. This is the monthly output corresponding to point A, at which $MR = MSC$. When that much output is available per month, its price will be P_M. This is the marginal social benefit of that monthly output, MSB_M. Because a monopolist's marginal revenue is less than the price of the product, marginal social cost of production also will be less than the price. Thus, at a monthly output level of Q_M, $P = MSB > MSC$, as shown in Figure 2.2. Efficiency is not attained because $MSB > MSC$ at Q_M.

Efficiency could be attained by forcing the monopolist to increase output until prices fell to a level equal to marginal social cost. The additional net benefits possible

Figure 2.2 ✦ LOSS IN NET BENEFITS DUE TO MONOPOLISTIC POWER

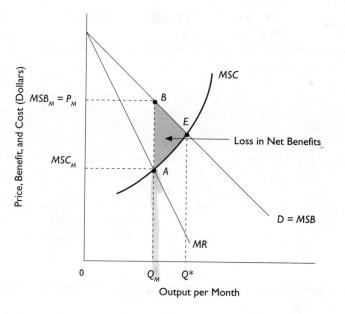

The monopolistic firm maximizes profits by producing Q_M units per month. At that output level, the marginal social benefit of the good exceeds its marginal social cost. Additional net benefits equal to the area ABE are possible if output were increased to $Q°$ units per month.

from increasing output from Q_M to $Q°$ units per month are shown by the triangular area *ABE* in Figure 2.2. This represents the extra social benefits over the extra social costs involved in increasing monthly output up to the point at which $MSB = MSC$. Government intervention in the market to increase output therefore would be prescribed by normative economists seeking to attain efficiency.

How Taxes Can Cause Losses in Efficiency in Competitive Markets

In Chapter 1 we discussed how taxes are used to reallocate resources from private to government use. Now that we know the marginal conditions for efficiency, we can begin to show how taxes impair the ability of competitive markets to achieve efficient outcomes.

When a product or a service is taxed, the amount that is traded is influenced by the tax paid per unit as well as the marginal social benefit and marginal social cost of the item. The tax *distorts* the decisions of market participants. For example, income taxes influence the decision workers make about the allocation of their time between work and leisure. Workers consider not only the amount of extra income they can get from more work, but also the extra taxes they must pay on that income when deciding how many hours per week or year to devote to work. When you work more hours, you receive less than the gross amount of wages paid to you. In deciding whether to work more when you have the opportunity to do so, you weigh the extra income *after taxes* against the value of the leisure time you give up. Taxes influence your decision to work by reducing the net gain from working.

A simple example shows how a tax can prevent a competitive market from achieving the efficient output. Suppose that the market for long-distance telephone service is perfectly competitive. The Figure 2.3 graph shows the demand and supply curves for long-distance telephone service. We assume that points on the demand curve reflect the marginal social benefit of any given number of message units and points on the supply curve reflect the marginal social cost of the service. The equilibrium output in the market, corresponding to point *E*, is 4 billion message units per month and the equilibrium price is five cents per message unit. The market output is efficient because it corresponds to the point at which the marginal social cost of long-distance telephone service is equal to its marginal social benefit.

Now suppose that the government levies a two-cent per-message-unit tax on sellers of long-distance services. Sellers must now consider the fact that each time they supply a message unit they must not only cover the marginal social cost of that unit,

Figure 2.3 ✦ TAXES AND EFFICIENCY

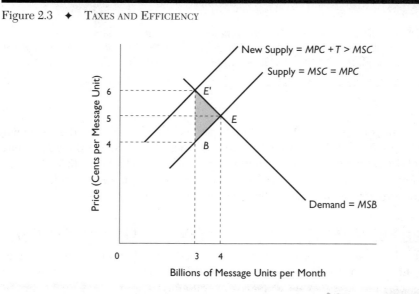

A tax on the sale of a product affects incentives to supply that product. In the graph above a tax on telephone service decreases the supply of the product. The price of a message unit increases from five to six cents. There is a loss in net benefits from telephone service because the marginal social cost of the new equilibrium output (corresponding to point E') is less than its marginal social benefit. The loss in net benefits is represented by the triangular areas E'EB. The tax costs more than the $0.06 billion in revenue collected when the loss in net benefits is added to the amount of revenue collected.

The Tax System and the Birthrate—An Example of Positive Economic Analysis

What does the tax system have to do with babies? The answer is quite a bit, according to recent positive economic analysis of the effect of the U.S. system of income taxation on the decision to have children.° The U.S. birthrate increased by 3 percent in 1990 and it will soon increase more, according to economists Leslie Whittington, James Alm, and H. Elizabeth Peters. These economists have examined how the U.S. tax system has indirectly subsidized the cost of raising children since 1917. They have set up a positive economic model of the choice to have children and then used the model to isolate the effect of the personal exemption of the U.S. income tax on the fertility rate in the United States from 1913 to 1984. The fertility rate measures the number of births per one-thousand women of childbearing age.

The personal exemption is a feature of the federal income tax that, as of 1994, allows most families to exclude $2,450 of income from taxation for each family dependent. For a family subject to a 28 percent tax rate, each additional child reduces the family's annual federal income tax bill by $686 = 0.28($2,450). The $686 annual tax reduction really amounts to a subsidy that varies with the number of children. Other factors considered equal, the greater the personal exemption, the greater the subsidy for having children. The value of that subsidy also depends on a family's tax bracket. For example, for a family in the 15-percent tax bracket, the annual subsidy resulting from a $2,450 personal exemption is merely $367.50. Finally, a low-income family that does not earn enough income to be subject to income taxation gets little benefit from the personal exemption. The benefit of the personal exemptions also is phased out for very high income individuals under current law.

For a middle-income family, the subsidy from the personal exemption ranges from 4 to 9 percent of annual child rearing costs. For additional children the subsidy amounts to as much as 14 percent of annual costs.† And the subsidy continues until a child reaches eighteen, or even longer if that child attends college. By reducing the cost of child rearing, the tax system therefore encourages families to have children; thus the positive economic analysis suggests that fertility rates, other factors remaining equal, varies directly with the value of the personal exemption.

Using actual data from 1913 to 1984, the researchers tested their hypothesis by conducting a statistical analysis of the relationship between the fertility rate in the United States, the personal exemption, and a set of other variables that influence the choice to have children. By statistically controlling for all other influences of the fertility rate, the researchers could isolate the relationship between fertility rates and the real tax reduction value personal exemption on average for all taxpayers.

The researchers concluded that an increase in the real tax value of the personal exemption will be associated with an increase in the number of births per thousand women. They then used their analysis to estimate the possible effect of recent increases in the personal exemption on fertility rates. The personal exemption increased from $1,080 in 1986 to $2,450 in 1994, and is adjusted each year for inflation. Using the historical relationship between the real tax value of the personal exemption and the birthrate, the researchers conclude that an 11 percent increase in the U.S. birthrate will result from this increase in the personal exemption. Their analysis suggests that middle-income families will get the greatest increase in the subsidy and their fertility rates will increase accordingly. On the other hand, the new law actually decreases the incentive of very low- and very high-income families to have children because many low-income families do not now pay any income tax and because the personal exemption is phased out for many families with very high incomes.

Some nations directly subsidize children through special family allowances. For example, the Japanese government gives families with more than one preschool child a monthly allowance. Many European nations also have family allowance systems that encourage families to have children. Although the U.S. government does not directly subsidize families with children, the federal tax system provides benefits that vary with family size and these benefits have been increasing in recent years!

°See Leslie A. Whittington, James Alm, and H. Elizabeth Peters, "Fertility and the Personal Exemption: Implicit Pronatalist Policy in the United States," *American Economic Review* 80, 3 (June 1990): 545–556.
†Whittington, et al., 546.

but also the two cent tax. The effect of the tax is to decrease the supply of the service as the price required by producers to expand service by one unit must equal the sum of the marginal private cost of the service and the tax per unit of service, T. In Figure 2.3, points on the new supply curve after the tax is imposed correspond to $MPC + T$ for any given quantity.

As a result of the tax-induced decrease in supply, the point of equilibrium now corresponds to E'. At that point the price of telephone services has increased to six cents per message unit and the equilibrium output has fallen to 3 billion units per month.

It is now easy to show how the tax has prevented the market from achieving efficiency and resulted in a loss in net benefits from telephone service. At an output level of 3 billion message units per month the marginal social benefit of the service is six cents per message unit. However, the marginal social cost of that output is only four cents! As a result of the change in behavior caused by the tax, the marginal social benefit of telephone service now exceeds its marginal social cost. The loss in net benefits from telephone service is equal to the shaded area $E'EB$ in Figure 2.3. The tax will collect a total of $0.06 billion per month in tax revenue, which is equal to the two cent per unit tax multiplied by the 3 billion message units sold per month after the tax is imposed. The cost of the tax is not only the $0.06 billion per month paid by taxpayers. In addition, there is the loss in net benefits, called the *excess burden* of the tax, equal to the area $EE'B$ from telephone service that results from the distortion in the choices after the tax is imposed.

When evaluating the marginal cost of a new government program we therefore must add any loss in net benefits from distortions in market behavior to the dollar amount of additional tax revenue required to finance the program. Government spending programs can provide net benefits to citizens in the aggregate only when the marginal social benefits of additional spending exceed both the tax revenue collected and the dollar value of the loss in efficiency (the excess burden) in markets that occurs as a result of the distortions in choices caused by the tax.

How Government Subsidies Can Cause Losses in Efficiency

Governments often subsidize private enterprises or operate their own enterprises at a loss using taxpayer funds to make up the difference. Taxes can impair market efficiency and so can subsidies. Let's examine the effects of agricultural subsidies and the operation of agricultural markets. Suppose that the government guarantees farmers a certain price for their crops. When the market price falls below the "target" price guaranteed by the government, the government will pay eligible farmers a subsidy equal to the difference between the market price of the product and the target price. Growers of wheat, corn, and other grains in the United States have been eligible to participate in a target price subsidy program like the one described here.

Figure 2.4 shows how the target price program works and how it results in more than the efficient output of the subsidized grains when the target price is above the market equilibrium price. The Figure 2.4 graph shows the supply and demand curves for wheat in a competitive market for this product. We assume that the points on the demand curve for wheat reflect the marginal social benefit of any given quantity. Sim-

Figure 2.4 ✦ SUBSIDIES AND EFFICIENCY

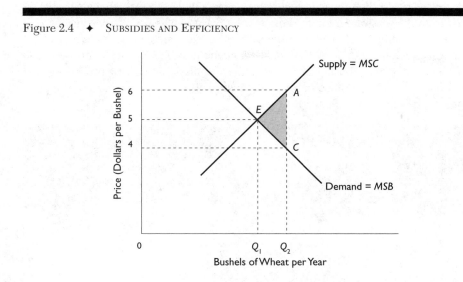

A target price of $5 per bushel is set by the government. Because this price exceeds the market price of $4 per bushel, the wheat farmers produce Q_2 bushels per year instead of Q_1. Q_2 is more than the efficient amount of wheat because its marginal social cost is greater than its marginal social benefit. The loss in net benefits from resource use is represented by the area EAC. The subsidy the government pays is $2 per bushel multiplied by the Q_2 bushels produced annually. After the subsidy the market price of wheat falls to $3, which is less than the marginal social cost of producing it.

ilarly, points on the supply curve of wheat reflect the marginal social cost of any given quantity. In the absence of any government subsidies, suppose that the equilibrium price of wheat would be $4 per bushel. At that price farmers produce Q_1 bushels of wheat per year because that is the level of output at which price equals their marginal cost. This would be the efficient output level because it corresponds to the point E at which the marginal social benefit of wheat equals its marginal social cost.

Now let's see how the availability of the subsidy will affect farmer decisions. Farmers know that they will receive a minimum of $5 per bushel of wheat. In deciding how much to plant, they will base their decision on the target price rather than the market price when they believe that the target price will exceed the market price. In Figure 2.4 they will produce Q_2 bushels of wheat per year because that quantity corresponds to point A on the supply curve for wheat where the marginal cost of wheat is equal to $5. The output level Q_2 is greater than the efficient amount because the marginal social cost of wheat exceeds its marginal social benefit at point A. As a result of the target price program, more than the efficient amount of resources are devoted to the production of wheat. Therefore the loss in net benefits from resource use is equal to the area *EAC* in the graph. In addition to this loss in net benefits that results from the subsidy-induced distortion in resource use, the target price program costs the government $2 per bushel of wheat multiplied by the Q_2 bushels of wheat produced per year. The overproduction of wheat relative to the efficient level that results from the program depresses the market price of wheat to $3 per bushel, corresponding to point *C* on the demand curve for wheat. The overproduction of wheat makes it seem cheaper than it would be without any subsidies. In fact, consumers end up paying only $3 per bushel of wheat while the marginal cost of producing that wheat is $5. The $2 difference between the marginal cost to producers and the price to consumers is paid by the government.

C H E C K P O I N T

1. Explain how a system of perfectly competitive markets can achieve efficiency.
2. How does the exercise of monopolistic power prevent efficiency from being attained?
3. Describe how taxes can affect incentives and cause losses in net benefits.

MARKET FAILURE: A PREVIEW OF THE BASIS FOR GOVERNMENT ACTIVITY

We cannot rely on markets to provide all goods in efficient amounts. Market failure to make goods and services available in cases for which the marginal social benefits of the goods outweigh the marginal social costs of those goods or services often results in demands for government action. The following forms of market failure to achieve efficient outcomes are commonly used as a basis for recommending government intervention in markets or government provision of services:

1. Exercise of Monopoly Power in Markets. When markets are dominated by only a few firms or by a single firm, the potential exists for the exercise of monopoly power. Firms exercising monopoly can add to their profits by adjusting prices to the point at which marginal revenue equals their marginal private costs without fear of new entrants into the market. To prevent monopoly control over price, governments typically watch over markets to ensure that barriers to entry do not act to encourage the exercise of monopoly power. Governments also often regulate the pricing policies of monopoly producers of such services as electric power, natural gas, and water.

2. Effects of Market Transactions on Third Parties Other Than Buyers and Sellers. When market transactions result in damaging effects on third parties who do not participate in the decision, the result will be inefficiency. This leads to demand for government policies to reduce the damaging effects of market transactions on third parties who do not participate in such decisions. For example, the exhaust fumes from cars, trucks, buses, heating systems, factories, and power plants decrease air quality and impair public health. In the following chapter the third-party effects resulting from market transactions are discussed, and government policies to deal with these problems are considered.

3. Lack of a Market for a Good with a Marginal Social Benefit that Exceeds its Marginal Social Cost.   In many cases useful goods and services cannot be provided efficiently through markets because it is impossible or difficult to sell the good by the unit. The benefits of such goods can be shared only. These goods are called "public" goods to distinguish them from private goods that are consumed by individuals and whose benefits are not shared with others who do not make the purchase. A distinguishing characteristic of public goods is that a given quantity of such goods can be enjoyed by additional consumers at no reduction in benefits to existing consumers. National defense is an example of a public good having this property. Increases in U.S. population occur daily and the additional population can be defended without any reduction in benefits to the existing population. Another characteristic of public goods is that their benefits cannot be easily withheld from persons who choose not to contribute to their finance. Even if you refuse to pay the costs of national defense, you still will be defended. This means that firms selling public goods like national defense will have great difficulty collecting revenue necessary to finance costs of production for such goods. Chapter 4 discusses the characteristics of public goods in detail and explain why it is likely that such goods will be supplied in less than the efficient amounts if markets are used to make them available.

In many cases government provision of goods is justified because of a conviction that the marginal social benefit of the good exceeds the marginal social cost at quantities that would result if the good were supplied through markets. For example, government provision of health insurance, deposit insurance, and flood insurance are common because many persons believe that these are useful services that cannot be provided profitably in efficient amount by profit-maximizing firms selling in competitive markets. Similarly, direct payments or subsidized loans to students attending institutions of higher education are often justified by arguing that government should encourage education because the marginal social benefits of its consumption exceeds the marginal private benefits received by individual students.

4. Incomplete Information.   We often demand that government intervene in markets because we have incomplete information about the risks of purchasing certain products or working in certain occupations. For example, we rely on government to test new drugs and to prevent hazardous products from being sold. We also rely on government to establish standards for safety in the workplace.

5. Economic Stabilization.   Market imperfections, such as downwardly rigid wages, give rise to excessive unemployment in response to decreases in aggregate demand. Governments engage in monetary and fiscal policies in an effort to stabilize the economy to correct for these market failures to ensure full employment. Governments also seek to avoid excessive and erratic inflation that can erode purchasing power and can impair the functioning of financial markets. Although the stabilization activities of government do not absorb significant amounts of economic resources, they do represent an important complement to the efficient functioning of markets. Economic stabilization programs are not discussed in this book. Modern public finance concentrates on the microeconomic aspects of government activity and finance rather than the macroeconomic aspects.

EQUITY VERSUS EFFICIENCY

Efficiency is not the only criterion that is used to evaluate resource allocation. Many citizens argue that outcomes also should be evaluated in terms of **equity,** that is, in terms of the perceived fairness of an outcome. The problem involved with applying criteria of equity is that persons differ in their ideas about fairness.

Economists usually confine their analyses of questions of equity to determinations of the impact of alternative policies on the distribution of well-being among citizens. For example, many people are concerned about the impact of government policies on such groups as the poor, the aged, or children. Positive economic analysis of the outcomes of market and political interaction is useful in providing information about the effects of policies on income distribution. In the field of public finance, analysts usually try to determine the effects of government actions on both resource allocation and the distribution of well-being, thus providing useful information that citizens can use to judge the equity of alternative policies in terms of their own notions of fairness.

The Trade-Off Between Efficiency and Equity: A Graphic Analysis

The trade-off between improvements in efficiency and changes in the distribution of welfare can be illustrated with a **utility-possibility curve.**[3] This curve gives the maximum attainable level of well-being (or utility) for any one individual, given the utility level of other individuals in the economy, their tastes, resource availability, and technology. Figure 2.5 gives all the efficient combinations of well-being between two individuals, A and B, per year.

If, for example, resources are allocated in such a way that the distribution of well-being between A and B is given at point E_1, then E_1 is efficient because, at that point, it is impossible to increase either A or B's utility without reducing the other's. Similarly, E_2 is also an efficient point. Points E_1 and E_2 differ in the distribution of well-being between A and B over a given period such as a year. Both, however, are efficient. Points above the utility frontier, such as Z, are unattainable. Given available resources and technology, the economy is simply incapable of producing enough goods and services to achieve the combinations of well-being represented by points outside the frontier. Points within the frontier are inefficient in the sense that it is possible to reallocate resources to improve one person's well-being without hurting another's.

At point X there would be incentives for either A or B to increase their individual utility by attempting to change resource allocation so as to arrive at some point on the section of the frontier E_1E_2. Whichever one makes the attempt, the other will not oppose it because that person would not be made worse off as a result of the change.

[3]The utility-possibility frontier is derived in Francis M. Bator, "The Simple Analytics of Welfare Maximization," *American Economic Review* 47 (March 1957): 22–59.

Figure 2.5 ♦ A UTILITY-POSSIBILITY CURVE

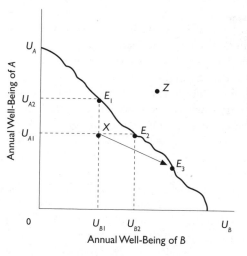

Points on the utility-possibility curve give the maximum level of well-being for any one person, A, given the level of well-being of any other person, B. Points E_1, E_2, and E_3 are efficient. Point Z is unattainable. Point X is inefficient. However, a movement from X to E_3 will be opposed by A because it would make him or her worse off.

The only reason a move from X to a point on E_1E_2 might be opposed would be if one individual were ill-informed about the impact of such a move.

Suppose, however, that B wants to move to point E_3. This will be opposed by A because that move would reduce A's well-being. A move from an inefficient resource allocation, such as that represented by point X, to an efficient one, represented by E_3, results in losses to certain groups. The movement from X to E_3 will make B better off at the expense of making A worse off.

Those improvements in efficiency represented by the movement from point X to point E_3 are vigorously opposed. Often the losing groups are effectively organized and work tirelessly through political institutions to block the change. It is no surprise that the policy recommendations of many normative economists for elimination of minimum-wage laws and international trade restrictions, on grounds that such elimination would improve efficiency, are continuously defeated in the political arena. These restrictions provide significant benefits to certain groups that prefer to resist losses in income. To understand why inefficient government policies and functions persist, it is necessary to investigate the opportunities that exist for both gainers and losers to protect their interests through political action.

The Trade-Off Between Equity and Efficiency in a System of Competitive Markets

A perfectly competitive market system can be given high marks because it is capable of achieving efficiency. The efficient outcome in a market system is a point on the utility-possibility curve. In a market system, each person's money income will depend on the amount of productive resources owned and the returns obtained from selling productive services to others in markets. The distribution of income will determine the willingness and ability to pay for the various goods and services that the economy can produce with available resources and technology.

Many critics of the market system argue that it cannot be given high marks on the basis of equity criteria. They complain that many participants in the system cannot satisfy their most basic needs because low incomes provide them with little capacity to pay for market goods and services. Poverty in the midst of wealth is regarded as inequitable by many. The market system caters to those with the ability to pay, which depends on earnings. This, in turn, depends on the marginal social benefit of resources that a person owns. The poor lack resources. Often they are unskilled and uneducated, and, as a result, the quality of their labor service is low. In many cases, the poor are unemployable or employable only at low wages. In addition, they usually own no land or capital, meaning that their nonlabor income is also low.

Critics of the market system also argue that these poor persons should receive transfers financed by taxes on more fortunate members of society. The incomes of the poor, and therefore their level of annual well-being, thus would be kept from falling below minimum standards. This, however, creates a dilemma. Often, as is shown throughout this book, the taxes and subsidies used to alter the distribution of income distort incentives to produce in ways that prevent achievement of efficiency. Policy makers are confronted with the inevitable conflict between the quests for both efficiency and equity.

POSITIVE ANALYSIS TRADE-OFF BETWEEN EQUITY AND EFFICIENCY

Positive analysis can be used to evaluate the effectiveness of alternative policies in achieving any given change in the distribution of income. The positive approach attempts to explain why efficient outcomes are, or are not, achieved. It can also be used to predict how government intervention in private affairs affects the likelihood of achieving efficiency while avoiding any direct judgments on the desirability of efficiency as an outcome.

Rather than recommending changes that will result in efficient outcomes, the positive approach attempts to predict whether changes in government policy or spending will be agreed upon through existing political institutions. The analysis is firmly based on models of maximization of personal gains from exchange. For example, it is entirely reasonable to expect individuals to support and vote for inefficient policies if their income shares will be larger under such policies. In effect, these individuals are content with a larger share of a smaller pie. Achievement of efficiency would allow the given amount of resources in the economy to produce more net benefits, but the total shares of this larger pie accruing to groups opposing the change would be less than what they would have with the smaller pie.

Referring to Figure 2.5, person A is better off at point X compared with point E_3, even though point X provides less aggregate net social benefit in the economy. Individuals are not concerned with net social benefit. Rather, they maximize their net personal benefits. The trick in devising efficient policies is to make maximization of net personal benefits coincide with maximization of net social benefit.

In evaluating public policy it is important to understand both the efficiency and the distributive consequences of alternatives. Improvements in efficiency are often opposed vigorously by special-interest groups that would suffer losses if the improvements were enacted. These groups are concerned with protecting their income shares at the expense of reduced output and well-being in the economy as a whole. The actual policies and institutions that emerge reflect the conflict between groups of individuals seeking to protect and enlarge their income shares and the benefits of efficient resource use that accrue to individuals comprising the entire community. A further factor affecting the outcome is the effectiveness of economic institutions in allowing those who receive benefits from policy change to bargain with those who bear costs so as to reach a compromise agreement.

One problem in using the efficiency criterion as a normative tool is that the actual number of allocative changes that will satisfy the criterion might be few and quickly exhausted. Most debates concerning resource allocation (for example, how to allocate scarce resources between expenditures on defense and other uses) involve benefits to some groups and losses to other groups.

In such cases, no one can easily predict whether the change in resource allocation will be made, inasmuch as the results will be both gainers and losers. The efficiency criterion, strictly speaking, can only recommend changes when there are gainers only (and no losers) or when the gainers can compensate the losers at transaction costs that do not exceed the gains. Some normative theorists try to overcome this problem by using **compensation criteria,** which attempt to measure the value of the gains to gainers in dollar terms and compare these with the dollar value of the losses to losers. If the value of gains outweighs the value of losses, they argue that it is efficient to make the change, regardless of whether the losers are compensated for their losses.[4] Such a change, however, still will be opposed by the losers. Although some might argue that the change will improve efficiency, its approval cannot be predicted because it involves losses in income to some individuals. Most public policy issues involve trade-offs between gains in efficiency obtained at the expense of losses by certain groups.

The positive approach can make a genuine contribution by generating information on the gains, losses, and transaction costs associated with particular policy changes and on the distribution of such benefits and costs among citizens. Without such information, it would be impossible for the normative economist to make prescriptions for achieving efficiency in resource allocation and for attaining equity goals. Such information is indispensable to voters themselves when they are deciding how to vote on questions concerning the functions of government and the extent of its powers and expenditures.

---

[4]This is known as the Kaldor-Hicks criterion. See Nicholas Kaldor, "Welfare Propositions of Economics and Interpersonal Comparisons of Utility," *Economic Journal* 49 (September 1939): 549–552.

INTERNATIONAL VIEW

AGRICULTURAL SUBSIDIES, INTERNATIONAL TRADE RESTRICTIONS, AND GLOBAL EFFICIENCY

Farmers are a potent political force not only in the United States but also in Japan, South Korea, and nations in Western Europe. Governments have responded to the political power of agricultural interests by imposing barriers that prevent or limit imports of agricultural commodities. Price supports and subsidies to farmers cause global losses in efficiency by distorting the world prices of agricultural commodities and the global pattern of resource use. The subsidies waste resources when they protect high-cost domestic producers at the expense of domestic consumers and low-cost producers in other nations.

For example, farmers in the nations of the European Union (EU) have been protected by a complex set of import restrictions and government subsidies that insulates farmers from international competition. As a result, domestic food prices in Western Europe are higher than they would be if the borders of these European nations were open to competition. Japan has protected rice growers by restricting imports of rice. The restriction on imports of rice into Japan deprives the United States and other low-cost rice producers of a market for exports while making Japanese consumers pay very high prices for this staple of their diet.

The governments of the nations in the EU set high prices for a variety of agricultural products. These high prices have resulted in huge agricultural surpluses that have been exported with government subsidies making up the difference between the world price and the higher price guaranteed to European farmers. The export of surplus agricultural commodities by the EU nations also result in low incomes to more efficient agricultural producers elsewhere in the world by depressing the world price of the commodities sold by these nations.

As a result of agricultural protection policies, global efficiency in the use of resources is reduced. More than the efficient amount of resources is devoted to agriculture in high-cost areas while less land is devoted to agriculture in relatively efficient low-cost areas. If protectionist policies were eliminated, more resources would be devoted to manufacturing and other industries in Western Europe. In low-cost agricultural nations there would be an increase in resources devoted to agriculture and an increase in the exports of agricultural products.

All member nations of GATT agreed in 1993 to reduce the volume of subsidized agricultural exports by 21 percent over a six-year period. Bans on rice imports in Japan and South Korea have also been lifted. These and other reductions in agricultural subsidies and quotas under GATT could result in a very substantial fall in the price of food in nations that support the prices of agricultural commodities. As price supports are eliminated, the huge agricultural surpluses would be eliminated and the exports of crops from the high-cost nations would decline, causing the world market prices to rise. These higher world prices could increase the income-earning potential for farmers in many impoverished nations.

Summary

Resources are efficiently allocated when the well-being of any one person cannot be increased without harming another. This condition is attained when all goods are consumed over any period up to the point at which the marginal social benefit of each good equals its marginal social cost.

When prices in competitive markets reflect marginal social costs and benefits, market exchange achieves efficiency. In cases for which interaction between buyers and sellers in competitive markets does not result in an efficient outcome, government intervention can be prescribed to help achieve efficiency.

Changes in policy that move the economy toward efficiency are often opposed because they result in a change in income distribution. Individuals opposing actions that improve efficiency act rationally. They are simply better off with a larger share of a smaller pie. To predict outcomes in any political process, it is necessary to know the benefits of any changes proposed, to whom they accrue, and what changes in the distribution of income result.

A Forward Look

The appendix to this chapter develops a more rigorous model of efficient resource use. The following chapter further explores the implications of market failure to achieve efficiency. The causes, implications, and remedies for the failure of an unregulated system of markets to achieve efficiency are extensively discussed. The framework developed in Chapter 3 is further applied in the discussion of public goods in Chapter 4.

Important Concepts

Positive Economics
Normative Economics
The Efficiency Criterion
Marginal Social Benefit
Marginal Social Cost
Total Social Benefit
Total Social Cost
Marginal Net Benefit
Marginal Conditions for Efficient Resource Allocation
Equity
Utility-Possibility Curve
Compensation Criteria

Questions for Review

1. How are normative statements distinguished from positive statements? Look through a daily newspaper for articles on politics and make a list of statements regarding current issues; indicate which are positive and which are normative.
2. How does trading improve efficiency? Why are trades that apparently provide mutual gains to those involved not undertaken? Show how equating the total social benefit of a good with its total social cost will result in more than the efficient output of the good.
3. Suppose you have more books than you want but would like to have more sporting goods. Explain how your well-being would be affected if a law existed preventing the trading of books for sporting goods. How would such a law affect efficiency in the use of resources? Show how a law banning the sale of books will cause a loss in efficiency. How can these losses be measured?

4. Why might individuals support the status quo over policies that can be shown to improve efficiency? Examine your own views on issues relating to social policy and ask yourself whether you would support such policies as the elimination of tariffs and other barriers to international trade, which might improve efficiency in the use of productive resources. How would quotas on imports of Japanese cars affect you personally? Suppose you owned stock in General Motors or worked in an automobile factory; would that affect your support for the quotas?
5. Relate the concept of efficiency to points on a utility-possibility curve.
6. Suppose a politician asks consultants to calculate the total social cost and the social benefit of the activities in a government agency. The politician discovers that total social benefits exceed total social costs. Does this imply that the activities of the agency should be increased to achieve efficiency?
7. Suppose the marginal social cost of fighter aircraft each year exceeds their marginal social benefit. Are fighter aircraft being produced at an efficient level?
8. The marginal social benefit of college enrollments currently exceeds its marginal social cost. Use a graph to demonstrate the gain in efficiency that would result from an increase in college enrollment.
9. The price of automobiles currently equals both the marginal social benefit and the marginal social cost at existing annual output. A tax is levied on the sale of cars. Assuming that the tax increases the marginal private cost of sellers, show how it will cause a loss in efficiency in the automobile market.
10. Efficiency can correspond to more than one distribution of well-being. Can the efficiency criterion be used to rank one distribution over another?

Problems

1. The following table shows how the total social benefit and total social cost of summer outdoor concerts in Central City vary with the number of performances.

Number of Concerts	Total Social Benefit	Total Social Cost
1	$10,000	$ 5,000
2	$15,000	$11,000
3	$18,000	$18,000
4	$20,000	$26,000
5	$21,000	$36,000

What is the efficient number of concerts?

2. a. Suppose the marginal social cost of television sets is $100. This is constant and equal to the average cost of television sets. The annual demand for television sets is given by the following equation, $Q = 200,000 - 500P$. If television sets are sold in a perfectly competitive market, calculate the annual number sold. Under what circumstances will the market equilibrium be efficient?

   b. Show the losses in well-being each year that would result from a law limiting sales of television sets to 100,000 per year. Show the effect on the price, marginal social benefit, and marginal social cost of television sets. Show the net loss in well-being that will result from a complete ban on the sales of television sets.

3. A prominent senator has calculated the total social benefit of the current amount of space exploration at $3 billion per year. The total social cost of space exploration is currently only $2 billion. The senator argues that a net gain to society would result by increasing the amount of space exploration until total costs rise enough to equal total benefits. Is the senator's logic correct?

4. The market equilibrium price for rice in Japan would be $3 per pound in the absence of government subsidies to rice production. However, the government sets the price of rice at $5 per pound and agrees to buy all the rice produced by farmers at that price. Assume that points on the demand curve for rice equal the marginal social benefit of alternative quantities while points on an upward sloping supply curve equal the marginal social cost of various quantities. Show how the subsidy program will result in losses in efficiency.

Suggestions for Further Reading

Bator, Francis M. "The Simple Analytics of Welfare Maximization." *American Economic Review* 47 (March 1957): 22–59. A modern classic providing a clear and crisp exposition of the Paretian model of welfare economics.

Congress of the United States, Congressional Budget Office. *The Outlook for Farm Commodity Program Spending, Fiscal Years 1991–1996.* Washington, D.C.: U.S. Government Printing Office, June 1991. This report outlines the way the government subsidizes farmers in the United States and projects spending under the various agricultural support programs up to 1996.

Pasour, E. C., Jr. *Agriculture and the State.* Oakland CA: Independent Institute, 1990. An analysis of the impact of U.S. farm subsidy programs and agricultural policy in general on resource use.

Slemrod, Joel, ed. *Tax Policy and the Economy,* 8, Cambridge, MA: The MIT Press, 1994. A summary of recent research of the economic effects of taxation on economic performance in the United States. Includes analysis of both subsidies and taxes on market choices and efficiency.

Appendix
2

WELFARE ECONOMICS

Welfare economics is the normative analysis of economic interaction that seeks to determine the conditions for efficient resource use. This appendix develops a basic model to investigate how the economic well-being of persons is related to economic variables. Extensive use is made of graphic analysis. Efficiency conditions are derived from the analysis. A good background in microeconomics is necessary for understanding the material in this appendix. For those who skip the appendix, the basic notions of efficiency and the efficiency conditions derived in Chapter 2 are sufficient for understanding the analysis to follow in the rest of this text.

A MODEL OF EFFICIENT RESOURCE USE

Suppose two individuals annually produce and consume two goods produced with two inputs, given technology.[5] The consumption or production of each good is at costs that reflect the full social value of all resources used. The two inputs are labor and capital. These are used to produce food and clothing. The problem is to find the allocation of inputs to the alternative outputs and the allocation of outputs among individuals (A and B) that satisfy the efficiency conditions.

Production and Technology

Consider, first, the technological relationships within this economy. The two production functions are one for food and another for clothing. Such functions, by definition, give the maximum attainable output from any input combination. Call the annual output of food F and the annual output of clothing C. If L_F is the amount of labor used in the production of food and K_F is the amount of capital used in the production of food each year, then

$$F = F(L_F, K_F) \tag{2A.1}$$

is the production function for food.

---

[5]The model can easily be expanded to include many goods, inputs, and persons. A multidimensional model requires the use of calculus to derive the efficiency conditions.

Similarly, if C is the annual output of clothing and L_C is the amount of labor used in the production of clothing, while K_C is the amount of capital used in the production of clothing each year, then

$$C = C(L_C, K_C) \tag{2A.2}$$

is the production function for clothing.

The output of food depends only on the inputs used in producing food and not on those used in producing clothing. Similarly, the output of clothing depends only on the amounts of labor and capital used in the process of producing clothing.

In addition, all available labor and capital will be fully employed in the production of food and clothing. If L is the total annual available labor services and K is the annual available capital services, then this condition can be written as follows:

$$L = L_F + L_C \tag{2A.3}$$

$$K = K_F + K_C. \tag{2A.4}$$

L_F, L_C, K_F, and K_C are variables with values to be solved in the model. L and K are assumed to be in fixed supply

PRODUCTIVE EFFICIENCY

Productive efficiency exists if it is not possible to reallocate inputs to alternative uses in such a manner as to increase the output of any one good without reducing the output of some alternative good. For a two-goods world, this criterion will be met when, for any specified output level of one good, the maximum possible amount of the alternative good is being produced, given the community's endowment of inputs and technology.

The next step is to determine the condition that will lead to productive efficiency in the use of inputs. This may be accomplished by employing an *Edgeworth box*. The length of the horizontal side of the rectangle illustrated in Figure 2A.1 equals the total available labor services per year, L. The length of the vertical side of the box represents the total available capital services per year, K. Measure the amount of capital used in the production of food upward along the vertical side of the box, $0K$, and measure the amount of labor used in production of food along the horizontal side of the box, $0L$. If productive resources are presumed to be always fully employed, then it must follow that any labor or capital not used in the production of food must be used in the production of clothing. This can be seen by simply rearranging terms in Equations 2A.3 and 2A.4 as follows:

$$L_C = L - L_F \tag{2A.5}$$

$$K_C = K - K_F. \tag{2A.6}$$

The diagram accounts for Equations 2A.5 and 2A.6 by measuring the amounts of labor and capital used in the production of clothing from the origin $0'$. Any point

Figure 2A.1 ✦ PRODUCTIVE EFFICIENCY

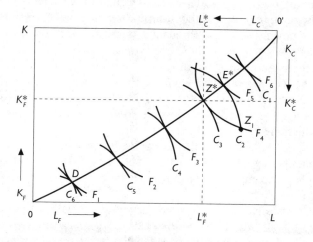

All input allocations corresponding to tangencies of the food and clothing isoquants satisfy the conditions for productive efficiency.

within the Edgeworth box therefore will correspond to certain values of the four variables L_F, K_F, L_C, and K_C. For example, at point Z^*, the four values are

$$L_F = 0L_F^\circ, L_C = 0'L_C^\circ$$

$$K_F = 0K_F^\circ, K_C = 0'K_C^\circ.$$

It is a simple matter to plot the isoquants corresponding to the production functions for food and clothing within the box. Use 0 as the origin for plotting the food isoquants labeled F_1 to F_6. The marginal rate of technical substitution of labor for capital diminishes as more labor is substituted for capital in the production of food. Through any point within the box will be, of course, an isoquant corresponding to some level of production of food. Isoquants farther away from the origin 0 represent higher production levels for food.

In the same fashion, isoquants corresponding to different levels of production for clothing can be plotted. Now, however, $0'$ is used as the origin. The isoquants for clothing, labeled C_1 to C_6 therefore are convex to $0'$, and those farther from $0'$ correspond to higher levels of production of clothing. Now, it easily can be seen that each point within the box corresponds to values for six variables. Referring again to point Z^*, it has already been shown that it corresponds to values of L_F, K_F, L_C, and K_C. As soon as the input mix is specified, so are the production levels of the two outputs (see Equations 2A.1 and 2A.2). Therefore, at point Z^*, the use of $0L_F^\circ$ labor and $0K_F^\circ$ capital in the production of food implies an annual output level of F_4 of food, where F_4 is the level of production of the good corresponding to the isoquant through Z^*. The annual output of clothing at Z^* is C_3.

At point Z_1 in Figure 2A.1, the input combination used results in an annual output F_4 of food and C_2 of clothing. The input mix at Z_1 is not efficient. Why? Because it is possible to increase the production of clothing to C_3, which represents a higher level of production for clothing, without decreasing the production of food. This is accomplished by moving along the isoquant F_4 until the highest clothing isoquant is reached. (Remember that even though they have not been drawn in Figure 2A.1, there is a clothing isoquant through every point on F_4.) The highest that can be reached is clearly C_3, where C_3 is tangent to F_4. To move from Z_1 to Z°, simply reallocate labor away from the production of food while replacing it with capital. Once point Z° is reached, it is no longer possible to increase the production of clothing while the production of food is held at F_4.

Similarly, it can be shown easily that, at Z_1, the production of food could be increased without decreasing the production of clothing if the production of clothing is held at C_2. This is accomplished by moving along the isoquant corresponding to C_2 until point E° is reached.

Similar exercises can be performed for any point within the box. Only those points corresponding to tangencies between food and clothing isoquants will fulfill the requirements of productive efficiency. The line 00′ has been drawn to connect all the points of tangency. Along 00′, it is impossible to increase the production of any one good without decreasing the production of the other. Accordingly, 00′ defines all values for F, C, L_F, K_F, and K_C that satisfy the requirement of productive efficiency. All the points of 00′ correspond to tangencies between some food isoquant and some clothing isoquant.

The slope of the food isoquant is its marginal rate of technical substitution of labor for capital multiplied by -1 in the production of food. Writing this slope as $MRTS_{LK}^F$, it follows that all points on the efficiency locus 00′ are defined by

$$MRTS_{LK}^F = MRTS_{LK}^C, \tag{2A.7}$$

where $MRTS_{LK}^C$ is the slope of any clothing isoquant multiplied by -1.

The Production-Possibility Curve

The economic information displayed in the efficiency locus may be summarized in alternative fashion. To do this, consider what the efficiency locus implies. Given the economy's resources (L and K), any point on 00′ gives the maximum amount of food that can be produced for any given level of production of clothing each year and the maximum amount of clothing that can be produced given any level of production for food each year. This is precisely the definition of an economy's production-possibility curve. Plotting the annual quantity of food on the vertical axis of Figure 2A.2, and the annual quantity of clothing on the horizontal axis, the curve TT' gives the economy's potential for producing combinations of food and clothing efficiently, given its endowment of resources (L and K). The production-possibility curve has the usual shape; that is, it is concave to the origin, implying that an increasing marginal rate of transformation of food into clothing as more resources are devoted to clothing production in a year.

Each point on TT' gives a different annual output allocation for the economy, that is, a different combination of F and C. This serves to emphasize that an infinity

Figure 2A.2 ◆ THE PRODUCTION-POSSIBILITY CURVE

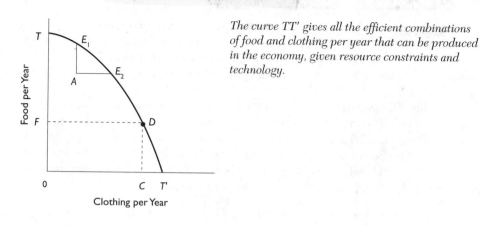

The curve TT′ gives all the efficient combinations of food and clothing per year that can be produced in the economy, given resource constraints and technology.

of output allocations satisfies the criterion of productive efficiency. However, no basis exists to decide whether a move from a point which is not efficient (a point within $T0T′$) to a point which is efficient (one on $TT′$) is desirable in all cases. Referring to Figure 2A.2, a movement from point A to any point on arc E_1E_2 can be said to be *desirable* because it increases the output of both food and clothing. However, no basis exists for saying that a movement from point A to a point off the arc E_1E_2, like D, is desirable. A movement from A to D increases the output of one good while reducing the output of the other. The same will hold for any movement from A to a point on $TT′$ off the arc E_1E_2. Only movements to points on E_1E_2 from A will be costless.

PARETO EFFICIENCY

Tastes and Utility

The welfare and tastes of individuals A and B are described by the following two utility functions:

$$U_A = U(F_A, C_A) \tag{2A.8}$$

$$U_B = U(F_B, C_B), \tag{2A.9}$$

where U_A is A's utility level taken as a function of the amount of food and clothing that A alone consumes each year. Similarly, U_B is B's utility level that is taken to depend on the food and clothing that B alone consumes each year. To derive the conditions for Pareto efficiency, it is again necessary to construct an Edgeworth box similar to that used for the case of production. However, a number of differences exist between the box to be drawn now and Figure 2A.2. The first difference concerns what goes inside the box. Now, instead of production functions for food and clothing, utility functions are plotted. Second, whereas the sides of the production box were taken to be fixed, the sides of the consumption box are variable; that is, the assumption was a fixed annual amount of labor and capital available to produce food and clothing. The side of the Edgeworth box for consumption represents the total amount of food and clothing available for consumption each year. It is clear that these are variables. One such box corresponding to the output of F and C, represented by point D in Figure 2A.2, is drawn as Figure 2A.3. An infinite number of boxes can be drawn—one for each point on TT'.

A's utility is measured from the origin 0; B's utility is measured from the origin D. Moving northeast from 0, A is successively better off as he moves to higher indifference curves. Similarly, B is placed on higher utility curves as she moves from D to 0. Any point within the box corresponds to values for the allocation of the total available supplies of food and clothing between A and B—F_A, F_B, C_A, C_B—such that the total available supply of food and clothing produced are consumed; that is,

$$F = F_A + F_B \tag{2A.10}$$

$$C = C_A + C_B. \tag{2A.11}$$

In addition, each such point within the box implies some level of utility for both A and B (this follows from Equations 2A.8 and 2A.9). It is not necessary to compare the utility levels of A and B; it is required only that A and B know when they are better, or worse, off.

Attainment of Efficiency

When it is no longer possible to make either A or B better without making one of them worse off, Pareto efficiency is attained. Assume that the output of food and clothing is fixed at F and C units per year.

Look at point E in Figure 2A.3. Is this point Pareto efficient? The answer is clearly no. Why? Because it is possible to make B better off without harming A by moving along the indifference curve labeled U_{A4} to point E^*. Moving from E to E^*, A receives more food at the expense of giving up some clothing each year while B gains clothing and loses food each year. At E^*, where the indifference curve corresponding to U_{A4} is tangent to that corresponding to U_{B4}, it is no longer possible to reallocate clothing and food between A and B so as to make one better off without making the other worse off. At point E^*, A consumes OC_A^* of clothing and OF_A^* of food while B consumes DC_B^* of clothing and DF_B^* of food. Point E^{**} is also a Pareto-efficient allocation of the fixed amount of food and clothing between A and B.

Points E^* and E^{**} are not the only positions of Pareto efficiency. There are many such points—one for each possible tangency between the two sets of indifference curves. Each tangency represents a different annual distribution of goods and well-being between A and B.

Multiplying the slope of any indifference curve in the box by -1 gives the marginal rate of substitution of clothing for food. MRS_{CF}^A measures A's willingness to exchange food for a unit of clothing. MRS_{CF}^B measures B's willingness to exchange food

Figure 2A.3 ✦ EFFICIENT ALLOCATION OF A GIVEN AMOUNT OF FOOD AND CLOTHING PER YEAR FOR TWO CONSUMERS

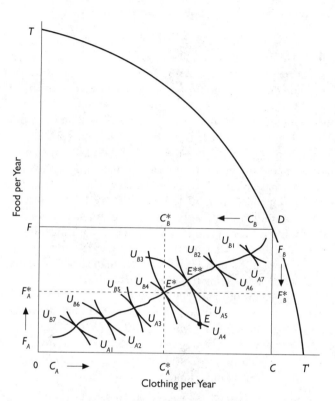

An efficient allocation of the two goods requires that the marginal rate of substitution of food for clothing be the same for both consumers.

for a unit of clothing. All points of efficiency within the box must satisfy the following criterion:

$$MRS_{CF}^A = MRS_{CF}^B. \qquad (2A.12)$$

Equation 2A.12 merely states that, in order for an allocation of the fixed amount of goods to be efficient, the two relevant indifference curves must be tangent, implying that their slopes are equal.

Now suppose that the annual outputs of food and clothing can be varied. It is now necessary to determine the efficient production levels of the two outputs, as well as the efficient allocation of goods among A and B. It is possible to "transform" food into clothing according to the terms implied by the slope of the transformation curve of Figure 2A.3 (the marginal rate of transformation of food into clothing). Not all the points on the locus of tangencies between the two sets of indifference curves in Figure 2A.3 are really efficient when the annual production of the two goods is variable. To understand this, suppose that at point E° in Figure 2A.3, the marginal rate of substitution of clothing for food is 1 for both A and B. Thus,

$$MRS_{CF}^A = MRS_{CF}^B = 1. \tag{2A.13}$$

Call the marginal rate of transformation of food into clothing MRT_{CF}, and suppose that its value is 2 at point D in Figure 2A.3. This implies that, at that particular point on the transformation curve, two units of food can be produced by diverting into food production the labor and capital used to produce one unit of clothing. But, by assumption, only one unit of food is necessary to replace one unit of clothing in order to keep A and B at the same level of utility at point E° in Figure 2A.3.

Therefore, if one unit of food is taken from A and replaced with one unit of clothing, he will not be made any worse off by this exchange. Needless to say, a unit of clothing taken from A has no effect on B's utility. Now, the resources that were previously employed to produce this unit of clothing for A can be diverted to food production, and, by assumption, two units of food can be produced. One of these must be given to A to compensate for the loss of a unit of clothing. But, this leaves one extra unit of food. The extra food can be given to either A or B or divided between them. In any event, either both of them will be better off than they were previously or one can be made better without making the other worse off. It follows that no allocation of resources can be efficient until all gains from exchange of this kind have been exhausted. This will occur only for those points where the rates at which A and B are willing to substitute food and clothing while retaining the same level of utility are precisely equal to the rate at which clothing may be transformed into food at the margin by diverting resources (labor and capital) from the production of one commodity to the other. That is, the following must hold:

$$MRS_{CF}^A = MRS_{CF}^B = MRT_{CF}. \tag{2A.14}$$

An Interpretation of Efficiency Conditions

A more intuitive interpretation of the efficiency conditions is made possible by allowing one of the two goods to be "money." Efficient substitution of money for clothing in Equation 2A.14 requires that A's willingness to substitute clothing for money be equal to B's willingness to substitute clothing for money, which, in turn, must equal the capability of the economy to transform money into clothing. The willingness to substitute clothing for money for both A and B is a measure of the marginal benefits they obtain from clothing. Assume as well that the marginal benefits obtained by each consumer reflect the marginal social benefit of the good. The capability to transform money into clothing is a measure of the value of alternative goods that must be forgone to produce another unit of clothing. This is the marginal social cost of clothing. Rewriting Equation 2A.14,

$$MSB = MB_C^A = MB_C^B = MSC_C. \tag{2A.15}$$

At least one output combination will satisfy the efficiency condition. The actual number of efficient output solutions depends on the differences in tastes among households. If A and B have different tastes, then any change in income distribution would alter relative demands and cause a change in the efficient output mix (that is, lead the economy to a new efficient point on the production-possibility curve).

Therefore, many allocations are likely to satisfy the efficiency criteria when tastes differ among households. Each one still differs in terms of the distribution of welfare. Insofar as A and B have different tastes, changes in income distribution alter the efficient-resource-use pattern. Thus, for any income distribution, the model specifies from the utility functions (Equations 2A.8 and 2A.9) the output demands of A and B. Given the income distribution, some efficient output mix (F, C) exists where $F = F_A + F_B$ and $C = C_A + C_B$, allowing both A and B to maximize their welfare within their income. The production functions (Equations 2A.1 and 2A.2) give the efficient allocation of inputs L_F, L_C, K_F, and K_C that are necessary to produce that mix. Thus, for any income distribution, the model produces a solution for the variables F, C, L_F, L_C, K_F, K_C, U_A, U_B, F_A, F_B, C_A, and C_B. All points satisfying the efficiency criterion of Equation 2A.14 are represented by the utility-possibility frontier (Figure 2.5 in Chapter 2).

Ranking Efficient Outcomes: Social-Welfare Functions

Some normative economists attempt to do more than simply specify the efficient outcomes. They try to develop criteria to rank alternative income distributions. No objective way exists to do this. Positive economists therefore have been extremely critical of attempts to rank alternative income distributions.[6]

The technique used by the normative economists is to postulate the existence of a social-welfare function. Social welfare, W, is taken as a function of individual welfare. Social welfare depends on the utility levels of A and B:

$$W = W(U_A, U_B). \tag{2A.16}$$

This function embodies ethical evaluation of the importance of A's and B's relative welfare in determining social welfare. The actual form of the function depends on the weights, or coefficients, that are applied to individual utilities. The function then can be used to choose among alternative efficient welfare distributions. Thus, the welfare distribution that maximizes social welfare is chosen as "best." Once the social-welfare maximizing values of U_A and U_B are known, the values of the other variables are determined easily from the utility and production functions.

EFFICIENCY AND ECONOMIC INSTITUTIONS

Pure Market Economy and Productive Efficiency

The efficiency criterion can be used to evaluate resource allocation in a pure market economy operating under conditions of perfect competition in all markets. Assume

---

[6]James Buchanan has argued, quite convincingly, that resorting to the social-welfare function is inconsistent with the basic value judgments of Paretian welfare economics precisely because it is based on a nonindividualistic ethic. See his *Demand and Supply of Public Goods* (Chicago: Rand McNally, 1968), 193–197.

that productive resources are privately owned and that no individual market participant has any power whatsoever to affect prices of the commodities or inputs that are
bought or sold. The price of any given commodity must be assumed to be identical
for all buyers and sellers of that particular commodity. This implies no distortions in
the marketplace, such as taxes, cause the price received by sellers to differ from the
price paid by buyers.

In a perfectly competitive market, producers take the prices of labor and capital
as fixed and behave in such a way as to minimize the cost of producing any output. If
the price of labor is P_L and the price of capital is P_K, then the total cost of producing
any given annual output is

$$C = P_K K + P_L L. \tag{2A.17}$$

As more labor and capital are used, the cost of production becomes greater. If cost is
held constant at C, Equation 2A.17 can be plotted on a set of axes, with capital measured on the vertical axis and labor on the horizontal axis. The resultant relationship
is an isocost line, defining all those combinations of labor and capital that cost C dollars. This is illustrated in Figure 2A.4. There will be one isocost line through every
point within the set of axes. Each isocost line corresponds to a different value of C.
Lines farther from the origin imply greater purchases of both L and K and therefore
greater total cost.

Now, consider the combinations of labor and capital that might be used to produce a particular amount of food, say $F = F_1$. The slope of the isoquant is the marginal rate of technical substitution of labor for capital in the production of food, say
$F = F_1$. This information is summarized in the isoquant corresponding to $F = F_1$
and is illustrated in Figure 2A.4. To produce this particular output of food at minimum cost, the input combination corresponding to the tangency of the isoquant with

Figure 2A.4 ✦ COST MINIMIZATION AND PRODUCTIVE EFFICIENCY

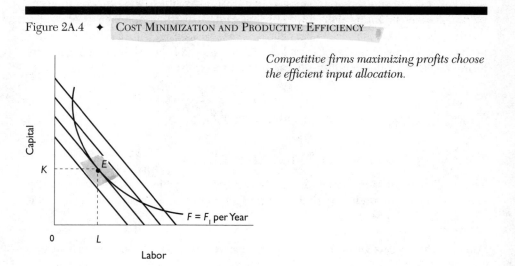

*Competitive firms maximizing profits choose
the efficient input allocation.*

some isocost line is chosen. At that point, the slope of the isocost line equals the slope of the isoquant corresponding to $F = F_1$. The slope of the isoquant is the marginal rate of technical substitution of labor for capital in the production of food multiplied by -1, while the slope of the isocost line is the ratio of the price of labor to the price of capital multiplied by -1. The cost of producing any output of food will be minimized when the isoquant corresponding to that level of production is tangent to an isocost line. Thus, the condition for minimizing the cost of production of any output of food is

$$MRTS_{LK}^{F} = \frac{P_L}{P_K}. \tag{2A.18}$$

A similar argument can be advanced for the production of clothing. The only necessary alteration is to draw the isoquant corresponding to a particular level of clothing production in Figure 2A.4. The conclusion is similar. To minimize costs of production for any output level, the clothing producer must set the marginal rate of technical substitution of labor for capital in the production of clothing equal to the ratio of the price of labor to the price of capital:

$$MRTS_{LK}^{C} = \frac{P_L}{P_K}. \tag{2A.19}$$

Now, assuming no distortions in the market, such as taxes, ratio of the price of labor with respect to capital (P_L/P_K) will be the same for producers of food and clothing. Because both producers adjust to equate their marginal rates of technical substitution to the same ratio of prices, it follows that they also adjust to set these rates of substitution equal to one another. Therefore, combining Equations 2A.18 and 2A.19 yields

$$MRTS_{LK}^{F} = MRTS_{LK}^{C} = \frac{P_L}{P_K}. \tag{2A.20}$$

Equation 2A.20 is the condition for efficiency in production. It follows that perfect competition in the markets for labor and capital implies that the criterion of productive efficiency will be satisfied; that is, the economy automatically will be led to a point on, as opposed to within, its production-possibility frontier.

A Pure Market Economy and Pareto Efficiency

Next, consider the decisions concerning the level of production for food and clothing. If P_F is the price of food and P_C is the price of clothing, the producers can maximize profits by selecting that level of output for which the price of each commodity is equal to the marginal cost of producing that output. Accordingly, profits are maximum for both food and clothing producers when they have adjusted their output to satisfy the following conditions:

$$P_F = MC_F \tag{2A.21}$$

$$P_C = MC_C, \tag{2A.22}$$

where MC_F and MC_C are the marginal costs of food and clothing, respectively. The information represented in these two equations may be combined into one equation by dividing Equation 2A.22 by Equation 2A.21:

$$\frac{P_C}{P_F} = \frac{MC_C}{MC_F}. \tag{2A.23}$$

It easily can be shown that the ratio of marginal costs in Equation 2A.23 represents the marginal rate of transformation of food into clothing.

The slope of the production-possibility curve can be interpreted as the amount of one commodity that must be foregone in order to produce one more unit of the other commodity. The value of the extra resources necessary to produce this one more unit is the marginal cost of producing that unit, as measured by the foregone alternative commodity output that could have been produced by them. In symbolic form, if ΔF is a change in food output and ΔC is a change in clothing output,

$$MC_F = \Delta C \tag{2A.24}$$

$$MC_C = \Delta F. \tag{2A.25}$$

Dividing Equation 2A.25 by Equation 2A.24 gives

$$\frac{\Delta F}{\Delta C} = \frac{MC_C}{MC_F} = MRT_{CF} = \frac{P_C}{P_F}. \tag{2A.26}$$

The bowed-out shape of the curve shows that marginal costs of production increase as the production of any good increases. To see the shape, move along the production-possibility curve from T to T' in Figure 2A.2, thereby increasing the output of clothing at the expense of decreasing the output of food. When this is done, the marginal cost of food will decrease because less is produced. The ratio of the marginal cost of clothing to food, therefore, increases, causing the slope of TT' to increase as point T' is approached.

Prices of food and clothing are given to persons A and B. Both A and B have a certain income level dependent both on the amount of labor and capital they own and on prices. This income level, together with the prices of food and clothing, determines their budget constraint. The tangency between their budget constraint line and an indifference curve in their indifference map defines the market basket of goods they choose in order to maximize their utility. This is illustrated in Figure 2A.5.

Given the budget line and indifference curves for A, point E represents A's equilibrium position, implying that he consumes F_A units of food and C_A units of clothing in order to maximize his utility. At E, the slope of an indifference curve is equal to the slope of the budget line. It follows that

$$\frac{P_C}{P_F} = MRS_{CF}^A. \tag{2A.27}$$

Similarly, for B at equilibrium, given B's indifference curve and budget constraint,

$$\frac{P_C}{P_F} = MRS_{CF}^B. \tag{2A.28}$$

Figure 2A.5 ✦ CONSUMER CHOICE

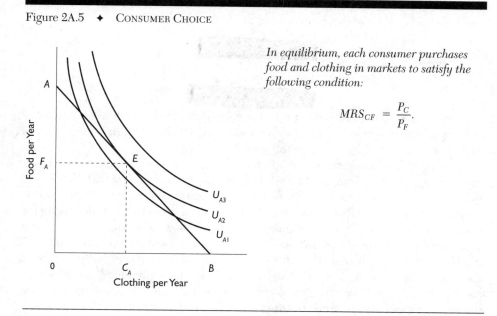

In equilibrium, each consumer purchases food and clothing in markets to satisfy the following condition:

$$MRS_{CF} = \frac{P_C}{P_F}.$$

If both producers and consumers react to the same price ratio, they will behave in a manner that will satisfy the condition for efficiency. To understand this, refer to Equations 2A.26, 2A.27, and 2A.28; the relevant slopes are equal to the same price ratio. It follows that these slopes must be equal to each other; that is

$$MRS_{CF}^A = MRS_{CF}^B = MRT_{CF} = \frac{P_C}{P_F}, \tag{2A.29}$$

which is the condition for efficiency. From a normative point of view, therefore, a perfectly competitive economy is desirable because it leads to efficiency.

Income Distribution

But many possible efficient resource allocations are likely if tastes differ between A and B. Which one will the market economy achieve? This depends on the initial income distribution between A and B, which, in turn, depends in part on the amount of productive resources owned by each individual. Their annual income is the sum of payments received by them in return for the services of the productive resources they own. Call the amount of labor and capital that A owns L_A and K_A, respectively. B's labor supply is L_B while K_B is B's capital. All the available capital and labor is distributed between A and B, so that

$$L = L_A + L_B \tag{2A.30}$$

and

$$K = K_A + K_B. \tag{2A.31}$$

Given the prices of labor and capital services, A's and B's annual income levels are I_A and I_B, respectively, and can be expressed as follows:

$$I_A = P_L L_A + P_K K_A \tag{2A.32}$$

and

$$I_B = P_L L_B + P_K K_B. \tag{2A.33}$$

If A and B have differing preferences, any change in the distribution of annual income will shift the relative demand for food and clothing, thereby resulting in a change to a new efficient annual output mix.

Under certain circumstances, A and B might agree to an alteration in the distribution of income. For example, A's welfare might be interdependent with that of B's. In this case, A might be able to improve his own welfare by making B better off. It would be in his interest, therefore, to give some of his income to B without asking for any service to be given in return. While such mutually beneficial transfers are easy to administer in a two-person world, they might require a more sophisticated administrative mechanism when many individuals are involved, each with different ideas about what constitutes a desirable distribution. Under these circumstances, a government might emerge from the community's political institutions to act as an agent for redistributing income according to an agreed plan that allows mutual gains (due to interdependent utility functions) to be realized through income redistribution. This implies that some households will pay taxes while others will receive transfer payments.

The kind of taxes that the government uses must be of a special type, and the government must be careful not to destroy the identity of relative prices, as seen by producers and consumers; that is, the taxes must not be reflected in any of the relative prices of outputs or inputs so as to distort them in such a way as to make the attainment of efficiency impossible.

Alternative Economic Institutions and Efficiency

Alternative economic institutions could conceivably satisfy the efficiency criteria. Productive resources might be owned by the state and could be allocated according to a central plan devised by a managerial agency. In such a Socialist economy, resource allocation would be efficient if the planners succeed in setting prices of resources and commodities that equal their marginal social benefits and marginal social costs. Given the prices, households and plant managers would then proceed to maximize their returns from trade. In the same way as described in the market economy, this would lead to an efficient outcome and would satisfy Equation 2A.14. The actual efficient resource allocation that would emerge under such a set of institutions would depend again on the income distribution. Because resources are not privately owned, the income distribution would have to be determined by the planners, and stipends would have to be paid to all citizens to achieve both that distribution and its implied resource allocation.

However, it's reasonable to believe that such a planned Socialist economy would not attain efficiency in a dynamic or rapidly changing environment. In such a world, knowledge about productive relations and consumption possibilities is likely to be a scarce good. Prices represent an avenue for communication of such knowledge. If a natural disaster occurs that destroys half of the world's oil supply, this information eventually gets to the citizen through an increase in the price of oil products, even though, at first, the disaster might be known only to a few. The market economy, with its allowance for rapid price changes, provides a mechanism for economizing on such scarce knowledge.[7] The complex interrelationships between and among markets, however, will permit rapid communication of occurrences in other markets.

In a planned economy, the managerial committee would require knowledge of changes in all markets simultaneously so as to achieve the same result and, likewise, the ability to change prices rapidly. If knowledge is costly to acquire, then it can be difficult for the planners both to acquire it and to use it to adjust prices in a way that would accommodate shifts in supply and demand. Thus, when knowledge is a scarce "good," a market economy then, in fact, might be preferable to a planned one, on the basis of the efficiency criteria.

MARKET IMPERFECTIONS

A number of conclusions can be reached concerning the desirable market structure in terms of the efficiency criteria. When producers possess a degree of monopoly power, they might influence the price of their output by manipulating their production. Prices can no longer be taken as given for these producers. To maximize their profits, producers no longer set prices equal to marginal costs. Instead, they produce that amount of output that corresponds to a point where marginal cost of output is less than price.

Because the demand curve slopes downward, the marginal revenue is always less than the price of the product. To reach the output level that maximizes profits, the monopolist must restrict the amount of production per time period to a level below that which would prevail if the monopoly were organized as a perfectly competitive industry. When the monopolist firm equates marginal revenues with marginal costs, it finds that marginal revenues are less than prices because the demand curve is not infinitely elastic (as is the case for firms operating under conditions of perfect competition).

If the producer of, say, food, has a monopoly, it produces that output corresponding to

$$MR_F = MC_F, \tag{2A.34}$$

where MR_F is the marginal revenue of food ($P_F > MF_F$) and MC_F is the marginal cost of producing food. If perfect competition remains in the production of clothing, the following will be true for the profit-maximizing output of clothing:

$$P_C = MC_C. \tag{2A.35}$$

---

[7]For a classic discussion of the knowledge problem and alternative economic institutions, see Friedrich A. Hayek, "The Use of Knowledge in Society," *American Economic Review* 35 (September 1945): 519–530.

Dividing Equation 2A.35 by 2A.34 gives

$$\frac{P_C}{MR_F} = \frac{MC_C}{MC_F} = MRT_{CF}. \tag{2A.36}$$

Because consumers set their MRS_{CF} equal to the ratio of prices P_C/P_F, it follows that, for any consumer,

$$MRS_{CF} > MRT_{CF}; \tag{2A.37}$$

that is, the independent maximizing behavior of producers and consumers no longer acts to achieve efficiency automatically. For this reason, monopoly is considered undesirable by normative economists. To maximize profits, a monopolist produces less, relative to a perfectly competitive industry producing the same good; in doing so, the monopolist prevents the market from attaining an efficient resource allocation.

Similarly, monopolistic power in input markets results in less of the input, say labor, being offered for sale, so that the sellers of the input might maximize their return. Monopolistic power in input markets prevents the attainment of efficiency in production. The normative economist, therefore, often recommends governmental regulation of competition insofar as this is necessary to attain an efficient resource allocation.

3

EXTERNALITIES AND
GOVERNMENT POLICY

LEARNING OBJECTIVES

After reading this chapter you should be able to

1. Define an externality and explain how positive and negative externalities can prevent efficiency from being achieved even when markets are perfectly competitive.

2. Describe how corrective taxes and subsidies can be used to internalize externalities.

3. Explain the Coase Theorem and its significance.

4. Prove how a system of tradable pollution rights or emissions can work to reduce pollution at lower cost than emissions standards.

5. Discuss command and control methods of environmental protection, and compare the economic effects of these with such market-based alternatives as corrective taxes and marketable pollution rights.

The federal and state governments have been in the business of environmental protection now for many years. As a result of government regulations and other programs, emissions of sulphur dioxide, smoke, and other particulates have declined substantially. There also has been considerable progress in the United States and in other nations in cleansing rivers, lakes, and streams of pollutants. However, environmental pollution remains a serious health and social problem.

Many citizens believe that they have the right to a clean environment and they naturally look to government to protect that right. Cleaner air will result in many benefits, including a reduction in diseases from pollution and a decrease in the medical costs to treat those diseases. A decline in smog and acid rain will preserve the beauty of natural resources that provide recreational benefits to millions of Americans.

Some of you undoubtedly have some very strong feelings about environmental protection and many of you regard it as a moral rather than an economic issue. However, environmental protection is an issue that has an important economic dimension because it boils down to a question of resource use and the legal rights to use the air, water, and land for disposal of wastes. Because it is technologically impossible to recycle all wastes (such as residues and gases that result from burning of fuels), a complete ban on the emissions of wastes in the environment could grind modern industrial societies to a screeching halt.

Business firms in the United States spent more than $30 billion in 1990 on air pollution control, and new legislation could increase this sum to $50 billion or more annually to meet new environmental standards. Some state governments are adopting even more stringent emissions control legislation than the new federal rules. The increased costs of pollution control ultimately will result in higher prices for many products.

But is it possible to improve the quality of the environment to the same degree at lower cost? To find out we need to examine how competing uses for resources results in pollution and the issues involved when governments limit the rights to emit wastes. We begin by demonstrating how the rights of some resource users are sometimes ignored as buyers and sellers go about their business in the marketplace.

EXTERNALITIES: A CLASSIFICATION AND SOME EXAMPLES

Let's examine some of the reasons why buyers and sellers in markets sometimes fail to consider their effects on third parties. **Externalities** are costs or benefits of market transactions not reflected in prices. When an externality prevails, a third party other than the buyers or sellers of an item is affected by its production or consumption. The benefits or costs of the third party (either a household or a business) are not considered by either buyers or sellers of an item whose production or use results in an externality.

The third parties are people like you who bear the costs of polluted air and water. These third parties often organize politically through groups such as the Sierra Club to lobby legislators and public officials to protect their rights to a clean environment. In the United States and other industrial nations, environmentalists have emerged as a potent political force to effectively induce governments to pass laws that limit the rights of producers and consumers to emit wastes that pollute the air, water, and land.

Market prices do not accurately reflect either all the marginal social benefit or all the marginal social cost of traded items when an externality is involved. **Negative externalities,** also called *external costs,* are costs to third parties, other than the buyers or the sellers of an item, not reflected in the market price. An example of a negative externality is the damage done by industrial pollution to persons and their property. The harmful effects of pollution are impairments to good health and reductions in the value of business and personal property and resources. Another example of a negative externality is the dissatisfaction caused by the noise of low-flying aircraft as experienced by residents who are located near an airport. Those bearing pollution damages are third parties to market exchanges between the buyers and the sellers of goods or services. Their interests are not considered by the buyers and sellers of goods and services when an externality is present.

Positive externalities are benefits to third parties, other than the buyers or the sellers of a good or service, not reflected in prices. Buyers and sellers of goods that, when sold, result in positive externalities do not consider the fact that each unit produced provides benefits to others. For example, a positive externality is likely to exist for fire prevention, because the purchase of smoke alarms and fireproofing materials is likely to benefit those other than the buyers and sellers by reducing the risk of the spread of fire. Buyers and sellers of these goods do not consider the fact that such protection decreases the probability of damage to the property of third parties. Fewer resources are devoted to fire prevention than would be the case if it were possible to charge third parties for the external benefits that they receive.

Effects of market exchanges on third parties are not externalities when those effects are included in prices. For example, if a person's hobby is photography, increases in the demand for photographic equipment by others could make that person worse off by increasing the price of the equipment. These higher prices, however, merely reflect the fact that such goods have become scarcer, relative to the demands placed on them. The higher price serves to transfer income from buyers to sellers and to increase incentive to produce these goods, while existing production is rationed through higher prices. Some economists refer to these as *pecuniary externalities*, that is, the effects of increases (or decreases) in the price of a good on existing consumers as a result of changes in the demand or supply of a good. Pecuniary externalities merely result in changes in real income of buyers or sellers. *Real externalities* are unpriced costs or benefits. They are the effects of market exchanges external to prices.

Externalities and Efficiency

Why do externalities pose problems for resource allocation in a market system? Unregulated competitive markets result in prices that equal the marginal costs and marginal benefits that sellers incur and buyers enjoy. When an externality exists, the marginal costs or marginal benefits that market participants base their decisions on diverge from the actual marginal *social* costs or benefits. For example, with a negative externality, business firms producing a product for sale in the marketplace neither pay for nor consider the damage the production or consumption of that product can do to the environment. Similarly, with a positive externality, buyers and sellers of a product in the marketplace do not consider the fact that their production or consumption of the item benefits third parties.

We can now apply the framework developed in Chapter 2 to understand why externalities prevent competitive markets from achieving efficient outcomes. Once this is understood, we can look at alternative government policies to correct the resource allocation problems that result from externalities.

Negative Externalities

When a negative externality exists, the price of a good or service does not reflect the full marginal social cost of resources allocated to its production. Suppose, for example, that in the production of paper, each unit of output results in cost to parties other than the buyers or the sellers of the product. Neither the buyers nor the sellers of the good consider these costs to third parties. The **marginal external cost (MEC)** is the extra cost to third parties resulting from production of another unit of a good or service. *MEC* is part of the marginal social cost of making a good available. However, it is *not* reflected in the price of the good.

A negative externality might be associated with paper production because of damages done by pollutants emitted into streams and rivers. The pollutants decrease the benefit obtained by other users of streams, rivers, or lakes. For example, industrial pollution from paper production could decrease the catch of commercial fishers. It also could reduce the benefit that recreational users of lakes and streams can receive from swimming, boating, and other activities.

Assume that the paper industry operates under perfect competition, implying that market power is diffused and that no one seller or buyer can influence price. The market equilibrium price and quantity in the competitive market corresponds to point *A* in Figure 3.1. The current price of paper is $100 per ton, and the industry produces 5 million tons per year at that price. The demand curve, *D*, is based on the marginal benefit that buyers receive from each ton of paper, also assumed to be the marginal social benefit of paper. The supply curve is based on the marginal cost actually incurred to produce additional units, such as additional wages and material cost,

Figure 3.1 ◆ Market Equilibrium, a Negative Externality, and Efficiency

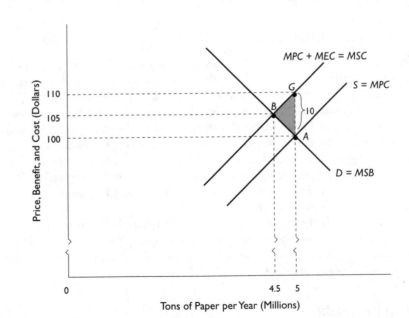

The market equilibrium output of 5 million tons per year is inefficient because MSC > MSB at that output. The efficient output corresponds to point B, where the annual output of paper is 4.5 million tons per year. The price of paper would have to rise to $105 to move to the efficient output. This will reduce the marginal social cost of paper from $110 to $105 per ton and result in net gains equal to the area BGA.

as firms in the industry produce more. But the marginal cost curve, as seen by producers, does not include all the cost incurred in producing extra units of paper. Suppose that a marginal external cost of $10 is associated with each ton of paper produced. In reality the marginal external cost could increase with output either because emissions per ton increase as more output is produced or because the damages done by the fixed amount of emissions per ton of output are greater when more is emitted per year. When the marginal external cost of production increases with output, the pollution damages per ton of paper are a more serious social problem at higher levels of paper output than at lower levels of output. For simplicity in this example we assume that the marginal external cost associated with each ton of paper is constant.

The marginal external cost of $10 per ton is not considered in the producers' choice of output. But external cost is as much a part of the opportunity cost of making paper available as are wages and materials cost. If the stream had no other use, then dumping wastes into it would cause no problem inasmuch as the usefulness of the stream to others would not be impaired. The negative externality in this case stems from the fact that dumping industrial wastes in the stream decreases its usefulness to other users.

The marginal cost that producers base their decisions on is the **marginal private costs (MPC)** of producing paper. To obtain the marginal social cost, the marginal external cost of output, MEC, must be added to the marginal private costs, MPC:

$$MPC + MEC = MSC. \tag{3.1}$$

When a negative externality exists, the marginal private cost of a good falls short of its marginal social cost of output. To obtain the marginal social cost of paper in Figure 3.1, MEC must be added to MPC for each possible output. Because $MEC = \$10$ at all output levels, the MSC curve is above the MPC curve. The distance between the MPC curve and MSC curve in Figure 3.1 is therefore $10, independent of annual output. If, instead, MEC were to increase with annual output, the distance between the MPC curve and the MSC curve would increase as annual output increased.

The competitive market equilibrium corresponds to point A, at which

$$MPC = MSB. \tag{3.2}$$

Efficiency requires that the full marginal social cost of a good be considered in the productive decision. As shown in Figure 3.1, the efficient equilibrium will be at point B rather than at point A. At point B, the following condition is satisfied:

$$MSC = MPC + MEC = MSB. \tag{3.3}$$

The marginal social cost of the good, including the marginal external cost, must be equal to its marginal social benefit in order to attain efficiency.

The market equilibrium output of 5 million tons of paper per year is inefficient because its marginal social cost equals $110 per ton at point G, while its marginal social benefit is only $100 per ton at point A. Because the marginal social cost of paper production exceeds it marginal social benefit, too much is being sold in the competitive market relative to the efficient amount. A gain in net social benefit equal to the triangular area BGA is possible by reducing annual output from 5 million tons to 4.5

million tons. The price of paper would have to increase to $105 per ton to induce consumers to cut back consumption from 5 million tons to 4.5 million tons per year. *When a negative externality exists, too much output is produced and sold in a competitive market relative to the efficient amount.*

Positive Externalities

When a positive externality is present, prices do not fully equal the marginal social benefit of a good or service. For example, suppose inoculation against a disease results in a positive externality. Those who are vaccinated benefit themselves, of course, by reducing the probability that they will contract a contagious disease. But they also provide benefits to those who do not receive inoculations by reducing the number of persons who will become hosts for the disease. This, in turn, reduces the probability of outbreaks of the disease for the entire population, including those who are not vaccinated. Eventually, if the disease is eradicated in this way, the entire world population will benefit. The external benefit of inoculations is the reduction in the probability that those other than the persons purchasing vaccinations will contract the disease.

Figure 3.2 illustrates how the sale of inoculation services in a competitive market will result in less than the efficient annual number if a positive externality exists. The market equilibrium occurs at point U. At that point, 10 million inoculations are sold per year at a price of $25 per inoculation. Suppose that the **marginal external benefit,** that is, the benefit of additional output accruing to parties other than buyers or sellers of the good, is $20 for each inoculation. The marginal benefit that consumers base their decisions on is the **marginal private benefit.** In Figure 3.2, market equilibrium corresponds to the equality of each person's marginal private benefit, MPB_i, of an inoculation with the marginal social cost of providing it. Assume that the marginal private cost of an inoculation to sellers accurately reflects its marginal social cost. At the market equilibrium, point U, the actual marginal social benefit of an inoculation exceeds the $25 price each consumer uses in deciding whether to be inoculated. The actual marginal social benefit of an inoculation, when 10 million are purchased per year, is $45. This equals the sum of the marginal private benefit received by consumers and the marginal external benefit (MEB) to others of $20.

$$MPB_i + MEB = MSB. \tag{3.4}$$

In general, when a positive externality exists, marginal private benefit will fall short of marginal social benefit at each level of annual output.

Less than the efficient output results from market interaction because the marginal social benefit at the market equilibrium exceeds the marginal social cost. The efficient output of inoculations corresponds to point V in Figure 3.2. At that point, the marginal social benefit of inoculations equals the marginal social cost incurred to produce them. The marginal conditions for efficiency are met at that point because

$$MPB_i + MEB = MSB = MSC. \tag{3.5}$$

At V, the marginal social cost of an inoculation would be $30. To get to that point, the price of inoculations to consumers would have to *decrease* to $10, which corresponds to point H on the market demand curve for inoculations. At that point, the quantity of

Figure 3.2 ✦ Market Equilibrium, a Positive Externality, and Efficiency

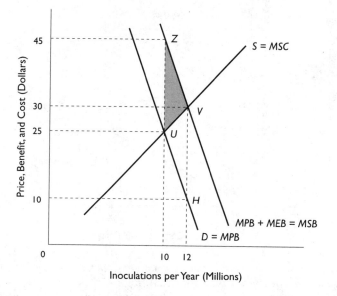

The market equilibrium corresponds to point U, at which MPB$_i$ = MSC. The resulting output of 10 million inoculations per year is inefficient because MSB > MSC at that point. The efficient annual output corresponds to point V, at which 12 million inoculations would be consumed per year. The price to consumers would have to fall from $25 to $10 per inoculation to move to that point. Moving to the efficient point allows net gains equal to the area UZV.

inoculations demanded by consumers per year would be the efficient number of 12 million. The marginal social benefit of inoculations, MPB_i + MEB, equals their marginal social cost of production at the efficient output. The increase in net benefits that would be possible by movement to point V is represented by the shaded triangular area UZV in Figure 3.2.

In actuality, the marginal external benefit per inoculation is likely to fall as more of the population is inoculated, because fewer people will be susceptible to the disease. If this were the case, the marginal external benefit would eventually fall to zero when enough persons were inoculated. Suppose that MEB gradually declined, eventually becoming zero at 16 million inoculations per year. In Figure 3.3, MSB exceeds MPB_i only if annual output is less than 16 million inoculations per year. The MSB curve gives the sum of the marginal private benefit and the marginal external benefit at each level of output. The distance between the MSB and the MPB_i curves decreases because MEB declines with output, as shown on the graph.

The implications of this type of externality for market failure are quite important. For example, suppose that the marginal social cost curve was S. This would also be the supply curve under conditions of perfect competition. Under these circumstances,

Figure 3.3 ✦ A POSITIVE EXTERNALITY FOR WHICH *MEB* DECLINES WITH ANNUAL OUTPUT

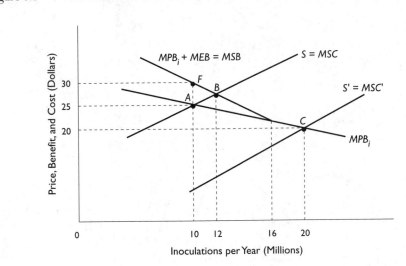

In this case, MEB declines as more persons are inoculated per year. If market price is $25 per inoculation, a loss in efficiency occurs because MEB > 0 at the corresponding output of 10 million inoculations per year. However, when the market price is $20, the market equilibrium is efficient because MEB = 0 at the corresponding output of 20 million inoculations per year.

the market equilibrium would correspond to point *A*, at which the price would be $25 per inoculation and the annual quantity consumed would be 10 million per year. This would be inefficient because the marginal social benefit of an inoculation exceeds its marginal social cost at that annual output. The efficient output would correspond to point *B*, at which $MSC = MSB = MPB_i + MEB$ and annual output is 12 million inoculations. Thus, a market failure exists.

Suppose, instead, supply were $S' = MSC'$. Under those circumstances, the market equilibrium would correspond to point *C*. At that point, the price per inoculation would be $20, and the quantity consumed per year would be 20 million. Is the market equilibrium inefficient in this case? The answer is no! This is because *MEB* = 0 at an annual output of 20 million. Therefore, no divergence exists between marginal social cost and marginal social benefit. For positive externalities such as these, with a marginal value that declines with output, competitive markets fail to perform efficiently only at low levels of output.

INTERNALIZATION OF EXTERNALITIES

Internalization of an externality occurs when the marginal private benefit or cost of goods and services are adjusted so that the users consider the actual marginal social benefit or cost of their decisions. In the case of a negative externality, the marginal external cost is added to marginal private cost for internalization. For a positive externality, the marginal external benefit is added to marginal private benefit to internalize the externality. Internalizing an externality results in changes in prices to reflect full marginal social cost or benefit of a good.

Internalization of externalities requires *identification* of the individuals involved and *measurement* of the monetary value of the marginal external benefit or cost. The data required for such identification and measurement are often difficult to obtain. Economic policy toward externalities is sometimes controversial because of strong differences of opinion concerning the actual value of the external cost or external benefit. For example, how can all the sources of air pollution be identified? How are the damages done to property and personal well-being evaluated? This is a formidable scientific, engineering, and economic detective problem. Because strong disagreement exists among physical and biological scientists as to the costs of pollution, the necessary information required for internalizing the externality can be elusive.

Corrective Taxes: A Method of Internalizing Negative Externalities

A **corrective tax** is designed to adjust the marginal private cost of a good or service in such a way as to internalize the externality. The tax must equal the marginal external cost per unit of output to achieve this objective. In effect, a corrective tax is exactly like a charge for emitting wastes. It is designed to internalize a negative externality by making sellers of the product pay a fee equal to the marginal external costs per unit of output sold.

Suppose a corrective tax were levied on producers of paper to internalize the negative externality resulting from their output. Figure 3.4 shows the impact of such a tax. The marginal external cost per unit of output is assumed to be $MEC = \$10$. The corrective tax, T, is therefore

$$T = MEC. \tag{3.6}$$

In this case, the tax would be set at $10 per ton of paper, the marginal external cost of paper per year. This tax is levied on each unit produced and will be treated by producers as an increase in the marginal private cost of production. Consequently, the supply curve shifts up from S to S', where S' reflects the full marginal social cost of producing paper. The increase in cost caused by the tax changes the point corresponding to the market equilibrium from A to B. The market price of paper increases to $105 per ton and the equilibrium quantity of paper consumed declines from 5 million tons to 4.5 million tons per year. This is exactly equal to the efficient annual output.

The tax of $10 per ton will collect $45 million of revenue per year at the equilibrium output of 4.5 million tons. This is represented by the area $FBJH$ in Figure 3.4. After the tax is imposed, the annual value of pollution costs to alternative users of the stream declines. Initially, these costs were $50 million per year, equal to the $10 per ton cost of pollution multiplied by the annual output of 5 million tons. Because annual output declines to 4.5 million tons after the tax, the annual cost of pollution from paper produced declines to $45 million.

Figure 3.4 ◆ A CORRECTIVE TAX

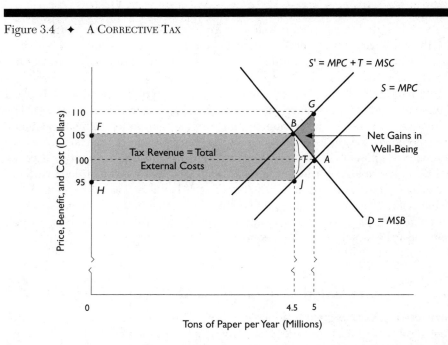

A corrective tax of T = $10 per unit output increases marginal private cost by an amount equal to the marginal external cost and results in the efficient annual output of paper. The tax revenue collected is represented by the area FBJH. This revenue equals the total external costs at the efficient output, provided that MEC does not vary with output. The tax allows net gains in well-being equal to the area BGA.

The corrective tax does *not* reduce the pollutants in the streams to zero. It merely raises the cost of using the stream to reflect the marginal damage done to alternative users of the stream. Paper producers that use the stream now compare this extra cost ($10 per unit output) with other alternatives of waste disposal and then decide how much of the stream's services to use at that cost. It is unlikely, though possible, that all producers will completely stop dumping in the stream. But, given the costs of alternatives, including the recycling of any wastes, purifying the wastes before disposal, reducing output, or going out of business, most certainly fewer wastes will be emitted. The actual amount of that reduction will depend on the availability and cost of alternative disposal methods relative to the corrective tax and on the impact of the tax on the profitability of producing paper. The tax is designed to force the producer to compare the marginal benefit (in terms of profits) of dumping wastes in the stream with the marginal external cost of emitting untreated wastes. It does so by adding the marginal external cost to producers' marginal private cost.

The tax revenue collected can be used for a variety of purposes. If the competing users of the stream are easily identifiable, the tax revenue collected, $45 million, could be used to compensate other users of the stream for $45 million in damages that remain after the externality is internalized by the corrective tax.[1] Alternatively, paper producers might argue that they should receive compensation for their losses in the form of a once-and-for-all payment to each producer. This payment would compensate them for the loss of their free right to dump. Finally, the revenue collected could go toward a reduction in other taxes or an increment in government services.

In summary, the corrective tax causes the following results:

1. An increase in the price of paper and a reduction in the quantity demanded, to the efficient level, where the marginal social cost equals the marginal social benefit of paper.
2. A consequent transfer of income away from paper producers and consumers in favor of individuals who use the recreational services of streams and of others who might have their taxes reduced or enjoy the benefit of increased government services if the revenue collected is used for those purposes.
3. A reduction in, but not the elimination of, use of the stream for disposal purposes and a consequent reduction in damage to alternative users of the stream.

In view of these results, the following predictions can be made concerning political support for enactment of such a corrective tax:

1. Paper producers, employees, and consumers will be likely to vote against it to the extent to which they are not involved in alternative uses of the stream and will not be compensated for their losses.
2. Recreational and commercial users of the stream, as well as taxpayers in general, will vote in favor of the corrective tax to the extent to which they have few interests in paper production or consumption.

To internalize the externality through the use of a corrective tax therefore will result in some groups receiving benefits at the expense of other groups bearing the costs. In other words, the internalization of the externality also will result in income redistributive effects, which, in turn, will influence the willingness of the individuals involved to support the scheme.[2]

The gain in efficiency resulting from the corrective tax is represented by the triangular area BGA in Figure 3.4. This area measures the increase in net social benefits when annual paper output is reduced to the point at which its marginal social benefit equals its marginal social cost.

---

[1]Compensation for damages in this way is likely to cause allocational problems if the number of alternative users of the stream is not fixed. Under those circumstances, new users would be able to enter without considering the effect of their presence on the paper producers' cost. For this reason, many economists argue against the use of tax funds for compensation.

[2]Refer to the utility frontier in Chapter 2. Unless paper producers are compensated for the loss of their unlimited right to dump, they will oppose the corrective tax and attempt to block benefits to those groups that use the stream for alternative purposes. Lack of compensation would imply a move such as the one from X to E_3 in Figure 2.5.

How a Corrective Tax Could be Used to Reduce Global Warming

A corrective tax on the emission of carbon wastes is one possible way to reduce the economic costs associated with global warming. Global warming results from the "greenhouse effect" of carbon dioxide and other gases that trap energy in the atmosphere. Carbon dioxide is a waste from the burning of fossil fuels such as coal, oil, and gasoline. The costs and extent of global warming are issues of enough concern to world leaders that delegates to a United Nations Conference on Development and the Environment in 1992 agreed to recommend a goal of reducing carbon dioxide emissions. Some scientific forecasts suggest that the amount of carbon dioxide in the atmosphere could double in the future, causing average temperatures to increase by as much as 9 degrees. The resulting global warming could then have high costs including reduced agricultural productivity, increased flooding from rising sea levels, and other damage to the natural environment. In 1990, 1.5 trillion tons of carbon were emitted in the United States alone!

A corrective tax on carbon emissions could hold U.S. emissions of carbon to the 1990 level.[3] The tax could initially be set at $2 per ton of carbon waste. The tax will have to grow with the demand for fuel to encourage conservation in later years. Because coal has the highest carbon content of all fuels its tax would have to be highest amounting to $11.46 per ton in 2020. In the same year the tax on oil would be $2.41 per barrel and the tax on natural gas would be 29 cents per thousand cubic feet. The higher taxes on coal are likely to raise its price by about 40 percent and, based on the elasticity of demand assumed by the researchers, the quantity demanded would decline by 25 percent. Higher coal prices would raise the price of electricity and induce power generating firms and users of electricity to conserve energy. The corrective tax on carbon also would raise the prices of gasoline, heating oil, and natural gas.

The tax on carbon could double current U.S. pollution control costs. To decide whether these additional costs are worthwhile requires a comparison of the marginal benefit of preventing global warming. Unfortunately, scientists themselves disagree on the possible effects of global warming, making calculation of such benefits difficult.

Internalizing Negative Externalities Associated with Goods Sold in Imperfectly Competitive Markets

Such economic problems as externalities are typically looked at one at a time. In many cases, however, two or more factors contributing to losses in efficiency might exist in a single market. Suppose that a negative externality is associated with output sold by a monopoly. Also assume that the transactions costs (through political or other action) involved in attempting to break it up are too high to make this a feasible alternative.

---

[3]See Timothy Tregarthen, "Economists Propose Taxes to Avert Global Warming," *The Margin* 8, Spring 1993, pp. 32–33. The tax levels are based on research by Dale W. Jorgenson of Harvard University, Daniel T. Slesnick, and Peter J. Wilcoxen, both of the University of Texas at Austin.

In this case, two distortions prevent the attainment of the efficient output. The firm's monopolistic power results in less than the efficient output. On the other hand, because the monopoly causes negative externalities, other things being equal, it produces more than the efficient output. A "first best" solution would be to break up the monopoly, thereby increasing output as competition among firms in the industry lowers price to a level that equals marginal social cost. The output of the competitive industry then could be taxed to internalize the negative externality. This would increase price in the industry and decrease output.

However, an alternative way exists to achieve the same efficient outcome. The monopoly initially is producing an annual output level lower than the one corresponding to the equality between price and marginal social cost. This is equivalent to saying that it is behaving as a perfectly competitive industry for which marginal cost has been increased to account, say, for a negative externality. In effect, the monopolistic distortion can offset part, or all, of the distortion resulting from the negative externality.

Figure 3.5 shows a monopoly producing output Q_M per year, corresponding to point C, at which its marginal private cost equals its marginal revenue. This output

Figure 3.5 ✦ A Second-Best Efficient Solution

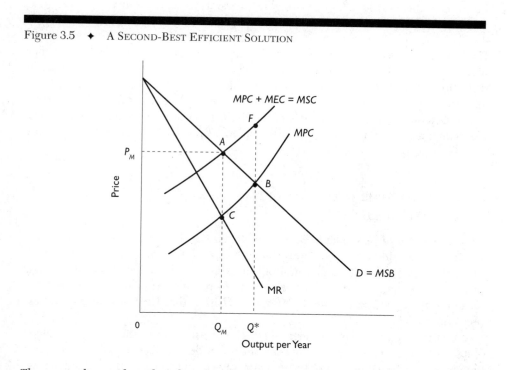

The monopolist produces less than the efficient output under normal circumstances. Here, however, the monopolist also generates external costs. The loss in well-being due to monopoly power is the area ABC. This is offset by a gain in well-being equal to the area AFB that would be lost if a competitive industry produced this output.

level is inefficient when the marginal private cost is also the marginal social cost. The efficient output would be Q^*, which corresponds to point B. The exercise of monopolistic power would result in a loss of net benefits corresponding to the area ABC.

If, however, a negative externality is also associated with the monopolist's output, marginal social costs would be $MPC + MEC$ at any output and therefore would exceed marginal private costs. The output Q^* would not be efficient because its marginal social cost would exceed its marginal social benefit. The efficient output, as shown in Figure 3.5, would be Q_M, corresponding to point A, at which $MSC = MSB$. As the graph is drawn, the monopolistic output *is* the efficient output!

In actuality, the efficient output could be greater or less than the monopolist's output. To emphasize the point being made, the graph assumes that the monopolist's output is, in fact, the efficient one when the externality is present. The monopolist's power thereby allows net gains in well-being equal to the triangular area AFB. This would not be possible in a competitive market. These gains offset the social losses from monopolistic power. A "second best" alternative to achieve efficiency is to allow the monopoly to continue operating. Efficiency could be attainable without even taxing the monopolist's output if the output reduction due to monopolistic power exactly offsets the external cost. In general, a corrective tax on the monopolist's output must be *less* than the corrective tax that would be necessary to achieve efficiency if the good were produced by a competitive industry.

This example illustrates an application of the **general theory of second best.**[4] Essentially, the theory states that, when two opposing factors contribute to efficiency losses, they can offset one another's distortions. If it is costly to eliminate a market distortion associated with some given economic activity, then, to achieve efficiency, an offsetting distortion in another economic activity by departing from the standard efficiency conditions in that activity is required. In evaluating resource allocations, the economist has to treat each problem on an ad hoc basis to see if there are any "second best" problems present.

Corrective Subsidies: A Means of Internalizing Positive Externalities

A corrective subsidy is similar in conception to a corrective tax. Figure 3.6 shows how a corrective subsidy for inoculations can result in the efficient output of this good. The competitive market equilibrium output would be 10 million inoculations per year at the competitive market price of $25 per inoculation. This is inefficient because the marginal social benefit ($MPB_i + MEB$) at that level of consumption exceeds the marginal social cost.

A corrective subsidy is a payment made by government to either buyers or sellers of a good so that the price paid by consumers is reduced. The payment must equal the marginal external benefit of the good or service. In this case, $20 is the marginal external benefit associated with each person inoculated. Suppose the government an-

---

[4]Richard G. Lipsey and Kelvin Lancaster, "The General Theory of Second Best," *Review of Economic Studies* 24 (1956): 11–32.

Figure 3.6 ◆ A CORRECTIVE SUBSIDY

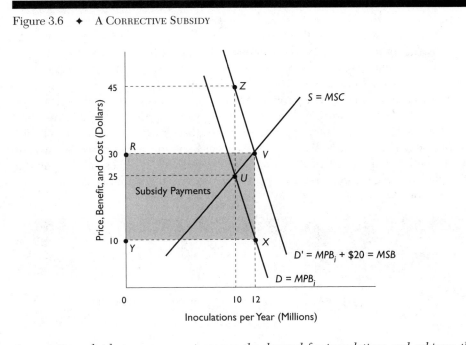

A corrective subsidy to consumers increases the demand for inoculations and achieves the efficient output. After subsidy payments are received by consumers, the net price of an inoculation falls to $10, inducing them to purchase the efficient amount of 12 million per year. The area RVXY represents the total subsidy payments at the efficient output.

nounces that it will pay each person inoculated a subsidy of $20. This subsidy adds $20 to the marginal private benefit of each inoculation. The demand curve for inoculations shifts upward from $D = MPB_i$ to $D' = MPB_i + \$20$. As the demand for inoculations increases, the market equilibrium moves from point U to point V in Figure 3.6. At that point, the market price of an inoculation *increases* to $30 to cover increased marginal costs of production. However, the *net price after receiving the subsidy declines for consumers*. The net price is now $30 − $20 = $10 per inoculation. This reduction in the net price to consumers increases the quantity demanded to 12 million per year, the efficient output.

The effect of the subsidy is to increase the benefit of inoculations accruing to those other than the buyers or the sellers of inoculations from $200 million per year to $240 million per year ($20 per person inoculated multiplied by 12 million inoculations per year). The government accomplishes this by making a total of $240 million in subsidy payments to the 12 million persons inoculated each year. This is represented by the area *RVXY* in Figure 3.6. The subsidy is paid from tax revenues.

Examples of corrective subsidies include the provision of certain government services at levels below the marginal cost of such services. For example, many municipal governments make special pickups of trash and such large waste items as discarded furniture at prices well below marginal cost. The difference between the actual price and the marginal cost of the pickup can be regarded as a corrective subsidy designed to avoid accumulation of trash and unauthorized dumping. Some city governments also subsidize property owners who plant trees by the curbs of their property. They might, for example, pay half the price of those trees. This is designed to internalize the positive externality associated with property beautification.

Many citizens believe that positive externalities are associated with college enrollments. Some states provide subsidies to students attending both public and private colleges. Governments often provide services that result in positive externalities free of charge and establish minimum levels of consumption, as is commonly the case for elementary and secondary schooling. However, not all subsidies are designed to internalize positive externalities. Many subsidies are based on other goals, such as alleviating poverty.

C H E C K P O I N T

1. What are externalities? Use a supply-and-demand analysis to show how a negative or positive externality prevents a perfectly competitive market from achieving efficiency.
2. What does it mean to internalize an externality?
3. Explain how corrective taxes and subsidies can be used to internalize an externality.

PROPERTY RIGHTS TO RESOURCE USE AND INTERNALIZATION OF EXTERNALITIES: THE COASE THEOREM

Let's look more closely into the causes of externalities. Externalities arise because the property rights of some resource users are not considered in the marketplace by buyers or sellers of products. The willingness of persons to engage in market transactions involving property or goods and services depends on both the gains expected from the transactions and the costs involved in acquiring those gains. **Transactions costs** include the time, effort, and cash outlays involved in locating someone to trade with, negotiating terms of trade, drawing contracts, and assuming risks associated with the contracts. Transactions costs depend, in part, on property rights to use resources. Government has the power to change property rights. By doing so, transactions costs will be affected, as will the potential net gains realizable through market exchanges. If a government lowers transactions costs, efficiency will be improved in cases for which new gains from trading outweigh the costs involved in establishing or modifying preexisting property rights.

Governments can and have modified the right of business firms to emit wastes in the air and water and can lower the transactions costs involved in trading existing rights to dispose of wastes in the environment. For example, users of a lake or stream could be granted the right to unpolluted water. Suppose an industrial firm can purchase the right to pollute from those who have been granted the right to a pollution-free lake. If the firm's owners can still be better off after purchasing the right to pollute, and users better or at least no worse off than they would otherwise have been, a gain in net benefits is possible. Provided that the transactions costs of the exchange do not outweigh the net benefits possible to the parties, exchange of these property rights will help achieve efficiency. By establishing property rights and seeking to lower the transactions costs associated with their exchange, governmental authority can increase net benefits to citizens.

The **Coase Theorem** states that governments, by merely establishing the rights to use resources, can internalize externalities when transactions costs of bargaining are zero.[5] Once these property rights to resource use are established, the Coase Theorem holds that free exchange of the established rights for cash payments among the affected parties will achieve efficiency. This result holds irrespective of which of the involved parties is granted the right.

For example, suppose that only two competing uses exist for a stream: a convenient place to dump wastes in paper production and a site for recreation. Suppose that the transactions costs of trading established rights to use the stream between the paper factory and the recreational users of the stream are zero. Under these circumstances, the Coase theorem maintains that it makes no difference whether the factory is granted the right to pollute the stream or the recreational users are given the right to a pollution-free stream. In either case, an efficient mix of industrial and recreational uses of the stream will emerge from private bargaining between the factory and the recreational users. Corrective taxes or any other charges are not needed, because competition for use of the stream by the interested parties will internalize the externality.

If the factory is granted the right, it will be in its interest to reduce pollution if the recreational users will offer a payment that more than offsets the reduction in profits resulting from reduced polluting. If, instead, the recreational users have the right to a pollution-free stream, they would give up part of this right if the factory can offer them a payment in excess of the losses they incur from increased pollution. By creating the right, the government gives the user who receives it a valuable asset that can be exchanged for a cash payment from the other user. The exchange of those rights will lead to efficient resource use, provided that no third parties are affected by the exchange of the government-created rights.

The transactions costs of bargaining to exchange rights include the costs of locating a trading partner and agreeing on the value of the traded right. In general, these transactions costs tend to be close to zero when the parties involved in trading the right are few in number. Under such circumstances, those who are granted a right are likely to know who (if anyone) is willing to purchase it, and a price can easily be agreed upon to internalize any externality. Those who purchase the rights of others to pollute, for example, know that no other polluters will continue to cause damages after the deal is completed. The kinds of externalities for which the Coase theorem is relevant, therefore, are called **small-number externalities.** In dealing with externalities of this type, or any externality, for that matter, it is useful to divide the parties involved into two groups: emitters and receptors. The distinction is, however,

---

[5]Ronald Coase, "The Problem of Social Cost," *Journal of Law and Economics* 3 (October 1960): 1–44. The examples used in this section are similar to those used by Coase.

somewhat arbitrary because, as is shown below, the emitter could as well be designated the receptor and the receptor could be considered the emitter. The essential social problem that exists for any externality is the disputed use of a productive resource.

Exchange of Property Rights to Internalize a Negative Externality: An Example Illustrating the Coase Theorem

Suppose that a cattle rancher and a wheat farmer operate on two adjoining plots of land. Currently, the border between the two plots is unfenced. Both producers sell their outputs in perfectly competitive markets; therefore, they have no control over the prices they receive for their goods. The cattle occasionally stray into the wheat fields, thus damaging the crop. As the size of the cattle producer's herd increases, it is inevitable that more steers will stray into the wheat fields and more wheat will be damaged. Thus, an increase in the output of beef is obtainable only with a corresponding decrease in the output of wheat. Only the wheat farmer is harmed by the damage done by the cattle.

Assume that the governing authorities grant the wheat producer the right to cattle-free land, requiring that the cattle producer pay the wheat farmer for damages incurred by the cattle. This forces the cattle producer to take into account the external cost, measured in wheat damage, caused by the herd. In effect, the law acts to internalize the externality in such a way as to increase the cattle producer's marginal private cost to the point where it is equal to marginal social cost (the direct cost incurred by the cattle producer plus the value of the damage to the wheat crop).

Figure 3.7A shows how the beef producer behaves, assuming that his goal is to maximize profits. The current price per pound of beef, P_B, is established in a competitive market. The rancher can sell all the beef produced at that price. The profit-maximizing output of beef is Q_{B1} pounds of beef per year when the rancher is *not* liable for damages to the farmer. This is the output corresponding to the point at which the marginal private cost of beef equals the price per pound: $P_B = MPC$. At that output, the marginal social cost of beef produced on this ranch would exceed the price of beef by the marginal external cost to the wheat producer. For any given level of beef output, the marginal external cost to the wheat farmer is the loss in wheat output, Q_W, multiplied by the market price of wheat, P_W:

$$MEC = P_W Q_W. \tag{3.7}$$

Therefore, the cost of any given amount of physical damage to the wheat crop will become higher as the price of wheat goes higher.

In Figure 3.7A, the marginal social cost of beef is $MPC_B + MEC$. When liable for damage, the rancher must consider MEC as part of his marginal costs. He therefore produces the output Q_B^* per year, corresponding to the point where $P_B = MSC$, when the wheat farmer has the right to cattle-free land. The annual output Q_B^* is the efficient output because P_B also equals the marginal social benefit of beef in a competitive market.

If the maximum revenues that the rancher can earn when producing the efficient output, Q_B^*, per year fall short of the opportunity costs of production, the rancher will go out of business. The land adjacent to the wheat farm then will be converted to

Figure 3.7 ✦ THE COASE THEOREM

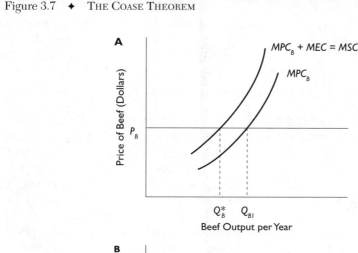

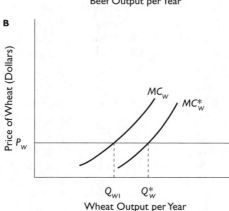

*The graph in **A** shows the marginal cost of producing beef and the price of beef, while that in **B** indicates marginal cost and price for a neighboring wheat farmer. The Coase theorem holds that the efficient output of beef, Q_B°, and the efficient output of wheat, Q_W°, will be produced on the adjacent lands, irrespective of who is liable for damages cattle cause to the wheat crop each year.*

some other use. If the rancher can increase profits by building a fence to eliminate the straying, the fence will go up. Building the fence increases average costs of production but does not affect marginal costs, because the amount of fencing does not vary with the size of the herd. After building the fence, the rancher therefore will produce output Q_{B1} per year because *MEC* will be zero at any level of output after the fence is constructed.

Finally, the rancher looks at the option of purchasing the wheat farmer's land. If the annual payment necessary to buy the land allows greater annual profits than available by producing output Q_B° and paying damages or building a fence, the rancher will choose that option. Buying the land eliminates the liability for damage and, in effect, results in the purchase of the right to cattle-free land from the farmer. Once again, this has no effect on marginal cost of beef and allows the rancher to produce output Q_{B1} without payment of damages. The rancher chooses the alternative that allows the greatest profit.

An Alternative Property Right Assignment

Suppose that the cattle rancher is *not* liable for damages. This means that the right to use unfenced land for grazing is granted to the rancher. How much will the wheat farmer be willing to pay to buy back any portion of the rancher's right of unlimited grazing? Such payments will act to reduce the size of the rancher's herd.

Figure 3.7B shows the problem faced by the wheat farmer. The marginal cost of producing wheat depends on the size of the neighboring cattle herd. The greater the size of the herd, the greater the marginal cost of producing any given quantity of wheat on the adjoining wheat farm. When the rancher produces Q_{B1} pounds of beef to maximize profits, the marginal costs of beef production are MC_W, as shown in Figure 3.7B. Under those circumstances, the farmer produces the output Q_{W1}, corresponding to the point at which the price of wheat, P_W, equals MC_W. A decrease in the output of the rancher to the efficient annual output Q_B^* will *reduce* the marginal costs of wheat, because it will take less seed, labor, and other variable inputs to harvest a given amount of wheat. If the rancher could be induced to cut back output to the efficient level, the marginal cost curve of producing wheat would shift downward to MC_W^*.

The rancher will accept a payment to reduce annual output of beef if it allows an increase in profits. The farmer is no worse off by making an annual payment up to the marginal external cost that would be caused by a given amount of annual beef output.

The maximum amount of money that the farmer would pay for each unit reduction in beef output by the rancher therefore is equal to the marginal external cost of beef. Making such a payment will increase wheat revenues per year by an amount exactly equal to MEC. In effect, this internalizes the externality. The payment that the farmer would be willing to make to prevent each increase in beef output becomes, in effect, part of the rancher's marginal costs. This is because the rancher forgoes receipt of this payment each time output is increased. The wheat damage is part of the opportunity cost of beef! The rancher now maximizes profits by setting $MPC_B + MEC = P_B$, where MEC is now the maximum payment per pound of beef received from the farmer. The rancher therefore reduces the size of his herd to the efficient amount Q_B^*. This is the same annual output that would prevail if the rancher were liable for damages! When the rancher produces the efficient annual output of beef, the farmer's marginal costs are lower. The farmer will therefore produce Q_W^*, corresponding to the point at which $MC_W^* = P_W$.

The mix of output produced on the adjoining lands will be exactly the same, independent of which party is liable for the damages. In this case, the farmer must make annual payments to the rancher, independent of the amount of wheat produced, to compensate the rancher for the reduction in the size of the herd. Therefore, the farmer's profits will be lower and the rancher's profits will be higher than was the case when the farmer had the right to claim damages from the rancher.

As was the case when the rancher was liable for damages incurred by his cattle, the wheat farmer can be expected to choose the option that will give maximum possible profits. The farmer will compare the alternative of annual payments to the rancher to reduce output or to build a fence with that of buying the rancher's land outright. Finally, the farmer will also consider the option of going out of business, choosing the option that maximizes profits.

Significance of the Coase Theorem

The remarkable conclusion of the Coase theorem is that the efficient mix of output will result simply as a consequence of the establishment of exchangeable property rights. It makes no difference which party is assigned the right to use a resource. Provided that the transactions costs of exchanging the right are zero, the efficient mix of outputs among competing uses of the resource (in this case, land) will emerge. When transactions costs of exchanging the right to resource use are low and the number of parties involved are few, a government need do no more than assign property rights. Bargaining among the interested parties will do the rest to achieve efficiency.

However, governments assigning property rights provide a valuable resource to those who get the rights. Although it makes no difference for resource allocation who gets the rights, it makes a big difference to the parties involved in terms of their incomes! Clearly a corporation is better off if it is granted the right to pollute. Under those circumstances those who wish cleaner air will have lower incomes because they will have to pay to get the corporation to reduce pollution. On the other hand, the corporation would be worse off if environmentalists and citizens at large were granted the right to pollution-free air. Under those circumstances the corporation would have to pay for the right to pollute and its annual income would be lower. *The users who are initially granted the right are better off, because then they own a valuable property right that can either be used or exchanged. Therefore, the assignment of the property right by the government affects the distribution of income between the two parties using the resource.*

The Coase theorem also points out that negative externalities are really disputes concerning the rights to use certain resources. The parties involved have conflicting claims on the use of certain resources for their own benefit. However, the use of the disputed resource for one purpose diminishes its usefulness for the other purpose. This emphasizes that the externality is a reciprocal relationship between the parties involved, with no need to label good guys or bad guys. The efficient solution, involving a trade-off between the social value of competing resource uses, strikes a balance between the net social value of both uses.

To make this point still stronger, consider the plight of the American farmer. In recent years, significant concern has arisen about the problem of agricultural runoff. Increased use of chemicals by farmers, as well as new methods of raising livestock in confined spaces, have resulted in external costs, because these chemical and organic wastes washed away by rains can cause offensive odors and illness stemming from contamination of drinking water. Thirty years ago, most farms were located in low-density, rural areas. Damages done by runoff would be borne by farmers themselves. These costs, therefore, would have automatically been considered in agricultural decisions, and no externality could be said to have existed. As urbanization increased, more homes were built on the periphery of urban areas, and, in many cases, land use in previously all-rural and agricultural areas became mixed with such nonagricultural uses as housing. Agricultural runoff now had the effect of decreasing the usefulness of the area for housing purposes because of the potential contamination of wells and the discomfort caused by offensive odors.

The introduction of a competing use of land in an all-agricultural area had the effect of externalizing an internal cost. As the number of homes built in the zone increases, the number of inhabitants with no direct interest in agriculture, as well as the external cost of any given amount of agricultural runoff, also increases. Establishing the rights of the parties involved in this case is no easy matter. The farmers might argue that they have disposed of waste through runoff for years and that the individuals who purchased homes in the area should have considered these costs before deciding to locate their residences in the vicinity of their farms. The home owners, on the other hand, could argue that they have a right to safe drinking water and sweet-smelling country air and that the farmers cannot infringe upon those rights.

If the liability for damages were assigned exclusively to farmers, and if they were required to compensate home owners for damages, little incentive would remain for developers to refrain from constructing homes in the area. New residents could expect to bear some costs of agricultural runoff if they chose to locate in the area, but they would receive full compensation for these costs. Damages paid by farmers would rise continually with increases in nonagricultural population, and if population continually increased, farmers eventually would be induced to sell their farms for nonagricultural use. This result is contingent on full payment of compensation to homeowners. If, however, the homeowners were forced to bear some, or all, of the costs of cleaning up the agricultural runoff, the process would be much slower. The issue of compensation for damages remains controversial in view of its influence on the dynamics of social change.[6] This example illustrates again how competing for the right to use certain resources (in this case, land) for alternative uses (in this case, runoff versus housing) results in an externality.[7]

---

[6]See, for example, William J. Baumol, "On Taxation and the Control of Externalities," *American Economic Review* 62 (June 1972): 307–322.

[7]The type of externality described here is often referred to as "undepletable." An undepletable externality is one for which the external costs borne by existing receptors are not affected by the number of receptors. In this case, no matter how many houses are built, the costs borne by each homeowner are not decreased as more homes are built. Depletable externalities are such that additional receptors decrease the costs borne by the existing receptors.

Applying the Coase Theorem: Pollution Rights

One possible market-based solution to the problem of controlling pollution is the establishment of transferable permits to pollute.[8] **Pollution rights** are transferable permits to emit a certain amount of particular wastes into the atmosphere or water per year. Regulatory authorities would issue a certain amount of these rights and monitor firms to make sure that only those with permits emitted the wastes. The permits would be offered for sale in a market. Firms that purchased the pollution rights then would be free to sell them to other firms if they wished. An advantage to permits over emissions charges or corrective taxes is that the regulatory authorities could strictly control the amount of emissions by issuing a fixed number of permits.

Suppose, for example, in the absence of any regulations or charges, the current amount of annual emissions of a certain type of air pollutant is estimated to be 100,000 tons. As illustrated in Figure 3.8, this is the amount that firms emit at zero price for emissions. The demand curve, *D*, represents the marginal social benefit of

[8]This scheme was first proposed by J. H. Dales. See J. H. Dales, *Pollution, Property, and Prices* (Toronto: University of Toronto Press, 1970).

Figure 3.8 ✦ POLLUTION RIGHTS AND EMISSIONS

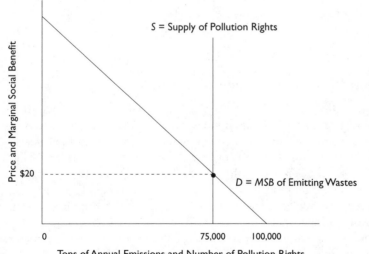

Tons of Annual Emissions and Number of Pollution Rights

If the fixed amount of pollution rights, one of which is required for each ton of emissions, is issued, the price of rights will be determined by the demand, which reflects the marginal social benefit of emitting wastes. In this case, competition for the 75,000 pollution rights issued results in a price of $20 per right.

emitting wastes to business firms. The current level of emissions corresponds to the point at which the demand curve intersects the horizontal axis.

If regulatory authorities wish to reduce emissions to 75,000 tons per year, they would issue 75,000 pollution rights, requiring that one right be purchased for the privilege of emitting one ton of waste per year. This might or might not be the efficient level of emissions. To determine the actual efficient level, authorities would have to estimate the marginal social costs of emissions and compare them with the marginal social benefits.

A pollution control board would auction off the rights to those firms that desire to emit wastes. The market price would correspond to the intersection of the fixed supply curve, S, and the demand curve, D, in Figure 3.8. Assuming that the scheme could be easily enforced, each polluter would have to buy one right per ton of waste emitted per year. As shown in Figure 3.8, the resulting price is $20 per pollution right. At that price, some firms find it cheaper to change their production methods, reduce output, or go out of business rather than purchase the rights. The result is an immediate reduction in emissions from 100,000 tons per year to 75,000 tons per year.

Changes in market conditions would change the price of pollution rights. For example, if the marginal social benefit of emissions were to increase, the demand for pollution rights would also increase. Provided that the supply of permits remained fixed, their price would increase. The regulatory authority could periodically increase the number of permits available. It could also purchase some of the permits of existing firms and remove them from circulation. This would affect the supply and thereby change the price. By controlling the number of rights in circulation, the authorities can strictly regulate the amount of pollution. Firms have the choice of paying the price to pollute or taking measures to reduce emissions.

Efficient Pollution Abatement Levels

How much pollution control is enough? Figure 3.9 illustrates the marginal social benefit and marginal social cost of pollution abatement. The marginal social cost of pollution abatement is likely to increase with increased abatement. Each successive 1 percent reduction in wastes emitted per year is likely to be more costly to achieve than the previously abated 1 percent. At the extreme, once abatement levels more than 95 percent are achieved, additional levels of improved environmental quality might be difficult, if not impossible, to achieve with given technology for recycling, cleaning, or collecting waste products before they are disposed of in the environment.

Similarly, the marginal social benefit of increased pollution abatement is likely to decline as more pollution is abated. The efficient level of pollution abatement will occur at point E. This is the point at which the marginal social cost of pollution abatement equals its marginal social benefit. The efficient amount of abatement is an A^* percent reduction in wastes emitted per year.

An ideal pollution abatement policy, therefore, is one that balances the forgone output that results from increased cost of pollution abatement with the added benefit of improved environmental quality. Failure to consider the opportunity cost of a cleaner environment can result in a cure more painful than the disease.

Figure 3.9 ✦ THE EFFICIENT AMOUNT OF POLLUTION ABATEMENT

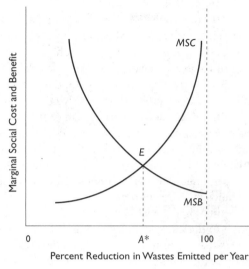

The efficient amount of abatement corresponds to the point at which the marginal social cost of additional reduction in wastes emitted just equals the marginal social benefit of that reduction. This corresponds to A° percent of abatement per year.

CHECKPOINT

1. What is the Coase Theorem? How is it significant to the understanding of social conflicts caused by externalities?
2. How can the sale of pollution rights reduce emissions by polluters and make them pay for the use of environmental resources?
3. Explain why the efficient level of pollution abatement is unlikely to be 100 percent.

ENVIRONMENTAL PROTECTION POLICIES IN THE UNITED STATES

In practice, the primary method of treating the problem of pollution in the United States is government regulation. Market-based corrective taxes or other pollution rights schemes that charge firms for the damages done by their emission are the exception rather than the rule in U.S. environmental protection policies. However, in recent years more market-based policies that allow trading of pollution rights have been initiated. Let's look at how government actually intervenes in the marketplace to deal with environmental pollution in the United States and compare the effects of regulation with those we might expect if emissions were reduced by corrective taxes or the issuance of a limited number of tradable pollution rights.

Emissions Standards Versus Corrective Taxes

The typical method used to control the external costs of pollution is the establishment of standards that limit the amount of pollutants that can be emitted into the air or water. For example, the 1970 Amendments to the Clean Air Act established stringent limits on automobile emissions per vehicle. Maximum levels of emissions of hydro-carbons, nitrogen oxides, and carbon monoxide per vehicle were specified. These limits led to the adoption of catalytic converters on vehicles, serving to increase the price of automobiles in this country. The emissions standards specify the maximum amount of grams per mile that can be emitted while driving.

Emissions standards differ from corrective taxes in that they *do not charge for emissions damages if the amounts emitted are less than legally established standards.* In effect, those who emit pollutants in amounts less than the standards can do so for free! Emissions levels that exceed the standards are strictly outlawed. When the marginal social benefit or cost of emissions varies among firms or locations, rigid emissions standards do not achieve an efficient outcome.

Figure 3.10 shows the marginal social benefit and marginal social cost of emission of a certain pollutant into the air by two firms, A and B. The marginal social benefit of the emissions reflects the maximum amount that a firm will pay for the right to emit those wastes. If no emissions charges currently exist at all, firms emit wastes up to the point at which the marginal social benefit is zero. Thus, firm A emits Q_{A1} tons of waste per year, while firm B emits Q_{B1} tons of waste per year. This would be efficient only if the marginal external cost associated with emissions were zero.

In Figure 3.10 we assume that the marginal external cost associated with each ton of emissions per year is $10 for each firm. This is also the marginal social cost of emissions. The efficient level of annual emissions is therefore Q_A° for firm A and Q_B° for firm B. This is the amount of emissions that would be observed per year if each firm were charged a fee of $10 per ton of emissions for the right to emit wastes. Notice that $Q_A^\circ > Q_B^\circ$ because the marginal social benefit of emissions is greater for any given quantity for firm A than it is for firm B. The marginal social benefit of emissions can vary from firm to firm or from region to region because of differences in the cost of reducing emissions or differences in the prices of output produced with inputs that pollute.

Now suppose that government emissions standards allow each firm to emit up to Q_R tons per year at no charge. Emission of more than Q_R tons per year is then strictly prohibited. Accordingly, firm A is forced to cut back wastes from Q_{A1} to Q_R tons per year. Similarly, the regulations force firm B to cut back emissions from Q_{B1} tons to Q_R tons per year.

These standards do not achieve efficiency. They result in *less* than the efficient level of annual emissions for firm A. At Q_R, the marginal social benefit of emissions exceeds their marginal social cost for A. If, instead, this firm were charged $10, the marginal social cost of the damages per ton of emissions, it would choose to emit $Q_A^\circ > Q_R$ tons of waste per year. The extra net gain in well-being made possible by using an emissions charge is represented by the triangular area ABC in Figure 3.10.

Standards set at Q_R result in more than the efficient amount of emissions from firm B. The efficient amount of emissions corresponds to $Q_B^\circ < Q_R$. This is the

Figure 3.10 ✦ REGULATING EMISSIONS: LOSSES IN EFFICIENCY FROM DIFFERENCES IN THE MARGINAL SOCIAL BENEFIT OF EMISSIONS

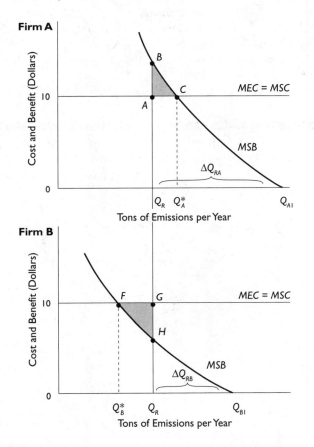

When the marginal social benefits of emissions differ among firms, uniform emissions regulations at Q_R result in less than the efficient level of emissions for firms such as A and more than the efficient amount of emissions for firms such as B.

amount that firm *B* would choose to emit per year if it were charged according to the marginal external cost of $10. The extra net gain possible by using the $10 emissions charge is represented by the area *FGH*.

From another perspective, uniform standards result in a greater *reduction* in emissions than is efficient for firm *A*. **Pollution abatement** is the reduction in pollution that results from reduced emissions. As shown in Figure 3.10, under uniform standards of emissions, firm *A* reduces emissions by ΔQ_{RA} tons per year. This results in *more* than the efficient amount of pollution abatement. Similarly, reduction in emissions of ΔQ_{RB} by firm *B* is *less* than the efficient amount of abatement by this firm.

Similarly, uniform regulations would not achieve efficiency if the marginal external cost of emissions varied by region in a nation. Suppose the marginal external cost per ton of emissions were \$20 in urban areas but only \$5 in rural areas. These represent the marginal social costs of emitting wastes in the two regions. Assume as well that the marginal social benefit of any given quantity of a certain type of pollutant that is emitted is the same for all firms, irrespective of their location. Figure 3.11 shows that the efficient amount of emissions for firm C, located in an urban area, is Q_C°. This is the amount for which MSB of emissions = \$20. The efficient amount of emissions for firm D, located in a rural area, is Q_D°. This is the level at which MSB of emissions = \$5.

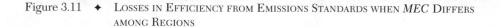

Figure 3.11 ✦ LOSSES IN EFFICIENCY FROM EMISSIONS STANDARDS WHEN MEC DIFFERS AMONG REGIONS

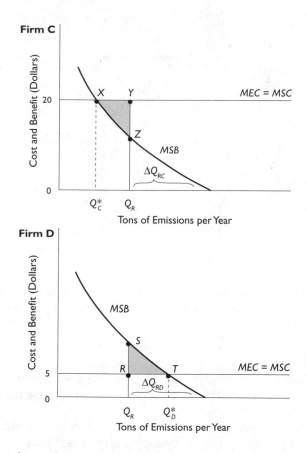

The marginal social cost of a ton of emissions is greater for firm C, located in an urban area, than for firm D, located in a rural area. A uniform standard of emissions of Q_R tons per year results in more than the efficient amount of emissions from firm C and less than the efficient amount from firm D.

If all firms, irrespective of their location, are subject to the same emissions standard of Q_R tons, the efficient level of emissions will not be achieved. The standard would allow all firms to emit Q_R tons of emissions per year at zero cost and prohibit more than this amount. This results in *more* than the efficient amount of emissions by the firm in the urban area because $Q_R > Q_C^*$. On the other hand, *less* than the efficient amount of emissions are allowed in the urban area because $Q_R < Q_D^*$.

The efficient amount of emissions could be attained by an emissions charge of $20 per ton in the urban area and $5 per ton in the rural area. The loss in net benefits when uniform emissions standards, and not charges, are used is the sum of the areas *XYZ* for firm *C*, and *RST*, for firm *D*. The amount of pollution abatement for the urban firm is ΔQ_{RC}. This is *less* than the efficient amount of abatement for that firm. On the other hand, *more* than the efficient amount of abatement occurs under uniform emission standards for firms in the rural area, where ΔQ_{RD} tons of emissions are abated.

Uniform standards for controlling emissions that result in negative externalities therefore are unlikely to achieve efficiency. Use of a standards approach to controlling negative externalities such as pollution will have to be flexible to achieve an efficient outcome. This can be accomplished by adjusting for differences in the marginal social benefit and marginal external cost of pollution among firms and regions. However, a disadvantage of using standards, as compared to corrective taxes, is that standards do not generate any revenue.

Command and Control Policies and Environmental Quality

The standards approach has given the federal government both the power and the responsibility of regulating the emissions of every polluter in the nation. Such direct controls often result in the Environmental Protection Agency (EPA) specifying rigid standards and techniques for coping with emissions, without duly considering the special conditions and difficulties encountered by certain industries in meeting those standards. **Command-and-control regulation** is a system of rules established by government authorities that requires all emitters to meet strict emissions standards for sources of pollution and requires the use of specific pollution control devices. In other words, under this system, the government not only tells emitters how much they can emit, it also tells them which technology they must employ to reduce emissions.

The rigid command-and-control regulation discourages private innovation in pollution control and entails an administrative burden that cannot possibly be carried out effectively, given the enormous amount of information required to specify the "best" way of treating the variety of environmental pollutants already in existence.[9]

William Baumol and Wallace Oates have argued persuasively for a more flexible system of pollution control:

> It is of great importance that our environmental policy include effective inducement for the development and introduction of superior pollution-abatement techniques.

---

[9]See Baumol and Oates, *Economics*, 338.

Where direct controls involve the requirement of particular equipment or techniques such as sound-absorbing materials in aircraft or scrubbers in chimneys, there is little inducement for industry to seek a better way to do the job.[10]

Standards imposed by the EPA have experienced considerable delays in implementation due to court challenges by private business interests. The costs of complying with the new regulations and standards often run into the hundreds of billions of dollars, and it is not surprising that various political forces are developed to oppose the standards, both through the courts and through standard political channels.

It is also naive to assume that regulations, merely because they exist, can be enforced. It is costly to police emissions standards, and the standards are often exceeded by businesses that know that the EPA cannot monitor emissions of all polluters in the nation. When a business is caught exceeding the standards it often denies any wrongdoing and, more often than not, it is difficult to prove in court that the standards were violated. In many cases, even when a polluter is found guilty in court, the fines paid are low. For example, in a 32-month period ending in early 1986, the state of Virginia in enforcing its water pollution laws managed to obtain only one court-ordered fine—hardly an admirable enforcement record.[11]

More on Market-Based Approaches to Pollution Control: How Trading Pollution Rights can Reduce the Cost of Environmental Protection

We have discussed two market-based approaches to dealing with negative externalities: corrective taxes and pollution rights. Both the approaches are similar in that they offer firms an opportunity to pay for the damages done by their emissions. When this is the case, the emitters weigh the marginal benefit of continuing to emit against the marginal cost of doing so, which in a market-based approach to pollution control would be either the corrective tax associated with more emissions or the pollution rights (or emissions permits) they must buy to pay for additional emissions. Many environmentalists oppose the idea of giving firms a "license to pollute" by offering them the option to pay for the damage their emissions cause. However, the remarkable fact is that market-based approaches like corrective taxes or marketable pollution rights can lower the cost of a given amount of emissions reduction.

Both tradable pollution rights and corrective taxes provide incentives to reduce pollution at the minimum possible cost. However, corrective taxes generate revenue for the government that can be used for other purposes or to compensate the victims of the efficient level of pollution. Tradable pollution rights result in the creation of a valuable asset for those who can clean up pollution at a cost per unit less than the pollution right. The tradable pollution rights provide incentives to clean up pollution by adding to the profits of some firms.

Rigid standards, such as those established by the EPA for ambient air quality, could constrain economic growth substantially for certain regions. Suppose that a city

---

[10]Ibid., 339.
[11]See Alan S. Blinder, *Hard Heads, Soft Hearts* (Reading, MA: Addison-Wesley, 1987), 143.

MARKETABLE POLLUTION RIGHTS FOR ELECTRIC POWER GENERATION

In July of 1991 the nation's largest commodity market, the Chicago Board of Trade, voted to create a market for the rights to emit sulfur dioxide. This historic decision was made possible by provisions of the Clean Air Act of 1990 empowering the Environmental Protection Agency to issue marketable rights to emit sulfur dioxides to electric power-generating companies. The pollution rights provide these firms with a new way of complying with emissions reductions of this compound, which is a major cause of acid rain.

By a stroke of the pen, Congress established the property rights necessary to create a market. Under the new law, electric power-generating firms must reduce their emissions of sulfor dioxide by 50 percent of current levels by the year 2000. The EPA has allocated rights to dump limited amounts of the compound to the power companies. Each right will grant the buyer the right to dump one ton of sulfur dioxide into the atmosphere per year. Firms that clean up their wastes and do not use all their allotted pollution rights can sell their remaining rights in the new market to other companies that want to emit more than their allotment of pollution rights allows or to anyone else willing to pay the price.

Power-generating firms will now be under pressure by their stockholders to compare the cost of continuing to emit sulfur dioxide with the price they can get for their pollution rights. The higher the market price of the pollution rights, the greater the incentive to reduce emissions. In this way the cost of polluting becomes a factor in the profit calculation of the power companies.

The trading of the pollution rights is likely to allow electric power companies to meet the new emissions reductions requirements at lower costs than would otherwise be possible. For example, suppose the market price of a pollution right to emit a ton of sulfur dioxide is $150. If a firm can recycle or remove that ton of wastes from its smokestack for only $75 it can add $75 to its annual profits by reducing the emissions and selling one pollution right for $150 on the market. Power companies can also reduce their emissions by shifting to low-sulfur coal. The only plants that would want pollution rights would be those for which the cost of cleaning up one ton of emissions would be greater than the $150 market price of the right. Naturally, the price of the pollution right will vary with the value of emitting wastes. As new technologies for reducing emissions develop, the price of the pollution rights could fall. Increases in the demand for electricity would be likely to increase the price of the pollution rights.

The new scheme also encourages electric power companies to develop new technology for reducing emissions. By doing so, they can add to their profits by selling their pollution rights! This new market-based approach to emissions reduction is a great improvement over the old command-and-control approach that required all firms to reduce their emissions by the same percentage and often dictated the technology they must use to achieve that result. The first auction of pollution rights was in 1993. Bidders at the Chicago Board of Trade auction bought rights to emit 150,010 tons of sulfur dioxide that year at prices that ranged from $122 to $450 per ton. The Chicago Board of Trade now runs auctions for these pollution rights every three months on behalf of power-generating utilities and other owners of the rights who want to sell them. The first auction generated $21 million in proceeds that will go to the power generating companies that sold their pollution rights on the market at that time. The largest single buyer at the first auction was Carolina Power & Light Company, which purchased 85,103 one-ton rights at prices ranging from $122 to $171.

Anybody can buy these pollution rights. Groups interested in cleaning up the environment can purchase the pollution rights and hold them. For example, a Cleveland-based group called the "National Air License Exchange" bought one license at the first auction for $350 and will hold the license to keep one ton of sulfur dioxide from being emitted each year!

exceeds the standard for a certain pollutant. A new firm that emits even small amounts of such pollutants into the air wants to locate in the city. Under rigid standards, the firm would not be allowed to do so. As a result, employment opportunities and economic growth in the city would be curtailed.

Concerns about the difficulties of meeting standards, and the social costs of doing so, have led to innovations in EPA policies, which recently move in the direction of the pollution rights scheme. The EPA now uses an "emissions offset policy" in most regions of the United States. Under this policy, new firms can enter an area in which standards are already met or exceeded, provided that they pay other firms to reduce their pollutants in an amount equal to, or greater than, that to be generated by the new firms. For example, suppose a new factory will discharge 500 pounds of sulfur dioxide per day in an area that already exceeds EPA ambient air standards. Without an offset, the firm would be unable to obtain a permit for operation from state authorities. If, however, the owners of the factory would be able to persuade, or pay, other polluters to reduce pollution by 500 pounds of sulfur dioxide per day, they would obtain the necessary offset for approval of the permit. For example, the EPA allowed construction of a new General Motors plant in Oklahoma City after the local chamber of commerce arranged for a reduction in hydrocarbon emissions from oil companies in the area.[12] The offset policy is similar to the pollution right policy in that it allows firms to "purchase" the right to emit wastes by paying other firms to reduce emissions.

Another scheme recently used by the EPA is the "bubble." Under this approach, an imaginary bubble is placed over the firm. Subject to an overall emissions limit, the firm is allowed to exceed emissions standards for one type of pollutant if it compensates for this by reducing emissions by more than the required standard for another pollutant. This is another approach designed to add flexibility to rigid standards and to decrease the costs of attaining a given level of environmental quality.

Finally, the EPA has allowed "banking" of emissions reductions in excess of current standards. Firms that exceed current standards are given credits that will allow them to fall short of the standards at some point in the future. The firm is even allowed to sell these credits to other firms that wish to exceed current standards. This is another move in the direction of a system of transferable pollution permits.

Let's examine how a trading approach can make it cheaper to obtain a given amount of emissions reduction. Suppose a new regulation requires all firms in your city to cut emissions of particulates, such as smoke, by one ton a day. An electric power-generating plant in the region finds that the marginal cost of meeting the new standards will be $1,000 per day. A steel manufacturer producer in the region finds that it can meet the new standard at a daily cost of only $100. Under the command-and-control regulation, the marginal social cost of the two tons of particulate emissions reduction will be $1,100 per day. If, instead, the same 2-ton daily reduction emissions were obtained by allowing the power plant to continue to emit wastes while requiring the steel manufacturer to reduce emissions by 2 tons, the marginal social cost of obtaining the given reduction in emissions would be only $200 per day—daily savings of $900!

It would, however, be wishful thinking to expect the regulators to be able to assign the cleanup to the least cost sources—it would require more information than a

---

[12]Joseph J. Seneca and Michael K. Taussig, *Environmental Economics*, 3d ed. (Englewood Cliffs, NJ: Prentice-Hall, 1984), 232.

GLOBAL POLLUTION: EXTERNALITIES THAT CROSS BORDERS

Are you worried about depletion of the earth's ozone layer? Will continued reduction of stratospheric ozone increase your risks of getting skin cancer? Will global warming result from continued use of fossil fuels and from deforestation of the Amazon in Brazil? Do we need more intergovernmental cooperation on the international level to save the planet?

Let's first look at the issue of ozone depletion. Chlorofluorocarbons (CFCs) and other chemicals used in the production of solvents and insulation materials disperse into the atmosphere no matter where they are used. The use of these chemicals increases the concentrations of chlorine and bromine in the atmosphere that then create chemical reactions that deplete ozone. Ozone depletion means that more ultra-violet radiation will reach earth, increasing the risk of skin cancer and cataracts. The depletion of the ozone layer also will reduce agricultural yields and have unfavorable effects on fishing and industrial materials.

It is clear that externalities do not stop at the borders of a nation. Even if the United States develops policies to reduce the emissions of CFCs, which are used in refrigeration, aerosol propellants, and fire extinguishers, the continued use of these and other chemicals in other nations will continue to threaten the ozone layer. It is going to take action by more than one government to internalize the externalities associated with the use of CFCs. Some progress has already been made through international agreements that will result in a sharp reduction in CFC production by 1998.

Global warming is another international problem that is aggravated by the fact that users of fossil fuels and timber do not consider the full social cost of their use of these products. The "greenhouse effect" results when concentrations of carbon dioxide and other gases increase in the atmosphere and absorb heat that then radiates down toward earth. The concentrations of these gases do not depend only on the amounts emitted. They also depend on the vegetation cover of the earth because vegetation naturally absorbs carbon dioxide. Much of the world vegetation cover is forest. In recent years deforestation in Africa and in Brazil has contributed to fears that the greenhouse effect would become worse. However, harvesting of timber is a key source of income and well-being to citizens in low-income regions of the world. The governments of these nations naturally resist calls for them to restrain from clearing and harvesting their forest resources. This has led to calls for international cooperation to compensate Brazil and nations in Africa in return for their promises to reduce harvesting of forest resources.

Of course, another way to reduce the risk of global warming is to discourage the use of fossil fuels, which spew forth the gases that create the greenhouse effect. This could be accomplished through very high corrective taxes on the use of these fuels. The high taxes could slow world economic growth unless alternative fuels that are cleaner burning can be developed.

Externalities have a very important international dimension that cannot be ignored in social policy. Effectively dealing with the problems of protection of our environment will ultimately require coordinated actions by all governments of the world. A United Nations sponsored Conference on Environment and Development in Rio de Janeiro in 1992 has made some progress in such coordination. The conference resulted in 160 nations signing an agreement that commits richer nations to assisting poorer nations to develop while minimizing environmental damage. In exchange for international aid and technology transfer, poorer nations will pursue policies that reduce high birth rates.

central agency could expect to have. No one knows the costs of reducing emissions better than the emitters themselves and they cannot be expected to volunteer that information to the government if they know they are going to be ordered to increase the amount of their emissions reductions as a consequence! A better approach is to let the firms trade rights to pollute among themselves. For example, by allowing trading of the right to pollute, the steel manufacturer can make a profit by offering to reduce emissions by an extra ton per day so that the power plant manager can avoid the $1,000 daily cost of cleaning up an extra ton of particulates. As long as the steel manufacturer gets more than $100 marginal cost of reducing emissions from the electric power plant to clean up an extra ton, it would be more advantageous to offer to reduce its emissions still further. Similarly, the power plant manager will agree to pay to have its ton of emissions reduced by the steel manufacturer as long as the amount paid for that ton is less than the $1,000 marginal cost incurred by reducing emissions itself. If the two firms can strike a mutually agreeable bargain to trade, the two tons of emissions can be obtained for a cost of less than $1,100. For example, if the power plant pays the steel manufacturer $200 to reduce emissions by one additional ton per day, the marginal cost of two tons of emissions reduction would only be $300.

C H E C K P O I N T

1. What are the major differences between emissions standards and market-based approaches, such as corrective taxes and marketable pollution rights, to pollution abatement?
2. What is command-and-control regulation?
3. How can market-based approaches to pollution control work to obtain a given amount of emissions reduction at the minimum possible social cost?

Summary

Externalities are costs or benefits of market transactions not reflected in prices. They are a dominant form of market failure to achieve efficiency in industrial economies. When externalities are present, market prices fail to equal the marginal social cost or benefit of goods. Exchange of goods and services in an unregulated system of competitive markets fails to achieve efficiency when externalities prevail. When the marginal external cost or benefit is priced so that buyers and sellers consider it in their decisions, an externality is internalized.

Externalities can be negative or positive. Negative externalities result in costs, while positive externalities result in benefits to third parties of market exchanges. To internalize an externality, the parties involved must be identified and the marginal external cost or benefit must be measured.

In some cases, particularly that of few individual emitters and receptors, private action through informal bargaining can be expected to internalize the externality without recourse to collective action through political institutions. The Coase theorem shows that, in such cases, government assignment of rights to resource use, along with facilitation of free exchange of those rights, achieves efficiency, independent of which party is granted the right. When larger numbers of individuals are involved, a solution will require collective action to internalize the externality. Among the techniques used for this are corrective taxes and subsidies, regulations, and the establishment of standards.

A Forward Look

The following chapter discusses the nature of public goods and shows that their market provision results in positive externalities. The difficulties involved in efficiently supplying public goods through markets make government a logical candidate for their production and distribution.

Important Concepts

Externalities: Negative and Positive
Marginal External Cost
Marginal Private Cost

Marginal External Benefit
Marginal Private Benefit
Internalization of an Externality
Corrective Tax
Effluent Fees
Pollution Abatement
General Theory of Second Best
Corrective Subsidy
Transactions Costs
The Coase Theorem
Small-Number Externalities
Pollution Rights
Command-and-Control Regulation

Questions for Review

1. Explain why externalities prevent the attainment of efficiency when goods are traded in competitive markets.
2. Do you agree with the following statement? "Efficiency cannot be achieved when externalities exist." Explain your view.
3. Why do prices fail to represent the opportunity costs of resources when externalities exist?
4. How can a corrective tax adjust costs to reflect externalities? What effects will a corrective tax have on prices, output, and pollution?
5. Suppose a positive externality is associated with college enrollment. Assume that college instruction is sold in a competitive market and that the marginal social cost of providing it increases with enrollment. Show how a corrective subsidy to college students will increase the market price of instruction. Show the net gain in well-being possible from the subsidy and the amount of tax revenue required to finance its costs on your graph.
6. What kinds of information must be gathered to internalize an externality?
7. Why do limits on pollution emissions fail to internalize the externality that generates the pollution?
8. Under what conditions are externalities likely to be internalized without the necessity of government intervention?
9. Why might it be argued that the distinction between emitters and receptors of an externality involves an arbitrary judgment?
10. What criteria can be used to determine if a small-number externality exists? Why is it undesirable to compensate receptors of external damage in cases where there are few emitters and many receptors?

Problems

1. The supply of paper is described by the following equation:

$$Q_S = 5,000P$$

where Q_S is tons supplied per year and P is the price per ton. The demand is described by

$$Q_D = 400,000 - 1,000P$$

where Q_D is tons demanded per year.
Because of the pollution associated with paper production, marginal external costs of $20 are associated with each ton of paper. Assuming that paper is sold in a competitive market, what is the market price? How many tons of paper will be produced per year at that price? What is the efficient annual output of paper? How can a corrective tax achieve efficiency?

2. The following data show how the marginal external benefit and marginal private benefit associated with a soil treatment agent to control Japanese beetles vary with the gallons of the control agent sold per year:

GALLONS PER YEAR (IN MILLIONS)	MPB	MEB
20	$30	$10
30	25	6
40	20	2
50	15	0

Draw the demand curve for the control agent and show how the marginal private benefit differs from the marginal social benefit. Suppose that the supply of the agent is infinitely elastic at the current price of $25 per gallon. Will the market equilibrium be efficient? How would your answer differ if the market supply were infinitely elastic at a price of $15 per gallon? What policies could you suggest to achieve efficiency?

3. The EPA wants to reduce emissions of sulfur dioxides from electric power general plants by 20 percent during the next year. To achieve this goal, the EPA will require each power-generating plant in the nation to reduce emissions by 100 tons per year. Suppose five power plants emit sulfur dioxides and serve a given metropolitan area. The following table shows the cost

per ton of reducing emissions for each of the five plants:

PLANT	COST PER TON OF EMISSIONS REDUCTION
1	$600
2	$500
3	$500
4	$400
5	$200

Assuming that the cost per ton of emissions reduction is constant and that the improvement in the air for the metropolitan area is the same no matter which plant reduces emissions, calculate the following:

a. The cost of meeting EPA regulations

b. The least-cost method of achieving the EPA goal of reducing emissions of sulfur dioxides from power plants in the metropolitan area.

4. Instead of using regulations to achieve the 20-percent reduction in emissions discussed in the preceding problem, suppose the EPA requires each of the five emitters to pay a fee of $450 for each ton of sulfur dioxide it dumps in the air during the year. Use the data from the table for problem 3 to predict which companies will purchase pollution rights, the total cost of achieving the reduction in sulfur dioxide emissions, and the revenue generated from sale of pollution rights in the area.

Suggestions for Further Reading

Barthold, Thomas A. "Issues in the Design of Environmental Excise Taxes," *Journal of Economic Perspectives,* 8, 1 (Winter 1994): 133–151. An analysis of some of the practical problems involved in the implementation of corrective taxes to deal with pollution control.

Baumol, William J., and Oates, Wallace E. *The Theory of Environmental Policy.* Englewood Cliffs, NJ: Prentice-Hall, 1975. A technical application of the theory of externalities to environmental problems.

Blinder, Alan S. *Hard Heads, Soft Hearts.* Reading, MA: Addison-Wesley, 1987. Chapter 5 discusses issues in environmental policy and bemoans the fact that sensible policies proposed by economists have not been implemented on a broad scale.

Coase, Ronald. "The Problem of Social Cost." *Journal of Law and Economics* 3 (October 1960): 1–44. A modern classic on the nature of externalities and the nexus between economics and the law.

Cropper, Maureen L. and Oates, Wallace, E. "Environmental Economics: A Survey," *Journal of Economic Literature,* 30, 2 (June 1992): 675–740. A survey of the state of knowledge in environmental economics along with analysis of recent economic policy to deal with environmental problems in the United States and other nations.

Dahlman, Carl J. "The Problem of Externality." *Journal of Law and Economics* 22 (April 1979): 141–168. A discussion of transactions costs, efficiency, and externalities.

Economic Report of the President. Washington, D.C., U.S. Government Printing Office, 1990. Insights into issues in environmental policy are offered in Chapter 6 of this report.

Hahn, Robert W. "Economic Prescriptions for Environmental Problems: How the Patient Followed the Doctor's Orders." *The Journal of Economic Perspectives* 3, 2 (Spring 1989): 95–114. In this article Hahn discusses how market-based pollution-control policies have actually been implemented in several nations.

Poterba, James M. "Global Warming Policy: A Public Finance Perspective," *Journal of Economic Perspectives* 7, 4 (Fall 1993): 47–63. An analysis of use of corrective taxes and other policies to deal with the problem of global warming.

4

PUBLIC GOODS

LEARNING OBJECTIVES

After reading this chapter you should be able to

1. Define public goods and discuss their characteristics.
2. Explain the difference between pure public goods and pure private goods.
3. Derive the demand curve for a pure public good and explain how it differs from the demand curve for a pure private good.
4. Determine the conditions for efficient

output of a pure public good and explain why positive externalities associated with the production of pure public goods imply that market provision of the good is likely to be inefficient.
5. Discuss cooperative methods of supplying pure public goods and the characteristics of the Lindahl equilibrium.
6. Analyze the free-rider problem.

*I*n 1993 the federal government spent $303 billion on national defense—an amount equal to one out of every five dollars of federal outlays. However, with the end of the cold war, which has dominated U.S. defense policy for most of the post-World War II era, we can expect sharply declining defense spending in the years to come.

When the federal government provides national defense, it must employ labor and procure capital in the form of weapons systems, aircraft, naval vessels, and land to use as military bases and airfields. The production aspect of national defense is very similar to that of any business operation: labor must be hired, work rules must be established, research and development contracts must be negotiated for new capital equipment and new products such as the Patriot missile, which was successfully employed for the first time in Operation Desert Storm. However, the similarity with business ends on the output side of the picture. The output of the agencies of the federal government that supply national defense are not sold in the market to buyers like cars, cookies, or clothing. In fact, it is inconceivable to imagine defense services being packaged into neat bundles that can be sold over the counter to eager buyers. Although the production of national defense is similar to that of any other good, its *consumption* is fundamentally different. Products such as national defense are *collectively consumed.* As soon as we defend any one person, we defend all.

Because defense is not sold by the unit in the market and cannot be parceled out to individuals to enjoy in greater or smaller amounts according to their tastes, we all consume the total amount produced. We all pay taxes to finance the production of national defense and we must consume the amount made available even though we might prefer to have more or less than the government makes available. An issue that concerns us all is how much of our resources we allocate to services such as national defense. As the world changes and the risk of nuclear conflict is reduced, it is likely that the efficient level of national defense for the United States also will be reduced.

This chapter explores the characteristics of goods that are collectively consumed. We evaluate alternative methods of supplying public goods and show why it is efficient for persons to *share* the costs of producing goods with shared benefits.

The Characteristics of Public Goods

Chapter 3 shows how markets tend to fail to produce efficient amounts of goods that result in externalities when exchanged. Many of the goods and services actually provided by governments, such as national defense, would result in positive externalities were they made available for sale to individual buyers in markets. To repeat, goods such as national defense cannot be sold as easily as candy bars in markets for the exclusive benefit of individual consumers. An entire class of goods, including environmental protection, roads, and public safety, have benefits that must be shared by large groups of individuals. The production of these goods for sale in the marketplace would be accompanied by positive externalities because any such items purchased for individual use would provide external benefits to a large number of third parties as well. Market provision of goods with benefits shared by persons other than those who purchase them for their own use is unlikely to result in an efficient amount of output.

Goods with benefits that cannot be withheld from those who do not pay and are shared by large groups of consumers are **public goods.** Public goods are usually made available politically through the ballot box as people vote to decide how much to supply rather than through the marketplace where those who care to pay the price can buy as much as they like for their own exclusive use. In most cases, government provision of public goods, such as national defense, implies that the goods are freely available to all rather than being sold in a market. The costs of making the good available are usually financed by taxes.

Let's begin our analysis of public goods by examining their characteristics more closely. Public goods are **nonrival in consumption,** meaning that a given quantity of a public good can be enjoyed by more than one consumer without decreasing the amounts enjoyed by rival consumers. For example, television and radio transmissions are nonrival in consumption. A given amount of programming per day can be enjoyed by a large number of consumers. When an additional viewer switches on a television set, the quantity of programming enjoyed by other viewers is not reduced. Similarly, the benefits of national defense services are nonrival. When the population of a nation increases, no citizen suffers a reduction in the quantity of national defense as a result of the increased numbers of people being defended at any time.

Goods that are rival in consumption are called **private goods.** A given quantity of fish available on a dock is said to be rival in consumption. As the number of fish made available to any one consumer increases, the quantity available for rival consumers who desire the fish decreases. Except when externalities are present, prices can efficiently allocate goods that are rival in consumption. The price serves the purpose of making any one person who desires a unit of the good consider the decrease in benefits to rivals who wish to consume that unit.

Pricing a good that is nonrival in consumption serves no useful purpose. After all, an additional consumer of a nonrival good does not reduce the benefit to others who wish to consume it. In other words, the marginal cost of allowing additional persons to consume a given amount of a good with nonrival benefits is zero. It is therefore inefficient to price goods that are nonrival in consumption.

In most cases, it is also infeasible to price units of a public good. This characteristic of public goods is called **nonexclusion,** which implies that it is too costly to develop a means of excluding those who refuse to pay from enjoying the benefits of a given quantity of a public good. For example, it is infeasible to exclude those who refuse to pay for cleaner air from enjoying the benefits of a given amount of air quality improvement once it has been supplied for the benefit of other persons. Air quality improvement therefore has the property of nonexclusion.

From a practical point of view, goods that are nonrival in consumption need not necessarily be subject to nonexclusion. Television broadcasting services, as was pointed out above, are nonrival. However, it is feasible to exclude those who refuse to pay from the benefits of transmissions through cable provision of the broadcasts or use of signal coding. Similarly, the benefits of roads are often nonrival. However, it is feasible to use tolls to exclude those who refuse to pay. The characteristics of nonrival consumption and nonexclusion therefore vary in degree from good to good. Much, however, can be learned from further investigation of the problems involved in making available efficient amounts of a good that is *both* nonrival in consumption and whose benefits are nonexclusive.

Pure Public Goods and Pure Private Goods

A **pure public good** is nonrival in consumption for an entire population of consumers and its benefits have the characteristic of nonexclusion. A given quantity of a pure public good is consumed by all members of a community as soon as it is produced for, or by, any one member. In contrast, a **pure private good** is one that, after producers receive compensation for the full opportunity costs of production, provides benefits *only* to the person who acquires the good, and not to anyone else. A pure private good is rival in consumption, and its benefits are easily excluded from those who choose not to pay its market price.

Market exchange for pure private goods results in neither positive nor negative externalities. A pure public good, instead, results in widely consumed external benefits to all persons, even if it is made available only for one particular person. These two extremes can be considered as poles on a continuum, where goods are ranked according to their degree of publicness or privateness in terms of the range and extent to which their production or consumption generate externalities.

Pure public "bads" can also exist. These are activities that result in external costs affecting a wide range of the population. The quantities of public bads is of concern to all individuals. Air pollution, for example, is a pure public bad if pollutants diffuse in the atmosphere, thereby affecting all individuals, independent of the location of their residence. At the other extreme, national defense can be considered a pure public good, insofar as it is impossible to protect any one individual against harm from a foreign invasion or attack without protecting, at the same time, all other individuals in the nation.

The marginal cost of distributing a pure public good to an additional consumer is zero for a given amount of the public good. This follows from the nonrival characteristic of pure public goods. Figure 4.1A shows that the marginal cost of allowing additional persons to consume a certain amount of a pure public good falls to zero after the good has been made available for any one person. Be careful not to confuse distribution cost with production cost. The marginal costs of accommodating an additional consumer will be zero for a *given quantity* of a pure public good. However, the marginal cost of producing *additional units* of the public good will be positive, as is the case for all economic goods, because increasing the quantity of a pure public good requires additional resources. This is illustrated in Figure 4.1B, where the average cost of a pure public good is assumed to be constant. Two units of the public good cost twice as much as one unit. In this case, if the average cost of the public good is $200 per unit, the marginal cost will also be $200.

The distinction between pure public goods and pure private goods can be emphasized in still another way.[1] A pure public good is not divisible into units that can be apportioned among consumers. A given quantity of a pure public good can be only shared, rather than individually enjoyed. Its benefits are collectively consumed by the entire population. A unit of a pure private good, on the other hand, can be enjoyed only by a single consumer. The more units of a given amount available consumed by one person, the less is available to rival consumers.

An Example: Bread Versus Heat

A simple example will help to clarify the distinction between pure public goods and pure private goods. Suppose a community of a certain number of persons is confined to a room. Decisions made in that room affect only those in the room and no one else. Each day, residents of the room receive a fixed quantity of bread and a certain amount of fuel to heat the room. The bread is a pure private good in the sense that it is possible to slice it and divide it among the individuals. The total amount of bread available each day equals the sum of the amounts consumed by persons in the room. If more bread is allocated to any one person, less will remain available per day for the others. Bread could be easily sold in a market where the price would be established each day by the interaction of demand and supply. Given the daily price of bread, persons in the room could adjust their consumption of bread according to their preferences and economic circumstances.

---

[1]This point is emphasized by Samuelson in his classic papers on pure public goods: Paul Samuelson, "The Pure Theory of Public Expenditure," *Review of Economics and Statistics* 36 (November 1954): 387–389 and "Diagrammatic Exposition of the Theory of Public Expenditure," *Review of Economics and Statistics* 37 (November 1955): 350–356.

Figure 4.1 ✦ MARGINAL COSTS OF CONSUMING AND PRODUCING A PURE PUBLIC GOOD

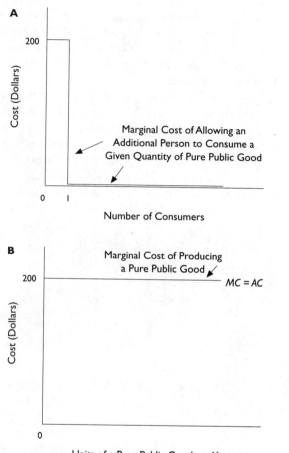

The diagram in **A** shows that the marginal cost of allowing an additional person to consume a given quantity of a pure public good falls to zero after it is made available to any one person. The graph in **B** shows that the marginal cost of producing the good is always positive. In this case, the marginal cost of each extra unit of the good is $200.

On the other hand, it is impossible to divide among persons in the room the extent to which it is heated. All individuals in the room at any point in time experience the same temperature level. Assume that the room is large enough so that the effect of the heat emitted by additional bodies on the amount of fuel needed is negligible. Therefore, additional persons can be accommodated in the room at a given temperature without using more or less fuel. It is impossible for one person to consume more heat in such a way as to reduce the amount made available to others. Finally, it is impossible for different people in the room to consume different quantities of heat; that is, the level of heat produced for any one individual is the level that all individuals must consume. Individual consumers of heat therefore will lack the ability to adjust the amount of heat they consume in accordance with their own tastes and economic circumstances. It is impossible for two individuals simultaneously to occupy a room in which the temperature is both 65 degrees and 78 degrees Fahrenheit. The level of heat in the room therefore will have all the characteristics of a pure public good for those who occupy the room.

An important consideration in discussing public goods is the range of their benefits. Some public goods, such as world peace, conceivably might provide collectively consumed benefits to every single individual, no matter where on the face of the earth. Some goods are collectively consumed within the confines of given nations, although others might produce collectively consumed benefits that are locally consumed. The geographic range of shared benefits influences the desirability of having public goods supplied by various levels of government (for example, federal, state, or local). This problem is extensively investigated in the last part of this book.

CHECKPOINT

1. What are the characteristics of public goods?
2. How do pure public goods differ from pure private goods?
3. Why is the marginal cost of allowing another consumer to enjoy the benefits of a pure public good always zero, even though the marginal cost of producing the good is positive?

PROVISION OF PRIVATE GOODS AND PUBLIC GOODS: MARKETS AND GOVERNMENT

The supply of goods and services and the mechanisms of distributing these among individuals reflect collectively agreed-upon institutional arrangements that have emerged in a community. It is difficult to make generalizations about the most appropriate means for making goods and services available. Private goods that are individually consumed are sometimes supplied through markets by government, as is the case for certain transportation services, electricity, and other public utility services. On the other hand, many goods that are nonrival in consumption, and therefore have characteristics of public goods, are privately produced and supplied through markets. This is the case for certain recreational services sold through private clubs, television and other communication services, and private police protection. In many cases, goods and services are supplied both through markets under private production and by governments through political institutions. For example, both private and public schools are available. Recreational services and facilities, such as parks, tennis courts, and golf courses, are supplied by both the government and the private sector.

It is possible to imagine, at the extreme, pure private goods being supplied through government and financed through taxation. For example, citizens could agree collectively to supply clothing through government and allow every person one identical suit of clothes per year at no direct charge, financing the production and distribution of the clothing through taxation. Similarly, it is possible to envision goods that have the characteristics of public goods being produced privately and sold through markets when the costs of exclusion are not very high. This is the case for cable television services, in which programming that is nonrival in consumption is produced by profit-maximizing firms that sell monthly subscriptions to their programming services. The fee serves as an exclusion device, making the service available only to those who sign a contract and agree to pay.

In practice, it is not possible to draw a neat line between pure private goods and pure public goods. Many intermediate cases exist in which external benefits or costs accrue only to some persons and the transactions costs associated with trading goods with collectively consumed benefits are not prohibitive. In those cases, both private supply and government supply are feasible, and it is often difficult to determine which method of supply is appropriate.

Congestible Public Goods and Private Goods with Externalities

Government supply through political institutions and private supply through markets are alternative means of making any good available. These two alternatives can be evaluated according to the extent to which externalities are associated with either the production or consumption of the good and the extent to which it is possible to develop a means of selling rights to use the good or service.

Congestible public goods are those for which crowding or congestion reduces the benefits to existing consumers when more consumers are accommodated. The marginal cost of accommodating an additional consumer is not zero after the point of congestion is reached. For example, an additional user of a congested road decreases the benefits to existing users by slowing down traffic and increasing the risk of an accident. This is illustrated in Figure 4.2. After N^* users of a road have been accommodated per hour, the marginal cost of allowing another user on that road becomes positive.

Price-excludable public goods are those with benefits that can be priced. Private clubs are often set up to share facilities such as tennis courts, swimming pools, and dining areas for small groups. Membership rights, which are sold in the market, are sometimes negotiable and can be sold by their holders to others. By joining clubs and paying dues, members share in the cost of facilities and services that they otherwise would be unable to afford. Dues and limits on the number of members are determined by collective agreement of existing members.[2] The dues ration the facilities of the club to avoid the effects of congestion. Other price-excludable public goods include such public facilities as schools and hospitals. These goods can be priced, but their provision results in positive externalities.

---

[2]See Todd Sandler and John T. Tschirhart, "The Economic Theory of Clubs: An Evaluative Survey," *Journal of Economic Literature* 18 (December 1980): 1481–1521.

Figure 4.2 ◆ A CONGESTIBLE PUBLIC GOOD

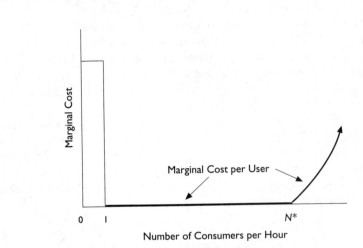

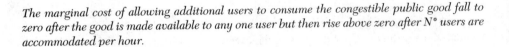

The marginal cost of allowing additional users to consume the congestible public good fall to zero after the good is made available to any one user but then rise above zero after $N°$ users are accommodated per hour.

Table 4.1 summarizes alternative means for producing, distributing, and financing goods and services. Goods and services have been divided into four categories:

1. Pure private goods
2. Price-excludable public goods
3. Congestible public goods
4. Pure public goods

The first category represents goods that approximate the ideal of a pure private good that is individually consumed and subject to low-cost exclusion from benefits for those who do not pay for the right to receive such benefits. The production of these goods usually does not generate an externality, but some individuals believe that external benefits are associated with others who consume these goods. Such private goods might be sold in markets either by private firms or government. When sold in markets, their costs of production are financed by the revenue obtained from sales to individual buyers. Alternatively, they may be produced by government or purchased by government from private firms, distributed free of direct charge to eligible recipients, and financed by taxes. Such is the case for public welfare programs that give medical services, food, housing, and other services to low-income citizens who meet certain eligibility tests. These services also could be sold at subsidized prices, with losses made up from tax-financed subsidies.

Second, some goods can be individually consumed and are subject to exclusion but their production or consumption is likely to generate externalities. These are price-excludable public goods. Again, such goods can be distributed through markets

Table 4.1 ◆ ALTERNATIVE MEANS OF PRODUCING, DISTRIBUTING, AND FINANCING GOODS AND SERVICES

CHARACTERISTICS OF THE GOOD OR SERVICE	MEANS OF PRODUCTION	METHODS OF DISTRIBUTION	METHODS OF FINANCE	EXAMPLES	
				PRIVATE	PUBLIC
PURE PRIVATE GOODS No externality; low-cost exclusion	1. Private firms; government	Markets; direct unit charge	Revenue from sales	Food; clothing; cars	Government liquor stores; government tobacco monopoly
	2. Government; private firms under contract with government	No direct unit charge; eligibility to consume various amounts, determined politically	Taxes		Government distribution of medical services and food to low-income citizens
PRICE-EXCLUDABLE PUBLIC GOODS External benefits when produced or consumed; low-cost exclusion	1. Private firms; government	Markets; direct unit charge (may be subsidized)	Revenue from sales; taxes	Schools; hospitals; transportation	Transit facilities; public hospitals
	2. Government; private firms under contract with government	No direct unit charge; consumption available or required only at collectively chosen quantity and quality	Taxes		Public schools; public sanitation; inoculations
CONGESTIBLE PUBLIC GOODS Collectively consumed benefits subject to crowding; possibility of exclusion	1. Private firms; government	Fees for the right to use the facility sold in markets	Revenue from sales	Clubs; theaters; amusement parks; sporting events	Public golf courses; roads
	2. Government; private firms under contract with government	No direct user charge (or partial charge)	Taxes; revenue from sales		Public parks; public recreation; roads, bridges
PURE PUBLIC GOODS Collectively consumed benefits not subject to crowding; high-cost exclusion	1. Private firms; government	No direct unit charge; quantity dependent on amount collected	Fees; contributions	Private charity	Public television and radio
	2. Government; private firms under contract with government	No direct unit charge; quantity and quality of service collectively chosen	Taxes		National defense; environmental protection

when produced either by private firms or government. The production or consumption of these goods can be subsidized to account for the positive externality associated with their sale. The good, therefore, would be financed by both the revenue from sales and the taxes used to finance the subsidy. Such is the case for private and public hospitals, mass transit facilities, and schooling. These goods also can be produced by government and distributed with no direct charge. In such cases, however, the quantity and quality of the service would be determined collectively through political institutions, and costs would be financed through taxation. This is the case for public schooling, public sanitation service, and government-supplied inoculations that are available at public health facilities.

Congestible public goods are nonrival in consumption only up to a certain point. After the number of consumers exceeds a certain amount, the goods become at least partially rival in consumption. Therefore, an increase in the use of the good by one consumer decreases the benefits from a given amount of the good that can be enjoyed by others. Exclusion from benefits of these goods is often possible through application of certain fees. Congestible public goods, in some cases, therefore are also price-excludable public goods. These goods are often in the form of services flowing from shared facilities that can be distributed in markets either by government or by firms through the sale of admissions, memberships, or other use-related fees; these might receive public subsidies. Privately supplied examples include clubs for sharing recreational or other facilities, amusement parks, theaters, and sporting events. Government-supplied goods of this type might be partially or fully financed by taxes. Public parks are an example, as are other forms of public recreation, civic centers, auditoriums, roads, bridges, and similar public facilities.

Pure public goods result in collectively consumed benefits that are not subject to crowding and are subject to high-cost exclusion. It is difficult to sell use rights to the benefits of these goods, and markets are unlikely to provide a convenient mechanism for distributing them. Conceivably, they could be produced privately through voluntary contributions, with the quantity and quality of service provided being contingent on the amount of revenue collected. Private charity is often provided and financed in this manner. However, goods resembling pure public goods are most likely to be distributed free of direct charge by governments, with the quantity and quality of the service determined through political institutions and financed by taxes. Such is the case for national defense, environmental protection, and other goods resembling pure public goods.

Really, semipublic goods exist in a continuum ranging from pure private goods to pure public goods. Figure 4.3 shows how goods could be categorized according to the degree of rivalry in consumption and the degree of excludability. The horizontal axis of the graph plots the extent to which the benefits of the good are rival on a scale of zero to one. A pure private good with benefits that are fully rival in consumption would rate a value of one on the horizontal axis while a pure public good with benefits that are completely nonrival in consumption would rate a zero on the horizontal axis. A congestible public good with benefits that are only partially nonrival would be assigned a number of between zero and one on the horizontal axis depending on the degree of its congestibility.

Figure 4.3 ◆ Classifying Goods according to the Degree of Rivalry and Excludability of Benefits from Their Use

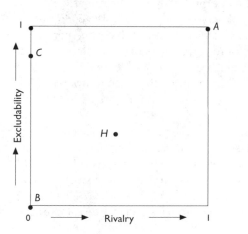

A pure public good corresponds to point B, where there is no rivalry for benefits and excludability from benefits is impossible. A pure private good corresponds to point A on the graph. A nonrival good, such as TV transmissions, for which exclusion is possible corresponds to a point like C. A congestible public good for which it is possible to charge for use, such as a limited access highway, corresponds to a point like H.

The vertical axis measures the excludability of the good on a scale of zero to one. A pure private good, which is perfectly excludable because its benefits can be fully withheld from someone who does not pay, would be assigned a one on the vertical axis. Similarly a pure public good that is not price excludable would be assigned a zero. Goods such as highways for which tolls can be charged and other price-excludable goods would be assigned a number between zero and one, depending on the ease to which the benefits of the product can be priced.

According to this classification scheme, a pure private good would correspond to point *A* on the graph. At that point there is full excludability and full rivalry for the benefits of the good. Similarly a pure public good would correspond to point *B* at which the benefits are fully nonrival and price excludability is impossible. Some goods such as cable TV transmissions would correspond to a point on the vertical axis like *C*. For such a product the benefits are nonrival but price exclusion is relatively easy because signals can be scrambled and those who decline to pay for a hookup can be denied the benefits. A highway subject to congestion would correspond to a point like *H* where there is a degree of rivalry, and price exclusion is possible through tolls.

C H E C K P O I N T

1. How do congestible public goods differ from pure public goods?
2. How do price-excludable public goods differ from pure public goods?
3. Give some examples of "semipublic goods" that are provided through the marketplace by profit-motivated businesses. Discuss the characteristics of these goods in terms of the excludability of their benefits and the rivalry among consumers for the benefits of given amounts of the goods.

THE DEMAND FOR A PURE PUBLIC GOOD

The demand for a pure public good must be interpreted differently from the demand for a pure private good. The market demand curve for a pure private good gives the sum of the quantities demanded by all consumers at each possible price per unit of the good. The market demand curve for a pure private good, such as bread, is illustrated in Figure 4.4. For any given price, a point on the market demand curve for a pure private good is found by simply adding the quantity that each individual would purchase at that price. The individual demand curves, therefore, are added laterally over the horizontal axis to obtain the market demand curve.

In Figure 4.4 there are only three consumers of the private good. At a price of $3 per loaf, the person whose demand curve is D_A purchases one loaf per week. That is the quantity for which the price equals his marginal benefit per week (MB_A = $3). The person whose demand curve is represented by D_B purchases two loaves per week at a price of $3 per loaf. At that amount of weekly purchase of bread, MB_B = $3. Finally, the person with demand curve D_C purchases three loaves per week at a price of $3 per loaf because MB_C = $3 at that amount of weekly consumption. The total market quantity demanded by these three consumers is therefore six loaves per week at a price of $3 per loaf. This is represented by point E on the market demand curve. Until the price falls below $4 per loaf, the only individual purchasing the good will be the one whose demand curve is represented by D_C. At lower prices, the other individuals whose demands are represented by D_B and D_A progressively enter the mar-

Figure 4.4 ◆ DEMAND FOR A PRIVATE GOOD

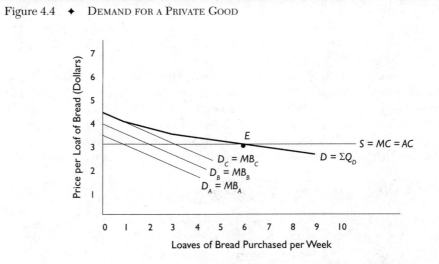

The demand for a private good is obtained by adding the quantities demanded by each consumer at each possible price. The efficient output is six units per week, which corresponds to point E. At a price of $3 per loaf, MB_A = MB_B = MB_C = MC.

ket, and the quantities that they demand as prices are lowered are added to that of the consumer whose demand is D_C. The market demand curve for the private good is labeled $D = \Sigma Q_D$.

For a pure public good, all consumers *must consume the same quantity of the good*. Purchasers of a pure public good would not be able to adjust their consumption so that one person had one unit per week while another person enjoyed two units per week and still another had three units per week. If consumer A had three units per week, all other persons would consume three units per week. For a pure public good, consumers cannot adjust the amounts purchased until the price of the good equals their marginal benefit from the good per week. In fact, a pure public good cannot be priced because of its nonexclusion property.

How then can a demand curve for a pure public good be derived? The variables on the vertical axes are not market prices. Instead, they are the maximum amounts that persons would pay per unit of the pure public good as a function of the amount of the good actually available. For example, suppose the three consumers live together in a small community and desire to provide themselves with security protection. The quantity of security protection can be measured by the number of security guards hired per week to patrol their community. Security guards represent a pure public good for these three consumers. No way exists for any one person in this community of three to hire a security guard for his own benefit without benefiting his neighbors.

Figure 4.5 shows each person's demand curve for security guards. A point on any of the individual demand curves represents the maximum amount that the consumer

Figure 4.5 ✦ DEMAND FOR A PURE PUBLIC GOOD

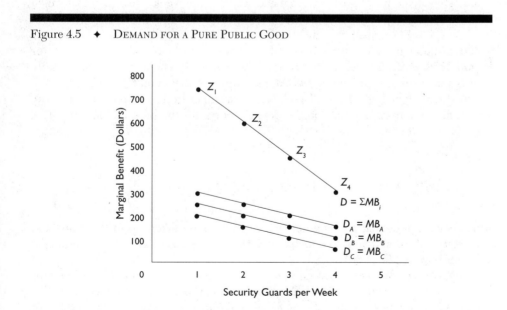

The demand curve for a pure public good is obtained by summing the individual marginal benefits at each quantity.

would pay to get *each unit* of the corresponding quantity of the public good. This maximum amount is the marginal benefit of security protection at each quantity. Each individual's demand curve shows how the marginal benefit of security guards declines as more are made available.

The total amount that would be given up per security guard hired per week is the sum of the annual weekly marginal benefits of each of the three consumers. Points on the aggregate demand curve for a pure public good could be obtained by adding each person's marginal benefit at each possible quantity. The demand curve for a pure public good therefore is obtained by summing the individual demand curves vertically. The marginal benefit, or demand price, that each person would pay per unit of the public good is summed at each quantity of the good, because all persons must consume the same quantity.

For example, the person with the demand curve D_A would pay a maximum of $300 per security guard if only one guard were provided per week. Similarly, the maximum amounts the persons with demand curves D_B and D_C would give up per security guard if only one were provided per week would be $250 and $200, respectively. A point on the market demand curve therefore is obtained by adding these maximum amounts. Because the maximum amounts reflect the marginal benefit of security protection, the point on the market demand curve represented by point Z_1 corresponds to the sum of the marginal benefits of all three consumers. This equals $750 per year when only one security guard is provided.

The marginal benefit of additional units of a pure public good declines in the same fashion as do those of pure private goods. The amount per security guard that could be collected if two guards were made available per week is less than that which could be collected per guard when only one is provided per week. This, too, is shown in Figure 4.5. The maximum amount per guard that each of the three consumers would give up when two guards are made available per week is $250 for A, $200 for B, and $150 for C. Therefore, the sum of the marginal benefits when two security guards per week are provided is $600, as represented by point Z_2 in Figure 4.5. Adding the marginal benefit received by each consumer from any number of security guards in this way gives points on the demand curve for the pure public good. This curve is labeled $D = \Sigma MB_i$.

EFFICIENT OUTPUT OF A PURE PUBLIC GOOD

Efficiency requires that all economic activities be undertaken up to the point that their marginal social benefit is equated with their marginal social cost. This principle holds for pure public goods as well.

Suppose a person were to attempt to produce or purchase a pure public good for her own use. By making a unit of the public good available in the community, this person will generate benefits not only for herself but also for every other member of the community in which she resides. The marginal social benefit of this good therefore will be more than the extra benefit to its purchaser. Additional benefits will accrue to each and every other person who will simultaneously enjoy each unit made available. Summing up these benefits to all persons in the community gives the marginal social benefit for each extra unit of output produced. The marginal social benefit of any given amount of a pure public good is therefore the *sum of the individual marginal benefits received by all consumers.*

The efficient quantity per time period of a pure public good therefore corresponds to the point at which output is increased so that the sum of the marginal benefits of consumers equals the marginal social cost of the good. The efficiency conditions for a pure public good therefore are

$$MSB = \Sigma MB = MSC. \tag{4.1}$$

Market sale of a pure public good for individual purchase would generate wide-ranging positive externalities, because a purchaser of the good would consider only *his* marginal benefit in deciding how much to buy. The marginal external benefit would be the sum of the marginal benefits to all other consumers. When individual buyers do not take the marginal external benefit into account, sale of the good to individuals in a market is likely to result in less than the efficient annual quantity. A pure private good has no external benefits of additional production. In evaluating the benefit of extra production, it is necessary to count only the benefit received by the individual who actually purchases and consumes the extra output.

The efficiency conditions for a pure public good can also be written as follows:

$$MSB = MB_i + \sum_{j=1}^{n-1} MB_j = MSC. \tag{4.2}$$

Equation 4.2 states the marginal social benefit of a unit of a pure public good as the sum of the benefits accruing to any one person acquiring it (MB_i) and of the extra benefits that accrue to the remaining ($n - 1$) members of the community (ΣMB_i). The marginal social benefit is the sum of an individual benefit and an external benefit accruing to all other members of the community. The summation term

$$\sum_{j=1}^{n-1} MB_j$$

therefore represents the marginal external benefit of a unit of a pure public good made available to any one person. The production of a pure public good generates external benefits that are positively valued by all members of a community.

A Numerical Example

Table 4.2 provides data on the marginal benefits of three consumers who desire security protection in a community. These data summarize the numbers used to derive the demand curve for security protection in Figure 4.5. In the table, the marginal benefits of as many as four security guards per week are shown for each consumer.

Suppose that the weekly cost per security guard is $450. If as many guards as desired can be hired at that rate, the average cost of security protection would be constant at $450 per unit. In this case, a unit of security protection per week is presumed to be perfectly correlated with the services of one security guard per week. Because

Table 4.2   ✦   HYPOTHETICAL MARGINAL BENEFITS OF SECURITY PROTECTION FOR A
COMMUNITY OF THREE PERSONS

	NUMBER OF SECURITY GUARDS PER WEEK			
	1	2	3	4
MB_A	$300	$250	$200	$150
MB_B	250	200	150	100
MB_C	200	150	100	50
ΣMB_i	$750	$600	$450	$300

average cost is constant, it is also equal to the marginal cost. Assuming no negative externalities associated with security protection, the marginal social cost of security protection also will be constant and equal to $450.

Table 4.2 also shows the sum of the marginal benefits, ΣMB_i, of security guards for the three consumers at each weekly quantity. Figure 4.6 plots the marginal benefit curve of each of the three consumers on the same set of axes as the marginal social cost curve. This latter curve is a straight line drawn at $450. Also plotted on the axes is the sum of the marginal benefits for the three consumers at each level of output. This latter curve gives the marginal social benefit of alternative weekly amounts of security protection.

The efficient number of security guards for the three members of the community is three per week. At that level of supply, corresponding to point *E,* the sum of the marginal benefits equals the marginal social cost. At that level of weekly supply, the marginal social benefit equals the marginal social cost for members of the community.

Figure 4.6 can show quickly why market provision of security protection would not result in the efficient output. If the services of security guards were available to individuals only through market purchases, the quantity supplied to this community would be zero! This is because it costs $450 per week to hire each security guard. No single resident alone values the services of the first security guard that highly. The most any one person would pay for a security guard is $300 per week. The marginal benefit of the first security guard for any one buyer falls short of the market price per unit necessary to cover the marginal costs of sellers.

However, an output of zero is inefficient. The market equilibrium would be inefficient because, as is shown in Figure 4.6, the sum of the marginal benefits of the three consumers when one security guard per week is provided exceeds the marginal social cost of making that guard available. The marginal social benefit of the first guard is $750, while the marginal social cost is only $450. Therefore, it is certainly inefficient not to hire *at least* one security guard per week. The efficient output is actually three security guards per week, corresponding to point *E* in Figure 4.6. At that point, the sum of the individual marginal benefits equals the marginal social cost of security protection.

Figure 4.6 ✦ EFFICIENT OUTPUT OF A PURE PUBLIC GOOD

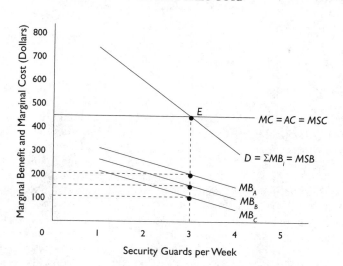

The efficient output occurs at point E, which corresponds to three security guards per week. At that point, $\Sigma MB_i = MSC$. The Lindahl equilibrium is also at point E. At that point, voluntary contributions of the three persons would cover the cost of the public good. Each person would demand three security guards per week at a price per unit equal to the marginal benefit received from three guards per week.

A Cooperative Method of Efficiently Supplying Pure Public Goods: Voluntary Contributions and Cost Sharing

To achieve the efficient output of three guards per week, members of the community will have to cooperate to share the costs per unit of security protection. By sharing the costs, members can pool their resources to enjoy public goods that they could not afford if they had to purchase them on their own in a market. In small communities, pure public goods conceivably could be made available in the efficient amounts and financed by voluntary contributions. Understanding why this is unlikely to occur in larger communities is the key to understanding the reasons that citizens resort to governments to provide many public goods. It also helps provide insights into the reasons governments finance most of their activities with compulsory taxes instead of voluntary contributions.[3]

---

[3]A classic model of a cooperative mechanism for supplying public goods was developed by Erik Lindahl in the early 1900s. See Erik Lindahl, "Just Taxation: A Positive Solution," in *Classics in the Theory of Public Finance*, eds. Richard A. Musgrave and Alan T. Peacock (New York: Cromwell-Collier, 1958), 168–177. Also see Cecil Bohanan, "McCaleb on Lindahl, Comment," *Public Finance* 38 (1983): 326–331.

PUBLIC POLICY PERSPECTIVE

DEFENSE SPENDING IN THE UNITED STATES AND THE "PEACE DIVIDEND"

National defense is a classic public good. Defense services provide nonrival benefits to all in a nation regardless of whether they pay. In the 1980s, defense spending in the United States increased dramatically, growing at a rate of nearly 6 percent per year, after adjustment for inflation, from 1981 to 1988. From 1980 to 1987, federal government purchases to provide national defense increased from 23.2 percent to 27.5 percent of annual federal outlays. Much of the spending during this period reflected investment in new military hardware and systems including the electronic marvels that were used in Operation Desert Storm. In 1986, defense spending in the United States amounted to 6.3 percent of GDP. The graph below shows defense spending variation as a percent of GDP from 1960 to 1993. During the period 1966–1971 defense expenditures were a relatively large portion of GDP because of the Vietnam War.

The marginal social benefit of national defense varies with the threat to national security. The elimination of the Soviet threat in Eastern Europe has reduced the marginal social benefit of defense spending. By 1993 defense spending had fallen to 4.75 percent of GDP and was likely to continue to absorb a smaller share of national output in the future because the demise of the former Soviet Union diminished the threat of nuclear attack.

Let's take a look at the implications of reduced output of national defense. Cuts for defense spending brings reductions in U.S. military troop strength. Through 1995, U.S. troop strength will be reduced by 100,000 with troop reduction in Europe amounting to 50,000. Many U.S. bases will be closed and defense

DEFENSE PURCHASES AS A PERCENTAGE OF GDP, 1966–1993

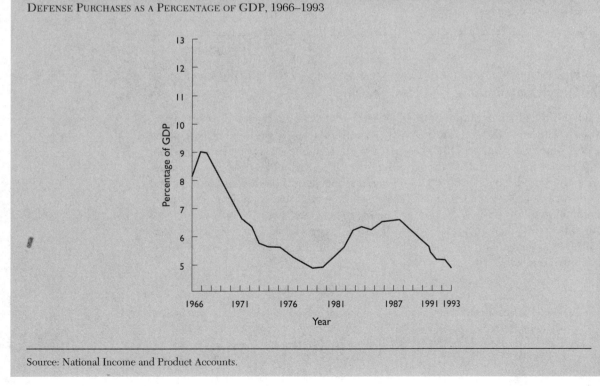

Source: National Income and Product Accounts.

spending is expected to decline to less than 20 percent of federal spending.

If international relations with our former adversaries continue to improve, the pressure to cut back on naval forces and reduce our nuclear arsenals will increase. Little rationale or benefit would remain in maintaining a large nuclear arsenal aimed at dismantled former Soviet nuclear capabilities. We also could abandon expensive defense schemes such as the B-2 bomber, the strategic defense initiative (SDI), and the Sea Wolf Attack submarine, which was specifically designed to defend against a Soviet fleet in the Arctic seas.

The decline in military spending will allow resources in both the United States and Russia as well as other former Soviet republics to be diverted to other uses. However, because the former Soviet Union devoted much higher percentages (about twice as much as the United States) of its GDP to defense in the past, the amount of resources that will be made available from reduced spending, the so-called "peace dividend," is likely to be much greater for the Russians than for the United States. That peace dividend is vital to the peoples of the former Soviet Republics who are struggling to transform their crippled economy by introducing free markets. By reducing defense spending, they can reallocate resources to create new industries that the Russians and other former Soviet people could use to provide consumer goods and export products to earn sorely needed foreign currencies. For example, if the Russians reduce their defense spending from 12 percent to 4 percent of GDP, as much as 8 percent of their current production can be reallocated from military goods to consumer goods.

In the United States, where the share of output devoted to national defense amounted to less than 5 percent in 1993, there will also be a reallocation of resources. However, because defense spending is not expected to decline to much less than 4 percent of GDP, the peace dividend will amount to little more than 1 percent of national output. With the transition toward reduced defense spending, there will be some short-term economic dislocation in the United States. Communities in which military bases and defense-related industries currently provide jobs will suffer from increased unemployment. Assembly line workers and engineers with defense-related skills will have to find new work, often at lower wages and at another location, as government purchases of aircraft, ships, military vehicles, and missiles are cut.

As the marginal social benefit of spending for defense declines, the efficient level of output devoted to defense also will be less. As politicians respond to the reduced demand for defense, it is reasonable to expect the share of output devoted to military goods and services also to decline.

Suppose that the three persons previously discussed try to cooperate to satisfy and finance their desires for security protection. These persons are confronted with the problem of financing a pure public good that is collectively consumed by them alone. All three persons must consume the identical quantity of security protection per week and must voluntarily contribute to cover the annual costs of making the protection available. Remember, it costs $450 per week for each security guard, and no member of the community will purchase security protection service if he or she has to pay for it alone.

Suppose the three persons pool their resources to hire security guards. If they can obtain enough funds in this way, they will be able to make themselves better off by acquiring benefits none of them can individually afford. They will continue to cooperate in this way by hiring guards up to the point at which their pooled contributions can no longer finance additional guards.

Suppose they try to hire one guard per week. How much would they collect in contributions? Figure 4.6 shows that A would contribute $300 for the first guard, B would contribute $250, and C would contribute $200. These amounts represent the marginal benefits for these persons when only one guard per week is hired. Because the sum of the voluntary contributions exceeds the marginal cost of the first guard, the members conclude that it might be worthwhile to try to finance two guards per week instead. Hiring only one guard per week leaves a budget surplus for security protection. The budget surplus therefore indicates that the marginal social benefit of the first security guard in the community exceeds the marginal social cost of providing the protection.

The sum of the marginal benefits of two security guards per week is $600. The members of the community therefore would contribute $600 per guard if two would be hired per week. This also exceeds the marginal cost of making two guards per week available. The members of the community therefore would collect more than enough funds to finance two units of security protection per week. The community security budget still has a surplus as long as each member faithfully contributes an amount equal to the marginal benefit per guard. The total cost of two guards per week would be $900. Because each person contributes an amount equal to the marginal benefit *per* guard, the total amounts collected to finance two security guards would be $500 from A, $400 from B, and $300 from C. The total revenue therefore would be $1,200. The surplus is $300 per week.

The marginal benefits when three guards per week are available are $MB_A = $200, $MB_B = 150, and $MB_C = 100. The sum of the marginal benefits exactly equals the marginal cost of the third guard, $450. The community therefore can finance still another unit of security protection. The total cost of three security guards per week is $1,350. Person A contributes $200 per guard, or $600 per week for three guards. Person B contributes $150 per guard and thereby pays $450 per week for three guards. Finally, C contributes $100 per guard, making a total weekly contribution equal to $300 for three guards. The total contributions exactly equal the total cost of $1,350 per week for three guards. This occurs at point E in Figure 4.6, where the ΣMB_i curve for the public good intersects the marginal cost curve for the good. At point E, $MSB = \Sigma MB_i = MC = MSC$ for the three consumers.

Any output greater than three could not be financed with voluntary contributions, because the sum of the marginal benefits of security protection in excess of three guards per week would fall short of the marginal cost of that level of security. Voluntary contributions therefore would fail to collect enough to finance more than three security guards per week.

The equilibrium achieved through voluntary contributions results in the support of three security guards per week, which is efficient. This is because $MSB = MSC$ at the equilibrium number of guards per week. Thus, voluntary contributions, in small groups, can achieve the efficient output of a pure public good.

The Lindahl Equilibrium

Point E in Figure 4.6 is called a **Lindahl equilibrium,** after the Swedish economist, Erik Lindahl.[4] The voluntary contribution per unit of the public good of each member of the community equals his or her marginal benefit of the public good at the efficient level of output. These equilibrium contributions per unit of the public good

---

[4]Erik Lindahl, "Just Taxation."

are sometimes called **Lindahl prices.** If the good were made available at these prices per unit for each of the consumers, the quantity demanded by *each* consumer would be the efficient amount of three security guards per week.

In effect, the Lindahl equilibrium also could be achieved by assigning each participant a Lindahl price per unit of the public good. Each person would have to be assigned a price that equals his or her marginal benefit at the efficient output of the good. In equilibrium, all three individuals would unanimously agree on the efficient quantity of the good to be made available, given their assigned Lindahl prices. In the preceding example, the Lindahl prices for each security guard would have to equal each community member's marginal benefit at the efficient output of three guards per week. If disagreement about the quantity of the good arises, the Lindahl prices per unit of the good will have to be adjusted until all individuals demand the quantity for which $MSB = MSC$. If disagreement ensues about the Lindahl prices, the quantity of the good will have to be adjusted until all individuals accept their share and no surplus or deficit in the budget exists at the efficient output.

The solution to the model is similar to a market equilibrium, because it results in a set of price shares per unit of the good that are unanimously accepted to finance the cost of production of a simultaneously agreed-upon quantity. No one is forced or coerced to enter into the agreement. Given the distribution of income and other factors that affect the demands (or willingness to pay) of the three individuals for security protection, the outcome is a determinate quantity of the public good and an associated cost-sharing scheme. The voluntary cooperation model presented is one in which contributions are accepted for alternative quantities of the public good, which, in turn, are compared with the marginal cost of additional production. Other similar models have auctioneer-announcing schemes for the division of the cost per unit of a public good in terms of the percentages to be borne by each individual, independent of the number of units produced. This ensures that the budget will always be in balance. Such tax-sharing schemes continually are called out until the quantity demanded of the public good is the same for all individuals.[5] The result in both cases is identical: The public good is produced at the level where the sum of the marginal benefits is equal to the marginal social cost and each individual's Lindahl price in equilibrium reflects that person's marginal benefit at the equilibrium level of production.

Generalizing the Results

The Lindahl equilibrium consists in an agreement on the division of the costs of producing the equilibrium quantity of a pure public good. The conditions for equilibrium can now be generalized. Call t_i the amount contributed by each person for any quantity of a pure public good made available and Q^* the equilibrium annual quantity of the pure public good. The equilibrium under the model of voluntary cooperation meets the following conditions:

1. The amount contributed per unit of the public good by each person, t_i, must be adjusted so that each individual desires the identical amount of the public good. This requirement stems from the nature of public goods. It is impossible for any

---

[5]This is the approach used by Lindahl in his classic model.

one member of a community to consume, for example, more security protection than another, assuming that protection is truly a public good.

2. The sum of the amounts contributed by each member of the community per unit must equal the marginal social cost of producing the public good. When marginal social cost equals the average cost of the good, this implies that the voluntary contributions will constitute amounts sufficient to finance the good without any surplus or deficit.[6] The revenue collected can be expressed as the sum of the cost shares per unit of the public good, Σt_i, multiplied by the number of units produced in equilibrium, Q°. The total cost of production is average cost, AC, multiplied by the quantity produced, Q°. It follows that

$$\Sigma t_i Q^\circ = MC(Q^\circ) = AC(Q^\circ) \tag{4.3}$$

or

$$\Sigma t_i = MC = AC.$$

3. All individuals must agree voluntarily, with no coercion whatsoever, on the cost-sharing arrangement and the quantity of the good. The equilibrium must occur under unanimous consent. This ensures an efficient outcome, because any individual made worse off by any arrangement can block its approval.

THE FREE-RIDER PROBLEM

A system of voluntary contributions for reaching agreement on the financing and quantity of a pure public good could work well when a community comprises only a few individuals. In fact, a great deal of similarity exists between voluntary agreements on the supply of pure public goods and the Coasian small-number externalities discussed in Chapter 3. When the number of persons involved in reaching the voluntary agreement is small, the transactions costs are likely to be low. In small groups, individuals know each other well and have a good idea of each other's benefits from the availability of a public good. Persons in the community are well aware of the common benefit of the shared good. Any attempts by individuals to conceal their actual marginal benefits from the good can be easily detected.

For example, persons living in a condominium often meet to determine the extent of maintenance on roads jointly owned by the owners of individual apartments. They might also meet to pool their resources so as to provide security protection. Members of the association are likely to be sufficiently aware of the tastes and incomes of their neighbors to have a good notion of their true marginal benefits of additional maintenance services. Under such circumstances, individual members have little incentive to

---

[6]When marginal costs of producing the pure public good are increasing, $MC > AC$ at any given quantity. This implies that $\Sigma MB_i > AC$ at the efficient output for which $\Sigma MB_i = MC$. In this case, the sum of voluntary contributions per unit exceeds the average cost of production in equilibrium. The equilibrium budget therefore will have a surplus, which could be returned as a lump-sum payment to the members of the community after the cost of the public good is financed.

conceal their preferences in the bidding process. Similarly, in small communities, moral obligations of members might act as strong constraints in preventing inaccurate preference revelation. For this reason, churches and many civic clubs successfully finance projects of common benefit to their members through donations.

However, as the number of persons involved in the decision increases, and information about neighbors' tastes and economic circumstances becomes scarcer, the likelihood that individuals will inaccurately reveal their preferences becomes higher. This is because no one person in a large group is likely to have accurate information on the actual marginal benefits of others.

If persons know that they are required to pay a share of the unit cost of the public good dependent on their marginal benefits, they have an incentive to understate their true marginal benefits. To do this is in their interest because it conserves their incomes. At the same time, they do not have to forgo all the benefits of public goods because these benefits are nonexclusive. A person might, in fact, choose to contribute nothing toward the financing of government activity in the hope of enjoying benefits made possible by other person's contributions. Clearly, if all citizens behave in this way, no source of finance for the budget exists, and therefore no benefits. But the individual who behaves in this manner assumes others will continue to contribute.[7]

A good example of this problem is public television and radio programming. Listener- and viewer-financed stations fund a good portion of their operations from voluntary contributions. Many of the viewers and listeners who receive benefits from the station give nothing or contribute amounts below their marginal benefits from existing programming. A likely result is less than the efficient amount of programming.

A **free rider** is a person who seeks to enjoy the benefits of a public good without contributing anything to the cost of financing the amount made available. The free-rider problem stems from the incentive persons have to enjoy the external benefits financed by others, with no cost to themselves. Free riding can be a reasonable strategy for any one individual, provided that no penalty exists and that only a few individuals choose the strategy. If all members of the community choose the free-rider strategy, no vehicle is available to hitch a ride on because no production of the public good would be forthcoming. Everyone would be worse off under this strategy, because the benefits of the public good will be foregone completely.

Under a system of voluntary contributions when large numbers of persons are involved, attempts by individuals to play the free-rider strategy almost guarantee that the equilibrium amount of pure public good will be less than the efficient amount. Therefore, voluntary cost sharing of pure public goods will result in insufficient amounts of the public good being produced relative to the efficient amounts.

Individuals members of the community can be made better off by engaging in free-rider strategies. Suppose person C, whose marginal benefit curve is drawn in

---

[7]This problem can be avoided if a collectively agreed-upon mechanism can be established to provide artificial incentives for individuals to reveal their true preferences. For a review of this literature, see Martin Loeb, "Alternative Versions of the Demand Revealing Process," *Public Choice* 29 (Spring 1977): 15–26. Also see O. Kim and M. Walker, "The Free-Rider Problem: Experimental Evidence," *Public Choice* 43 (1984): 3–24.

Figure 4.6, tries to be a free rider. To see how he can gain, calculate his net benefits from security protection at the efficient output of three guards per week. His total benefit, $450, is the sum of his marginal benefit from each of the three guards. If he truthfully reveals his marginal benefit for three guards per week, his cost share per guard will be $100. His total cost for the three guards therefore will be $300, and he will enjoy net benefits of $150 at the efficient output.

If he were to be a free rider, he would contribute zero per guard. The cost of a third guard therefore could not be covered even if the other two members truthfully contributed their marginal benefits. This is because $MB_A + MB_B = \$350$ at three guards per week. However, two guards per week could be financed because $MB_A + MB_B = \$450$ at two guards, barely covering the marginal cost of the second guard. At that level of weekly output, person C would enjoy net benefits of $350 (the sum of $200 for the first guard and $150 for the second guard) without contributing a cent. Because his net benefit while pursuing the free-rider strategy exceeds his net benefit from truthfully contributing, he is better off. Other members of the community also could gain by pursuing a free-rider strategy. However, if more than one person were to attempt to be a free rider, not enough would be contributed to finance even one security guard per week! All three persons would be worse off under those circumstances because they would forgo security protection completely.

The free-rider problem tends to become more acute as the size of the group benefiting from a pure public good becomes larger. This is because each individual member of a small group reasons that if he or she withholds his or her contribution, the result could be a significant reduction in the quantity of the good that is supplied in equilibrium. In the three-member group example, the individuals know that if more than one of them is a free rider, no security protection is possible. This provides a strong incentive for them to cooperate. If, on the other hand, 10,000 members are in the community, C's attempt to be a free rider might reduce the equilibrium amount of security only slightly if enough of the others still contribute. In large groups, the incentive for any one person to be a free rider is greater because each person might reason that the vast multitude of other beneficiaries will contribute enough to finance the good. Therefore, the probability of the free-rider problem reducing the actual contributions to zero is all the greater in a community with a large number of members.

Compulsory Finance

In view of the free-rider problem, communities commonly require compulsory payments to help finance the costs of public goods made available to large groups. This leads to government supply of public goods and financing of the cost by taxation. Of course, not all goods supplied by governments are pure public goods. Some government services, such as schooling, roads, and postal services, can be priced and, in fact, could be sold in markets to individuals. However, it is common for government services that involve some degree of collective consumption to be financed through a compulsory tax scheme to avoid the possibility of free riding.

However, an important lesson remains from the model of voluntary cost sharing of public goods. Under compulsory taxation, a voter is told, not asked, to contribute.

The Marginal Cost of the Persian Gulf War to the United States and How International Cost Sharing Financed It

World security is an international public good. Conflicts that affect the supplies of essential resources, such as crude oil from the Middle East, can play havoc with the economies of most industrial nations. When Iraq invaded Kuwait in August of 1990, and stood poised to invade Saudi Arabia, the industrial nations of the world and many Arab nations who saw their security at risk were quick to unite against Iraqi aggression. With the Soviet Union and other old U.S. adversaries no longer opposed to U.S. intervention, the stage was set for a massive military buildup in the region to counter the Iraqi threat to other nations.

Although the bulk of the military effort came from the United States, millions around the world saw not only unprecedented cooperation among the many nations in the conflict but also commitments of cash and materiel from industrial nations that did not send troops to the region. The voluntary contributions to finance the U.S. cost of Operation Desert Storm is a classic case of cooperation in the supply of a public good.

Let's take a look at the numbers to see how the U.S. cost of the war was shared by the group of nations threatened by the Iraqi aggression. The Office of Management and Budget of the federal government has calculated the "incremental" costs of the war. These costs reflect the additional resources that were used to transport and supply troops during Operations Desert Shield and Desert Storm. These incremental costs are an indication of the marginal social cost of the war. Additional wages for military personnel and military operations are included in the estimate of the marginal social cost. Other costs include the transport of personnel and equipment by sea and by air to the Persian Gulf, support operations once there, fuel for military vehicles, and military construction.

According to the Office of Management and Budget, weapons and other nonpersonnel costs amounted to 70 percent of the total costs of the war. About one-third of the costs were for personnel, including the difference between reserve pay and active duty pay for reservists called to active duty, combat pay, and long-term costs such as increased veterans benefits for soldiers who served in the conflict.

As of May 1991, the official estimate of the incremental costs of Operations Desert Shield and Desert Storm was a total of $61 billion. However, much of these costs have been offset by contributions of foreign nations that voluntarily pledged to contribute to costs incurred by the United States. Here is an example of the Lindahl model at work on an international scale: Total pledges by allies of the United States amounted to $54 billion! Of this total, $48 billion were monetary contributions and the remainder were contributions of fuel and other materials to the war effort. These contributions have been allocated to the Defense Department to offset war-related expenses. The net cost of the war to the U.S. taxpayers was therefore expected to amount to only $7 billion.

The following table shows the pledges of the major allies:

Voluntary Contributions to Finance the Marginal Social Cost of Operations Desert Shield and Desert Storm (Billions of Dollars, Rounded to the Nearest Whole Number)

NATION	CONTRIBUTION
Saudi Arabai	17
Kuwait	16
Japan	11
Germany	7
United Arab Emirates	4
Total Pledged	54
U.S. Share	7
Total	61

Source: Office of Management and Budget and Congressional Budget Office.

However, in democratic nations, because political outcomes are determined by voting, the willingness of any voter to vote in favor of a proposal depends on his or her tax share per unit of the good. As demonstrated in the following chapter, a person decides how to vote in an election by comparing the tax share per unit of a public good with the marginal benefit at the proposed output.

CHECKPOINT

1. How does the demand for a pure public good differ from that of a pure private good? How can the demand curve for a pure public good be derived?
2. Under what conditions is the output level of a pure public good efficient?
3. What are the characteristics of the Lindahl equilibrium for cooperative supply of a pure public good? How does the free-rider problem affect the effectiveness of voluntary cooperative methods in achieving efficient levels of output for pure public goods?

Summary

A pure public good is one that is consumed by all members of a community as soon as it is produced for any one member. Its benefits are nonrival and nonexcludable to consumers. The market supply of such a good would result in positive externalities to all members of the community. Therefore, its benefits are collectively consumed, and the exclusion of any one member from those benefits is costly. A pure private good is one that generates no externalities, neither when produced nor when consumed.

Efficiency requires that the production of pure public goods be undertaken to the point where the sum of the marginal private benefits is exactly equal to the marginal social cost of production. Market supply of public goods for individual purchase is likely to be inefficient. This results from the positive externalities associated with market provision of such goods. Persons often attempt to consume the benefits of others' purchases of pure public goods while bearing no costs themselves. These people try to become free riders.

Ideally, an efficient output of a pure public good could be achieved if each person contributed an amount equal to the marginal benefits received per unit of a public good. This is known as the Lindahl equilibrium. However, problems in inducing households to reveal their true preferences for public goods resulting from free-rider effects make this solution difficult to implement.

In actuality, many goods and services fall between the extremes of pure public goods and pure private goods. In evaluating the alternatives of government and market supply for intermediate cases, the external benefits of the good and the efficiency of alternative methods of exclusion have to be considered.

A Forward Look

Public goods supplied through political institutions require collective agreement on the quantity to produce and the means of finance. The following chapter examines the public choices and the political process.

Important Concepts

Public Goods
Nonrival in Consumption
Private Goods
Nonexclusion
Pure Public Good
Pure Private Good
Congestible Public Goods
Price-Excludable Public Goods
Lindahl Equilibrium
Lindahl Prices
Free Rider

Questions for Review

1. What are the essential differences between pure public goods and pure private goods?
2. Although the marginal cost of producing a pure public good is always positive, some consumers can enjoy the benefits of pure public goods at zero marginal costs. Explain the apparent paradox, if there is one!
3. Why does the definition of a pure public good imply that its benefits are not subject to congestion?
4. How does the condition for efficiency differ between pure public goods and pure private goods?
5. What problems are likely to arise if persons try to supply public goods for themselves without cooperating and sharing costs?
6. In what sense does the demand curve for a pure public good differ from that of a pure private good?
7. How will shares in the finance of public goods vary among contributors in a model of voluntary cooperative supply of such goods?
8. Give some examples of goods sold by governments in markets. Think, as well, of examples of partially public goods produced and distributed by private firms for profit.
9. Suppose the price of hiring a security guard increases from $450 to $600 per week. Using the data in Table 4.2, show how this will affect the Lindahl equilibrium.
10. Use the data in Table 4.2 to show how a decrease in the demand for security protection by any one voter will affect the Lindahl equilibrium.

Problems

1. Suppose that the marginal cost of a pure public good increases as more is purchased by a community. Prove that the Lindahl equilibrium will result in a budget surplus at the efficient annual output of the pure public good.
2. Suppose that the services of a road are subject to congestion after 50,000 vehicles per hour enter the road. Assume that it is feasible to price road services on an hourly basis. Use a graph like that drawn in Figure 4.2 to show how the services of the road should be priced per hour when less and more than 50,000 vehicles per hour are expected so as to achieve efficiency.
3. The following table shows how the marginal benefit enjoyed by John, Mary, Loren, and all other consumers from outdoor rock concerts varies with the number made available by a city government per summer.

Marginal Benefit of Number of Rock Concerts per Consumer (in Dollars)

| | NUMBER OF CONCERTS | | | |
	1	2	3	4
CONSUMERS				
John	150	125	100	75
Mary	125	100	75	50
Loren	100	75	50	25
All others	600	400	200	100

a. Derive the demand curve for rock concerts assuming that it is a pure public good.
b. If the marginal cost of producing rock concerts is $1,000, no matter how many are produced, then what is the efficient number of concerts to have each summer? What would be the efficient number of concerts to produce if the marginal cost of production were $425 instead of $1,000?

4. Suppose that the marginal cost of producing rock concerts is only $250 per concert no matter how many are produced. Use the data from the previous question to calculate the efficient number of concerts. If a Lindahl scheme is used to finance the concerts, what prices of admission should be charged to John, Loren, and Mary?

Suggestions for Further Reading

Buchanan, James M. *The Demand and Supply of Public Goods.* Chicago: Rand McNally, 1968. A pioneering work applying principles of exchange to the public sector and attempting to formulate a theory of supply as well as demand for public goods.

Collender, Stanley E. *The Guide to the Federal Budget: Fiscal 1995.* Washington, D.C.: Urban Institute Press, 1994. Analysis of what is in the federal budget.

Hanusch, Horst, ed. *Public Finance and the Quest for Efficiency.* Detroit: Wayne State University Press, 1984. Includes a number of essays on the demand for public goods and government activities.

Head, John G. *Public Goods and Public Welfare.* Durham, NC: Duke University Press, 1974. A readable exposition of the theory of public goods.

Mueller, Dennis C. *Public Choice II.* Cambridge, Eng.: Cambridge University Press, 1989. A good integration of the theory of public goods with the notion of collective choice.

5

PUBLIC CHOICE AND THE
POLITICAL PROCESS

LEARNING OBJECTIVES

After reading this chapter you should be able to

1. Define a public choice and the concept of political equilibrium.
2. Explain how voting decisions are influenced by tax shares.
3. Discuss incentives to vote.
4. Discuss the characteristics of political equilibrium for a single public good under majority rule, the importance of the median voter, and how cycling of outcomes can result when all voters do not have single-peaked preferences.
5. Describe the role of political parties and special interest groups in the political process.
6. Show how logrolling can influence political equilibrium.
7. Analyze how bureaucrats behave and how they can influence political outcomes.

*H*ave you ever thought about how many decisions affecting your daily life are made through the political process? Everything from quality of your local public educational system and road network to the commitment of U.S. military forces to war are determined through political decisions. Politics also influences the amount of taxes you pay and how the burden of financing government programs is distributed among citizens. The process is also used to compete for the favors of government. Politics also determines who gets income support from the government and which businesses are the fortunate recipients of government subsidies.

The political process is based on rules embodied in a nation's constitution. In democratic nations citizens have the opportunity to vote on issues or for candidates who take positions on those issues. The outcome of the process depends on voting and the behavior of a host of characters including politicians, elected officials, special interest groups, and bureaucrats.

The political process involves more than merely counting votes and deciding on the rules for reaching agreement. Agendas for political action are drawn up by political parties, and alternative proposals are placed before Congress and legislatures. A variety of groups then seek to provide voters with information on the costs and benefits of alternatives so they can decide how to vote.

The theory of *public choice* studies how decisions to allocate resources and redistribute income are made through a nation's political system. The political process is, of course, influenced by factors other than economics, including ideology. However, from an economic point of view, the purpose of politics is to provide citizens with useful goods and services. The theory of public choice examines how the political process is used to determine the quantity of goods and services supplied by governments.

THE SUPPLY OF PUBLIC GOODS THROUGH POLITICAL INSTITUTIONS: THE CONCEPT OF POLITICAL EQUILIBRIUM

A **public choice** is one made through political interaction of many persons according to established rules. The supply of a public good through political institutions requires agreements on the quantity of the public good and the means of finance. Political institutions rarely require unanimous agreement on both the quantity of the public good to produce and the cost-sharing scheme. In fact, a variety of public choice rules are used to make decisions in communities, the most familiar of which is majority rule.

The model of voluntary cooperation for supplying public goods discussed in Chapter 4 is useful in gaining insights into the factors that influence the actual political choices. Under government supply of goods and services, taxes, rather than voluntary contributions, are usually used to finance the goods and services provided. Citizens who vote against an outcome that is enacted must abide by the results. This differs from the voluntary cost-sharing model for supplying public goods, for which individual citizens could veto proposed outcomes if they were dissatisfied with their share of the costs.

Political Equilibrium

A **political equilibrium** is an agreement on the level of production of one or more public goods, given the specified rule for making the collective choice and the distribution of tax shares among individuals. **Tax shares,** sometimes called *tax prices*, are preannounced levies assigned to citizens and are equal to a portion of the unit cost of a good proposed to be provided by government. To a voter, these tax shares represent price per unit of a government-supplied good. The sum of the tax shares must equal the average cost of the public good to avoid budget surpluses or deficits. If t_i is the share of the cost per unit of a pure public good for voter i, then Σt_i for all the voters must equal the average cost of the good.

The cost of producing a public good influences the amount of taxes that citizens must pay to finance the production of each unit of the good. Given the distribution of tax-shares per unit of a public good among individuals, an increase in average cost of producing the public good will increase the individual's tax bill per unit of the public good. Unless such increases in cost are accompanied by increases in benefits, the increased taxes likely will serve to diminish support for increases in the output of the public good.

In reality, information on costs of producing the good is difficult to obtain. Debates preceding an election may influence the willingness of voters to support various levels of output of the public good. Political campaigns provide information on both the cost and the benefit of the alternative programs being offered to voters for their consideration. Control over information concerning the cost and benefit of public goods is an important factor influencing collective choices and their efficiency.

The actual outcome depends, in part, on the particular public choice rule used to make the decision. Proposals that cannot gain approval under unanimous consent might very well be approved under majority rule. In general, the smaller the proportion of the community required to approve any given issue, the greater the probability the issue will be approved. The analysis in this chapter concentrates on choices made through **simple majority rule,** under which a proposal is approved if it receives more than half the votes cast in an election.

Elections and Voting

Public choices are made formally through elections, in which each individual is usually allowed one vote. The economic analysis of the political process assumes that persons evaluate the desirability of goods supplied by government in the same way they consider market goods and services. They are presumed to vote in favor of a proposal only if they will be made better off by its passage.

A rational person's **most-preferred political outcome** is the quantity of the government-supplied good corresponding to the point at which the person's tax share is exactly equal to the marginal benefit of the good. This level of output of the good provides the maximum possible satisfaction to the person. Increasing the quantity of the government-supplied good a fraction of a unit over this amount would make the person worse off.

The most-preferred political outcome for the person whose marginal benefit curve and tax share are illustrated in Figure 5.1 is Q^* units of the good per year. This is the output corresponding to point Z, at which $MB_i = t_i$, where t_i is the voter's tax per unit of the public good. Increments in output of the good up to Q^* per year make this voter better off because the extra benefit of those units exceed the extra taxes the voter must pay to make those units available. If, however, output were to increase above Q^* units per year, the extra taxes would exceed the extra benefit and the voter would be made worse off. In effect, the voter acts as though the public good could be bought at price t_i in a market. A voter will vote in favor of any quantity of a public good as long as the marginal benefit of that quantity is not less than the marginal tax he must pay to finance that amount.

For a given public choice rule, the outcome of an election will depend, in part, on the distribution of tax shares among individuals. Proposals to increase the output of public goods that cannot gain approval under a certain distribution of tax shares might be approved under a different distribution of tax shares, because a change in tax shares will change the most-preferred outcomes of voters. Similarly, the political equilibrium will depend on the distribution of benefits among individuals. A change in the distribution of benefits for a given public project alters its chances of approval, because it changes the most-preferred outcomes of voters. The distribution of bene-

Figure 5.1 ✦ THE MOST-PREFERRED POLITICAL OUTCOME OF A VOTER

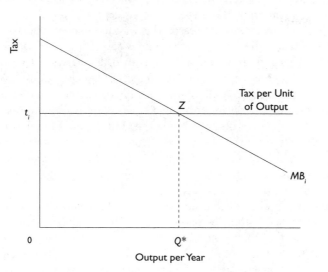

The voter achieves maximum net satisfaction at point Z. This is the point at which $MB_i = t_i$. The voter's most-preferred political outcome corresponding to this point is Q^* units of the public good per year.

fits of such programs as military installations in the United States is often a crucial factor influencing congressional approval of increases or decreases in spending. Politicians, by manipulating the distribution of benefits of certain programs, can alter the chances of those programs being enacted.

To Vote or Not to Vote

A person's decision to vote depends on the benefits and costs of doing so, as well as on the probability that voting will help to achieve the anticipated benefits. The individual also might receive benefits from voting that do not necessarily depend on whether the desired alternative is approved. One such benefit is the pleasure received from exercising the duties of being a citizen.

One of the costs involved in voting is the time and effort it takes to go to the polls. Other costs include those of gathering the information necessary to make a choice. This involves reading newspapers and going to meetings to understand the issues and the positions of the candidates. This can be a time-consuming process.

Many citizens quite rationally believe that their votes will not make any difference in the outcome of an election. Indeed, any given citizen's choosing not to bother to vote very likely does not affect the outcome of any given election. Voters reason that the probability of their votes influencing the election will be close to zero when the number of voters is large. Because the costs of voting are positive while the expected benefits, in terms of influencing the outcome, are close to zero for an individual voter, it is rational not to vote. In effect, nonvoters try to become free riders on the time and effort put in by those who do vote.

However, if all voters were to reason this way, a democratic nation would not be able to function as such because no one would vote! In fact, some democratic nations make voting a legal requirement for citizens in order to avoid free riding by nonvoters. However, even in nations where voting is not legally required, voters turn out to the polls in surprisingly large numbers. This indicates that other forces, such as the pleasure of exercising the duties of being a citizen or social pressures, motivate citizens to vote. Nevertheless, voter turnout in the United States has decreased in recent years. The Committee for the Study of the American Electorate estimated that only 50 percent of eligible voters actually voted in the 1988 presidential election! Voter turnout in presidential elections has been declining in the United States since 1960, when 62.8 percent of the electorate voted.

Some evidence indicates that incentives to vote in the United States are influenced by the existence of the electoral college. Voters in states dominated by a single party often reason that their votes make no difference in presidential elections because all the state electoral votes go to one candidate. In fact, one economist has concluded that the existence of the electoral college discourages voting in *all* elections in states that are dominated by a single political party.[1]

In general, the closer the alternatives are, the less the benefit obtained from choosing one alternative over another. In these cases, the net benefit of voting is likely to be very low, even if the probability of influencing the result of the election is significantly greater than zero. Therefore, some might argue that voters are less likely to vote when they see little or no differences between the alternatives considered in the election.

In other cases, a given voter's most-preferred position might be so far from the alternatives being offered that the probability of receiving any net benefits as a result of casting a vote is very low. The voter will choose to stay away from the polls under these circumstances. The decision to vote therefore depends on the cost and the expected benefit of that action, as is the case for any economic activity.

Some voters who do vote do so on the basis of scanty information and their votes might be different if they knew more about the issues. When an individual casts a vote based on poor information it is doubtful that the social benefit obtained is any greater than if the voter had stayed away from the polls. To vote intelligently, voters must have information on the marginal costs, including extra taxes, that they will bear if the issue under consideration passes. They also must know the marginal benefits they will receive if the issue passes. A voter cannot vote rationally in an election to increase the quantity of a public good, such as more roads, without accurate information on the extra taxes and marginal benefits that will result if the issue wins. Unfor-

---

[1]Richard J. Cebula, "A Note on Voter Participation Rates in the United States," *Public Choice* 41 (1983): 449–450.

tunately, because information on taxes paid and the benefits of many public programs is hard to obtain, many voters do not take the time to become fully informed. **Rational ignorance** is the lack of information about public issues that results because the marginal cost of obtaining the information exceeds the apparent marginal benefits of doing so. When voting for congressional representatives, few people take the time to find out where candidates stand on all the issues and what taxes the candidates support. As a result, many voters who do vote may be making decisions that are not in their own interests. For example, voters who do not research their decisions might actually vote in favor of extensions of public services such as roads beyond the point at which marginal benefits to them fall to equal the marginal costs they must bear as a result of the public choice.

Determinants of Political Equilibrium

In summary, all of the following factors influence whether a public choice will result in approval or disapproval of any proposal regarding the level of production of a public good (or any other issue of collective interest):

1. The public choice rule itself, that is, the proportion of yes votes in relation to the number of votes required for approval of the issue.
2. The average and marginal costs of the public good.
3. The information available to voters on the cost and benefit associated with the issue.
4. The distribution of tax shares among voters and the way in which extra taxes vary with extra output of the good provided. In the models developed here, the marginal tax per unit of output is assumed to be constant.
5. The distribution of benefits among voters.

If any one of these factors is changed, the equilibrium itself will respond accordingly.

In any presidential or congressional election, each of these determinants of political equilibrium affects the outcome. All candidates seek to formulate policies that will give them a majority of the votes cast. In recent elections the issue of tax increases and the distribution of the tax burden were important. Walter Mondale's pledge to raise taxes might very well have been a major fact contributing to his defeat in the 1984 election. In the 1988 election George Bush pledged not to raise taxes and emphasized that a great deal of uncertainty surrounded the costs and benefits of programs proposed by Michael Dukakis, who argued that proposals for tax changes by Bush would alter the distribution of tax shares to favor the rich. Dukakis argued that his programs for spending and taxation would provide more benefit to middle-income groups. Both candidates argued that they would cut federal spending to reduce the deficit but remained vague about which programs would be cut for fear of suggesting that they would alter the distribution of benefits of spending in a way that would harm their chances of being elected. In the 1992 presidential election Bill Clinton promised to raise taxes on upper income groups to help reduce the budget deficit. This combined with an economy barely recovering from a recession helped

Clinton win the election over George Bush who once again promised not to raise taxes (a pledge he did not keep in his term in office after the 1988 election).

A MODEL OF POLITICAL EQUILIBRIUM UNDER MAJORITY RULE

To illustrate political equilibrium under simple majority rule, assume that citizens must decide on the quantity of a pure public good to produce. Given the average cost of producing the good, a tax-sharing scheme is announced whereby each individual will pay the same tax per unit of the good. If the good can be produced under conditions of constant costs and there are n individuals in the community, each individual will pay a tax equal to AC/n per unit of the public good. Assuming seven voters, Figure 5.2 shows the marginal benefit curves of the voters, the marginal (and average) cost line for the public good, and the tax share per unit of the public good of each of the voters.[2]

Suppose that the seven voters, whose marginal benefit curves are subscripted, A, B, C, M, F, G, and H, respectively, constitute a community of persons trying to provide themselves with security protection. Assume that the quantity of protection provided varies with the number of security guards hired per week to patrol their neighborhood. Security protection services have all the characteristics of a pure public good for the seven members of the community. Given their tax shares per guard, each of the seven individuals has his or her own most-preferred output level, corresponding to the point where each marginal benefit curve crosses the tax share line, t, in Figure 5.2. Suppose that the cost of each security guard is $350 per week. This represents both the average and the marginal cost of security protection. The weekly tax share of each voter per security guard therefore will be $50, if the tax shares are to be equal for each voter. This is because $AC/n = \$350/7 = \$50$.

If security protection were a private good available at price t per unit, each person would be able to consume the most-preferred amount of the good, which ranges from one to seven security guards per week. However, because it is a pure public

---

[2]This analysis follows the classic model of political equilibrium developed by Howard R. Bowen in "The Interpretation of Voting in the Allocation of Economic Resources," *Quarterly Journal of Economics* 58 (February 1943): 27–48; reprinted in *Readings in Welfare Economics,* Kenneth Arrow and Tibor Scitovsky, eds. (Homewood, IL.: Irwin, 1969), 115–132.

Figure 5.2 ✦ Political Equilibrium Under Majority Rule with Equal Tax Shares

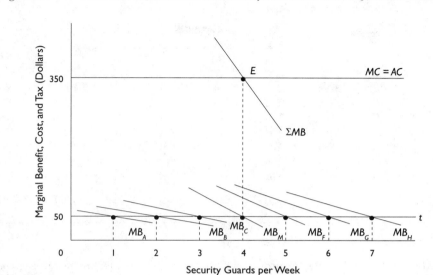

The political equilibrium occurs at the median most-preferred outcome of four security guards per week under simple majority rule. Each voter pays a tax share of $50 per guard per week. In equilibrium, the weekly tax bill of each voter therefore is $200.

good, all must consume the same quantity. That quantity is the number of security guards per week that can gain approval under majority rule.

Election Results Under Majority Rule

Elections now will be held to approve or disapprove successive increases in the output of the public good. Proposals to increase production from zero to any positive amount will be successively voted on. As long as a proposal to increase the amount of guards per week by one more unit achieves more than half the seven votes, it will pass. Therefore, at least four votes are required for a proposal to pass. Assume that all members of the community vote.

Table 5.1 shows the vote tallies for each election and the results, as referenda to increase output from zero to seven are successively held. The election held to increase output from zero to one unit of security protection passes unanimously, because the marginal benefit of the first unit is not less than the tax cost of that unit for any of the voters. As shown in the tally sheet, all vote yes.

A proposal then is made to increase weekly security protection by increasing the number of guards from one to two per week. This proposal also passes under majority rule. Only voter *A* votes against this proposal. She does so because the marginal benefit of the second security guard falls short of the extra taxes she will have to pay

Table 5.1 ◆ VOTING TO PROVIDE SECURITY PROTECTION AND ELECTION RESULTS UNDER
SIMPLE MAJORITY RULE

		INCREASE SECURITY GUARDS PER WEEK TO:						
		1	2	3	4	5	6	7
VOTERS	A	Yes	No	No	No	No	No	No
	B	Yes	Yes	No	No	No	No	No
	C	Yes	Yes	Yes	No	No	No	No
	M	Yes	Yes	Yes	Yes	No	No	No
	F	Yes	Yes	Yes	Yes	Yes	No	No
	G	Yes	Yes	Yes	Yes	Yes	Yes	No
	H	Yes	Yes	Yes	Yes	Yes	Yes	Yes
RESULTS		Pass	Pass	Pass	Pass	Fail	Fail	Fail

per week to finance that extra protection ($MB_A < \$50$). Under majority rule, the
proposal to increase output to two guards per week passes 6 to 1, even though an individual is made worse off by the move. Similarly, expansion in the output of the public good to three and four units per week obtains the majority necessary for passage.
This is because at least half the members of the community will be made better off
when the number of security guards increases up to four per week.

Increases in the output of the public good beyond four security guards per week,
however, will not receive a majority of votes. The election to expand output to five
guards per week, for example, will receive only three yes votes. The other four voters
will have reached levels of consumption at which marginal benefits are less than their
tax shares and therefore vote no.

The political equilibrium under majority rule and equal tax shares, given the
marginal benefit curves shown in Figure 5.2, therefore will be four security guards
per week. If voters were asked to choose between this number of guards and any alternative number, four would win. This is because four guards per week is closer to
the most-preferred outcome of a majority of voters. As long as the alternative of four
guards per week is put on the ballot, it will emerge as the political equilibrium under
simple majority rule.

The Median Voter

The **median voter** is the one whose most-preferred outcome is the median of the
most-preferred outcomes of all those voting. In Figure 5.2, the voter with the marginal benefit curve MB_M is the median voter. The most-preferred outcomes of all voters range from one to seven security guards per week. Voter M's most-preferred outcome is the median of four guards per week. Three voters have a most-preferred
outcome of less than four guards per week, and three voters have a most-preferred alternative of more than four guards per week.

The median voter ends up consuming the same amount of the public good that she would choose to consume if it were sold in a market at a price $t = \$50$. In equilibrium, under majority rule, voters A, B, and C consume more than their most-preferred levels of security protection, given the tax shares. Similarly, voters F, G, and H end up consuming less than their most-preferred levels, under the majority rule equilibrium.

If the marginal benefit of a public good declines for all voters, the median most-preferred quantity of the good always is the political equilibrium under majority rule. As shown below, this holds even if each voter does not pay the same tax share. Voters whose most-preferred outcomes deviate from the median must consume either more or less of the public good than they would choose independently, given their tax shares.

The greater the dispersion of most-preferred outcomes from the median, the more likely to be dissatisfaction with public choices under majority rule. At one extreme, all voters could have the *same* most-preferred outcome. If this were the case, *all* voters would agree unanimously on the quantity of the good to supply. Any one voter could be regarded as the median voter in this case. The other extreme is the one shown in Figure 5.2, for which each voter has a different most-preferred outcome. The more voters whose most-preferred outcomes are clustered toward the median voter's most-preferred outcome, the greater the satisfaction with the political equilibrium under majority rule. This emphasizes an important point about majority rule. When more than two outcomes are possible, majority rule does not necessarily ensure that 51 percent of the voters will receive their most-preferred outcomes. *Only the median voter obtains his most-preferred outcome.* Differences in the most-preferred outcomes of voters can be explained either by differences in the marginal benefits they receive from alternative quantities of the public good or differences in their assigned tax shares.

Political externalities are losses in well-being that occur when voters do not obtain their most-preferred outcomes, given their tax shares. Political externalities would be zero if the tax shares of all voters of government goods and services were adjusted until they equaled the marginal benefits received from government output. When political externalities prevail, additional gains to voters are possible either through changes in the output of government goods or changes in voters' tax shares.

Do not confuse political externalities with market externalities. Market externalities, as defined in Chapter 3, are costs or benefits of market exchanges not reflected in prices. Political externalities are costs borne by those who would like to have either more or less of a government good or service, given their tax shares, than the amounts agreed upon through political interaction. If all decisions were made under unanimous agreement, political externalities would not exist. This is because any single voter could veto a proposal if she did not attain her most-preferred political outcome.

If political externalities were the only costs of political interaction, unanimous agreement would minimize the costs of the political process. In fact, some proponents of democracy argue that more inclusive majorities (for example, two-thirds majority) required for approving government programs would more adequately protect minorities. However, other costs also are involved in actually reaching an agreement. **Political transactions costs** measure the value of time, effort, and other resources expended to reach and enforce a collective agreement. These are additional costs of the political process that must be considered in evaluating the efficiency of government supply compared with market supply. Political institutions that require high percentages of agreement in the population before increments in government activity can be undertaken are likely to result in a minimal amount of political externalities. On the other hand, rules that require close to unanimous agreement are likely to take a great deal of time and effort before an agreement can be achieved. In choosing political institutions, citizens must weigh the political externalities associated with these rules against the political transactions costs of the rules.

The prevalence of representative government in all democratic nations is best explained by an effort to economize on political transactions costs. In a large nation, decisions never would be made (or be made too late) if the entire nation had to vote before action could be undertaken. Other costs of political interaction are those resulting from bureaucratic inefficiency. If bureaucrats do not produce their output at minimum possible cost, or if they succeed in getting more than the efficient amount approved, losses in net benefits to citizens will occur.

UNIQUENESS AND CYCLING OF OUTCOMES UNDER MAJORITY RULE

Under certain circumstances, a unique political equilibrium cannot emerge under majority rule. When this is the case, for any output of the public good that can achieve a majority of the votes, another output level will exist that also can achieve a majority.

When no equilibrium exists, the outcome of elections decided under simple majority rule can depend on factors other than the benefits of the proposed changes in output and the costs to voters. These other factors could include the order in which alternatives are presented to voters or the addition or subtraction of an alternative to the ballot. This possibility is particularly disturbing because it suggests that the outcome under majority rule could depend on factors other than the merits of the proposed changes. For example, it implies that skillful politicians might be able to manipulate the results of elections by controlling the order in which proposals are considered by the electorate.

Single-Peaked and Multiple-Peaked Preferences

To illustrate the problems associated with simple majority rule, consider the following hypothetical election. A community of three citizens must vote to decide on the number of fireworks displays to have per year. Each display costs $200. Voter A must pay a tax, t_A, of $100 per display. Voter B's tax share per display is $t_B = \$75$, and voter C pays a tax share of $t_C = \$25$ per display. The voters agree to consider three alternatives: one display per year, two displays per year, and three displays per year. The results of an election between any pair of alternatives will be determined by simple majority rule. Table 5.2 shows how each of the voters rank the three alternatives.

Table 5.2 ◆ VOTER RANKINGS FOR FIREWORKS DISPLAYS PER YEAR

VOTERS	FIRST CHOICE	SECOND CHOICE	THIRD CHOICE
A	3	2	1
B	1	3	2
C	2	1	3

Given their tax shares, the three individuals are presumed to rank these alternatives in terms of highest-to-lowest levels of net benefits received. In other words, the rankings are obtained for each voter by subtracting the taxes paid from the benefit gained from availability of each alternative. The net benefit of each output for a voter is the difference, as evaluated by the voter, between the total benefit of the output and the total costs of the output measured by taxes.

In Figure 5.3, the information contained in Table 5.2 is used to plot the net benefits of the three voters, A, B, and C, for each of the three alternatives. A's preferences are apparently such that, for the three alternatives available, her net benefit increases with the number of displays per year. B obtains the greatest net benefit when only one display is provided per year. However, his second-ranked alternative is three displays per year, the greatest number of displays being considered by the voters. The moderate alternative of two displays per year apparently gives him the least net benefit. B is an individual who prefers the extremes to the moderate alternatives. Finally, C's preferences are such that she gets the greatest net benefit from two displays per year and lower net benefits when either one or three displays are provided per year.

Single-peaked preferences imply that individuals behave as if a unique optimum outcome exists for them. The further away from their optima, either in the positive or negative direction, the worse things are. **Multiple-peaked preferences** imply that persons who move away from their most-preferred alternative become worse off at first *but eventually become better off as the movement continues in the same direction.* Of the three voters whose rankings are shown above, B is the only one with multiple-peaked preferences. As shown in Figure 5.3, B becomes worse off as fireworks displays are increased from one to two per year. However, this voter becomes *better off* as output is increased from two to three displays per year. Voters A and C both have single-peaked preferences. If output is reduced below three displays per year, A is made continually worse off. If displays per year deviate in any direction from C's most-preferred outcome of two, she is made worse off.

Pair-Wise Elections: The Phenomenon of Cycling

Pair-wise elections are those held between any two alternatives when three or more alternatives are possible. Begin with one display per year against the alternative of two displays per year. The tally sheet for that election is given in Table 5.3. Each voter is presumed to vote for the alternative that gives the highest net benefit. Because the

Figure 5.3 ✦ Voter Rankings of Alternatives

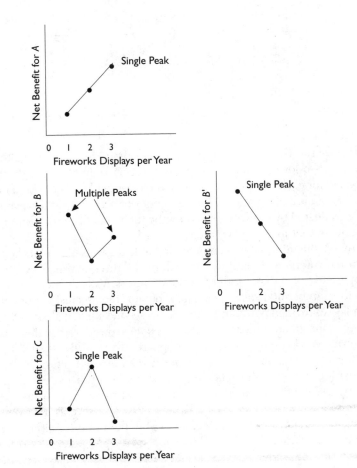

All voters have single-peaked preferences except for voter B, who becomes worse off as he moves from his most-preferred outcome of one display per year but then better off as he moves to three displays per year.

alternative of two displays per year receives two votes against only one vote for one display per year, it receives the simple majority and is declared the winner.

Now, suppose the next pair-wise election were held between the losing alternative of one display per year and the remaining alternative of three displays per year. As shown in the tally sheet for election two, the alternative of one display per year would win. Finally, suppose an election were held between the alternative of three displays per year and two displays per year. The result, under simple majority rule, would be three displays per year.

Table 5.3 ◆ ELECTORAL TALLY SHEETS FOR PAIR-WISE ELECTIONS (BASED ON RANKINGS IN TABLE 5.2)

ELECTION 1	1 DISPLAY PER YEAR	2 DISPLAYS PER YEAR
VOTERS		
A		X
B	X	
C		X
Totals	1 Vote	2 Votes

RESULT: 2 displays per year wins.

ELECTION 2	3 DISPLAYS PER YEAR	1 DISPLAY PER YEAR
VOTERS		
A	X	
B		X
C		X
Totals	1 Vote	2 Votes

RESULT: 1 display per year wins.

ELECTION 3	2 DISPLAYS PER YEAR	3 DISPLAYS PER YEAR
VOTERS		
A		X
B		X
C	X	
Totals	1 Vote	2 Votes

RESULT: 3 displays per year wins.

The result of pair-wise voting in this fashion among the three alternatives is a never-ending cycle. In the three elections held, two displays per year defeats the alternative of one display per year; then one display per year emerges as the winner, when paired against three displays per year; and, finally, three displays per year wins, when paired against two displays per year. Each loser can become a winner when paired with another alternative. The outcome of the election between pairs of alternatives is arbitrary. Depending on the order in which the elections are held, any of the three alternatives can emerge as the winner under simple majority rule. This phenomenon is called *cycling*. In pair-wise elections, no political equilibrium exists. No one alternative can defeat all others *wherever* it appears on the ballot.

Elections could be held for any pair of alternatives. The winner of that election then could be paired against the remaining alternative. In a series of such elections, any of the three alternatives can win the runoff elections, depending on the order in which the alternatives are presented to the voters.

The phenomenon of cycling is very disturbing to our confidence in the democratic institutions of voting and majority rule to reach public choices because it suggests that perhaps no rhyme or reason explains the choices that emerge. Cycling implies that public choices can be influenced by such factors as the order in which issues are placed on the agenda for consideration by voters and legislatures. It also suggests that with three or more alternatives on the agenda, elimination of one of the alternatives can change the way the remaining two are ranked in a public choice.

Arrow's Impossibility Theorem generalizes the results discussed here for majority rule by stating that it is impossible to devise a voting rule that meets a set of conditions that can guarantee a unique political equilibrium for a public choice. To prove his theorem, Kenneth Arrow, who received a Nobel prize for his groundbreaking work on the properties of political equilibrium, sets up a number of conditions for "collective rationality." These conditions require that public choices meet the same criteria we expect for rational individual choices. Arrow's conditions can be roughly summarized to include the following[3]:

1. All voters must have free choices among alternatives in elections and the public choices cannot be made by any one individual who would act as a dictator.
2. A unique political equilibrium must be attained no matter what the preferences of individuals comprising the electorate. We cannot rule out the possibility that some voters have multiple-peaked preferences.
3. If all voters change their rankings of a particular alternative (either moving it up or down), the public choice that emerges must not move in the opposite direction. For example, if all voters now prefer less national defense, we would not expect a public choice to emerge in which more national defense is chosen.
4. Public choices and political equilibrium must not be influenced by the order in which alternatives are presented to voters.
5. Public choices must not be affected by the elimination or addition of an alternative to the ballot. If voters choose A over B in an election when A and B are the only alternatives, then they must not choose B over A when a third alternative, C, enters the race.
6. Public choices should be transitive: if A is chosen over B and B is chosen over C then A should be chosen over C.

Arrow's conditions imply that no "paradox of voting" should exist such that a third-party candidate can act as a "spoiler" in an election. For example, suppose a Republican candidate for president runs against a Democrat and that the Republican would win if the Democrat and the Republican were on the ballot alone. However, a third-party Conservative candidate who enters the race takes votes away from the Republican and the Democrat wins. This means that the ranking between Republicans and Democrats changes when the third-party candidate enters.

Arrow's theorem is disturbing because it implies that any alternative could emerge as a political equilibrium. It also implies that strategies such as controlling the agenda for political debate or manipulating the order in which issues are discussed in a legislature can influence political outcomes. However, Arrow's theorem does not

---

[3]See Kenneth Arrow, *Social Choice and Individual Values*, 2d ed. (New York: Wiley, 1963). Arrow's work is expressed in terms of mathematics. The analysis here simplifies the theorem.

imply that public choices are always inconsistent. It merely points out that no voting rule, such as majority rule, can always be relied on to reach a unique political equilibrium. However, a given voting rule can produce unique public choices when voters themselves have preferences that meet certain properties. To find out the conditions under which public choices *are* consistent under simply majority rule, we need to examine the cases of the cycling phenomenon we have discussed.

The Cause of Cycling

Cycling and the lack of a political equilibrium under pair-wise voting in majority rule is caused by multiple-peaked preferences. When all voters have single-peaked preferences, simple majority rule is capable of achieving a political equilibrium for a single-issue election at the median peak for all voters.[4]

This theorem can be illustrated with the preceding example. Simply replace voter *B*, who has multiple-peaked preferences, with voter *B'*, whose preferences are single-peaked at the fewest number of fireworks displays per year. Assume that voter *B'* pays the same tax share per display as did voter *B*. The net benefit from fireworks displays for voter *B'* declines as more are provided. This is shown in Table 5.4. The net benefit functions of the three voters, *A*, *B'*, and *C*, are plotted together in Figure 5.4, which now shows three single peaks (or maxima) for each of the three voters. Voter *A* would enjoy maximum net benefit at three displays per year. Voter *B'* would enjoy maximum net benefits if one display per year were provided. Finally, voter *C* would have maximum net benefit if two displays per year would emerge as the political equilibrium. For each voter, now, movement away from his or her most-preferred outcome in any direction results in decreased net benefit over the range of the possible outcomes. All voters have single-peaked preferences. The median peak is at two

Table 5.4 ◆ Voter Rankings for Fireworks Displays per Year: All Voters with Single-Peaked Preferences

	First Choice	Second Choice	Third Choice
Voters			
A	3	2	1
B'	1	2	3
C	2	1	3

[4]This is sometimes called the Black theorem, after Duncan Black, who first developed it. Duncan Black, *The Theory of Committees and Elections* (Cambridge, England.: Cambridge University Press, 1958). Also see his "On the Rational of Group Decision Making," *Journal of Political Economy* 56 (February 1948): 23–34 and "The Decisions of a Committee Using a Special Majority," *Econometrica* 16 (July 1948): 245–261.

Figure 5.4 ♦ THE MEDIAN PEAK AS THE POLITICAL EQUILIBRIUM UNDER MAJORITY RULE

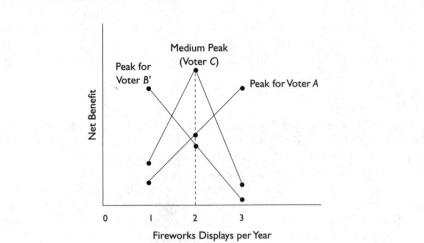

The median voter is C, whose most-preferred outcome of two fireworks displays per year is the political equilibrium under majority rule.

displays per year. Because voter *C* is the one whose first choice corresponds to the median peak, this voter is the median voter.

Now hold elections between pairs of alternatives as before but base the votes on the preferences in Table 5.4. The electoral tally sheets for these elections are given in Table 5.5. In this case, the alternative of two displays per year emerges as the political equilibrium. In elections 1 and 3, in which two displays per year is paired directly with the alternatives of one display per year and three displays per year, two displays per year receives a simple majority in both cases. In election two, between the alternatives of one and three displays per year, one display per year is victorious. But this alternative will lose when paired with the most-preferred outcome of the median voter: two displays per year.

The median peak of two displays per year is the political equilibrium. When all preferences are single-peaked, neither cycling of outcomes nor arbitrariness is involved in the collective choice. One, and only one, outcome of the three emerges as victorious: the one corresponding to the median peak. This is the median most-preferred outcome of all voters, and is sometimes called the **median voter rule.** The rule holds for any tax-sharing arrangement as long as voter preferences are single peaked.

Existence of Multiple-Peaked Preferences

Economists typically assume that the marginal benefit of any good tends to decline as more of the good is made available. It easily can be demonstrated that multiple-

Table 5.5 ✦ ELECTORAL TALLY SHEETS FOR PAIR-WISE ELECTIONS (BASED ON RANKINGS IN TABLE 5.4)

ELECTION 1	1 DISPLAY PER YEAR	2 DISPLAYS PER YEAR
VOTERS		
A		X
B'	X	
C		X
Totals	1 Vote	2 Votes

RESULT: 2 displays per year wins.

ELECTION 2	3 DISPLAYS PER YEAR	1 DISPLAY PER YEAR
VOTERS		
A	X	
B'		X
C		X
Totals	1 Vote	2 Votes

RESULT: 1 display per year wins.

ELECTION 3	2 DISPLAYS PER YEAR	3 DISPLAYS PER YEAR
VOTERS		
A		X
B'	X	
C	X	
Totals	2 Votes	1 Vote

RESULT: 2 displays per year wins.

peaked preferences are inconsistent with declining marginal benefit of public goods. Figure 5.5A plots the net benefits received by a voter whose tax share and marginal benefit curve for a pure public good is shown in Figure 5.5B. When the voter's marginal benefit exceeds her tax per unit of the good, her net benefit increases. The net benefit is at a maximum when Q^* units of output per year are provided. If more than Q^* per year are made available, the marginal benefit would be less than taxes per unit, and net benefit therefore would decline. It follows that the net benefit curve for any voter with declining marginal benefit for the good will have an inverted U-shape, as shown in Figure 5.5A. This is a single-peaked net benefit function, with the peak at the output corresponding to $MB = t$.

Unfortunately, the possibility of multiple-peaked preferences cannot be ruled out. For example, individuals voting in a school budget election can have multiple-peaked preferences. Suppose the voters have the alternative to send children to private schools. In part, the incentive depends on the quality of public schools, which presumably is correlated with the size of the public school budget.

Figure 5.5 ✦ Declining Marginal Benefit of a Pure Public Good Meaning that Preferences Are Single Peaked

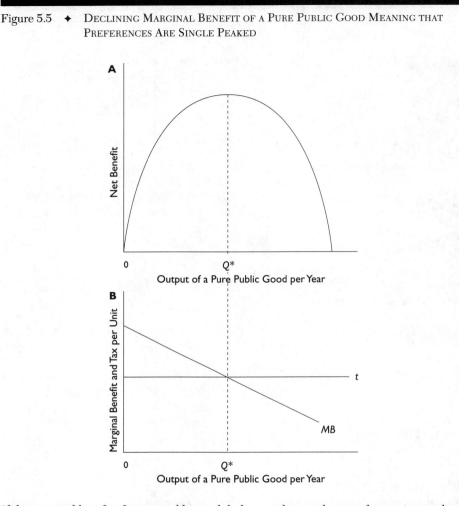

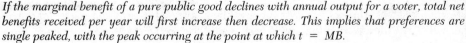

If the marginal benefit of a pure public good declines with annual output for a voter, total net benefits received per year will first increase then decrease. This implies that preferences are single peaked, with the peak occurring at the point at which t = MB.

The voter's first choice might be to send his children to private schools. If he does this, it is in his interest to keep the size of the public school budget as small as possible, because he will receive no direct benefit from public schooling for his taxes. His first choice therefore will be a budget that allows minimum-quality public schooling. If it is assumed that the taxes necessary to finance a school budget that allows only moderate-quality schooling will make it difficult for the voter to afford private schooling, his second choice may very well be the budget that allows the highest-quality public schooling. Under such circumstances, he might view the quality of public schools adequate enough to forgo sending his children to private schools. His least-favored alternative will be a school budget that allows only moderate-quality public schooling. The taxes required to finance moderate-quality public schooling will not leave him enough income after taxes to afford private schooling. Thus, given the alternative of private schooling, multiple-peaked preferences might be quite reasonable for a voter who seeks to maximize the quality of schooling for his children.

During the 1960s and the early 1970s, multiple-peaked preferences by U.S. citizens were prevalent on the issue of the Vietnam War. Many citizens argued that wars, if fought, should be fought to win. They preferred the alternative of all-out war (including the use of nuclear weapons) or no war at all to the alternative of a limited war that did not use the full military capability of the armed forces for the purposes of winning territory and subduing the enemy. Again, these individuals were expressing preferences for an extreme, and not moderate, solution. Multiple-peaked preferences might be common, therefore, on a wide variety of issues. This leaves open the specter of absence of political equilibrium under majority rule as a possibility.

CHECKPOINT

1. What are single-peaked preferences?
2. What can cause cycling of outcomes under majority rule?
3. What is the median voter rule?

THE POLITICAL PROCESS: POLITICIANS, LOGROLLING, AND BUREAUCRACY

Individuals with similar ideas on the role of government and other issues often group together to form **political parties.** Politicians seek elective office for a variety of reasons: power, prestige, desire to serve others, and pecuniary returns. They are influential in formulating the alternatives that are presented to voters and in dispersing information on the relative merits of alternative measures and candidates on the agenda for approval. When information is scarce, the behavior of politicians can be influential in determining the actual political equilibrium that emerges. Competition among political parties, particularly under a system of majority rule, has been analyzed by economists in an attempt to gain a better understanding of the political process.[5]

Thus far, little has been said about the role of political parties in the formulation of the alternatives presented to the electorate. Clearly, political parties play an important part in defining issues and in attempting to influence the results of elections. For the individual voter, the marginal benefit of any particular budget proposal will depend not only on the level of expenditures but also on the mix of types of expenditures within the budget. The willingness of any citizen to vote favorably on any given budget also will depend on the particular tax-sharing plan proposed to finance the

---

[5]See Anthony Downs, *An Economic Theory of Democracy* (New York: Harper & Row, 1957).

PUBLIC POLICY PERSPECTIVE

PUBLIC CHOICE IN U.S. CITIES: DO POLITICAL INSTITUTIONS MATTER?

In the United States, municipal government takes two basic forms. One form relies heavily on a professional city manager who, along with a staff, makes the day-to-day decisions about how to run the city and plays an important role in advising elected public officials on expansion of public facilities. The city-manager form of government typically involves non-partisan elections for mayor and city council members. In the second form, a mayor, deputy mayor, and other public officials are elected directly, usually in partisan elections (in which candidates are members of a political party). In this form of government the mayor and city council members wield considerably more power than they do under the city-manager form of government.

Does the form of city government affect the public choices made in municipalities? Some scholars have argued that politicians under partisan governments respond to different incentives than city managers. For example, one researcher has argued that city managers act as technicians who view city capital and labor simply as inputs for the production of city services. However, partisan mayors view these inputs partly as political assets that can affect their power base and ability to be reelected.°

To test the hypothesis that the form of city government makes a difference for public choices, Kevin Duffy-Deno and Douglas R. Dalenberg collected data from twenty-six large U.S. cities chosen at random.

Half were city-manager governments and half were run by elected mayors.[†] Using estimates of the capital stock for each city, the researchers sought to explain difference in city capital per person and capital-labor ratios between cities. City capital included police and fire facilities, parks, recreation centers, highways, water and sewer systems, and health and welfare facilities. Among the variables used to explain these differences were the number of facilities located in the metropolitan area of each city of the sample, municipal population density, the number of manufacturing firms in the city, per capita personal income, percentage of owner-occupied homes, median age of city residents, the city's region, population change in the preceding five years, percentage of homes built in or before 1950, and the number of services offered by the city.

After accounting for the influence of all variables, the researchers found that the per capita stock of capital was 12.5 percent greater in those cities managed by elected mayors than those with the city-manager form of government. The capital-labor ratio was also higher in the cities run by elected mayors rather than city managers. Although the form of government did not seem to influence total municipal expenditures, it did seem to influence the means by which services are produced. Public choices in cities managed by elected mayors appear to result in more capital-intensive production methods and larger stocks of capital relative to population. Therefore, public choice rules do seem to matter when it comes to choices of input mixes of U.S. cities!

°See J. S. Zax, "Economics Effects of Municipal Government Institutions," working paper no. 1657, National Bureau of Economic Research, 1985.

[†]See Kevin T. Duffy-Deno and Douglas R. Dalenberg, "Do Institutions Matter? An Empirical Note," *National Tax Journal*, 43, 2 (June 1990): 207–215.

expenditures. In some ways, political parties act as brokers to encourage vote trading among voters. Political platforms often include proposals for programs that benefit only a minority of voters. However, by including these benefits and spreading the costs over the majority, the party can gain votes.

Economists characterize political parties as vote maximizers, because they tend to put together political programs and tax-sharing arrangements designed to maximize the votes that they receive. Under majority rule, the party that is most successful at maximizing votes wins the election. Therefore, vote maximization is a prerequisite to successfully obtaining political power in a democracy.

The Median Voter, Political Parties, and Political Equilibrium Under Majority Rule

Suppose the positions of political parties can be ranked according to a scale that measures the quantity of government activity per year. For example, conservatives who argue that government activity should be reduced or curtailed would rank low according to this scale. Liberal candidates who propose more government activity would rank high on the scale.

Political candidates tend to take a position that represents the median on the scale. Political parties and candidates who take extreme positions are likely to lose elections. The candidate who most accurately approximates the median most-preferred outcome will emerge as the victor.

This is illustrated in Figure 5.6. The graph plots the net benefit (after paying taxes) that each voter receives from each possible political platform on government activity. Assume that the greater the quantity of government goods and services per year, the more liberal is the platform.

The graph assumes that the most-preferred outcome of voters varies considerably. Some conservative voters' most-preferred outcome occurs at zero government goods and services per year. The most-preferred outcome of more liberal voters corresponds to higher amounts of government goods and services per year. In Figure 5.6, the net benefit curves of nine voters are drawn. The median most-preferred outcome is Q^*,

Figure 5.6 ✦ THE MEDIAN VOTER AND POLITICAL PLATFORMS

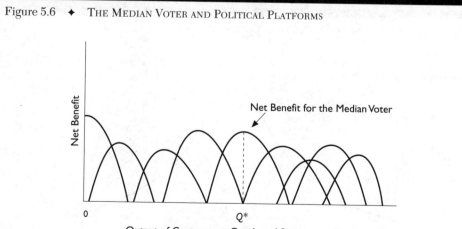

Given tax shares, the political party proposing Q^* units of government goods and services per year will win an election over any other party proposing an alternative quantity. This is because Q^* is closer to the most-preferred outcome of a simple majority of the voters.

which corresponds to the peak of the net benefit function of the median voter. Assuming that each voter has a single-peaked net benefit function, Q° will emerge as the political equilibrium. This is because the net benefits of more than half of the voters will be higher under Q° than for any alternative quantity of government goods and services, given tax shares.

Figure 5.7 shows that, if the most-preferred outcomes of voters are normally distributed, a political party can maximize the number of votes by taking a center position corresponding to Q°. The implication of this analysis is that political parties or candidates who take extreme positions on issues are doomed to lose elections. Political parties that seek to maximize votes will always have an incentive to straddle the median position.

Ample evidence exists to prove that when political candidates in the United States take extreme positions, they do, in fact, lose. For example, in the 1964 presidential election, Barry Goldwater, a presidential candidate, proposed a platform that was apparently far more conservative than the one preferred by the median voter of that time. The result was a landslide victory by his Democratic opponent, Lyndon Johnson. Similarly, in 1972, the Democrats chose George McGovern as their candidate but his position was apparently far to the left of the median peak. The result was a landslide victory by the Republican candidate, Richard Nixon. In 1976, in the Jimmy Carter versus Gerald Ford race, both candidates proposed platforms close to the median most-preferred position. As a result, the election was very close.

Over time, the median most-preferred outcome can change. For example, a movement to a more conservative point of view by voters can provide opportunities for candidates who propose conservative platforms to win elections. Perhaps the landslide victory of Ronald Reagan in 1984 can be interpreted as the result of a move-

Figure 5.7   ✦   NUMBER OF VOTERS AND GOVERNMENT OUTPUT

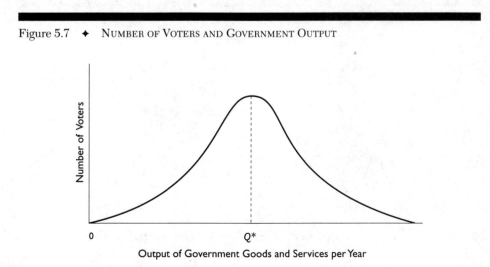

The annual output, Q°, is the political equilibrium under majority rule because it can obtain more votes than any other alternative.

ment to a more conservative median most-preferred outcome. In 1992 the victory of the more liberal Bill Clinton over a conservative George Bush reflected a movement to a more liberal median most-preferred outcome. In any event, political issues are seldom, in fact, single-dimensional. In presidential elections, in particular, many issues are bundled together in the platforms of the political parties. Often, ranking of candidates along a single dimension is impossible. For example, a candidate might be regarded as conservative on domestic policy but liberal on foreign policy.

The Effect of Nonvoting on Political Equilibrium

Politicians seek to offer a political platform in line with the median most-preferred outcome of all *voters*. If all citizens do not vote, this outcome can differ from the median most-preferred outcomes of all *citizens*.

Voters might abstain from voting because they are indifferent to the platforms of two competing political parties. Barry Goldwater's campaign slogan in 1964 was "A choice, not an echo!" Perhaps he hoped that a significant number of conservative citizens who had not turned out in the past because they were indifferent to the positions of the candidates might turn out in hordes to support his position even though it was to the right of that espoused by the median voter. Apparently, he was mistaken.

When voters do not vote because the platforms of the candidates appear to be similar, the impact on political equilibrium depends on the number of voters on each end of the political spectrum that do not vote. Assume that candidates can be ranked on a single-dimensional scale, such as the liberalness of their positions. The median most-preferred outcome of citizens still will be the political equilibrium, provided that as many conservative citizens as liberal citizens do not vote because of indifference. Only in the case in which nonvoters are predominantly conservative or liberal will the median most-preferred outcome of all citizens diverge from the median most-preferred outcome of all actual voters.

Another reason for abstaining from voting is alienation. Citizens might find the positions of the candidates too far from their own most-preferred positions to bother to vote at all. The effects of alienation on the outcome of elections are complex. Assume, once again, that the positions of voters can be ranked according to a single scale of liberalness. When voters choose not to vote because they are alienated, the tendency for political parties is to move toward the mode rather than the median of the most-preferred outcome of citizens. If the distribution of the most-preferred outcome of voters is symmetric (as is the case for the familiar bell-shaped normal distribution shown in Figure 5.7), then the median and the mode will coincide. Under these circumstances, the median most-preferred outcome of all citizens still will dominate, provided that the distribution is unimodal. When the distribution of most-preferred outcomes is either asymmetric or multimodal (one that has two peaks), alienation can result in political equilibriums that differ from the median most-preferred outcome of all citizens.[6]

---

[6]Otto A. Davis, Melvin J. Hinich, and Peter C. Ordeshook, "An Expository Development of a Mathematical Model of the Electoral Process," *American Political Science Review* 64 (June 1970): 426–448.

VOTING ON MORE THAN ONE ISSUE AT A TIME: LOGROLLING

When more than one issue is voted on simultaneously as a package—as is commonly the case—voters are sometimes confronted with political packages that include both favorable and unfavorable items. If the voter feels more strongly about some issues compared with others, or if he is better informed on some issues than on others, then his vote may be a function of the extent to which the package supports those issues he strongly favors. When intensities of preference differ on issues, there are incentives for groups to trade votes for those issues of great interest to them. Such a vote-trading process is called **logrolling.**

Suppose, for example, the ballot contains two issues, neither of which can pass separately because each issue provides benefits to only a minority of voters. One of the issues significantly benefits oil producers, and the other greatly benefits shoe manufacturers. Suppose that oil producers can gain considerably when their issue passes, and these gains outweigh any losses they might incur by voting for the issue favored by the shoe manufacturers. They then will have incentives to offer to vote for the issue of interest to shoe manufacturers in exchange for the shoe manufacturers' positive vote on the issue of interest to the oil producers. The shoe producers will agree to such a trade, provided that passage of both issues, simultaneously, will provide them with net benefits.

The incentives to trade votes exist when an asymmetry of gains on the issues is involved. If the oil producers' gains resulting from passage of their issue were exactly offset by losses from passage of the legislation of interest to shoe manufacturers, the incentive to trade votes disappears.

Trading votes might not be successful in accumulating enough votes to pass an issue. However, opportunities for logrolling clearly result in passage of some issues that otherwise could not command a simple majority.

Incentives to engage in logrolling depend on the relative intensities of voters' preferences on issues. If voters felt the same about all issues, the gains from passage of any one issue would be exactly offset by the losses expected as a result of passage of any other paired issue. Again, no incentive to trade votes exists under those circumstances.[7]

Implicit Logrolling

Implicit logrolling occurs when political interests succeed in pairing, on the same ballot or the same bill, two (or more) issues of strong interest to divergent groups. This is a common practice in legislatures, where riders are often attached to bills. For example, two unrelated issues, such as import quotas for textiles and the funding of a new bomber, might be included on the same ballot. By doing so, legislators will have to vote for each of the issues together even if they would gain from the passage of one

---

[7]See James S. Coleman, "The Possibility of a Social Welfare Function," *American Economic Review* 57 (December 1967): 1311–1317.

issue only. Each issue, if voted on separately, would be defeated because each alone provides benefits only to a minority of voters. However, the combined package might succeed in passing by a simple majority if each minority special interest group votes for it to get its favored program. In effect, each special interest group is induced to support the program of another special interest group in order to receive benefits from its most-favored program.

Again, the willingness of each special interest group to vote for the combined package is a function of the relative intensity of preference on the two issues. If the gains on the most-favored issue were balanced equally by the losses resulting from passage of the issue most favored by the other group, no incentive exists to muster support for the combined package. Citizens will have incentives to engage in implicit logrolling only to the extent to which it provides them with positive net benefits.

Many argue that logrolling is a positive safety valve in a democratic society because it allows citizens an opportunity to express their intensity of preference for particular outcomes in terms of their willingness to trade votes. A problem often overlooked in democratic societies is that allowing one vote per voter on each issue provides no direct basis for individuals to express their intensity of preference on issues. A vote is a vote. It says nothing about the extent to which a citizen is made better or worse off by a given political change. Under simple majority rule, a coalition of individuals can succeed in defeating issues about which certain minority groups have extremely strong feelings. If the minorities have no outlet for venting these intense preferences, the result might very well be social instability and, eventually, a revolution to change political institutions. Thus, logrolling can be thought of as such a safety valve.

Although logrolling has the potential to account for intensity of preference, the danger remains that it will be used by skillful politicians as a means of gaining approval for programs with purely redistributive benefits. In fact, the common judgment is unfavorable toward logrolling because of its reputation as a mechanism for members of Congress to use the political system to gain benefits that accrue only to their constituents. Those who argue against logrolling believe that it extends the size of the public sector over and above what would be the case in its absence. Many believe that this extension is primarily in programs that redistribute income to certain groups, rather than providing positive net benefit.

Logrolling and Efficiency

Suppose that citizens in a community vote to decide whether to support both security protection and community entertainment. Both these goods are pure public goods for the citizens. Security protection is measured by the number of security guards hired per week. Entertainment is measured by the number of fireworks displays per week. Assume three voters who agree to share equally in the unit costs of these two goods. Assume that each fireworks display costs $300 per week and the cost of a security guard is also $300 per week. The marginal and average costs of each of these public goods is therefore $300. At first, these issues are voted on separately, and no logrolling agreements are made. Each voter is assigned a tax share of $100 for each unit of the good. The collective decisions are made according to majority rule.

In Figure 5.8, the marginal benefit, tax per unit, and marginal cost of each of the goods are shown. Figure 5.8A assumes that the marginal benefit received by voters A and B is zero at one fireworks display per week. The MB_A and MB_B curves intersect the horizontal axis at one display per year. However, voter C receives a marginal benefit of $250 from the first fireworks display. C is the only person whose tax does not exceed the marginal benefit of the first display. She will cast the only favorable vote.

Figure 5.8 ✦ LOGROLLING

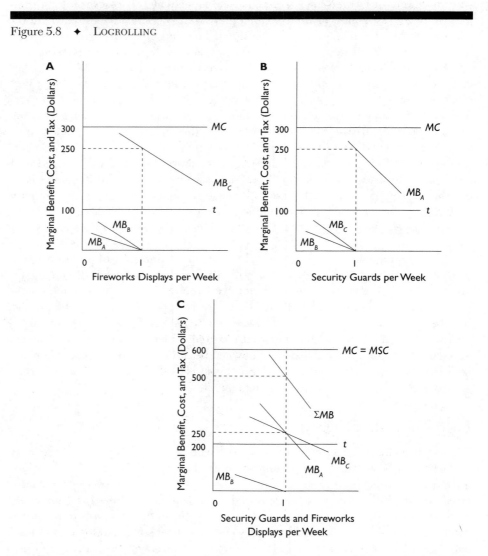

Logrolling can result in the passage of two issues together that could not pass if voted on separately.

Under majority rule, no fireworks displays will be provided because *A* and *B* vote against the first unit, given their $100 tax per display.

Figure 5.8B shows the marginal benefit, marginal cost, and tax per unit of security guards. In this case, voter *A* is the only one whose marginal benefit does not fall short of the $100 tax per guard. The marginal benefit that *A* receives from the first security guard is $250. Voters *B* and *C* are presumed to have zero marginal benefit at a weekly level of protection corresponding to one security guard per week. It follows that, given their $100 tax shares, they vote no. No security protection will be provided under majority rule. Given the assumptions, neither security protection nor fireworks displays will be provided under majority rule. The median most-preferred outcome of the three voters is zero in both cases.

Now suppose that *A* and *C* collude to get fireworks displays and security guards paired together as an issue. The election now consists of approval of a budget that includes one fireworks display per week for each security guard hired per week. In Figure 5.8C, the total output of security and fireworks is plotted against the marginal cost, benefit, and tax shares. A budget of $600 is proposed. All voters understand that this budget consists of one fireworks display and one security guard per week. The tax share for each voter is $200 for each combined security guard and fireworks display per week. Voter *B*, who evaluates the marginal benefit of both of these goods as zero, votes against the proposed budget. However, both voters *A* and *C* will vote in favor of this budget because the sum of the marginal benefits of fireworks and security protection exceeds their taxes. For voter *A*, the marginal benefit of the budget is $250, which consists entirely of the benefit received from security protection. For voter *C*, the marginal benefit of the budget is also $250 and consists entirely of the marginal benefit received from fireworks displays. When they agree to pair the issues, both *A* and *C* are better off than they otherwise would have been, were the issues voted on separately. Thus, pairing of the issues results in passage of both, while neither would pass if voted on alone on its own merits.

The same result would emerge if voters *A* and *C* agree to trade votes if each of the issues were voted on separately. That is, *C* would agree to vote in favor of security protection, even though that would make her worse off, provided that *A* agreed to vote in favor of fireworks displays. The net weekly gain to *A* from agreeing to vote for security protection would be $50. This is the difference between the weekly marginal benefit of $250 from one security guard and the weekly tax bill of $200 that would finance *both* fireworks and security. Similarly, voter *C* also would get a net weekly gain of $50 by agreeing to trade votes. The big loser in this process is voter *B*, who ends up paying $200 per week in taxes to pay for both a security guard and a fireworks display, neither of which provide positive marginal benefit to him!

Notice how the result depends on the intensity of preferences of voters *A* and *C*. Suppose that the marginal benefit of the first fireworks display was only $125 for voter *C*. She would still vote in favor of it if it were proposed on its own merits, because her marginal benefit would exceed her $100 tax share. However, under these circumstances, she would have no incentive to engage in logrolling, because the sum of her marginal benefits for the first fireworks display and the first security guard would be only $125, assuming again that she receives zero marginal benefit from one security guard. Because this falls short of the $200 tax share necessary to support both programs together, she would vote against the combined budget of one fireworks display and one security guard per week.

Logrolling also can cause losses in efficiency. At the political equilibrium budget of $600 per week, the marginal benefit received by A and C from both security protection and fireworks is $500. Because the marginal benefit from both of these public goods is zero for voter B, the sum of the marginal benefits for all three is only $500 in equilibrium. This is less than the marginal cost of $600 necessary to provide both goods. Because the marginal social cost of the budget exceeds its marginal social benefit by $100, approval of the budget means that more than the efficient amount of public spending occurs.

However, logrolling does not always cause losses in efficiency. For example, if B and A were each to get $25 in positive benefits from fireworks displays, then it would be efficient to have one display per year. But one display per year would not pass when voted on alone because both B and A still would vote against the program that would cost each of them $100 per week in taxes for $25 per week in benefits. However, the sum of the marginal benefits in this case would equal the $300 marginal cost. Similarly, if both B and C were to get $25 per week in marginal benefits from security guards, it would be efficient to have one guard per week because the sum of the marginal benefit of the guards would be $300, which equals the marginal cost. Pairing the two issues as before still would result in B voting against the two goods, because his $200 tax share would fall short of the $50 benefit he got from the two goods. However, A and C would each get $275 in benefits from passage and would both vote in favor of it, given a $200 tax share for each. The sum of the marginal benefits of the combined programs would be $275 + $275 + $50 = $600, which equals the marginal cost of $600.

It is not possible to reach an unequivocal conclusion about the impact of logrolling on efficient use of resources. In some cases logrolling can allow improved efficiency by contributing to passage of programs with a marginal social benefit that equals or exceeds their marginal social costs. In other cases logrolling results in an overallocation of resources to government use by allowing passage of government programs with marginal social costs that exceed their marginal social benefits.

SPECIAL INTEREST GROUPS AND THEIR IMPACT ON POLITICAL EQUILIBRIUM

Special interest groups are lobbies that seek to increase government expenditures that benefit their constituents. They differ from political parties in that their leaders do not actually run for political office. They do, however, seek to put pressure on political candidates, bureaucrats, and, ultimately, on voters to support issues that benefit the members of their groups. Special interest groups can apply pressure to politicians by threatening to tell their constituents to vote against them. They also can make campaign contributions to politicians who support their positions and finance advertisements against candidates who do not support their interests.

Special interest groups exist to promote policies favorable to workers, particular industries, regions, racial minorities, ethnic groups, environmental preservation, and taxpayers in general. The Sierra Club, for example, often acts as a special interest group in trying to persuade environmental protection agencies to preserve wilderness areas. In recent years, such groups as the Sierra Club and the Moral Majority have become potent political forces. Many of these special interest groups have used their power to influence the votes of those who are not members or direct beneficiaries of their efforts. In effect, special interest groups in modern democracies often campaign with as much zeal and actual expenditure of money and resources as do the political candidates themselves. The technical efficiency of the group in influencing the votes of nonmembers can make small groups, such as those representing automobile workers, farmers, or environmentalists, formidable and powerful influences on voters and therefore on the political equilibrium. Research on the effectiveness of several special interest groups in Switzerland in achieving their objectives measure their influence and suggests that they have influenced the political equilibrium in that nation.[8]

Gary Becker has analyzed how special interest groups affect political equilibrium.[9] Successful pressure groups succeed in manipulating taxes, government subsidies, and government regulations to raise the well-being of their members. Becker points out that pressure groups that succeed in obtaining increased benefits from government must make the members of competing pressure groups worse off. This is because an increase in government spending for one group increases taxes, or imposes other costs, on other groups. Increased influence of any one particular group is also assumed to decrease the influence of competing groups. The pressure groups themselves compete for political influence by spending time, effort, and some of their income on the production of political pressure. The number of members in a group and the resources spent per member in supporting the group's pressure activities determine the political pressure that a group can deliver. To the extent to which those who benefit from the special interest group's efforts try to be free riders, the effectiveness in producing pressure declines. By spending money to reduce free riding, the leaders of the groups can increase pressure on political agents.

Becker's model can be used to gain some insights into the success or failure of competing special interest groups. *Successful special interest groups are likely to be small, relative to the portion of the population that pays taxes to support their subsidies.* This result might seem surprising, but it is really very logical. After all, the greater the number of citizens who pay taxes to support even a rather large subsidy to a group with only a few members, the lower is the tax per citizen, relative to the subsidy per beneficiary. Becker points out that this result is consistent with empirical observations. For example, agriculture tends to be heavily subsidized in nations where it is a small sector, as is the case in the United States and in Japan. It tends to be heavily taxed in nations where it is a large sector, as is the case in Poland and in many African nations.

---

[8]F. Schneider and J. Naumann, "Interest Groups in Democracies—How Influential Are They?: An Empirical Examination for Switzerland," *Public Choice* 38 (1982): 281–303.

[9]Gary S. Becker, "A Theory of Competition among Pressure Groups for Political Influence," *Quarterly Journal of Economics* 98 (August 1983): 371–400.

INTERNATIONAL VIEW

TARIFFS AND IMPORT QUOTAS ON TEXTILES AND APPAREL IN THE UNITED STATES: SPECIAL INTEREST GROUPS IN ACTION

The U.S. textile and apparel industries, concentrated in the Southeast, are special interest groups that have been successful in protecting their constituents from foreign competition through tariffs and import quotas since the 1930s. These industries are quite labor-intensive, and although they pay below average wages, they have difficulty in competing with imported products produced in foreign nations with lower-priced labor. In recent years, productivity gains in these industries have increased supplies and put downward pressure on price. Employment in the industries has declined in part because fewer workers are required to produce output with newer technologies and current levels of demand.

In the early 1930s, the average tariff rates on cotton goods were 46 percent, while wool products were subject to an average tariff of 60 percent. Currently, tariffs on textile imports average three to six times higher than the average of 3.4 percent for all U.S. merchandise imports. In 1936, quotas on textile and apparel imports were first imposed on imports from Japan. As of 1992, various informal "voluntary export restraints" negotiated between the United States and other nations, mostly developing countries with low-wage labor, restricted imports from forty-one countries that accounted for 69 percent of U.S. textile imports and 88 percent of U.S. apparel imports.[*]

A study by the International Trade Commission in 1987 concluded that U.S. quotas on textile imports were equivalent to a 21.8 percent tariff while apparel quotas matched a 28.3 percent tariff. The combined effect of tariffs and quotas on textile prices equaled a 32 percent tax on textiles and a 46 percent tax on apparel. The imported suit or dress you would pay $200 for in the absence of trade restraints costs $292 dollars based on the effective tariff rate of 46 percent!

The study concluded that elimination of all tariffs and quotas on textiles and apparel in the United States would reduce employment by 60,000. The workers whose jobs would be eliminated would eventually find other employment. Displaced workers in these industries could be compensated for their loss of wages while searching for new jobs at much lower cost per job than the current cost of tariffs and quotas in these industries.

It costs the United States as much as $52,000 per year to save a job that on average pays less than $20,000 per year. Estimates from various studies indicate that the total cost of each job saved in the apparel industries as a result of tariffs and quotas ranges from $39,000 to $46,000 per year. Estimates of the cost of protecting jobs of workers in the textile industries range from $50,000 to $52,000 per year for each job saved. These estimates include the higher consumer costs for textiles and apparel that result from the trade restrictions that transfer well-being from consumers to workers and owners of capital in these industries. Also included in the estimates is the net welfare cost of the trade restrictions that measure the amount by which costs to consumers exceed benefits to special interests in the industry. These estimates range from $9,000 to $38,000 per job retained in the industries.[†]

The power of the textile and apparent industries in the United States appeared to be waning in the early 1990s. Two trade liberalization treaties at that time, the North American Free Trade Agreement (NAFTA), and a new General Agreement on Trade and Tariffs (GATT) negotiated in 1993 were expected to eliminate import quotas on textiles and apparel and significantly lower tariffs by the turn of the century.

The influence of special interest groups in this case has contributed to inefficient resource use. We pay higher prices for textiles and apparel and devote more than the efficient amount of resources to their production because of the power exerted by special interest groups.

[*]See Congress of the United States, *Congressional Budget Office, Trade Restraints and the Competitive Status of the Textile, Apparel, and Nonrubber-Footwear Industries,* Washington, D.C.: Congress of the United States, December 1991.
[†]See ibid., xvi.

Persons are often members of more than one special interest group. For example, a person could be a member of an occupational pressure group and of a group that supports regional growth. This person could spend money and effort as a member of her occupational pressure group in ways that result in increases in the costs of obtaining the benefits desired for her special interest in regional growth. In effect, the activities of various special interest groups often result in both taxes and subsidies for their constituents. Many persons could be equally as well off if both their taxes and subsidies from each pressure group were reduced in equal amounts. If the effect of these taxes and subsidies is to cancel each other, members of the various special interest groups will not be harmed. But, because taxes and subsidies to particular activities result in efficiency losses, the result will be net gains from reducing taxes and subsidies.

BUREAUCRACY AND THE SUPPLY OF PUBLIC OUTPUT

The establishment of a government also implies the development of a **bureaucracy** that is in charge of implementing public choices made through political institutions. The bureaucracy itself influences the actual delivery of services and the efficiency with which such services can be produced.[10] Insofar as bureaucrats influence the cost of producing public goods, their behavior is an important determinant of the actual terms on which such goods can be produced and offered to citizens. In other words, bureaucrats influence the terms of supply of public goods and thus influence the resulting political equilibrium.

A basic problem exists in measuring the efficiency of production by bureaucrats. In most cases, the output produced is neither easily quantifiable into units nor easily sold for profit in markets. Therefore, it is difficult to determine whether government bureaus produce their output at minimum possible cost. For a private firm competing with other firms producing a similar output, such information is rapidly made available to owners through the firm's profit and loss statement. A business firm with costs of production that are higher than those of competing firms will quickly discover that it will be difficult to make a profit unless costs are lowered. Bureaucrats do not directly own the inputs they use for production. Funding comes from an external source (such as Congress), and any net financial gains to bureaucrats who produce efficiently are rare.

Bureaucratic Behavior

Among the most significant contributions by economists who have analyzed bureaucracy in recent years is the work of William Niskanen.[11] He has argued that bureaucrats

---

[10]See Thomas E. Borcherding, ed., *Budgets and Bureaucrats* (Durham, NC: Duke University Press, 1977).

[11]William A. Niskanen, Jr., *Bureaucracy and Representative Government* (Chicago: Aldine-Atherton, 1971) and "Bureaucrats and Politicians," *Journal of Law and Economics* 18 (December 1975): 617–643.

seek to maximize the power associated with holding public office. Such power is likely to be correlated with the resources that the bureaucrat has under command. This, in turn, is related to the size of the bureau's budget. Niskanen therefore assumes that the bureaucrat seeks to maximize the size of the bureau's budget. The implication of Niskanen's analysis is that attempts by bureaucrats to maximize their budgets lead to a general overextension of the government sector, in excess of the efficient level of output.

Figure 5.9 shows the bureaucratic incentive to supply more than the efficient amount of output. The marginal social benefit and marginal social cost of the bureau's output per year are shown in Figure 5.9A. The output could be the number of new missiles deployed per year for a military bureau, such as the air force. For a civilian agency such as a bureau of public roads, the output could be measured as the miles of new road supplied per year. The efficient output, $Q°$ units per year, corresponds to point E, where the marginal social benefit of output just equals its marginal social cost. The bureaucrats, however, seek to maximize the size of their budgets. They therefore seek to obtain as much funding as possible for their output. If they reason that they can obtain additional funds as long as the *total social benefit (TSB)* of the output exceeds its *total social cost (TSC)*, they will try to increase output beyond the efficient level of $Q°$ units per year. This is illustrated in Figure 5.9B, where the total social benefit and total social cost of the bureau's output are plotted. The efficient output corresponds to the point where the slope of the total social cost curve equals the slope of the total social benefit curve. At that output, $MSB = MSC$ in Figure 5.9A. The output that the bureau will try to get approved is Q_B, which corresponds to the point where $TSC = TSB$. The bureau's desired level of output therefore exceeds the efficient amount.

Figure 5.9A shows the loss in well-being that results if the bureaucrats succeed in getting their desired level of output approved. The loss in net benefits is the triangular area EAB.

An additional problem with managing bureaucracies to achieve efficiency is that bureaucrats often have monopolistic power. Single agencies provide such services as environmental protection, defense, and social insurance. In many cases, the bureaucrats themselves have specialized information not available elsewhere. The bureaucrats could seek to attain the budget-maximizing output by trying to make politicians believe that the social benefit of their output is greater than it is in fact. This would shift the TSB curve up to the TSB' curve in the eyes of funding agencies, as shown in Figure 5.8B. The maximum output that the agency could fund would increase to Q_B'.

A funding agent often has difficulty monitoring the activities of its bureaus because of high transactions costs. Budgeting and managerial improvements that lower these transactions costs would contribute to better monitoring of bureaucrat behavior and therefore would help achieve efficient output levels.

Bureaucrats can increase the size of their budgets in two ways. They can seek to convince governing authorities that their output needs to be increased, as in the preceding analysis. Alternatively, they can increase the amounts of input necessary to produce any given amount of output by using inefficient production techniques. In this latter case, the loss in efficiency results from misuse of input rather than excessive production of the bureau's service. Bureaucrats do not achieve efficiency because they maximize a utility function that depends not only on net benefit to their

Figure 5.9 ✦ BUREAUCRACY AND EFFICIENCY

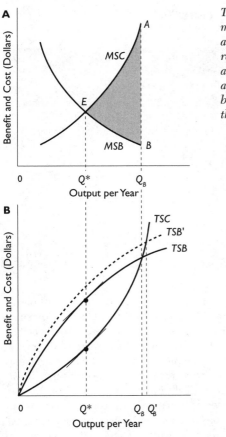

The efficient output is $Q^°$ per year. A budget-maximizing bureau tries to get its sponsor to approve Q_B units per year. This amount would result in a decrease in well-being equal to the area EAB. A bureau could try to get Q'_B approved if it convinced its sponsor that its benefits at any given output level were given by the curve TSB' instead of TSB.

"sponsors" (funding authorities) but also on the growth of their budget, fringe benefits, job security, and reduced work load.[12] Some empirical studies have provided evidence on the relative inefficiency of bureaus by comparing the costs of production of the same output produced by public (nonprofit) and private firms. In such cases, the private firm was shown to be more efficient.[13]

[12]Dennis C. Mueller, *Public Choice II* (Cambridge, Eng.: Cambridge University Press, 1989), 262–263.

[13]William Orzechowski, "Economic Models of Bureaucracy: Survey, Extensions and Evidence," in *Budgets and Bureaucrats*, ed. T. E. Borcherding (Durham, NC: Duke University Press, 1977), 229–259.

The behavior of bureaucrats depends on the constraints that they face. Most of the models of bureaucracy presume that sponsors are at the mercy of the bureaucrats. In fact, however, adequate budgeting procedures can establish a set of constraints that could govern the tendencies of bureaucrats to overexpand or produce inefficiently.

C H E C K P O I N T

1. What is logrolling?
2. How can logrolling result in approval of extensions of public services that could not be approved under majority rule when they are voted on as single issues?
3. How does bureaucratic behavior influence public spending? How can bureaucrats influence information in ways that increase government spending beyond the efficient levels?

Summary

A political equilibrium is an agreement on the level of production of one or more public goods, given a specified rule for making the public choice and the distribution of tax shares among individuals. The political equilibrium is also influenced by the cost of production of the public good or goods and information available to voters on both costs and benefits. Individuals base their votes on a comparison of their marginal benefits and tax shares for proposed increases in output. A voter's most-preferred outcome corresponds to the point at which the marginal benefit of a given quantity of a public good is equal to the extra taxes that must be paid for that quantity.

Collective, or public, choices are agreements resulting in political equilibriums on issues of common concern. The most commonly used public choice rule is simple majority rule. Under certain circumstances, when two or more alternatives are to be decided upon, majority rule might be incapable of achieving a unique political equilibrium. However, when all voters have single-peaked preferences, majority rule will produce a unique political equilibrium at the median most-preferred outcome. Single-peaked preferences exist when a unique optimum outcome exists for each individual, such that movement away from the optimum always makes that individual worse off.

Political equilibriums are influenced by politicians and bureaucrats. Models of political behavior presume that political parties attempt to maximize votes. When all voters have single-peaked preferences, parties will tend to move to the median position to win elections.

When all voters do not vote, the median most-preferred outcome of all citizens could differ from the median most-preferred outcome of all voters. Voters might choose not to vote because they believe that their votes will have no effect on the outcome of an election. The costs of voting might outweigh the expected benefits of doing so.

Political parties have incentives to propose less than the efficient amount of government services when voters are better informed on costs than on benefits of those services. However, vote-maximizing behavior also provides incentive for politicians to engage in logrolling.

Logrolling is the explicit trading of votes on issues of great interest to voters. When two or more issues are voted on simultaneously, implicit logrolling can occur. Under these circumstances, two issues that could not be approved if voted on separately could pass. Logrolling offers an outlet to express intensity of feeling on an issue in a one-person, one-vote democracy. However, logrolling also can cause losses in efficiency.

Models of bureaucratic behavior presume that bureaucrats attempt to maximize the size of their budgets. If they face no competition and no restraints from budgeting procedures, this leads to a tendency of oversupply of government output or inefficient production techniques. Special interest groups also influence political outcomes by seeking to increase government subsidies to their constituents that are financed by taxes on others.

A Forward Look

The next chapter examines some practical techniques for evaluating the costs and benefits of government programs. We show how the budgeting process can be used to help achieve the least-cost means of providing public goods and how government projects to increase the output of government goods and services can be evaluated with cost-benefit analysis.

Important Concepts

Public Choice
Political Equilibrium
Tax Shares
Simple Majority Rule
Most-Preferred Political Outcome
Rational Ignorance
Median Voter
Political Externalities
Political Transactions Costs
Single-Peaked Preferences
Multiple-Peaked Preferences
Arrow's Impossibility Theorem
Median Voter Rule
Political Parties
Logrolling
Implicit Logrolling
Special Interest Groups
Bureaucracy

Questions for Review

1. What factors influence the costs of supplying such public goods as police protection and national defense? What might cause these costs to go up or down, and how would such change affect your taxes?
2. How does a person decide to vote on any issue that proposes to change the amount of public goods supplied by the government?
3. What factors influence the political equilibrium?
4. Using the data in Table 5.1, show that the median most-preferred outcome will defeat any other alternative in elections decided by majority rule.

5. Given tax shares, explain why only the median voter consumes his most-preferred quantity of a public good under majority rule. Show how other voters are prevented from obtaining maximum satisfaction from the public good. Show the losses in well-being that can be prevented if the tax paid by *each* voter equaled that voter's marginal benefit.
6. Use Figure 5.2 to show how an increase in weekly wages of security guards to $420 will affect the most-preferred outcome of each voter and the political equilibrium under majority rule.
7. When does majority rule lead to the possibility of public choices that result in the outcome of an election being contingent on the order in which alternatives are presented to the electorate? Under what conditions will a unique collective choice result from simple majority rule?
8. Under what conditions will the median peak correspond to an extreme outcome, such as no output of a good?
9. What is logrolling? Under what conditions is logrolling likely to emerge? How can logrolling prevent the attainment of efficiency?
10. Show how an increase in the average cost of supplying a pure public good will reduce the output resulting from simple majority rule. Is the median voter always the same person? Show how a change in tax shares could change the identity of the median voter.

Problems

1. The average cost of landscaping services for members of a condominium community is $350 per week. Assume that the quantity of landscaping services is perfectly correlated with the number of gardeners per week. Suppose that the community consists of seven residents, each with the identical marginal benefit curve for landscaping services. The marginal benefit of the first gardener is $100 per resident.
   a. How many gardeners would be hired if their services were sold in a market to individual buyers at a price of $350 per week? Explain why the market arrangement is inefficient.
   b. Assume that the efficient number of gardeners is three per week. What is the political equilibrium under majority rule if each voter is assigned a tax share of $50 per gardener per week? How will the political equilibrium differ from the Lindahl equilibrium?
2. The example of logrolling used in the text assumes that the transactions costs of vote trading are zero.

Suppose, instead, voters A and C have to incur expenditures equal to $60 per week to reach agreement on the vote-trading scheme. Show how this would prevent successful logrolling. Also show how logrolling would be impossible if the marginal benefit of the first security guard were only $150 to voter A and transactions costs were zero.

3. Suppose that the positions of political candidates on all issues can be ranked on a scale of conservative to liberal. The more conservative a candidate, the less the quantity of public goods he will supply. Suppose, as well, that all voters favoring liberal candidates will vote while only 50 percent of those favoring conservative candidates will vote. Use a graph like the one drawn in Figure 5.6 to show how the political equilibrium will differ from an election in which all citizens vote.

4. Suppose the military bureaucracy consistently misinforms Congress on the total costs of producing military hardware. Assume that it underestimates the actual costs and that the political representatives believe these estimates. Show how this is likely to cause a loss in efficiency. Show the efficient output of military hardware, the output desired by the military bureaucracy, and how the output chosen will differ from the efficient output even if Congress attempts to achieve efficiency. In your answer, assume that the military seeks to maximize the size of its budget.

Suggestions for Further Reading

Arrow, Kenneth. *Social Choice and Individual Values*. 2d ed. New York: Wiley, 1963. A treatise on collective choice that led to a Nobel prize in economics for the author. Requires a strong background in mathematics.

Becker, Gary S. "A Theory of Competition among Pressure Groups for Political Influence." *Quarterly Journal of Economics* 98 (August 1983): 371–400. A pathbreaking technical application of economic theory to political interaction. It analyzes the behavior and impact of special-interest groups on political equilibrium.

Black, Duncan. *The Theory of Committees and Elections*. Cambridge, Eng.: Cambridge University Press, 1958. A classic in the theory of collective choice.

Breton, Albert. *The Economic Theory of Representative Government*. Chicago: Aldine, 1974. An analysis of the demand and supply of government output and policy.

Buchanan, James, and Tullock, Gordon. *The Calculus of Consent*. Ann Arbor: University of Michigan Press, 1962. An application of economic theory to political interaction in constitutional democracy.

Downs, Anthony. *An Economic Theory of Democracy*. New York: Harper & Row, 1957. A pioneering application of techniques of economic analysis to political interaction. Very readable.

Hanusch, Horst, ed. *Public Finance and the Quest for Efficiency*. Detroit: Wayne State University Press, 1984. Proceedings of a conference on political interaction and government. It includes many essays on the political process and on the impact of government on efficiency.

McLean, Iain and Urken, Arnold B., eds. *Classics of Social Choice*. Ann Arbor: The University of Michigan Press, 1993. A collection of classic articles on public choice issues.

Mueller, Dennis C. *Public Choice II*. Cambridge, Eng.: Cambridge University Press, 1989. A summary of the literature on public choice.

Niskanen, William A., Jr. *Bureaucracy and Representative Government*. Chicago: Aldine-Atherton, 1971. A modern classic that analyzes bureaucratic incentives and the influence of bureaucracy on public policy.

Government

Expenditures and

Policy in the

United States:

Selected Issues

II

6

COST-BENEFIT ANALYSIS
AND GOVERNMENT
INVESTMENTS

LEARNING OBJECTIVES

After reading this chapter you should be able to

1. Discuss cost-effectiveness analysis and explain how it can be used to help government select the least-cost means of achieving given objectives.

2. Describe how cost-benefit analysis can be used to help government choose among alternative investment projects.

3. Explain how benefits and costs of government investment projects can be measured and list some of the difficulties involved in doing so.

4. Define the social rate of discount, the difficulties involved in estimating it, and how it is used to obtain the present value of future net benefits of government investments.

5. Put all the steps of cost-benefit analysis together and show how a typical cost-benefit tableau can be set up.

6. Analyze the role of cost-benefit analysis in government investment budgeting and in the political process.

*H*ow many times have you heard political candidates claim that the problem with government is that it is not run like a business? The average citizen believes, perhaps for good reason, that considerable waste and mismanagement exists in government that would not be tolerated in a profit-maximizing business. You have all heard about outrageous prices for screwdrivers and other components in defense contracting, and many believe that federal and state bureaucracies are inflated with workers whose productivity is low.

It would be nice if government could be run like a business, but some fundamental differences between the nature of government and the nature of business make this impossible. First, governments do not sell their products for a profit. Because they do not earn profits they do not receive very good signals about how well they are doing in satisfying the demands of the citizens they serve. Second, governments do not usually face competition. Even if they are doing a poor job because they are supplying a product or service that has little value or because their costs are excessively high, no competing producer can quickly enter to produce a better service or one that costs less. Finally, government projects and programs are often chosen through the political process because of their effects on the incomes of special-interest groups rather than their contribution to the efficient allocation of resources.

Many government programs involve investment in roads, water and sewer facilities, air and sea ports, education, and other projects that provide social capital that enhances the productivity of inputs employed by both government and the private sector. For example, roads provided by governments in the United States are used as inputs into trucking services and provide transportation benefits to many segments of the U.S. population. The air traffic control system run by the federal government makes it possible for both businesses and households to enjoy the benefits of safe air travel. The government investments usually take several years to develop and construct, but once completed yield a stream of benefits to citizens for many years to come. However, because the government projects do not usually result in output sold in the marketplace by governments, it is difficult to compute the return earned on the government funds invested. We need a way of estimating net return to government investments to determine whether they provide net benefits to society. This chapter discusses some practical techniques that can be used to help government economize the use of resources and rank alternative investment projects according to their net benefits.

ECONOMIC ANALYSIS FOR THE BUDGET PROCESS: ACHIEVING THE LEAST-COST MEANS OF ACCOMPLISHING AN AUTHORIZED OBJECTIVE

In this section we discuss some budgeting techniques that can be used to help government choose the best mix of programs to accomplish various objectives, such as providing children with a certain amount and quality of schooling. We then discuss techniques to help government choose among alternative investment projects. Governments are like enormous multiproduct firms. To choose among alternative products we must evaluate both the marginal social benefits and marginal social costs of additional investments and rank projects according to their marginal social net gain.

Program Budgeting

A **program** is a combination of government activities producing a distinguishable output. **Program budgeting** is a system of managing government expenditures by attempting to compare the program proposals of all government agencies authorized to achieve similar objectives. The **mission** of a government agency is comparable to a business firm's product. Program budgeting seeks to measure the outputs of agencies in quantitative terms. Then the goal is to choose the combination of programs that achieve the mission at minimum cost. The minimum-cost combination of programs is sometimes called the cost-effective program mix.

An advantage of program budgeting is that it has the potential to allow budget managers to see trade-offs that are not immediately obvious when agency or department budgets are viewed in isolation. For example, suppose all agencies with the basic function of improving health and safety are required to submit their proposed programs to a central budget office. The programs of many agencies in such diverse departments as Health and Human Services and Transportation are designed to accomplish similar objectives. For example, highway safety, cancer research, antipollution controls, and medical subsidies all ultimately serve the purpose of prolonging human lives. Under program budgeting, each agency would estimate the years of human life that their programs will produce over time. The budget managers then would seek to achieve a given number of years of life prolongation by choosing the cost-effective mix of programs.

Trade-offs between the programs of agencies with similar missions in the two departments would not be as easily discovered under a *line budgeting system,* which compares the budget proposals of agencies in a given department with each other, even though those agencies have very different missions. Consistent use of program budgeting techniques, and skillful grouping of alternative programs according to the actual outputs produced, can result in considerable tax savings by allowing choice of least-cost mixes of programs achieving given objectives.

Cost-Effectiveness Analysis

Cost-effectiveness analysis is a technique for determining the minimum-cost combination of government programs to achieve a given objective. The first step in implementing a cost-effectiveness analysis would be to choose an objective that alternative government programs can achieve. For example, suppose we decide that we want to achieve the objective of reducing deaths from disease or accidents by 5,000 per year on average over the next ten years. We can choose from many programs, all of which help reduce deaths. We can use tax funds to provide more information about the risks of smoking, drinking alcohol, or having a diet high in fat. We also could require that all buildings be equipped with smoke detectors and provide them for free in low-income neighborhoods where the quality of housing is so poor that the incidence of deaths as a result of residential fires is high. We could provide subsidies to improve the cardiac care facilities of hospitals in the nation. Finally, we could invest funds in improving the safety of our highways so as to reduce accidental traffic deaths or improve air traffic control techniques to reduce aircraft accidents.

Let's look at two programs: government provision of free smoke detectors to urban neighborhoods and government provision of free inoculations against the flu to the same neighborhoods. The objective of both programs is to save an extra 5,000 lives per year. The problem is to choose the mix of the two programs that achieves this objective at minimum possible cost.

The first step to solve the problem is to find all the combinations of the two programs in appropriate amounts that can be used to save 5,000 lives per year. In this way we can derive an isoquant for the two programs. Such an isoquant is illustrated in Figure 6.1; each point on the isoquant shows a specific combination of the two programs that will save 5,000 lives per year. For example, point *A* corresponds to 20,000 smoke detectors and 10,000 free inoculations per year. Point *B* corresponds to 10,000 smoke detectors and 20,000 free inoculations. Because both points are on the isoquant, they

Figure 6.1   ✦   Cost-Effectiveness Analysis

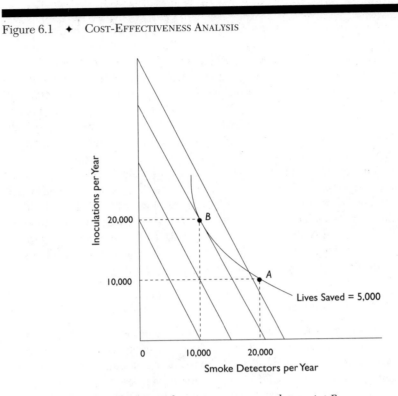

The minimum cost combination of programs corresponds to point B.

are both equally effective in achieving the objective of saving 5,000 lives per year. To actually construct the isoquant, budget analysis requires estimates of the marginal product of each of the two programs in terms of lives saved and information on how the marginal products will vary with the level of the program, which in this case is easily measured by the number of smoke detectors and inoculations provided.

With information on the marginal products we also can calculate the slope of the isoquant at each point. The slope provides information on the marginal rate of technical substitution of one program for the other. It tells us, for example, how many more inoculations we will have to provide to keep the number of lives saved at 5,000 when we reduce the number of smoke detectors by any given amount. The marginal rate of technical substitution ($MRTS$) is the slope of the isoquant multiplied by -1 and equals the ratio of the marginal product of smoke detectors (SD) to the marginal product of inoculations (I):

$$MRTS = \text{Marginal Product of } SD/\text{Marginal Product of } I. \qquad (6.1)$$

To determine the cost-effective mix of the two programs, we must then get information on the prices of the two alternatives. If the price of a smoke detector is P_{SD}

while the price of an inoculation is P_I then the cost of any combination of smoke detector and inoculation can be calculated as follows:

$$C = (SD)P_{SD} + (I)P_I. \tag{6.2}$$

This equation defines a family of isocost lines. The slope of each isocost line is the price of smoke detectors divided by the price of inoculation multiplied by -1. (See the appendixes of Chapters 1 and 2 for a review of isoquant analysis.) Suppose that each smoke detector installed costs \$30 and each inoculation costs \$15. The equation of the family of isocost lines therefore would be

$$C = 30(SD) + 15(I). \tag{6.3}$$

Figure 6.1 plots a hypothetical isoquant for the two programs giving all the combinations of smoke detectors and inoculations per year that can be used to save 5,000 additional lives per year. Also plotted on the same set of axes is the family of isocost lines.

The cost-effective mix of the two programs occurs at point B, where 20,000 free inoculations are provided and 10,000 free smoke detectors are installed. At that point the isoquant becomes tangent to an isocost line. No other combination of programs other than that at point B can save lives at lower annual cost. At the point of tangency the slope of the isoquant is equal to the slope of the isocost lines and the following condition is therefore satisfied:

$$MRTS = P_{SD}/P_I. \tag{6.4}$$

Remember the $MRTS$ depends on the marginal productivities of both programs. The analysis shows that the cost-effective mix of the two programs depends both on their productivity in terms of lives saved and the prices of units of services provided by the programs themselves.

Cost-effectiveness analysis allows policymakers to see tradeoffs between programs by budgeting together for all agencies with similar missions. In this way governments can lower the costs of achieving certain goals such as improving health or reducing delays from congestion in travel. By encouraging government agencies to compete for scarce budget funds through the development of more effective programs, this system also can reduce taxpayer expense further by encouraging innovation that reduces the cost of government programs or increases their productivity. The trick in making the government more cost-effective is to group all agencies having similar goals together for budgeting purposes. For example, programs in the Department of Transportation and the Department of Health and Human Services and even the Department of Urban Affairs could all serve similar purposes. By budgeting together for these agencies we can help reduce the costs of achieving such objectives as reducing deaths each year or improving health.

Performance Measures and Government Budgeting in Practice

Program budgeting has had only limited use in the United States. At the federal level variants of program budgeting and cost-effectiveness analysis were used in the 1960s and 1970s. In the 1960s the variant used by the Johnson administration was called the "planning-programming-budgeting system" (PPBS). In the 1970s under the Carter administration a system called "zero-based budgeting" (ZBB) was used. These systems both failed to change the process by which resources were allocated to federal programs largely because the information they generated was ignored by Congress. The federal bureaucracy also had considerable difficulty in generating the information necessary to effectively implement these program budgeting schemes. Currently no system of program budgeting is being used by the federal government.

Systems of program budgeting are still used in several state and local governments in the United States. As of the early 1990s Florida and Oregon used variants of the program budgeting system to try to improve efficiency of allocation of resources. The system has also been adopted by some local governments in the United States.

In an assessment of the value of such systems currently in use, the Congressional Budget Office (CBO) in the United States has argued that they have only limited ability to improve resource allocation but that they do improve management and finance reporting.[1] The study also indicated that federal agencies today do attempt to measure results of their programs in various ways to determine their effectiveness. However, none of the agencies surveyed by the CBO used cost-effectiveness analysis to make decisions about how to allocate resources among programs.

Although program budgeting techniques are not currently being used in a consistent manner in the United States, political concern does exist about improving resource allocation within the federal government sector. Under the Clinton Administration the Vice President's National Performance Review represented an attempt to find techniques to implement quality management and program budgeting for federal programs.

C H E C K P O I N T

1. What is program budgeting?
2. What information and procedures are required to implement a cost-effectiveness analysis of government programs?
3. How can cost-effectiveness analysis help keep government spending down?

COST-BENEFIT ANALYSIS

Cost-benefit analysis represents a practical technique for determining the relative merits of alternative government projects over time. Use of cost-benefit analysis can contribute to efficiency by making sure that new projects for which marginal social cost exceeds marginal social benefit are not considered for approval. Cost-benefit analysis, if done well, provides essential information to be used by government authorities and citizens in making choices among alternative government projects.

---

[1]See Congress of the United States, Congressional Budget Office, "Using Performance Measures in the Federal Budget Process," July 1993.

Cost-benefit analysis is not a new tool. It has been used in the United States since 1900 by the Army Corps of Engineers to evaluate the desirability of alternative water resource projects. In commonsense terms, cost-benefit analysis is nothing more than a statement of the pros and cons of a particular activity over a period of time. It is a very systematic way of gathering information.

Since 1981 all new regulations proposed by the federal government must be subjected to a cost-benefit analysis. This practice was instituted by the Reagan administration to control the growth of new social regulations in the 1980s. Cost-benefit analysis is applied to new social regulations dealing with product, job safety, and environmental protection.

Essentially, the three steps involved in a cost-benefit analysis are:

1. Enumerate all costs and benefits of the proposed project.
2. Evaluate all costs and benefits in dollar terms.
3. Discount future net benefits. This allows future benefits and costs to be reduced to their present values, so that they can be compared with the dollar amount of budget authority necessary to finance the project.

Although the steps may seem simple, an adequate analysis demands a great deal of ingenuity. It might require the combined talents of economists, engineers, and scientists to correctly enumerate and evaluate costs and benefits. Benefits must include all indirect effects (externalities) generated by the project. Costs must be defined correctly as alternative benefits forgone if the project is adopted (the opportunity cost). An appropriate discount rate must be chosen to compare present and future returns from alternative projects.

Enumerating Benefits and Costs

The preliminary step is to define both the project under consideration and its output. Once this is done, the analysts can proceed to enumerate the costs incurred and the benefits generated over the life of the project.

Benefits can be divided into two categories: direct and indirect. Direct benefits are those increases in output or productivity attributable to the purpose of the project. For example, in an irrigation project, the purpose is to increase the fertility of a particular tract of land. The direct benefits, in this case, will be the net increase, over time, in agricultural output on the tract of land being irrigated. Indirect, or spillover, benefits are those accruing to individuals not directly associated with the purpose of the project. In an irrigation project, spillover benefits might include the improved fertility of adjoining land that is not actually irrigated by the scheme, resulting from changes in the height of the water table in the area.

In enumerating benefits, only real increases in output and welfare are considered. Care must be exercised not to double count benefits of a particular project. For example, agricultural land values are likely to increase as a result of an irrigation project. However, such appreciation merely reflects the increased output potential of the land. Counting the increase in land value, along with the value of the increase in agricultural output, results in double counting the benefits of the project. Unfortunately, this is not always understood by those undertaking cost-benefit analyses, and, on occasion, double counting does occur.[2]

Another problem is the definition of indirect, or spillover, effects of a project. In some cases, analysts include as a benefit the extra profits of third parties not directly affected by a project. For example, retailers will sell more goods in a region where incomes rise as a result of a government project. In a full-employment economy, these extra retail sales and profits merely reflect changes in the distribution of income as a result of the project; that is, they reflect increases in income to owners of resources, attracted from alternative uses rather than from increases in output. The increase in retail sales in the area that benefits from the project is balanced by a *reduction* in retail sales elsewhere, because the taxes to finance the project reduce incomes elsewhere. The practice of counting extra profits of third parties has been common in some cost-benefit analyses of irrigation projects.[3] In these cases, the profits of businesses that process the increased agricultural outputs, as well as the profits of firms that supply goods to farmers, have been included in the enumeration of benefits.

For some projects, enumeration of benefits is difficult. How are the benefits of an education program or a health program defined? Again, the answer must give a quantifiable result that avoids double counting. In a particular vocational education program, benefits might include the increased output as reflected in the higher earnings of those who attain new skills as a result of the program. In an accident prevention project, benefits might include the increased output that results from reduced injuries and fatalities.

In enumerating costs of a project, listing direct resource costs gives only a partial account of real costs when external costs also will occur. Any costs not reflected in the prices of inputs must be included. Suppose, for example, that a new project in a given area will have the effect of reducing water resources available to nearby agricultural land. The corresponding reduction in agricultural output must be included as a cost of the project.

Evaluating Benefits and Costs

After all costs and benefits have been satisfactorily enumerated, the next step is to evaluate these costs and benefits in dollar terms. Valuing output requires an estimate of the demand for increased production and calculation of consumer surplus.[4] When the outputs of particular programs are not sold in markets, the problem of valuation is difficult. Surrogate measures of the willingness of beneficiaries to pay for outputs that are not sold must be obtained. For example, although the benefits of many public health programs are consumed collectively, the value of these benefits might be reflected in

---

[2]Examples of double counting are offered by Alan R. Prest and Ralph Turvey, "Cost-Benefit Analysis: A Survey," in *Surveys of Economic Theory*, 3 vols. (New York: St. Martin's, 1966), 3:155–207.

[3]Prest and Turvey, "Cost-Benefit Analysis," 181.

[4]For a discussion of consumer surplus, see Edward J. Mishan, *Cost-Benefit Analysis* (New York: Praeger, 1976), Chapter 7.

increased earnings of those whose health is improved by the project. An estimate of such increased earnings, over time, can be a good reflection of the value of the benefits for the project. Similarly, the benefits of an education program might be measured by an estimate of the increased earnings accruing, over time, to former students.

An additional problem occurs with outputs and inputs that are marketable but have prices that do not reflect their true social value. This results when any output attributable to a project is sold in monopolistic markets, when external effects are generated by production of the output, or when distortions due to subsidies or taxes are present. Under such conditions, prices must be adjusted to reflect the actual marginal social cost or benefit. For example, if the prices of increased agricultural outputs of an irrigation project reflect the price supports of U.S. agricultural policy, then the prices must be adjusted downward to reflect the actual marginal social benefit of the output to consumers. If the prices of inputs used are distorted upward from actual marginal social cost by the monopolistic power of sellers, then a downward adjustment must be made in the input prices. The elimination of such price distortions might require some arbitrary estimating decisions by the analysts.

Discounting Future Net Benefits

The next step after enumerating and evaluating costs and benefits is to discount all future net benefits. The choice of an appropriate discount rate is of crucial importance here. The need to discount stems from the existence of positive interest rates in the economy. Positive interest rates imply that a dollar of benefits in the future will be worth less than an equivalent dollar of present benefits, because it takes less than a dollar of resources invested today to produce a dollar of resources tomorrow (say, one year from today), when interest rates are positive.

For example, if the interest rate is 5 percent per year, then only $95.24 needs to be invested today to obtain $100 one year from today. That is to say, $100 received one year from today is worth only $95.24 today. The $95.24 is called the *present value*, PV, of $100 to be received in one year. At the end of the year, $95.24 will be equal to $95.24 + (0.05)($95.24) = $100.

In general, the present value of X dollars to be received n years from now at simple interest rate, r, is obtained by solving the equation $X = PV(1 + r)^n$.

$$PV = \frac{X}{(1 + r)^n}.$$ (6.5)

The higher the interest rate used to discount a certain amount of future income, X, the lower the present value of X. The interest, r, called the **social rate of discount,** is used to compute the present value of X. If a particular project yields benefits over a number of years, the net benefits, X_i, per year must be discounted in each year as follows:

$$PV = \sum_{i=1}^{n} \frac{X_i}{(1 + r)^i}.$$ (6.6)

For example, if a project yields X_1 dollars in net benefits after the first year and X_2 dollars after the second year, its present value is

$$PV = \frac{X_1}{(1 + r)^1} + \frac{X_2}{(1 + r)^2}. \tag{6.7}$$

How the Discount Rate Affects the Present Value of Projects

Why is the choice of an appropriate discount rate important? First, it is no more important than the proper enumeration and evaluation of costs and benefits. An analysis that uses the correct discount rate but a serious miscalculation of costs and benefits will give results as misleading as a study that uses a zero discount rate. All phases of cost-benefit analysis are equally important if such studies are to yield useful information. However, the choice of the discount rate affects the ranking of alternative projects and the number of projects that can be approved. A low discount rate tends to favor projects that yield net benefits further into the future, relative to projects that yield current net benefits.

An arithmetical example illustrates this effect. Consider two alternative projects. Project 1 yields $90 in net benefits immediately. Project 2 yields $100 two years after it is undertaken but nothing at present or after one year. The present values of net benefits from these two projects can be calculated with a variety of discount rates and then ranked according to their present values. Consider three alternative discount rates: 0 percent, 5 percent, and 10 percent. The present value of project 1 is always $90 because it yields only present net benefits. The present value of project 2 will vary with the discount rate. Table 6.1 gives the present values of net benefits for project 2 under the alternative discount rates.

As shown in the table, the present value of project 2 is greater than that of project 1 under a discount rate of 0 percent and 5 percent. But if a discount rate of 10 percent is chosen, the result is such that project 1 is ranked above project 2. In general, the higher the discount rate, the less is the weight given to the value of future net benefits.

Furthermore, higher discount rates result in fewer government projects that can be approved. Insofar as the discount rate reflects the return to private consumption and investment, a higher rate implies that the opportunity cost of government expen-

Table 6.1 ✦ THE DISCOUNT RATE AND PROJECT RANKINGS

DISCOUNT RATE	PRESENT VALUE OF PROJECT 1	PRESENT VALUE OF PROJECT 2
0%	$90	$\dfrac{\$100}{(1 + 0)^2} = \$100$
5	90	$\dfrac{\$100}{(1 + 0.05)^2} = \$90.7$
10	90	$\dfrac{\$100}{(1 + 0.1)^2} = \$82.6$

diture, in terms of private satisfaction forgone, is greater. This, in turn, implies that efficiency requires a relatively smaller amount of government expenditure as a percentage of GDP. Some projects that yield a positive value for the present value of net benefits under low discount rates will have negative net present benefits at higher discount rates.

Choosing the Social Rate of Discount

The social rate of discount should reflect the return that can be earned on resources employed in alternative private use.[5] This is the opportunity cost of funds invested by the government in a project. To avoid losses in well-being, resources should not be transferred from the private sector to government use if those resources can earn a higher social return in the private sector.

Setting the discount rate equal to the **social opportunity cost of funds** ensures that misallocations do not occur. The social opportunity cost depends on the rate at which savers and investors are willing to give up either consumption or investment to finance the government project. For example, if the rate of interest in the economy is 10 percent, a government project must yield at least that much to justify the transfer of funds from private to government use.

Because of the existence of distortions (the corporate income tax, for example), the net return that savers can earn often is different from that earned by investors. For example, with a 50-percent tax on corporate profits, the return to investments in the corporate sector of the economy is only one-half of the actual gross percentage rate of return. If investors must pay 10 percent interest to borrow funds, they will require a return in excess of 20 percent to undertake any project. A gross return greater than 20 percent is necessary to earn a positive net return after paying 10 percent interest. The existence of such taxes causes investors and savers to adjust to different interest rates.

This is illustrated in Figure 6.2. The curve D represents the demand for funds for investment in the absence of any taxes. Points on this curve give the gross return to investors for any quantity of funds invested per year. S is the supply curve of investible funds. It gives the rate that would have to be paid to savers to induce them to supply any given amount of funds per year. In the absence of any taxes, the market equilibrium would be at point E. The gross return to investors, r_G, would equal the interest rate paid to savers. Suppose this rate is 16 percent.

Now suppose that investors are subject to a 50-percent tax on the return to investment but that the interest earned by savers is not subject to taxation. The tax causes the *net return* to investors to fall short of the gross return by a factor of 50 percent. In Figure 6.2, this is represented by a downward shift of the investment demand curve from D to D'. Investors now make their decisions according to points on D', which give the net return to investment after the 50 percent is paid. The new market equilibrium corresponds to point E'. As the amount of funds invested declines from

---

[5]For a comprehensive discussion of the discount rate, see Raymond F. Mikesell, *The Rate of Discount for Evaluating Public Projects* (Washington, D.C.: American Enterprise Institute, 1977).

Figure 6.2 ✦ A TAX ON INVESTMENT INCOME
AND THE SOCIAL OPPORTUNITY COST OF CAPITAL

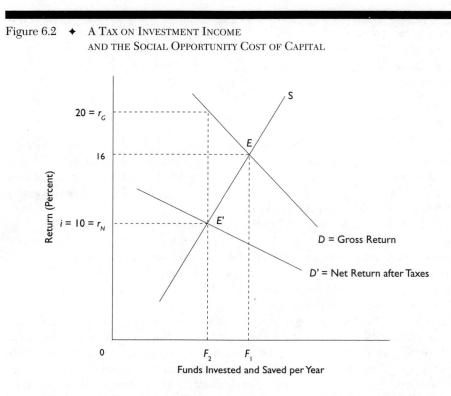

A tax on investment income causes the gross return to investment r_G to exceed the market rate of interest earned by savers, i. The social opportunity cost of government investment is 20 percent if private investment funds are displaced. However, the social opportunity cost of government funds will be only 10 percent if taxes displace private saving.

F_1 dollars to F_2 dollars per year, the gross return rises to $r_G = 20$ percent. However, the net return after payment of the tax is only $r_N = 10$ percent. The net rate of return is also the market rate of interest necessary to induce savers to supply F_2 dollars per year for investors to use. If the funds used to finance the project displace investment, the appropriate discount rate is 20 percent. If, however, they displace consumption, the opportunity cost is only the 10 percent that those funds could have earned had they been saved.

An ideal technique for determining the social rate of discount is to ascertain the kind of private expenditures that are displaced by a government activity and to use an average of the return on displaced expenditures.[6] However, such an estimate of the distribution of expenditure displaced may be difficult to obtain.

---

[6]For an analysis that yields such an estimate, see Arnold C. Harberger, "On Measuring the Social Opportunity Cost of Public Funds," *Project Evaluation* (Chicago: Markham, 1972), 94–122.

From a pragmatic point of view, it is often convenient to estimate the social rate of discount by considering a variety of factors. These factors include the riskiness of displaced investment and taxes.[7] For example, if risk and other complications are ignored, assume that the market rate of interest would be 10 percent. With a 50-percent tax on business profits, the gross actual return on business investment must be 20 percent before taxes, as shown in Figure 6.2. This results in a *net return* after taxes of 10 percent. The opportunity cost of displaced business investment therefore will be 20 percent. Similarly, risk and inflation often result in higher returns on private investment. If higher returns are required on private investment in equilibrium to compensate investors for risk and expected inflation, then these must be added into the opportunity cost of government use of those displaced funds.[8]

Weighting and Disaggregating Net Benefits

Cost-benefit analysis is primarily a tool designed to aid in choosing government projects that are efficient. However, some practitioners attempt to modify its techniques to build in equity as well as efficiency criteria in ranking projects. The effects of a given project on the distribution of income can be built in by weighting the costs or benefits according to whom or where they accrue.[9] This technique would disaggregate both benefits and costs according to income of recipients and also would weight those benefits and costs borne by low-income groups relatively higher. No unique set of weights to apply exists; the weights would reflect either the opinions of those who do the analysis or some consensus on the relative deservingness of individuals according to their income. Universal agreement on a set of norms to do this remains difficult and requires interpersonal comparisons of utility.

A variant of the weighting of benefits according to income of recipients is to weight net benefits according to their regional location. Many argue that a legitimate function of government is to base decisions on which public expenditures to undertake according to the region in which benefits and costs would flow and that the higher weight should be placed on benefits and costs in depressed or declining regions.

Attempts to formalize distributional considerations through weighting of benefits and costs might not be in accord with the distributional goals of all citizens. For this reason, formal weighting of benefits and costs might serve only to confound the distribution and efficiency aspects of projects by confusing net increases in welfare with their distribution. Separate consideration of efficiency and distributive consequences allows the trade-offs between net benefits and their distribution to be more clearly seen.

Another proposal that would allow cost-benefit analysis to take into account distributional considerations is to disaggregate benefits according to demographic, income,

---

[7]For an analysis using the opportunity-cost approach, see William J. Baumol, "On the Social Rate of Discount," *American Economic Review* 58 (September 1968): 788–802.

[8]Some controversy exists as to whether a risk premium should be added to the social rate of discount. For a discussion of the desirability of using a riskless versus a risk-adjusted discount rate, see Mikesell, *The Rate of Discount,* 28–32.

[9]See Arnold C. Harberger, "On the Use of Distributional Weights in Social Cost-Benefit Analysis," *Journal of Political Economy* 86 (April 1978): S87–S120.

and other social characteristics of the citizens who will receive benefits and bear the costs. This avoids the problem of how to weight benefits and provides direct information on the distribution of costs and benefits among citizens. Insofar as this provides information on the distribution of marginal benefits of increased government expenditure and on the manner in which costs are distributed among citizens, it allows both citizens and their political representatives to vote on a more informed basis.

Treatment of Inflation

Inflation creates a problem in cost-benefit analysis by making the measuring rod of money a poor standard for comparing benefits over time. There are two alternative ways of dealing with the problem of inflation. First, both benefits and costs could be measured in nominal values, through time, by estimating the rate of inflation, over time, and inflating both future benefits and costs accordingly. If this is done, the analyst must take care to use the nominal interest rate, as well, in discounting future net benefits. The *nominal interest rate* is the sum of the real interest rate and the rate of inflation. If inflated values of net benefits are used, they must, in turn, be deflated by the nominal interest rate to account for the inflation.

Similarly, if benefits and costs, over time, are measured in real terms, meaning that future benefits and costs are deflated, then one also must use the real interest rate (the nominal interest rate less the rate of inflation) to discount future benefits and costs.[10]

Ranking Projects

Projects are usually ranked according to the present value of their discounted net benefits $(B - C)$ or according to the ratio of the present value of benefits to the present value of costs. All projects with positive net benefits are considered for approval. Similarly, all projects with benefit-cost ratios in excess of a value of 1 are considered for approval. These two criteria are shown below.

$$\text{Net Benefit Criterion:} \quad B - C = \sum_{i=1}^{n} (B_i - C_i)/(1 + r)^i, \tag{6.8}$$

$$\text{Benefit-Cost Ratio:} \quad \frac{B}{C} = \frac{\sum_{i=1}^{n} B_i/(1 + r)^i}{\sum_{i=1}^{n} C_i/(1 + r)^i} \tag{6.9}$$

where B_i are benefits in year i, C_i are costs in year i, n is the life of a project, and r is the discount rate.

---

[10]For proof of this, see Edward M. Gramlich, *A Guide to Benefit-Cost Analysis,* 2d ed. (Englewood Cliffs, NJ: Prentice-Hall, 1990).

Use of these rules can ensure that inefficient projects will not be considered for approval. In any given year for any agency, a certain level of service has already been provided. It is difficult to determine in fact whether this level of service is the efficient amount. For example, in a given year, a certain amount of interstate highways exists. Proposed projects for new highway construction represent additional units of this transportation service. The new highway construction will improve efficiency only if its marginal social benefit exceeds its marginal social cost. Projects are ranked according to the net social gain they provide.

Figure 6.3 shows the marginal social benefit and marginal social cost of highways, measured in miles available each year. Suppose the amount of highway mileage currently existing is Q_1 miles of four-lane, limited-access roads. A new project is proposed that will increase road mileage to Q_2. The project will add an additional ΔQ_1 miles of road to available highways. Suppose that a cost-benefit analysis of the project finds that the ΔQ_1 miles has a positive net benefit (or a benefit-cost ratio greater than 1). This would imply that the area Q_1ABQ_2, representing the marginal social benefit of the project, would exceed the area Q_1CDQ_2, which represents the marginal social cost of the extra highway miles. Approval of the project moves output closer to the efficient level Q^*, at which $MSB = MSC$.

Suppose, instead, Q_3 miles of highways already exist. If proposals to increase miles available to Q_4 are made, the increment in roads supplied, ΔQ_2, will be inefficient, because the marginal social cost of ΔQ_2 miles of road, Q_3FGQ_4, exceeds the marginal social benefit of Q_3HJQ_4. This is because at an output of Q_3, more than the efficient amount of roads, Q^*, exists. A correctly executed cost-benefit analysis of the project resulting in ΔQ_2 units of road should reveal a negative net benefit or a benefit-cost ratio less than 1.

Figure 6.3 ✦ COST-BENEFIT ANALYSIS AND EFFICIENCY

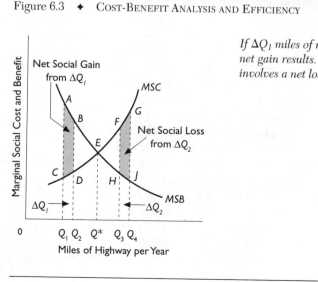

If ΔQ_1 miles of new roads are made available, a net gain results. However, the increment ΔQ_2 involves a net loss.

ANALYSIS OF GOVERNMENT INVESTMENTS: COST-BENEFIT ANALYSIS IN PRACTICE

Governments supply a considerable amount of capital used in production. A nation's **physical infrastructure** is its transportation and environmental capital including its schools, power and communication networks, and health care system. Much of the capital that constitutes a nation's physical infrastructure is supplied by governments. In the United States, both the private sector and governments provide infrastructure. Most of the communication and power supply networks are provided for profit by business firms, and the output is sold through the marketplace. Local governments are active in supplying educational and health care facilities, although some of these facilities also are provided by business firms motivated by profit. The federal government in the United States is active in providing and helping to fund highways, bridges, mass transit facilities, railways, airports and airways, and water resources, including fresh water supply and waste water treatment plants. Government-provided infrastructure accounts for a significant portion (about one-fifth) of U.S. nonresidential capital stock. Governments also invest in *human* capital through programs designed to improve the skills and education of its citizens.

Government-provided infrastructure complements private capital and improves its productivity. Better roads and bridges reduce travel time and make private cars and trucks more productive. Government-provided airports and air traffic control systems improve both the performance and the safety of private air carriers. Similarly, the Intracoastal Waterway as well as public ports, locks, and dams make shipping more productive. Government facilities for water waste treatment lower the costs of production for business and help improve the environment.

In the United States, roads and bridges are aging. The nation's physical infrastructure is in need of repair. Federal spending for roads, mass transit, railways, airports and airways, water resources, and water treatment has grown little after adjustment for inflation since 1980. In 1990 the federal government spent $26.2 billion on the nation's infrastructure and more than half of that amount was allocated to highways. Real spending on infrastructure in the United States grew rapidly between 1956 and 1966, then stagnated throughout much of the 1970s during a massive reallocation of federal spending to transfer programs including Social Security. Some growth in federal spending for infrastructure occurred in the late 1970s, but on average spending during the 1980s did not increase at all.

I N T E R N A T I O N A L   V I E W

GOVERNMENT INFRASTRUCTURE INVESTMENT IN LESS-DEVELOPED NATIONS

Governments have been very active in less-developed nations in recent years by providing infrastructure for agricultural development. Cost-benefit analysis of government investment projects that create agricultural infrastructure in less-developed nations concluded that the economic rate of return on those projects averaged 17 percent. This return was considerably higher than the 10 percent social opportunity cost of capital in those nations.[*] Improved agricultural infrastructure increases the productivity of inputs used in agriculture. Water resource projects, particularly irrigation, have been especially effective in reducing variability of agricultural output in South and East Asia.

However, many large-scale projects, particularly those involving construction of dams, disrupt the lives of inhabitants of regions where reservoirs are created. It is important to include the relocation costs and loss of income of these displaced people in the cost of the projects to compute the social return accurately. For example, in thirty-nine projects financed by the World Bank in twenty-seven nations between 1979 and 1985, three-quarters of a million people had to be relocated to make room for reservoirs. The relocation often entailed loss of output, stress, and even environmental damage.[†]

Considerable evidence indicates that development of infrastructure provides benefits to the poor. A study of sixteen villages in Bangladesh, one of the poorest nations in the world, shows that villages that benefited from new government-provided infrastructure enjoyed a 33-percent increase in average household incomes after adjustment for other factors influencing household incomes. Investments in agricultural infrastructure in Bangladesh increased crop income by 24 percent and increased income from wages by 92 percent according to the study. Income from livestock and fisheries increased by 78 percent. Much of the increased income from sale of the extra agricultural output accrued to poor households.[‡]

Investment in roads, electricity, and other types of infrastructure in Bangladesh also increased agricultural output and encouraged the growth of small-scale industries. The increase in labor demand resulting from the increased output also contributed to higher wages and a reduction in poverty.

Although investment in infrastructure in less-developed nations often disrupts lives and has environmental costs, the projects do have high net return. The evidence indicates that past projects have resulted in benefits that outweigh the costs.

[*]The World Bank, *World Development Report, 1990* (Oxford, Eng.: Oxford University Press, 1990), 58–59.
[†]See World Bank, 59.
[‡]World Bank, 60.

Is it economically desirable to spend more than we are currently spending on government investment projects for transportation and water resources? Is the return to additional government investment higher than the return to private investment that will be foregone if more funds are allocated to government investment? Unfortunately the answers to these questions are not easy, but cost-benefit analysis is useful in providing a framework to help guide economic policy decisions on the mix of investment spending.

Additional investments in infrastructure or government education and research programs result in net benefits to society if the return on these investments exceeds the opportunity cost of the private funds that must be diverted to government use to finance the government projects. Cost-benefit analysis is a useful tool to analyze the net benefits and social return provided through government investments that yield a stream of net benefits through time. This section shows how cost-benefit analysis can be used to help calculate the net benefits of government investments in infrastructure and human capital and provide information on the social return to government investment relative to the private investment that must be sacrificed when funds are diverted from private to government use.

In practice, cost-benefit analysis is more of an art than a science. Many simplifying assumptions must be made to obtain measures of benefits of both marketable and nonmarketable goods resulting from projects. In addition, when projects involve negative externalities, considerable differences of opinion often exist among experts about how they should be valued. Economists can develop principles to use as guidelines in enumerating and evaluating costs and benefits. In practice, actual enumeration and valuation requires a cooperative effort of scientists, engineers, and other experts. Differences of opinion are common. A few examples can illustrate these problems.

Water Resource Development: An Irrigation Project

Irrigation increases the supply of water for agricultural and other purposes. The direct benefits of the project include the increase in water available to farmers. Estimates must be made of the value of the increased annual flow of water from the project over the life of the facility. Ideally, the water should be valued on the basis of the price that farmers would be willing to pay for extra units. However, in the absence of a market for water or water rights, such evaluation is difficult.[11] Instead, with the help of agronomists and other scientists, it is possible to approximate the amount that farmers would be willing to pay by estimating the increase in agricultural yields attributable to the increased water supply. This represents an estimate of the marginal productivity due to the increased water supply. Multiplying this estimate of increased agricultural output over the life of the project by the appropriate price will give an estimate of the value of the marginal product of the increased water supply, which, in turn, can be used as a proxy for the price that farmers would pay for the extra water.

For example, a proposed project for Nebraska by the Bureau of Reclamation would have irrigated 44,000 acres of dry farming lands. The bureau, in 1967, used data based on cropping patterns, input costs, farm yields, and other information to estimate that benefits from the project totaled nearly $2.5 million. This was 43 percent of the total benefit from the land reclamation project for the area. However, the prices that the bureau used to calculate the agricultural benefit included the effect of agricultural support programs. These programs caused prices to be higher than they would have been otherwise. Therefore, part of the price of the output included a subsidy to farmers that represents a transfer to them from taxpayers rather than a benefit of the project. In addition, some of the inputs used to produce the goods were also subsidized. In particular, farmers in the area were eligible for subsidized loans for their crops. Finally, those doing the cost-benefit analysis underestimated the value of

---

[11]For a method of actually evaluating the water, see Harberger, *Project Evaluation,* chap. 11.

labor of owner-operators, relative to the opportunity cost of that labor. Adjusting for these effects, a critical analysis found that the value of increased agricultural output falls from $2.5 million to only slightly more than $1 million. This illustrates the pitfalls in doing cost-benefit analysis incorrectly, even in cases in which marketable output exists.[12]

Suppose an artificial lake is created as part of the irrigation system. The lake will have the potential for recreational use. If it is feasible to exploit the lake for recreational purposes, the resulting recreational benefits should be included as part of the project. As is always the case, the test for benefits on the national level involves answering the question of whether the proposed benefits represent a net increase in potential well-being not offset by reductions in well-being elsewhere. If new recreational facilities result from the project, they qualify as a real benefit. Such benefits might include fishing, picnicking, boating, swimming, and so forth. If the lake is available for use free of charge, the evaluation of benefits becomes difficult. Usually, rough estimates are made concerning potential use of the recreational resource and the willingness of users to pay for a day of recreation, on average, at the new facility.[13]

The cost of the project would include all labor costs necessary to construct and maintain the irrigation facility and the lake; all capital that would need to be acquired, such as pipes, or rented, such as backhoes and derricks, in the process of construction and maintenance; and all land acquisition costs, right-of-way costs, and rental payments that would be required for construction of the facilities. These are the direct costs of the project.

One issue of dispute concerns the proper valuation of labor costs when the economy suffers from unemployment. Some economists argue that in periods of unemployment, the social costs of using labor should be set at zero because the project provides work that would not otherwise be available. This argument is faulty for two reasons. First, unless deficit finance is used, with no effect on the price level, the revenues necessary to finance the project withdraw effective demand from the private sector, thereby further decreasing the ability of the economy to provide jobs. Increased employment on the irrigation project therefore is offset by at least some decrease in employment opportunities elsewhere in the economy. Second, the labor skills required to construct the irrigation facilities might not be those possessed by workers currently unemployed. This being the case, the irrigation workers would have to be attracted from other employment, with no net increase in employment to workers currently out of work. For both these reasons it is good practice, in computing project costs, to value labor resources positively, even in periods of unemployment.

Indirect costs include lost agricultural output on land that has to be flooded as a result of the project, provided that these costs were not already included in the price paid by the government to acquire that land. Similarly, if the project diverts water, it

---

[12]See Steve H. Hanke and Richard A. Walker, "Benefit-Cost Analysis Reconsidered: An Evaluation of the Mid-state Project," in *Public Expenditure and Policy Analysis*, 3d ed., Robert H. Haveman and Julius Margolis, eds. (Boston: Houghton Mifflin, 1983).

[13]On valuing recreation, see Marion Clawson and Jack Knetsch, *Economics of Outdoor Recreation* (Baltimore: Resources for the Future, 1966).

can reduce the water table in locations not served by the irrigation system, with the consequent effect of a reduction in agricultural output not otherwise reflected in land acquisition costs. If wilderness areas are harmed as a result of the project, with a consequent loss in the recreational services provided by the wilderness (hunting and fishing, for example), estimates must be made of these costs and included as a cost of the project.

Cost-Benefit Tableau

When all costs and benefits have been enumerated and evaluated, a tableau that lists all such costs and benefits over the life of the project can be drawn up. Assume that, in this case, the expected life of the irrigation system is fifty years. In a capital-intensive project, such as the construction of an irrigation system, costs in early years are likely to be high, relative to benefits (for example, no benefits at all until the system is completed, which might take a considerable number of years). In later years, benefits might be high, relative to costs, as construction costs fall to zero and only maintenance costs are required.

The tableau for the irrigation project is shown in Table 6.2. The costs and benefits for this hypothetical example are shown symbolically rather than as actual dollar amounts. Costs are likely to be very high in the first five years of the project, as con-

Table 6.2 ◆ Cost-Benefit Analysis of a Hypothetical Irrigation Project

				Year				
Costs[a]	1	2	3	4	5	6	...	N
Engineering and Planning Studies	E	—	—	—	—	—		—
Building and Construction								
Labor								
Pipes								
Heavy Equipment	F_1	F_2	F_3	F_4	F_5	—		—
Land Acquisition								
Easements (Right-of-Way)								
Maintenance	—	—	—	—	—	M_6		M_N
Loss in Agricultural Output on Other Lands	A_1	A_2	A_3	A_4	A_5	A_6		A_N
Loss in Recreation Due to Destruction of								
Wilderness	R_1	R_2	R_3	R_4	R_5	R_6		R_N
Total Costs	C_1	C_2	C_3	C_4	C_5	C_6		C_N
Benefits[a]	1	2	3	4	5	6	...	N
Increased Agricultural Output	—	—	—	—	—	A_6		A_N
Increased Recreation	—	—	—	—	—	R_6		R_N
Total Benefits	—	—	—	—	—	B_6		B_N

[a]A dash indicates either zero benefit or zero cost in that year.

struction is carried on. These costs then are likely to decline rapidly in the sixth year, when construction will have been completed, so that only maintenance costs and indirect losses (agricultural output having declined on lands suffering from the effects of declines in the water table, and reduced benefits from wilderness destroyed) will be incurred. In Table 6.2, F, construction costs, fall to zero in the sixth year. On the other hand, no direct benefits occur until the project is completed. Thus, in the first five years, the total benefits in the tableau are zero, as indicated by a dash. Only in the sixth year will benefits accrue. To account for inflation, all projections would have to be done in constant dollars.

Finally, because the decision to approve the project must be made today, the stream of benefits and the stream of costs over the life of the project must be collapsed down to their present values by discounting with an appropriate discount rate, as discussed previously. Typically, cost-benefit analysis done by the federal government computes a cost-benefit ratio, B/C, and considers those projects for which B/C exceeds 1. Projects then are ranked according to the magnitude of their benefit-cost ratios.

The tableau does not include any secondary benefits, such as increased purchases of farm equipment and consumer goods by farmers whose incomes are increased as a result of the project. As discussed, these are transfers, rather than real benefits produced by the irrigation project. Nothing in the project increases the capability of the economy to produce tractors or consumer goods; hence, any increased purchases of these items by farmers merely represent a transfer of resources from elsewhere to the area of the project. No net gain in national well-being is to be had.

Transportation: Widening an Existing Highway

To evaluate the benefits of adding two more lanes to a highway, an estimate must be made of the demand for travel between the points involved as a function of the average cost per trip. The average cost per trip includes fuel, depreciation, vehicle maintenance, and, most important, the value of time involved. Improvement of the facility makes trips between two points faster. This will result in cost savings to existing users and will encourage new users to take trips on the road. The major benefit of the improved facility therefore will be the cost saving on existing trips, plus the net benefits on new trips along the improved route.

Assuming enough information is available, these benefits can be estimated from the demand for travel between the points involved. This is illustrated in Figure 6.4. D_T is the demand for travel. The current average cost of travel per trip for points served by the existing road is C, and the current number of trips per year is measured as T. Widening the facility is estimated to lower the average cost of a trip to C' and increase the number of trips per year to T'. The annual cost saving on existing trips is CC' multiplied by T, or the area $CBAC'$. The net increase in trips is TT'. The cost of making these new trips is, on average, C'. The net benefits on new trips is additional consumer surplus over and above the cost of making the new trips.[14] This is the area

---

[14]For a discussion of valuation of travel time, see Gramlich, *Benefit-Cost Analysis,* 72–74.

Figure 6.4 ✦ THE BENEFITS OF WIDENING A HIGHWAY

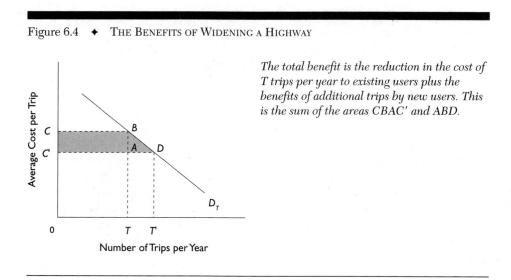

The total benefit is the reduction in the cost of T trips per year to existing users plus the benefits of additional trips by new users. This is the sum of the areas CBAC' and ABD.

ABD. The net benefits from widening the road are therefore the sum of the two areas, *CBAC'* and *ABD*.

Cost of the project would include all labor, capital, and land costs to construct the new facility, as well as maintenance costs over the life of the facility after construction is completed. Any external costs, such as destruction of wilderness or increased pollution due to the increased traffic generated on the road (less any pollution reduction elsewhere, if some of the new traffic previously used alternative routes), would have to be included as a real cost of the project.

After all such costs, over time, are estimated, a tableau, similar to that of the irrigation project, would be constructed, giving the flow of both costs and benefits over the life of the project. Both benefits and costs could then be discounted, and the present value of net benefits, or a benefit-cost ratio, could be calculated to evaluate the project.[15]

Health: How is Human Life Valued?

Among the most difficult projects to evaluate, using cost-benefit analysis, are those involving human resources. The problem is particularly difficult for health programs of various kinds that involve benefits in the form of a decrease in mortality rates and reduced loss of human welfare due to injury or illness. Many programs seek to prolong life by avoiding accidental death. For example, suppose a proposed project seeks to reduce accidents by redesigning dangerous superhighway access points. The benefit-cost ratio for this project should be compared with other projects, more tra-

---

[15]For a more complete and detailed analysis, see Harberger, *Project Evaluation*, Chapter 10.

ditionally thought of as health programs, those with major goals of reducing mortality, injury, or disabling illness. These would include inoculation programs, research, and various preventive medicine programs.

The primary benefit of redesigning a highway access will be a reduction in accidents. Fairly good data might exist on the current accident rate for various fatalities, and estimation of the decrease in accidents could be fairly easy. In all cases, such estimates would have to adjust for the possibility that improved access might increase traffic on the road, which, in turn, will offset some of the benefits by contributing to increased accidents, unless a corresponding decrease occurs in accidents on alternative routes.

The basic problem encountered in such a cost-benefit analysis, after the accident reduction is estimated, is to place a value on the lives saved and the reduction in injuries. A number of techniques have been used to estimate the value of human life saved. A common technique is to value lives saved according to the discounted present value of future earnings. This requires estimates of the number of lives that would be saved and the ages of individuals whose lives are likely to be saved (for two individuals of equal earning capacity, an older life will be worth less than a young life). One problem with such an approach is that is places a zero value on the leisure time of the potential lives saved and a higher value on lives of persons with high earnings, relative to those with low earnings.

An alternative approach to valuing life argues that it is not really necessary to value or identify the lives saved to get meaningful data on the benefits of various health-related programs. This approach argues that public programs that save lives really produce a public good, which, in turn, reduces the probability that any given individual will die or suffer harm as a result of a particular hazard—in this case, accidents upon entering a highway. The benefits of such programs therefore should be measured in terms of the willingness of individuals affected by the programs to pay for such reduction in hazards or risks to which they are exposed. Such information, however, might be difficult to obtain because of the familiar free-rider problems associated with public goods. Some attempts have been made to get estimates of the willingness of individuals to pay for reduction in the risk of death and injury by sending questionnaires to a random sampling of the population.

The questionnaires specify the odds of a person being exposed to the hazard in question (an accident upon entering a highway) and surviving the accident. The person then is presented with an estimate of the impact of the proposed project on those odds and asked how much he would be willing to pay in taxes for improvements in the odds. The average dollar response then is calculated and used as a crude index of the willingness to pay, or, in other words, the benefits per taxpayer of the project in terms of saved lives.[16]

Whichever method is used, the outcome will be a dollar value of benefits for the project in terms of reduced mortality and disability, which will be estimated over

---

[16]See Steven E. Rhoads, "How Much Should We Spend to Save a Life," *The Public Interest* 51 (Spring 1978): 74–92.

PUBLIC POLICY PERSPECTIVE

A COST-BENEFIT ANALYSIS OF THE JOB CORPS PROGRAM

Cost-benefit analysis is valuable to evaluate the success or failure of programs that have been in operation for a while. Data for existing programs are usually easier to obtain and more accurate than data for programs under proposal. One such study was done for a controversial federal program designed to increase the future earnings of disadvantaged teenagers: the Job Corps.

The Job Corps was still in operation in 1991 providing education and training in a residential setting to about 70,000 young people in that year. The cost of the program was about $12,000 per participant per year at that time. Have the costs of this program been worth the social benefits received in return? To find out, the U.S. Department of Labor commissioned a cost-benefit analysis of the program in the late 1970s and early 1980s.° To estimate the impact of the program, information was collected from interviews with about 5,000 participants in the Job Corps in 1977 and with other youths of similar background who had not been enrolled in the program. The researchers then analyzed differences between the two groups to determine the impact of the Job Corps on the earnings of the participants and to analyze other benefits from the program.

In 1977 the cost for the average participant in the Job Corps program was $10,000 measured in 1990 dollars.† These costs consisted of a bit more than $8,000 in government funds per participant for the operation of the residential centers and the compensation of teachers and other staff members. Most of the participants in the program were poor teenagers who had dropped out of high school and had few job opportunities. The researchers therefore assumed that their forgone earnings for participating in the program were quite low—less than $2,000 per year.

A major benefit from the program was the increased output produced by those enrolled in the program as a result of their Job Corps training. Based on their interviews and statistical analysis, the researchers concluded that over the four-year period they studied after participants left the Job Corps their earnings averaged about $1,000 higher per year (measured in 1990 dollars) because of their training. Assuming that their earnings reflected the value of the extra goods and services they produced and that this extra output was a net addition to GDP that resulted from the program, the researchers measured the return to the investment in the Job Corps per worker as the increment in their earnings. They calculated this return for four years after the participants left the program.

However, the Job Corps yielded additional major benefits to society besides increased output. The study concluded that the program contributed to a reduction in crimes committed by young people while they were enrolled in the program and after they left it. Part of the benefit of the program therefore consisted of a reduction in the costs of crime including reduced property damage and values, reduced personal injury, and reduced legal costs. The researchers concluded that a decrease in murders was a major result of the program! Finally, the researchers also estimated the reduction in the costs of operating other government welfare programs that resulted from the success of the Job Corps.

The following table provides a cost-benefit tableau for the costs and benefits of the Job Corp per participant in 1977 measured in 1990 dollars. Using a dis-

---

°The study was conducted by Mathematica Policy Research Inc. See *Evaluation of the Economic Impact of the Job Corps Program: Third Follow-Up Report* (Washington, D.C.: Mathematica, September 1982).
†See U.S. Congress, Congressional Budget Office, *How Federal Spending for Infrastructure and Other Public Investments Affects the Economy* (Washington, D.C., U.S. Government Printing Office, July 1991).

---

time, adjusting for any changes in traffic flow as a result of the project.[17] The costs will be any capital, labor, and right-of-way acquired to improve the facility and any subsequent maintenance. As before, a tableau can be constructed, and both benefits and costs can be discounted to calculate a benefit-cost ratio.

count rate of 5 percent the present value of the benefits of the program over the 5 year period 1977 to 1981 were estimated to be close to $15,000 per participant. The cost of obtaining these benefits were only about $10,000 per participant. The present value of the net benefit per participant was estimated at $4,660 indicating that the Job Corps program was well worth the costs over the period studied!

RESOURCES INVESTED IN THE AVERAGE JOB CORPS PARTICIPANT IN 1977 AND THE ECONOMIC RETURNS ON THE INVESTMENT (IN 1990 DOLLARS)

SOURCE OF IMPACT	PRESENT VALUE[a]	IMPACT DURING PROGRAM	IMPACT FOLLOWING TERMINATION			
			FIRST YEAR	SECOND YEAR	THIRD YEAR	FOURTH YEAR
Costs to the Economy						
Program Operating Costs (Other than Transfers	8,380	8,380	0	0	0	0
Forgone Output of Participants	1,760	1,760	0	0	0	0
Total Costs	10,140[b]	10,140[b]	0	0	0	0
Benefits to the Economy						
Increased Output of Participants	8,080	1,520	600	1,500	1,300	940
Reductions in Cost of Crime-Related Activities	5,840	2,020	1,200	940	1,260	780
Reductions in Costs of Operating Other Programs	880	540	160	20	40	80
Total Benefits	14,800	4,080	1,960	2,460	2,600	1,800
Net Impact on the Economy	4,660					

Note: Amounts are expressed in 1990 dollars by adjusting the original estimates for inflation since 1977.

[a]Present value is based on a 5-percent real discount rate and assumes that the impact on earnings estimated for the fourth year will decline by 14 percent per year, falling below $100 by the eighteenth year.

[b]Excludes about $2,800 in costs the government incurred for cash or in-kind payments to participants, such as food and clothing, that Mathematica considered to be transfers between the government and the participants, rather than costs to society.

Source: Estimates by the Congressional Budget Office based on data from Mathematica Policy Research, *Evaluation of the Economic Impact of the Job Corps Program: Third Follow-up Report* (Washington, D.C.: Mathematica, September 1982).

---

[17]An additional method is the use of wage differentials in risky occupations as an indicator of the amount of payment necessary to induce individuals to bear the risk of loss of life. However, a number of difficulties are involved in using such data to calculate willingness to pay. See Gramlich, *A Guide to Benefit-Cost Analysis*, 67–71.

THE ROLE OF COST-BENEFIT ANALYSIS IN BUDGETING

Cost-benefit analysis is a valuable tool for evaluating the net benefits of proposed government projects. It can be used to organize information in a way that aids citizens, politicians, and bureaucrats. However, it remains difficult to measure the benefit of government goods and services accurately. Difficulties also arise in accurately measuring social costs. Differences of opinion exist regarding what benefits and costs to include and how to value the output of various projects.

It is also difficult to reduce the problem of selecting government goods and services to a few simple, objective criteria. Political interaction is influenced by many factors. As has been pointed out many times in this book, not all citizens benefit when efficient outcomes are chosen. Some are often better off when the less efficient mix of government goods and services are produced. Very few politicians or citizens will abandon their favorite proposed government projects because those projects have benefit-cost ratios that are lower than competing projects.

CHECKPOINT

1. What are some of the difficulties involved in actually implementing a cost-benefit analysis?
2. How would you estimate the benefits and costs of an irrigation project?
3. How would you estimate the benefits and costs of a project to widen the beltway that surrounds a city?

Summary

Program budgeting and cost-benefit analysis can be used to improve efficiency by lowering the cost of government activities and assuring that only programs for which marginal social benefits exceed marginal social costs are considered for approval. Cost-effectiveness is achieved when governments achieve their missions by choosing a combination of programs with the minimum cost. Cost-benefit analysis is a technique for determining net increases in well-being that result from alternative government projects. Cost-benefit analysis is particularly useful in evaluating government investment projects that will yield a stream of benefits through time. A cost-benefit analysis lists and evaluates all benefits and costs of a project and discounts all future net benefits. The discount rate should reflect the opportunity costs of funds used to finance the project. Projects are ranked according to the discounted present values of net benefits or the ratio of discounted benefits to costs.

A Forward Look

Modern governments allocate a considerable amount of the funds they raise to the transfer of income among citizens. The next two chapters evaluate two major types of transfer programs: transfers to the poor and transfers to the elderly. The next chapter looks at the problem of poverty in the

United States and how government subsidies programs designed to alleviate poverty affect resource use.

Important Concepts

Program
Program Budgeting
Mission (of a Government Agency)
Cost-Effectiveness Analysis
Cost-Benefit Analysis
Social Rate of Discount
Social Opportunity Cost of Funds
Physical Infrastructure

Questions for Review

1. What are the steps necessary to implement a program budgeting system? How does program budgeting differ from line budgeting?
2. What information is required to find out whether a given combination of programs designed to achieve the same objective is cost-effective?
3. Explain how program budgeting systems seek to improve efficiency within government. How are decisions made under program budgeting similar to those made by profit-maximizing business firms?
4. Explain how the cost-effective mix of government programs to provide national security can be determined. How does approval of programs that are not cost-effective prevent the attainment of efficiency?
5. Why would counting retail sales that result from increased farmer income resulting from an irrigation project overstate the benefits of the project? When should increases in land values that result from government projects be included as a benefit of the project?
6. Suppose that investment income is taxed at a higher rate than the interest that consumers earn on their savings. Explain why the social opportunity cost of funds used for government projects will depend on whether investment or consumption will be displaced as a result of the project.
7. How does the social rate of discount used affect the number of projects that can be approved and their ranking in cost-benefit analysis?
8. Suppose more than the efficient number of hydroelectric power projects have already been approved. Show why a properly executed cost-benefit analysis would result in a benefit-cost ratio that is less than 1.

9. Suppose that a new project to expand air traffic control facilities will allow reductions in the cost of air travel and increases in the volume of travel. How would you measure the benefits of the new facilities?
10. What are some of the problems involved in measuring the value of human life? Explain why saying that each life is priceless is likely to result in more than the efficient amount of investment in life-saving programs.

Problems

1. Two alternative programs to save fifty more lives per year entail providing more cardiac intensive care facilities and redesigning dangerous highway interchanges. The price of a new cardiac intensive care unit is $500,000 and the price of redesigning and renovating a highway interchange is $1 million. One combination of the two programs that can save five-hundred lives is five cardiac units and three highway exit renovations. If five cardiac units are built, the marginal product of this program will be ten lives saved per year. If three highway interchanges are redesigned, the marginal product of this program also will be ten lives saved per year. Is the mix involving five cardiac units and three highway exit renovations cost effective? Assuming that the marginal products of both programs decline, what needs to be done to achieve the cost-effective mix of programs?
2. Suppose a proposed new road to be constructed in North Carolina between Raleigh and Morehead City will lower the average cost per trip by car from $5 to $4. Currently, 500,000 trips are made between the two cities per year. An estimate indicates that, other things being equal, the new road will increase the number of trips per year to 600,000. Calculate the annual benefits to motorists of the new road as based on their willingness to pay.
3. A new tax is levied on airline profits to finance improvements in the nation's airports. The current market rate of interest is 8 percent. However, airline profits are subject to a 50-percent tax. A cost-benefit analysis calculates the percent return to the investment in new air facilities to be 12 percent. Will net benefits from resource use increase as a result of construction of new air travel facilities?
4. A cost-benefit analysis of a new irrigation project indicates that the net benefits $(B - C)$ of the project in each of the first four years will be −$2 million. Thereafter, the project will yield positive net benefits of $750,000 for the next twenty years. Calculate the

present value of benefits minus costs when the social rate of discount is 10 percent. If you have access to a microcomputer, you can use spreadsheet software to get the computer to do this calculation for you. Does the program merit approval? How would the present value of the net benefits change if the social rate of discount were 15 percent?

Suggestions for Further Reading

Anderson, Lee G., and Settle, Russell F. *Benefit-Cost Analysis: A Practical Guide.* Lexington, KY: D. C. Heath, 1977. A practical "how-to-do-it" approach to cost-benefit analysis.

Gramlich, Edward M. *A Guide to Benefit-Cost Analysis,* 2d ed. Englewood Cliffs, NJ: Prentice-Hall, 1990. A comprehensive treatment and guide to all aspects of cost-benefit analysis.

Haveman, Robert H., and Margolis, Julius, eds. *Public Expenditure and Policy Analysis,* 3d ed. Boston: Houghton Mifflin, 1983. A collection of readings on the analysis of public expenditures and efficiency in government.

Hulten, Charles R. and Schwab, Robert M. "Infrastructure Spending: Where Do We Go From Here," *National Tax Journal* 46, No. 3, September 1993. A review of the literature and controversy about spending trends on infrastructure in the United States and the impact of the decline in infrastructure spending on productivity and economic growth.

Lynch, Thomas D. *Public Budgeting in America.* Englewood Cliffs, NJ: Prentice-Hall, 1979. A descriptive account of budgeting procedures for both the federal and nonfederal governments in the United States.

Mishan, Edward J. *Cost-Benefit Analysis.* New York: Praeger, 1976. A complete discussion of theoretical and practical aspects of cost-benefit analysis. Contains many examples.

Sassone, Peter G., and Schaefer, William A. *A Cost-Benefit Analysis: A Handbook.* New York: Academic Press, 1978. A manual illustrating techniques of cost-benefit analysis.

U.S. Congress, Congressional Budget Office, *How Federal Spending for Infrastructures and Other Public Investments Affects the Economy.* Washington, D.C., U.S. Government Printing Office, July 1991. An analysis of federal investment spending in the United States.

Zerbe, Richard O. Jr., and Dively, Dwight D. *Benefit-Cost Analysis in Theory and Practice.* New York: HarperCollins College Publishers, 1994. An advanced and highly detailed text on techniques of cost-benefit analysis and use of the tool in practice.

7

GOVERNMENT SUBSIDIES
AND INCOME SUPPORT FOR
THE POOR

L E A R N I N G   O B J E C T I V E S

After reading this chapter you should be able to

1. Discuss the extent of poverty in the United States.
2. Understand the basis for government assistance to the poor and the major government programs that benefit the poor in the United States.
3. Explain the difference between cash assistance, price-distorting subsidies, and in-kind allotments of benefits and

discuss their effects on incentives and resource allocation.
4. Analyze the impact of transfer payments to the poor on work incentives.
5. Examine the negative income tax, wage rate subsidies, and the Earned Income Tax Credit as alternative programs to aid the poor.

As of early 1992 one of every five children in the United States was living in poverty. Nearly 36 million Americans were classified as poor by the federal government in that year—more than 14 percent of the U.S. population. Despite the vast wealth of the United States, poverty remains a serious social problem, the signs of which are visible to us daily in large cities and rural areas. Many live in dilapidated substandard housing. Children go to bed hungry. Many of the poor lack access to adequate health care and education.

Poverty breeds crime and social unrest. Many citizens believe that it is their moral responsibility to help the poor through charitable contributions. Philanthropic organizations and religious institutions have traditionally acted as intermediaries to channel such contributions to the poor. However, charitable contributions are unreliable and unstable as a means of providing income support for the poor. Many citizens do not contribute in the belief that others will take up the slack. During recessions, when the ranks of the poor swell, charitable contributions typically decline because the incomes of the nonpoor decline.

25

Support for the poor has evolved into a government function in the United States and most other industrialized nations. Today one of every ten dollars spent by governments in the United States is allocated to programs that support the poor. Some think we should spend more to aid the poor, and others believe that existing government programs to assist the poor are ineffective and actually trap the poor in an endless cycle of poverty that runs from generation to generation. Government programs to aid the poor in the United States have been criticized for doing little to provide a decent living standard for the poor while discouraging them from working. The government programs are commonly accused of encouraging illegitimate births and the dissolution of families. Finally, as explained in this chapter, many government programs assist the poor by providing them with services including housing and medical care that cost more to taxpayers than these services are worth to recipients.

Almost every recent President has had a plan to reform the patchwork of federal programs that has emerged as a system of government support for the poor. However, aside from minor changes, no fundamental revision has occurred in the U.S. system of support for the poor in nearly thirty years. The most recent plan by the Clinton administration proposed to pump more funds into child care, child support enforcement, education and job training for mothers of dependent children receiving income support and to limit eligibility for such payments. The Clinton plan was designed to reduce the amount of time younger mothers could remain on welfare by requiring them to attend school or enroll in training programs and also requiring them to accept offers of work. The Clinton plan also proposed programs to reduce teenage pregnancy. The Clinton administration also was instrumental in proposing programs that were enacted in 1993 to increase support to the working poor.

All programs of support to the poor and proposals to reform these programs must come to grips with the tradeoff between providing minimum living standards to those who are poor—a group that comprises an alarming increase in the number of children—while trying to minimize the work disincentive for those who are eligible for support.

In this chapter we examine the major government programs that assist the poor in the United States. We also develop a general framework for analyzing the impact of subsidies and transfers to individuals on the allocation of resources. Government assistance to the poor requires redistribution of income from the nonpoor to the poor. The generosity of the programs affects the tax burdens on those who must finance their costs. Of course, social costs of programs designed to redistribute income are inevitable. Transfer programs that subsidize the consumption of particular goods, such as food or medical services, are likely to affect the choices of recipients in ways that cause losses in efficiency. The availability of transfers also can affect the incentives of eligible recipients to work. The social losses from distortions in work and spending decisions of transfer recipients are matters of concern to those who finance the programs.

Economic analysis of transfer and subsidy programs provides insights into their effects that are not immediately obvious. Much of this chapter is devoted to an in-depth analysis of the impact of the major transfer programs on incentives of those eligible, or potentially eligible, for the benefits.

POVERTY IN THE UNITED STATES

Federal statistics classify as poor those persons who live in households having annual income below the established poverty level. According to a definition developed by the Social Security Administration, persons are poor if their income is less than three times the cost of a "nutritionally adequate diet." This method of measuring poverty assumes that a poor family does not have enough income to purchase a low-cost diet and twice that amount to spend on other goods and services. The official poverty level income varies with size of the family and whether the family lives on a farm or has a head of household older than 65. A two-person household headed by a person older than 65 is classified as poor at a lower level of income than a two-person household not headed by an elderly person. Larger households are classified as poor at higher levels of income than smaller households.

The **poverty threshold** is the level of income below which a household is classified as poor in the United States. The poverty threshold is adjusted each year by multiplying the previous year's threshold by the change in the Consumer Price Index and adding the increase to the previous year's threshold. In 1991, the poverty threshold for a single person under the age of 65 living alone was $7,086. The poverty threshold for a family of four in 1991 was $13,924.

The definition of poverty is arbitrary, and many would argue that it is either too low or too high. Be that as it may, this definition has become the poverty standard for statistical purposes.

If only cash income is counted, including government cash transfer payments received, 35.7 million persons were living below the poverty level in 1991. This amounted to 14.2 percent of the population. Families with children have a greater likelihood of living in poverty in the United States than those with no children. Approximately 40 percent of the persons classified as poor are children. More than one-third of the poor live in families headed by a female with no husband. The elderly have lower poverty rates than other demographic groups. Approximately 12 percent of the elderly (those over 65 years of age) in the United States are poor.

Table 7.1 and the accompanying charts show the extent of poverty in the United States from 1960 to 1991. The official rate of poverty in the United States declined from 22.2 percent of the population in 1960 to 11.1 percent in 1973. From 1973 to 1983, the official poverty rate increased to more than 15 percent of the population in that recession year. From 1984 to 1989, the poverty rate declined from 15.2 percent to 12.8 percent of the population. The chart accompanying Table 7.1 shows that the poverty rate in the United States fell significantly in the 1960s but rose sharply between 1977 and 1983, then falling again after 1983. However, partly as a result of a recession, the poverty rate increased again in 1990 and 1991.

One problem with the official poverty statistics is that they measure only cash income. They do not include government transfers of goods and services received by the poor. This is significant, because, as shown in the following discussion, transfers of goods and services, rather than cash, are the dominant means of aiding the poor in the United States. However, these figures can be adjusted to account for such transfers.

Table 7.1 ✦ PERSONS BELOW THE POVERTY LEVEL, 1960–1991 (PERSONS AS OF MARCH OF THE FOLLOWING YEAR)

YEAR	NUMBER	PERCENTAGE OF POPULATION
1960	39,851,000	22.2
1961	39,628,000	21.9
1962	38,625,000	21.0
1963	36,436,000	19.5
1964	36,055,000	19.0
1965	33,185,000	17.3
1966	28,510,000	14.7
1967	27,769,000	14.2
1968	25,389,000	12.8
1969	24,147,000	12.1
1970	25,420,000	12.6
1971	25,559,000	12.5
1972	24,460,000	11.9
1973	22,973,000	11.1
1974	23,370,000	11.2
1975	25,877,000	12.3
1976	24,975,000	11.8
1977	24,720,000	11.6
1978	24,497,000	11.4
1979	26,072,000	11.7
1980	29,272,000	13.0
1981	31,822,000	14.0
1982	34,398,000	15.0
1983	35,266,000	15.2
1984	33,700,000	14.4
1985	33,064,000	14.0
1986	32,370,000	13.6
1987	32,341,000	13.4
1988	31,745,000	13.0
1989	31,534,000	12.8
1990	33,534,000	13.5
1991	35,000,000	14.2

The gray bars indicate recession periods.

Source: U.S. Bureau of the Census, *Characteristics of the Population below the Poverty Level,* Current Population Reports, Series P-60, various years.

How Protectionism in Industrialized Nations Contributes to Increased Poverty in Less-Developed Countries

It might surprise you to learn that protectionist trade policies of industrialized nations, including those of the United States, contribute to increased poverty in less-developed nations. The United States and most nations of Western Europe have pursued farm trade policies through price supports, subsidies, tariffs, and import quotas. These programs benefit domestic farmers by increasing their incomes as a result of higher farm prices and by discouraging imports while encouraging exports. Exports of surplus farm products from industrialized nations depress world agricultural prices. By depriving the poor in rural areas of less-developed countries (who earn their income mainly through agriculture) of markets for their products and by lowering the prices they receive for what they do sell, the protectionism of industrialized nations makes it harder for these people to escape from poverty.

Nontariff barriers such as import restrictions on sugar, dairy products, and rice are common in industrialized nations. One estimate indicates that about one-third of the agriculture exports of developing countries have been affected by these trade barriers.[*] For example, U.S. sugar import quotas have harmed the urban poor in the Dominican Republic. The U.S. sugar import quotas sharply reduced sugar exports from the Dominican Republic between 1982 to 1987 as its quota for exports to the United States was slashed. At the same time exports of subsidized sugar from the European Union (EU) resulted in much lower prices for sugar on world markets. The world price for sugar during the 1980s averaged only about one-third of the U.S. support price for sugar. As a result of the policies of the industrialized nations, sugar production in the Dominican Republic, a very efficient low-cost producer of sugar, fell drastically and four sugar mills had to be closed by 1990 as a result of the 40 percent reduction in production.

Because of the decline in domestic sugar production, the average real income of cane cutters, the poorest people in rural areas, fell and many Haitian cane cutters who worked in the Dominican Republic lost their jobs. Those Dominican workers were forced back to subsistence farming or had to migrate to urban areas in search of work, thereby increasing the supply of labor in the cities and bringing down urban wages and incomes.

Restrictions on imports of textiles and clothing in the United States and other industrialized nations also harm low-income groups in developing nations while keeping the prices of clothing high to protect domestic producers. World trade in textiles and clothing has been dominated mainly by the "Multifibre Arrangement" that is used to negotiate import quotas. These import quotas on textiles harm low-cost producers and workers in less-developed nations. For example, Bangladesh, a less-developed nation where poverty is extreme, had a thriving garment industry as of the mid-1980s, thanks to foreign investment in the nation by Korean manufacturers whose exports of textiles were limited as a result of the Multifibre Arrangement. In the mid-1980s the Bangladesh garment industry was contributing to higher incomes for many poor households by providing employment opportunities in a labor-intensive industry.

However, in 1985 the United States imposed more restrictive import quotas on textiles from Bangladesh. By 1987, additional restrictive quotas for Bangladesh were imposed and several factories had to be closed there, contributing to increased unemployment and lower incomes. Quotas were eased after 1987, but by 1988 exports from Bangladesh to the United States were once again coming close to the quota amounts and production had to be curtailed. The Multifibre Arrangement and the negotiated trade quotas that result from it therefore contribute to reduced employment opportunities in less-developed nations such as Bangladesh that are low-cost producers of clothing. By restricting growth of the textile industry in Bangladesh, U.S. trade policies limit the opportunities of the poor for increasing their incomes in this nation. Fortunately, the new GATT trade agreement, when fully implemented, will remove many of the barriers to trade that harm less-developed nations.

[*]World Bank, *World Development Report, 1990* (Oxford, England: Oxford University Press, 1990) 121–122. This section is based on information in the World Development Report.

For example, by adding the market value of noncash assistance in food, housing, and medical care and other forms of noncash income in 1991, the overall rate of poverty would be reduced to 10 percent in that year.

GOVERNMENT PROGRAMS TO AID THE POOR: THE BASIS AND THE TRADE-OFFS

Needs Versus Earnings and the Equity-Efficiency Trade-Off

Government programs to aid the poor establish minimum standards of living for those eligible for assistance. A common justification for establishing minimum standards of well-being through transfers is that market outcomes can result in households earning less than the minimum level required for survival. The result is low-income families who cannot earn enough to support their children and otherwise meet their needs. Such outcomes are viewed as unacceptable by many citizens and provide a basis of support for a program of "safety net" measures to prevent citizens' incomes from falling below minimally acceptable levels. This approach justifies programs and policies that provide the transfers to the poor discussed in this chapter.

Disagreement on what is minimally required for survival would have to be resolved to implement such policies. At the extreme, if it were agreed that needs do not differ among individuals, policies that distribute income according to need would call for an equal distribution of income. This notion, however, conflicts with the belief that persons should be rewarded according to their abilities and the value of their work. A compromise solution would allow persons to obtain earnings in line with the value of their work but to provide minimal income support. This could be coupled with policies that provide equal opportunity in labor markets and schooling. In the United States in 1991, approximately 21 percent of households classified as poor had the equivalent of at least one person working full-time all year. Nearly two-thirds of all poor families with children have some family members who work during the year. A substantial number of poor families are poor because of insufficient earnings rather than inability to work.

A pragmatic approach to the problem of altering income distribution to alleviate poverty is one that considers the impact of transfers on efficiency. This approach recognizes that transfers to low-income persons can decrease their incentive to work and distort the pattern of consumption, so that the net benefits from resource use is less than would be possible if resources were efficiently utilized. In effect, this approach recognizes that the way the "pie" is divided can ultimately affect its size. Under such circumstances, losses in efficiency decrease the economy's potential for producing goods and services and jobs. Insofar as transfers cause such losses, these losses must be weighed against the gains of improved equity. At the extreme, many argue that the best way to improve the lot of the poor is to pursue efficient policies because these maximize job opportunities. However, many of the poor are not employable because of age or health, so that programs that create jobs do little to help them. In fact, as shown in this chapter, many of the transfer policies in the United States are designed to help persons incapable of working or to benefit children who are poor.

Collective Benefits Resulting from Aid to the Poor: Social Stability and Safety Nets

Changes in the distribution of income that reduce the incidence of poverty can result in benefits that are collectively enjoyed. From this perspective income redistribution to the poor can be viewed as a public good. Many persons who support government efforts to redistribute income do so because they believe that they, and other nonpoor citizens, will benefit when poverty is reduced. They might also believe that government programs that establish a safety net to prevent personal income from falling below certain levels provide them with insurance; that is, if individuals should suffer a financial or health-related catastrophe, government policies would prevent them from becoming destitute. In 1991 and 1992, a period of recession and slow growth in the United States, the number of people receiving such benefits increased substantially.

In addition, persons could have genuine compassion for those who are unfortunate enough to be unable to provide for their own needs, and, indeed, experience satisfaction when the government provides subsidies to the poor. Income redistribution also can provide collective benefits through social stability. Many persons reason that a society in which poverty is prevalent breeds discontent and revolution, with the potential for chaos and violence. Upper-income groups tend to support income transfers to the poor to secure the benefits of social stability, thereby reducing the probability of revolutionary upheaval.

But why do we rely on government rather than on private charity to provide assistance to the poor? The answer lies in the public-good nature of charity. Voluntary donations to the poor are likely to result in an undersupply of income redistribution to low-income groups relative to the efficient amount because of the free-rider problem discussed in Chapter 4. Government action to redistribute income can establish uniform standards of eligibility for aid. Such standards might not be ideal from the point of view of all citizens, but these government standards reflect the political compromise necessary to obtain a public program of ensured tax-financed income redistribution.

GOVERNMENT PROGRAMS OF ASSISTANCE TO THE POOR IN THE UNITED STATES

Eligibility

One of the crucial concerns in the development of programs to aid the poor in the United States has been the effect of transfers on the work incentive of the recipients. As a result, the major welfare programs for the poor in the United States mainly assist those who, for one reason or other, cannot work. These groups include the disabled, the aged, and families of needy children headed mainly by women. Those falling into these demographic categories satisfy the **status test** for public assistance. The status test ensures that they belong to one of the particular groups that is eligible for poverty relief. Because persons in these groups are not usually in the labor force, transfers to them are believed to have minimal effects on work incentive. In effect, this policy "tags" certain groups of limited work capacity and makes them eligible for government assistance.

The status test provides only a crude indication of the extent to which candidates for public assistance are capable of working. Use of health, age, or other arbitrary criteria to determine whether a person is able to work provides only an imperfect indication of the actual capacity to work. For example, tagging poor children who are not expected to work as eligible for government assistance means that their parents also will receive assistance. To prevent adverse work incentive effects on parents in poor families with dependent children, most state welfare programs provide aid only to families with a single parent—primarily female-headed families. However, with increased labor force participation of women in the United States in recent years, the notion that single mothers are not expected to work has come under scrutiny. Concern has increased about the effect of government assistance programs assisting children on the incentives of single parents to seek work. In 1988 new legislation was enacted by Congress to increase incentives for welfare mothers to join the labor force and work.

To be eligible for cash and other forms of assistance in the United States, recipients also must pass a **means test,** which establishes that those passing the status test have incomes and asset levels that are below the minimally required amounts to be eligible for aid. Those meeting both the means test and the status test are *automatically entitled to the transfers.* For this reason, these transfer programs are often called **entitlement programs,** which are those that require payments to all those persons meeting eligibility requirements established by law.

Government programs to aid the poor consist of direct cash transfers, direct provision of such basic goods and services as medical care, subsidies to assist the poor in obtaining housing and food, and various programs designed to aid children and provide incentives to the poor to become self-sufficient. The bulk of the aid, however, is in direct provision of goods and services or subsidies to assist the poor in obtaining goods and services.

Cash Transfers to the Poor: Aid to Families with Dependent Children and Supplemental Security Income

When most people discuss welfare assistance in the United States, they are usually referring to this country's major cash transfer program for the poor: **Aid to Families with Dependent Children (AFDC).** AFDC began as a relatively minor program authorized by the Social Security Act of 1935. The program provides cash assistance to families from which one parent is absent and to two-parent families in which one parent is disabled or unemployed if these families have dependent children. Most families who receive aid under this program are headed by females without spouses or whose spouses are absent. The program is jointly administered and financed by the federal government and state governments. The level of benefits and eligibility requirements are determined by the states under federal guidelines. Benefits vary widely from state to state, reflecting public choices made in those states rather than the differences in the cost of living among states.

In 1990, the average monthly benefit paid to AFDC recipient families in various states ranged from a low of about $114 per month in Alabama to a high of $651 per month in Alaska. The national average monthly benefit payment under AFDC was $377 per family in 1990. The actual amount received by a family depends on the income earned and the number of dependents. About 11.5 million persons benefited from this program in 1990 and total government outlays amounting to about $19.5 billion were allocated to the AFDC program in 1990. Of this total, $10.5 billion were expenditures by the federal government. Since 1970, AFDC support payments to families have not kept up with inflation and have fallen substantially in real terms.

Another major program of assistance to the poor is **Supplemental Security Income (SSI).** SSI is a federally funded and operated program that provides cash transfers to the aged, the blind, and the disabled who pass a means test. Most states supplement the basic SSI payments made to individuals by the federal government. Because of the state supplements, SSI benefits vary considerably; the payments received by the individuals also vary with their income from other sources. The monthly benefit levels for a typical elderly couple in 1990 ranged from $610 to $1,312. In that year, government outlays for this program totaled $16 billion, of which $12 billion were outlays by the federal government; 4.8 million received SSI payments in 1990. The benefits are adjusted for inflation each year.

In addition, state governments have programs of *general assistance* to the poor, which provide financial aid to couples without children and unrelated individuals who pass a means test but are ineligible for benefits under SSI or AFDC. The federal government provides additional assistance to the poor through the **Earned Income Tax Credit (EITC)**, which is a program that provides assistance to families who work and have children in the form of supplements to earnings that are transfers paid out when eligible recipients file appropriate federal income tax forms. The maximum credit per family was $1,998 in 1994. The EITC has emerged as a major means of support to the poor in the United States. The features of the EITC are discussed at the end of this chapter.

In-Kind Aid to the Poor: Food Stamps, Medicaid, Housing Assistance, and Other Programs

The federal and state governments also assist the poor through **in-kind benefits,** which are noncash benefits that increase the quantities of certain goods and services that will be consumed by the recipients. In-kind benefits are those received in some form other than money that improve the well-being of recipients. These benefits consist of medical services, food, housing, and other services provided either directly to recipients or at subsidized prices to eligible families and individuals. In dollar terms, in-kind subsidies are much more important than cash transfers to the poor. Some poor also receive subsidies that lower the prices they pay for services such as housing that they purchase in the marketplace.

Medicaid was enacted by Congress in 1965 to provide, at government expense, medical care services for the poor under the age of 65. The program is jointly financed by the federal and state governments but administered by state governments.

It provides benefits for all those eligible for AFDC and SSI cash subsidies and others who pass a means test. Under Medicaid, all states (except Arizona) provide basic health services to eligible recipients. Each state determines eligibility requirements under Medicaid and can provide benefits above the minimum established by federal law. Each state establishes its own reimbursement policies to medical providers who supply services to Medicaid patients. The fees of the providers of the service are billed directly to the various state governments.

Medicaid has become the most expensive of all programs of public assistance to the poor. Total government expenditures for the Medicaid program in 1990 amounted to $72.5 billion or 3.8 percent of total spending by all levels of government in that year. The federal government alone spent $41 billion on Medicaid in 1990, which amounted to 3.2 percent of its total outlays that year. Medicaid costs have been rising rapidly and are expected to continue to do so at an even more rapid rate. In 1992, Medicaid outlays were more than $100 billion. The Medicaid program benefits about 24 million recipients. Beneficiaries under the program receive a card that they can use in lieu of cash to pay for medical services from physicians and hospitals. Approximately 60 percent of families living in poverty receive Medicaid benefits.

The **food stamp program** is a federally financed subsidy program that began in 1971. The program is administered by state governments. Recipients receive food coupons that can be redeemed for food and related items at stores. An eligible recipient must pass a means test. The actual amount of stamps received per month varies with a person's earned income, less allowable deductions. The benefits received by recipients decline as earned income increases. In 1990, more than 20 million persons received food stamps. Total government outlays for the food stamp program in 1990 were nearly $18 billion, of which $16.5 billion were expenditures by the federal government.

Housing assistance programs are administered by governments to provide subsidized housing to low-income families. Only about one-fourth of the population eligible for these subsidies actually receives them because of limited resources allocated to housing programs. The programs consist of public housing at subsidized rents, rent supplements for those renting private housing, and subsidies designed to make more housing available to low-income persons. These programs cost the federal government about $18 billion in 1990.

Finally, various other programs, including those for employment and training, social services (such as child care, rehabilitation, supplementary educational services for disadvantaged children, and legal aid) and energy assistance, are also available to those who meet both means and status tests.

Expenditures for Assistance to the Poor in the United States

Table 7.2 shows federal government and total expenditures under the major programs of government aid to the poor in the United States in fiscal year 1990. Total expenditures under the major transfer programs to low-income persons in the United States accounted for 8.8 percent of total expenditures by all levels of government and 10.3 percent of federal government expenditures in 1990.

Table 7.2 ✦ Major U.S. Government Expenditures to Aid the Poor, 1990

CASH TRANSFERS	FEDERAL		ALL GOVERNMENTS	
	AMOUNT $ BILLIONS	PERCENTAGE OF TOTAL FED. EXP.	AMOUNT $ BILLIONS	PERCENTAGE OF GOVT. EXP.
AFDC	11.5	0.78	21.2	0.89
SSI	13.6	0.92	17.2	0.72
EITC	5.9	0.40	5.9	0.25
Other[a]	6.0	0.40	10.8	0.45
Total Cash	37.0	2.50	55.1	2.31
IN-KIND TRANSFERS				
Medicaid	41.2	2.78	72.2	3.03
Food Stamps	16.5	1.11	17.7	0.74
Housing	17.5	1.18	17.5	0.73
Other[b]	40.0	2.70	48.1	2.02
Total In-Kind	115.2	7.77	155.5	6.52
TOTAL BENEFITS TO POOR	152.2	10.27	210.6	8.83

[a]Includes pensions for needy veterans, general assistance to the poor, and assistance to the working poor.
[b]Includes education aid, job training, energy assistance, and other medical and nutritional assistance.
Source: *Statistical Abstract of the United States,* 1993.

Cash transfers to the poor accounted for only 24 percent of total spending to aid the poor by governments in 1990. The remainder, 76 percent, is accounted for by in-kind benefits. Cash transfers consist of AFDC and SSI benefits paid to individuals and families and such other programs as pensions for needy veterans, general assistance to the poor by state and local governments, and assistance to the working poor through the earned income tax credit. Total cash payments to the poor accounted for only 2.5 percent of total government spending in 1990.

In-Kind Versus Cash Transfers

As the data in Table 7.2 demonstrate, the welfare system of aid to the poor in the United States is heavily weighted toward provision of goods and services and subsidies for consumption of housing. The reasons for this are complex. Political realities make it more likely that a given dollar amount of in-kind assistance can gain approval while equivalent amounts of cash assistance cannot. Apparently, assistance to the poor is more likely to obtain votes when a particular issue is clarified. For example, programs of food assistance to the poor were expanded after an investigation of the extent of hunger in the United States in the 1960s. It also appears that programs of in-kind assistance to the poor are more easily approved during periods of high unemployment.

The rationale for many in-kind benefits to the poor is that they allow some control over the spending patterns of recipients. Many persons who support such programs as food stamps, public housing, and government-supplied training and schooling argue that these programs ensure that the recipients will spend their grants on necessities rather than luxuries. However, in-kind benefits free up cash that would have been spent on the subsidized items. This cash then can be spent on nonsubsidized items. In other words, in-kind subsidies, like cash subsidies, allow increased purchases of all goods.

C H E C K P O I N T

1. How is poverty officially defined in the United States? Based on the official definition of poverty, has any progress been made in reducing its incidence in the United States since 1960?
2. How is eligibility determined for government programs designed to assist the poor in the United States?
3. What are the major types of government programs that provide support for the poor in the United States?

SUBSIDIES AND TRANSFERS TO INDIVIDUALS: ECONOMIC ANALYSIS OF THEIR EFFECTS

A major concern about all transfer programs is their effect on resource allocation. In-kind programs of assistance can distort the behavior of the recipients in ways that cause losses in efficiency. The programs can result in consumption of goods or services by recipients beyond the point at which the marginal benefit of the item to the consumer falls to equal its marginal social cost. In addition, the availability of the programs themselves could result in changes in the behavior of those who would take advantage of eligibility requirements. Finally, those who are already receiving government assistance might lose their incentive to work if earning income results in a loss of cash and in-kind benefits. The effects of government assistance programs to the poor on resource allocation highlight the realities of the equity-efficiency trade-off.

All forms of assistance to the poor in the United States can be regarded as subsidies. In effect, subsidies are the opposite of taxes. They are payments to individuals, usually from governing authorities, subject to certain terms and conditions. Economic analysis of in-kind and cash subsidies help to isolate their impact on efficiency.

Price-Distorting Subsidies

Let's begin our analysis with a discussion of subsidies that decrease the price of consuming a good or service to the recipient. For example, poor people often are eligible for housing subsidies that allow them to rent apartments at monthly rents below the market equilibrium rent for similar housing. The government then pays the difference between the actual rent and the amount that the tenant pays. The difference between the market rent paid to the landlord and the tenant's rent is the subsidy. Some government programs subsidize payments on mortgage loans to enable low-income individuals to acquire their own homes. Similarly, some poor persons also receive subsidies that reduce the price of energy and other services.

Subsidies that reduce prices to consumers below the market price are called **price-distorting subsidies,** which (other things being equal) are likely to result in losses in efficiency as individuals act to substitute the subsidized good for other goods in their annual budgets. Figure 7.1 illustrates the impact of a price-distorting subsidy for housing services. Suppose, for example, the government agrees to pay a certain fraction (such as 40 percent) of monthly rents of low-income citizens. Initially, before the subsidy is available, the person (whose indifference curves are drawn in Figure 7.1) is in equilibrium at point E_1. At that point, she purchases H_1 units of housing services (measured in terms of, say, square feet or number of rooms rented per month) and spends N_1 on other goods each month. Total expenditure on housing per month is represented by the distance N_1I.

Figure 7.1 ✦ A PRICE-DISTORTING SUBSIDY

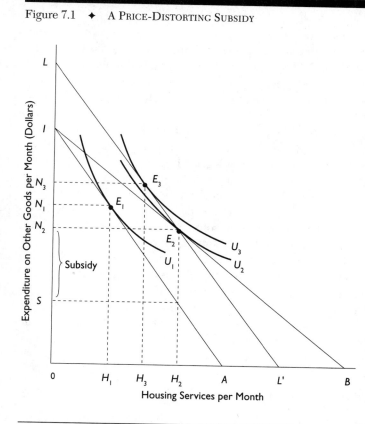

A price-distorting subsidy to housing services moves the recipient from equilibrium at point E_1 to equilibrium at point E_2, as the price that must be paid for such services declines. If, instead, the recipient were given N_2S per year as a cash subsidy, she would be in equilibrium at point E_3. The person is better off at E_3 than at E_2 because she achieves utility level $U_3 > U_2$.

The government subsidy reduces the price of housing services to the recipient and therefore swivels the budget line outward from IA to IB. The consumer now is in equilibrium at point E_2, at which she consumes H_2 units of housing per month. Her total monthly expenditure on housing services now is represented by the distance IS. However, only a portion of this comes out of her income. Of the total annual expenditures on housing after receipt of the subsidy, IN_2 is paid by the recipient and N_2S is paid by the government. The total amount of the subsidy received by the individual is therefore N_2S per year. After receipt of the subsidy, then, she enjoys H_2 units of housing services each month and spends N_2 on other goods each year.

Suppose, instead, this consumer were given a monthly cash subsidy exactly equal to the amount that would be received under the price-distorting housing subsidy. The amount of the monthly cash subsidy would be N_2S. The budget line would now be LL'. This budget line goes through point E_2, with the result that the consumer could still buy the combination of housing services and other goods that would be affordable under the price-distorting subsidy. However, the increase in cash income now enables the consumer to purchase more of all goods, not only housing services. The equilibrium under the cash subsidy is at point E_3, where the consumer chooses to purchase H_3 units of housing services per month and to spend N_3 on other goods each month. This result will hold as long as the marginal rate of substitution of housing services for expenditure on other goods, which is the marginal benefit of housing services to the person, declines. Because the slope of the budget line LL' is steeper to the left of point E_2, the equilibrium must be at a point on an indifference curve that is also steeper. The consumer must substitute expenditure on other goods for housing to increase the marginal benefit of housing, thereby moving to a steeper point on the indifference curve at point E_3. The price-distorting subsidy induces the consumer to purchase a larger amount of housing services than would be the case if she received an equivalent cash grant.

A cash grant to an individual equal to the amount received under the price-distorting subsidy would therefore allow the person to enjoy a higher level of utility. After all, the consumer could always use the cash grant to purchase the combination of housing and other goods at point E_2. The cash subsidy gives the recipient greater freedom of choice, thereby allowing the achievement of a higher level of satisfaction. The difference between the utility level U_3 and the utility level U_2 is a loss in utility to the recipient from the N_2S dollars of subsidy compared to the unrestricted cash grant. This **deadweight loss** of price-distorting subsidy is the extra benefit a recipient can enjoy from the dollar amount of the price-distorting subsidy if instead the grant was received in a lump sum. Here the deadweight loss of the subsidy is the difference in well-being of the individual at point E_2 compared to what she can enjoy at point E_3 for the same dollar amount of subsidy. A net gain would result if each individual receiving a price-distorting subsidy were able to get the same sum in the form of a lump-sum unrestricted cash transfer. Naturally, with the cash transfer, the individuals would choose to consume less of the subsidized good.

The Excess Burden of a Price-Distorting Subsidy: Market Effects

Now let's examine the effect of a price-distorting subsidy on the market for a product like housing services. To make the analysis simple, assume that the housing industry operates under conditions of constant costs so that the long-run supply curve of housing is perfectly elastic. Figure 7.2 shows the long-run market supply curve for a standard one-bedroom apartment along with the demand curves for these apartments by low-income tenants. Because the supply curve is perfectly elastic, the rent for the apartments is independent of the demand by low-income tenants. The marginal social cost of making one-bedroom apartments available to tenants is assumed to be $400 per month. Assuming no externalities in the production or consumption of housing, and perfect competition in the housing market, the supply curve of housing gives the marginal social cost of any given number of apartments, which is constant at $400 per month.

The demand curve shows that the marginal benefit of one-bedroom apartments to low-income tenants varies with the number rented. In the absence of any subsidy, the market equilibrium rent would be $400 per month for the apartment and the number of apartments rented would be Q_1. This would be efficient because at point E the marginal benefit of the apartments equals their marginal social cost to low-income tenants. Assuming no positive externalities are associated with housing consumption to low-income tenants, the marginal benefit they receive from renting a one-bedroom apartment is also the marginal social benefit of making that apartment available to them.

Now suppose that the government agrees to pay one-half the rent for low-income tenants. As a result of the subsidy, the price to low-income tenants falls to $200 and the quantity demanded by these tenants increases to Q_2 corresponding to

Figure 7.2　◆　EXCESS BURDEN OF A SUBSIDY

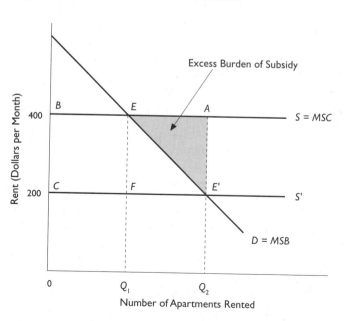

The cost of a subsidy to low-income tenants to taxpayers is represented by the rectangular area BAE'C. The net benefits to recipients of the subsidy are represented by the area BEE'FC. The excess burden of the subsidy is the difference between its costs to taxpayers and the benefits to recipients represented by the triangular area EAE'. The subsidy causes more than the efficient amount of resources to be devoted to housing because the marginal social cost of housing after the subsidy exceeds the marginal social benefit received by tenants.

point E'. At that point tenants pay only $200 per month rent but landlords receive $400. The $200 difference between the market rent and the rent paid by tenants is the price-distorting subsidy per tenant represented by the distance AE'. Naturally, the price-distorting subsidy to housing induces low-income tenants to increase their consumption of housing services. Families who would normally live in small one-room apartments or with relatives now move into one-bedroom apartments and are made better off as they consume more housing. Because of the price-distorting subsidy, more resources are devoted to making one-bedroom apartments available to low-income tenants. When Q_2 units are supplied each month to these tenants, the $400 marginal social cost of the apartments exceeds the marginal social benefit to tenants of only $200. Too many apartments are being supplied to low-income tenants relative to the efficient number. The marginal social cost of making the additional apartments available exceeds the marginal social benefit, which is the value that tenants place on additional apartments. In effect, the subsidy program induces a reallocation of resources toward housing, but the value of the resources used exceeds the benefits that they provide to the tenants. The result is a loss in net benefits from resource use because the subsidy induces tenants to consume housing beyond the point at which its marginal benefit to them equals the marginal social cost of the service.

Now let's look at the cost of the subsidy to taxpayers and compare those costs with the net increment in benefits low-income tenants enjoy as a result of the subsidy. The monthly cost of the subsidy to taxpayers is the $200 subsidy per apartment multiplied by the Q_2 apartments rented by the recipients of the subsidy. This is represented by the area $BAE'C$ in Figure 7.2. The total value of the subsidy to recipients can be calculated as follows:

1. Those low-income tenants who would rent one-bedroom apartments even without the subsidy enjoy a $200 per month net gain as the net rent they pay is cut from $400 to $200. The total net monthly gain to these individuals is $200 multiplied by Q_1 apartments, which is represented by the area $BEFC$ on the graph.
2. As a result of the subsidy, the number of apartments rented to low-income tenants increases. The monthly net gain to each of these tenants is the difference between the monthly marginal benefit they place on housing and the monthly $200 rent. The total monthly net gain for these tenants is represented in the graph as the triangular area $EE'F$.

The total increase in net benefits to recipients of the subsidy is therefore the sum of the rectangular area $BEFC$ and the triangular area $EE'F$. The sum of the two areas is the area $BEE'FC$.

The area $BEE'FC$ is *less* than the area $BAE'C$ representing taxes paid to finance the subsidy to tenants. The subsidy costs more to taxpayers than it is worth to those who receive it. The difference between the cost of the program to taxpayers and the gain in net benefits to the tenants is called the **excess burden of the subsidy.** The excess burden of the subsidy is the triangular area EAE'. The excess burden measures the additional cost over and above the taxes paid for the subsidy. This additional cost is the loss in efficiency in housing markets that results because the subsidy results in overconsumption of housing beyond the point at which its marginal social benefit equals its marginal social cost.

Price-distorting subsidies result in an excess burden because of the fact that they encourage recipients of the subsidy to consume the subsidized good beyond the point at which its marginal social benefit falls to equal its marginal social cost. A smaller lump-sum cash subsidy (in this case equal to the area $BEE'FC$) can be substituted for the dollar value of the price-distorting subsidy that would make recipients equally as well off and cost taxpayers less in taxes. If we wish to preserve efficiency in the marketplace, then lump-sum transfers to the poor are preferable to price-distorting subsidies.

Medicaid: A Price-Distorting Subsidy that Lowers the Price to Zero

The analysis of the effects of subsidies on resource use is pertinent to the economic effects of Medicaid, which is the largest program of assistance to the poor in the United States. Medicaid, basically, is a government-financed health insurance plan for the poor under the age of 65. Although its actual provisions are quite complex, the program can be viewed in general as reducing to zero the money price of medical services to most eligible low-income persons.

Figure 7.3 analyzes the effect of such a medical subsidy program as Medicaid on consumption of medical services by the poor. Assume that the annual quantity of medical services consumed can be measured by office or hospital visits to medical practitioners. Medical services are presumed to be supplied by a perfectly competitive industry. In Figure 7.3, the marginal social costs of supplying medical services do not increase as more are made available to the poor. In the absence of any subsidies, the poor would have to pay the market equilibrium price of an office visit. This price would equal the marginal social cost of medical service of $P^* = \$25$. Given the

---

Figure 7.3 ✦ FULL SUBSIDIZATION OF MEDICAL SERVICES

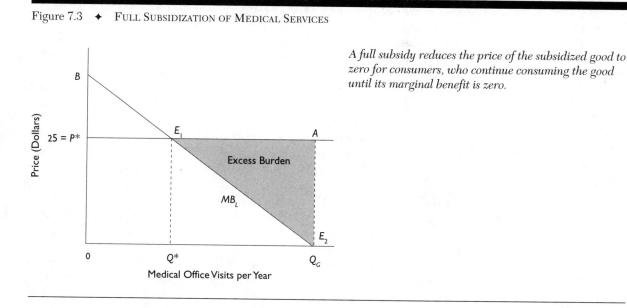

A full subsidy reduces the price of the subsidized good to zero for consumers, who continue consuming the good until its marginal benefit is zero.

demand for medical services by low-income persons, the quantity that they would consume at the market price would be Q°. The demand curve for medical services by the poor reflects their willingness to pay, given their low incomes. This is their marginal benefit for medical services. The equilibrium at P° would be efficient because $P^\circ = MC = MB_L$ of medical services.

When eligible for Medicaid, the price of medical services to low-income persons becomes zero. At zero price, the quantity demanded by Medicaid recipients is Q_G. At this level of annual consumption, recipients of Medicaid are consuming medical services beyond the point at which their marginal benefits equal the marginal cost of the service. At point E_2, the marginal social cost of providing medical service to low-income persons exceeds the marginal benefit that they obtain. This is because, at zero price, recipients of the subsidy consume medical services up to the point at which their marginal benefit (MB_L) is zero.

The total annual cost of the Medicaid program to taxpayers is represented by the area $P^\circ AE_2 0$. However, the dollar value of the gain in well-being for recipients of Medicaid is *less* than the cost of the program to taxpayers. In the absence of a subsidy, low-income persons would consume Q° units of medical services (a certain number of office visits per year). The difference between the maximum amount that they would pay for that amount of medical services and the market price of $25 per office visit is represented by the triangular area $P^\circ BE_1$. This is the consumer surplus that they earn on Q° office visits per year. The gain in consumer surplus to recipients of the Medicaid program is the area $P^\circ E_1 E_2 0$. This represents the net gain in well-being to recipients of Medicaid (see the appendix to Chapter 1 for a discussion of consumer surplus).

Part of the increase in consumer surplus is the extra net benefit on the Q° units of medical service that would have been purchased anyway. This is represented by the rectangular area $0P^\circ E_1 Q^\circ$. The remainder is the area $Q^\circ E_1 E_2$. This is the consumer surplus on the extra medical services consumed after the price falls to zero.

The excess burden of the Medicaid subsidy is represented by the triangular area $E_1 AE_2$. This is a measure of the loss in efficiency due to the in-kind subsidy as the recipients consume medical services beyond the point at which their marginal benefit falls to equal the marginal social cost of the services. The recipients of Medicaid could be made as well off with a cash subsidy, which would be less than the amount the government would have to pay to finance the program!

A cash subsidy to the poor would increase their ability, and therefore willingness, to pay for medical services. In Figure 7.3, this would shift the demand curve for such services outward. The advantage of the cash subsidy to the recipients is that it could be used to purchase not only medical services but also other services or goods. In the case of Medicaid, the subsidy is enjoyed only if more medical services are purchased. Because the average value of Medicaid services provided to an eligible family of four in the United States is more than $2,000 per year, the gain in purchasing power from a cash grant equivalent to Medicaid benefits would be substantial. For example, the U.S. Bureau of the Census estimated that the average market value of medical services received by a single parent with two children under Medicaid was $2,166 in 1987. However, based on ability and willingness to pay, the bureau estimated that these benefits were worth on average only $652 in 1987 for such a family if its income were $10,000 per year. Instead of receiving Medicaid, the recipient could be given an unrestricted lump-sum grant of the $652 and be as well off as with Medicaid while taxpayers would save $1,514!

Additional Effects of Subsidies: The Case of Increasing Costs

Suppose the long-run supply curve of medical services is upward sloping. This would imply that the prices of inputs, such as the services of physicians and hospitals, would increase as a result of increased annual production of medical services. Figure 7.4 shows that, in this case, the market for medical services would be affected by the Medicaid program.

The market demand for medical services, again measured as office visits per year, is D_M in Figure 7.4. This demand curve is the lateral summation of the demand curve for medical services for low-income persons, D_L, and everyone else, D_O. The market price, $25 per office visit, corresponds to the point at which D_M intersects the upward-sloping supply curve, at point E_1. At that price, low-income persons consume Q_L visits per year and others consume Q_O visits per year, for a total of Q_1.

The Medicaid program reduces the price of an office visit to zero for low-income persons only. As a result, their quantity demanded increases to Q_G. The total market demand curve is now the sum of the quantity demanded by all others at any given price and Q_G where Q_G is independent of price because $P = 0$ to Medicaid recipients. The new market demand curve, D'_M, intersects the market supply curve at point E_2. The market price *increases* to $35 per office visit. At that higher price, those who are not receiving Medicaid decrease the quantity of medical services demanded per year to Q'_O. Total quantity demanded is $Q_2 = Q'_O + Q_G$.

It follows that, when the supply of medical services is upward sloping, the government subsidy program will cause the price of medical services to increase. This

---

Figure 7.4 ✦ THE IMPACT OF THE MEDICAID PROGRAM ON PRICE: THE CASE OF INCREASING COST

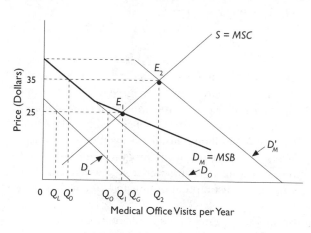

The initial market equilibrium corresponds to point E_1, at which the market demand curve D_M intersects the market supply curve, S. If low-income persons are eligible for Medicaid, their quantity demanded increases to Q_G. The market demand curve D'_M, is obtained by adding Q_G to the demand curve D_O. Given the new increased demand by the poor for medical services, the price of an office visit increases from $25 to $35.

means that those paying the taxes to finance the program *also* will pay more for their own medical services but that owners of specialized inputs necessary to provide medical services, such as physicians and hospitals, will enjoy increases in income. Consumers of medical services who are ineligible for the subsidies therefore suffer a reduction in real income, while medical practitioners are likely to enjoy an increase in real income. This points out how price-distorting subsidies, in addition to causing losses in efficiency, also can cause changes in the distribution of income through changes in the market price of the subsidized goods or services.

Concern about the impact of Medicaid and other government subsidy programs for medical care, such as those enjoyed by the elderly and veterans, on the prices of medical services has led to recent cutbacks in coverage offered by the program. These cutbacks have reduced the subsidy received by the poor by limiting the kinds of medical services that are provided free. Cost-containment measures that limit reimbursement to hospitals and physicians decrease incentives to offer such services to Medicaid patients.

We discuss the economics of health care and the role of government in providing medical services in greater detail in Chapter 9.

C H E C K P O I N T

1. What is a price-distorting subsidy? Why do price-distorting subsidies result in a deadweight loss?
2. What is the excess burden of a subsidy?
3. Explain why the Medicaid program contributes to an overallocation of resources to health care in the United States relative to the efficient amount. Under what circumstance does subsidized medical care contribute to increases in the price of medical services?

SUBSIDIES TO HOUSING AND FOOD

Public Housing

Let's return to the issue of housing subsidies. Some housing subsidies for the poor in the United States reduce the price of housing only if the poor agree to move into specially constructed government-supplied housing reserved for low-income families. This housing is usually rented to eligible citizens at rates considerably below those prevailing in the market. In 1989, about 1.4 million households lived in government-supplied low-income housing projects. The public housing programs are expected to increase the recipient's consumption of housing. Unfortunately, the availability of these programs could actually *reduce* the consumption of housing by restricting the freedom of choice of the consumer.

Suppose, for example, a government program makes available a standard three-room apartment at a rental rate of $30 per room per month. The total rent paid by those eligible for the government housing is therefore $90 per month. Assume the housing can be measured in standardized rooms per unit. This, of course, is a simplification because housing can vary greatly in quality and other characteristics (such as the neighborhood in which it is located). Assume that the market rent for a standardized room (the same size and quality as that provided in public housing) is $100 per month. The three-room public housing apartment therefore would cost $300 per month if rented on the free market. The cash equivalent of the public housing subsidy to eligible tenants is therefore $210 per month, which is the difference between the market rent and the subsidized rent.

Figure 7.5 shows that a person who is eligible for public housing could be induced to move from a larger privately rented apartment to a smaller government-subsidized unit. This person therefore *would reduce* monthly consumption of housing as a result of the availability of the subsidy. Those taking advantage of the subsidy have no choice in the size or quality of their apartments. They must accept the standardized three-room units offered in the public housing projects or forgo the subsidy.

The person whose indifference curves are illustrated in Figure 7.5 is currently in equilibrium at point E_1. He currently rents a four-room apartment at the going market rent of $400 per month. After paying rent, he has $0F$ remaining to spend on other goods. For example, if his monthly income were $800, he would spend $400 on housing and have $400 left over each month to spend on other goods.

Now suppose the person becomes eligible for a new public housing program. He can move into a standardized three-room public housing apartment at the subsidized

Figure 7.5 ✦ ELIGIBILITY FOR PUBLIC HOUSING AND THE EFFECT ON HOUSING CONSUMPTION

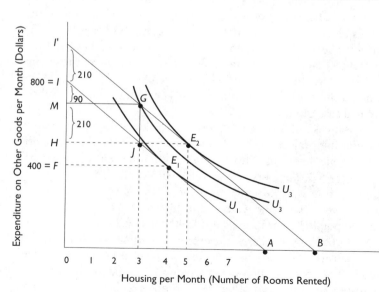

A person eligible for a standardized three-room apartment at a subsidized rent whose indifference curves are shown in the graph reduces consumption of housing from four to three rooms per month. If the person were given the monthly cash value of the in-kind subsidy, $210, he would increase housing consumption.

rent of $90 per month if he chooses. Point *G* on the graph represents this alternative. At that point, the tenant would be consuming for only $90 a three-room apartment that normally would cost $300. He spends only *IM* = $90 a month for this apartment. The remainder is paid by government as a subsidy represented on the graph by the distance *MH* = $210. If the eligible recipient chooses to move to public housing, he will spend $90 per month on housing and, assuming a $800 monthly income, have $710, represented by the distance *M*0, left over to spend on other goods.

The analysis shows that the eligible tenant, in fact, will choose to move out of the nonsubsidized four-room apartment and into the subsidized three-room apartment, because he is better off at point *G* compared with his initial equilibrium at point E_1. If he were to remain in the four-room apartment, he would achieve utility level U_1 at point E_1. By moving into the subsidized three-room apartment, he can increase his utility level to U_2 at point *G*. Therefore, given the choice, he accepts the subsidized apartment and *reduces* the amount of housing consumed per month.

The analysis also shows that, if the person were to receive the cash value of the housing subsidy, he *would increase* his consumption of housing. The subsidy of $210 per month is represented by the distance *GJ* = *MH* on the graph. If this amount were given in cash each month to the person, the budget line would become *I'B*. With the monthly cash grant, he would be in equilibrium at point E_2. He would move from his four-room apartment into a five-room apartment. He therefore would spend $500 per month on housing. His total income would be $800 (monthly earnings) plus $210 (monthly grant), for a total of $1,010. He would spend $510 on other goods. This person therefore would consume more housing and be better off (because $U_3 > U_2$) at point E_2 than at point *G*.

Thus, for some persons, a public housing program could have results opposite to those intended. Some persons would not want to reduce the quantity of housing if they were eligible for public housing. For example, a person currently in equilibrium consuming the services of a three-room apartment per month would clearly be made better off by the subsidy. She would gladly move into the government-supplied three-room apartment, provided that it were of the same quality as her current residence. This is because the subsidy would enable her to have more of other goods while consuming the same amount of housing per month. For this person, the housing subsidy would be equivalent to a cash grant.

Figure 7.6 shows the case of a person who will turn down the opportunity to enter a government housing project even with no differences in the quality of government- and market-supplied housing. This person's indifference curves are steeper than those drawn in Figure 7.5. The person is originally in equilibrium at point E_1 in a four-room apartment. If he were to move to point *G*, the government-supplied three-room housing, he would be made worse off, achieving utility level $U_1 < U_2$. He therefore remains at point E_1 by refusing subsidized housing.

In fact, many argue that, in some cases, government housing is of lower quality than market housing, because the housing projects have been concentrated in low-income neighborhoods. The concentration of poverty-level households in deteriorating neighborhoods results in crime and other social problems that plague tenants. Public housing is also an expensive subsidy. One estimate is that new construction of

Figure 7.6 ◆ REFUSING A PUBLIC HOUSING SUBSIDY

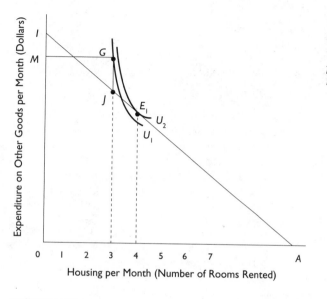

The person whose indifference curves are drawn is better off remaining in his four-room apartment than moving into the three-room public housing at point G. This person does not accept the offer of subsidized public housing.

public housing in 1984 required a federal subsidy of $5,000 per unit per year![1] Given the magnitude of that subsidy, few new public housing projects have been built in recent years. An equivalent cash grant of that amount would clearly contribute greatly to pull many low-income persons out of poverty.

The Housing and Community Development Act of 1987 authorized a new voucher program that gives low-income households coupons, like food stamps, that can be used to rent housing. These vouchers provide subsidies to rent privately owned housing units instead of limiting the subsidy to public housing.

Food Stamps: A Fixed Allotment Subsidy

Some subsidy programs do not distort prices. **Fixed allotment subsidies** give eligible recipients the right to consume a certain amount of a good or service each month either through direct allotment of the item or the issuance of vouchers that can be used only to buy a specific item. An example of a fixed allotment subsidy is the food stamp program.

The food stamp program grants low-income persons the right to purchase a certain amount of food per month through the issuance of special stamps. For most

---

[1]See Sar A. Levitan, *Programs in Aid of the Poor,* 5th ed. (Baltimore: Johns Hopkins University Press, 1985), 72.

INTERNATIONAL VIEW

FOOD SUBSIDIES IN LESS-DEVELOPED COUNTRIES

A common way of subsidizing the poor in less-developed nations is through food subsidies.[*] The governments of Brazil, China, Colombia, Egypt, Mexico, Morocco, Pakistan, Sudan, Thailand, and Tunisia subsidize food and place no restrictions on who can buy the subsidized food and how much can be bought at the subsidized prices. Government outlays to finance food subsidies range from less than 1 percent of total outlays to as much as 17 percent. Although the food subsidies provide benefits to all who consume food, they amount to a higher percentage of the income of the lowest income groups in these nations. The value of the food subsidy to the poorest fifth of households in Egypt in the early 1980s was estimated to be 8.7 percent of the income of the urban poor and 10.8 percent of the rural poor.[†] In Egypt most of the subsidy is given to bread and wheat flour sold through normal retail outlets. General food subsidies are often criticized because they provide benefit to the rich as well as the poor. In some nations, where rural consumers have little or no access to markets, the bulk of the subsidies accrue to the urban poor and barely reduce the poverty concentrated in rural areas.

To better target the poor, some nations subsidize only those foods that are mainly consumed by low-income groups. For example, Mexico subsidizes maize tortillas sold in markets. However, because rural consumers, who live far from organized markets, tend to make their own tortillas at home, this subsidy benefits the urban poor more than the rural poor.

In some nations households receive a limited amount of food at subsidized prices while food is generally sold in markets at prices determined by supply and demand. The food ration system allows all citizens to purchase a minimum amount of food at low prices while allowing those who wish to purchase more to do so on the open market at nonsubsidized prices. These schemes provide less benefit to upper-income groups than do general food subsidies.

Some nations, such as Sri Lanka, operate food stamp programs similar to those used in the United States. Households with low income are given food stamps to purchase both food and kerosene. In Sri Lanka, about 50 percent of the population benefits from these food stamps.

Finally, some governments sponsor specific food distribution schemes that distribute free or highly subsidized food through special government or health centers to groups that suffer from malnutrition. These programs are often designed to benefit children and pregnant women.

[*]See World Bank, *World Development Report 1990* (Oxford, England: Oxford University Press, 1990) 92–97.
[†]World Bank, 93.

---

recipients of food stamps in the United States, the stamps received are equivalent to a cash transfer. This is illustrated in Figure 7.7.

The person whose indifference curves are illustrated in Figure 7.7A has a current monthly income equal to $0I$. Given the price of food, the person is initially in equilibrium at point E_1, where she purchases Q_{F1} units of food per month and spends M_1 per month on other goods. Suppose that this person now becomes eligible for a monthly grant of food stamps that will allow her to purchase Q_F units of food each month.

The cash value of these stamps, given the current price of food, is F. This represents the amount of cash necessary to purchase Q_F units of food per month. For example, the maximum value of food stamps for a family of four in 1991 was $352 per month in 48 states and the District of Columbia. A monthly cash grant of F would

Figure 7.7 ✦ THE IMPACT OF AN IN-KIND TRANSFER: FOOD STAMPS

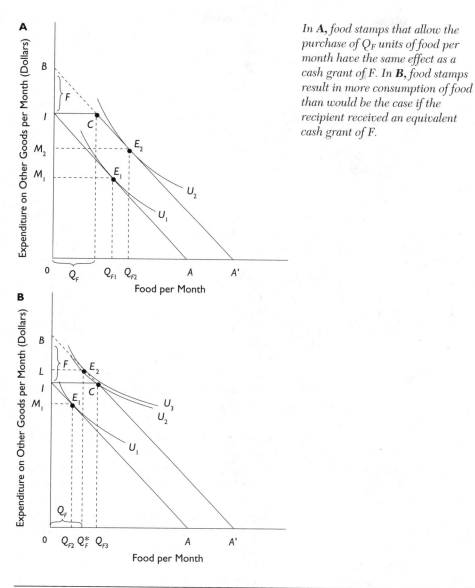

A

In **A,** *food stamps that allow the purchase of Q_F units of food per month have the same effect as a cash grant of F. In* **B,** *food stamps result in more consumption of food than would be the case if the recipient received an equivalent cash grant of F.*

allow the recipient to increase her purchase of other goods by *IB*. However, because the stamps can be used only to purchase food (and related items), the budget constraint, after the monthly food stamp grant, becomes *ICA'*. If instead, a monthly cash grant of *F* were given to the recipient, the budget line would be *BA'*. Under the food stamp grant, the market baskets of goods represented by the section *BC* on the budget line BA' cannot be purchased. This is because food stamps can be used to buy only food while cash can buy anything. With an equivalent cash grant of $300 per month, the person could purchase *all* the market baskets along the budget line BA'.

Suppose the person is in equilibrium at point E_2 after receiving the monthly grant of food stamps. At that point, she consumes Q_{F2} units of food each month and spends $0M_2$ on other goods. The effect of the grant in this case is to increase *both* the quantity of food consumed per month and monthly expenditure on other goods. In effect, the recipient spends the equivalent of F in stamps received per month on food, along with some of her own money. However, because the grant frees some of her own monthly income that would have been spent on food, she is able to increase her consumption of other goods as well. The equilibrium at E_2 in Figure 7.7A is exactly the same as that which would occur if the recipient were given a cash grant of F per month instead of the food stamps. The effects of the cash grant and the food stamp grant on consumption are identical in this case.

Figure 7.7B illustrates the case of a person who, under a cash grant, would be in equilibrium along the line segment BC. This person is initially in equilibrium at point E_1. A cash grant of F would move him to point E_2, which, in Figure 7.7B, falls on BC and he would consume Q_F° units of food per month. If, instead, he were given a monthly amount of food stamps valued at F per month, he would be forced to point C. At that point, his maximum possible monthly utility is U_2, which is less than U_3, obtained with the equivalent cash grant. This is because he cannot use the stamps to purchase combinations of food and other goods on the line segment BC. At C, he consumes Q_{F3} units of food per month, which is greater than Q_F° units that he would choose to consume each month if he were given a cash grant. For this person, the food stamps do increase food consumption above the monthly level he would choose with an equivalent cash grant. He is also forced to spend F per month on food. He would spend only BL on food (and $0L$ on other goods) with the cash grant. However, this person is worse off with food stamps than he would be with an equivalent monthly cash grant.

It is commonly believed that the cash value of food stamps is so low that recipients would be likely to spend at least that much on food, even if they were given cash. For example, the maximum cash value of food stamps for a family of four amounted to less than $1 per person per meal in 1987 dollars. Given that most recipients are likely to spend more than this amount per person per meal, food stamps can be regarded as equivalent to a cash grant. Contrary to common belief, this program is unlikely to increase the consumption of food over the levels that would prevail if recipients were given the cash value of the stamps.

Does the food stamp program contribute to an increase in the price of food? Keep in mind that although the program provides more than $15 billion for food expenditures (based on 1990 expenditures), it does not increase actual expenditures by that amount because recipients normally would spend some of their own cash on food, even in the absence of the program. Part of the food stamp grants increases expenditures on other goods. Total expenditures on food in the United States exceed $400 billion per year. It is therefore unlikely that the injection of only a portion of the $15 billion from the food stamp program into the food market is likely to have a major effect on the price of food.

THE IMPACT OF GOVERNMENT ASSISTANCE PROGRAMS FOR THE POOR ON THE WORK INCENTIVE OF RECIPIENTS

A program that grants cash or in-kind subsidies on the basis of a means test is likely to distort the recipient's choice of work or leisure. The subsidies granted to the poor in the United States are likely to diminish their willingness to work. Potential and existing recipients possibly will refuse offers of employment in order to retain their welfare benefits. In addition, most transfer programs available to the poor reduce the benefits paid as a person's earned income increases. In effect, the reduction in benefits that occur as earnings increase amounts to a tax on the earnings of recipients. This tax further affects work incentives. Of course, if an individual earns enough income, eligibility for transfers approved through the means test will be terminated under this system.

Welfare benefits in cash or in kind assure the recipient of a minimum level of real income independent of work. The more generous the grant, the greater the disincentive to work. In other words, a transfer results in an income effect that is unfavorable to work. This is illustrated in Figure 7.8. The indifference curves drawn illustrate a person's preference for leisure or income. Leisure per day is plotted on the horizontal axis. The maximum hours of leisure that a person can enjoy per day is twenty-four. Leisure is defined as engaging in any activity other than work for pay.

The line AB shows a person's opportunity for giving up leisure for income by working, assuming that the only way the person can obtain income (or goods and services) is by working for an employer. In other words, the line AB assumes that nonwage income is zero. If the person can work at a wage of w per hour, the equation of the budget line is

$$I = w(24 - L), \tag{7.1}$$

where I is income per day and L is leisure hours per day. If $L = 24$, along AB, the person's income will be zero.

The slope of the budget line is $-w$. The person whose indifference curves are illustrated is in equilibrium at point E_1, where he enjoys L_1 hours of leisure per day. He therefore works $(24 - L_1)$ hours each day.

If the person were to receive a transfer payment of $BD = AC$ per day, his income per day would increase by that amount. Even if he took twenty-four hours per day in leisure, he would enjoy positive income. The increase in income leads to an

Figure 7.8 ✦ THE INCOME EFFECT OF A TRANSFER

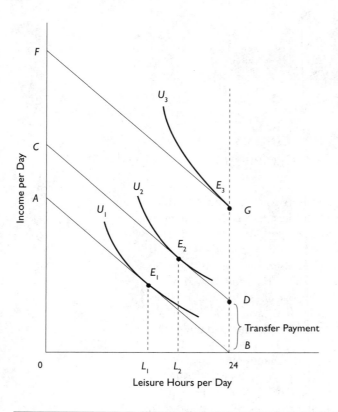

If leisure is a normal good, an increase in income caused by a transfer increases leisure hours per day. The income effect of the transfer therefore is unfavorable to work. A transfer of BG dollars per day will reduce hours worked per day to zero for the person whose indifference curves are illustrated.

increase in the consumption of all normal goods. If leisure is a normal good, the person will increase the amount consumed. In Figure 7.8, the transfer payment to the person shifts the budget line upward to CD and results in a new equilibrium at E_2, where the individual increases hours of leisure per day by L_1L_2. He therefore decreases hours worked per day. If the person were eligible for a transfer of ($BG = AF$) per day, he would be in equilibrium at point E_3, where he would consume twenty-four hours per day in leisure, therefore not working at all. Eligibility for a subsidy of that amount would cause the person to drop out of the labor force!

Another work disincentive effect results from the way in which benefits are reduced as the recipient earns more income. This is illustrated in Figure 7.9. Given the wage rate that a person can earn, the amount of the transfer for which the person is eligible varies with hours worked per day (or any other time period). In Figure 7.9, the maximum subsidy per day a person is eligible for is BD. This is granted if the person does not work at all. As the person works, the subsidy steadily declines. At point C, where the person works $(24 - L°)$ hours per day, the daily transfer would be zero.

Figure 7.9 ✦ A TRANSFER THAT DECLINES WITH EARNED INCOME

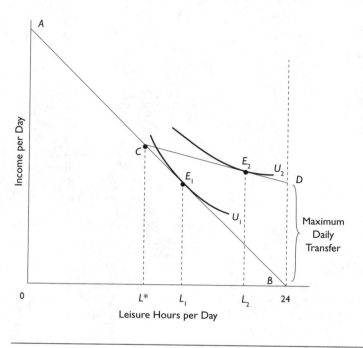

Transfer income per day declines as the recipient's earned income per day increases. At point C, the subsidy per day would be zero. The subsidy reduces the net wage if the person takes more than $L°$ hours of leisure per day. This transfer reduces the incentive to work because it generates both income and substitution effects unfavorable to work.

This subsidy program shifts the person's budget line up to *CD* and *decreases its slope* at points corresponding to more than $L°$ hours of leisure per day. This means that the net effect of the program is to *reduce* the person's real wage rate if he works less than $(24 - L°)$ hours per day. In Figure 7.9, the person is in equilibrium at point E_2 after the subsidy. The subsidy program reduces hours worked per day from $(24 - L_1)$ to $(24 - L_2)$. This type of subsidy has a *substitution effect* in addition to an income effect for persons who work less than $(24 - L°)$ hours per day. It decreases work incentive by causing the wage a recipient can earn to decline, because working increases earned income but *decreases* transfer income. As a result, the recipient has an incentive to substitute leisure for work. In effect, the subsidy decreases the opportunity cost of an hour of leisure by reducing the wage when more than $L°$ hours per day are enjoyed. In this case, both the income and the substitution effects of the transfer act to decrease hours worked per day.

When AFDC recipients work, their transfer payments are reduced by 67 cents for each dollar of earnings for a period of four months after the recipient begins working. However, during the first four months various adjustments for such expenses as child care result in an effective reduction in AFDC benefits of 50 cents or less for each dollar of earnings.

After four months of working, AFDC benefits are reduced by $1 for each dollar of earning, which subjects workers to a nominal 100 percent tax rate on their earnings!

PUBLIC POLICY PERSPECTIVE

Work and Welfare Benefits: The Bitter Trap

It is often very difficult for the poor on welfare to better themselves by working because of the way in which government assistance is reduced with earnings. A simple example based on a typical case illustrates the trap faced by the poor and demonstrates the work disincentive effects of the U.S. welfare system. A female-headed family with two children in the state of Pennsylvania received a monthly AFDC payment of $421 per month in 1991 if the mother had no earnings. This household therefore received annual AFDC cash benefits of $5,052 if the mother did not work at all. In addition, this family is eligible for food stamps with a market value of $2,166 per year in 1991 if earnings for the year are zero. Finally, Medicaid benefits to the family are estimated to be worth about $2,300 at market value in 1991. The $2,300 value is an estimate of the price the family would have to pay for a health insurance policy similar to Medicaid. This gave the family annual disposable income and in-kind transfers equal in value to $9,518 in the year 1991 when the mother had no earnings.° This is shown in the last column of the first line of the accompanying table.

If the female head of the family begins to work, her AFDC payments will decline. Most states will allow welfare recipients to earn a standard allowance of $120 per month ($1,440 per year) before they start reducing welfare benefits during their first year of work.† Allowances are also made for child care costs equal to 20 percent of earnings up to a maximum of $350 per year for two children. Assuming that the mother incurs maximum permissible child care costs, she can earn up to $1,790 per year before her welfare benefits will be reduced. After earnings increase above that level, AFDC payments will decline by approximately 67 cents for each dollar earned during the first four months for which the welfare recipient is employed. In addition, the worker will pay Social Security tax on her wages.

After the welfare recipient has been employed for four consecutive months, AFDC benefits are reduced

by $1 for each $1 of earnings after the standard $120 allowance and allowances for child care expenses. Even if the worker quits her job, she will be subject to the $1 reduction in AFDC for each $1 in earnings if she becomes employed again during the next twelve months. By working, the welfare recipient also incurs expenses for commuting, child care, clothes, and other work expenses that she would not have if she were not employed. The table subtracts an estimate of such work expenses from earnings when calculating income available for spending (disposable income).

There is, however, some good news for the worker. She will be eligible for the *earned income tax credit (EITC)* as she works. These payments are phased in as the worker starts earning income. The benefit of the program begins to be phased out after earnings increase over a certain level. The table shows that the sum of the worker's disposable income and welfare benefits change as her annual earnings increase from zero to $10,000 per year. The calculations in the table assume that when she does work she has been on the job for more than four consecutive months so that she is no longer eligible for the 67 percent phaseout rate of AFDC benefits.

After the worker earns slightly more than $7,000 per year, her AFDC benefits drop to zero. After earnings exceed $10,000 per year, most workers lose their Medicaid coverage! This results in a further reduction in transfers worth about $2,300 per year. Her food stamp benefits also will vary as income increases. With $10,000 annual earnings she will receive only $1,881 in food stamps and will no longer be eligible for Medicaid. She will pay $765 per year in Social Security tax. After getting and holding a job that pays $10,000 per year, the worker has lost her Medicaid benefits and will no longer have health insurance unless it is provided by her employer. The total of her earnings and food stamps after taxes will be equal to $9,141 as shown in the last column of the table, which is $377 less than the sum of her AFDC and in-kind benefits when she did not work at all! And it could be even worse. She might lose government housing subsidies if the rent she pays

---

°Pennsylvania pays AFDC benefits slightly above the national average. The value of the Medicaid coverage is a rough estimate.
†This amount falls to $90 per month after one year on the job.

EARNINGS, TRANSFERS, AND DISPOSABLE INCOME FOR A TYPICAL AFDC MOTHER WITH TWO CHILDREN, 1991[a]

| | | | | | TAXES | | | | DISPOSABLE INCOME, |
EARNINGS	EITC	AFDC[b]	FOOD STAMPS	MEDICAID[c]	SOCIAL SECURITY	FEDERAL INCOME	STATE INCOME	WORK EXPENSES[d]	FOOD STAMPS, AND VALUE OF MEDICAID
$ 0	$ 0	$ 5,052	$ 2,166	$ 2,300	$ 0	$ 0	$ 0	$ 0	$ 9,518
2,000	346	4,892	1,854	2,300	153	0	0	600	10,639
4,000	692	3,299	1,974	2,300	306	0	0	1,200	10,752
5,000	865	2,492	2,030	2,300	383	0	0	1,500	10,808
6,000	1,038	1,692	2,094	2,300	459	0	0	1,800	10,865
7,000	1,211	892	2,154	2,300	536	0	0	2,100	10,921
8,000	1,235	0	2,254	2,300	612	0	0	2,400	10,764
9,000	1,235	0	2,061	2,300	689	0	38	2,700	11,169
10,000	1,235	0	1,881	0	765	0	210	3,000	9,141

[a]The family resides in Pennsylvania. Calculations assume that, when working, the mother has been on the job for at least four consecutive months. Phaseout of benefits is based on law prevailing January 1991.

[b]Assumes the $120 monthly standard allowance and child care costs equal to 20 percent of earnings up to a maximum of $320 for two children.

[c]Estimate for 1991. The family qualifies for Medicaid for nine additional months after it is removed from the AFDC rolls under 1984 federal law, until earnings exceed $9,000 per year.

[d]Assumed to equal 10 percent of earnings up to a maximum of $100 monthly, plus child care costs equal to 20 percent of earnings up to the maximum allowed by AFDC, and food stamps ($350 for two children).

Source: Committee on Ways and Means, U.S. House of Representatives, *Overview of Entitlement Programs with the Jurisdiction of the Committee on Ways and Means*, 1991 Edition.

is tied to her income. Also, the earned income tax credit will begin to phase out as annual earnings increase greater than $10,000.

The welfare system therefore severely dampens the incentive to work by reducing the net gain from work. As this typical case shows, welfare recipients can actually decrease their material well-being by taking a full-time job. This is a bitter trap for the poor.

Concern about this welfare trap led to passage of the *Family Support Act of 1988*. This act requires states to set up programs of training, education, and job preparation programs for the welfare mother whose youngest child has reached three years of age, provided that the state has day care facilities for the children. These programs are funded in part by the federal government. States will be required to have at least 20 percent of eligible welfare parents enrolled in such train-ing programs by 1995. The act also toughens child support laws to make absent fathers provide income for their children. The child support program would automatically deduct such payments from the absent fathers' paychecks. The act also requires states to provide Medicaid and child care assistance for one year after a welfare family leaves the welfare rolls. States, however, have the option of charging for a portion of these benefits under the new law six months after the family leaves the welfare rolls. These provisions are designed to reduce the grips of the welfare trap and provide the poor with more work incentives. These innovations will not come without cost. Federal outlays to finance training programs alone were expected to reach $1.3 billion per year by 1995. Also, other costs will be incurred to fund extended Medicaid payments and child care for those who succeed in breaking out of the welfare trap.

However because of liberal deductions for child care and other expenses of working, the tax rate on earnings by AFDC recipients is effectively 70 percent, which is still a very high tax rate on earnings, equal to nearly twice the top tax rate for the federal income tax.[2] For example, suppose a recipient is eligible for a $300 per month transfer if she has no earnings at all. Suppose her transfer is reduced by 70 cents for each dollar of earnings. At any level of earned income, I_E, her monthly transfer, T, can be calculated from the following formula:

$$T = \$300 - .7I_E. \tag{7.2}$$

For example, if she earns $300 per month, her transfer would be reduced from $300 to $90 per month. The transfer eventually would be terminated if she earns sufficient income. To calculate this level of income, set T equal to zero in the preceding equation and solve for I_E. In this case, I_E is equal to $428.57 per month. This would correspond to the level of earned income at point C in Figure 7.8.

Many low-income persons receive benefits under more than one program and have their transfers reduced under all programs as their earnings increase. In some cases, sufficient increase in income causes tenants to be evicted from subsidized public housing.

The fact that most recipients of welfare in the United States are out of the labor force acts to minimize these unfavorable effects on work incentive. The cash benefits of many programs are often at values low enough to minimize their income effects. Most states, for example, pay AFDC benefits that are insufficient to raise a recipient's income above the poverty level, even at the maximum monthly amounts. Evidence does indicate that recipients are more likely to work in states where welfare benefits are minimal than in states where benefits are more generous.[3] In some states, work incentive programs and other motivational plans exist to encourage welfare recipients to work.

Work and Welfare: Empirical Evidence

Numerous empirical studies and even some experiments have attempted to measure the impact of welfare programs on the work incentive of recipients. One research study has concluded that, in the absence of AFDC, women whose families received these benefits would have worked between ten and fifteen hours per week more than they actually did in the early 1980s.[4] However, because most welfare recipients are unskilled and earn very low wages, this extra work would have increased their disposable income by a mere $1,500 per year—hardly enough to bring them out of poverty and certainly not enough to take the place of the AFDC stipends. Most of the exper-

---

[2]See Gary Burtless, "The Economist's Lament: Public Assistance in America," *Journal of Economic Perspectives* 4, 1 (Winter 1990): 64.

[3]Frederick Doolittle, Frank Levy, and Michael Wiseman, "The Mirage of Welfare Reform," *The Public Interest* 47 (Spring 1977): 62–87.

[4]Robert A. Moffitt, "Incentive Effects of the U.S. Welfare System: A Review," *Journal of Economic Literature,* 30, 1 (March 1992): 1–61.

imental evidence also suggests that means-tested transfers have an effect on work effort but that the effect on low-income men and women with dependent children is small.[5] A 10-percent increase in cash transfers will reduce hours worked by less than 2 percent according to estimates based on these experiments. These findings suggest that even if welfare benefits were to be reduced substantially or if the rate at which they are phased out with earnings is reduced, work would increase but the increase would not be sufficient to bring the workers out of poverty.

PROGRAMS WITH NO STATUS TESTS: THE NEGATIVE INCOME TAX AND SUBSIDIES TO THE WORKING POOR

Critics of the U.S. system of assistance to the poor argue that the status tests are demeaning to the recipients. They also argue that the "patchwork quilt" overlap of programs lacks consistent goals. Some have proposed scrapping the system in favor of a **negative income tax (NIT)**.[6] This would be a cash assistance program that would provide a minimum income guarantee for all Americans. All those with income below the floor would receive cash subsidies from the government while those above the floor would pay taxes. A negative income tax plan would integrate the system of government assistance with the federal income tax.

How a Negative Income Tax Would Work

The first step in developing a negative income tax plan is to decide on the income guarantee. This represents a floor on family income. A person with zero earnings would be guaranteed the standard of living represented by the floor. Suppose the floor is set at I_G = $5,000 per year for a family of four. This is about half the poverty income level for such a family. The floor, of course, would vary with household size.

The second step in the plan is to determine the rate, t_N, at which the transfer received by those with zero income would be phased out as recipient's annual earnings increase. Assuming t_N = 50 percent, for every $2 earned the transfer to eligible recipients from the government will be reduced by $1.

The annual transfer, T, received by any eligible family can be expressed as

$$T = I_G - t_N I_E, \tag{7.3}$$

where I_E is earned income per year. For example, if I_E is zero, the family will receive a transfer of I_G = $5,000. As the family's annual earnings increase, the annual transfer will be reduced accordingly. Table 7.3 shows how the transfer will decline with income.

---

[5]Ibid.

[6]See Milton Friedman, "The Case for the Negative Income Tax," in *Republican Papers*, Melvin R. Laird, ed. (New York: Praeger, 1968).

Table 7.3 ✦ NEGATIVE INCOME TAX: DISPOSABLE INCOME OF RECIPIENTS IN RELATION TO EARNED INCOME

EARNED INCOME (I_E)	TRANSFER FROM GOVERNMENT $(T = I_G - t_N I_E)$	DISPOSABLE INCOME $(I_D = I_E + T)$
$ 0	$5,000	$ 5,000
1,000	$5,000 - [0.5 \ (1,000)] = 4,500$	5,500
2,000	$5,000 - [0.5 \ (2,000)] = 4,000$	6,000
3,000	$5,000 - [0.5 \ (3,000)] = 3,500$	6,500
4,000	$5,000 - [0.5 \ (4,000)] = 3,000$	7,000
5,000	$5,000 - [0.5 \ (5,000)] = 2,500$	7,500
6,000	$5,000 - [0.5 \ (6,000)] = 2,000$	8,000
7,000	$5,000 - [0.5 \ (7,000)] = 1,500$	8,500
8,000	$5,000 - [0.5 \ (8,000)] = 1,000$	9,000
9,000	$5,000 - [0.5 \ (9,000)] = 500$	9,500
10,000	$5,000 - [0.5 \ (10,000)] = 0$	10,000[a]

[a]Break-even income.

If the family earns enough, the transfer will fall to zero, and the family will begin to pay taxes instead of receiving transfers (which are negative taxes) from the government. The level of income at which this occurs is called the *break-even income* and can be determined from Equation 7.3 by setting $T = 0$ and solving for I_E. This gives the annual earned income, designated as I_B, at which $T = 0$:

$$0 = I_G - t_N I_B \tag{7.4}$$

$$I_B = I_G/t_N. \tag{7.5}$$

I_B is the annual income at which the taxpayer is neither paying taxes nor receiving transfers. As shown in Table 7.3, when $I_G = $5,000$ and $t_N = 50$ percent, $I_B = $10,000$.

The disposable income, I_D, of a family receiving a transfer is obtained by adding earned income and the transfer, as shown in Table 7.3. For example, the disposable income of a family of four with $2,000 earned income is $2,000 + [$5,000 − .5($2,000)] = $6,000$. A family of four with income *greater than* the break-even level of $10,000 per year would pay positive taxes. Its disposable income would be earned income *minus* taxes paid.

A crucial step in implementing a negative income tax comes after a family reaches the break-even level of annual income. If income is taxed at a flat rate of, say, 20 percent, after the break-even point, the effective tax rate paid by taxpayers would actually be lower than that paid by transfer recipients whose income declines by 50 percent with earnings! Figure 7.10 shows that disposable income would vary with earned income assuming that t_N is 50 percent and that income above the break-even level is taxed at 20 percent.

Figure 7.10 ✦ A NEGATIVE INCOME TAX PLAN

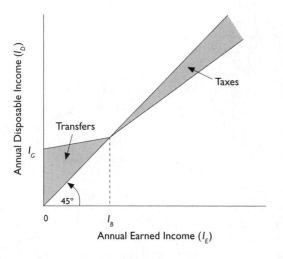

All persons with less than the break-even level of income, I_B, would receive transfers. The annual disposable income of these persons therefore would exceed their annual earned income. All persons with annual earned income greater than I_B will pay taxes. Disposable income for these persons therefore will fall short of earned income.

A problem with a national income guarantee plan such as NIT is that it can end up being very expensive if the income guarantee is set at any reasonable level, because the plan requires no status test. For example, suppose the income guarantee is set at the level of about $10,000 for a family of four and at correspondingly lower levels for smaller families and higher levels for larger families. With t_N equal to 50 percent, all families of four with income of less than $20,000 per year would be transfer recipients. This could be a substantial portion of the population! Needless to say, the taxes on the remaining portion of the population would have to be quite high to finance the transfers and other government services. If a lower t_N is used to encourage work effort, it would be even worse. If $t_N = 0.2$, and $I_G = $10,000$, the break-even income level would be $I_B = $50,000$. Therefore, all families of four with income of less than $50,000 per year would receive transfers! As this is likely to include more than 80 percent of American families, who would pay the taxes?

Wage Rate Subsidies

Concern about the work disincentive effects of existing transfer programs for the poor has led to proposals for **wage rate subsidies (WRS)** as a means of both supporting the incomes of the working poor and providing them with incentives to work. Under a WRS plan, minimum-wage legislation would be repealed and workers would be induced to search for jobs at the market-determined wage. Those working at the lowest wages would receive subsidies from the government to raise their incomes to some minimum level. The subsidy would vary with hours worked and would be phased out as a worker's hourly wage rate increased.

Table 7.4 ♦ WAGE RATE SUBSIDIES

WAGE PAID	SUBSIDY (PER HOUR)	TOTAL WAGE RECEIVED
$2.00	$1.50	$3.50
2.50	1.25	3.75
3.00	1.00	4.00
3.50	.75	4.25
4.00	.50	4.50
4.50	.25	4.75
5.00	.00	5.00

For example, if a worker earned $2.00 per hour, the government might subsidize the hourly wage at the rate of $1.50, bringing up actual take-home wages per hour to $3.50 for the worker. Employers would still pay $2.00 per hour. The lower wages made possible by the plan would provide more employment opportunities but maintain the worker's income and incentive to work. Table 7.4 shows how the wage rate subsidy might vary with hourly wages. For a worker earning wages of, say, $3.00 per hour, the subsidy might be reduced to only $1.00 per hour, giving the worker a net wage of $4.00 per hour. The subsidy might decrease with an increase in wages until it fell to zero at, say, wages of $5.00 per hour.

The subsidization schedule would have to be designed to provide incentive for workers to move on to higher-paying jobs. The subsidy also would have to be phased out at some reasonable level of wages to keep the costs of the plan down.

An obvious advantage of WRS is that it directly increases wages and therefore encourages low-income persons to seek and find work. It also encourages employers to hire low-income workers, assuming that wages under the plan would be below those that would prevail under minimum-wage laws.

The Earned Income Tax Credit

The Earned Income Tax Credit (EITC) has emerged in the United States as a form of wage subsidy that is a major means of income support for the working poor. The EITC has only minimal status tests. Unlike AFDC and SSI, which require that the recipient have some characteristics that prevent them from participating in the labor market to be eligible for transfers, the EITC is available *only* to those who work.

The EITC is actually part of the Federal Income Tax code. It was first introduced in 1975 as a modest program to stimulate consumption when the U.S. was in recession. The program provides a *negative tax payment* (actually a transfer of income) to low-income earners. Notice that this is not a tax refund—it is a payment from the federal government to workers who file income tax returns. Persons eligible for the EITC file a regular income tax return but instead of paying taxes or receiving a full or partial refund on taxes already paid they actually get a payment from the federal government! The EITC works to reduce some of the work disincentive effects of the tax system on AFDC and other welfare recipients who take a job, and it also reduces the burden of Social Security taxes that all workers must pay when they have earnings.

The EITC was expanded as an income support program for the working poor in 1979 and 1986. Legislation enacted in 1990 raised the maximum credit to $1,998 per year in 1994 and simplified eligibility for the EITC. The amount a household can receive under the EITC is dependent on its income, the number of children in the household, payments the family makes for health insurance, whether a new child was born during the year, and whether the family receives other tax benefits. The benefits under the program are phased out as a family's income rises over a certain threshold amount, like the negative income tax plan discussed in the preceding sections.

The EITC was greatly expanded as a result of legislation enacted in 1993.[7] In 1996, when the new provisions enacted in 1993 become fully effective, the EITC for a family with two children will be 40 percent of the first $8,425 of income. The maximum credit therefore will be $3,370 per year (measured in 1994 dollars—actual amounts will be indexed for inflation to keep the real amount constant). The maximum payment is paid until income reaches $11,000 annually. After income increases greater than $11,000 per year, the tax credit is reduced by 21.06 percent of income (see Table 7.5). The break-even level of income under the EITC for a family with two children is therefore $27,000.

The EITC was estimated to benefit 15 million families in 1994. It typically can increase the money income of a family with one earner working full time at the minimum wage to a level above the poverty threshold. Prior to 1993 only workers with children were eligible for credits. The new legislation makes single workers also eligible

---

[7] For analysis of the changes see Alicia H. Munnell, "The Coming of Age of the Earned Income Tax Credit," National Tax Association, *NTA Forum*, Winter 1994.

Table 7.5 ✦ THE EARNED INCOME TAX CREDIT: TWO-EARNER, TWO-CHILD FAMILY IN 1996 (ALL AMOUNTS IN 1994 DOLLARS)

EARNINGS	EITC
0	0
2,000	800
4,000	1,600
6,000	2,400
8,000	3,200
10,000	3,370
15,000	2,654
20,000	1,601
27,000	0

for the EITC. However, payments to single workers is limited to a portion of the workers Social Security tax up to a maximum of a $306 credit per year. An estimated 5 million individuals will benefit from this new extension of the EITC.

The changes in the EITC introduced in 1993 represent an increase in the cash support for the poor and an increased federal commitment to support the working poor. Payments under the EITC are entirely the responsibility of the federal government, but AFDC payments are financed by federal, state, and local governments.

EITC Versus a Negative Income Tax

A common criticism against the negative income tax as originally proposed by Friedman was that it would discourage work effort. The EITC is more favorable to work effort than the NIT because it is available only to those who work. In that sense it is more like a wage rate subsidy than an NIT. In effect, the EITC turns a $4.25 per hour minimum wage into a $6.00 hourly wage (a 40-percent increase) for workers eligible for the full credit. The EITC therefore can also be viewed as a substitute for an increase in the minimum wage. Also, because the credits are a percentage of income earned, tax rates at low levels of income are actually negative, which encourages recipients to work more. Notice that for the program the tax rate is *minus* 40 percent of earnings up to $11,000 for a two-parent, two-child family.

The EITC differs from the NIT plans already discussed in that the basic income guarantee is a percent of earnings and increases as earnings increase until it reaches the maximum amount allowed. Also the negative tax rate for phasing out benefits when income is greater than $11,000 is only slightly more than 20 percent. This low tax rate is much more conducive to encouraging work than is the case for a system with a 50-percent negative tax rate. However, the break-even level of income is much higher, which adds to the cost of the plan. Under existing legislation, all two-parent, two-child families with income less than $27,000 per year will receive EITC *payments* from the federal government rather than paying taxes! Also, recipients with incomes greater than $20,000 per year are subject to both payroll and income taxes that increase the effective taxes they pay on additional earnings to as much as 50 percent.

When combined with other programs such as food stamps and Medicaid, which, in effect, provide an income guarantee for those with zero income who are eligible for these programs, the EITC represents a way of increasing support for the poor in the United States while increasing their incentive to work.

C H E C K P O I N T

1. What is the income effect of a transfer on incentives to work?
2. How does the AFDC program diminish the incentive to work in the United States?
3. How would a negative income tax program with no status test differ from the current U.S. system of public assistance to the poor? What is the advantage of a wage rate subsidy plan to assist the poor?

PROGRAMS TO AID THE POOR AND THE DISTRIBUTION OF MONEY INCOME IN THE UNITED STATES

How effective have U.S. transfers to the poor been in changing the distribution of income in the United States? Table 7.6 shows the distribution of annual money income before taxes for selected years from 1947 to 1991. The money income of each one-fifth of households includes cash transfers. The table provides some indication of the degree of inequality in the distribution of money income among these households. If the distribution of income were perfectly equal, each one-fifth of households would receive one-fifth, or 20 percent, of total aggregate annual money income. The data in the table indicate significant inequality of income in the United States.

The 1970s were marked by a sharp increase in the importance of transfers and aid to the poor, as associated with President Johnson's "war on poverty." The data, however, seem to indicate that during the 1970s, these programs had little impact on the actual distribution of money income. These data do not include the impact of the many income in-kind transfers for which the poor are eligible. Adjustment can be made for in-kind transfers. If assumed that each dollar's worth of in-kind benefits is worth a dollar to the recipient, inclusion of in-kind transfers would increase the share of income of the lowest group by about 2 percent.[8] This indicates that in-kind

---

[8]Alan Blinder, "The Level and Distribution of Economic Well Being," in *The American Economy in Transition*, ed. Martin Feldstein (Chicago: University of Chicago Press, 1980).

Table 7.6 ✦ PERCENT SHARE OF AGGREGATE MONEY INCOME OF EACH ONE-FIFTH OF HOUSEHOLDS INCLUDING CASH TRANSFERS, SELECTED YEARS, 1947–1991

YEAR	LOWEST FIFTH	SECOND FIFTH	THIRD FIFTH	FOURTH FIFTH	HIGHEST FIFTH
1947	5.0	11.9	17.0	23.1	43.0
1967	4.0	11.1	17.6	24.6	42.7
1969	4.1	11.0	17.5	24.5	42.8
1971	4.1	10.7	17.3	24.5	43.4
1973	4.3	10.6	17.2	24.4	43.5
1974	4.4	10.6	17.0	24.5	43.5
1976	4.3	10.4	17.0	24.7	43.6
1978	4.3	10.3	16.9	24.7	43.9
1983	3.9	10.0	16.5	24.6	45.0
1987	4.6	10.8	16.9	24.1	43.7
1989	4.6	10.6	16.5	23.7	44.6
1991	4.5	10.7	16.6	24.1	44.2

Source: U.S. Department of Commerce, Bureau of the Census, *Money Income of Households in the United States*, Current Population Reports, Series P-60, various years.

transfers have reduced income inequality. Nonetheless, the shares going to each one-fifth of these households ranked according to their incomes remained remarkably stable during the period shown in the table. Despite the sharp increases in spending to aid the poor, their income shares have not substantially increased.

One explanation for this could be that the growth in transfers has been accompanied by an increase in the number of poor persons.

Summary

Many government subsidies benefit low-income persons. Eligibility for these subsidies is determined by a status test and a means test. The status test determines whether a person belongs to one of the demographic groups eligible for government assistance. The means test determines whether the person's income and wealth are low enough for eligibility for government assistance.

In the United States, both in-kind and cash subsidies are used to assist the poor. In-kind subsidies include transfers in the form of food, medical services, and housing to the poor. They account for about 75 percent of federal assistance to the poor in the United States. In some cases, in-kind subsidies can actually decrease consumption of the subsidized goods. In most cases, in-kind subsidies free enough cash for other uses by recipients that they can be regarded as equivalent to cash transfers.

Most transfers reduce the incentive to work. In evaluating transfer programs, the desire to obtain changes in the distribution of income favored by some voters must be weighed against the decreases in efficiency and work incentive resulting from the subsidy programs.

A Forward Look

The following chapter looks at social insurance programs. These programs transfer income to persons who need not pass a means test. The major social insurance program in the United States is the Social Security pension system, and its functions are closely analyzed.

Important Concepts

Poverty Threshold
Status Test
Means Test
Entitlement Programs
Aid to Families with Dependent Children (AFDC)
Supplemental Security Income (SSI)
In-Kind Benefits
Earned Income Tax Credit (EITC)
Medicaid
Food Stamp Program
Housing Assistance Programs
Price-Distorting Subsidies
Deadweight Loss of a Subsidy
Excess Burden of a Subsidy
Fixed Allotment Subsidies
Negative Income Tax (NIT)
Wage Rate Subsidies (WRS)

Questions for Review

1. List the major programs of government assistance to the poor in the United States. What percentage of the population is poor? Do all the poor qualify for government assistance programs?

2. What is a means test? How does it differ from a status test? What are entitlement programs, and how are the expenditures under these programs related to means tests and status tests?

3. Suppose the government gave away heating oil free to eligible low-income citizens. Use a graphic analysis to show the excess burden in the market for this good. Under what circumstances will the subsidy cause the market price of fuel oil to increase?

4. What are the possible collective benefits of government assistance to the poor? Why are in-kind benefits to the poor more prevalent than cash benefits?

5. Explain why, in many cases, in-kind transfers to the poor are likely to be equivalent to cash transfers in their effects.

6. Suppose a person receives stamps from the government that allow the purchase of $300 worth of clothes per year. These stamps cannot be used to buy any other items. Show how these stamps affect the person's budget line. Show the various market baskets of goods that could be purchased with a $300 cash grant that *cannot* be purchased with the stamps.

7. Explain how cash and in-kind transfer programs can reduce the incentive to work by recipients.

8. Suppose a person will receive $50 per day as a transfer if he does not work at all. This transfer is reduced by 60 cents for each $1 of earned income. How much daily earned income will reduce the transfer to zero?

9. Has poverty in the United States been eliminated as a result of transfers to the poor? What are some of the problems involved in measuring poverty?

10. Explain why the negative income tax plan is likely to be more expensive than the current system of assistance to the poor. What are the advantages of wage rate subsidies?

Problems

1. Suppose bread is subsidized in a small Caribbean nation with a high percentage of citizens who live in poverty. The subsidy is paid to suppliers of bread by the government in the amount of 50 pesos per loaf. In the absence of the subsidy the price of bread would be 100 pesos per loaf. Assuming that the supply of bread is perfectly elastic at the 100 peso price, show the effect of the subsidy on the market equilibrium price of bread. Assuming no externalities, show that the subsidy will result in more than the efficient amount of bread being produced. Show the excess burden of the subsidy on your graph. Explain why the subsidy will provide benefits to the nonpoor as well as the poor.

2. Suppose low-income people are given vouchers worth $200 per month that they can use only to pay rent on housing. Use indifference curve analysis to show how the person could be made as well off with a $200 cash transfer. Would the consumer's choice of the amount of housing to rent be any different if he receives cash instead of housing vouchers? Use indifference curve analysis to show under what circumstance the $200 per month housing vouchers would cause the recipient to increase the amount of housing rented (measured in square feet) compared to what would be rented if the recipient received $200 in cash each month in lieu of the housing vouchers. Would this recipient be as well off under the housing voucher scheme as she would be with a cash transfer of equal value?

3. An AFDC family consisting of a mother and three children currently receives cash benefits that average $12 per day. The mother of this family is allowed to earn an average of $4 per day before her AFDC benefits begin to decline. After that, for each dollar earned, AFDC cash benefits decline by 67 cents for each dollar earned. Plot the recipient's money income–leisure trade-off (budget) line under these circumstances. Assume that she can find work at $4 per hour. How many hours will she have to work per day before her AFDC benefits are eliminated? Assuming that her indifference curves for work and leisure are convex, show her equilibrium allocation of time between work and leisure per day. Show that it is possible to have *more* than one most-preferred outcome.

4. A proposal for a negative income tax is designed to provide an income guarantee for each person, irrespective of his age or status, of $3,000 per year. Thus, a family of four would have an income guarantee of $12,000 per year. The transfers under the program will be phased out at a rate of 25 percent as earned income increases. Calculate the break-even level of income for a family of four. If all families above the break-even level of income pay a flat-rate 25 percent tax on their earnings, plot disposable income as a function of earned income. Comment on the costs of this plan.

Suggestions for Further Reading

Burtless, Gary. "The Economist's Lament: Public Assistance in America." *Journal of Economic Perspectives* 4, 1 (Winter 1990). An excellent review of how cash transfer programs to aid the poor work in the United States and an analysis of their economic effects.

Committee on Ways and Means, U.S. House of Representatives. *Overview of Entitlement Programs.* Washington, D.C.: U.S. Government Printing Office, published annually. This book contains everything you could want to know about the way federal assistance programs to the poor operate and lots of useful data on poverty and income in the United States.

Levitan, Sar A. *Programs in Aid of the Poor,* 6th ed. Baltimore: Johns Hopkins University Press, 1990. A compendium and analysis of all major government assistance programs for the poor in the United States.

Moffitt, Robert A., "Incentive Effects of the U.S. Welfare System: A Review," *Journal of Economic Literature,* 30, 1 (March 1992): pp. 1–61. A review of economic analysis of the effects of the U.S. system of support to the poor on their incentives to work and engage in other economic activities.

8

SOCIAL SECURITY AND
SOCIAL INSURANCE

LEARNING OBJECTIVES

After reading this chapter you should be able to

1. Discuss the Social Security system and how it is financed by payroll taxes in the United States.
2. Explain how the Social Security retirement system differs from private pension systems and how Social Security retirement benefits are computed.
3. Describe the concepts of gross and net replacement rates for retirees and how these rates vary for Social Security pensions with preretirement earnings and other factors.
4. Examine the intergenerational aspects of the Social Security system and how changing demographic factors, Social

Security tax rates, and changes in gross replacement rates affect the effective return on taxes paid into the system by retirees.
5. Analyze the impact of the Social Security system on work incentives and labor force participation of the elderly.
6. Estimate the possible impact of the Social Security system on savings rates in the United States.
7. Discuss social insurance provided by the Medicare system of health insurance for the elderly and unemployment insurance in the United States.

*O*ne of every five dollars spent by the federal government each year is used to provide Social Security pensions. In 1993 more than 40 million U.S. citizens received Social Security pensions. The amount spent for such pensions is likely to grow rapidly in the next century as the elderly fraction of the population eligible for pensions increases. The elderly (sixty-five and older) accounted for 11 percent of the U.S. population in 1980, and are forecasted to account for about 25 percent of the U.S. population by the middle of the twenty-first century. As the number of retirees increases relative to the total population, the Social Security system will have greater demands placed on it to support a larger number of elderly persons who, thanks in part to improved health care, will live longer.

Social Security is the most expensive federal government program. In 1993, for the first time, Social Security surpassed national defense as the government program absorbing the most resources. The Social Security Act of 1935 remains one of the most significant and enduring mandates for government activity in the United States. Originally proposed by President Franklin D. Roosevelt as part of his New Deal, the act provided, for the first time in the United States, a system of compulsory taxation to finance pensions to the aged and the disabled and their survivors, and unemployment benefits to workers (in most occupations) who, laid off from their jobs, are temporarily out of work. The system is designed to ensure adequate income security to individuals during periods of unemployment, in the event of disability, and in old age. The pension system is financed through a tax on payrolls, up to a certain limit for each worker's annual wages. The tax is split between the workers and the employers. The proceeds of the payroll tax are earmarked for a special trust fund to be used to finance pensions for the aged. An additional payroll tax finances health insurance for people older than sixty-five, and a tax paid only by employers finances unemployment insurance benefits.

Social insurance and Social Security programs provide income and health benefits financed by taxes to eligible individuals. The United States, compared to major European countries, was relatively tardy in passing social insurance legislation. The first social security legislation had been enacted in Germany in 1889. Similar plans were established in the United Kingdom in 1908; in France, 1910; in Sweden, 1913; and in Italy, 1919. Social insurance in the United States is still not as comprehensive as it is in some other countries. More than 140 countries have some form of social security system today, many of them providing sickness and maternity benefits (national health insurance) and family allowances (subsidies for child expenses, most often payable to families with two or more children). The first national health insurance system was established in 1912 by the United Kingdom.

Social Security pensions have had a profound effect on the well-being of the elderly in the United States. The average age of retirement of Americans has fallen sharply since 1965. From 1970 to 1987, the average real income of the elderly increased by 28 percent while the average real income of the rest of the population increased by only 10 percent. On average, the elderly are less likely to be poor than the rest of the population. Research on the economic status of the elderly in the United States suggests that they are at least as well-off as the nonelderly and their living standards might in fact be much better than the nonelderly.[1] Social Security, which accounts for an average of 40 percent of the earnings of the elderly in the United States, has vastly improved the economic status of the aged.

This chapter shows how social insurance programs, particularly those that aid the elderly, operate in the United States. The economic effects of the benefit programs on incentives to work and save are highlighted.

SOCIAL SECURITY IN THE UNITED STATES

Social Security in the United States is a rubric that includes many programs benefiting diverse groups of citizens. In general, **social security and insurance programs**

---

[1]Michael D. Hurd, Research on the Elderly, "Economic Status, Retirement, and Consumption and Saving," *Journal of Economic Literature* 28, 2 (June 1990): 565–637.

INTERNATIONAL VIEW

SOCIAL SECURITY THROUGHOUT THE WORLD

Social security is a general term for a number of programs established by governments to insure individuals against interruption or loss of earning power and to meet costs resulting from marriage, maternity, children, sickness or injury, unemployment, or death.

The most common form of social security protection is the replacement of a portion of income resulting from retirement. Most nations have social security old-age pension systems similar to those in the United States. However, some countries pay retirees a fixed pension that is not related to prior average earnings as are Social Security pensions in the United States. Other nations do not provide pensions but instead give a large lump-sum payment to workers on retirement, which is equal to a refund of the employees' and employers' contribution to a fund plus the accumulated interest on those contributions.[*]

Unemployment insurance is not as common as social security old-age pensions. As of the early 1990s, only about 40 nations had unemployment insurance programs. Most of these nations were industrialized and had well organized labor markets. In less-developed nations the family and in some cases the tribe or community have informal mechanisms for providing support to the unemployed. However, in many of these less-developed nations labor markets are not developed and much of the work is carried on within the household through subsistence farming.

Other programs that are common to social security programs throughout the world, but not available as part of the U.S. Social Security system, are universal health insurance and systems of allowances to families to assist them with the expenses of rearing children. The U.S. government does provide the elderly and the poor with health insurance. However, in many nations including Great Britain and Canada health insurance is provided universally to all citizens as part of the system of social security. Many nations also supplement their health insurance programs to pay medical costs with sickness and maternity benefits. These programs offer cash benefits to replace earnings lost as a result of short-term illness or maternity leaves.

Some nations offer citizens a lump-sum "demogrant" payment, which is a flat cash payment to citizens irrespective of their income, employment, or wealth. These payments are basic no-strings-attached subsidies designed to help all citizens, but they generally account for a higher percentage of the incomes of the poor than the rich. The United States does not have a similar program, but it does provide cash assistance to the poor through various means-tested programs such as AFDC and SSI (see Chapter 7).

Family allowances are regular cash payments for families with children. In some nations this form of so-

[*]See U.S. Department of Health and Human Services, Social Security Administration, *Social Security Programs throughout the World* (Washington, D.C.: U.S. Government Printing Office, periodically issued).

include government-provided pensions, disability payments, unemployment compensation, and health benefits. As pointed out in the previous chapter, many of the government assistance programs for the poor in this country are administered by the Social Security Administration. This chapter confines the discussion exclusively to social insurance and pension programs administered under the Social Security Act. This category of expense includes a multitude of other programs, such as railroad retirement, public employee retirement, disability insurance, and worker's compensation. However, the most important programs, from the point of view of public policy, are (1) old-age, survivors, disability, and insurance (OASDI)—the system of government-supplied pensions; (2) Medicare (HI)—the system of health insurance for the elderly; and (3) unemployment insurance (UI). This chapter emphasizes government pension programs.

cial security protection includes grants for birth expenses, for schooling, and for prenatal, maternal, and child care services. The family allowance system originated in several European nations in the 1920s and 1930s. As of the early 1990s, more than 60 countries had family allowance systems that subsidized the cost of having and nurturing children. The programs typically consist of monthly payments to families with children irrespective of the family's income and wealth. Some systems, such as that of Italy, pay allowances for an unemployed dependent spouse but most begin payment only with the arrival of the first child. The payments commonly terminate when the child reaches a certain age—usually between fourteen and eighteen years (although in some nations the payments terminate as early as age five). In nations desiring to increase their population, no limit is placed on the number of children that can be covered with the allowances. For example, as of the late 1980s, Canada gave family allowances in excess of $30 Canadian per month per child. Some nations, however, reduce the payment per child as the family size increases.

As the twenty-first century approaches many of the social security systems around the world are under stress because of demographic change. Government-financed pensions represent a vast public enterprise in most nations. In almost all cases the pay-as-you-go social security pensions systems require higher tax rates to pay benefits at promised levels when the ratio of the working age population to retirees declines. In the United States this support ratio has declined from 7.1 workers for each retiree in 1950 to only 4.7 workers per retiree in 1990. By the year 2020, projections indicate that there will only be 3.3 workers per retiree in the United States. In other nations, particularly those with very low birth rates like Japan, projections indicate that there will be only 2 workers paying taxes to support each retired worker by the year 2020!

Declining death rates combined with low birth rates spell trouble for many social security pensions systems throughout the world. As the populace ages, the cost of financing pension benefits at any given per capita level imply higher taxes imposed on relatively fewer workers. This problem has led some nations to seek alternatives to the traditional pay-as-you-go government pensions plans. For example, Chile in the 1970s forecast that a whopping 65 percent tax rate would be required on earnings of workers to finance social security benefits at promised replacement rates to workers in the future. To avoid the incentive problems that would result from such high tax rates Chile took the radical step of privatizing its social security pension system. It accomplished this by mandating retirement contributions into special accounts and then allowing private pension plans to compete for the right to manage these accounts. Older workers in Chile were given the option to remain in the old system and receive pensions at the promised replacement rates or to receive a bond, equal in value to their past contributions, to be invested in the new privatized system. Most workers opted out of the old system. The new system has been quite successful in that in has resulted in an annual real return on retirement contributions of 12 percent![†] This is much better than the 2-percent average return that U.S. workers can expect on their retirement contributions.

[†]See Gary S. Becker and Isaac Ehrlich, Social Security: Foreign Lessons, *The Wall Street Journal*, March 30, 1994.

Eligibility for benefits payable under the Social Security system and other social insurance programs is usually contingent on paying a tax or having that tax paid on one's behalf by virtue of employment in a job for which coverage is required. In the United States today, self-employed individuals are required by law to pay Social Security taxes for the pension program (OASDI) and for Medicare (HI) and thereby are covered by the Social Security system. The taxes paid are in accordance with the provisions of the Federal Insurance Contribution Act (FICA), established to finance Social Security pensions, and are usually deducted from employee wages and salaries. In addition, employers also pay the tax based on their payrolls. In 1993, the tax rate was 7.65 percent for workers and 7.65 percent for employers. The combined rate therefore was 15.3 percent and was levied on wages up to $57,600 per year per worker for OASDI and up to $135,000 maximum for HI in 1993. The maximum amount of wages per worker subject to the Social Security payroll taxes is adjusted for inflation each year. Beginning in 1994, the HI tax has no maximum earning limit.

To be eligible for benefits, a worker must have worked and paid the tax on a certain minimum amount of earnings. For example, in 1991 a quarter of coverage was earned for taxes paid on a minimum of $540 earnings over a three-month period. Forty quarters of coverage (ten years of covered work) qualifies a worker for Social Security retirement benefits. The monetary amount of the pension that a worker receives depends on previous earnings history, marital status, dependents, and the amount of time that Social Security taxes have been paid by the worker.

Unemployment insurance benefits are financed by a special tax on payrolls levied on employers alone. They are administered by state governments, and some variation in eligibility and benefits paid exists among the states. On average, however, the unemployment benefits equal about one-half of the wages previously earned, up to a certain limit. Benefits are usually paid for a maximum period of twenty-six weeks; However, they can be extended automatically during a period of high unemployment. In periods of deep recession, and other extraordinary circumstances, Congress can enact legislation that extends benefits for even longer periods. Benefits are available to all workers who, through no fault of their own, involuntarily lose their jobs and whose previous employers paid unemployment insurance taxes on the workers' behalf. No means test is required to be eligible for benefits.

Social insurance and Social Security pensions are transfer programs open to all workers, regardless of their income. However, the way in which benefits are paid can affect the income distribution somewhat, because they are distributed according to the worker's wages. Low-income workers receive benefits that are higher proportions of their preretirement earnings than higher-income workers or workers for whom nonwage sources of income are relatively important. All workers in jobs covered by the Social Security system must pay the Social Security tax, as must their employers, regardless of their own personal circumstances or evaluation of the program's future benefits.

THE SOCIAL SECURITY RETIREMENT SYSTEM

Pay-As-You-Go Versus Fully Funded Pension Systems

The government-supplied retirement benefits under Social Security are financed in a radically different manner than are the benefits under most private retirement systems. A **fully funded pension system** is one in which benefits are paid out of a fund built up from contributions by, or on behalf of, members in the retirement system. The dollar value of the fund must equal at least the discounted present value of pensions promised to members of the system in the future.

A member of a fully funded private pension system contributes monthly to the pension plan (or the employer contributes along with or instead of the employee). When the workers retire, they receive a pension based on the amount of contributions (a form of saving) plus the return earned (net of administration costs) on those contributions over the period of time the money was held (and invested) by the retirement system.[2] The administrators of fully funded retirement systems invest the funds of the pension system in various financial obligations, seeking to obtain reasonable rates of return on the fund while balancing the return earned with any risks associated with their investments.

The Social Security retirement system uses revenues collected from the payroll tax to provide pensions for the aged, the disabled, and their survivors eligible for benefits.[3] The **Old-age, Survivors, and Disability Insurance (OASDI)** program is a **tax-financed pension system;** retirement benefits are financed through taxes levied on the working population.

A **pay-as-you-go pension system** is one that finances pensions for retired workers in a given year entirely by contributions or taxes paid by currently employed workers. Because the bulk of payroll taxes collected to finance Social Security pensions in recent years has been used to pay pensions of currently retired workers, the Social Security system has been characterized as a pay-as-you-go retirement system. A special trust fund invests revenue in federal government securities. However, in the 1970s and early 1980s, the amount in this fund equaled less than two months of annual pension benefits. In recent years, the Social Security retirement system has been one that is financed by directly transferring taxes collected from those working to those who are retired. The Social Security pension system represents an implicit contract between workers and retirees. It is this "contract" that keeps the system functioning.

As the twenty-first century approaches, the Social Security trust fund will begin to grow because of increases in the payroll tax collections and other changes in the Social Security system made in 1977 and 1983. Without these changes, the Social Security system would have been unable to pay promised pensions benefits from payroll taxes. As the trust fund builds up, some current workers will be contributing not only to finance the pensions of currently retired workers but also to fund their own future retirement benefits.

In 1991, the balance in the Social Security trust fund after payment of annual pension benefits was equal to a bit less than eleven months of pension benefits. The Social Security trust fund is projected to increase until sometime in the first quarter of the twenty-first century. Thereafter, as the proportion of retirees in the population increases, revenues taken into the fund are projected to fall below outlays from the fund, and the trust fund will begin to decline. From now until the time the trust fund is depleted, the U.S. Social Security system will not be strictly on a pay-as-you-go basis. If it were to return to such a basis, payroll tax rates could be reduced from their

---

[2]This is called a *defined-contribution pension plan,* under which the worker (or the employer) contributes a certain amount per year and receives a pension based on the contributions, the earnings of the pension fund, and the fund's pay-out experience. *Defined-benefit plans* promise the employee a certain pension. To be fully funded, these plans must collect contributions to finance a fund that will amass adequate earnings to pay the promised pensions.

[3]Taxes collected from any portions of Social Security pensions subject to the federal income tax are also used to finance Social Security retirement benefits.

scheduled levels until about the first quarter of the twenty-first century. However, these rates would be much higher later on in the twenty-first century if the system were to remain pay-as-you-go.

Currently, workers who are paying the payroll tax expect that future generations of workers also will be taxed in a similar way so that, when they retire, they too will receive a pension under Social Security. In simple terms, the Social Security system pays benefits today only because of the government's ability to tax and because of the willingness of individuals to agree collectively to such taxes in exchange for the promise of future retirement benefits.[4]

How Retirement Benefits are Computed Under Social Security

The monthly pension benefits that a particular worker receives upon retirement depend on a benefit formula used by the Social Security Administration. Such personal information as a person's earnings history and age are considered. The formula calculates an employee's **average indexed monthly earnings (AIME),** which are based on the worker's average monthly earnings (on which payroll taxes are paid). The thirty-five years of highest actual earnings prior to retirement, adjusted for changes in the general price level each year, are used in the formula. In effect, AIME is a measure of workers' real average taxable monthly earnings, up to a certain maximum, over a lifetime in jobs covered by Social Security benefits. The formula varies with the worker's age of retirement.

After AIME has been calculated, it is used in another formula to determine a worker's *primary insurance amount* (PIA). This represents the basic monthly pension for which a worker who is retiring at sixty-five is eligible. The amount then is adjusted according to the worker's actual age at retirement, marital status and dependents, and other personal circumstances.

The Social Security pension for which a person qualifies is considered an *earned right*. This means that it is paid regardless of the worker's wealth and nonlabor income. However, retired workers between sixty-two and sixty-nine years of age are subject to an **earnings test,** which reduces Social Security benefits by $1 for each $3 of earnings (for those between 65 and 69) over a certain maximum amount of earnings that is adjusted each year. For example, the maximum earnings amounted to $10,560 per year in 1994. This implies that if a worker earns enough wages in a given year, the Social Security pension benefit will become zero. Workers younger than seventy earning more than the maximum permissible wages are considered as delaying retirement. For these workers, AIME is adjusted upward to allow a higher monthly retirement benefit after the worker actually does retire after age seventy.

Social Security benefits are also paid to a worker's family under certain circumstances. Dependent spouses older than sixty-five are entitled to one-half a worker's

---

[4]To the extent to which a private pension system is not fully funded, it, too, might be forced to use pay-as-you-go means of finance or forgo paying full promised benefits to retirees. For a discussion of private pensions and their problems, see Bruno Stein, *Social Security and Pensions in Transition* (New York: Free Press, 1980).

basic monthly benefit. In addition, in most cases, widows and widowers receive the amount to which their spouse would have been entitled. Benefits are also paid to dependent children of retirees.

Workers who have twenty quarters of their past forty quarters of earnings in a job covered by the Social Security system are eligible for disability pensions if they become severely disabled. These pensions are also available for disabled workers younger than thirty-one if they have worked a certain number of quarters after turning twenty-one. These pensions require proof of disability and are paid after a five-month waiting period.

The Gross Replacement Rate

A useful measure of the standard of living allowable under Social Security retirement benefits compared with that enjoyed prior to retirement is the extent to which these benefits replace preretirement earnings. The **gross replacement rate (GRR)** is the worker's monthly retirement benefit divided by monthly earnings *in the year prior to retirement:*

$$\text{GRR} = \frac{\text{Monthly Retirement Benefit}}{\substack{\text{Monthly Labor Earnings in the} \\ \text{Year Prior to Retirement.}}} \tag{8.1}$$

Table 8.1 shows 1993 gross replacement rates for three typical workers who retired at sixty-five in January 1993. The average earner has had average earnings in relation to all retiring workers covered by Social Security pensions in the year of retirement. The low earner had earnings equal to 45 percent of the amount earned by the average earner. The maximum earner had earnings equal to the maximum taxable wage which was $57,600 in 1993.

Notice how the gross replacement rate declines with the level of earnings in Table 8.1. A single, low-earner worker who retired at sixty-five in 1993 with gross earnings of $840 per month in 1992 would be eligible for a $497 monthly pension. The gross replacement rate for this worker is therefore 59 percent. The average

Table 8.1 ✦ Gross Replacement Rates under Social Security (Percent for Workers Retiring at Age 65 in January 1993)

Worker Status	Gross Replacement Rate
Low Earner[a]	59
Average Earner	44
Maximum Earner[b]	25

[a]Earnings equal 45 percent of average earner.
[b]Earnings equal the maximum wage taxable for Social Security purposes.
Source: Office of the Actuary, Social Security Administration.

earner retiring in 1993 had annual earnings of $22,393 in 1992 and received a monthly Social Security pension of $821. The gross replacement rate for the average earner was therefore 44 percent. Finally the replacement rate for the maximum earner was only 25 percent.

Workers with dependent spouses older than sixty-five have higher gross replacement rates than do single workers with the same income because their Social Security pensions are adjusted upward. For example, a low earner with a dependent spouse would enjoy a gross replacement rate equal to 90 percent of preretirement earnings.

Two-earner households receive benefits based on the earnings histories of both spouses (with a floor on the benefits available to the one spouse with lower earnings equal to 50 percent of the benefits due the spouse with higher earnings). For example, a two-earner household in which both earners retired at sixty-five in January 1993, and both received the maximum possible monthly benefit, would have a monthly pension of $2,262, assuming that both are receiving the maximum possible monthly Social Security benefits. This represents twice the maximum single pension of $1,131 per month.

Social Security pensions are based on "need" as well as earnings histories. Adjustments for family size reflect the underlying belief that married couples, and households with dependents, will require greater retirement income than single-person households. Therefore two workers with identical earnings histories may well receive pensions of different amounts, based on their marital status and the number of dependents they support.

Social Security pensions also have a redistributive element built into their calculation. The pensions are designed to provide higher benefits, as a proportion of preretirement income, to lower-income workers, relative to higher-income workers. Therefore, for workers with earnings histories over the same number of years, the gross replacement rate for the worker with higher average wages earned will be lower than that for the worker earning less over his lifetime. Figure 8.1 shows that gross replacement rates decline steadily with monthly preretirement earnings.

The Net Replacement Rate: A Better Measure of the Generosity of Social Security Pension Benefits

The gross replacement rate underestimates the extent to which Social Security pension benefits replace a retiree's actual disposable earnings. Disposable income is gross income less taxes paid on those earnings. Social Security pension benefits are nontaxable for most retirees.[5] Therefore, for most workers, the entire Social Security pension is disposable income.

---

[5]Workers whose income plus one-half of their Social Security pensions exceeds $25,000 ($32,000 for married couples who file joint returns) do pay income tax on a portion of their Social Security pensions. Income taxes collected on Social Security pensions are used to finance Social Security benefits. As of 1995, 85 percent of pensions for these workers are subject to income tax.

Figure 8.1 ✦ How Gross Replacement Rates for Social Security Pension Recipients Vary with Preretirement Earnings

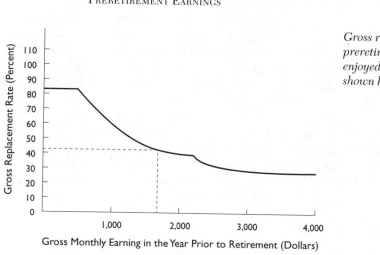

Gross replacement rates decline with monthly preretirement earnings. In 1993, the average earner enjoyed a gross replacement rate of 44 percent, shown by the dashed line.

A better measure of the generosity of the pension benefits is the **net replacement rate (NRR):**

$$\text{NRR} = \frac{\text{Monthly Social Security Pension Benefits}}{\text{Monthly Labor Earnings after Payment of Taxes in the Year Prior to Retirement.}} \qquad (8.2)$$

Net replacement rates are higher than gross replacement rates. To see this, consider the case of the average earner. This worker is likely to have paid a total of 20 percent of labor earnings in federal and state (and possibly local) income taxes and Social Security payroll taxes in 1993. Assume that the retiree with average earnings has no income other than a Social Security pension. This worker's monthly preretirement earnings were $1,866 in 1990. Taxes due on these earnings would therefore be $373 per month.

The average earner in 1993 with no dependent spouse would have received a monthly Social Security pension of $821. Therefore, the net replacement rate would be

$$\text{NRR} = \frac{\$821}{\$(1,866 - 373)} = \frac{\$821}{\$1,493} = 55\% \qquad (8.3)$$

which exceeds the 44 percent gross replacement rate for the worker shown in Table 8.1. Net replacement rates decline with monthly preretirement earnings in a fashion similar to that shown for gross replacement rates in Figure 8.1.

Other Pension Income and the Well-Being of the Elderly

Social Security pensions are the most important source of income to the elderly. Nearly 60 percent of the elderly rely on Social Security pensions to provide at least half of their income. Less than half of the elderly have income from government or private pensions. In 1990, private and government pensions amounted to only 18 percent of the income of the elderly. Income from past saving accounted for 26 percent of income of the aged in 1990.[6]

Most studies of the rate of growth of income for the elderly show that, on average, they have fared very well since 1967. The average rate of growth of real household income for households headed by a person older than sixty-five from 1967 to 1984 was 42.4 percent. During the same period, real income in families headed by the nonelderly grew by only 10.7 percent. Undoubtedly, the well-being of the elderly has increased relative to the rest of the population since 1967, and the growth of Social Security pensions and increases in the replacement rates for those pensions during that period have helped improve the economic status of the elderly in the United States. After adjustment for size of household and other factors that affect the budgets of the elderly relative to the rest of the population, many studies conclude that on average the elderly in the United States are now at least as well off as the nonelderly, using income as a measure of well-being.[7]

Cost-of-Living Adjustments

Since 1972, the Social Security pensions received by retired workers have been directly indexed to consumer prices. The retirement benefits of the elderly therefore are protected against erosion by inflation. This implies that, unless the method of calculating benefits is changed, the retiring worker will have the net replacement rate obtained in the year of retirement maintained in real terms over the full period of retirement. Nominal benefits will increase with the rate of inflation.

The method of indexing retirement benefits is often criticized as being overgenerous, because many claim the consumer price index is based on a basket of goods more typical for young, rather than elderly, households. In particular, changes in mortgage interest rates, included in the index as an estimate of housing costs, might have little impact on the elderly.

Other sources of income to the elderly are also likely to vary with the price level. For example, the value of government-provided medical care through the Medicare program also increases with inflation. Further, some private pensions are indexed for inflation, and for elderly home owners, inflation increases the return on their investments in their homes. In short, inflation erodes but little of the income of the elderly.

C H E C K P O I N T

1. How are Social Security pensions financed in the United States? Is Social Security a fully funded pension system?
2. How is eligibility for Social Security pensions determined? What factors will influence a retiree's Social Security pension?
3. How do gross and net replacement rates of Social Security pensions vary with preretirement income in the United States?

---

[6]See John A. Turner and Daniel J. Beller, eds. *Trends in Pensions 1992* (Washington, D.C.: Department of Labor, Pension and Welfare Benefits Administration, 1992).

[7]Hurd, 578.

The Return to Workers: How do Pension Benefits Compare with the Taxes that Workers Pay?

What is the rate of return to retirees who pay Social Security taxes over their lifetimes? In other words, if the total Social Security taxes paid by the worker and his employer had been invested, what rate of interest would produce the stream of retirement benefits for which the retiree is eligible? This return varies from worker to worker, depending on the worker's earnings history and personal circumstances. However, it is interesting to perform this calculation in the aggregate to see how the ability of a pay-as-you-go retirement system, which pays benefits in excess of the taxes paid by workers, depends on certain economic variables.

To calculate the average rate of return to retirees, as a percentage of their taxes, requires a number of simplifying assumptions. First, assume that the payroll tax rate on worker's wages is fixed over time. Also assume that the size of the work force is constant. Finally, assume that the rate of inflation is zero.

In a pay-as-you-go system, the taxes paid by workers in any one year go directly into the pockets of retired workers. Given the assumptions, the annual increase in aggregate taxes collected and, therefore, total pensions paid equal the annual growth of labor earnings subject to the Social Security tax. This is because, in any given year, revenue available to pay benefits will be tW, where t is the Social Security tax rate and W is total aggregate labor earnings subject to the tax. With t fixed, revenues available to pay pensions will increase only if W increases. The growth of revenues therefore depends on the annual rate of growth of labor earnings subject to taxation.

Adjusting for inflation, the rate of growth of wages per worker in the United States has averaged about 2 percent per year since the Social Security system has been in operation. This is the average return on taxes paid that workers can expect, provided that the size of the work force and tax rates are fixed. Because net replacement rates vary with preretirement income, some workers receive a higher return and some a lower return.

However, until the late 1970s, retiring workers were able to enjoy a much higher average return on the taxes they paid during their lifetimes because during that period the number of workers paying Social Security payroll taxes steadily increased. In addition, the tax rates paid by workers were steadily increased by Congress. From 1950 to 1975, the segment of the U.S. population older than sixteen rose at an annual rate of 1.4 percent, labor force participation rates of workers increased, and Social Security taxes were levied on workers in many new industries and jobs and on the self-employed, as these workers were made eligible for pension benefits.

Until the late 1970s, on average, workers who were retiring under the Social Security system received a relatively high return on their taxes paid, compared with what they could have earned, on average, had their Social Security taxes been invested in a fully funded system. More generous Social Security benefits, and their indexing for inflation, were enacted into law in the 1970s and financed by a growing amount of taxable wages earmarked to finance benefits and only modest increases in tax rates paid by workers.

From 1950 to 1975, the average return that a conservative portfolio manager could have earned, in real terms, on a fully funded pension system was about 5 percent. This is based on real (adjusted for inflation) yields of about 8 percent on common stocks and 3 percent on high-grade corporate bonds. A less conservative portfolio (one subject to more risk) could have earned considerably more. A common estimate of the postwar real rate of return in the corporate sector is about 12 percent through 1976.[8]

Martin Feldstein has estimated that the real rate of Social Security tax receipts (excluding the portion of the tax used to finance health benefits for the elderly) grew 10.4 percent per year from 1950 to 1975.[9] This compares very favorably with the 12 percent achievable on a conservative portfolio in the corporate sector over the same period. (Social Security taxpayers bore little risk over this period, because they were guaranteed a pension by the taxing power of the federal government.)

This favorable past performance of the Social Security system is not likely to be repeated in the future. Any future increase in Social Security receipts to pay pensions over and above the value of taxes paid will be limited to the annual growth rate of real wages. This is because taxable wages are no longer growing through increases in the number of workers covered. Most economists predict that this rate will be no more than a mere 2 percent in real terms.

Intergenerational and Distributive Effects of Social Security

An interesting intergenerational aspect of Social Security benefits is the inevitable result of starting up a pay-as-you-go retirement system. Workers who reached retirement age in the early years of the Social Security system received a better deal than do workers currently retiring and those who will retire in the future. This is because the first workers who received pensions had not paid Social Security taxes over their entire working lives. For example, Ida Fuller of Brattleboro, Vermont, the first Social Security pension recipient in the United States, paid approximately $22 in Social Security taxes over her lifetime. Ms. Fuller died at the ripe old age of 99, after collecting a grand total of approximately $20,000 in Social Security benefits—not a bad return on $22!

Workers who retired through 1990 have paid taxes over a long period when tax rates under Social Security were quite low. For example, workers who had median earnings and who had retired in 1971 earned pension benefits three times greater than they could have enjoyed had their Social Security taxes paid over their lifetimes been returned to them at 6 percent interest on retirement.[10] A middle-income person who retired in 1970 with no dependents received a pension with a discounted present value of $25,000 more than the taxes paid during the retiree's lifetime—a good deal! However a person in the exact same circumstances retiring in the year 2020 will pay

---

[8]Martin Feldstein, "Facing the Social Security Crisis," *The Public Interest* 47 (Spring 1977): 88–100.

[9]Ibid., 91.

[10]Donald Parsons and Douglas Munro, "Intergenerational Transfers in Social Security," in *The Crisis in Social Security,* ed. Michael J. Boskin (San Francisco: Institute for Contemporary Studies, 1977).

THE RISE AND FALL OF GROSS REPLACEMENT RATES UNDER SOCIAL SECURITY PENSIONS

Social Security began as a program with modest gross replacement rates for retirees. During the period from 1937 to 1970, the gross replacement rate for a worker earning the average wage ranged from 30 to 35 percent. As a result of the Social Security Amendments of 1972, Congress instituted a procedure to index Social Security benefits to the rate of inflation. Prior to 1972, Congress periodically adjusted the benefit formula used to determine pensions to reflect changes in the price and wage levels.

Unfortunately, the formula used to adjust benefits beginning in 1972 had a flaw that caused benefits to rise more quickly than intended. The error resulted in a substantial increase in real pension benefits. In other words, the flaw more than compensated retirees for inflation!

To correct the error, the Social Security Amendments of 1977 reduced replacement rates by instituting a new formula, which became effective in 1982. However, before the correction was made, gross replacement rates had climbed for all retirees to levels much higher than those initially used by the Social Security system. A worker without dependents retiring with average earnings of all retirees in 1981 was enjoying a gross replacement rate of 55 percent. The net replacement rate for workers with dependent spouses earning average wages prior to retirement rose to an astounding 96 percent in 1981.

As a result of the 1977 amendments, gross replacement rates for workers with average wages prior to retirement were reduced. By 1993, the gross replacement rate for a worker with average earnings prior to retirement fell to 44 percent. Decreases in income tax rates in the 1980s also reduced the gap between the gross and net replacement rates that prevailed in the 1970s. Under current legislation, the gross replacement rate for retirees with average earnings of all retirees in a given year will stabilize at about 42 percent. This gross replacement rate is one-third more generous to retirees than the 30 to 35 percent replacement rate that prevailed from 1937 to 1970. As a consequence, the economic well-being of the elderly as a group in the United States has improved drastically since 1970. Today, the elderly are less likely to be poor than the rest of the population.

$88,000 more in taxes over a lifetime of work than the discounted present value of the Social Security pension received at that time—a bad deal![11] Workers who are entering the labor force now will pay, during their entire careers, high tax rates earmarked for current Social Security benefits. In addition, some of those taxes will be used to build up the trust fund to prepare for the increase in Social Security outlays in the future, as the proportion of retirees in the population increases. This makes the Social Security system a much poorer deal, on average, for workers today than it has been for their parents and grandparents.

Finally, the way in which Social Security gross replacement rates vary with family status and income also affects the benefits received by retired workers. In general, as the analysis of replacement rates has shown, Social Security retirement benefits, compared with taxes paid, are a better deal for low-income workers than for upper-income

[11]See Michael D. Hurd and John B. Shoven, "The Distributional Impact of Social Security," in *Pensions, Labor, and Individual Choice,* ed. David A. Wise (Chicago: University of Chicago Press, 1985) 193–215.

workers. In addition, married workers with dependent spouses are better off than single workers or workers with employed spouses eligible for their own Social Security benefits.

The Social Security system, then, affects the distribution of income by transferring income from workers to retirees, from single workers to married workers with dependent spouses, and from high-income workers to low-income workers.

DEMOGRAPHIC CHANGE AND THE FUTURE OF SOCIAL SECURITY

Maintenance of gross replacement rates at legislated levels has required sharp increases in payroll tax rates since 1970 to provide the revenue for current and future pensions. The tax increases will result in the Social Security trust fund growing until the end of the first quarter of the twenty-first century. This means that the Social Security system will be less of a pay-as-you-go system for current workers, who will pay taxes not only to finance the pensions of current retirees but also to accumulate reserves that will pay some of their own pensions. However, as the second half of the twenty-first century is approached, the Social Security trust fund will be drawn down rapidly, because payroll tax revenues will fall short of expected outlays for pensions at that time. By the mid-twenty-first century, the fund is forecast to have a large negative balance, which could require that more tax revenues be devoted to paying pensions at that time.

The basic problem is that the proportion of retirees relative to the working population has been, and will continue to be, increasing. Since 1957, the birthrate in the United States has fallen. In 1990, there were 4.7 workers for each retiree in the United States. Demographic projections by the Social Security Administration indicate that by the year 2030 there will be only 2.8 workers for each retiree.

From 1967 to 1973 changes in legislation sharply increased Social Security benefits by more than 70 percent (see the accompanying Public Policy Perspective). The expansion of Social Security benefits paid to retirees led to concerns that the system would have difficulty in meeting its future commitments. But given the political popularity of the system and the fact that the system's ability to pay benefits is based on the taxing power of the federal government, fears of the system's collapse are unwarranted.

The solution was new legislation sharply increasing both the maximum taxable wages per worker and the tax rate applied to wages for the collection of the Social Security payroll tax. In 1977, Congress passed a number of significant amendments to the Social Security Act, allowing these tax increases, along with certain changes in the way in which Social Security benefits will be calculated in the future, to reduce replacement rates. Additional reforms, enacted by Congress in 1983, accelerated the rate of increase of Social Security taxes; increased the tax rates applied to self-employment income; and placed new federal employees under coverage of Social Security, thereby subjecting these workers' wages to Social Security taxes. In addition, the changes decreased the benefits to early retirees and increased the bonus paid to workers delaying retirement. The retirement age at which the retiree is eligible for full benefits will be raised gradually from sixty-five to sixty-seven beginning in 2003. By the year 2027, the retirement age will have reached sixty-seven.

Table 8.2 shows the tax rate schedule and maximum taxable wages per worker for selected years from 1937 to 1993. The combined employee-employer tax rate has nearly doubled since 1966, totaling 15.3 percent in 1993. This tax rate includes a 2.9 percent combined employer-employee tax that finances health insurance for the elderly (Medicare). The maximum taxable wages per worker for OASDI have increased from $3,000 in 1937 to $57,600 in 1993. Starting in 1991, the maximum taxable wages for the health insurance tax (HI) was increased above that for OASDI. In 1993, maximum taxable wages for the combined 2.9 percent HI tax was $135,000. Beginning in 1994, *all labor earnings,* without limit, are subjected to a 2.9 percent HI tax. The maximum taxable wages per worker are indexed with the rate of inflation. The sharp tax increases are designed to ensure that the Social Security Administration can continue to pay benefits based on existing replacement rates.

Table 8.2 ✦ SOCIAL SECURITY TAX RATES, MAXIMUM TAXABLE WAGES, AND TAXES, SELECTED YEARS, 1937–1993

YEAR	BASIC OASDHI TAX RATE	COMBINED EMPLOYER-EMPLOYEE TAX RATE	MAXIMUM TAXABLE WAGES PER WORKER[a]	MAXIMUM TAX BASED ON COMBINED TAX RATE
1937	1.00%	2.00%	$ 3,000	$ 60.00
1957	2.25	4.50	4,200	189.00
1967	4.40	8.80	6,600	528.00
1977	5.85	11.70	16,500	1,930.50
1978	6.05	12.10	17,700	2,141.70
1979	6.13	12.26	22,900	2,807.54
1980	6.13	12.26	25,900	3,175.34
1981	6.65	13.30	29,700	3,950.10
1982	6.70	13.40	32,400	4,341.60
1983	6.70	13.40	35,700	4,783.80
1984	7.00	14.00	37,800	5,292.00
1985	7.05	14.10	39,600	5,583.60
1986	7.15	14.30	42,000	6,006.00
1987	7.15	14.30	43,800	6,263.40
1988	7.51	15.02	45,000	6,759.00
1989	7.51	15.02	48,000	7,209.60
1990	7.65	15.30	51,300	7,848.90
1991	7.65	15.30	53,400[b]	10,246.00[c]
1992	7.65	15.30	55,500[d]	10,657.80[c]
1993	7.65	15.30	57,600[e]	11,057.40[c]

[a]Automatically adjusted upward each year. Excludes earnings subject to additional HI tax.
[b]Combined HI tax (2.9%) levied on wages and self-employment income up to a maximum of $125,000.
[c]Includes additional HI tax levied on the maximum amount of wages subject to HI tax.
[d]Combined HI tax (2.9%) levied on wages and self-employment income up to a maximum of $130,200.
[e]Combined HI tax levied on wages and self employment income up to a maximum of $135,000.
Source: Social Security Administration.

Many workers currently have more payroll taxes for Social Security withheld from their wages than they pay in federal income taxes. For example, a married worker earning $20,000 per year income in 1993 would have had $1,530 withheld in payroll taxes that year. The same worker could expect to pay only slightly more than $1,000 in federal income taxes that year.

Table 8.2 shows the combined maximum tax paid by both employees and employers. The employer's share of tax is paid out of compensation that the worker could otherwise receive as wages. Almost all of the portion of the tax paid by employers represents a cost in terms of forgone wages to employees. The combined employee-employer tax of a worker earning $57,600 in 1993 was $8,812.80. A married couple each earning the maximum taxable wages therefore will have their salaries generate nearly $18,000 in payroll tax revenue in 1993—nearly enough to pay the Social Security pension of a typical high-income worker with a dependent spouse in that year! Workers earning $135,000 in 1993 paid more than $11,000 in Social Security taxes, including the incremental tax for Medicare on wages between $57,600 and $135,000 in that year. Currently the Medicare (HI) tax has no limit.

If demographic and economic growth projections are correct and if replacement rates for Social Security pensions remain as currently legislated, then the proportion of GDP devoted to Social Security pensions will increase through the first half of the twenty-first century. The initial Social Security legislation was passed during the height of the Depression of the 1930s. Economic conditions and the general quality of life in the United States have changed drastically since that time. In view of the financial problems anticipated by the Social Security retirement system in the future, many economists have begun to reassess some of the basic assumptions underlying government-supplied retirement benefits financed by compulsory taxation.

Government-supplied retirement systems can be viewed as a means of forcing citizens to save for their own retirement. By forcing workers to pay Social Security taxes in exchange for the promise of retirement benefits at some point in the future, the government, in effect, assures the public at large that the elderly will have at least some minimal means of support after their working years. This frees children from the necessity and worry of supporting their parents in their old age and reduces the probability that the elderly will require additional government assistance. An underlying presumption behind this justification for the Social Security system is that a substantial number of workers will fail to set aside an adequate amount of savings to support themselves in their old age.

If current replacement rates are maintained, many workers at or below the median income level might find that, at retirement, their real income rises relative to their wages earned when they were thirty to fifty years old. This might seem a pleasant state of affairs, if it were a costless development. However, workers typically have more expenses in their middle years, when they are raising families and furnishing households. Many workers might not realize how high the replacement rates are and how much the increased tax burden that they bear to finance Social Security benefits to others reduces their own real incomes during their working years.

Three alternatives that have been suggested to prevent Social Security tax rates from rising as much as they are already scheduled to be in the late 1990s are to lower existing average replacement rates, change the structure of replacement rates, or increase the retirement age.

As noted, recent legislation has been passed to raise the retirement age to sixty-seven by the year 2027. An increase in the retirement age at which a worker becomes eligible for Social Security benefits is equivalent to a reduction in replacement rates.

Changes in the replacement rates are likely to be unpopular with persons who are approaching retirement. The elderly are a potent and effective political force. Elderly people have more leisure time and probably are more likely to vote than younger citizens. They also have more time to inform themselves about current political issues. In future years, demographic change will result in the elderly constituting an ever-increasing percentage of the total population, as the children of various postwar "baby booms" reach old age. This effect might be even more pronounced if the life span of the elderly is lengthened as a result of medical advances. As the median voter ages, political support for reducing Social Security benefits might prove difficult to pass by majority rule. Some nations, such as Chile, have privatized their social security systems to deal with the problem of an aging population (see International View).

C H E C K P O I N T

1. What influences the average rate of increase in funds collected to pay Social Security pensions?
2. Why are Social Security pensions on average a much worse deal for workers who will be retiring in the next ten years than they were for their parents?
3. Why are demographic change and declining economic growth rates likely to increase the share of GDP allocated to pay Social Security pensions throughout the first half of the twenty-first century?

THE IMPACT OF SOCIAL SECURITY ON SAVINGS AND WORK INCENTIVES

Among the issues of greatest concern in the recent upsurge of criticism against the Social Security system is the impact of government-supplied retirement benefits on incentives to save and work. This is an area of considerable controversy and disagreement. Although economic theory suggests that a pay-as-you-go system of retirement distorts both savings and work choices, no conclusive evidence confirms this nor does any measure the actual effect. The impact of Social Security retirement benefits on economic incentives is the combined effect of its influence on the choices of both recipients of benefits and those who finance the benefits. Those who pay the payroll taxes to finance Social Security pensions and other benefits will have their economic choices influenced by Social Security taxes. Those already receiving Social Security benefits, or who are close to receiving such benefits, likewise have their choices influenced by the system. The analysis of work incentives in this chapter considers only the effect of Social Security benefits on the work incentive of the elderly eligible for pensions.

Work Incentives

Social Security affects the size of the work force by influencing the willingness of workers and spouses to participate in the labor force and by controlling the age of retirement. Social Security benefits reduce the incentive that older workers might have to work beyond the age of sixty-five. In many cases, net replacement rates for workers with dependent spouses are more than 85 percent of previous earnings and tend to be supplemented with benefits from private pensions. Little financial incentive to work beyond the age of sixty-five exists for workers who realize net replacement rates close to 100 percent. Since 1961, male workers have had the option to retire at age sixty-two with reduced benefits. Women have had this option since 1956. Many workers have taken advantage of this alternative since it was first introduced, apparently because they value the three extra years of benefits and leisure time more than the reduction in annual benefits.

Also, an annual earnings test can affect the amount of benefits received, regardless of the amount to which the retiree is entitled. Although the reduction of Social Security retirement benefits, with earnings, had been moderated somewhat since the passage of the 1977 and 1983 amendments, the effects still can significantly influence the older worker's incentive to work.

For example, in 1994, retired workers aged sixty-five to sixty-nine could earn $10,560 per year with no reduction in benefits. The amount of retiree earnings exempt of the earnings test is indexed with the rate of inflation. The maximum permissible earnings is somewhat less for retirees less than sixty-five. After the maximum earnings of $10,560 are achieved, retirees' Social Security benefits will be reduced by $1 for each $3 of earnings for those older than the normal retirement age but less than seventy. The earnings test is not applied to workers older than seventy. Retired workers also must pay Social Security payroll tax and federal and state income taxes on their earnings.

Figure 8.2 shows the impact of Social Security pensions and the earnings test on workers' incentives. The worker's leisure time per day is plotted against income, given the wage rate per hour for the worker. Each graph shows a retired worker's indifference curves for income and leisure and the income-leisure budget line. The slope of the income-leisure budget line is equal to w, where w is the net wage that the worker can earn.

In Figure 8.2A, the distance BG represents the worker's daily pension benefits, which for a worker with average income would be approximately $30 per day in 1994 dollars. This would be his income if he took twenty-four hours per day in leisure. In 1994, assume that a typical worker could earn, on average, up to $30 per day without being subject to the earnings test. Assuming that the worker could find employment at $6 per hour, on average he could work five hours per day without having his pension reduced. This would occur at point H, which corresponds to nineteen hours of leisure and five hours of work per day. Daily income at point H will be $60, which equals $30 in wages and approximately $30 of pension benefits. If the worker works more than an average of five hours per day, his Social Security pension, BG, will be reduced by $1 for each $3 of earnings. If, for example, BG = $30 per day, the worker who earns $120 per day would have his Social Security pension reduced to

Figure 8.2 ◆ Social Security Pensions and the Work-Leisure Choice

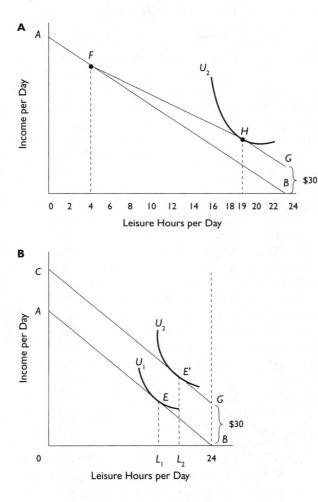

A

Income per Day

Leisure Hours per Day

B

Income per Day

Leisure Hours per Day

*The worker whose budget line and indifference curves are shown in **A** is subject to the earnings test. This worker encounters a substitution effect when he works more than five hours per day. Given his preferences, he is in equilibrium at point H. The worker whose choice to work is shown in **B** is not subject to the earnings test. His work-leisure choice is not affected by a substitution effect unfavorable to work.*

zero. This is because after the $30 per day not subject to the earnings test is deducted, the worker would have $90 in earnings. This would reduce his pension by the full $30 per day. Because this worker who earns $6 per hour would have to work twenty hours per day (leaving only four hours of leisure per day) to have his pension benefits reduced to zero, it is unlikely that the worker would lose all his pension. If the worker chose to work a standard eight-hour day, he would earn $48 per day on average. Because these earnings are $18 more than the wages not subject to the earnings test, his pension would average $(30 − 18/3) = $24 per day and his gross daily income would average $48 in earnings plus $24 in pension benefits, or $72. The number of hours of work that would reduce the worker's pension to zero would be less if the worker's hourly wage were higher.

Pension benefits allow the worker some income, equal to the distance BG, even without work. This results in an income effect that increases the demand for leisure. In addition, after a certain point the earnings test reduces the net wage that the retiree can earn until $(24 - L°)$ hours per day are devoted to work. This decrease in the net wage results in a substitution effect that is also unfavorable to work. In Figure 8.2A, the worker is in equilibrium when eligible for pension benefits at point H. At that point, the worker takes nineteen hours in leisure and therefore works, on average, only five hours per day, up to the point at which the earnings test begins. This result depends on worker preferences and wage rates. A worker with weaker preferences for leisure or a higher net wage works more hours, even though additional work will reduce Social Security benefits. Finally, a worker with strong desires for leisure might be in equilibrium at point G. This worker would drop out of the labor force and enjoy twenty-four hours per day of leisure.

Naturally, the number of hours of work per day at which the pension benefits will fall to zero depends on the worker's pension per day relative to the wage the worker can earn. For workers with low pensions relative to their hourly wages, the point F in Figure 8.2A would lie further to the right and would therefore correspond to more leisure and less work per day. Workers with strong desires for work or money income might actually be in equilibrium on the section AF of the budget line, at which they forgo their Social Security pension completely and remain in the labor force working full-time.

Figure 8.2B shows the impact of Social Security pensions on the work choices of a retiree older than seventy, not subject to the earnings test. The worker is in equilibrium at point E prior to retirement. When this worker retires, the budget line shifts up, parallel to itself, from AB to CG. The worker's income is increased by the same amount, BG, independent of the hours worked. Here there is only an income effect, which is unfavorable to work. Because there is no substitution effect, the worker has greater incentive to work, other things being equal, than would be the case if the earnings test applied. The worker is in equilibrium at point E', at which he continues to work $(24 - L_2)$ hours per day. Workers with stronger preferences for leisure might choose to drop out of the labor force.

Participation of the elderly in the labor force has declined steadily since 1940, when 59.6 percent of men aged 65 to 69 were in the labor force. In 1991, only 16 percent of men sixty-five and older were in the labor force. It is impossible to attribute all, or even part, of this decline to the availability and increase in Social Security benefits. Clearly, the decline was influenced by the increased availability of private pensions and the general trend, experienced since 1940, to increasing real income. It is likely, however that Social Security pensions and other benefits played a significant part in the reduced work incentive of the elderly. A number of empirical studies have provided some evidence of the effect of Social Security benefits on retirement choices and labor force participation. These have indicated a very strong negative relationship between labor force participation and the availability of Social Security benefits.[12] Similarly, others have found strong association between increased Social

---

[12]Joseph F. Quinn, "Microeconomic Determinants of Retirement: A Cross-Sectional View of White Married Men," *Journal of Human Resources* 12 (Summer 1977): 329–346.

Security benefits and coverage and the declining labor force participation of older workers.[13]

The U.S. income tax system also results in high rates of taxation for persons older than sixty-five who choose to continue working. In addition to being subjected to the earnings test, which results in a reduction in Social Security pension benefits to workers younger than seventy, retirees who work also must pay payroll taxes and regular income taxes on their earnings. In addition, elderly workers who earn more than $25,000 if they are single, or $32,000 if they are married, who still have Social Security pensions (as would be the case for workers older than seventy) will pay income tax on one-half to 85 percent (depending on their total income) of their Social Security benefits. For some retired workers, a dollar of earnings will result in both taxes and loss of Social Security benefits that will exceed the dollar of earnings! This results in very little incentive for the elderly to work. Only those elderly who enjoy working and are willing to work for much less than their gross compensation actually choose to remain in the labor force.

Saving Incentives

Among the most serious criticisms of the Social Security system is the assertion that it significantly reduces the rate of saving and capital formation in the economy. This could reduce both economic growth and the potential of the economy to provide jobs and raise incomes. The basic concern is that a pay-as-you-go system of retirement pensions has created the illusion that the tax contributions are placed in a trust fund and invested to provide retirement benefits to workers who belong to the system. As previously emphasized, the tax contributions of workers have been paid, by and large, directly to existing retirees until recently. The opportunity cost of such a system of paying pension benefits is the forgone return to capital that could have been earned had the taxes collected been invested in a true trust fund.

In effect, those who pay Social Security taxes receive as their return a claim, not against any capital asset, but against the earnings of future workers who will finance the current worker's pension when she retires. This line of reasoning remains correct even though the Social Security trust fund will grow substantially in the future, because much of the growth of the trust fund will be interest credited to its account by the U.S. Treasury. This interest will not constitute net income to the federal government because the credit of interest income to the fund will be offset by a debit of interest to the Treasury. When, however, the interest buildup is drawn on to pay cash benefits to retirees in the twenty-first century, the Treasury will have to use general fund revenues to pay out the benefits. Unless economic growth permits such revenues to be allocated without a general tax increase, the federal government might have to choose between increasing tax rates, cutting other government programs, or cutting Social Security replacement rates to meet its commitments.

---

[13]Michael J. Boskin, "Social Security and Retirement Decisions," *Economic Inquiry* 15 (January 1977): 1–25. For a summary of recent studies on retirement decision see Hurd, 1990, 590–606.

Although the effects of Social Security retirement benefits on saving are not clear-cut even in theory, the worker's incentive to save is affected in two different ways. First, the promise of a pension ensures an income for the worker's retirement years, thereby reducing the necessity of saving for old age. Second, by enabling the worker to retire earlier and discouraging work after retirement, Social Security increases the retirement years of the worker. This provides incentives to save more in order to provide the resources to finance various activities associated with a greater period of nonwork and more leisure time.[14] In the United States, since the end of World War II, the percentage of national income saved (in the aggregate) has been remarkably stable. Evidence is still scanty and somewhat conflicting, so no consensus has yet emerged among economists as to the actual effects of the Social Security system on saving.

The most controversial of the studies was conducted by Martin Feldstein and first published in 1974.[15] Feldstein's empirical work showed a significant impact of Social Security "wealth" (current value of promised pensions) on the rate of saving. Subsequent research by Leimer and Lesnoy found an error in Feldstein's calculation and concluded that the impact of Social Security wealth on saving could not be verified.[16]

The Asset-Substitution Effect

The promise of a Social Security pension results in what Feldstein calls an **asset-substitution effect,** reducing the incentive to save. In addition, the Social Security tax directly reduces the worker's income, so that the ability to save is reduced, and this, in turn, lowers the rate of saving still further.

Figure 8.3 illustrates the asset-substitution effect for two cases. In Figure 8.3A, a worker's indifference curves for consumption per year prior to retirement and consumption per year after retirement are drawn. If no government retirement system exists, the worker must save to provide retirement income. The line AB shows the worker's opportunity to give up annual preretirement consumption for annual postretirement consumption. The slope of the line reflects the rate of interest that the worker can earn. In the absence of a retirement system, the worker whose indifference curve U_1 is illustrated in Figure 8.3A is in equilibrium at point E. At that point, he gives up CB of annual preretirement consumption each year, which is saved to provide annual postretirement consumption of R per year.

---

[14]Another effect also might increase saving. If Social Security retirement benefits did not exist, and if the law provided for public assistance to the elderly poor, incentives might exist to avoid saving for one's old age, so as to be eligible for a means-tested poverty benefit at the time of retirement. The existence of Social Security pensions offsets the incentive to avoid saving so as to be eligible for public assistance at retirement.

[15]Martin Feldstein, "Social Security, Induced Retirement, and Aggregate Capital Accumulation," *Journal of Political Economy* 92 (September–October 1974): 905–926.

[16]Dean R. Leimer and Selig D. Lesnoy, "Social Security and Private Saving: New Time-Series Evidence," *Journal of Political Economy* 90 (June 1982): 606–629.

Figure 8.3   ✦   THE ASSET-SUBSTITUTION EFFECT

A

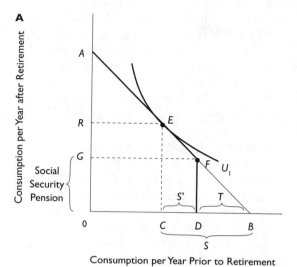

In **A,** the annual Social Security tax, T, reduces annual savings from S to S'. In **B,** the annual Social Security tax exceeds annual saving. For this worker, saving falls to zero. He is worse off than if no Social Security system existed and he were allowed to retain enough current income to save for retirement. His utility level is reduced from U_2 at point E without Social Security to U_1 at F with Social Security.

B

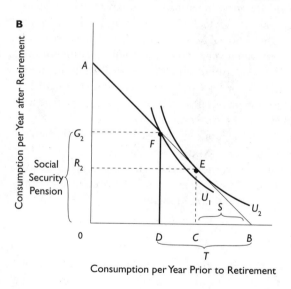

Now suppose that the government institutes a payroll tax of T dollars per year and promises the worker a pension of G per year at retirement. Assume that this tax is less than the amount the worker would otherwise save annually for retirement ($S = CB$). The distance DB represents the tax T. The payroll tax reduces the maximum amount of current annual consumption to $0D$ per year but guarantees the worker an annual pension at retirement of $0G$ even if the worker does not save. The worker's opportunities to trade current consumption for saving for retirement is now described by AFD. The worker whose indifference curves are illustrated in Figure 8.3A is still in equilibrium at point E. However, he now is saving only CD per year. The reduction in saving from CB to CD represents the asset-substitution effect. The worker saves less because he is promised a pension of G, even in the absence of any saving. In addition, the payroll tax reduces the person's current income, further reducing the ability of the worker to save. However, this worker is no worse off because he still enjoys $0C$ of current consumption and postretirement annual consumption of $0R$. The annual retirement income is equal to the government pension plus GR, from the worker's annual savings of CD.

Figure 8.3B shows the case of a worker who is made worse off as a result of the Social Security system. This worker would be in equilibrium at point E, where S per year is saved to provide postretirement annual consumption of R_2. For this worker, the annual payroll tax, T, exceeds the amount that she normally would save for retirement. However, this tax guarantees the worker a pension of G_2 per year, which is greater than the R_2 income her savings would have financed. The worker's opportunities for allocating consumption between preretirement and postretirement years are now represented by AFD. The government pension system does not give the worker the opportunity to give up part of her pension for more current consumption. The worker's highest level of well-being is now at point F, at which she receives utility level U_1, less than the U_2 that would be possible without Social Security benefits. This worker's saving falls to zero because the payroll tax of T per year and the overgenerous government pension (relative to the worker's preferences) remove both the capacity and the incentive to save for retirement. Also, an excess burden exists in this case due to the distortion between preretirement and postretirement consumption. This distortion results in the loss in well-being, from U_2 to U_1, for the worker.

In both cases, the reduction in saving by workers causes a decline in the rate of saving in the economy. This is because a pay-as-you-go government pension system does not replace lost private saving with government saving. Instead, the payroll taxes collected from individual workers are used to finance the postretirement consumption of retired workers. The result is a net reduction in savings.

The Induced-Retirement Effect

The negative impact of the asset-substitution effect on saving could be offset, however, by other possible effects of the Social Security retirement system. The **induced-retirement effect** results from the fact that Social Security benefits and the earnings test for such benefits tend to provide incentives for early retirement and less work during retirement years. This, in turn, provides incentive for workers to save more for a more lengthy period of retirement.

Feldstein has argued that the asset-substitution effect outweighs the induced-retirement effect. If this is true, the resulting reduction in saving reduces investment and tends to make capital scarcer than it would otherwise be. The scarcity of capital results in workers having fewer machines and other tools to work with than they would otherwise have. This reduces their productivity and results in lower wages than they would otherwise be earning.

It now is generally agreed that Feldstein's original model overestimated the reduction in saving caused by the asset-substitution effect of Social Security wealth. Subsequent research by Alicia Munnell found the induced-retirement effect for increased saving being roughly offset by the asset-substitution effect of Social Security wealth on reduction in saving. Munnell points out, however, that participation of the elderly in the labor force might increase in the future; this would result in a decrease in the reliance on saving to finance retirement. This could increase the relative importance of the asset-substitution effect and cause a net reduction in saving attributable to the existence of Social Security pensions.[17]

The Bequest Effect

Further analysis by Robert J. Barro suggests a theoretical basis for believing that Feldstein's asset-substitution effect is offset by still another influence of Social Security pensions on saving incentives.[18] Barro argues that strong incentives exist for parents to leave bequests to their children. This is the **bequest effect.** Social Security is, in effect, an agreement between generations to finance retirement by taxes on the working population. The transfer from the working population to the retired population, inherent in tax-financed Social Security benefits, increases the capability of the retired generation to put aside funds for bequests to their children. Barro believes that the existence of Social Security pensions provides incentives for the elderly to increase their saving to provide bequests to their children. He has also argued that Social Security pensions decrease the need for children to make payments to support their retired parents. This tends to increase their saving over their working life.[19]

Others have argued that the uncertainty over the future of the Social Security system, due to its financial difficulties and the decline in the expected return on tax contributions, is likely in the future to increase incentives to save for retirement. To the extent to which the yield on Social Security wealth declines in the future and market interest rates rise above the return on Social Security, increased saving will result. The net effect of the existence of government-supplied retirement benefits on saving remains indeterminate.

CHECKPOINT

1. How are Social Security pensions affected when retirees younger than seventy have earnings from work?
2. Explain why both the income and substitution effects of Social Security pensions are unfavorable to work incentives.
3. Why is it difficult to predict the effect of Social Security pensions on saving?

[17]Alicia H. Munnell, *The Future of Social Security* (Washington, D.C.: The Brookings Institution, 1977), chap. 6.

[18]Robert J. Barro, "Are Government Bonds Net-Worth?" *Journal of Political Economy* 82 (November/December 1974): 1095–1117.

[19]Robert J. Barro, *The Impact of Social Security on Private Saving* (Washington, D.C.: American Enterprise Institute, 1977).

HEALTH INSURANCE FOR THE ELDERLY: MEDICARE

The elderly have had government-supplied health insurance benefits since 1965, when amendments to the Social Security Act were passed. Under this health insurance plan, called **Medicare,** the elderly are covered by hospitalization insurance, which is financed by a special payroll tax amounting to a combined rate of 2.9 percent for employees and employers in 1994 on all labor income.

Medicare is a two-part program (A and B) of health insurance for persons older than sixty-five and some disabled workers. Medicare also pays for dialysis and kidney transplants for victims of renal disease no matter what their age. Part A of Medicare is a program of hospital insurance financed by a special payroll tax, the proceeds of which go into the Medicare Hospital Insurance (HI) Fund. Hospital benefits are subject to a deductible and cover only services that are considered medically necessary. Only reasonable charges are paid, and in some cases, Medicare patients end up paying part of the costs of covered services. Part B of Medicare is supplementary medical insurance for doctor's services, diagnostic tests, and some home health care services.

The supplementary medical insurance program under Part B is voluntary and is available to all Americans older than sixty-five who can purchase the coverage at subsidized rates. The monthly premium for Medicare Part B covers only about one-third of the costs of the program with the remainder financed by federal revenues. In 1991 the monthly premium was $29.90, with a $100 deductible per year before benefits were paid. The program pays 80 percent of covered services with certain maximum payments per medical service.

Why should government provide medical insurance to the elderly? One reason is the "adverse selection problem." *Adverse selection* is a process by which persons who have the greatest probability of obtaining benefits seek to obtain insurance and conceal information about their adverse conditions. In general, insurance companies can pool risks to avoid large payouts due to adverse selection by covering large groups rather than by offering their services to individuals. However, individuals who are no longer employed or do not belong to a clearly definable, insurable group will have to pay higher premiums, because insurance companies must protect themselves from high payouts that might result from adverse selection. Private insurance companies, therefore, might be reluctant to provide health insurance to the elderly on an individual basis because of the adverse selection problem. This provides a basis for government to pool insurance risks by providing compulsory insurance for a large group such as the elderly and financing the costs through taxation. The argument for government supply of medical insurance is therefore based on the presumption that government can provide such coverage to large groups at a lower cost than can be achieved if the insurance were provided through the market.

Expenditures under the Medicare program in 1991 were $104.5 billion, equal to 8 percent of total federal spending in that year. A modest amount of deductible expense must be incurred by the recipient before benefits are paid. Hospitalization benefits are paid for stays of up to ninety days for each benefit period. In effect, Medicare operates like a private health insurance program providing benefits to all its enrollees independent of their ability to pay for medical services.

Medicare, like its companion program for the poor, Medicaid, discussed in Chapter 7, encourages the consumption of medical services by reducing the price of such services to patients. The effects of government subsidization of consumption of medical services are analyzed in Chapter 7. As pointed out there, upward pressure on the price of medical services to those not covered by the public health plan can result from medical subsidies, and an excess burden will arise from the subsidy when it induces recipients to consume medical services beyond the point at which marginal benefit equals marginal cost.

The Medicare program and other issues in government provision of health care are discussed in greater detail in the following chapter.

UNEMPLOYMENT INSURANCE

Benefits from **unemployment insurance,** which provides income support for those temporarily out of work, are managed by individual states. Each state has its own separate trust fund; however, tax collections to support the program, as well as the trust funds, are managed by the federal government. Unemployment insurance was enacted into law as part of the original Social Security Act of 1935. Unemployment insurance is financed by a payroll tax, levied entirely on employers, on taxable wages up to a maximum of $7,000 per worker. The tax rate paid by each employer is based in part on the firm's layoff experiences, with firms that have relatively higher numbers of layoffs paying higher tax rates. This tax is collected by the federal government, but most of the funds are returned to the states, which administer the unemployment insurance program. The individual states levy their own unemployment taxes on wages. The taxable wage base varies by state but in no case is it less than the federal taxable wage base of $7,000 per year. State unemployment tax rates also vary considerably. In 1991, thirty-seven states had a taxable wage base for unemployment insurance that was higher than the federal tax base; the taxable wage base ranged as high as $22,400 (in Alaska).

Unlike medical insurance, unemployment insurance benefits are not commonly provided by private insurance firms. Unemployment insurance can increase the risk of unemployment. It is, after all, difficult to determine whether a worker actually is blameless for losing a job. In addition, workers in industries in which unemployment is most probable are likely to demand a disproportionate share of such insurance. Little private unemployment insurance is available, perhaps because the adverse selection problem prevents this service from being profitably supplied by private sellers.

Unemployment insurance benefits vary from state to state, with some states replacing as much as two-thirds of the workers' previous wages and paying dependent allowances. However, in recent years benefits paid have been declining and now average only 35 percent of previous earnings, not keeping pace with inflation rates. Gross replacement rates have declined on average from 50 percent to the current average of 35 percent. Normally, benefits last for a maximum of twenty-six weeks. However, since 1970, it has been possible to extend benefits for another thirteen weeks automatically, if the unemployment rate exceeds a certain level or during a recession.

In times of exceptional unemployment, Congress has the power to extend unemployment insurance benefits for even longer periods. The average period of unemployment for U.S. workers, however, is only eight weeks, so workers seldom collect benefits for the full period.

Unemployment insurance mainly benefits workers who are laid off or who lose their jobs when businesses shut down or reduce the scale of their operations. Unemployment insurance benefits are not available to new entrants or reentrants into the labor force. For example, a college student who graduates and enters the labor force to look for a job is classified as unemployed until he or she finds a job. However, even if it takes this new entrant into the labor force a year to find the job, the graduate is not eligible for unemployment insurance benefits.

Unemployment insurance is one of the automatic stabilizers in the federal budget. Its designers expected the system to maintain aggregate demand in periods of recession, when the demand normally falls due to unemployment.

Unemployment benefits are available to all workers who are covered by unemployment insurance, or about 88 percent of the work force. The benefits received are positively related to previous earnings. Since 1986 unemployment insurance benefits have been fully taxable as personal income under the federal income tax.

In recent years the proportion of the unemployed actually receiving unemployment insurance benefits has declined substantially. For example, in early 1990 only about one-third of the unemployed were collecting unemployment insurance benefits. In 1975, on average, three-quarters of the unemployed collected such benefits. The reason for the decline is that the contemporary economy includes more service workers and part-time workers, and many of these workers change jobs frequently. The workers do not stay in one job long enough to become eligible for UI benefits. In addition, state governments now require workers to work longer and earn more wages before they can collect benefits. Even though nearly 90 percent of workers are covered by unemployment insurance benefits, the proportion of workers who actually work in covered jobs long enough to get those benefits has been declining.

Research on the economic effects of unemployment insurance has concentrated on its impact on the duration of unemployment. Some have argued that the availability of generous unemployment insurance benefits subsidizes unemployment and job search by workers who lose their jobs, and therefore, this availability lengthens the period of unemployment desired by workers.

As was the case for Social Security retirement benefits, the net replacement rate is a key factor influencing the choices of those receiving unemployment insurance benefits. One study found that a 10 percentage point increase in the replacement rate increased the duration of unemployment by 1 ½ weeks.[20]

However, unemployment insurance benefits have not kept up with inflation since the 1970s. Average benefits paid have declined to only about one-third of previous earnings. In fact, the low current replacement rates under unemployment insurance have led to widespread criticism that the program no longer effectively cushions

---

[20]See Bruce D. Meyer, "Unemployment Insurance and Unemployment Spells," *Econometrica* 58, 4 (July 1990): 757–789.

the costs of unemployment. The decline in net replacement rates is likely to reduce the duration of the unemployment period.

Although unemployed workers are required to register for employment at local offices of the various state employment services, they cannot lose their unemployment benefits unless they refuse the offer of a suitable job. It is, however, difficult to force unemployed workers to accept jobs that pay considerably less than their previous jobs, or that have substantially poorer working conditions. For most workers, therefore, the registration requirement is merely a formality that requires them to spend a certain amount of time waiting in lines to receive their benefits. Workers have some control over the amount of time they remain unemployed. Their incentives to search for work and to accept lower-paying jobs depend on their replacement rates, the duration of unemployment insurance, and the availability (during their unemployment) of such subsidiary benefits as food stamps, relative to what they could earn on a new job. The decline in replacement rates since 1970 are likely to have increased incentives for the unemployed receiving unemployment insurance benefits to search for new jobs. The length of the period of job search associated with unemployment, however, has some positive aspects in that, in many cases, it allows workers to find higher wages and more stable employment.[21] We cannot, therefore, conclude that reduction in the duration of unemployment is necessarily a good thing.

CHECKPOINT

1. How does the Medicare program operate in the United States?
2. Why does "adverse selection" make it difficult or expensive for the elderly to obtain private health insurance?
3. How does the unemployment insurance system operate in the United States? Why has the proportion of the employed who actually receive such benefits been declining in recent years?

---

[21]For a review of studies on the effects on unemployment insurance, see Anthony B. Atkinson and John Micklewright, "Unemployment Compensation and Labor Market Transitions: A Critical Review," *Journal of Economic Literature*, 29 (December 1991): 1679–1727.

Summary

The Social Security Act of 1935 is the basis for most forms of social insurance in the United States today, including government-supplied retirement benefits, disability and survivors' insurance, health insurance for the elderly, and unemployment insurance. Social insurance is more comprehensive in many European countries, where health insurance, family allowances, and maternity benefits are supplied to all residents and financed through tax contributions.

The Social Security retirement system is tax financed and has been on a pay-as-you-go basis. Benefits are financed by a payroll tax on both employees and employers on wages paid up to a certain maximum amount per worker. Because of increases in tax rates, the Social Security trust fund has begun to grow, with the result that current workers will be paying taxes for a portion of their own pensions as well as those of current retirees. However, the trust fund will rapidly decline as the second half of the twenty-first century is approached.

The gross replacement rate measures the percentage of preretirement earnings replaced by pension benefits. This rate tends to decline with preretirement income. The net replacement rate is the percentage of preretirement after-tax earnings replaced by pension benefits.

Demographic changes anticipated in the twenty-first century have necessitated increases in Social Security taxes to finance benefits to future retirees at existing replacement rates. The amendments to the Social Security Act, passed by Congress in 1977 and 1983, scheduled significant increases in the payroll tax that will finance Social Security retirement benefits.

The return earned on Social Security by retirees, given rates of taxation to finance benefits, depends on the rate of growth of the taxable wages. In turn, the growth of taxable wages depends on the growth of labor force subject to Social Security taxes and the growth of real wages, with the latter being dependent on productivity. Little growth is expected in the labor force during the next few years; the rate of productivity growth is expected to be no more than 2 percent. Given the increased ratio of retirees per worker expected in the future and the indexing of retirement benefits with the rate of inflation, payroll tax rates have risen to finance current and future Social Security pensions.

Considerable concern has been expressed about the impact of Social Security retirement benefits on incentives to work and save. The availability and structure of Social Security benefits can discourage the elderly from working. The earnings test for retired workers between the ages of sixty-two and seventy reduces retirement benefits per dollar earned, after a certain allowable amount of earnings.

The effect of Social Security retirement benefits on saving is controversial. Because Social Security guarantees workers a pension, the incentive to save for retirement is diminished. On the other hand, insofar as Social Security benefits enable the worker to retire early, the incentive to save, and thus to provide for a longer period of retirement, is increased. The net effect on saving is indeterminate. The actual impact of the Social Security system on saving has not been unequivocally determined by empirical research.

Other forms of social insurance in the United States include health insurance for the elderly and unemployment benefits for workers. Medicare subsidizes medical expenses incurred by persons older than sixty-five. Unemployment insurance is available to workers who are laid off their jobs. The replacement rate averages about 35 percent of previous wages. Because unemployment insurance subsidizes those workers who are between jobs, concern has been expressed about its impact on the length of unemployment desired by workers.

A Forward Look

The next chapter presents a discussion of health and medical expenditures in the United States and discusses the role of government in providing health benefits. The current system of provision of health insurance in the United States is discussed and the costs and benefits of an expanded government role in the provision of health insurance services are analyzed.

Important Concepts

Social Security and Insurance Programs
Fully Funded Pension System
Old-Age, Survivors, and Disability Insurance (OASDI)
Tax-Financed Pension System
Pay-as-You-Go Pension System
Average Indexed Monthly Earnings (AIME)
Earnings Test
Gross Replacement Rate
Net Replacement Rate
Asset-Substitution Effect
Induced-Retirement Effect
Bequest Effect
Medicare
Unemployment Insurance

Questions for Review

1. What are the basic distinctions between social insurance and government assistance programs for the poor?

2. How do Social Security benefits increase the incomes of low-income workers relative to upper-income workers? Discuss the distinction between the net and gross replacement rates for workers. What does a net replacement rate of 100 percent imply about the standard of living of a retiree relative to preretirement earnings?

3. What are the fundamental differences between fully funded and pay-as-you-go tax-financed retirement

systems? How can the Social Security system continue to pay pension benefits even if its trust fund is depleted?

4. Under what conditions will the growth of tax revenues to pay Social Security benefits equal the rate of growth of labor earnings in the economy? Why have payroll tax rates been increased in recent years?

5. How can lowering replacement rates or increasing the retirement age affect the Social Security tax rate?

6. Many economists assert that Social Security pensions redistribute income from single workers to married workers with dependent spouses and from high-income workers to low-income workers. Why is this likely?

7. Use indifference curve analysis to show how the availability of Social Security pensions and the application of the earnings test are likely to decrease hours worked and labor force participation of the elderly.

8. Use indifference curve analysis to show how a pay-as-you-go Social Security retirement system can decrease a worker's savings per year from a positive amount to zero. Under what circumstances will the system make a worker worse off than would be the case if there were no such system?

9. In what sense are Social Security pension benefits based on "need"?

10. How can the bequest effect and the induced-retirement effect offset the asset-substitution effect?

Problems

1. A middle-income worker with a dependent spouse older than sixty-five will retire in January 1997. In the year prior to retirement, her gross monthly earnings are $1,500. Her Social Security pension benefit is $1,000 per month. Prior to retirement, she was subject to total taxes on her labor earnings amounting to 20 percent. Calculate her gross and net replacement rate. Suppose the cash value of Medicare subsidies that she expects to receive during retirement amount to $2,000 per year. Recalculate the replacement rates including the Medicare benefits.

2. Suppose the real rate of growth of wages subject to Social Security taxes is expected to average 1 percent per year during the next forty years. Assuming that the Social Security tax rate remains constant, prove that the average return on Social Security taxes paid into the Social Security trust fund also will be 1 percent. Explain why workers with high incomes can expect negative returns on their Social Security taxes during this period.

3. Use the data from Problem 1 to plot the worker's daily money income-leisure trade-off line. To do so, calculate her daily pension and assume 150 working hours in a month. Assume that the worker is allowed to earn $8,000 per year before her Social Security benefits are reduced by $1 for each $3 of labor earnings. Show how it is possible for the retiree to be indifferent between not working at all and working enough to give up all her Social Security benefits.

4. Use indifference curve analysis to show how the Social Security pension system can reduce annual consumption for some workers who have strong preference for current versus future consumption. What factors will influence the effect of the Social Security system on an individual's well-being and savings rate?

Suggestions for Further Reading

Congress of the United States, Congressional Budget Office, *Baby Boomers in Retirement: An Early Perspective* (Washington D.C.: U.S. Government Printing Office, September 1993). An analysis of how the baby-boom generation is likely to fare in retirement compared with their parents.

Detlefs, Dale R. and Myers, Robert J. *Guide to Social Security.* Louisville, KY: William M. Mercer–Meidinger-Hansen, Inc. A concise booklet explaining the nuts and bolts of the Social Security system. Revised annually.

Hurd, Michael D. "Research on the Elderly: Economic Status, Retirement, and Consumption and Saving," *Journal of Economic Literature* 38, 2 (June 1990): 565–637. A review and summary of many research articles on the economics of aging, retirement decisions, and the impact of Social Security pensions on choices.

Munnell, Alicia H. *The Future of Social Security.* Washington, D.C.: The Brookings Institution, 1977. A good overview of the Social Security system, with analysis of the effect of the system on saving.

Rejda, George E. *Social Insurance and Economic Security,* 3d ed. Englewood Cliffs, NJ: Prentice-Hall, 1988. A comprehensive analysis of the many social insurance programs commonly provided by industrial nations.

Stein, Bruno. *Social Security and Pensions in Transition.* New York: The Free Press, 1980. A comprehensive analysis of both government and private pension systems. Discusses the history of the Social Security system, the development of private pensions, and the basic problems faced by both types of retirement systems. The book is written well and does not require a strong background in economics.

Thompson, Lawrence H. "The Social Security Reform Debate," *Journal of Economic Literature* 21, 4 (December 1983): 1425–1467. A review of the Social Security system and research by economists regarding its effects on incentives of workers and savers. It contains an extensive bibliography.

9

GOVERNMENT AND
HEALTH CARE

LEARNING OBJECTIVES

After reading this chapter you should be able to

1. Explain the unique features of the market for health care in the United States and how these impair efficiency of operation of the market.
2. Discuss trends in health care spending in the United States.
3. Analyze how third-party payments for health care services affect incentives to purchase and provide such services.
4. Evaluate the role of government in regulating and providing health care services.
5. Discuss the basic benefits of the Medicare and Medicaid programs in the United States.
6. Analyze alternative government policies for controlling the growth of health care costs and extending health insurance coverage to all citizens of a nation.

*I*n the United States we spend much more per person for health care than do citizens of other nations—one-third more than Canada, twice as much as Japan, and three times as much as the United Kingdom. Yet despite the high spending on health care, dissatisfaction with the system is widespread. Rapidly rising prices for medical services is a serious concern—during the 1980s, prices for medical services rose at more than twice the rate of prices for other goods and services on average.

Governments are playing an increasingly active role in the finance of health care in the United States. In 1991, federal, state, and local governments paid 43 percent of the $751.8 billion of health care bills incurred by Americans in that year. The federal government's budget is allocating more and more funds to finance health care expenditures. In 1970, the federal government allocated 7.1 percent of its budget to health care spending; by 1991 it was allocating 14.1 percent of its budget to health. The Congressional Budget Office expects that under policies prevailing in 1993 health care spending will account for a 25 percent share of the federal budget by 2000. Governments are under pressure to pursue policies both to control the rate of increase in prices for medical services and to extend health insurance coverage to the uninsured.

President Clinton made health care reform a key goal of his administration. His health reform proposal sought to provide universal health insurance coverage to all Americans coupled with policies designed to slow the rate of growth of health care spending. As of 1992 an estimated 35 million Americans had no health insurance coverage. An important objective of the President's plan was to convert health insurance into a government mandated right for American citizens so that they could not be denied health insurance because of preexisting conditions and to ensure that they would not lose their health insurance coverage when they changed or lost their job. It also would have modified existing government programs like Medicare and Medicaid to provide new services such as long-term care and prescription drugs for the elderly. The controversy that greeted the President's proposal and his plans for funding it is only one indication of the many thorny issues involved in reforming the system of both providing and financing health care that has evolved in the United States since 1950.

In this chapter we examine the market for health care in the United States with special emphasis on the role of government in that market. We examine how a system of third-party payments for medical services affects incentives to consume and supply such services. We then examine mechanisms and policy alternatives that can result in a more efficient allocation of resources to health care and stem the growth of rising health care expenditures. Finally, we look at alternative means of financing and rationing medical and health care services, including universal entitlement, national health insurance, and government-provided health care.

CHARACTERISTICS OF THE U.S. MARKET FOR HEALTH CARE

Buying health care is not like buying pizza or jeans. Purchases of most medical services are not made to provide immediate gratification or to satisfy a person's desire to accumulate possessions. By and large, medical services are purchased when a person is ill or injured. A great deal of uncertainty surrounds an individual's own demand for medical services because no one can predict an illness or an injury. However, when such services are needed, the individual can expect potentially high treatment costs—in some cases of catastrophic illness or injury, these costs could exceed the ability of the individual to pay and force the person into bankruptcy. Because of both the uncertainty and potentially high cost individuals rationally seek to purchase insurance for their health care costs.

The system that has evolved in the United States is one in which health insurance is provided as part of the compensation of most employees while the elderly and the poor who qualify are covered under Medicare and Medicaid, which are government-provided health insurance programs. Those who do not receive health insurance benefits from their employers, or do not qualify for either Medicare or Medicaid, can purchase health insurance in the marketplace if they choose to do so.

No system of national, or government-provided health insurance is offered in the United States financed by taxes such as that which exists in the United Kingdom. Recent proposals by the Clinton administration for a government guaranteed entitlement to health insurance for all Americans would have left the current system of employer and government insurance plans intact but would have mandated benefits for all workers and subsidized health insurance for others.

As of 1994 in the United States, health insurance was not a right guaranteed to all Americans. Many individuals who either did not receive health insurance benefits from an employer, or who did not qualify for Medicare or Medicaid, chose not to insure themselves. These people made this decision either because they were willing to bear the risk of incurring high medical costs or because the insurance available to them in the marketplace was priced beyond their ability or willingness to pay. An estimated 35 million Americans in 1992 were not covered by health insurance. However, about 85 percent of the U.S. population as of 1994 was covered by some form of health insurance. Health insurance has become the ticket for health care services in the United States. Those without health insurance coverage run the risk of being refused service when then need it unless they can convince the providers that they can somehow pay their bills.

The insurance-dominated market for medical care has reduced the price consciousness of the public. On average, consumers of medical care pay only about one-fifth of the market price of services they consume. This encourages both the provision and consumption of medical services. The bulk of our bills for medical services are paid for by insurance and the premiums we or our employers pay are not necessarily related to the quantity of such services we as individuals consume. However, as we all consume more services and are offered better quality (and therefore higher cost) services, our health care spending rises. And as spending on health care increases so do insurance premiums. In other words, the insurance-based payment system for medical services has impaired the ability of prices to ration medical services efficiently and this in turn has increased insurance premiums so that many individuals choose not to purchase insurance. Many employers, especially those who employ unskilled workers, find that to offer health insurance to their workers would raise their labor costs enough to impair their competitiveness in their product markets. Therefore, under the current system, many small firms often choose not to include health insurance as part of the compensation of their workers.

The host of other imperfections in markets for medical services includes problems of dispersing accurate information to consumers, a tax system that has encouraged some large employers to compensate workers with general health insurance plans while making it difficult for small businesses to get insurance for their employees, and an array of private and government insurance plans that pay different prices for the same medical services thereby affecting the incentives of medical providers. All these imperfections naturally result in demands for government action to alter both the function and outcomes in the market for medical services and health care.

Before we examine the role of government in this market, we must examine how some of its unique features affects the way it functions. Let's first examine spending trends in the market for health care services and then look at some of the possible explanations for these trends.

Health Care Spending in the United States

Expenditures on health care in the United States have been rising rapidly. In 1960 we allocated only 5.3 percent of the value of our national production to health care—total national spending, including hospital care, professional services, drugs, and a variety of other health services including research and the construction of medical facilities, amounted to 14 percent of GDP in 1993. The share of GDP allocated to health care therefore has nearly tripled since 1960. Figure 9.1 shows how health care spending has increased as a percentage of GDP since 1965. Health care spending is projected to absorb nearly 20 percent of GDP by the year 2000 based on estimates by the Congressional Budget Office.

The pie chart (Figure 9.2) shows how total health expenditures in the United States were financed in 1991. Of the total amount spent in 1991, 43 percent was paid for by governments, with the federal government accounting for the largest share (about 70 percent) of total federal, state, and local government spending on health care in the United States. The strong government presence in the market for these services in the United States has been growing at a rapid rate as has the overall rate of increase in spending on health care in the nation. However, expenditures by governments in the United States are low compared to health care spending by governments in other industrialized nations. Most European nations have extensive government provision of health care and governments typically foot more than 70 percent of the

Figure 9.1 ✦ U.S. HEALTH EXPENDITURES AS A PERCENTAGE OF GROSS DOMESTIC PRODUCT, 1960–2000

Expenditures on health care in the United States have risen very rapidly since 1965, absorbing nearly 14 percent of GDP in 1991.

Source: Congressional Budget Office (CBO) calculations based on data from the Health Care Financing Administration, Office of the Actuary, 1992, and CBO baseline data for gross domestic product (GDP), January 1993.

Figure 9.2 ◆ FINANCING HEALTH CARE EXPENDITURES IN THE UNITED STATES, 1991

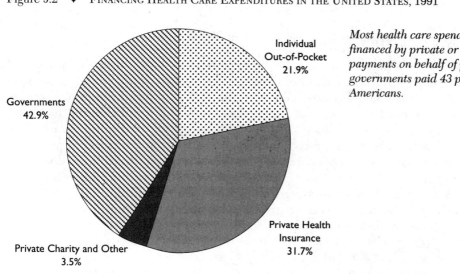

Most health care spending in the United States is financed by private or government health insurance payments on behalf of patients. In 1991 governments paid 43 percent of the medical bills of Americans.

bill of health care and finance those costs with taxes. For example, Norway has an extensive publicly financed system of health care and pays 97.6 percent of all the health expenditures of Norwegians. Yet at the same time Norway allocates only 7.5 percent of its GDP to health care compared to 14 percent in the United States as of 1993.

Private health insurance finances 31.7 of health care expenditures in the United States. Only 21.9 percent of Americans' health care bills are paid for directly by the individuals as out-of-pocket household costs. The portion of health care expenses directly paid for by Americans has been declining as a result of increased insurance coverage of major and minor health problems since 1965. In that year, out-of-pocket costs of health care to individuals financed 46 percent of expenditures in the United States. We have been spending less and less of our own funds on health care during the past 25 years with more of our medical bills being paid for by various insurance programs. This is a very significant factor in the rise of health care spending in the United States that we analyze in depth.

Total spending on health care per person in the United States amounted to slightly more than $3,000 in 1991. Government expenditures for health care in the same year were $329.9 billion, with more than 80 percent of that amount accounted for by the nation's two major government-provided health insurance programs, Medicaid and Medicare. As pointed out in the preceding two chapters, Medicaid provides health insurance mainly for the poor receiving welfare benefits and Medicare for the elderly and the permanently disabled.

Per capita spending for health care by governments was $1,200 in 1991—and rising rapidly. Expenditures for health care in the United States include hospital services; professional services such as those of physicians, dentists, and nurses; drugs;

health care equipment and buildings; the cost of administering the system; and the cost of research.

Asymmetric Information

One possible explanation for rising health care spending concerns the methods of providing information in the marketplace for medical services. The market for medical care is one of *asymmetric information* in which the sellers of medical care are better informed about cost and quality than are the buyers with whom they trade. Usually, consumers of medical care are patients whose only source of information on the benefits of medical procedures and products is the medical-care providers, mainly physicians. Often, information on the costs of treatments, especially emergency treatment, is difficult or impractical to obtain in advance. In effect, patients allow physicians to make decisions for them. The physician in most cases is trained to and has the incentive to maximize the quality of care provided to the patient.

However, medical care, like any other good or services is provided in efficient amounts only when it is consumed to the point at which its marginal benefit to the consumer falls to equal its marginal cost to the provider. The problem under asymmetric information in the market for health care is that the consumer must rely on the provider for information on both the marginal benefit and the marginal cost of the health care. If the marginal benefit of medical procedures is overstated or if physicians, in their attempt to provide the highest quality care, prescribe procedures for which marginal benefits fall short of marginal costs, then more than the efficient amount of resources will be devoted to medical care.

Some evidence indicates that asymmetric information does lead to overspending on health care. For example, a study of Medicare patients who underwent a procedure to remove plaque from their carotid arteries to avoid blockage found that one-third of the operations involved costs that exceeded benefits. The problem was that patients were not adequately informed about the complications possible from the procedure such as the risk of stroke. In fact, about 10 percent of the persons undergoing the procedure died within a month after the surgery!

Similarly, many life lengthening procedures for terminally ill patients could cost more than their benefits to patients. Remember that physicians are trained to provide benefits to their patient. The weighing of the benefits of such life lengthening procedures against the costs can be done only by the patient receiving the benefits. Further, under an insurance-based health care system, the patient rarely bears the full cost of such procedures. Instead the costs are shared by many individuals, to the extent to which services to individuals increase health care spending and insurance premiums.

Risk and the Market for Health Insurance

In a risky world, individuals desire health insurance to cushion the costs of unplanned and uncertain medical expenses. Private insurance companies can provide such coverage for individuals while earning profit because they are able to pool the risks incurred by a large group of individuals. Because you do not know in advance that you might be unfortunate enough to become ill or have an accident that forces you to incur very high medical bills for the year, you are likely to seek insurance. Most people are **risk averse,** meaning that they prefer to incur a certain modest cost for insurance rather than to risk high costs as a result of an unforeseen prospect. For example, you might be perfectly health this year and incur no medical expenses at all. On the other hand, suppose there is a 1-percent probability that you will contract a major illness requiring you to spend $100,000 in medical bills. The expected costs of your medical expenses are $1,000. A risk-averse person prefers the certain outcome of spending $1,000 or even more for $100,000 of health insurance as opposed to running the risk of getting ill and having to pay $100,000 for treatment.

Companies that provide health insurance to a large and diverse group of clients, on the other hand, can easily predict their expenses. If they know the historic probabilities of recent diseases and other medical problems, they can charge premiums that cover the costs of the medical expenses they insure and can add on additional administrative costs for processing claims and still make a profit by selling the policies to risk-averse consumers. For example, if the company provides $100 million worth of insurance per year for which the average probability of payout is 1 percent, then it can finance payouts if it collects premiums from enrollees of $1 million per year. To cover administrative costs and earn a profit, the company will charge a bit more, say 10 percent.

The system of health insurance in the United States does not, however, insure only against low probability medical expenses. Instead, virtually all expenses are covered up to certain limits after patients meet their deductibles. Our insurance system insures against low-cost treatment as well as high-cost treatment. By insuring treatment of high probability expenses, such as treatment of minor ailments including the common cold and most routine visits to a physician for minor health problems, health insurance in the United States has reduced price consciousness of the public and has impaired the ability of the marketplace to ration health care services. Many employer-provided health insurance plans also pay for routine dental expenses and eyeglasses.

The extension of health insurance to cover both high probability and relatively low-cost risks has resulted in high insurance premiums. The coverage costs more, simply because more is being covered. In addition, the risks associated with sale of private health insurance have made health insurance providers more cautious when taking on new business. In deciding to provide insurance to a group of individuals or an employer, insurance firms weigh the marginal cost of providing that insurance against the marginal return. If the marginal revenue from sale of the policy falls short of the marginal cost, the insurance firm will not sell the insurance. Given the rising cost of health care and the high expenditures associated with major illnesses, many health insurers have been reluctant to expose themselves to the risk of high payouts. The insurers have moved from "community rating," which charges premiums based on the expected costs of serving a population, to "experience rating." Under experience rating, insurance firms base premiums for a group on the expected costs of serving *that particular group.* Under this method of pricing, relatively healthy groups pay low prices for health insurance. On the other hand, a group with a poor experience rating, or for which one member has incurred very high medical expenses during the year because of an illness, will pay much higher premiums than would be the case if community rating was used.

Third-Party Payments

The system of health care that has evolved in the United States is based mainly on private provision of services with a mix of private and government health insurance programs reimbursing health care providers for their services. Those who have health insurance pay only a small portion of their health care bills. In 1991, only about one-fifth of the total expenditures for health care was paid for by individuals out of their own pockets. Instead, most medical and health care costs are paid for by an insurance company or a government program such as Medicare or Medicaid on behalf of the patients. U.S. businesses, as of 1993, were paying on average more than $3,000 per year per employee for health insurance costs.

The system of health care provision in the United States is financed by **third-party payments,** where the third party is neither the purchaser nor the seller of the service. Third-party payments have important effects on the incentives of patients to use medical services and on the incentives of health care providers to supply those services. When an insured person needs health care services, all but a small portion of the bill is typically paid by the insurer. The typical insurance plan requires patients first to incur a certain amount of health care expenditures, called the **deductible,** before the plan starts paying benefits. After this initial amount is paid by the patient, the plan takes care of most of the additional expenses incurred during the year up to a certain maximum that varies from plan to plan. The amount paid as an out-of-pocket cost by the individual is called **coinsurance** and varies from plan to plan but is typically 20 percent of the cost. After a patient incurs the deductible expense of the plan, the insurance plan pays 80 percent of covered expenses.

The system of third-party payments increases the incentive to both consume and provide health care services. Figure 9.3 shows that having health insurance increases spending on health care. The graph shows both the demand and supply curves for health care services. Without health insurance, each patient would have to pay his or her own medical bills, the equilibrium price of health care services on average would be P°, and the equilibrium quantity sold per year would be Q°. Assuming that the demand for health care services reflects the marginal social benefit of such services and the supply reflects the marginal social cost, the efficient quantity of these services would be produced because at P° the marginal social benefit of health care equals its marginal social cost. However, with both private- and government-provided health insurance, the price per unit of health care services will be lower than P°. The explanation is that after patients meet their deductible, they pay only a small fraction of the actual charge for various health care services including surgery, hospital stays, and prescription drugs. Suppose that, on average, availability of health insurance reduces the price per unit of service from P° to P_1 to patients. As a result of the price decline in out-of-pocket costs, the quantity of health care service demanded increases from Q° to Q_1. As the quantity demanded increases, the quantity supplied also must increase to prevent shortages in the market. However, to attract the additional resources required to increase the availability of medical services, the price paid to the

Figure 9.3 ✦ HEALTH INSURANCE AND THE MARKET FOR HEALTH CARE

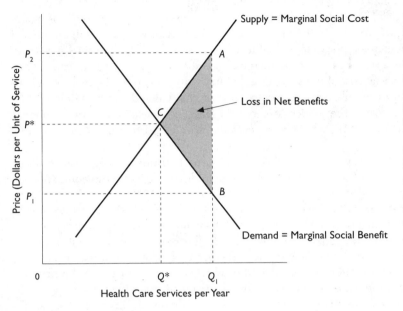

The third-party payment mechanism of health insurance lowers the out-of-pocket cost of health care to insurees. The price of health care is effectively reduced to consumers from $P°$ to P_1. As the quantity demanded increases from $Q°$ to Q_1, the price to health care providers must rise to P_2 to prevent shortages in the market. Third parties pay the difference between the price to buyers and the price received by providers. The system encourages an overallocation of resources to health care beyond the point at which the marginal social benefit of such services falls to equal the marginal social cost.

supplier must increase. As shown in Figure 9.3, the price to medical providers per unit of service on average must increase from $P°$ to P_2 to induce providers to make Q_1 units of service available per year. The system of third-party payments has both re-duced the price of services for patients and increased the price of services received by health care providers while increasing the amount of resources devoted to health care!

The system reduces people's incentive to economize on the use of health care services. The quantity of services demanded does not increase because people are becoming ill more often. It increases because individuals visit physicians more often for minor ailments they might choose to treat themselves if they had to pay the full price for such services. In addition, because physicians and other medical practition-ers know that patients pay only a fraction of the price for services, they prescribe more tests and other services than they would otherwise. Naturally, because the price paid per unit of services to providers increases as a result of health insurance while the quantities demanded and supplied also increase, total expenditures on health care also increase. As shown in Figure 9.3, total expenditures per year on health care services increase from $P°Q°$ to P_2Q_1. Health insurance therefore increases spending on health care. Total out-of-pocket expenditures by consumers are, of course, much lower after health insurance—an amount represented by the area $0P_1BQ_1$ in the graph. However, the bulk of the expenditures for health care are paid directly to med-ical providers by the private and government health insurers. The amount paid by third parties is represented by the area P_1P_2AB. These expenditures are financed by the health insurance premiums employers and their employees pay for coverage and the taxes that finance the government insurance programs of Medicare and Medicaid.

As a result of third-party payments, more than the efficient amount of health care services are provided in the marketplace. Health insurance results in Q_1 units of health care demanded per year. At that level of consumption the marginal social cost of health care services exceeds the marginal benefit of such services to consumers. The marginal social cost of the services at point A is P_2 while the marginal social benefit of Q_1 units of service per year (see point B on the demand curve) is only P_1. The marginal social cost of the services exceeds the marginal social benefit by an amount equal to the distance AB, which represents the average portion of services paid by third parties.

The area ABC represents the loss in net benefits from resource use resulting from overallocation of resources to health care production beyond the point at which MSB falls to equal MSC.

The **moral hazard of health insurance** is the increase in the incentive to consume and supply health care services that results from the reduction in price to consumers when third parties pay the bulk of medical expenses. Because out-of-pocket costs for medical services are low to insured consumers, they more readily agree to more procedures and prescriptions than they would in the absence of insurance. Another reason for the increase in the quantity demanded is the effect that coverage by insurance reduces incentive to take adequate precautions against incurring an insured expense. For example, those with theft insurance might take few precautions (such as locks and burglar alarms) to discourage thieves than would be the case if no insurance was available. Persons with health insurance might take fewer precautions to protect their health than they would if they had to pay the full price of medical care resulting from illnesses that they could avoid through changing their life-style. The magnitude of the moral hazard of health insurance would depend on the elasticity of demand for health care services. The more elastic the demand the greater the magnitude of the moral hazard.

Concern about the moral hazard problem associated with reduced-price provision of a good that is price excludable, such as medical care, has resulted in the development of various schemes to make consumers more price conscious. The deductible amount of an insurance policy, as previously discussed, requires a certain amount of expense to be incurred for health care before the company will start to pay benefits. Deductibles for many private health insurance plans run between $150 and $1,000 per year. The deductible reduces the incentive to seek medical care for minor problems. Because consumers who do not exceed the deductible in medical care costs will pay the full price of service, they must compare the marginal benefit of such services with the marginal social cost of the services. These individuals will be more careful in planning their health care expenditures than other individuals whose expenditures exceed the deductible.

Coinsurance, as mentioned, requires consumers to pay some share of the price of the health care services they consume while the remainder is paid by the insurance company. Coinsurance is commonly used together with deductibles to make insured consumers more price conscious.

Finally, insurance companies often limit their payments to fixed amounts for certain services. If this amount does not cover the full costs, the insured has to make up the difference or the provider will have to absorb the difference. This technique of limiting payout provides incentives for both the consumers and providers of medical care to economize on the quantity and quality of services they consume. Sometimes health insurance companies reimburse providers for "usual, customary, and reasonable" charges for certain medical procedures. The patient has to pay any differences between these charges and actual charges.

OTHER FEATURES CONTRIBUTING TO INEFFICIENCY AND HIGH COST

Malpractice Insurance

Another factor influencing the cost of medical services has been the soaring cost of malpractice insurance for physicians in recent years. These costs have, in part, been passed on to patients as higher fees. To reduce their risks of malpractice suits and to keep their malpractice insurance premiums under control, many physicians have resorted to more testing of patients, more office visits, and maintaining more extensive records to protect themselves in case of a malpractice suit. Furthermore, high malpractice insurance rates and the effect of a malpractice suit on those rates have also resulted in some physicians refusing to treat high-risk patients or perform high-risk procedures.

Service to Uninsured Patients

Another important characteristic of the market for health care is that many of the health care facilities, such as community hospitals or nursing homes, are nonprofit institutions or are run by governments. Many of these institutions are obligated to serve uninsured patients who cannot afford to pay for their health care. Naturally the costs incurred on behalf of these uninsured patients must be covered to prevent the institution from suffering losses. Providers of medical care often cover their losses while providing services to the uninsured by charging higher prices to the insured. This "cross-subsidization" of patients unable to pay by those who can pay through health insurance and out of their own pockets implies that health insurers pay more, as the cost of treating the uninsured is transferred to the insured. Because the insured consumers of health care pay only a small share of the price of those uninsured, the higher prices do not reduce the quantity of health care demanded substantially. However, the higher medical expenses of the insurance firms are transferred to employers and other providers of health insurance through higher insurance premiums. In effect, when nonprofit institutions treat uninsured patients who cannot pay their own bills, health insurance costs for all the insured rise, meaning that the insured end up paying for the treatment of the uninsured.

Technological Advance and Lack of Price Competition

Rapid technological change in health care has certainly improved the quality of service to patients. However, because third-party payments encourage overuse of new technology, new technology has likely been overdeveloped, beyond the point at which its marginal benefit equals its marginal cost. If new technology is developed and utilized beyond the efficient level, then more than the efficient amount of capital will be employed in the health care industry. In fact, hospitals often compete to attract patients by offering the latest technologies and comfortable rooms. They seek to attract patients by capital investments that improve the quality of care (and contribute to higher cost) rather than seeking to economize on costs and keep prices for services down to the minimum possible.

An eagerness on the part of physicians to supply and prescribe the wonders of modern technology has also contributed to rising health care expenditures in the United States. Federal, state, and local governments spend more than $10 billion per year on medical research that provides the basic knowledge to develop new equipment and treatment that improve the effectiveness of medical treatment. The system of third-party payments for medical treatment in the United States encourages doctors and their patients to utilize the new technology. As new technological equipment and procedures are disseminated through the marketplace, their very existence provides incentives for the owners (often physicians themselves) to utilize the equipment. Many small hospitals in the United States obtain equipment and finance its costs easily through third-party payments on behalf of insured patients. For example, in the late 1980s the United States had 3.7 magnetic resonance imagers per million persons. During the same period the area comprising the former West Germany had only 0.9 of the machines per million persons while Canada had 0.5 of the machines per million persons. The abundance of such marvels of medical technology as open-heart surgical units in the United States has led to a vast demand for use of these facilities not only by Americans but by foreigners as well, many of whom (such as those from Canada) live in nations where governments rather than the marketplace determine the allocation of resources to new medical technology. The scarcity of the new medical technology in many countries results in long waiting periods for patients to use the facilities.

Abundance of new technological marvels does not necessarily imply efficiency in their use. When the facilities are purchased in numbers for which their marginal benefits exceed marginal costs, more than the efficient amount of resources is utilized in providing the services of these new facilities. The third-party payment system encourages exactly such an overuse of all medical services.

Some studies have suggested that new technologies are overused in the United States. However, in nations where government controls limit the spending for and availability of new technologies, as in Canada and the United Kingdom, there are long waiting lists for access to the marvels of modern technology. The U.S. system encourages overuse of new technology and more than the efficient number of facilities; however, those insured patients who require access to the new technology can generally be accommodated without delay. If you require special medical equipment, you can get it readily in the United States. However, the opportunity cost of this abundance is a reduction of the availability of alternative health services (such as preventive care) or expenditures on other goods and services for which the marginal social benefit might be higher.

C H E C K P O I N T

1. What are some of the unique features of the market for health care in the United States that contribute to overallocation of resources to medical services?
2. How does the system of third-party payments through health insurance affect the market for health care?
3. What is the moral hazard of health insurance?

GOVERNMENTS AND HEALTH CARE: COMPENSATING FOR MARKET FAILURE

The imperfections in the markets for health care services result in demands for government activity in such areas as research, provision of information, and the distribution of services.

Certain aspects of the provision of health care often are difficult to sell. Pure medical research with no ready or current commercial application could be underfunded by organizations that seek profits from their operations. For this reason many argue that medical research should be like a public good, financed by government and made freely available to all who seek to use it. This view would prevent the patenting of basic medical advances resulting from pure research. By preventing ownership of and the right to charge royalties for the use of basic advances in medical knowledge, the cost of new medical technology and procedures would be lower.

Also, some positive externalities are associated with reducing contagious diseases. To internalize these externalities it is reasonable to subsidize the provision of vaccines. The Public Health Service of the U.S. government monitors contagious diseases and has the power to enforce regulations pertaining to vaccinations and quarantining individuals with contagious diseases. The service also provides information on the health effects of such activities as smoking and drinking. In recent years, the Public Health Service also has been active in providing information about AIDS and encouraging personal health practices that limit the spread of AIDS.

The general belief that individuals, because of inadequate information, tend to underconsume medical services also has led to government subsidization of medical expenditures through tax exclusion of employer-provided health insurance benefits. However, as our analysis in this chapter has shown, the system of health care provision in the United States leads to an overconsumption, rather than underconsumption, of medical services because of reduced price consciousness on the part of consumers.

The government also plays an active role in helping protect patients against incompetent physicians. Physicians must be licensed by state governments and they

WHY WORRY ABOUT GROWTH IN
HEALTH CARE COSTS?

Health care spending is expected to account for close to a whopping one-fifth of our GDP by the year 2000 unless current trends in spending are reversed. Why should public policy be affected by the fact that health care spending in the United States has absorbed sharply increasing shares of our Gross Domestic Product since 1960? As we devote increasing shares of our resources to health care, less will be available to spend on alternative good and services. In other words, the opportunity cost of spending more on health care is a decrease in alternative goods and services. Health care spending in the United States is likely at a point at which the marginal costs of health care exceed the marginal benefits and still further increase in the allocation of resources to health care will add to the inefficiency with which resources are used. For this reason, many are demanding more government intervention in the market for health care to control growth in spending.

The rising cost of health insurance policies provided by employers has probably resulted in lower money wages and less generous nonmedical benefits to workers in the United States. During the past twenty years average real wages paid to workers in the United States have been stagnant but the share of workers compensation accounted for by health insurance benefits has been rising. Much of this is the result of the favorable tax treatment of health insurance benefits that has encouraged corporations to overallocate resources to health insurance. The growth in worker money pay has consequently lagged behind the growth in payments for their health insurance. Bidding up of health care prices and an increase in prescribed treatments as a result of the growth of third party payments also has pushed the price of health insurance policies beyond the ability to pay of many individuals who do not receive such benefits from their employers.

Other labor market effects of the system of health insurance also have evolved. In general, skilled, high-wage employees of large companies tend to be the beneficiary of good employer-provided health insurance while those without health insurance benefits are low-wage unskilled workers employed by small firms and who often drift in and out of the labor force. For low-wage workers, the cost of a health insurance is a higher proportion of their money wage than for high-wage workers. As a result, the labor market forces work to exclude low-wage workers from health insurance benefits. Many employers avoid putting low-wage workers on their full-time payroll to avoid having to pay health insurance benefits for them. When added to low-wages, health insurance premiums often makes the labor more expensive than it's worth to the firm. Some firms hire independent contractors employing low-wage workers without health insurance benefits to do janitorial work and other low-skill jobs. The employer-provided health insurance system also impairs the fluidity of labor markets by reducing the incentive to change jobs as workers often fear that they will lose their health insurance or not be covered for pre-existing illness if they move to a better paying or more suitable job than the one they currently hold.

From the government's point of view, rising health care costs cause more difficulty in balancing budgets or funding other programs. The federal government could be spending one of every four dollar of revenues on health care by the year 2002 unless current trends and policies change. Medicaid payments are likely to devastate the budgets of state governments by the year 2002 by absorbing 12 percent of their revenues and preventing them from pumping more funds into schooling and infrastructure as well as other high priority programs including crime control. Unless other programs are cut to finance increasing government spending on health care we can expect higher taxes or increased deficit spending to finance the growth in government health care spending.

In short, imperfections in the market for health care probably result in more than the efficient allocation of resources to its provision. Our institutions for financing health care spending have caused health insurance premiums to increase, which has put such insurance out of the financial reach of many Americans and has contributed to increased government spending to finance Medicare and Medicaid. Real wages have not grown as employers compensate workers with funds to pay their health insurance and labor market fluidity has been impaired. We are giving up more than the efficient amount of other goods and services for health care. Correcting these inefficiencies will cause pressure for government intervention in the market for health care in the years to come.

must pass a test and go through a number of procedures to assess their professional skills. The federal government also plays a role in assessing and guaranteeing the competency of physicians through a process of peer review of physicians who treat Medicare patients. Physicians whose competency is in question can be denied reimbursement under Medicare.

Income Inequality and Health Care

Assuring access to medical services to all citizens irrespective of their ability to pay or employment status is viewed by many as a desirable government function. According to this view, health care should be a guaranteed right equally available to all as if it were a public good. For example, those who support this view would argue that it is acceptable for lack of income or wealth to prevent a person from buying a luxury car but that same lack of ability to pay should not prevent individuals from receiving a needed heart transplant. Under the current health care system in the United States, ability to pay is chiefly determined by health insurance coverage rather than income. Some insurance plans do cover expensive procedures such as transplants while others do not. The ability of a given patient to obtain expensive care that will prolong life, therefore, depends not only on whether the patient has insurance but also on the extent of that insurance.

For example, as of 1991, a liver transplant cost $200,000 in the United States. A person younger than sixty-five, whose insurance did not cover the transplant, could not receive it unless he or she could afford the $200,000 expenditure. Typically, the person would not qualify for Medicaid to pay for the procedure if household assets exceeded $3,000 and income was more than about $500 per month. A person older than sixty-five, could be covered by Medicare, which pays for liver, kidney, and heart transplants as medical therapy.

A system of free access to medical care has existed in the United Kingdom since the end of World War II. Such a system provides health care benefits to all, rich or poor, at zero price. The government system shifts the responsibility of rationing medical services from the market, where ability to pay (determined mainly by health insurance coverage) would determine priorities, to committees that decide who should obtain treatment and the priority list for deciding who get the treatment first. The system is more equitable than that in the United States but it still does not prevent those with higher incomes from consuming more or better quality medical services because those individuals can purchase such services in either the domestic or international marketplace. However, such rich people would pay the full marginal cost of such services out of their own pockets.

As an alternative to equal care for all, many individuals argue that all citizens should be guaranteed a minimum level of health care regardless of their income. The Medicaid program in the United States is designed to achieve such a goal by guaranteeing medical care at zero price to the poorest members of society. However, as of 1994 many of the near poor did not qualify for Medicaid, and others qualify only after they have exhausted the bulk of their income or assets as a result of catastrophic medical expenditures. Governments can extend health insurance to many of the near poor as well by providing health insurance to those workers who are not covered by employer-provided health insurance policies. These persons could be provided with health insurance similar to that available through employers with a certain deductible and a reasonable rate of coinsurance. The cost of the insurance could be financed by taxes on employers through a payroll tax or out of general tax revenue.

Because many of the uninsured are employed, one way to accomplish this would be to mandate that all employers provide health insurance. This method could, however, be particularly burdensome to small firms where insurance premiums based on experience ratings are very high. Mandating insurance as a fringe benefit by these firms could make it impossible for them to operate profitably and force them out of business. Mandated insurance could also be a great burden for firms that employ unskilled workers. Unskilled workers typically earn relatively low wages. For these workers health insurance payments would be a substantial portion of the wage bills—about $3,000 per year—to employers. The $3,000 per employee bill amounts to only 10 percent of the wage bill of a $30,000 per year worker but is a 30 percent of the wage bill for a $10,000 per year worker. The increase in the cost associated with employing these unskilled workers could reduce employment opportunities for them. This insurance could be financed by increased payroll taxes. However, if the payroll taxes are levied on the employers, the effect will still be to increase the cost of labor and this could still reduce the quantity of labor employed.

Finally, another proposal is for the government to provide catastrophic health insurance. This type of insurance could supplement private health insurance by kicking in only after patients have exhausted any private health insurance benefits they have and after they have paid a certain amount of medical expenses our of their own pockets. In effect, this would be insurance with a very large out-of-pocket deductible. The deductible could vary as a percent of household income.

Because the incidence of catastrophic medical expenses is of low probability and quite predictable from year to year for the whole population, this type of insurance could be provided at relatively low cost per person for all and financed through taxation. By establishing an insurance pool of the entire nation, the government could provide this coverage to all at low cost and fill a gap in the insurance protection of most Americans, including Medicare enrollees, who are not insured against catastrophic medical expenses.

Direct Government Expenditures on Health Care in the United States

Governments in the United States support health expenditures with a number of programs that directly fund health programs. Governments are directly involved in medical and health research and also provide some funding for the construction of such medical facilities as hospitals. You should be familiar with the work of the surgeon general of the United States, who supervises the Public Health Service and occasionally publishes reports on health issues and provides information about contagious diseases such as AIDS. However, it might surprise you that the bulk of government expenditures for health care are made through direct payments to physicians, hospitals, and other health care provided through the country's two major public health insur-

Table 9.1   ✦   PUBLIC HEALTH EXPENDITURES IN THE UNITED STATES, 1991 (MILLIONS OF DOLLARS)

Medicare	122,803
Medicaid (and other public assistance)	104,941
Public Health Services	24,533
Workers Compensation Medical Payments	17,793
Defense Department Hospital and Medical	12,809
Veterans Hospital and Medical	12,185
State and Local Government Hospitals	12,697
Medical Research	11,674
Medical Facilities Construction	2,365
Other	8,160
Total	329,960

Source: *Statistical Abstract of the United States,* 1993.

ance programs, Medicare and Medicaid. Medicare alone accounts for 39 percent of government direct spending on health care in the United States. Public assistance to the poor in meeting health care expenditures, mainly through the Medicaid program, accounts for another 33 percent of government health expenditures. Therefore nearly three-quarters of all government spending on health is accounted for by government-provided health insurance.

Governments also pay medical expenses of disabled workers through various workers' compensation programs provided by governments and provide medical services to military personnel and veterans. State and locally run hospitals and their activities are subsidized through government payments financed by taxes.

Table 9.1 summarizes public expenditures for health care in 1991 and shows that the bulk of these expenditures are accounted for by government-financed health insurance programs. Like overall spending for health care, government spending in this field has been rising at a very rapid rate since 1965, when Medicaid and Medicare were introduced as government health insurance programs. Figure 9.4 shows how government expenditures for health care have grown since 1965.

The federal government also provides health benefits to veterans at hospitals run by the Veterans Administration. The costs of providing medical services to veterans has been increasing as those who served in World War II have aged.

Medicare

Much of the growth of federal spending is accounted for by the largest federal health program, Medicare. Medicare reimburses health care providers for much of the medical costs incurred by those older than sixty-five, and some disabled people in the United States. As pointed out in Chapter 8, Medicare is a government entitlement program available to all those eligible regardless of their income. All eligible persons receive hospital insurance through Medicare and all are eligible for

Figure 9.4   ◆   GOVERNMENT HEALTH SPENDING, 1965–1991 (SELECTED YEARS)

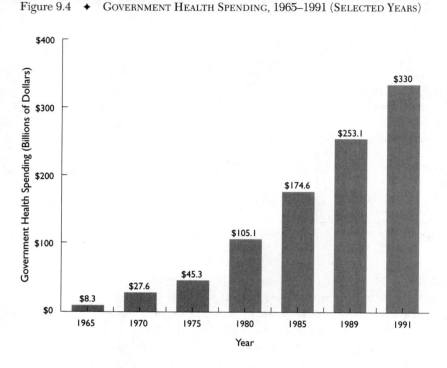

Government spending for health care has increased rapidly since 1965. Amounts include government spending for research and medical facilities.

Medicare's supplementary medical insurance, which makes payments to physicians and other medical providers. Those enrolled in the supplementary insurance program pay a modest monthly fee. The amount collected from these fees is not sufficient to cover the costs of the supplementary health insurance and the difference is made up with government funds obtained through taxation. In other words, Medicare's supplementary health insurance is heavily subsidized. However, Medicare benefits are subject to strict limits that are less generous than most private health insurance programs. For example, (as of 1994) Medicare does not cover prescription drugs nor does Medicare cover long-term care for the elderly in nursing homes. Many individuals older than sixty-five in the United States also are covered by private health insurance plans to fill in the gaps of their Medicare coverage.

Aging of the population has contributed to rising Medicare spending. A number of steps already have been undertaken or proposed to keep the costs of the Medicare program down. Since January 1992 reimbursement to physicians under the program has been based on a Medicare fee schedule (MFS) that sets payments according to the time, skill, and intensity of the service rendered. The fee reimbursement schedule for physicians is based on complicated formulas designed to limit payments. The system is designed to reimburse physicians on the basis of the value of resources that go into the services they provide to Medicare patients. Under the new MFS system, the reimbursement rate for a service can increase only if the cost of providing it goes up. Some critics of the new system fear that if MFS rates lag behind reimbursement rates paid by private insurers, the quantity of medical services provided to Medicare patients will decrease.

Currently Medicare limits payments for specific hospital providers to certain amounts independent of the actual costs of the procedures. The current law pays hospitals a flat fee for each of 474 illnesses classified into Diagnosis Related Groups (DRGs). Under the DRG system, payment for a medical procedure is the same regardless of any complications that might develop during the medical procedures. For example, a hospital treating a heart attack patient will be eligible for a certain flat fee no matter how much is actually spent caring for the patient. Some argue that the system provides incentives for hospitals to keep costs down so as to maximize profit. However, the DRG system does not completely curb the incentive to cut costs, because doctors and hospitals can charge the elderly who are able to pay for those services that are not covered by Medicare. This means that the elderly end up paying more for their medical care. The DRG system has not been politically popular among the elderly. Some also fear that the DRG system could result in a reduction in the quality of medical care to the elderly who lack the ability to pay for services not covered by Medicare.

The payment for each DRG is based on the average cost of treatment for the illness in all U.S. hospitals, adjusted for differences in local wage costs, the greater cost of providing care for Medicare patients in hospitals with teaching programs, and the higher costs related to treating a disproportionately large share of low-income patients. Some low-cost hospitals could be compensated at rates that exceed their average costs. The DRG system could cut hard into high-cost hospital profits and lead to a curtailment of services. At the extreme, the DRG system could cause hospitals in certain regions to shut down if they have a high proportion of elderly patients.

Like any third-party payment system, even one with copayment, Medicare encourages the consumption of medical services beyond the efficient level (see the analysis of the Medicaid program in Chapter 7). The federal government has chosen to limit the incentives to overconsumption mainly through programs that place limits on reimbursement to medical providers. Medicare increases the quantity of medical services demanded by the elderly. The DRG system acts to limit the quantity of medical services supplied to the elderly by capping the price per unit of service to medical providers.

Medicaid

Medicaid is also an entitlement program that is available to all persons eligible for government assistance through the AFDC program discussed in Chapter 7 and other poor persons who meet eligibility criteria. Medicare is administered by the federal government, Medicaid by state governments. Eligibility for Medicaid varies from state to state, as do the benefits provided to those eligible under this program. Like Medicare, Medicaid operates basically like an insurance program that reimburses hospitals and those providing medical and health services to individuals enrolled in the program according to guidelines and limits that vary from state to state. In recent years, the costs of the Medicaid program, like the costs of most other health insurance programs, have been soaring and many state governments have sharply reduced benefits available to Medicaid patients. The Medicaid program was designed to guarantee a minimum level of health care primarily to those receiving public assistance through AFDC or SSI (See Chapter 7). Medicaid also can be considered an insurance program that is part of a "safety net" for all. After a household's income and assets are literally exhausted by an illness or other catastrophic health problem, that household can become eligible for Medicaid. Medicaid finances both medical expenses and nursing home care to those who qualify. However, many of those classified as poor are not eligible for Medicaid. For example, in 1989, only 42.3 percent of the poor in the United States had Medicaid coverage.

The Medicaid program is designed to make sure that the poor receiving public assistance and those who become poor because of catastrophic medical expenses will be able to obtain medical care. Much of the cost of the Medicaid program is paid for by state governments, many of which have experienced severe financial problems in recent years. As Medicaid absorbs an increasingly large share of state government budgets, the states are seeking ways to control expenditures by reducing benefits they pay on behalf of Medicaid patients.

Medicaid is the health insurer of last resort—it takes many of the cases that no other insurance program pays for: crack-addicted babies, the homeless with disabilities, and the AIDS patient who runs out of private insurance and exhausts all other financial means of paying medical bills. Medicaid also pays for long-term care for elderly patients who can no longer take care of themselves and have used up all their savings. In fact, one of every three dollars spent under Medicaid pays for health care for the elderly. Many elderly Americans are becoming skilled in concealing their financial assets from government authorities so they can get their medical and nursing home bills paid through Medicaid before they go broke!

Enrollment in the Medicaid program has been soaring in recent years. The rise in spending comes at the same time states have been cutting their reimbursement rates to hospitals and physicians in an attempt to control the rising costs. For example, in Vermont in 1989, Medicaid reimbursed a physician performing a hysterectomy on a Medicaid patient an amount equal to less than half what the doctor might have received if performing the same operation on a Medicare patient. In Michigan, Medicaid paid obstetricians less than half the amount that private insurers paid for a normal delivery.

Because of reduced reimbursement rates, many physicians refuse to treat Medicaid patients. Even though we are spending more for Medicaid, more impoverished patients are finding it harder to obtain medical care from physicians and must resort to hospital emergency rooms for routine medical problems.

Other problems loom ahead for Medicaid. A number of health care providers have initiated legal action against the Medicaid program. Providers argue that payments made to them for their services to Medicaid patients are not "reasonable and adequate," as is required by law. In 1991, a federal judge in the state of Washington ruled that the Medicaid program was not reimbursing hospitals in that state at a reasonable rate.

It is going to require more resources to perfect Medicaid's role as the insurer of last resort. Recent suggestions that all the uninsured be covered under Medicaid irrespective of their income level would cause enrollment in the program to soar along with costs.

Indirect Government Finance of Health Care

Thus far we have discussed only the direct government expenditures for health spending—those that involve outlays of funds by governments. However, a surprisingly large amount of health care spending is financed by indirect government subsidies to private health insurance. Instead of involving spending by governments, these subsidies take the form of reduced revenues through favorable tax treatment of employee and employer contributions for private health insurance.

Employer-sponsored health insurance programs cover about 60 percent of Americans and pay about one-third of all medical expenditures in the United States. Federal, state, and local governments give favorable tax treatment to employee compensation in the form of health insurance premiums paid by employers. The amount that employers pay for health insurance to employees is neither taxable as payroll nor is it considered part of the taxable income of employees. Also, in many cases, when employees themselves pay a portion of their employer-provided health insurance premiums for themselves or their dependents, they receive favorable tax treatment for those expenditures. Many employers, under current tax rules, set up special plans that allow their employees to exclude the amount they pay for health insurance for themselves and their dependents from their taxable income.

By excluding employer-paid fringe benefits in the form of medical insurance premiums from the taxable income of employees, governments forgo the opportunity to collect taxes on this income. The reduced income tax collections constitute a subsidy to private health insurance by governments. Exclusion of employer-paid health insurance benefits from the taxable incomes of employees in the United States cost federal, state, and local governments between $56 and $58 billion in revenue in 1991 with an estimated cost of nearly $80 billion in 1994.

This subsidy encourages employers to provide employees compensation in the form of health insurance as opposed to cash income. The health insurance is worth more to employees than the cash income because it is available tax free. In other words, the employee can get health insurance at a lower price than using taxable income to reimburse employers for the costs. For example, suppose that on each extra dollar of earnings an employee pays income taxes amounting to one-third of earnings. Suppose that the cost of employer-provided health insurance is $150 per month for this employee. If the employer, instead of directly providing the insurance at no charge, charged the employee $150 for it each month and increased the employee's salary by the same amount, the employee would be worse off, assuming that she still wanted to purchase $150 worth of insurance. This is because the $150 would be taxable and the tax due would be $50. If the employee wanted to buy the $150 of coverage, she would have to earn more than $150 in money income to pay the bill! The employee would have to earn $225, which, after paying one third of that in taxes, would provide after-tax income of $150 that could be used to buy health insurance from the employer at the rate of $150 per month. In effect, the special tax treatment of employer-provided health insurance lowers the price of the insurance to employees and increases the quantity of health insurance demanded as a form of labor compensation.

The federal government also allows limited deductions for direct out-of-pocket medical expenses paid by individuals. Taxpayers can deduct medical expenses in excess of 7.5 percent of their adjusted gross income from their taxable income. This preferential tax treatment of medical expenses was estimated to cost the federal government $3.5 billion in revenue in 1994, which is only a small fraction of the amount given up from nontaxation of insurance premiums. Additional revenue is lost through exclusion of Medicare benefits to the elderly as part of their taxable income.

Figure 9.5 shows that the preferential treatment of health insurance premiums by the U.S. tax system increases the quantity of employer-provided health insurance services demanded. The figure shows the demand curve for health insurance in the nation. Suppose that on average employers can make employees as well off by giving them health insurance that costs $150 per month instead of paying them $225 in money wages before taxes. The employer can save $75 per employee per month in wages by providing health insurance instead of the money income. In effect, by reducing the price of health insurance to the employee, when it is provided by the employer, and by making it cheaper for employers to compensate employees in health insurance, the tax system encourages (and subsidizes) employer health insurance.

The graph shows that the tax treatment of insurance effects the quantity of health insurance demanded. In this case the employee gets health insurance as a non-taxable $150 per month fringe benefit. The average employee would have to earn $225 per month to pay for the policy if it were purchased from the employer for $150.

Figure 9.5   ◆   The Effect of Preferential Tax Treatment of Employer-Provided Health Insurance

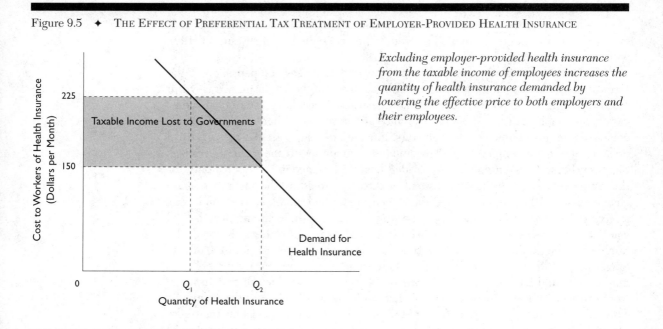

Excluding employer-provided health insurance from the taxable income of employees increases the quantity of health insurance demanded by lowering the effective price to both employers and their employees.

The effective reduction in price from $225 to $150 for workers increases the quantity of insurance demanded and the income corresponding to the shaded rectangle in the graph is not taxed.

C H E C K P O I N T

1. How much of the GDP in the United States was allocated to health care as of the early 1990s?
2. Who pays the U.S. health care bills?
3. What are the major government programs of health care finance in the United States? How do governments indirectly subsidize private health insurance in the United States?

HEALTH CARE REFORM: ISSUES AND POLICIES

In the United States the controversy around health care reform and the role of government in that process has centered around two issues.

1. Controlling the growth of health care spending so as to prevent health care from absorbing ever increasing shares of our gross domestic product.
2. Moving toward universal coverage for Americans by making health insurance a government guaranteed right for all citizens.

Rather than discussing particular proposals or complicated details of new legislation to help deal with these issues, the following sections examine general principles involved in coping with the problems of extending health insurance benefits to all while limiting the rate of increase of spending on health care. Remember, as with any public policy issue, both gainers and losers are likely to emerge as we tinker with any existing health care system in the United States. Special interest groups geared up advertising campaigns for and against Clinton's proposals for health care reform in 1993 and 1994. Medical-care providers, private insurance companies, small and large businesses, as well as groups such as the elderly, labor unions, and workers in large corporations who have enjoyed very generous health insurance benefits all were concerned about the way the president's plan would affect their standard of living.

No reform of our health care system is possible without some redistribution in benefits among consumers and providers of health care. The two preceding issues are not unrelated. As we guarantee health insurance to all, spending on health care is likely to increase. To prevent costs from spiraling as we move to universal coverage we must institute new policies that ration health care. As we do this, some individuals will find it more difficult or more expensive to obtain some services that they previously could obtain easily or at low cost.

The desire to control the rate of growth of spending on health care is getting stronger and stronger. The system of third-party payments in the United States encourages an overallocation of resources to health care beyond the point at which the marginal social benefits of medical services fall to equal the marginal social cost of such services. Some critics of the U.S. health care system argue that increased government participation in the market for health care in the United States is desirable both to curb the growth of spending and remove inequities from the system. The problem is not only to control the growth of spending but also to improve efficiency within the mix of services provided by the system. Health care providers often favor certain costly treatments that are covered by insurance over less expensive alternatives that involve greater out-of-pocket expenses to patients. For example, coverage of inpatient psychiatric costs and exclusion, or limited coverage, of outpatient psychiatric visits encourages hospitalization of persons with psychiatric problems. The exclusion of preventive measures and tests such as mammograms from insurance coverage in many insurance programs discourages patients from taking these tests often at the risk of much higher third-party payments on their behalf at a later time. Finally, the fragmented nature of the health insurance system in the United States involves high administrative costs that could be reduced with centralized claims processing. In the late 1980s, administrative costs of health insurance were running at close to 5 percent of health spending in the United States. In Canada, where the claims processing is handled by government and is more centralized, administrative costs were only 2.5 percent of health spending.

Let's now examine policies that can be used to control the growth of spending on health care. We begin with a look at proposals to improve efficiency in the market for health care not only by reducing the allocation of resources but also by improving the mix of services provided by the health care industry. Then we will examine alternative means of providing universal coverage such as government-mandated coverage and national tax-financed health insurance like the system used in the United Kingdom.

Increasing the Price of Health Care to Consumers: Coinsurance and Deductibles

The most obvious way for controlling health care spending is to increase the out-of-pocket price of those services to the individuals who consume them. By increasing the price of medical care to consumers, the quantity demanded will decline. Increased cost sharing of medical costs by patients will provide incentives for economizing on the use of health care services. The declining share of medical costs paid by consumers of these services has, in fact, been a major cause of the increase in prices and increases in volume of medical services consumed. A classic study of health care spending by the RAND corporation in the late 1970s and early 1980s found that spending per person for health care was 45 percent higher in insurance plans that required no cost sharing compared to an alternative plan that required 95 percent cost sharing (meaning than health insurance paid only 5 percent of the medical bills of insurees) up to an annual maximum of $1,000.

Increased cost sharing in both private health insurance plans and such government plans as Medicare and health care benefits for veterans, in which the policy holders have the ability to pay (as opposed to Medicaid, in which the recipients of services are indigent and presumably incapable of paying) have great potential for reducing health care spending. However, for such plans to be effective, governments will have to ban the development of supplementary health insurance (such as the Medigap policies purchased by Medicare enrollees) that will turn the patient's share of costs into a third-party payment. In other words, increased cost sharing will have to be made mandatory and apply to all insurance plans—public and private. This would require increased government regulation of the health insurance industry.

Two ways exist to increase consumer cost sharing. One is to increase the deductible amounts that consumers must incur before they become eligible for insurance payments. This would make consumers who are relatively healthy, and therefore incur health care costs less than the deductible, more price conscious. These consumers would presumably compare their marginal health benefits with the marginal cost and consume health care services up to the point at which their marginal benefits equal the marginal social cost of health care services. One disadvantage of increasing the deductible amount is that it could discourage patients from seeking early medical care or tests for symptoms and this could result in high medical costs in the future.

The other way to reduce the incentive to consume medical services is to increase the coinsurance rate paid by consumers. As this is done, the quantity of medical services demanded will decrease as will the quantity supplied. The effect of increasing the coinsurance rate is illustrated in Figure 9.6. Suppose the coinsurance rate is

Figure 9.6 ✦ How an Increase in Coinsurance Can Reduce Health Care Spending and Improve Efficiency in the Market for Health Care Services

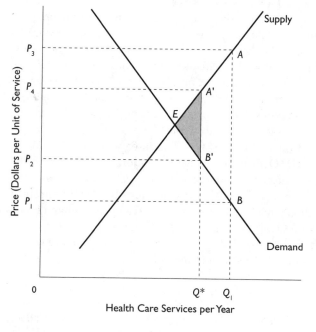

Increasing the coinsurance rate for insurees increases the price from P_1 to P_2 to patients and results in a decrease in the quantity of medical care demanded. As this occurs the price to providers also declines from P_3 to P_4. The reduction in both the quantity consumed and the price paid to providers decreases expenditures on health care. This reduces the overallocation of resources to health care, and the loss in net benefits from this overallocation declines from the amount represented by the triangle ABE to the amount represented by the smaller triangle A'B'E.

initially set at 20 percent after the deductible is met. At that level of coinsurance, third-party payers absorb 80 percent of the price of medical services for the insurees. If the coinsurance is increased to 40 percent, the quantity of medical services demanded will decline thereby reducing the quantity supplied. The share of the price of the services absorbed by third parties will be reduced to 60 percent. As a result of the increased coinsurance the market price of medical services on average will also decline.

Both the decline in the quantity of medical services demanded and the decline in price contribute to a decline in health care expenditures, causing a reduction in the overallocation of resources to medical services. The loss in net benefits from inefficient use of medical services will decline from an amount represented by the area ABE to an amount represented by the smaller area $A'B'E$.

Managed Care: HMOs and Other Means of Limiting Freedom of Health Care Providers to Prescribe Services and Patients Choosing Providers

Another way to control the rate of increase of medical services is to intervene in the decisions of medical care providers and patients directly through a system of managed care. Under managed care, the decisions of physicians and other health care providers are reviewed to determine whether they are appropriate for the patient. The patients themselves are required to purchase health care services from a specified network of providers and their freedom of choice in both treatments and physicians is limited. Finally, the means of paying the providers is often specified by the insurance firms sponsoring the managed care facilities. Patients often are charged no direct price for the services they consume. However, the providers frequently receive **capitation payments,** which are fixed amounts per patient per year. This fixed amount encourages providers to economize their use of medical resources. Their profits are higher when they do not prescribe inappropriate procedures or procedures for which the marginal benefit to the patient exceeds the marginal cost. A number of studies of medical procedures have provided evidence that insurance plans using a capitation fee have lower rates of hospitalized surgical procedures than insurance plans providing similar coverage but reimbursing physicians on a fee-for-service basis.[1]

A **health maintenance organization (HMO)** is an integrated delivery and finance system for health care. HMOs usually receive capitation payments from the health insurers with whom they contract. For the fixed fee per patient, the HMO provides comprehensive medical care for those it serves. Because the HMO's profit is the difference between capitation payments and the cost of its services, it has a financial incentive to minimize the cost of medical care. The number of HMOs in the United States more than doubled in the 1980s, and, as of 1990, 35 million patients were enrolled in HMO plans linked to their health insurance.

---

[1]See Paul J. Feldstein, *Health Care Economics*, 3d ed. (New York: John Wiley & Sons, 1988), 92–93.

Some holders of traditional health insurance plans obtain medical services from a "Preferred Provider Organization" (PPO), for which coinsurance payments by the patient are lower than with other health providers. PPOs still operate on the basis of fees for services and their patients are free to choose their own health care providers. However, the services provided by PPOs are monitored by the health insurance company, thereby giving it some control over services prescribed.

HMOs are apparently effective in reducing use of medical care. However, such organizations tend to have higher administrative costs because of the process of reviewing the decisions of health care providers. Although transfer of patients to HMOs does reduce the overall cost of health care at the time the transfer is made, the growth of spending on health care through HMOs has been as rapid as overall growth of health care spending.[2]

Regulation of Pricing, Competition, and Reimbursement of Hospitals and Physicians

The most direct and drastic ways of government intervention in the market for health care services to control expenditures are direct controls on prices and regulation of the volume of services supplied. Direct controls set limits on the amount of reimbursement to physicians for the services they provide. Private insurance companies typically limit reimbursement to physicians for procedures provided. During the mid-1980s the Medicare program froze physician fees.

Unless implemented by all third-party payers and accompanied by controls on the ability of health care providers to increase the quantity of procedures supplied, price controls are not very effective in limiting the growth of spending. During the 1984–1986 period for which physician reimbursement rates were frozen by Medicare, the rate of physician expenditures per enrollee continued to increase at a rate of about 10 percent. Apparently physicians were able to increase the volume of services they supplied to Medicare patients to offset the effect of the price freeze on their incomes.

Medicare has also experimented with some innovative pricing mechanisms designed to economize on the use of hospital facilities. The **Prospective Payment System** used by Medicare gives hospitals a fixed payment per patient for the expected costs of treating patients with specific illnesses called "diagnosis related groups" (DRGs). The fixed payment does not vary with length of stay in the hospital and it thereby provides the hospitals with the incentive to discharge patients as soon as is medically advisable. During the first five years of this payment system, the average length of hospital stay for Medicare patients declined by 10 percent. The system is supplemented with a hospital utilization review process that limits admission of Medicare patients to hospitals. In 1992, Medicare extended this payment system to physicians and limits reimbursement to them on the basis of estimates of reasonable costs and charges associated with given diagnoses.

---

[2]See Congressional Budget Office, *Rising Health Care Costs: Causes, Implications, and Strategies* (Washington, D.C., Congress of the United States, Congressional Budget Office, 1991).

The Medicaid program in the United States also has limited reimbursement to hospitals and physicians on behalf of patients in the program. State governments limit their reimbursement to hospitals for Medicaid patients to covering the minimum possible average cost of hospital services. The average reimbursement rate under Medicaid is about 80 percent less than hospital costs of services. Physicians who provide services to Medicaid patients are also reimbursed at lower rates. In 1989, for example, the average reimbursement to physicians under Medicaid was only about 70 percent of the amount reimbursed for similar procedures under the Medicare program.

Unfortunately, low rates of reimbursement under Medicaid have reduced access to medical care for those enrolled under the program. Many doctors are unwilling to accept Medicaid patients and some hospitals are reluctant to admit Medicaid patients. Because of difficulties in finding physicians to treat them, Medicaid patients often seek treatment at hospital emergency rooms where cost of treatment is more expensive to third-party payers.

To be effective, price controls and review procedures have to be instituted on a national basis and apply to all third-party payers. In nations with government-provided health insurance, such as Canada, health care providers are reimbursed on a fee-for-service basis with fees negotiated by the government authorities who administer the health plan. All providers are paid according to the same schedule for all patients so no incentive exists to refuse to treat patients as is the case under the Medicaid price controls. In the United States, four states—Maryland, New Jersey, New York, and Massachusetts—have "all-payer rate-setting programs" for hospital reimbursement. Under this system the states establish fees for hospital services and all third-party and consumer charges are based on those rates. These programs have been effective in controlling the rate of growth of hospital expenditures compared to what would be the case without the system.[3]

Finally, governments can directly intervene in the market for health care services to increase competition among providers. For example, the growth in HMOs since 1980 in the United States is in part a result of federal requirements that employers offering health insurance include an HMO option for their enrollees. By offering more than one plan to their employees, health insurance companies have the incentive to keep prices low so as to compete for enrollees. Another technique to lower costs is to change laws to allow more providers who might not necessarily be physicians to supply services. Recently many public and private insurance companies have allowed such medical practitioners as optometrists and chiropractors to treat patients and be eligible for third-party payments. New laws enacted in the 1970s and 1980s allow advertising by health care providers to encourage competition and price consciousness among consumers.

One of the major causes of increased health expenditures in the United States has been the rapid diffusion of new technology and new capital equipment and facilities. Many therefore argue that controls on capital investment to avoid overallocation of resources to new technology and duplication of facilities in an area are warranted. Such policies will control the growth of capital costs in health care at the expense of

---

[3]See Congressional Budget Office, *Rising Health Care Costs,* 50.

making it more difficult for patients to obtain access to the technology when they demand it. In Canada and other nations where governments play a more direct role in health care there are limits on capital acquisition by hospitals. Although this does keep costs down it limits access to the new technology often creates long waiting lists for scans and for complicated procedures such as open heart surgery as a result of the limits on capital acquisition.

CHECKPOINT

1. How would the market for health care be affected if the federal government required all health insurance companies to increase their coinsurance rates from current levels by 50 percent?
2. How do capitation fees affect the incentive of suppliers to provide health care services?
3. What techniques have been used by the Medicare and Medicaid programs to control the growth of health care expenditures?

UNIVERSAL COVERAGE

In light of what we now know about the market for health care services and how incentives to consume health care services are influenced by the price system, health care providers themselves, and the institutions for paying for health care services we can examine alternative means of extending guaranteed health care to all. Any plan of universal coverage must involve more extensive government intervention in the market for health care than has prevailed in the United States through the early 1990s. First let's examine the gaps in coverage in the United States as of the early 1990s.

Gaps in U.S. Health Insurance Coverage in the 1990s

The U.S. health insurance system provides health insurance benefits to the bulk of the employed, the indigent, and the elderly. However, there are significant gaps in coverage. As of 1992, it was estimated that 35 million people younger than sixty-five had no health insurance. This total amounted to 14 percent of the U.S. population. This gap in health insurance coverage is a matter of serious concern. Naturally, those without insurance face the prospect of financial ruin if they are struck by a major illness. However, because many of the uninsured will obtain treatment in nonprofit hospitals, the costs of the treatment will be borne by the rest of the population as hospitals cover their losses by increasing fees paid by insured patients. Finally, some of these uninsured will be reduced to poverty status as a result of illness or other medical problems. If this is the case, their health care will be paid for by others through higher taxes as these people become eligible for the Medicaid program.

The proportion of the uninsured in the United States has grown from 12.5 percent in 1980 to about 16 percent of the population younger than sixty-five in 1992.

One cause of the decline in coverage has been a reduction in the number of employees who are covered with health insurance by their employers. Between 1982 and 1987, the percentages of full-time workers with employer-provided health insurance fell from 77.2 percent to 73.8 percent. Similar declines in coverage occurred for part-time workers. The shift in jobs to the service sector of the economy accounts for most of the decline because service workers are less likely to enjoy coverage than industrial workers.

About one-half of the uninsured younger than sixty-five have jobs and relatively low incomes, but their income levels are not low enough to qualify them for Medicaid benefits. Another 30 percent of the uninsured are dependents of uninsured workers. Many of those who lack health insurance coverage are part-time workers and young adults. One of every four persons between the ages of eighteen and twenty-four in the United States lacked health insurance coverage in 1990! Workers employed by smaller firms are less likely to have health insurance than workers employed by large firms. Almost all U.S. firms with 100 or more employees provide health insurance. However, less than half of the firms with fewer than twenty-five employees provide their employees with health insurance.

Even in large firms, substantial numbers of employees are not eligible for employer-provided health insurance. Part-time workers who make up about 20 percent of the U.S. labor forces generally are not eligible for employer-provided health insurance even in large firms. New employees typically have to wait for a period before they become eligible for employer-provided health insurance coverage. Workers who change jobs frequently and work only for a short time at a job, even one in a large firm, often are without health insurance coverage for long periods.

The uninsured are generally quite sensitive to the price of medical services because they pay the full costs of such services out of pocket. Those without health insurance are generally more reluctant to use physician services and much less likely to use inpatient hospital services than the insured.[4] Physicians and hospitals also are less likely to provide the uninsured with expensive medical procedures that are readily available to the insured.

About one-fifth of the people without health insurance coverage in 1990 in the United States were not part of the labor force. Many of these people were ill and could not obtain insurance at all from private insurers or could obtain such insurance only at very high rates that they cannot afford. Private insurers underwrite health insurance to individuals only after obtaining assessments of the individual's health and other factors influencing the risk of providing insurance. Individuals with such diseases as AIDS, coronary artery disease, cancer, diabetes, or alcoholism often find it difficult to obtain coverage.

The relatively large number of uninsured in the United States has led to demands for government policies to extend health insurance to all, either through mandated employer-based coverage or new government health insurance that fills in the

---

[4]See S. Long and J. Rodgers, *The Effects of Being Uninsured on Health Care Service Use: Estimates from the Survey of Income and Program Participation,* Bureau of the Census, SIPP Working Paper #9012, 1990.

gaps between Medicare, Medicaid, and employer-provided benefits. Even if this gap is filled, other gaps remain in health insurance coverage in the United States. For example, the considerable diversity in coverage for catastrophic medical expenses ranges from private insurance policies that put caps on lifetime benefits available to the uninsured to many insurance policies that place limits on annual benefits available to policy holders.

Although Medicaid covers virtually all the costs of its beneficiaries, Medicare pays only 45 percent of the total health costs of the aged and disabled eligible for coverage. Also, many private insurance plans place annual limits on out-of-pocket costs once an enrolled individual has incurred a certain amount of medical expenditures, but Medicare patients have no such cap. Medicare enrollees therefore are at much greater risk than the rest of the U.S. insured population for the effects of catastrophic medical expenses. About 80 percent of Medicare enrollees, however, have either supplementary health insurance from their former employers or through a "medigap" policy purchased from a private insurer. Medicare patients who are medically indigent also are eligible for benefits under the Medicaid program.

In general, much of the U.S. population faces limits to its annual and lifetime benefits under their employer-provided health insurance. This leaves many individuals vulnerable to the effects of catastrophic medical expenses that could result from long hospital stays and the need for care in a nursing home. Most private insurance plans limit annual insurance coverage for hospitalization to about sixty days for an illness. Limits also are in place on payments for expensive medical procedures, such as organ transplants. However, those with extensive out-of-pocket medical expenses in excess of 7.5 percent of their income can deduct that amount from their income in computing the amount subject to income tax. For taxpayers who can itemize their deductions, the result is that the federal government pays part of their catastrophic medical expenses by forgoing tax revenue.

Finally, employer-based health insurance does not provide benefits for long-term nursing home care. **Long-term care services** are medical, support, and rehabilitative services for patients who have functional limitations or chronic health problems and need daily assistance with the normal activities of living. Most private insurance and Medicare do not cover long-term care services. Currently governments pay half the total cost of long-term care in the United States through the Medicaid program. However, this provides little protection for the average family because, to be eligible for such payments, it must first be literally bankrupted by its long-term care expenditures. In view of the aging U.S. population, increased demands are likely for insurance coverage for long-term care or through Medicare or other means. As of 1990, long-term care services absorbed $58 billion in resources for the nearly 2 million U.S. nursing home residents. Projections indicate that nursing homes in the United States will have more than 5 million residents by the year 2050, three-fifths of which will be over the age of 85!

Moving to Universal Coverage

Should health insurance be provided as a public good—one that is freely available to all, the costs of which would be financed by taxes rather than revenue from the sale of services? Should the government be more involved in the market for medical and health care services?

Let's recap the problems with the system of health care delivery in the United States:

1. The system of third-party payments results in an oversupply of health care services relative to the efficient amount. Reduced price of consciousness on the part of consumers of health care and medical services has impaired the ability of the price system to ration health care services.

2. The ability of physicians, hospitals, and other health care providers to influence the demand for health care has contributed to sharply increasing expenditures on health care in the United States.

3. A relatively large portion of the U.S. population has not been covered by health insurance. These individuals have found it increasingly difficult to obtain health care services when they need it. Financing of the cost of health care to those unable to pay is shifted to those who have health insurance through higher insurance premiums. To become eligible for government-supplied health insurance, people younger than sixty-five must first draw upon most of their own financial resources.

These three problems have increased demands for governments to intervene in the markets for health care to achieve the objectives of more equitable distribution of access to medical care, regardless of ability to pay. Governments have also been called on to develop policies to more effectively ration health care and stem the rising rate of growth of health care expenditures.

Universal Entitlement Systems with Managed Competition

One way to provide universal coverage in the United States is to build on the current system of employer-provided insurance and government programs by using the power of government to mandate that all employers provide insurance. The government would then fill in the gaps through new programs and subsidies to help those who are unemployed, choose not to participate in the labor force, or otherwise do not have health insurance. A plan like this was proposed by the Clinton administration in 1993. The plan was coupled with new proposals to manage competition in the health care industry so as to limit the growth of health care costs thereby trying to put a lid on both private insurance premiums and government costs for provision of health insurance. The extremely complicated plan was greeted with both praise and harsh criticism by the various special interest groups who would have been either positively or negatively affected by its provisions. Let's now examine some general issues involved in mandating universal coverage through government authority while keeping the responsibility for provision of health insurance mainly with employers.

Using government authority to provide a universal entitlement to health insurance while maintaining the existing employer-based provision of such insurance involves an increase in labor costs for at least some employers while other employers might find their health insurance cost falling. Because many employers already will be providing such coverage at some minimum level, they would not have their labor costs increased. So, a system of universal entitlement to health insurance through employment would be equivalent to a tax on some employers who currently provide no health insurance or supply it at levels below the universal standards that the government mandate would require. Some small companies could find this tax high enough to force them out of business. Alternatively, forcing these firms to provide insurance could result in decreases in money wages to their employees. Smaller firms could be subsidized by the government to help them finance health care benefits to their employees so as to minimize the effects in their profits and the wages they pay.

With subsidies and incentives to reduce more generous health insurance plans to a standard level, a universal entitlement system could actually reduce total health insurance premiums the employers pay. However, if a goal of the universal entitlement is to ensure that all employees (and all citizens) have the same level of coverage so as to make health insurance more like a public good, then some workers who currently have more generous health insurance plans than the government mandated plan could suffer either a decrease in health benefits or an increase in costs of such coverage. For example, a universal entitlement could set up a standard insurance plan and tax those workers (or their employers) if their plan provides higher than standard benefits. Benefits in excess of the standard policy could be treated as taxable income to recipients. Further, a system of universal entitlement would have to find a way of financing health insurance to non-employees who would otherwise have no coverage. These people could be required by law to buy a standard policy and pay at least part of the premiums for the insurance. The remainder of the premium could be subsidized by the government at a rate that would vary with the individuals' ability to pay. The guarantee of government subsidized individual health insurance could induce some workers to leave the labor force which would increase the cost of universal entitlement to the government as subsidy payments increased. All enrollees, including those who receive insurance under such programs as Medicaid would have the standard policy, and physicians serving them would be reimbursed at the same rate. Persons on welfare who fear losing their Medicaid insurance benefits if they accept a job would have greater incentive to work because a government subsidized health insurance program would be available to them when they no longer were covered under Medicaid, which would still be available to the qualifying poor at no cost to them or their families.

To keep costs down, a universal entitlement program, such as the one proposed by President Clinton, would have to organize large groups of insurees (Clinton called these groups "Alliances") that would bargain with health care providers to keep prices of medical services down. The alliances of insured workers would seek to establish "fair" prices for medical procedures that would limit payment to providers and allow providers to compete for the right to sell services at or below those rates to insurees. The universal mandate would require insurance companies to provide insurance to all those who applied irrespective of their health status. No one could be denied health insurance under a universal entitlement programs. Under the Clinton plan a number of standard policies were proposed and individuals could choose among these plans according to their preferences. However, employees would have incentives to select less expensive plans because the payments their employers would make would be independent of the plan selected, and if they chose a more expensive plan they would have to pay the difference between that plan and the standard plan. Thus,

I N T E R N A T I O N A L   V I E W

NATIONAL HEALTH INSURANCE AND HEALTH SERVICES IN GREAT BRITAIN AND CANADA

Government plays a much more active role in the provision of health insurance and health care in many foreign nations than is the case in the United States. All these nations have national or regional budgets for health care that attempt to cap or at least target total annual health care spending. Most of these nations also limit the supply of health care provided through their budgets and limit the acquisition of medical equipment and facilities. Also review systems are in place to monitor and control the supply of medical care to keep costs down.

Let's examine the role of government in health insurance and health care in two nations with extensive government participation in health care: Great Britain and Canada.*

GREAT BRITAIN

Perhaps the most famous government health insurance system is the British National Health Service (NHS), which was set up after the end of World War II to provide and finance health care for British citizens. In Britain the government operates and supplies the bulk of health care services produced in the nation. The NHS provides universal coverage for physician and hospital services, long-term care, and prescription drugs and funds those services almost entirely through taxes, which pays for 97 percent of NHS services. British citizens pay little or no fees directly for the health care services they consume.

Private health insurance is also available in Great Britain to finance elective surgery and nursing home care that is not covered by the NHS. But only a bit more than 10 percent of British citizens carry private insurance. Some private provision of hospital services is available. However, the NHS has a virtual monopoly on the supply of hospital services accounting for nearly 80 percent of the hospital beds in the nation.

British citizens have very little choice among health care providers. To obtain health care services, a British citizen must register with a general practice (GP) physician who is currently accepting patients. The GP serves as the patient's access to the health system in much the same way as GPs control access to health care services in an HMO in the United States. GPs refer patients to specialists who can order tests and admit patients to hospitals. Once hospitalized, a patient is treated by salaried NHS specialists on the staff of the hospital.

GPs receive capitation payments for their patients. This practice provides incentives to economize on the use of medical services because each physician receives a fixed payment from the NHS per patient regardless of the number and kind of services provided to the patient. NHS specialists are salaried government employees of regional health authorities. However, some physicians do receive fee-for-service payments for such services as preventive medicine and family planning services. Physicians who serve private hospitals also are paid on a fee-for-service basis.

Budgeting for capital expenditures is done by the government. Regional boards participate in decisions to acquire such new equipment as CAT scanners. The budgetary limits on capital expenditures and payments to physicians often result in shortages of services and long waiting lists. Typically, getting emergency care in Great Britain is no problem, but long waits (weeks and even months) to obtain an appointment with a specialist are common. Doctors classify patients according to their needs for hospitalization and surgery and the classification system determines their place in line to be admitted to hospitals. As of early 1991, more than 700,000 were on waiting lists for surgery in Great Britain. Of

*For a more detailed analysis of health care programs in these and other foreign nations, see Congressional Budget Office, *Rising Health Care Costs*, Appendix C, 81–90.

the plan would encourage competition among insurers to keep the costs of their insurance down. Only community ratings could be used under this system. Premiums for insurance could vary only with the number of people in a family or location of the family being insured, not with the current health status of members of the family.

this number, about 200,000 were on the list for more than a year! It typically takes about a year to get to the top of the list for such common operations as hernia repair, varicose veins, hip replacements, and cataract removals. Limitations on the hospital budgets to pay surgeons has resulted in the waiting lists growing.[†]

Many British citizens are frustrated by the waiting to obtain services and often choose to go to private hospitals for operations where they must pay the *full cost* of the services. A heart bypass operation coupled with a valve replacement costs $26,250 at a private hospital, and some patients of modest means choose to pay such a large sum rather than risk the chance of dying while waiting to be admitted to an NHS hospital![‡] Britain spends about 6 percent of its GDP on health care—approximately half the amount spent in the United States. However, there are not enough services to go around and the services are rationed by long waiting lists. The services are free to all but not readily available. The NHS physicians control access to health care for the bulk of the population, while the rich who can afford to pay the full price of medical services can purchase those services at private hospitals.

CANADA

Canada's health insurance system is often cited as a model to be used to reform the U.S. system. Unlike the British, the Canadians do not operate the health care system. Instead each province administers its own health insurance plan under a system of universal health insurance and federal Canadian guidelines. The system has been in operation since 1972. The provincial insurance plans guarantee minimum standards of health care for all Canadians and are financed in part by federal income taxes. Most provinces finance the remainder of the costs of the plans with their own tax revenues.

The Canadian health care plans cover physician and hospital services in much the same way that private health insurance plans do in the United States but do not cover prescription drugs and long-term care. However, most provinces do have their own plans that pay the bills for these uncovered services for the elderly and the poor. Private health insurance provides benefits for services not covered by the provincial health care plans. Most of the health care bills of Canadians are therefore paid by governments. Because the Canadian provinces act as the health insurers in Canada, the administrative costs of the system are lower than those in the United States, where there are many private insurers, each with its own claims-processing facility.

Governments budget for health care in Canada. Many Canadian provinces establish expenditure targets for physician services and adjust the fees to physicians downward if the targets are exceeded. Physicians in Canada are reimbursed on a fee-for-service basis, which is negotiated with the provincial governments, who are, in effect, the single purchasers of physician services. The fees are also, in effect, controlled by the provinces. Hospitals face stiff budgetary constraints under the Canadian system and receive fixed annual allocations that vary with such criteria as the number of hospital beds and the types of services provided. The federal government also places limits on its own annual health spending. These federal limits have, in recent years, increased the share of health care costs borne by the provinces.

Hospitals in Canada must request funding for capital acquisitions—including those for new structures, equipment, and other capital outlays—from a provincial ministry of health. Most of the new funding of capital equipments comes from the provincial governments, but hospitals also bear some of the costs. Canadian provinces also have committees to review physician patterns and budgets and limit the number of physicians available to the public. As is the case for the British system, shortages of medical services and facilities in Canada are common, resulting in long waiting lists for medical procedures and hospital beds.

[†]See Craig R. Whitney, "British Health Service, Much Beloved but Inadequate, Is Facing Changes," *New York Times*, Sunday, June 9, 1991, 11.
[‡]*Ibid.*

Extension of insurance to the large numbers of people who have none is likely to result in higher costs for health care, at least in the short run, that would have to be financed in some way. The additional funds could come from new or higher taxes, premiums paid by individuals, reductions in the costs of already existing government health programs such as Medicare and Medicaid, taxes on insurance benefits that exceed minimum standards. In the long run constraints on the growth of health care spending would have to be instituted through the price system either by limiting payments to health care providers or by increasing coinsurance and deductibles in the standard plan. For example, the Clinton plan proposed to limit the growth in spending by putting annual caps on insurance premiums for a standard policy. However, his estimates of the effectiveness of the alliances in keeping health care costs down was greeted with widespread skepticism in 1993 and 1994.

National Health Insurance

A system of comprehensive national health insurance in the United States would fill the gaps in coverage and assure all Americans access to at least a minimal amount of health care. At one extreme, the government could become the sole health insurer: It would finance its expected payouts and administrative costs through taxation. By becoming the sole insurer, the government would use a vast community rating system to determine its expected payouts of claims during the year and would finance the costs through either general taxation (the personal income tax for example) or through payroll taxes levied on employers and employees. Coverage would be uniform for all Americans.

However, a national insurance system would face the same issues of rationing of health care we have discussed within the context of our current system. Without deductibles or coinsurance, some means would have to be found to overcome the moral hazard of overconsumption of health care services beyond the point at which marginal social benefit equals the marginal social cost. Rationing could be accomplished by limiting reimbursement to physicians and hospitals and reviewing procedures through one of the techniques discussed. Alternatively, the government health insurance plan could be set up to have deductible and coinsurance components.

Typically, national health insurance schemes that allow free health care to all citizens have severe problems with shortages. Medical care can be provided as if it were a pure public good but, in fact, it is price excludable and divisible. The more health care services provided to and given to individuals, the less that are available to others over a given period. Waiting times for complex medical procedures and expensive diagnostic tests are typically quite high in the United Kingdom, where health care is provided free but rationing is by waiting in line with priorities for service established by review committees of medical professionals. In the United Kingdom there is also typically a long waiting period merely to be admitted to a hospital for a nonemergency medical procedure. Freedom to choose practitioners and modes of treatment are limited under a system of government-provided health care. In short, a national health insurance system for the United States will not necessarily stem the rate of growth of medical expenses. Such a system must face the same issues we have discussed in relation to our current mix of private and government provision of health insurance. However, the system could insure coverage to all Americans at a cost that will not depend on the experience rating of a particular group. National health insurance financed through taxation will benefit some Americans at the expense of others—some will be newly covered, some will get better coverage than they have now, and still others would find that the coverage they received from their employers was superior. A shift to a tax-financed system will influence both the burden of financing health insurance and the quality of medical care available to particular individuals.

The international view in this chapter discusses national health insurance in Great Britain and Canada and how health care is rationed in these systems.

Summary

Health care expenditures have been claiming an increasing share of GDP in the United States in recent years. Governments have been playing an increasingly more active role in the financing of health care expenditures in the United States since 1965. Federal, state, and local governments currently pay more than 40 percent of the health care bills of Americans, mainly through Medicaid and Medicare the two major government health insurance programs. Medicaid pays the health care bills of those on public assistance and other qualifying individuals whose resources have been exhausted by medical bills. Governments also indirectly subsidize private health insurance by excluding employer-provided health insurance from taxation.

The system of health insurance that prevailed in the United States in the early 1990s was a mix of government and private insurance programs. Most private health insurance is provided by employers; 60 percent of Americans are covered by such programs. Significant gaps in coverage remained in the U.S. system that prevailed in the early 1990s—about 15 percent of Americans had no health insurance coverage. This group included low-income workers and many young adults who do not receive health insurance benefits through employment and whose incomes are too high to make them eligible for Medicaid.

Under the U.S. health insurance system, most Americans pay only a small portion of the price of medical services. Out-of-pocket costs for health care services cover only 21 percent of the costs. Third-party payments by private insurance firms and the government cover the bulk of health care costs. Because the third-party payments reduce the price of medical services to consumers, the quantity demanded increases. The price of health care services must rise to increase the quantity supplied, assuming an upward sloping supply curve. Third-party payments therefore contribute to an increase in the quantity of medical services demanded and the price of those services, thereby increasing health care expenditures. The moral hazard of health insurance is the increase in the quantity of health care demanded that results when insurance companies pay most of the bills of consumers.

Health care expenditures are difficult to control because health care providers can influence the demand for such services. Health insurance seeks to control expenditures by establishing deductibles and coinsurance to make consumers more price conscious. Some insurance companies provide service through HMOs, where the physicians receive capitation payments that vary with the number of patients rather than services provided. The capitation payments provide incentives for the providers to economize on the use of health care resources.

In addition to a large portion of the population being uninsured, other gaps exist in the U.S. health care system. Few private health insurance policies provide long-term care coverage and many Americans lack coverage for catastrophic health care expenditures. In other nations, national health insurance schemes provide universal health insurance coverage and finance the coverage through taxation. In those nations governments budget for health care spending and control reimbursements to hospitals and physicians to achieve spending targets. Control of spending for capital facilities in most nations with national health insurance limits access to these facilities and often results in long waiting lists for admission to hospitals and for surgical procedures. Recent proposals for reform in the United States have sought to guarantee universal coverage by mandating benefits while trying to set up mechanisms to control the growth in health care spending.

A Forward Look

Taxation is the major means of financing government expenditures. Part III develops techniques to analyze the economic effects of taxes. The following chapter discusses taxation and alternative methods of financing government goods and services.

Important Concepts

Risk Aversion
Third-Party Payments
Deductibles
Coinsurance
Moral Hazard of Health Insurance
Capitation Payments
Health Maintenance Organization (HMO)
Prospective Payment System
Long-term Care Services

Questions for Review

1. How are health care expenditures financed in the United States?
2. What is the role of governments in providing health insurance and financing health care in the United States?
3. What are third-party payments and how do they result in an overallocation of resources to the provision of health care?
4. Show how the moral hazard of health insurance varies with the coinsurance rate. How can an increase in deductibles reduce the moral hazard of health insurance?
5. What are capitation payments? How can capitation payments of HMOs help control health care spending?
6. Discuss some of the major aspects of the Medicaid and Medicare systems in the United States and techniques used by these programs to control government health care spending in recent years.
7. What are some of the problems involved with providing health care as a public good free of charge and in equal amounts to all consumers?
8. Which groups in the United States were not covered by health insurance as of the early 1990s? How does the lack of health insurance affect those who are not covered and others?
9. How are health care services rationed in Great Britain and Canada, where universal health insurance is available?
10. How is health care spending controlled in Great Britain and Canada?

Problems

1. The current tax rate paid by employees in a company on their income is 30 percent. Currently the employer provides workers with a health insurance policy that is worth $3,000 per year.
   a. Assuming that the company has 1,000 workers, what is the indirect government subsidy for health insurance for workers in the company?
   b. Suppose that instead of providing the workers with health insurance as a fringe benefit, the employer sold them the policy for a $3,000 annual premium? How would this change in the arrangement affect the typical worker, assuming that he or she still wants $3,000 worth of insurance under the new arrangement?

2. The following graph below shows the supply and demand for health care in the nation. The demand curve reflects the marginal social benefit of health care while the supply curve reflects the marginal social cost.

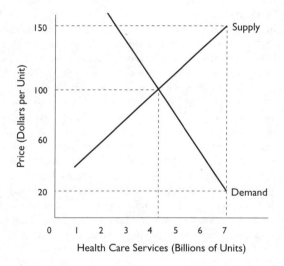

a. What is the efficient amount of health care expenditures?
b. Suppose that under current arrangements health insurance reduces the price of health care to the population from an average of $100 per unit to $20 per unit. Show how the third-party payments will affect the market for health care by affecting the quantity demanded and quantity supplied. Assuming that the price must increase

to \$150 to accommodate the new quantity demanded, calculate the increase in expenditures for health care. Is efficiency now attained in the market?

3. Use the graph from problem 2 to show the loss in efficiency that results from third-party payments. Show how the loss in net benefits from overallocation of resources to health care can be reduced by increasing coinsurance from \$20 per unit of health care services to \$50 per unit.

4. How do health care providers control the demand for health care? Suppose reimbursement rates to physicians under all payers is limited by law. Use supply and demand analysis to show how the limit in reimbursement need not decrease expenditures for health care if health care providers succeed in increasing the demand.

Suggestions for Further Reading

Feldstein, Paul J. *Health Care Economics,* 3d ed. New York: Wiley, 1988. A textbook covering the major economic issues in health care, including health insurance and health care financing.

Fuchs, Victor R. *The Future of Health Policy,* (Cambridge, Mass.: Harvard University Press, 1993). A collection of essays on health economics and health care policy by an eminent economist who has specialized in health care economics.

Phelps, Charles E. *Health Economics,* New York, Harper Collins Publishers Inc., 1992. An up-to-date analysis of issues in health economics.

U.S. Congress, Congressional Budget Office. *Managed Competition and Its Potential to Reduce Health Care Spending.* Washington, D.C., U.S. Government Printing Office, May 1993. An analysis of how limits on payments to insurers and health care providers could reduce the rate of growth of health care spending.

U.S. Congress, Congressional Budget Office. *Policy Choices for Long-term Care.* Washington, D.C.: U.S. Government Printing Office, June 1991. A discussion of current provision of long-term care and alternatives to help finance the pending increase in demand for such care as the U.S. population ages.

U.S. Congress, Congressional Budget Office. *Restructuring Health Insurance for Medicare Enrollees.* Washington, D.C.: U.S. Government Printing Office, August 1991. A discussion of the gaps in Medicare coverage and alternatives to both extend coverage and control costs.

U.S. Congress, Congressional Budget Office. *Rising Health Care Costs: Causes, Implications, and Strategies.* Washington, D.C.: U.S. Government Printing Office, April 1991. A carefully organized study of the causes of rising health care expenditures in the United States and problems in the system of health care financing in the early 1990s.

U.S. Congress, Congressional Budget Office. *Selected Options for Expanding Health Insurance Coverage.* Washington, D.C.: U.S. Government Printing Office, July 1991. A discussion of the gaps in coverage for health insurance in the United States and recent proposals to extend health insurance to all in various ways.

Financing

Government

Expenditures

III

10

INTRODUCTION TO
GOVERNMENT FINANCE

LEARNING OBJECTIVES

After reading this chapter you should be able to

1. Discuss alternative means of financing government expenditures, the effects they have on the economy, and issues relating to the distribution of the burden of government finance.
2. Understand the basic terminology used to analyze the impact of taxes on

the economy, including the tax base and the tax rate structure.
3. List the criteria used to evaluate alternative means of financing government expenditures.
4. Examine alternatives to taxation as means of government finance.

Federal, state, and local governments in the United States spend more than $2 trillion annually. To raise the funds necessary to finance their expenditures, governments tax economic activities, including income-earning activities and consumption of goods and services. Those who own homes and other property also are taxed according to the value of their property. The average U.S. worker allocates more than four months of annual earnings to pay federal, state, and local taxes. You name it, some government usually taxes it—everything, including gasoline, alcoholic beverages, jewelry, electricity, not to mention your earnings from work and savings, and, if you are fortunate enough to own one, your home!

Although taxation is the main source of revenue for governments in the United States, accounting for 75 percent of total government revenue, governments obtain some funds from fees and charges, including tolls, and tuition charges at state-run colleges and universities. Governments also raise funds from enterprises they operate such as public utilities (water, gas, and electricity) and the liquor stores operated by many state governments. State governments even operate gambling enterprises that raise revenue from lotteries and legal off-track horse race betting! Governments must borrow funds when they cannot cover all their expenditures from tax and nontax receipts. In recent years the tax revenue collected by the federal government has fallen far short of an amount sufficient to pay for all federal spending. To meet its expenses, the federal government has had to borrow to cover enormous budget deficits, such as the one in 1991 that was more than $260 billion!

This chapter begins an exploration of the means and consequences of government finance. We develop the vocabulary necessary to analyze tax systems and such alternatives to taxes as user charges for government provided services and borrowing. We also discuss the criteria that are used to evaluate systems of government. In most cases, funds to pay for government-provided goods and services are obtained in a way that is fundamentally different from that used to finance goods and services in markets. Buyers and sellers interact in markets to establish prices that provide sales revenue to pay the costs of making goods available. The prices simultaneously ration the goods and services and provide the revenue necessary to finance the costs that sellers incur in providing the goods to consumers. Taxes do not ration goods and services in this way because payment of taxes is not a prerequisite for enjoying the benefits of most government-supplied goods and services. So although these benefits are financed by taxes, the absence of a direct link between taxation and enjoyment of government-provided goods and services complicates the analysis of government finance.

THE PURPOSE AND CONSEQUENCES OF GOVERNMENT FINANCE

Government activity requires the reallocation of resources from private to government use. To accomplish this, individuals must be induced to surrender their right to command resources for their own private uses, so that government authorities can then obtain those rights for the purpose of providing goods and services.

The particular method of finance that is either proposed for a community or actually used can affect a number of important economic and political variables. These include the following:

1. The political equilibrium: The equilibrium quantity and mix of government-provided goods and services depend on the distribution of tax shares per unit of those goods and services, because citizens' tax shares influence their voting choices.
2. The overall market equilibrium and the efficiency with which resources are employed in private uses: The particular method of finance used can distort the prices of goods and services in ways that prevent competitive markets from achieving efficiency.
3. The distribution of income: Alternative financing schemes affect the distribution of income by reducing the income that persons have to spend on private goods and services and by influencing prices and the amounts of private goods exchanged in markets. In fact, many citizens advocate the use of particular methods of public finance precisely for the purpose of redistributing income.

The impact of the method of finance on political equilibrium is discussed in the chapters on public goods and choices. This chapter, and those to follow, therefore concentrate on the impact of government finance on private choices and on the distribution of income.

Principles of Taxation

What Are Taxes?

Taxes are compulsory payments associated with certain activities. The revenues collected through taxation are used to purchase the inputs necessary to produce government-supplied goods and services or to redistribute purchasing power among citizens.

Taxation reallocates resources from private to government use in two distinct steps. First, the ability of individuals to command resources is reduced, because taxation reduces income for spending on market goods and services. Second, the revenues collected by government then are used to bid for resources necessary to provide government goods and services and to provide income support payments to recipients of government transfers such as Social Security pensions. For example, a family whose annual income is $30,000 and who pays $6,000 in taxes must necessarily curtail either annual consumption or saving. The $6,000 could have been used to purchase home furnishings or to help finance private investment. The private goods and services that could have been bought with the $6,000 is the opportunity cost of government-supplied goods and services for this particular family.

Under tax financing, the resources released and made available to government as a result of taxes do not always correspond to the resources required to produce the politically chosen government-provided goods and services. In such cases, government demands on resources, coupled with the reduction in private demands caused by the taxes themselves, cause the relative prices of some inputs to change. For example, if taxation results in a reduction in the demand for blue-collar workers while government spending increases the demand for white-collar workers, the net effect will be an increase in the wages of white-collar workers relative to blue-collar workers, if full employment is to be maintained.

A single-step alternative to taxation is the use of government power to acquire resources directly. The most common example of this is the military draft. When resources are acquired directly, their owners bear the cost of finance by losing the opportunity to use them in the way that maximizes their income or satisfaction.

The Tax Base

The **tax base** is the item or economic activity on which the tax is levied. The most commonly used tax bases can be grouped into three broad categories: income, consumption, and wealth. These are economic bases; their values depend on decisions made by individuals. For example, individuals make daily choices that affect their income. They also can control the allocation of their income between saving and consumption. Because most individuals must save to accumulate wealth, their decisions regarding consumption also affect their wealth.

A person's income is the sum of the value of his annual consumption of goods and services and annual saving. Income is often regarded as a good index of the ability to pay taxes. Total annual income in a nation is equal to the value of the total consumption and saving of all persons and organizations in the country. A person's annual consumption is his annual income less the amount of that income saved that year. Finally, wealth represents the value of a person's accumulated savings and investments at any point in time. The annual flow of income from the stock of accumulated wealth in a nation is the annual return to saving.

The three major tax bases are related. Consumption is the portion of income that is not saved, while wealth is the net value of a person's stock of accumulated savings or investments.

Because income is believed to be a good index of the ability to pay taxes, many economists use this broad economic base as a benchmark for evaluating the fairness of taxes. The amount of taxes paid is generally computed as a percentage of annual income. The way a particular tax varies as a percentage of income per year is often used to make judgments about the fairness of the distribution of taxes among taxpayers.

Taxes on economic bases can be general or selective. A **general tax** is one that taxes all of the components of the economic base, with no exclusions, exemptions, or deductions from the tax base. For example, a general income tax would tax all sources of income and would not allow any sort of deduction from total income in computing tax liability. All income, irrespective of its source or use, would be taxable. Similarly, a general wealth tax would tax all forms of holding wealth.

A **selective tax** is one that taxes only certain portions of the tax base, or it might allow exemptions and deductions from the general tax base. For example, an **excise tax** is a tax on the manufacture or sale of a particular good or service. Excise taxes are selective taxes on production or sales. Similarly, a tax on real estate in an example of a selective tax on a particular form of wealth. A tax on profits is a selective income tax, because it taxes only a particular form of income.

The Tax Rate Structure

The **tax rate structure** describes the relationship between the tax collected during a given accounting period and the tax base. In evaluating taxes on such economic bases as income, the tax rates are calculated as the ratio of taxes paid to the various values of the base. The **average tax rate (ATR)** is simply the total dollar amount of taxes collected divided by the dollar value of the taxable base.

$$ATR = \frac{\text{Total Taxes Paid}}{\text{Value of the Tax Base}}. \tag{10.1}$$

The **marginal tax rate (MTR)** is the additional tax collected on additional dollar value of the tax base as the tax base increases.

$$MTR = \frac{\Delta\text{Total Taxes Paid}}{\Delta\text{Value of the Tax Base}}. \tag{10.2}$$

A **proportional tax rate structure** is one for which the average tax rate, expressed as a percentage of the value of the tax base, does not vary with the value of the tax base. For example, an income tax of 20 percent would tax all income at 20 percent. Thus, a person with an income of $10,000 and a person with an income of $100,000 would each be subject to the same rates of taxation. The tax on $10,000 at 20 percent would be $2,000, and the tax on $100,000 of income at 20 percent would be $20,000.

Under proportional taxation, the average tax rate, but not the amount of tax, is independent of the size of the base. A tax with a proportional rate structure is sometimes called a **flat-rate tax.**

For a proportional tax rate structure, both the average and marginal rates of taxation are the same. Because the rate of taxation does not vary with the annual value of the base, additional increments in the tax base, such as additional earnings under an income tax, are taxed at the same rate as that applied to previous values. This is illustrated in Figure 10.1.

When a **progressive tax rate structure** is used, the average tax rate increases with the size of the base. The larger the tax base, the larger the average tax rate applied. The **tax bracket** gives the increment of annual income associated with each marginal tax rate. The marginal tax rates and associated tax brackets for a progressive income tax are illustrated in Figure 10.2.

For progressive taxation, the marginal rate of taxation eventually exceeds the average rate of taxation as the marginal tax rate increases. The dichotomy between the two rates is important, because the marginal tax rate is more crucial in determining behavior changes that can cause losses in efficiency than is the average rate. Therefore, when the average and marginal rates of taxation vary from each other, it is necessary to carefully delineate the two in order to ascertain properly the effect of the tax on individual behavior. For example, if a person is deciding to work more hours, the net gain for doing so would be the net income she can keep after taxes. If her income is subject to a 50 percent marginal tax rate, she will be able to retain only half of her extra income. However, because only income after a certain amount is subject to the 50 percent rate, the person's average tax rate will be lower than 50 percent. The difference between average and marginal rates of taxation for a typical progressive tax is illustrated in Figure 10.2.

Figure 10.1 ✦ A PROPORTIONAL TAX RATE STRUCTURE

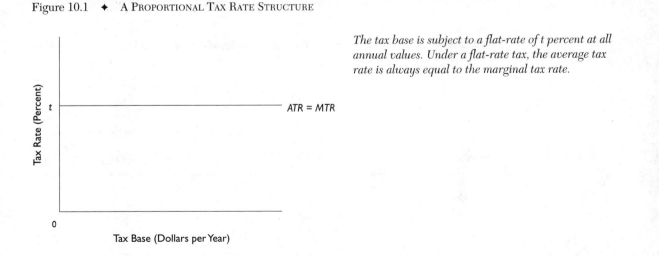

The tax base is subject to a flat-rate of t percent at all annual values. Under a flat-rate tax, the average tax rate is always equal to the marginal tax rate.

ATR = MTR

Tax Rate (Percent)

t

0

Tax Base (Dollars per Year)

Figure 10.2 ✦ A PROGRESSIVE TAX RATE STRUCTURE

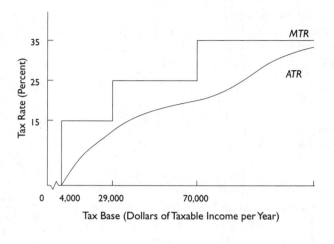

Under a progressive tax rate structure, the average tax rate increases with the size of the tax base. The marginal tax rate exceeds the average tax rate after a point. These curves are based on Table 10.1.

Table 10.1 shows the marginal and average tax rates on which the graph in Figure 10.2 is based. All income up to $4,000 per year is subject to a zero marginal and average tax rate. This is the first tax bracket. Income between $4,000 and $29,000 per year is subject to a 15-percent marginal tax rate. Income between $29,000 and $70,000 per year is subject to a 25-percent rate. Finally, all income greater than $70,000 per year is subject to a 35-percent marginal tax rate. These are the marginal tax rates for each *bracket* of income.

Table 10.1 ✦ AN EXAMPLE OF A PROGRESSIVE TAX RATE STRUCTURE

TAX BRACKETS (TAXABLE INCOME)	MARGINAL TAX RATES (MTR)	AVERAGE TAX RATES (ATR)	
		BEGINNING OF BRACKET	END OF BRACKET
0–$4,000	0	0	0
$ 4,000–$29,000	15	0	13
$29,000–$70,000	25	13	20
Above $70,000	35	20	34[a]

[a]Calculated for $1,000,000 annual income.

Table 10.1 shows the average tax rates for income at the beginning and end of each tax bracket. For example, a taxpayer with a $4,000 annual income would pay a zero average tax rate, because only income greater than $4,000 would be taxable. A taxpayer with income at the end of that bracket would pay 15 percent on the amount of income greater than $4,000. This will be 15 percent of $25,000, which is $3,750 per year. Dividing this by that taxpayer's $29,000 annual income gives an average tax rate of 13 percent, which is less than the 15-percent marginal tax rate.

In each tax bracket, the average tax rate would steadily rise. Thus a taxpayer just entering the $29,000 to $70,000 bracket would be paying an average tax rate of slightly more than 13 percent. A taxpayer with a $70,000 annual income pays nothing on the first $4,000 of income, 15 percent on all income from $4,000 to $70,000, and 25 percent on income greater than $29,000 up to $70,000 per year. The total tax is therefore $3,750 + .25($70,000 − $29,000) = $14,000. The average tax rate for a taxpayer with $70,000 annual income therefore would be 20 percent. For the final tax bracket, which is open-ended, the table shows the average tax rate for a taxpayer with a million-dollar annual income. The average tax rate for taxpayers with higher annual income would rise steadily and approach, but never equal, the marginal tax rate. In Figure 10.2, a line is traced through the corresponding points on the average tax rates within brackets to show how average tax rates vary. Notice that the average tax rate is always less than the marginal tax rate at all levels of income.

Finally, taxes may have a **regressive tax rate structure,** in which the average tax rate declines as the size of the tax base increases. In a regressive tax rate structure, the marginal tax rate is less than the average tax rate for all those brackets above the lowest. A regressive income tax results in a lower annual average tax rate as income rises. More productive individuals would be rewarded with lower tax rates as they produced and earned more. However, the opposition to such a method of taxation is strong because it violates widely held belief that ability to pay increases with income. However, in many cases, a regressive tax rate structure can result in upper-income persons paying higher dollar amounts of taxes than lower-income persons.

An example of a tax with a regressive rate structure is the Social Security payroll tax. In 1991 this tax was levied at an initial combined employer and employee marginal tax rate of 15.3 percent on annual wages $53,400 and less. Wages in excess of $53,400 up to a maximum of $125,000 were then taxed at a combined employee-employer marginal tax rate of only 2.9 percent. Wages in excess of $125,000 were not subject to the tax at all, so the marginal tax rate for the payroll tax fell to zero for labor earnings in excess of that amount. The tax therefore had a three-bracket regressive tax rate structure as illustrated in Figure 10.3. A worker earning $53,400 in 1991, therefore, would generate tax revenue from the payroll tax of (.153)($53,400) = $10,246. The average tax rate paid on less than $53,400 annual labor earnings was also 15.3 percent. Workers earning between $53,400 and $125,000 were taxed at a rate of only 2.9 percent on their earnings in excess of $125,000. A worker with $125,000 earnings therefore would generate an additional $2,076.40 in payroll tax revenue from wages, equal to ($125,000 − $53,400)(.029). The average tax rate on the wages of a worker with $125,000 earnings therefore would be $(10,246.00 + 2,076.40)/125,000 = 9.9 percent. Because the marginal tax rate would fall to zero for earnings in excess of $125,000, the maximum Social Security tax on wages would

I N T E R N A T I O N A L   V I E W

Taxes and Tax Rates Throughout the World

You might think that taxes take a big bite out of incomes in the United States. However, taxes are a relatively small share of aggregate income in the United States compared to other industrial nations of the world. As of 1990, total federal, state, and local taxes in the United States amounted to 29.9 percent of U.S. gross domestic product (GDP), which is a measure of aggregate income generated from domestic production. The share of gross domestic product allocated to pay taxes provides a rough indication of the average tax rate for all taxes expressed as a percentage of aggregate domestic income.

Table A (below) shows average tax rates measured by tax revenues as a percent of GDP for major industrial nations in 1990. Almost all industrial nations have average tax rates in the aggregate of at least 30 percent of GDP. The highest tax rates are in the Scandinavian nations, which have extensive social programs administered by the government sector of the economy. Tax revenues amounted to a whopping 56.9 percent of

Table A   ◆   Average Tax Rates by Nation Measured by Tax Revenues as a Percent of Gross Domestic Product (GDP), 1990

NATION	TAX REVENUES AS A PERCENT OF GDP
United States	29.9
Australia	30.8
Austria	41.6
Belgium	44.9
Canada	37.1
Denmark	48.6
Finland	38.0
France	43.7
Germany	37.7
Greece	36.5
Ireland	37.2
Italy	39.1
Japan	31.3
Luxembourg	50.3
Netherlands	45.2
New Zealand	38.2
Norway	46.3
Portugal	34.6
Spain	34.4
Sweden	56.9
Switzerland	31.7
Turkey	27.8
United Kingdom	36.7

Source: Organization for Economic Cooperation and Development.

GDP in Sweden in 1990, 48.6 percent in Denmark, and 46.3 percent in Norway. European nations also have higher average tax rates than those of the United States. Tax revenues amounted to 36.7 percent of GDP in the United Kingdom, 43.7 percent of GDP in France, and 45.2 percent of GDP in the Netherlands. Japan, which devotes only a small amount of its GDP to defense (about 1 percent), in the past has had much lower tax rates than average. For example, in 1980, tax revenues in Japan amounted only to 25 percent of GDP. However, tax burdens have been growing rapidly in Japan and, as of 1990, Japan raised tax revenues amounting to 31.3 percent of GDP—slightly more than in the United States. Canada allocated 37.1 percent of its GDP to taxes in 1990.

Most tax revenues in industrial nations come from taxes levied on both personal and corporate incomes, from taxes on payrolls used to finance social security programs, and from taxes on goods and services. The United States, Canada, and Sweden rely heavily on the income tax base as a source of revenue. For example, in 1990, 43.2 percent of tax receipts in the United States came from taxes on personal and corporate income. In the same year payroll taxes on wages and salaries paid to employees accounted for 29.5 percent of tax receipts in the United States. Only 16.5 percent of tax receipts came from taxes on consumption of goods and services. France and Italy, on the other hand, relied more heavily on consumption taxes, which amounted to 28.2 percent of tax receipts in France and 28 percent of tax receipts for Italy. France also had very high payroll taxes. Canada relies very heavily on consumption as a tax base and has relatively low payroll taxes. Table B shows the percent distribution of tax receipts by type of tax for selected nations in 1990.

Table B ✦ DISTRIBUTION OF TAX RECEIPTS BY TAX BASE—SELECTED NATIONS, 1990 (PERCENT)

NATION	CORPORATE AND PERSONAL INCOME	PAYROLLS	CONSUMPTION	OTHER (INCLUDES WEALTH)
United States	43.2	29.5	16.5	10.8
France	17.3	44.2	28.2	10.3
Germany	32.1	36.8	27.4	3.7
Italy	36.5	32.9	28.0	2.6
Japan	48.3	29.2	13.2	9.3
Sweden	41.0	27.6	24.6	6.8
Canada	48.3	14.2	27.4	10.1

Source: Organization for Economic Cooperation and Development.

be $12,322 per year. The average tax rate of a corporate CEO with an annual salary of $500,000 therefore would be only 2 percent! Figure 10.3 shows the 1991 regressive rate structure for the Social Security payroll tax in the United States. Notice how the average tax rate falls for workers earning more than $53,400 per year.

Sales taxes in the United States are often labeled regressive by critics. Strictly speaking, the retail sales tax as used by most state and local governments in the United States is basically a tax with a proportional rate structure applied to the consumption base. However, because consumption as a percentage of income tends to fall as income rises, the proportional tax on consumption could be regressive with

Figure 10.3 ✦ An Example of a Regressive Tax Rate Structure

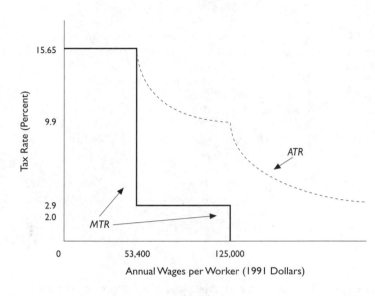

This is the tax rate structure used for the Social Security payroll tax for 1991. It is a three-bracket regressive rate structure. The maximum tax per worker is $12,322, and the marginal tax rate falls to zero for earnings in excess of $125,000.

respect to income (depending on the actual details of the tax and tax preferences allowed). Thus, those who argue that sales taxes are regressive are evaluating the taxes with respect to a base different from that on which the tax is actually levied. This is commonly done. They, in fact, believe that sales taxes are regressive with respect to the income base.

CHECKPOINT

1. What is a tax base? List three major classes of tax bases, and give an example of a particular type of tax levied on each of the three major bases.
2. What is a general tax? How does a general tax differ from a selective tax?
3. How does the relationship between the marginal tax rate and the average tax rate vary, depending on whether a tax rate structure is proportional, progressive, or regressive?

How Should the Burden of Government Finance be Distributed?

A basic problem in government finance is to distribute among citizens the burden of financing the costs of government-supplied goods and services. No way of distributing these costs will satisfy all citizens. However, some clearly defined principles, or "philosophies," have been developed regarding the ways of distributing the costs of financing government-provided goods and services. Two major approaches to use as principles in determining the distribution of the burden of government finance are discussed in this section.

The Benefit Principle

The **benefit principle** argues that the means of financing government-supplied goods and services should be linked to the benefits that citizens receive from government. From the point of view of those who favor the benefit approach, fees and charges are ideal forms of government finance. Charges, like prices, distribute the costs of goods and services among those who consume them.

A major advantage of the benefit approach is that, if successfully implemented, it links the cost per unit of government-provided services with the marginal benefits of those services. A distribution of tax shares per unit of a pure public good that reflects marginal benefits received by taxpayers induces individual citizens to vote for the efficient output of that good. Taxing all citizens according to their marginal benefits results in a Lindahl equilibrium, provided that the free-rider problem does not exist.

Most government-provided goods and services result in collectively consumed benefits that are difficult to assign to individuals. The only way to determine such benefits would be to ask individual citizens how much extra units of the good or service are worth to them. If individuals know that their share of the financial burden depends on their declaration of benefits, they might have little or no incentive to declare their true benefits. Only in communities that are fairly small, where individuals know each other's tastes, can a voluntary benefit approach work easily and without compulsion.

In some cases, the benefits from government-provided services can be correlated with a particular economic activity, which is taxed so that the amount paid varies according to benefits received by taxpayers. For example, the linking of gasoline taxes and road construction can be thought of as an attempt to apply the benefit principle by earmarking a particular tax for a particular use. The presumption behind the use of the gasoline tax to finance roads is that the benefits of road use vary directly with the consumption of gasoline. Most user charges, such as tolls for road and bridge use, fares for the use of public transport, and admission fees for the use of recreational and cultural facilities, are all based on the benefit principle.

The Ability-to-Pay Principle

The **ability-to-pay principle** maintains that taxes should be distributed according to the capacity of taxpayers to pay them. Citizens with greater ability to earn income, for example, should be taxed more heavily than those with less capacity to earn. Using this approach, the problem of distributing tax shares is viewed as independent of individual marginal benefits received from government activities. The implementation of a tax system based on the ability to pay requires some collective agreement concerning an equitable distribution of the taxes among citizens. Individual evaluations of the ability to pay are likely to differ among citizens whose preferences differ. In the United States, general consensus holds that the ability to pay varies with income.

Related to the ability-to-pay principle are the notions of horizontal equity and vertical equity. **Horizontal equity** is achieved when individuals of the same economic capacity (measured, for example, by income) pay the same amount of taxes per year (or over their lifetimes). **Vertical equity** is accomplished when individuals of differing economic ability pay annual tax bills that differ according to some collectively chosen notion of fairness. Both these concepts are subjective and are difficult to administer. Insofar as individual assessments of economic capacity differ, no consensus concerning horizontal equity is likely—and vertical equity requires judgments on income distribution that are even more subjective than those associated with horizontal equity.

Let's consider a few examples to illustrate the difficulties involved in determining whether a tax system achieves horizontal or vertical equity. The application of the principle of horizontal equity requires agreement on some measure of equality between individuals. For example, you might argue that two people who earn exactly the same income each year be considered equal for the purpose of deciding how much tax to pay. Suppose that both Mary and John earn $50,000 per year. However, John also owns a house valued at $500,000 that he was fortunate enough to inherit from a rich uncle, has no debts, and has $100,000 in the bank. Mary, by contrast, rents a small apartment, owns no property, and has little savings in the bank. Are these two people really equal in the sense that they have the same economic capacity to pay taxes? Although they have the same money income, John has more wealth (property and financial assets) than Mary and therefore really has more capacity to pay taxes than does Mary.

Consider another example: Suppose two physicians have exactly the same training and capacity to earn income. However, one physician, Dr. Jones, values her leisure time more than Dr. Smith and therefore spends more time on the golf course and on vacations. Because Dr. Jones spends less time in the office than Dr. Smith, she has less income. If you use income as the basis for determining horizontal equity, we would argue that it is alright for Dr. Jones to pay less taxes than Dr. Smith. However, if we use earning capacity rather than actual income earned as our measure of the ability to pay taxes, the two physicians should both pay the same tax even though their incomes differ.

Vertical equity is even more difficult to establish than horizontal equity. Even if a tax system is generally agreed to have satisfied criteria for horizontal equity, say, because people with equal income pay equal amounts in taxes, it might not satisfy everyone's ideal of how people of different economic capacity pay different amounts in taxes. For example, suppose you think that a tax system achieves vertical equity if all taxpayers make an equal sacrifice to pay for government services. But you might also reason that equal sacrifice does not mean that all taxpayers pay the same number of dollars in taxes. It is reasonable to assume that the marginal benefit of a dollar to a person varies with the number of dollars that person earns each year and the number of dollars stored up as wealth. Accordingly a dollar might be worth a whole lot to a person with little income and little wealth such, as a single mother with no savings or property who works in a factory earning $6 an hour and supporting two children. That same dollar might be worth much less to a billionaire such as Donald Trump, who has lots of income and wealth. Most people would therefore argue that equal sacrifice requires that the rich pay more dollars in taxes each year than the poor. But how much more should they pay? If, for example, both the working mother and Donald Trump paid the same percentage of their income in taxes, Mr. Trump would pay more dollars in taxes because a fixed percentage of several billion dollars will be more money than the same percentage of a modest annual income of $12,500. But for many this would not be sufficient to achieve vertical equity. Because the marginal benefit of a dollar falls with income, to achieve equal sacrifice of the benefits of income, a person as rich as Mr. Trump should pay a *higher percentage* of income in taxes than people with lower incomes. But how much higher a percentage should it be? We all might have different ideas about this, based on our own assessments of the way the marginal benefit of a dollar will vary with the person's income and wealth.

It is possible to derive technical rules for vertical equity by making specific assumptions about the way the marginal benefit of income declines as income (or wealth) rises.[1] To derive these rules, we also would have to make interpersonal comparisons of well-being among taxpayers—something that is difficult to do. You might think that a dollar to someone with $100,000 annual income is worth less than half as much as that to a person with only $25,000 annual income, but how do you really know? The person with the larger income might be ill and expect sharp declines in the future income because of inability to work and therefore values current income very highly. Determining the precise number of dollars that each taxpayer would have to pay for equal sacrifice is therefore a very difficult task.

Nonetheless, despite our inability to determine a precise rule for vertical equity, the consensus in the United States appears to be that the poor should pay less in taxes than the rich. For example, the federal income tax has provisions that keep the tax burden of the lowest income groups at or close to zero while tax rates are designed to increase as income increases to achieve vertical equity.

Actually assessing the fairness of tax systems according to the way tax burdens vary with ability to pay also is complicated by the fact that taxes affect prices and quantities of both inputs and outputs sold. Taxes therefore affect incomes in very complex ways. For example, a sales tax on boats might raise the price of the product, therefore reducing the real income of people who buy it. But the tax might not raise the price of the boat by the full amount of the tax per boat. Therefore, after selling the boat and paying the tax, the boat builder might have less revenue per boat. For example, imagine a $5,000 tax on a $100,000 boat. If the price of the boat rises to $102,000 after the decrease in supply that results from the tax, the net revenue per boat taken in by the builders after paying the tax will be only $97,000—that is, $3,000 less than before the tax. The boat builders, therefore, also are made worse off. The price increase caused by the tax also will reduce the quantity of the product

---

[1] The problem of equal sacrifice in taxation was considered in great detail by the English classical economist John Stuart Mill in his *Principles of Political Economy,* ed. W. I. Ashley (London: Longmans, 1921). For technical derivations of such rules, see Richard A. Musgrave, *The Theory of Public Finance* (New York: McGraw-Hill, 1959), chap. 5. For a modern interpretation, see Martin Feldstein, "On the Theory of Tax Reform," *Journal of Public Economics* 6 (July–August 1976): 77–104. Feldstein argues that the principle of horizontal equity requires that the posttax utilities of two persons with the same pretax utility levels be the same.

demanded, reducing revenue taken in by sellers. As this occurs, the sellers use less input to produce the product. If workers and owners of capital, who must find alternative uses for their resources because of the tax, cannot do so for the same rates of pay, their incomes will decline as a result of the tax. If skilled boat builders who lose their jobs because of the tax cannot find work that pays wages as high as they earned in boat building, their incomes will fall.

We need to trace out all the effects of a tax on prices and the quantities of outputs and inputs sold before we can accurately assess how much of it is directly and indirectly paid by different individuals. Once we have this information, we can then use it to see whether taxes vary according to commonly held notions of ability to pay.

CRITERIA FOR EVALUATING ALTERNATIVE METHODS OF GOVERNMENT FINANCE

No single criterion exists by which to evaluate alternative means of government finance. In reality, the system of government finance that emerges is one that makes trade-offs among such normative criteria as

1. Equity: The distribution of the burden of government finance should coincide with commonly held notions of fairness and the ability to pay.
2. Efficiency: The system of government finance should raise revenues with only minimal loss in efficiency in the private sector.
3. Administrative ease: A government finance system should be relatively easy to administer in a consistent manner, without excessive costs to collect, enforce, and comply with taxes and tax laws.

All these criteria must be considered in evaluating taxes. It is unlikely, however, that all can be achieved simultaneously. Efficient taxes are likely to be considered inequitable by many citizens, but equitable taxes might be costly to administer and could entail losses in efficiency.

Equity Versus Efficiency

Government finance often has significant and complicated effects on the private choices made by citizens. Taxes can affect the willingness of individuals to produce and invest. User charges affect the levels of consumption of those goods and services on which they are levied, with subsidiary effects on the consumption of substitutes for and complements to government-supplied goods and services. The use of debt finance can affect the market equilibrium rate of interest and the willingness of investors to make private investments.

Because the main function of government finance is to reallocate resources away from private use and toward government use, government must reduce private consumption and investment to accomplish its objective. The main concern in evaluating the efficiency of proposed taxes and methods of finance is the impact of any financial scheme on the total income and wealth available. Two alternative methods of financing a given dollar amount of government-provided goods and services can result in different levels of national income and well-being. The most efficient means of government finance raises that given level of revenue while, at the same time, it minimizes the loss in well-being from market production and exchange.

The goals of efficiency and equity in the distribution of taxes among citizens are likely to conflict. Methods of government finance that minimize losses in efficiency in markets are not always considered desirable by all citizens. Those who subscribe to the ability-to-pay approach, or who believe that the system of government finance should be used to redistribute income, often oppose taxes that involve minimal losses in efficiency on the grounds that the distributive effects are undesirable. For example, strong support for progressive income taxes exists in industrial nations mainly because many citizens believe that a progressive tax rate structure applied to income correlates taxes with the ability to pay.

The trade-off between an equitable and an efficient system of government finance must be resolved through political interaction. In reality, under a system of compulsory finance, such as taxation, the resulting structure of government finance likely will be neither efficient nor equitable from the point of view of all citizens. In particular, unless a general consensus exists on what is a fair and equitable distribution of taxes among taxpayers, a given system of finance will be unlikely to satisfy all citizens.

For most democratic nations, in fact, the tax systems that tend to emerge are full of exemptions and deductions that grant special favors to particular groups for a variety of reasons. Many economists have argued that tax systems should be as efficient as possible and that the questions of income redistribution should be treated separately through a system of transfers independent of the tax system.

Equity remains a subjective concept, and the economist's judgments are no better than anybody else's. The economist, however, can generate information on how taxes affect the distribution of income in a community. Quite often, taxes have rather subtle effects on relative prices that might not be immediately obvious to citizens when they are considering the impact of a proposed tax. The economist's estimates of effects that alternative taxes have on relative prices, incomes, and efficiency are useful for citizens in evaluating any particular tax in relation to their own concepts of equity, or fairness. Such estimates permit more-informed collective choices by participating citizens.

Tax Compliance and Evasion

A tax system must have rules for payment that are easily understood by citizens and are enforceable at low cost. **Tax evasion** is noncompliance with the tax laws by failing to pay taxes that are due. The question of tax compliance and evasion is essentially a legal problem with economic aspects. In the absence of strong moral constraints against noncompliance with tax laws and payment of government charges, the incentives for evasion by individuals depend on the costs and benefits expected from noncompliance. The benefits of evasion tend to increase with the amount of tax, or money in general, saved by not complying with the rules. This, in turn, tends to increase with the marginal tax rate and the amount of tax owed.[2]

The costs of tax evasion vary with the penalties involved and the probability of being caught by the authorities. Additionally, individuals consider the probability that they actually will be convicted of a crime after being caught, along with having to bear any costs of legal action necessary to defend themselves.

From the legal point of view, a distinction exists between the concepts of tax evasion and tax avoidance. **Tax avoidance** is a change in behavior to reduce tax liability. Taxpayers respond to the changes in prices caused by taxes by rearranging their personal affairs. High taxes on labor income might induce workers to refuse overtime work. Similarly, taking advantage of special provisions (sometimes called loopholes) in the tax code that reduce tax liability constitutes tax avoidance. Tax evasion is illegal, whereas tax avoidance merely involves adjusting the extent to which one engages in a taxed activity in response to the rate at which that activity is taxed. Tax avoidance is not illegal. However, tax avoidance is socially wasteful in that it results in distorted choices, made on a basis other than the marginal social cost and benefit of an economic activity.

To ensure proper compliance with a system of government finance, an administrative mechanism must be established to collect the tax and to enforce penalties against noncompliance.[3] This involves hiring personnel, establishing offices, acquiring such capital equipment as computers, building toll booths, and so on. To ensure low-cost administration, the taxed activity should be easily measurable, and the costs of collecting that information should be low. For example, the computerized system of tax withholding from employee' wages, so prevalent in many nations using the income tax, constitutes a simple and very inexpensive way of ensuring tax compliance.

Tax evasion has become a serious problem in the United States. Noncompliance with tax laws reduces revenues collected for any given tax rate structure. The greater the noncompliance, the higher the tax rates necessary to raise any given amount of revenues per year. Honest taxpayers therefore have to pay higher tax rates than would otherwise be the case. The Internal Revenue Service (IRS) estimates that revenue loss from noncompliance with the tax laws was $87.1 billion in 1988. This amount was equivalent to nearly two-thirds of the federal government's budget deficit that year. Of this amount, $64.3 billion represented unpaid personal income taxes and $22.8 billion represented taxes unpaid by corporations. The revenues lost due to tax evasion were estimated to be increasing at a rate of 14 percent per year from 1973 to 1981.[4]

Understanding the incentives for tax evasion provides a useful starting point to the development of policies to fight it. Assume that all taxpayers seek to maximize

---

[2]Tax evasion also can vary with the degree to which individuals consider the tax system "fair." See Michael W. Spicer and Lee A. Becker, "Fiscal Inequity and Tax Evasion: An Experimental Approach," *National Tax Journal* 33 (June 1980): 171–176.

[3]A formal model of tax administration and operation has been developed by Kenneth L. Wertz, "Allocation and Output of a Tax Administering Agency," *National Tax Journal* 32 (June 1979): 143–156.

[4]Ann D. Witte and Diane F. Woodbury, "The Effect of Tax Laws and Tax Administration on Tax Compliance: The Case of the U.S. Individual Income Tax," *National Tax Journal* 38 (March 1985): 1–13.

their expected income after taxes. To do so, other things being equal, they seek to minimize their tax payments. They are willing to take the risk of not complying with tax laws if the gains for doing so outweigh the expected costs. This, of course, is a simplification because some citizens feel that it is their duty to comply with the tax laws. However, many citizens reason that if they reduce their tax payments through non-compliance, the quantity and quality of government-supplied services that they receive will not be affected.

Both costs and benefits are associated with tax evasion. The benefit to the taxpayer is the reduction in taxes. The costs are the penalties, both monetary and otherwise, that the taxpayer will incur if caught.

For the taxpayer, the marginal benefit of tax evasion is the dollar amount of taxes not paid. This depends on the taxpayer's marginal tax rate. Assume that the taxpayer is subject to a progressive tax rate structure, as is the case under the personal income tax. In this case, the marginal benefit of a dollar of tax evasion declines as more taxable income is not reported, because tax evasion pushes the taxpayer into lower tax brackets. The marginal tax rate, and thus the marginal benefit in terms of taxes saved, therefore declines as more taxable income is not reported. This is shown in Figure 10.4A, where the marginal benefit of tax evasion is plotted against the amount of taxable income not reported.

The expected marginal cost of tax evasion is likely to rise, because taxpayers are likely to reason that both the probability of detection and the penalty will increase as more taxable income is not reported each year. Assuming that the taxpayer has no moral compunction against tax evasion, the optimal amount of tax evasion in the form of unreported income (shown in Figure 10.4A) corresponds to the point at which the marginal cost of tax evasion to the person equals the marginal benefit. This occurs when D^* dollars per year are not reported.

A reduction in marginal tax rates, such as that which resulted from changes in the U.S. tax law in 1986, reduces the marginal benefit of tax evasion. As shown in Figure 10.4B, this will result in a downward shift in the MB curve and a decrease in unreported income. Increasing moral pressures against tax evasion also could shift the MB curve down. In Figure 10.4B, tax evasion declines from D_1^* to D_2^* as MB_1 shifts to MB_2.

Increases in the marginal cost of tax evasion also will reduce the amount of tax evasion. This can be done by either increasing the probability of detection of increasing the penalties to taxpayers who are detected. This shown in Figure 10.4C. After the marginal cost curve shifts from MC_1 to MC_2, tax evasion declines from D_1^* to D_2^*. If the probability of detection were 100 percent, or if the penalties were severe, the optimal amount of tax evasion to any citizen could fall to zero.

One study of tax compliance for the income tax suggests two effective ways to decrease tax evasion: increases in the probability of IRS tax audits for taxpayers and increases in requirements for reporting of income to the IRS and for withholding of taxes from earnings. The researchers also conclude that much of the increase in tax evasion in the United States during the 1970s was accounted for by a reduction in the probability of audit of tax returns during that period.[5] However, little progress has been made in increasing audits during the 1980s. In 1987 the IRS examined 42

---

[5]See Witte and Woodbury, "The Effect of Tax Laws," 9–10.

Figure 10.4 ✦ REDUCING TAX EVASION

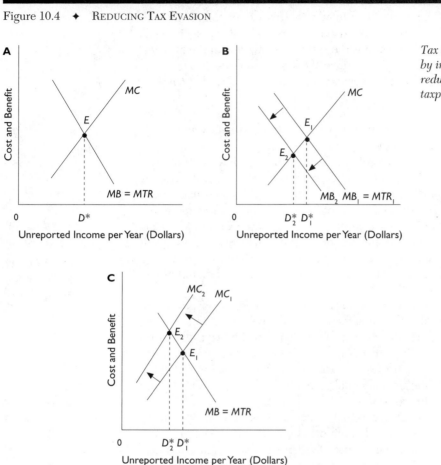

Tax evasion can be reduced either by increasing its marginal cost or by reducing its marginal benefit to taxpayers.

percent fewer returns than it did in 1978. In 1987 only 1.1 percent of returns filed were audited compared with 2.3 percent audited in 1978.

CHECKPOINT

1. What are the two major "philosophies" of taxation used to guide the way the burden of government finance is distributed?
2. What are some of the difficulties involved in determining whether a tax meets criteria of horizontal or vertical equity?
3. How could tax evasion in the United States be reduced?

ALTERNATIVES TO TAXATION

Although taxation is the dominant form of government finance, other alternatives are used, including debt finance, government-induced inflation, donations, user charges, and government-run enterprises such as state lotteries.

Debt Finance

Debt finance is the use of borrowed funds to finance government expenditures. Those who loan funds to the government for the purpose of financing government expenditures usually do so under their own free will. In return for the funds that they lend to the government, they receive a bond, or other note of government indebtedness, that embodies the promise of the government to repay the loan with interest at some future date. Presumably, the interest payment received by these individuals adequately compensates them for the consumption and alternative private investments that they could have enjoyed had they chosen not to buy the government securities. On the other hand, as the debt is paid off by the government, some form of alternative finance is necessary, unless the government decides to retire the debt through issuance of additional debt. If taxes are used in future periods to pay off the debt, citizens will be forced in those future periods to reduce their consumption and saving to compensate those who voluntarily gave up their income in the past to buy the government securities. In other words, debt finance can be used to postpone the burden of taxation.

Government borrowing often is used to finance capital expenditures made by government authorities. Under those circumstances, borrowing by government authorities allows the financing of projects with benefits that will accrue in the future, without excessive reduction in the purchasing power of citizens in the current period. For example, construction of a major public facility, such as a hospital or a road, can take years. If these facilities were to be financed immediately by taxation, individuals would be forced to forgo consumption and saving opportunities equivalent to the entire capital cost of the facility, without any benefits accruing until the facility was fully constructed and functioning. The use of debt finance allows government authorities to tax citizens in the future, as the facility is being constructed and after it is completed. This, in effect, spreads the costs over time and allows citizens to pay for the facility as it is being used, rather than at the initial point of construction. If debt finance is used prudently, it can improve the efficiency of the use of resources for the economy by linking the tax cost of public investments to the stream of benefits produced by those investments.

The implication for the use of debt finance by government on the distribution of well-being among generations is an issue of controversy among economists. In view of the increasing importance of debt finance by central governments in the United States and other nations, the debate on its effect on intergenerational equity has taken on added significance. Chapter 12 provides a detailed analysis of the issues involved in determining the burden of the government debt.

Inflation as a Means of Finance

Government-induced inflation is a sustained annual increase in prices caused by expansion of the money supply to pay for government-supplied goods and services.

Government authorities simply can print money to pay for costs of government-provided goods and services or take other measures to expand the money supply. The net effect of such continual increases in the money supply is, of course, sustained increases in the general level of prices—in other words, inflation. Increases in the market prices of goods and services caused by expansion of the money supply force citizens to curtail their consumption and saving, which, in turn, finances the reallocation of resources to public use over the long run. The burden of government-induced inflation varies according to the extent to which individuals succeed in adjusting their money incomes and assets, along with the rate of increase of retail prices.

Any increase in the money supply to finance government expenditures can result in inflation. If the central bank cooperates with government authorities by increasing the monetary base in response to government credit requirements, inflation is likely to result. An increase in the monetary base by the central bank is the equivalent of printing money. The impact of increased government borrowing to finance deficits on the rate of inflation is complex. Among the various factors that influence the effect of increased borrowing on the price level are (1) the extent to which the monetary reserves are increased by the central bank, (2) the maturity structure of the government debt, (3) the extent to which citizens substitute new government debt for existing private debt and consumption, and (4) the effect of government borrowing on the velocity of circulation of money.[6]

As illustrated in Figure 10.5, the use of inflationary finance can be considered an attempt to move outside the production-possibility curve. For example, creating

---

[6]For a discussion of inflation as a means of public finance, see Stanley Fisher, "Towards an Understanding of the Costs of Inflation: II," in *The Costs and Consequences of Inflation,* eds. Karl Brunner and Alan Meltzer (Carnegie-Rochester Studies on Public Policy 15, 1981), 5–42.

Figure 10.5 ✦ INFLATIONARY FINANCE

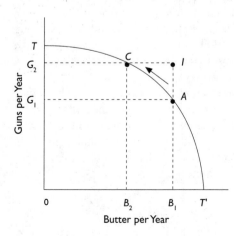

Using inflation as a way of financing government-supplied goods, such as guns, is an attempt to increase the output of these goods without decreasing the output of such private goods as butter. The government attempts to move to point I, but the increase in the price level decreases consumption of private goods, and the economy actually moves from point A to point C. The annual output of butter must decline to release the resources necessary to increase the annual output of guns.

money in times of war to increase the annual output of military goods, such as guns, is an attempt to increase their output with no reduction in annual output of such civilian goods as butter. In other words, inflationary finance attempts a move from point A to point I in Figure 10.5. The result is inflation, which moves the economy to a point such as C, where the increased annual output of guns causes a reduction in the annual output of butter to B_2. The higher prices effected by inflationary finance cause consumers to reduce their consumption of civilian goods. Inflation also can decrease the real value of accumulated savings held by citizens, thereby decreasing their wealth.

Donations

Donations are voluntary contributions to governments from individuals or organizations. These occasionally are used to finance particular programs. For example, governments might set up special funds to finance aid to victims of natural disasters and other individuals in difficulty, perhaps asking citizens to send contributions to such funds. In wartime, citizens of many nations have been invited to contribute both materials and their time in support of the war effort. Similarly, in peacetime, organizations such as the Peace Corps have been set up to induce individuals to volunteer their time, with little or no monetary remuneration, for providing specific public services for certain groups of individuals. Governments also could encourage businesses and individuals to provide public goods such as roads, sewers, and parks that would otherwise be provided by government.[7]

In communities where individuals have similar tastes or commonly shared goals, voluntary contributions of both funds and productive inputs might work well as a means of finance. However, such community consciousness or patriotism tends to diminish as the diversity of preference and population increases. In the United States, voluntary finance has been used extensively in the past in small communities, particularly in rural areas, for financing such services as fire protection, transportation of ill people to hospitals, and police protection. In many small towns today, a common form of supplying and financing fire protection is the volunteer fire department. Even in large cities, many individuals volunteer their time to serve as nurses' assistants in hospitals and convalescent institutions. However, voluntary donations remain only a minor source of finance in most nations.[8]

Grants from one level of government to another are similar to donations. However, these grants are financed by taxes levied on citizens of the grantor government. For example, federal grants to state and local governments financed 17 percent of expenditures of those governments in the United States in 1990. Of course, those who pay federal taxes finance the costs of these grants. Grants are not really an alternative to taxation. The impact of grants on recipient governments is discussed in the last part of this book.

---

[7]Corporate philanthropic contributions and provision of charitable services have received some analysis. See Ferdinand K. Levy and Gloria M. Shatto, "The Evaluation of Corporate Contributions," *Public Choice* 33 (1978): 19–28.

[8]For a formal analysis, see Clarence C. Morrison, "A Note on Providing Public Goods through Voluntary Contributions," *Public Choice* 33 (1978): 119–123.

User Charges

User charges are prices determined through political rather than market interaction. These charges can finance government-supplied goods and services only when it is possible to exclude individuals from enjoying their benefits unless they pay a fee. User charges often help to finance such government-supplied services as highways, bridges, and recreational facilities. Tolls for the use of superhighways and bridges are common in the United States and in many other nations. One advantage of user charges is that they make those who directly consume the services pay for at least part of the costs of producing those services, forcing individuals at least to compare some of the benefits of using the public services with the costs imposed by the user charge. In addition, user charges ration the use of public facilities in such a way as to avoid congestion.

User charges can take such forms as (1) direct prices associated with the consumption of particular goods and services, (2) fees for the option to use certain facilities or services provided by the government, (3) special assessments on privately held property, (4) licenses or franchises, and (5) fares or tolls. The distinction between such charges and market prices is that user charges do not necessarily reflect the interplay of supply and demand in markets. They reflect political and other forces.

Earmarked taxes are special taxes designed to finance specific government-supplied services. These taxes are similar to user charges. For example, the gasoline tax in the United States is a levy on the consumption of gasoline, the proceeds of which are used exclusively to finance roads and alternative public transport facilities. Although earmarked taxes do not serve the same rationing function as user charges, they can make it easier for citizens to compare the benefits of specific government-provided services with the taxes that they pay for those services. If the tax scheme is designed well, it can link tax payments with benefits received by taxpayers.

Typically, user charges are less than the average cost of providing the good or service. The difference between the average cost and the charge is a subsidy to users that is financed by taxes. It is often possible to arrange the subsidies of such goods in a way that varies the charge for use with the income of the consumer. Examples of government-supplied goods and services for which user charges are levied to at least partially finance consumption benefits include public housing; public transit; educational services; public recreational facilities; sewer and water services; and such public health services as inoculations, ambulance transport, and various hospital services.

Charges, in fact, often do cover the full costs of providing certain government-supplied services. This is often the case for water and sewer charges levied by municipal governments. The administrative costs for such services as processing applications (for example, for passports) are often financed by fees. In some European countries, citizens are required to purchase special stamped paper when making applications or inquiries to government authorities. The price of the paper is intended to cover some of the administrative costs of processing the citizens' requests.

A common criticism against user charges is that they prevent the poor from using government-supplied services. For example, many argue that publicly supplied cultural and recreational facilities should be made available free of charge to all citizens, so as not to prevent those who are unable to pay from enjoying these services. One problem with this argument is that, if such services are made available to all free of charge, a subsidy accrues, not only to the poor who use the service but also to the rich. Thus, tax financing of parks, museums, and concerts, with free admission, provides few benefits to poor people if attendance by people who can afford to pay is heavy. In fact, if the tax system is such as to weigh heavily on the poor, it is possible that such free admission policies, in fact, could redistribute income from the poor to the rich. For example, insofar as demands for use of public library and museum facilities are income elastic, and taxes used weigh heavily on low-income groups, tax financing will redistribute income from the poor to the rich.

Special reductions in user charges always can be allowed for low-income persons or for other groups singled out for special treatment, such as children or the elderly. The reduction in the cost accruing to these groups might take the form of direct price reductions upon presentation of a special document. This technique allows a user charge to generate revenue while still permitting those least able to pay to enjoy the services of such government-supplied facilities as museums and parks.

User Charges and Efficiency

Creative use of user charges as an alternative to tax financing improves the efficiency of use of productive resources and lowers the annual tax bills of citizens. In many cases, the goods provided by governments that are, in fact, price excludable generate external benefits. For example, goods and services such as schooling, inoculations, and cultural events are commonly believed to generate external benefits. The problem is one of determining whether it is desirable to charge users for at least some portion of their private benefits.

The problem of determining the appropriate user charge for a government-supplied good or service with external benefits is similar to that of determining a corrective subsidy. Figure 10.6 shows the marginal social cost and marginal social benefit of trash pickups in a city. The marginal social benefit has two components: a marginal private benefit for trash pickup service, MPB, and a marginal external benefit, MEB, to others. The external benefit could be in reduced risk of disease or simply a cleaner city. This is a public benefit that all citizens in the city enjoy. The efficient number of trash pickups per year, Q^*, corresponds to point Z^* at which $MSB = MSC$. This level could be attained by charging C^* per pickup. At that price, citizens demand Q^* pickups per year. This corresponds to point Z on the graph. However, a user charge of C^* per pickup falls short of the marginal social cost of that number of pickups per year. The difference must be made up by a subsidy of S^* per pickup. Taxpayers pay S^* for each pickup per year, while the citizens who order each pickup pay C^* per pickup.

User charges also can help in attaining efficiency if the benefits of government-supplied goods and services are subject to congestion. For example, if a road is subject to congestion, additional use of the road after the point of congestion decreases the benefits that all consumers obtain from the road. To attain the efficient level of traffic on the road, its services should be priced according to the marginal social cost imposed at any given level of traffic. A zero price is desirable only when the level of traffic is below the point of congestion. This is illustrated in Figure 10.7. If the road is a congestible public good, the marginal social cost of accommodating additional users

Figure 10.6 ✦ USER CHARGES AND EFFICIENCY

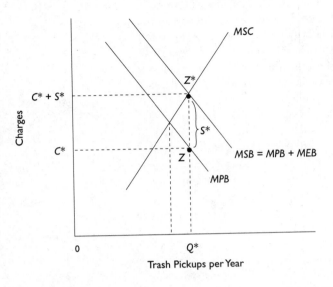

The efficient user charge is C° per trash pickup. However, because this does not cover the marginal social cost of pickups at the efficient level of Q°, a subsidy of S° per pickup must be provided by the government and financed by taxes.

Figure 10.7 ✦ USER CHARGES FOR A CONGESTIBLE GOVERNMENT-SUPPLIED SERVICE

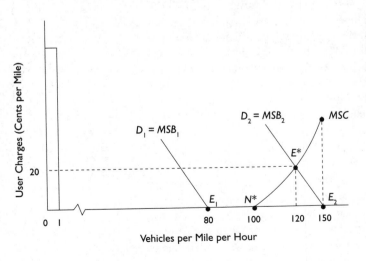

If the demand for road services is D_1, the efficient toll is zero. However, if demand increases to D_2, the efficient toll per mile is 20 cents. If a zero toll were charged when demand is D_2, equilibrium would be at point E_2, at which $MSC > MSB_2$.

falls to zero after the first user enters the road but eventually becomes positive. In Figure 10.7, the point of congestion occurs where the traffic on the road is 100 vehicles per mile per hour. If the demand curve for road use were D_1, a zero user charge would be efficient. This is because at zero price, the equilibrium would be at point E_1, at which $MSB_1 = MSC = 0$. This follows because the marginal social cost at the level of usage at E_1 is 80 vehicles per mile per hour, which is below that point of congestion, at N^*. If, however, the demand for road services were to increase to D_2, a zero user charge would no longer lead to efficiency. At zero price, the equilibrium would be at point E_2, at which 150 vehicles per mile per hour would be using the highway. Because the marginal social cost at that level of usage exceeds the marginal social benefit ($MSC > MSB_2$), more than the efficient amount of traffic would prevail per hour.

The efficient level of traffic corresponds to point E^* for which $MSB_2 = MSC$. This corresponds to 120 vehicles per mile per hour. To attain that level, government could impose a user charge of 20 cents per vehicle per mile.[9] Thus, a user charge of 20 cents per mile would serve to decrease traffic on the road to its efficient level while raising government revenues.

GOVERNMENT ENTERPRISE

Governments often run enterprises, selling private goods and services, to raise revenues. The difference between the revenues that are taken in by such enterprises and the costs can be used to reduce reliance on taxes. Many governments sell gambling services through operation of state lotteries and betting games. This type of government enterprise is quite popular in Latin America and also is used in a number of states in the United States. When a monopoly does not exist, governments must provide prizes and "odds" that are attractive enough to compete with the private supply of gambling. In addition, the amount of net revenues that the government unit collects from the lottery is limited by the demand for gambling services in the area.

Many government units also engage in retail sales of private goods, and some actually produce the private goods offered for sale. An example is the liquor stores run by many states. The profits of such stores often provide a significant amount of revenues to local government units. The markup on liquor by government-operated stores is equivalent to a tax on liquor.

Pricing the Output of Government Enterprise

Whatever the justification might be for government ownership of enterprises that produce items having the characteristics of private goods, the problem faced by government authorities is to price their output to cover costs in a collectively agreed-upon

[9]The toll could be set on the basis of the weight or horsepower of vehicles, as is common. Trucks therefore would pay a higher toll than passenger vehicles.

P U B L I C   P O L I C Y   P E R S P E C T I V E

USER CHARGES AND EFFICIENT ALLOCATION OF RESOURCES TO TRANSPORTATION INFRASTRUCTURE

There is a rising tide of demands for increased spending on such transportation infrastructure as roads and airports. If you have driven the nation's congested interstate highways or have missed a connection at a congested airport because of delays during periods of peak travel, you might well agree that we need more roads and airports. However, the demand for new roads and airport facilities depends in part on the prices charged for use of existing facilities. One economist has recently argued that our worn and congested roads and runways are in part a result of underpricing. If the marginal costs of road use and congestion costs were charged to users, not only would they generate lots of revenue to help pay for new facilities, they also would help ration the use of these facilities so as to reduce wear and tear and the funds required to replace or expand the facilities.[°]

Clifford Winston argues that "the belief of most economists that public infrastructure spending should be substantially increased as not based on efficient pricing and investment principles."[†] We often demand more and wider roads because the use of existing roads is free. When new roads are built and congestion is reduced it encourages more traffic from other routes. The road inevitably fills again at peak use periods because the congestion costs are rarely priced. Winston argues that efficient pricing based on marginal cost would decrease the demand for new transportation infrastructure and generate sufficient revenue to finance improvements on roads where congestion is a problem without the need to dip into tax funds.

An efficient pricing mechanism must calculate the marginal cost of using a facility based on both congestion and wear. For example, wear of a road varies with the vehicle weight per axle. A truck of a given weight with four axles does less damage to a road than one of equal weight with only two axles. Trucks therefore should be charged tolls to use roads and bridges according to their "equivalent standard axle loads" where the standard axle is one of 18,000 pounds. Currently some roads and bridges that do charge tolls charge vehicles

[°]See Clifford Winston, "Efficient Transportation Infrastructure Policy," *Journal of Economic Perspectives* 5, 1 (Winter 1991): 112–127.
[†]Ibid., 114.

manner. At the extreme, the services of the public facility can be priced at zero, as is the case for most road services provided by state and local governments. The costs can be completely financed through taxation or the use of such earmarked taxes as the gasoline tax. Alternatively, prices can be set equal to average costs, including a normal return on the capital invested in the government-owned facility, with no taxes imposed on the public.

The traditional normative approach to public finance argues that the output of public enterprises must be priced at its marginal cost in order to achieve efficiency. To implement marginal cost pricing correctly, all costs involved in using the facility, including congestion costs, must be measured. For example, once a road or bridge has been constructed, the capital costs that went into its construction budgets will not vary with traffic and will not be figured into the marginal costs. Therefore, marginal cost will be very low, relative to the average cost per mile traveled. However, if the price for using the facility is placed at zero, or an amount close to zero, overuse of the facility can occur if congestion exists. Pricing a congestible public good was discussed earlier in this chapter.

according to the number of axles, thereby discouraging truckers from adding more damage-averting axles per vehicle! Similarly, the fuel tax discourages truckers from adding axles because trucks with more axles get fewer miles per gallon. Winston also estimates that if road surfaces were built thicker and truckers were charged tolls according to the pavement wear damage they do, the result would be a sharp reduction in the rate at which roads wear out. According to Winston, a $1.2 billion investment in thicker road surfaces would yield an annual maintenance cost reduction of nearly $10 billion if coupled with axle-based tolls that would encourage truckers to distribute their loads on more axles. The higher tolls also would result in higher truck shipping charges, which would encourage more rail shipping and a reduction in truck traffic on the nation's roads.

Winston also points out that modern electronics can be used to vary toll charges with congestion on roads. An automated vehicle identification (AVI) system has already been tested successfully in Hong Kong. The system consists of an electronic number plate mounted underneath each vehicle. The plate transmits the vehicle's numbered identification to a control center as it passes over a power lock located in the pavement at a toll site. The vehicle owner is then sent a monthly bill for road use based on tolls in effect at the various times of day when the vehicle used a road. The Hong Kong test indicated that the system is accurate and that security features easily can detect fraud. Vehi-

cles without the toll plate that pass the control point can be apprehended and fined by police. Congestion charges can work to decrease demand for road use during peak use periods, thereby reducing both congestion and wear and tear. The charges also would generate much revenue in tolls that could be used to finance road maintenance and improvements.

A similar problem exists for the way airports charge for the use of their services. Currently airports charge fees to land based on aircraft weight. This means that the fee to land a large fully loaded Boeing 747 is much higher than the charge to land a small two-seat aircraft. However, the congestion cost of landing the small plane can be quite high if it delays a fully loaded large plane. If airports were to charge landing fees based on marginal congestion costs instead of aircraft weight, they could generate enough revenue to finance expansion by building additional runways. Passengers would enjoy fewer delays as a result of airport congestion and the value of their time saved would be $8 billion annually, according to Winston. Winston argues that airfares would actually fall under a congestion fee because landing fees would actually be lower after funds collected were invested in new runways. Passengers therefore would benefit from both lower fares and fewer delays with congestion-based landing fees used to finance new runways. However, the big loser in the shift to the congestion-based fees would be general aviation as the small planes would see their landing fees skyrocket.

In applying the principle of marginal cost pricing, the incremental cost in supplying additional facilities when demand increases must be considered. A problem with various government-supplied facilities is that investments can be made only in large lumps. It is true that capital costs do not vary with output once a facility, such as a road, actually opens. However, future capital costs involved in expanding capacity can be considered as long-run marginal costs. Therefore, long-run marginal cost should include funds for expansion of units of capacity after the facility reaches that point of congestion. Marginal cost should include a capital recovery cost, which can be used to finance extra units of capacity.[10] It is possible that these capital recovery costs may be correlated with congestion costs. Costs that are not marginal for an existing facility therefore can be considered marginal costs, with respect to the decision to add units of capacity.

[10] John V. Krutilla, "Is Public Intervention in Water Resources Development Conducive to Efficiency?" *Natural Resources Journal* 6 (January 1966): 72.

CHECKPOINT

1. What are some of the problems that result when a government prints money rather than raises taxes to pay their expenses?
2. Give some examples of donations used to finance public goods and services.
3. How should user charges for government-provided goods and services be set to achieve efficient outputs and usage rates of such products?

Summary

Government finance transfers use of productive resources from individuals and business firms to the government. Taxes are the major method of government finance. However, governments also can obtain resources through the use of police power to acquire resources directly and through user charges, inflation, and borrowing. Donations also can be used to obtain revenues.

The method of government finance used can have an impact on political and market equilibriums and on the efficiency with which resources are employed in the private sector. Different means of government finance have different effects on the distribution of income.

A basic problem in government finance is the distribution of the costs of financing public goods among citizens. No one best way of accomplishing this exists that will satisfy all citizens. The benefit approach argues that taxes should be distributed according to benefits received from government expenditures. The ability-to-pay approach argues that taxes should be dependent on one's economic capacity. As a matter of practice, application of these two concepts is difficult not only because of data problems but also disagreement on what constitutes the most applicable index of the ability to pay.

In addition to affecting the political equilibrium, the method of government finance chosen often has significant and complicated effects on the private choices made by citizens. In particular, taxes and other means of finance can affect production incentives in such a way as to impair the efficiency with which resources are used in private sector.

A Forward Look

The next chapter develops techniques of analysis for determining the impact of taxes on market prices, income distri-

bution, and the efficiency with which resources are used in the market. These techniques are applied in later chapters to evaluate specific taxes on economic bases of income, consumption, and wealth.

Important Concepts

Taxes
Tax Base
General Tax
Selective Tax
Excise Tax
Tax Rate Structure
Average Tax Rate (ATR)
Marginal Tax Rate (MTR)
Proportional Tax Rate Structure
Flat-Rate Tax
Progressive Tax Rate Structure
Tax Bracket
Regressive Tax Rate Structure
Benefit Principle
Ability-to-Pay Principle
Horizontal Equity
Vertical Equity
Tax Evasion
Tax Avoidance
Debt Finance
Government-Induced Inflation
Donations
User Charges
Earmarked Taxes

Questions for Review

1. In what important ways do taxes differ from prices as a means of finance and as a means of rationing goods and services?

P U B L I C   P O L I C Y   P E R S P E C T I V E

STATE LOTTERIES—A GOVERNMENT ENTERPRISE WITH A HIDDEN REGRESSIVE TAX ON GAMBLING

Government-run lotteries were used in the United States in colonial and revolutionary periods to raise funds for such purposes as the Jamestown settlement, the Continental Army, and to finance infrastructure, including bridges and schools. However, in the post-Civil War era Congress enacted a series of restrictive rules on the use of the mails to conduct lotteries and barred lottery activity in interstate commerce. From 1895 to 1963 every state in the union prohibited lotteries and shunned them as a source of revenue. Then, in 1963, the state of New Hampshire reintroduced the state lottery as a government enterprise and source of revenue. As of 1995 a majority of American states were running lotteries, and other states, hard-pressed for new sources of revenue, were under pressure to introduce lotteries as well.[*]

Lotteries are a form of government enterprise. In most states the government-run lottery is a monopoly on large-scale organized gambling. The only legal competition is often the lotteries of other state governments. Lotteries are profit-making enterprises that most states run like any business with heavy advertising and innovation in products to generate sales. The modern lottery offers instant-win game tickets, a computerized numbers game that allows players to pick their own numbers, and lotto—a game with long odds and enormous jackpots.

In fact, lotteries are very profitable for state governments; their net revenue generates enough funds to account for more than 3 percent of state revenue, on average. The percentage of lottery revenues that are returned as prizes is extremely low relative to commercial gambling. For example, horseracing and slot machine operations both return more than 80 percent of the revenue collected as prizes. The payout rate for lotteries in 1989 ranged from 45 percent in West Virginia to 60 percent in Massachusetts. After deduction of the costs of operating the lottery, including commissions to retail sales agents, most states lotteries generated net revenue (profit) that averaged a whopping 40 percent of sales! The low odds of winning in state lotteries contributes to the high profits of the enterprises.

The state profit from operating the lotteries really can be regarded as a tax on the tickets sold to the more than 60 percent of adults in a lottery state who pay to play the games. If the average 40-percent profit is deducted from the price of a ticket, and the tax collected is expressed as a percent of expenditures net of the revenues that are returned to the state treasuries, the effective tax rate on lottery tickets is 66 percent! Those who buy lottery tickets therefore pay high taxes on their purchases in return for pretty low odds of winning! Also, evidence suggests the lottery is a regressive tax when expressed as a percent of the income of those who play it. Much of the revenue generated from the lottery comes from the most active 10 percent of players who account for about half of the receipts. The average amount spent on lottery tickets by households making $10,000 is pretty much the same as that spent by households earning $60,000. Because expenditures on lottery tickets do not vary much with income, the implicit "lottery tax" is a smaller percentage of the income of upper groups than it is of the income of lower income groups.[†]

[*]See Charles T. Clotfelter and Philip J. Cook, "The Economics of State Lotteries," *Journal of Economic Perspectives* 4, 4 (Fall 1990): 105–119. The information presented here is based on research by Clotfelter and Cook.
[†]See ibid., 112.

2. How does government finance affect both political and market equilibriums?

3. How does the ability-to-pay philosophy of taxation differ from the benefit principle? What problems are encountered in implementing both these tax philosophies?

4. What is the difference between horizontal equity and vertical equity?

5. A tax rate schedule for the federal income tax is usually included with its instruction packet. Identify the marginal tax rates associated with each tax bracket. Plot the marginal tax rates associated with the taxable income in each tax bracket. Compute the average tax rate associated with the income corresponding to the beginning and end of each tax bracket. Plot the average and marginal tax rates associated with the ends of each tax bracket.

6. What is a flat-rate tax? Plot the marginal and average tax rates associated with a flat-rate tax of 5 percent on sales.

7. How can inflation be viewed as a form of taxation?

8. List alternatives to taxation as a means of financing government expenditures. Give an example for each alternative.

9. What are user charges? How can user charges be used to both finance government-supplied services and ration their use? How can user charges help achieve efficiency for consumption of price-excludable government-provided goods?

10. What criteria can be used to price the output of government enterprises?

Problems

1. Suppose that you currently earn taxable income of $100,000 per year. You are subject to a marginal tax rate of 50 percent. Currently, your average tax rate is 35 percent. Calculate your annual tax. Calculate the extra tax that you would pay per year if your annual income increased to $110,000 and your average tax rate when your annual income if $110,000.

2. The payroll tax for unemployment insurance in a certain nation taxes all wages up to a maximum per worker of $30,000 at a 5-percent flat rate. What are the marginal and average tax rates on the wages for each of the following three workers?
   a. A restaurant worker with annual wages of $18,000
   b. An assistant bank manager with wages of $35,000 per year
   c. A corporate CEO with an annual salary of $500,000

3. A large city currently provides free water service to residents. The marginal social cost of making a gallon of water available per month is estimated to be 5 cents, no matter how much water is used. Currently, city residents consume 500,000 gallons of water per month. The costs of making the water available are financed by a local tax on city residents.
   a. Draw a graph to show that the current monthly consumption of water is not efficient.
   b. Show the net gains in well-being possible by applying a user charge of 5 cents per gallon to residential users. Assume that monthly consumption declines to 400,000 gallons after the user charge

is imposed. Calculate the tax revenues that can be freed for other uses each month (including a reduction in taxes to local residents) after the user charge is imposed.

4. Indicate whether you agree with the following statement, and give your reasons for doing so:

   If the beltline surrounding the city of Raleigh were a pure public good, efficiency would require that the price to use the road be zero. However, during rush hour congestion, the road cannot be regarded as a pure public good and a toll should be charged for its use.

   If an AVI (automated vehicle identification system) were established for residents of the metropolitan area around Raleigh who use the beltline, how would you set tolls to achieve efficient use of the road? The AVI system would allow you to send a bill to each user of the road each month based on miles traveled on the road and the price you charge, which could vary by time of day.

Suggestions for Further Reading

Congress of the United States, Congressional Budget Office. *The Growth of Federal User Charges.* Washington, D.C.: U.S. Government Printing Office, August 1993. Analysis of the types of user charges used by the federal government, the growth of these as a means of finance, and issues relating to the charges.

Groves, Harold. *Tax Philosophers.* Madison: University of Wisconsin Press, 1974. A review of various philosophies of taxation as articulated by economists from Adam Smith to J. M. Keynes and J. K. Galbraith.

Musgrave, Richard A. *The Theory of Public Finance.* New York: McGraw-Hill, 1959. Chapters 4 and 5. A technical analysis of alternative philosophies of taxation.

Simon, Carl P., and Witte, Ann D. *Beating the System: The Underground Economy.* Boston: Auburn House, 1982. Contains an analysis of noncompliance with tax laws in the United States. Income tax evasion and evasion of excise taxes are analyzed.

Winston, Clifford. "Efficient Transportation Infrastructure Policy." *Journal of Economic Perspectives* 5, 1 (Winter 1991): 112–127. A discussion of issues relating to the pricing of road and airport services and how current price systems prevent efficient use of infrastructure.

11

TAXATION, PRICES, EFFICIENCY, AND THE DISTRIBUTION OF INCOME

LEARNING OBJECTIVES

After reading this chapter you should be able to

1. Define a lump-sum tax and explain why it is used as the benchmark standard against which other taxes are compared when analyzing the effects of taxation on resource use.
2. Explain the concepts of excess burden of a tax and to use indifference curve analysis to compare the effects of a lump-sum tax and a price-distorting tax on decisions and well-being of an individual.
3. Use supply and demand analysis to show the effects of unit and ad valorem taxes on equilibrium prices and quantities of goods or services traded in mar-

kets and to show how the total excess burden of a tax varies with the unit tax or tax rate and the price elasticities of supply and demand of the taxed item.
4. Calculate the efficiency loss ratio of a tax.
5. Describe how taxes are shifted, how the shifting of a tax affects its incidence, and how the incidence of a tax depends on the price elasticities of supply and demand of the taxed item and the extent of competition in the market.
6. Use a general equilibrium analysis to evaluate the total excess burden of several taxes and the incidence of taxes.

Taxes affect the decisions to buy and sell products and inputs. By shifting market supplies or demands of goods and services, taxes inevitably change their prices and thereby influence the pattern of resource use. However, the effects of taxes on prices are often quite misunderstood. For example, many motorists line up at the gas pumps to fill up their tanks before a new gasoline tax increase goes into effect. However, a good understanding of the economics of taxation would tell these people that it is unlikely that a gasoline tax increase would increase the price of gasoline by the full amount of the tax. Some of the tax would be absorbed by sellers as a reduction in the net price received after paying the tax. For example luxury car makers, such as Jaguar, subjected to increased competition because of the introduction of new luxury car brands such as the Lexus by Japanese sellers in the United States market, actually ran advertisements saying that they would absorb all of a luxury tax on their cars and not increase the price to cover the tax. The demand for Jaguars was simply too elastic to risk a rise in price to cover the cost of the luxury tax!

Taxes can cause a loss in efficiency in private use of income and resources. When taxes influence the prices of goods and services traded in competitive markets with no externalities, losses in efficiency are likely to result. This is because, as demonstrated in this chapter, prices that are distorted by taxes no longer simultaneously reflect the marginal social costs and benefits of goods and services. Simple techniques are developed in this chapter to measure the losses in well-being when taxes prevent the attainment of efficiency through market interaction.

No person enjoys paying taxes. Taxes, however, do provide revenues to finance government-supplied goods and services, which, in turn, benefit taxpayers. Although this is true, the impact of taxes on the well-being of those who pay them can be analyzed independently of the benefits received from the uses of tax revenues. This is the approach that is usually pursued in the economic analysis of taxes.

Finally, to evaluate the fairness of taxation, it is necessary to determine the actual impact of taxes on the incomes of citizens. This is no easy task. The persons from whom taxes are collected are not necessarily those whose incomes are reduced by taxation, because the impact of taxes on prices can result in a transfer of the payment of a tax from those groups from which the tax is collected. For example, an excise tax on gasoline is commonly collected from distributors of that product. However, if the tax has the effect of decreasing the supply of gasoline, it will increase the market price of that product. By doing so, the tax will make consumers of gasoline worse off by decreasing their real incomes. The analysis in this chapter shows how changes in prices caused by taxes can be considered to determine the distribution of taxes paid among buyers and sellers of goods. The techniques and terminology developed here are used to discuss important current issues in tax policy in Part Four.

LUMP-SUM TAXES: A BENCHMARK STANDARD FOR COMPARISON

A **lump-sum tax** is a fixed sum that a person would pay per year, independent of that person's income, consumption of goods and services, or wealth. The fixed annual payments by persons to government authorities do not depend on any controllable variable. Lump-sum taxes do not prevent prices from equaling the marginal social cost and benefit of any goods and services. Imposition of these taxes would reduce the ability of consumers to purchase market goods and services and to save. But these taxes influence choices only through income effects. As shown in this chapter, no substitution effects result from a lump-sum tax. (See the appendix to Chapter 1 for a definition of income and substitution effects.) Therefore, a lump-sum tax does not provide any opportunity or incentive to substitute one activity for another.

Lump-sum taxes, however, do force those bearing the burden of taxation to reduce consumption, saving, or investment. Yet, they accomplish this objective without distorting prices in ways that prevent marginal social costs of goods and services from being set equal to their marginal social benefits. For this reason, the lump-sum tax is used as the benchmark against which the effects of price-distorting taxes are compared. Lump-sum taxes do not prevent the attainment of efficiency in markets.

Lump-sum taxes are likely to affect the distribution of income; therefore, they move the economy to a new efficient allocation of resources, consistent with the pattern of demand that results from the new income distribution. A **head tax** is an example of a lump-sum tax that would require all adults to pay an equal amount each year to governing authorities. In no way could taxpayers rearrange their economic affairs to avoid or reduce the tax burden.[1] A head tax would not distort any prices in ways that prevent markets from achieving efficiency. Nevertheless, when a head tax is used, the after-tax distribution of income will be less equal than the before-tax distribution of income. Such a tax would necessarily be regressive with respect to income, because the tax, as a percentage of income, would fall as income rose.

For example, total revenues raised by the federal government in the United States in 1990 were $1.1 trillion. Given 100 million adults in the United States, raising that amount with a head tax would have required each of them, without exception, to pay a tax of $11,000 per year. The average tax rates would amount to 50 percent for a person whose annual income was $22,000 but only 10 percent for a person whose annual income was $110,000. The average tax rate, therefore, would decline with a person's annual income. The marginal tax rate associated with a lump-sum tax is *always* zero. Regardless of any change in a person's income, consumption, or wealth, a lump-sum tax causes no change in the tax due.

Lump-Sum Versus Price-Distorting Taxes: Indifference Curve Analysis

A **price-distorting tax** is one that causes the net price received by sellers of a good or service to diverge from the gross price paid by buyers. Indifference curve analysis can be used to compare the effects of a lump-sum tax and a price-distorting tax, each collecting the same amount from a person. Suppose that a price-distorting tax is imposed on some good, say gasoline, the proceeds of which are used to finance government-supplied services. In Figure 11.1, the tax is assumed to be added on to the current market price of gasoline, which swivels the consumer's budget constraint line from AB to AB'. The amount of tax paid by the person whose indifference curves are drawn in Figure 11.1 is influenced by the quantity of gasoline purchased per year. The gross price paid by the buyer includes the tax. The net price received by sellers is the gross price minus the tax. The tax-induced price increase affects the consumer's choice of consuming gasoline or spending available income on other goods. The consumer enjoys an annual income represented by the distance $0A$. This gives the dollar amount of expenditures on goods other than gasoline that the consumer could buy if she purchases no gasoline in one year.

The consumer is initially in equilibrium at point E, consuming Q_1 gallons of gasoline per year and spending Y_1 on all other goods per year. The amount spent on gasoline per year prior to the tax is AY_1. This is the difference between her total annual income and her annual expenditure on other goods. The tax-induced price increase causes her to move to a new equilibrium at E', where she reduces annual consumption

---

[1]This assumes that migration to another country to avoid the tax is impossible or that a person migrating would have to pay the discounted present value of future tax liabilities under the head tax before being permitted to migrate.

Figure 11.1 ✦ A PRICE-DISTORTING TAX VERSUS A LUMP-SUM TAX

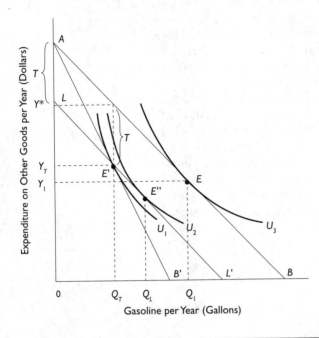

A lump-sum tax that collects T in taxes from a person allows that person to attain a higher level of well-being than a price-distorting tax that collects the same amount. The loss in well-being due to the substitution effect of the price-distorting tax is its excess burden.

of gasoline to Q_T gallons. The person now spends AY_T on gasoline each year at the price including the tax, leaving Y_T to spend on other goods each year. If the tax were not present, she would have to give up only $AY°$ of expenditure on other goods to obtain the same amount of gasoline per year. Of her total expenditure on gasoline, the distance $Y_T Y° = T$ represents the annual gasoline tax payments. This equals the difference between the amount of income she must give up to buy Q_T gallons of gasoline per year when the price includes the tax and the amount that she would give up for Q_T gallons in the absence of the tax. T is also the difference between the amount sellers receive for the Q_T gallons, $AY°$, and the amount the consumer actually spends, AY_T. The effect of the tax is to reduce the consumer's utility from U_3 to U_1, reduce her consumption of gasoline from Q_1 to Q_T gallons per year, and reduce her annual after-tax income from $0A$ to $(0A − T)$.

If T per year were collected from this person as a lump-sum tax, neither the price of gasoline nor the price of any other good would be distorted. No difference would result between the gross price paid by the buyer and the net price received by the seller. The lump-sum tax merely would reduce the income of the taxpayer by shifting her budget constraint line down, parallel to itself, from AB to LL'. All points along LL' collect T in tax by reducing the consumer's income by that amount, independent of the amount of gasoline per year that she purchases.

Figure 11.1 shows that the person is better off under the lump-sum tax than under the price-distorting tax if both collect T per year. With the lump-sum tax, the taxpayer attains an equilibrium at point E'', where she achieves utility level U_2 and

I N T E R N A T I O N A L   V I E W

THE LUMP-SUM TAX TAKES ITS LUMPS IN THE U.K.

It caused riots in Trafalgar Square and was instrumental in the fall of the reign of Maggie Thatcher as prime minister. What was it? Simply a lump-sum tax—the paragon of efficiency in raising revenue for government!

In the 1980s, Mrs. Thatcher's government replaced a local property tax with a form of lump-sum tax called "the community charge." The tax was supposed to be a means of financing local government services (such as schools and streets) and facilities—that fell equally on all taxpayers, irrespective of their personal income or property holdings. The level of the tax was set by each local council and was a fixed amount per adult taxpayer. The tax varied considerably among jurisdictions but because it was a fixed lump sum per taxpayer, it amounted to a higher percentage of the earnings of low-income than high-income taxpayers in each jurisdiction.

The tax was enormously unpopular in the United Kingdom. It was quickly dubbed a poll tax even though it was not a requirement for voting. Some 15 million Britons, including members of Parliament, actually refused to pay the tax and local governments estimated that they were only able to collect slightly more than 50 percent of the tax due. The very efficient lump-sum tax was viewed as so unfair by such a large percentage of taxpayers that they were willing to break the law and risk imprisonment by refusing to pay it.

By 1991, Prime Minister John Major's government threw in their hats and developed a plan to replace the hated poll tax with a new package of local taxes including increased sales taxes and increased central government responsibility for the financing of education.

The British version of the lump-sum tax and their problems with it illustrate the inevitable trade-off between equity and efficiency in tax policy. Although the lump-sum tax does not distort prices and does not impair efficient operation of markets, it results in a regressive distribution of tax burden with respect to income. Very regressive taxes, such as the lump-sum community charge, have proved to be politically unpopular. One politician in Great Britain estimated that three-quarters of the British public opposed the tax. The political opposition to the tax ultimately led to its recision.

---

consumes Q_L gallons of gasoline per year. Provided that gasoline is a normal good, the decrease in income caused by the lump-sum tax results in a decline in its consumption. However, because $Q_L > Q_T$, she consumes more gasoline per year than when she paid the price-distorting tax. Although the lump-sum tax reduces the taxpayer's income, it causes no substitution effects, because it does not affect the relative price of gasoline or any other good or service. The taxpayer consumes more gasoline than she did under the price-distorting tax, because the price she pays is lower under the lump-sum tax. Because the consumer has the same disposable income under the two taxes but consumes more gasoline per year under the lump-sum tax, it follows that she must be better off when paying T in annual taxes under the lump-sum tax. This is shown in Figure 11.1, in that the level of well-being at E'' under the lump-sum tax is $U_2 > U_1$. Thus, provided both taxes collect the same amount from the taxpayer, the lump-sum tax will be preferred by the taxpayer.

The loss in well-being of the taxpayer when she pays T in taxes under the price-distorting tax instead of under the lump-sum tax is the **individual excess burden of a taxation.** The excess burden measures the loss in well-being to a taxpayer caused by the substitution effect of a price-distorting tax. The excess burden of the price-distorting tax is the reduction in well-being of the taxpayer from U_2 to U_1 when the price-distorting tax is used instead of the lump-sum tax.

THE IMPACT OF TAXES ON MARKET PRICES AND EFFICIENCY

A Unit Excise Tax: Impact on Market Equilibrium

Suppose that a good such as gasoline is traded in a competitive market and that no externalities are associated with market exchange of gasoline. Under these conditions, market exchange of gasoline results in the efficient output of this good. This is illustrated in Figure 11.2, with a market price of gasoline at $1 per gallon. The demand curve, D, reflects the marginal social benefit of the good, while the supply curve, S, reflects its marginal social cost. The market equilibrium at point B corresponds to the efficient amount of gasoline per year. At the output Q^*, the marginal social benefit of gasoline is equal to its marginal social cost. The $1 price of gasoline

Figure 11.2 ◆ IMPACT OF A UNIT TAX ON MARKET EQUILIBRIUM

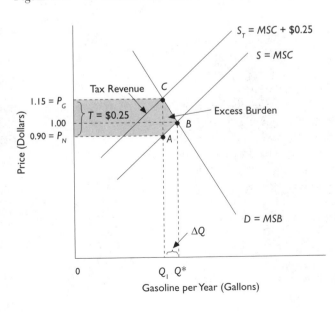

A unit tax of 25 cents on gasoline collected from sellers decreases the market supply of the good and increases the price. The market price, P_G, paid by buyers increases from $1.00 to $1.15. After payment of the tax, the net price received by sellers falls to 90 cents. If ΔQ is the reduction in output due to the substitution effect of the tax, then the area ABC measures the excess burden of the tax.

equals both the marginal social cost and marginal social benefit of gasoline ($P = MSB = MSC$).

A **unit tax** is a levy of a fixed amount per unit of a good exchanged in a market. Suppose that a unit excise tax of 25 cents per gallon of gasoline is levied on the sellers of gasoline. This fixed tax due on each gallon sold is independent of the price of gasoline. If the price of gasoline were to rise, the tax would not collect any more revenue per gallon. Taxes that are a percentage of the price of a good or service are analyzed later in this chapter.

When the tax is imposed, the marginal cost of selling gasoline increases by 25 cents per gallon because of the tax. In addition to covering all other variable costs of production, sellers also must cover the tax to avoid losses when selling gasoline. This shifts the supply curve (which is the marginal cost curve under perfect competition) upward, from $S = MSC$ to $S_T = MSC + 25$ cents at each level of annual output. The effect of the tax is therefore equivalent to an increase in the marginal cost to sellers that decreases the market supply of gasoline.

The decrease in supply results in a new posttax equilibrium at C, implying that the quantity sold decreases to Q_1 and that the equilibrium price rises to $P_G = \$1.15$. The price P_G is the new market price paid by consumers of gasoline. This is the gross price received by sellers. The sellers, however, must pay 25 cents of the gross price received as a tax. Their net price, P_N, is therefore only 90 cents per gallon after payment of the tax. In general, if T is the unit tax, the relationship between the gross price and the net price, P_N, received by sellers is

$$P_N = P_G - T. \tag{11.1}$$

The amount of revenue collected from the tax by the government is the amount of gasoline sold after the tax, multiplied by the tax per unit, TQ_1. This is represented by the rectangle $P_N P_G CA$ in Figure 11.2. The total revenue of producers is simply $P_N Q_1$. For example, if Q_1 is 10 million gallons of gasoline per year, the tax would collect \$2.5 million annually. The total revenue taken in by sellers after paying the tax would be \$9 million per year.

Excess Burden of a Unit Tax

When the excise tax of \$0.25 is imposed, buyers and sellers then base their decisions on their differing views of the price of gasoline. Buyers decide how much to buy by comparing P_G, the gross price, with their marginal benefit. Sellers, however, decide how much to sell by comparing their net price, P_N, with their marginal cost. In the absence of any externality, the marginal cost and benefit reflect marginal social cost and benefit. The tax prevents market interaction among buyers and sellers from automatically equating marginal social cost and marginal social benefit, as is required to attain efficiency. Because $P_G > P_N$ after the tax, it follows that $MSB > MSC$ at Q_1, as shown in Figure 11.2. As a result of the tax, less than the efficient annual output, Q^*, of gasoline will be sold in the market.

The **total excess burden of a tax** is an additional cost to society over and above the amount of dollars that citizens pay in a tax. The *excess* burden measures the loss in net benefits from private use of resources that results when a price-distorting tax prevents markets for taxed goods and services from attaining efficient output levels.

The total excess burden of a unit tax is the loss in well-being to buyers and sellers in a market over that which they would suffer if a lump-sum tax were used to collect the revenues. A lump-sum tax would not prevent the attainment of efficiency in markets because it causes no substitution effects. If this benchmark type of tax were used, no difference would result between the price paid by buyers and that received by sellers.

Figure 11.2 shows how the excess burden of the unit tax can be measured. Assume that the income effect of the tax-induced price increase on the consumption of gasoline is negligible. This implies that the observed reduction in the quantity of gasoline consumed entirely reflects the substitution effect of the tax-induced price increase. The efficient output is Q^*. This means that increasing output from Q_1 to Q^* would allow increments in well-being that exceed the incremental social costs. The price-distorting excise tax prevents the achievement of net gains, represented by the difference between the marginal social benefits and the marginal social costs of $\Delta Q = Q^* - Q_1$ gallons of gasoline. The total excess burden of the price-distorting tax can be represented by the area of the triangle ABC in Figure 11.2. This area represents the net loss in well-being to buyers and sellers of gasoline due to the substitution effect of the tax.[2] It is a measure of the loss in efficiency in the gasoline market attributable to the price-distorting gasoline tax.

When the excess burden is positive, the total burden of a tax on buyers and sellers in a market exceeds the tax revenues collected. Even if the total tax revenues collected were returned to buyers and sellers of gasoline as a lump-sum payment of TQ_1 (represented by the area $P_N P_G CA$ in Figure 11.2), the excess burden would not be recovered. For this reason, the total excess burden of a tax sometimes is called a *deadweight loss*. It is a loss in efficiency that cannot be regained even if tax revenues collected provide benefits equal in dollar amount to the amount paid by citizens in taxes.

Call W the area of triangle ABC. The area W is

$$W = \frac{1}{2}T\Delta Q \tag{11.2}$$

where T, the tax per unit, is the base of triangle ABC, and ΔQ, measuring the decrease in the consumption of gasoline because of the substitution effect of the tax-induced price increase, is its height. For example, if ΔQ is 2 million gallons per year, the excess burden of the tax would be $250,000 per year.

Excess Burden, Unit Taxes, and Price Elasticities

The excess burden actually varies more than proportionately with the unit tax, T, because ΔQ depends on the increase in price, ΔP, caused by the tax. Because ΔP

---

[2]When the income effects of tax-induced price changes cannot be ignored, ΔQ must be estimated along a compensated demand curve. The relationship between price and quantity demanded for which the income effect of price changes has been removed is the compensated demand curve. The appendix to this chapter shows how compensated demand curves are derived.

depends on the amount of the tax per unit, ΔQ also depends on T. The higher the unit tax, other things being equal, the greater is the annual reduction in gasoline (or any taxed good) sold. The reduction in output that results from the substitution effect of a price-distorting tax can be predicted with estimates of the price elasticities of demand and supply of the taxed goods.

A bit of algebraic manipulation (see the appendix to this chapter) can show how the excess burden of a tax depends on the unit tax, initial prices and quantities traded, and price elasticities of supply and demand. As derived in the appendix, the resulting formula for the excess burden of a unit tax is

$$W = \frac{1}{2}T^2\frac{Q^\circ}{P^\circ} \cdot \frac{E_S E_D}{E_S - E_D}, \tag{11.3}$$

where E_S is the price elasticity of supply, E_D is the price elasticity of demand, Q° is the pretax quantity, and P° is the pretax market price of the taxed good. Because the price elasticity of demand is a negative number, the change in well-being that results from the excess burden will be equal to or less than zero, indicating a loss.[3]

According to Equation 11.3, the excess burden of a tax varies quadratically with the unit tax. If the unit tax on a good such as gasoline were to double from 25 cents to 50 cents, the loss in well-being from the excess burden of a tax could be expected to increase fourfold! Other things being equal, the losses due to the excess burden of a tax increase at a faster rate than the rate of increase of a tax. The formula for the excess burden also indicates that, other things being equal, the loss in well-being due to the excess burden of a tax is greater the more elastic the demand for the good. Similarly, other things being equal, the greater the price elasticity of supply, the greater is the loss due to the excess burden of a tax. Assuming that income effects are negligible, any commodity for which either $E_S = 0$ or $E_D = 0$ has a zero efficiency loss. The most efficient taxes, therefore, are those levied on commodities or inputs that are in inelastic supply, demand, or both. In general, to minimize the excess burden of a tax, goods and services for which minimal substitution effects are likely should be taxed.

The algebraic result is in accord with commonsense reasoning. The less the opportunity or willingness to substitute other goods and services for those that are taxed, the less is the distortion introduced into the economy with respect to resource allocation. On efficiency grounds, the best taxes are those levied on goods that have few substitutes in either production or consumption.

The graphs in Figure 11.3 show that the excess burden of a tax would be zero if either the demand or supply of a tax product were perfectly inelastic. In the case of a perfectly inelastic demand shown in Figure 11.3A, the tax causes the price to rise, but because quantity demanded is not reduced, the change in output is zero and the excess burden is also zero. The more inelastic the demand for a taxed good or service, the smaller the area of the triangle that represents the excess burden of the tax.

---

[3]The elasticities must be based on changes in output due only to the substitution effects of tax-induced price increases in cases for which income effects of the price increases are not negligible.

Figure 11.3 ✦ Excess Burden When Demand or Supply Is Perfectly Inelastic

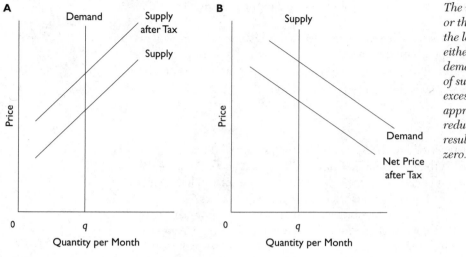

The more inelastic the demand or the supply of a taxed item, the lower the excess burden. As either price elasticity of demand or the price elasticity of supply approaches zero, the excess burden of the tax approaches zero because the reduction in quantity sold as a result of the tax approaches zero.

In Figure 11.3B, the tax is represented by a decline in the net price received by sellers and is subtracted from the price paid by buyers, which is represented by the market demand curve. When the market supply is perfectly inelastic, sellers suffer a net reduction in the price received for the item they sell, but they do not alter the quantity supplied in response. As a result, their net revenue from selling the product falls but no change occurs in the quantity of the product made available to buyers. Also, the excess burden is zero because the change in the amount of the product sold as a result of the tax is zero. In general, the more inelastic the supply of an item, other things being equal, the smaller the reduction in the quantity sold after the tax and the smaller the excess burden.

The Efficiency-Loss Ratio of a Tax

To compare the relative loss in efficiency of various taxes, economists often calculate the excess burden *per dollar of tax revenue*. The ratio of the excess burden of a tax to the tax revenue collected each year by that tax is called the **efficiency-loss ratio** of the tax (W/R):

$$W/R = \text{Excess Burden/Tax Revenue.} \tag{11.4}$$

An efficiency-loss ratio of 0.2 means that the excess burden of a tax is 20 cents for each dollar of revenue raised per year. The efficiency-loss ratio of a tax sometimes is called the *coefficient of inefficiency* of the tax.

Estimates of the efficiency-loss ratios of different kinds of taxes are extremely useful in achieving the goal of minimization of the total excess burden of taxation. By reducing use of taxes with high excess burdens per dollar of revenue while increasing use of taxes with lower excess burdens per dollar, the total excess burden of the tax system can be reduced without sacrificing revenues. For example, suppose that the efficiency-loss ratio for taxes on interest income is estimated to be 0.35, while the efficiency-loss ratio for taxes on gasoline is only 0.1. Each extra dollar of revenue gained from increasing gasoline taxes results in an excess burden of 10 cents. On the other hand, each dollar increment in revenue obtained from taxes on interest income is associated with an increase of 35 cents in excess burden. It follows that, on the margin, each dollar reduction in taxes on interest made up by a dollar increase in taxes on gasoline results in a *net reduction* of total excess burden equal to 15 cents. Using estimated efficiency-loss ratios for taxes thus can be used to recommend policy changes that will result in net gains in well-being.

One study of the U.S. tax system estimated that the excess burden per dollar of tax revenue in the U.S. tax system ranged from 13 cents to 24 cents per dollar of revenue in the mid-1970s and was running at about 18.5 cents in the mid-1980s.[4] Based on the tax laws and the tax rates effective in 1973, Ballard, Shoven, and Whalley concluded that the present value of the gain in well-being that would have been possible by replacing the tax system of 1973 with a system of lump-sum taxes would have been between $1.86 trillion and $3.36 trillion! The range of their estimates varies with assumptions made about price elasticities in their various simulations of the impact of taxes on the economy.

They found that the taxes on interest and investment income caused the greatest distortion in 1973. The average rate of taxation of capital income was about 45 percent in that year. Since that time, mainly as a result of the Economic Recovery Tax Act of 1981 and the Tax Reform Act of 1986, taxes on capital income have been reduced substantially compared with the levels that prevailed in 1973. Depending on the assumption made about the interest elasticity of supply of savings, the efficiency-loss ratio for taxes on industrial capital income in 1973 ranged from 15 to 35 cents per dollar of revenues collected.

The researchers concluded that savings would be 80 percent higher if a lump-sum tax collected the same revenue as that collected by the U.S. tax system in 1973. This estimate is based on tax rates of 1973 and on an interest elasticity of saving supply of 0.4. In their simulations, the higher savings would increase, over 100 years, the ratio of capital to labor in production by 31 percent. This would contribute to higher labor productivity and higher wages for workers.

Incidence of a Unit Tax

As illustrated in Figure 11.2, a unit tax can cause the market price of the taxed good to change. Tax-induced price change reduces the real incomes of groups other than

---

[4]Charles L. Ballard, John B. Shoven, and John Whalley, "The Total Welfare Cost of the United States Tax System: A General Equilibrium Approach," *National Tax Journal* 38 (June 1985): 125–140. Also see Don Fullerton and Diane Lim Rogers, *Who Bears the Lifetime Tax Burden?* (Washington, D.C.: The Brookings Institution, 1993), 163–170.

those from whom the tax is collected. The **shifting of a tax** is the transfer of the burden of paying a tax from those who are legally liable for it to others. When a tax is shifted, those liable for its payment succeed in recouping some of the reduction in their income caused by tax payments through changes in the prices of items that they either buy or sell. These changes in prices are caused by tax-induced shifts in either supply or demand.

Forward shifting of a tax is a transfer of its burden from sellers who are liable for its payment to buyers as a result of an increase in the price of the taxed good. For example, in Figure 11.2, the price of gasoline increases as a result of a tax levied on sellers, thereby shifting part of the burden to buyers. **Backward shifting** of a tax is a transfer of its burden from buyers who are liable for its payment to sellers through a decrease in the market price of the taxed good. For example, if employers are liable for payroll taxes on wages paid to workers, they will succeed in shifting part of the burden of the tax to sellers of labor services (workers) if wages decline as a result of the tax. The **incidence of a tax** is the distribution of the burden of paying it.

In Figure 11.2, the market price of gasoline increased from \$1.00 per gallon to $P_G = \$1.15$ per gallon at the posttax market equilibrium. As a result sellers succeeded in shifting 15 cents of the tax of 25 cents per gallon to consumers. The remaining 10 cents of the tax per gallon was borne by sellers, as the net price P_N, that they received declined from \$1 to 90 cents per gallon. The incidence of the tax per gallon was shared by buyers and sellers of gasoline. Although the entire tax of 25 cents per gallon is collected from sellers, they recoup 15 cents of the tax per gallon through the increase in the market price of gasoline. The total tax revenues collected can be represented by the rectangle $P_N P_G CA$. The upper portion of the rectangle represents the part of the total tax revenues that, in effect, is paid by buyers of gasoline. This is the 15-cents-per-gallon portion of the unit tax that is shifted to buyers multiplied by the annual consumption of gasoline. If, after the tax is imposed, 10 million gallons of gasoline are sold per year, consumers pay \$1.5 million of the \$2.5 million in tax revenue. The remaining \$1 million per year is paid by sellers.

Ad Valorem Taxes

Ad valorem taxes are levied as a percentage of the price of a good or service. For example, retail sales taxes are ad valorem taxes levied as a certain percentage of the price received by sellers of a good. Similarly, the payroll tax is an ad valorem tax because it is levied as a percentage of wages paid by employers. The higher the price of the taxed good or service, the greater the amount of the tax per unit under ad valorem taxation.

The preceding analysis for a unit tax is easily applicable to ad valorem taxes. Suppose consumers must pay a certain percentage of the market price of gasoline as a tax. In this case, the amount of tax collected *per unit of output, T,* is the tax rate, *t,* multiplied by the gross price paid by consumers of the product:[5]

---

[5]In many cases, the tax is levied on the net price, P_N, received by sellers. For example, under a retail sales tax the actual gross price paid by consumers includes the tax that is levied as a percentage of the net price received by retailers. In such cases, $T = tP_N$.

$$T = tP_G = \text{Tax Revenue per Unit of Output,} \qquad (11.5)$$

where P_G is the gross price paid by consumers. For example, if a flat-rate tax of 10 percent were levied on gasoline, the amount collected would be 10 cents *per gallon* if the market price of gasoline paid by buyers were $1 per gallon. However, if the market price paid by buyers were $2 per gallon, the same tax of 10 percent would collect 20 cents per gallon. An ad valorem tax therefore automatically collects more revenues per unit of the taxed item when the market price of that item increases.

Substituting Equation 11.5 for the tax per unit in Equation 11.3 for the excess burden of a unit tax gives

$$W = \frac{1}{2}t^2 P_G^2 \frac{Q^\circ}{P^\circ} \cdot \frac{E_S E_D}{E_S - E_D}. \qquad (11.6)$$

For taxes that result in very small changes in price so that the difference between the initial market price, P°, and the posttax market price, P_G, is negligible, the excess burden of the tax can be approximated by the following equation, which is derived from Equation 11.6, by setting $P_G = P^\circ$:

$$W = \frac{1}{2}t^2 (P^\circ Q^\circ) \frac{E_S E_D}{E_S - E_D}. \qquad (11.7)$$

$P^\circ Q^\circ$ is the total expenditure on the taxed commodity prior to the tax. Economists often use a formula like this one to estimate the excess burden that results from ad valorem taxes levied on the sale of goods or services.

As with the unit tax, the loss due to the excess burden of an ad valorem tax varies with the square of the tax rate. To predict the loss due to the excess burden of an ad valorem tax, Equation 11.7 requires estimates of the relevant price elasticities of supply and demand of the taxed item and data on current expenditures on the item to be taxed.

Ad Valorem Taxes on Labor

Figure 11.4 shows the impact of an ad valorem tax on market equilibrium. Suppose that all wages earned are subject to a flat-rate tax of 20 percent deducted from the wages of workers. The tax therefore is collected from workers rather than employers. The tax can be thought of as a reduction in the gross wage received by workers for each hour of work. This is similar to the payroll tax used to finance Social Security benefits.

In Figure 11.4, the actual demand curve for labor indicates the gross wage that employers would pay for each yearly amount of labor hours. The pretax equilibrium is at point E, where workers of given skill earn $5 per hour and Q° labor hours are employed per year. A tax of 20 percent would reduce the net wage received for any amount of work per week to 80 percent of the gross wage that employers actually pay. In Figure 11.4, the curve labeled Net Wage shows the actual wages received by workers after the tax has been deducted from the gross wage paid by employers. The tax per labor hour is represented by the difference between the gross wage curve and the

Figure 11.4 ◆ IMPACT OF AN AD VALOREM TAX ON LABOR

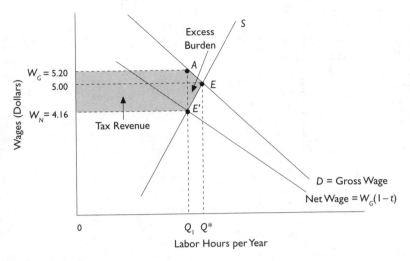

A payroll tax equal to 20 percent of wages collected from workers decreases the wages received by workers from W_G to $W_N = W_G (1 - t)$ for each hour worked per year. Workers respond to the reduction in their take-home wage by reducing the quantity of labor hours supplied per year. Part of the tax burden is shifted to employers as the market wage increases from $5.00 per hour to $5.20 per hour.

net wage curve. In general, the following relationship exists between the gross wage, W_G, at any level of employment and the net wage, W_N:

$$W_N = W_G(1 - t), \tag{11.8}$$

where t is the tax rate. As the gross wage increases, the actual tax per labor hour paid, tW_G, increases. This is why the difference between the gross wage curve and the net wage curve increases as gross wage increases. For example, if the market wage were only $2 per hour, the tax collected per labor hour would be only 20 cents under a tax rate of 10 percent. At a wage of $10 per hour, the same tax rate would collect $1 per labor hour at the same rate of 10 percent.

Workers base their work-leisure choices on the net wage; employers decide how much labor to hire on the basis of the gross wage. The posttax market equilibrium corresponds to point E', at which the quantity of labor that workers are willing to supply, based on their net wage, equals the quantity of labor that employers are willing to hire based on the gross wage. At the posttax equilibrium, the market wage, W_G, increases to $5.20 per hour but the net wage received by workers, W_N, is only 80 percent of that amount, or $4.16 per hour. The quantity of labor hired declines from $Q^°$ to Q_1 hours per year. Because workers decrease the quantity of labor hours supplied per year as a result of the tax, they succeed in shifting part of its burden of payment forward to employers as the market wage rises to $5.20 per hour.

The loss due to the excess burden of the tax could be estimated as the area of the triangle AEE' in Figure 11.4. Actual estimate of the tax would require an estimate of the reduction in hours worked due to the substitution effect of the tax-induced wage reduction.

Using Excise Taxes on Alcohol in the United States to Internalize Externalities

Excise taxes can cause losses in efficiency when they induce taxpayers to substitute untaxed or relatively lower-tax products for those subject to the excise taxes. Excise taxes cause a loss in net benefits from use of the taxed products. But what if the taxed product generates negative externalities? Remember products that result in negative externalities—whether through production or consumption—are overused relative to the efficient amounts in competitive markets. Excise taxes therefore can be used as corrective taxes: their distortions *balance* the distortions that result from negative externalities.

The idea of using taxes to internalize negative externalities often results in political support for such taxes as those on alcoholic beverages. For example, in 1991 federal taxes on liquor in the United States went up to $13.50 per gallon of 100 proof. The federal tax on beer was doubled to 32 cents per six-pack, and there were also increases in the taxes on wine. Because most of the federal taxes on alcoholic beverages in the United States are unit, as opposed to ad valorem, taxes, their bite as a percentage of the price of the product had been falling in recent years. Until the 1991 tax increases, federal taxes on beer and wine in the United States had not been increased since 1951. As the price of beer and wine has increased with inflation, the unit taxes fixed in dollar amounts per gallon of these products have become smaller and smaller percentages of the price. Similarly, except for a 19-percent increase in 1985, the federal unit tax on hard liquor had not been raised at all since 1951. But are we, even at current rates, taxing alcoholic beverages at a high enough rate to internalize the negative externalities associated with abusive use of alcohol?

The social costs involved in alcohol abuse are not borne completely by users of the product. Use of alcohol is a major cause of automobile accidents, often resulting in injury to others. The external costs of alcohol abuse include loss of life and property from alcohol-related accidents, costs of trials or other justice proceedings, taxpayer and other third-party payments for alcohol treatment programs, and other medical costs paid by third parties through health insurance.

In most studies of the social cost of alcohol, it is recognized that moderate consumption of the product does not necessarily cause harm to either the drinkers or others. Abusive drinking is defined as more than two drinks per day and this accounts for about 40 percent of annual consumption of alcoholic beverages. Based on data from studies, the economic costs of abusive drinking have been estimated to average 48 cents per ounce of alcohol consumed measured in 1986 dollars.[*] Currently, even with the recent increases, the federal tax on hard liquor amounts to about 21 cents per ounce of pure alcohol while the federal tax on beer is equivalent to a 10 cent per ounce tax on the alcoholic content of the product. Even when state and local taxes are figured in the average, combined tax per ounce of all alcoholic beverages (hard liquor, beer, and wine) averaged about 25 cents per ounce, which is about half the estimated external cost per ounce of 48 cents.

Therefore an opportunity exists to actually improve resource use while raising revenue for the federal government by levying still higher taxes on alcoholic beverages. These data suggest that the tax rate on pure alcohol could be doubled on average to help internalize the estimated external costs of abusive drinking.

Tax increases on alcohol are likely to have a nonregressive effect on income distribution because spending on alcoholic beverages tends to rise to greater percentages of income as family income rises. One study concludes that after offsetting change in income taxes and transfers to the poor, tax increases in alcoholic beverages would be borne proportionally as a percentage of posttax family income in the United States.[†]

---

[*]See Joseph J. Cordes, Eric M. Nicholson, and Frank J. Sammartino, "Raising Revenue by Taxing Activities with Social Costs," *National Tax Journal* 63, 3 (September 1990): 343–356. The estimates are based on a study cited in the article that appeared in the *Journal of the American Medical Association.*

[†]See U.S. Congress, Congressional Budget Office, *Federal Taxation of Tobacco, Alcoholic Beverages, and Motor Fuels* (Washington, D.C.: U.S. Government Printing Office, June 1990), xxii.

FURTHER ANALYSIS OF TAX INCIDENCE

Tax Incidence Is Independent of Legal Liability for Taxes

The final incidence of a tax is independent of whether the tax is collected from buyers or sellers of goods and services. To see this, suppose that the unit tax on gasoline discussed earlier in this chapter were collected from buyers instead of sellers. This would be the case if the tax were added on to the market price of gasoline. Buyers would pay the market price plus the tax for each gallon purchased. The tax can be thought of as being deposited in a box near each gas pump to be picked up each day or week by the tax authorities. The tax is the legal liability of buyers, not sellers.

When the tax is collected from buyers in this way, the marginal cost to sellers does not increase. Instead, the tax is subtracted from the marginal benefit that consumers get from each gallon of gasoline. Therefore, the maximum price that any buyer would pay for a gallon of gasoline, no matter how much was available, would fall by exactly 25 cents. Assume that the marginal benefit received by consumers also equals the marginal social benefit of the good.

Figure 11.5 shows that the demand curve D would shift downward to $MSB - T$. Subtracting T from the marginal social benefit of each quantity gives the net marginal benefit that consumers would get from gasoline after paying the tax. They now base their decision to buy gasoline on their net marginal benefit.

The pretax market equilibrium corresponds to point B. The decrease in demand caused by the tax results in a new market equilibrium corresponding to point A. At

Figure 11.5 ✦ INCIDENCE OF A TAX COLLECTED FROM BUYERS

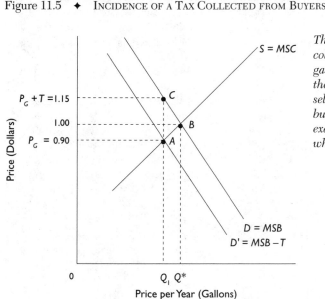

The incidence of a tax is independent of whether it is collected from buyers or sellers. Here a 25-cent unit tax on gasoline is collected from buyers. This causes a decrease in the demand for the good. The market price received by sellers falls to 90 cents per gallon. The total price paid by buyers, including the tax, goes up to $1.15. This results in exactly the same distribution of tax burden that prevailed when the tax was collected from sellers (see Figure 11.2).

that point, the market price of gasoline falls to 90 cents per gallon. This is now the gross price received by sellers, because they are not liable for the tax. This is exactly the amount that sellers received per gallon, after taxes, when they were liable for the tax (see Figure 11.2)! However, the total amount paid by buyers for each gallon is $1.15, because in addition to paying the market price of 90 cents per gallon, they also have to pay the tax of 25 cents on each gallon that they purchase. This corresponds to point C on the original demand curve, D. The total amount that buyers pay per gallon, including the tax, is exactly the same as the market price of gasoline that would prevail if the tax were collected from sellers!

When the tax is collected from buyers, the decrease in demand for gasoline caused by the tax results in backward shifting from buyers to sellers as the market price of gasoline declines. However, the distribution of the burden of the tax between buyers and sellers is exactly the same as when sellers were liable for the tax.

Tax Incidence and Price Elasticities of Demand and Supply

Other things being equal, the more inelastic the demand for a taxed good or service, the greater the portion of the tax borne by buyers. This is shown in Figure 11.6. The demand curve labeled D' is more inelastic at any price than the demand curve labeled D at each price. However, D' intersects the pretax supply curve, S, at point B.

Figure 11.6 ◆ THE MORE INELASTIC THE DEMAND, THE GREATER THE PORTION OF A TAX BORNE BY BUYERS

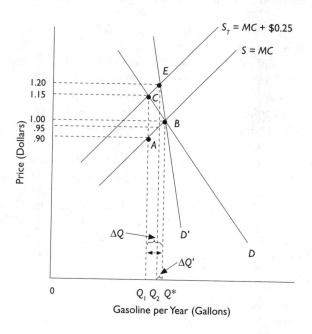

The demand curve D' is more inelastic than the demand curve D at each possible price. As a result, the same unit tax of 25 cents would result in a greater increase in market price when demand is D'. More of the tax is shifted to buyers when the more inelastic demand prevails.

Therefore, the pretax price would be the same, no matter which demand curve prevailed. Suppose the taxed good is, once again, gasoline. When the demand curve, D, prevails, a 25 cents per gallon tax increases market price to $1.15 and results in a 90-cent net price to sellers. The same tax of 25 cents per gallon that is collected from sellers would result in a sharper increase in market price when the more inelastic demand curve, D', prevails. The posttax market equilibrium would correspond to point E when the market demand curve is D'. The market price paid by buyers would be $1.20 per gallon under those circumstances. The net price that sellers would receive would be 95 cents per gallon. The more inelastic demand allows the sellers to shift 5 cents more of the tax per gallon to buyers than they could when demand was D, because buyers are less responsive to price increases when demand is more inelastic. In Figure 11.5, $\Delta Q'$, the reduction in quantity demanded due to the tax when the demand curve is D' is less than ΔQ, the corresponding reduction when the demand curve is D.

Also, other things being equal, the more elastic the supply of a taxed good or service, the greater is the portion of a tax borne by buyers. Suppose that a tax is levied on the sale of a good that is so elastic in supply in the long run that the supply curve is indistinguishable from a horizontal line. For example, suppose housing services can be produced under conditions of constant costs in the long run. Under those circumstances, the supply of housing services will be infinitely elastic.

Figure 11.7 shows the demand and supply for housing services. Empirical evidence does support the hypothesis that the long-run supply curve for this good is, in fact, a horizontal line.[6] This indicates that the marginal cost of producing housing in the long run is constant and equal to the long-run average cost. In Figure 11.7, the pretax market equilibrium corresponds to point E, where rent is 50 cents per square foot so a 600-square-foot apartment would rent for $300 per month in the absence of any taxes on housing.

Now suppose that a tax of 10 cents per square foot is levied on sellers of housing services. This would shift the supply curve up, from MC to $MC + T$, where T is the 10-cent tax. The new market equilibrium will be at point E', at which the equilibrium quantity falls from Q^* to Q_1 square feet rented per month. The gross price paid by buyers of housing services rises from 50 cents to 60 cents per square foot. The sellers of housing services succeed in shifting the entire tax of 10 cents per square foot to buyers. This has to be the case. Suppose that the market price did not increase by the full amount of the tax. The net price received by sellers then would be less than 50 cents per square foot per month, that is, the net price would fall below the average costs of production. Firms would leave the industry, and the quantity supplied would decrease until the market price rose enough to eliminate the losses. If price were to rise more than 10 cents per square foot per month, firms would earn economic profits and new firms would enter the industry. This would increase quantity supplied until market price once again was 60 cents per square foot. This would return the net price received by sellers to 50 cents per square foot after paying the tax. If this were

[6]See James R. Follain, Jr., "The Price Elasticity of the Long-Run Supply of New Housing Construction," *Land Economics* 55 (May 1979): 190–199.

Figure 11.7 ✦ IMPACT OF A TAX ON A GOOD WITH A PERFECTLY ELASTIC SUPPLY

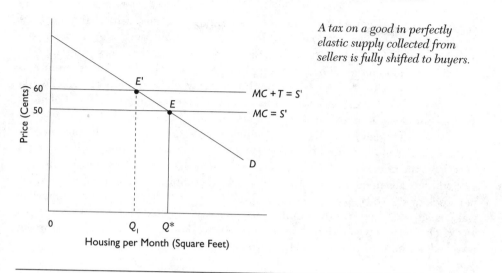

A tax on a good in perfectly elastic supply collected from sellers is fully shifted to buyers.

the case in the housing market, the tax of 10 cents per square foot would raise the monthly rental rate on a 600-square-foot apartment from $300 to $360.[7]

Generally, supply of most goods and services is much more elastic in the long run than in the short run. In other words, buyers are likely to pay more of a tax in the long run regardless of whether that tax is levied on buyers or sellers in a market. Industries in which, over a long period, resources can easily be shifted to other use, will have supply that is close to infinitely elastic over the long run, and prices will eventually rise by the full amount of taxes levied on the products of those industries. If the labor and capital employed in production can be reemployed easily elsewhere in the economy with no reduction in price received, then little backward shifting of taxes to suppliers of resources will occur. In the long run therefore, for industries of constant costs, it is quite likely that the prices of taxed products will rise to reflect the entire tax while the equilibrium output of the taxed products declines.

Suppose the supply of a taxed good or service were so unresponsive to changes in its price that its supply could be regarded as perfectly inelastic. For example, if the

[7]This conclusion holds as well for an ad valorem tax on sellers of housing services. This is because $P_N = MC = AC$, where P_N is the net price received by sellers in long-run equilibrium. An ad valorem tax on P_N increases MC to $MC' = MC + tP_N$ at all quantities. This will shift up the supply curve parallel to itself, because $P_N = MC = AC$. In the posttax equilibrium, $P_G = (1 + t)P_N$. Because $P_N = MC$ under constant costs, it follows that the posttax market price is $P_G = (1 + t)MC$. When an ad valorem tax is levied on P_G, market equilibrium price in posttax equilibrium is $P_G = MC/(1 - t)$ because $P_N = MC = (1 - t)P_G$.

supply of labor hours were perfectly inelastic, the amount of labor hours supplied per year would be fixed. Figure 11.8 illustrates the impact of a flat-rate tax, such as a pay-roll tax, on wages, under these conditions in a competitive labor market.

As shown in Figure 11.4, a tax on labor services deducted from the wages of workers causes the net wage received by workers to fall below the gross wage paid by employers. The flat-rate payroll tax on wages reduces the gross wage by tW_G for any given amount of labor hours supplied per week. The net wage, therefore, is $W_G(1 - t)$. Because the supply of labor hours per week is perfectly inelastic, work-ers do not respond to the tax-induced wage reduction by varying the amount of hours worked per week. Workers therefore cannot shift the burden of the tax backward to employers. The quantity of labor hours supplied must decline to result in an increase in the gross, or market, equilibrium wage paid by employers. In other words, the tax must have the effect of making labor scarcer for shifting to occur. As shown in Figure 11.8, the tax has no affect on either the market equilibrium quantity of labor hours per week or the wage. The pretax equilibrium wage is W_G^*. The posttax equilibrium wage is also W_G^* because the equilibrium quantity supplied remains Q^* hours per week. The entire tax per labor hour is borne by workers as a reduction in the wages received per hour to $W_N = W_G^*(1 - t)$.

Shifting Under Monopoly

A monopolist maximizing profits will choose that output level corresponding to the point where marginal revenue is equal to marginal cost. The marginal revenue curve for a monopolist is steeper than the average revenue (or demand) schedule, and falls

Figure 11.8 ✦ Tax Incidence When Market Supply Is Perfectly Inelastic

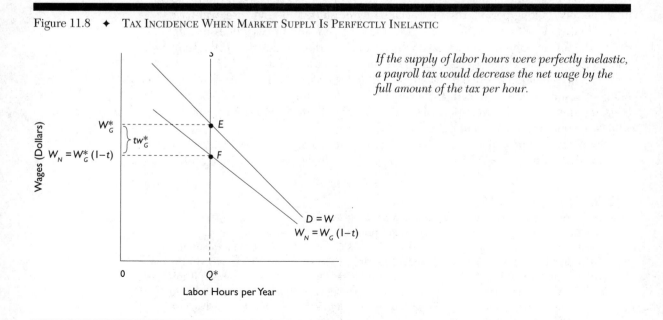

If the supply of labor hours were perfectly inelastic, a payroll tax would decrease the net wage by the full amount of the tax per hour.

below the average revenue curve. A unit excise tax on output produced by a monopoly increases marginal cost at each level of output by an amount equal to the unit tax. However, in this case, the effect on price is somewhat more complex.

To understand this, consider a perfectly competitive industry that has been transformed into a cartel and behaves as if it were a monopolist. This is illustrated in Figure 11.9. The demand curve for the industry's output is D, and the marginal revenue schedule corresponding to this demand is MR. The curve MC is the initial marginal cost schedule, while $MC + T$ is the marginal cost schedule after the imposition of the excise tax. If the industry were perfectly competitive, the initial price would be P^*, and the quantity sold would be Q^*. These are the price and quantity corresponding to the intersection of the MC curve and the demand schedule. But, under monopoly, the equilibrium price and quantity correspond to the intersection of the marginal revenue and marginal cost curves. The monopolist or cartel, therefore, would produce $Q_M < Q^*$ at price $P_M > P^*$. Accordingly, the cartel initially produces less than the perfectly competitive industry, and it charges more.

Now, the tax increases marginal costs from MC to $MC + T$ at all levels of output. Under conditions of perfect competition, the effect of the tax would be to reduce quantity sold from Q^* to Q_T^* and raise consumer prices from P^* to P_T^*. But, under monopoly, the effect of the tax is to reduce quantity sold by an amount less than the reduction that would prevail under perfect competition when the demand curve is linear. Thus, in Figure 11.9, when the monopolist readjusts output after the tax is

Figure 11.9 ✦ SHIFTING UNDER MONOPOLY

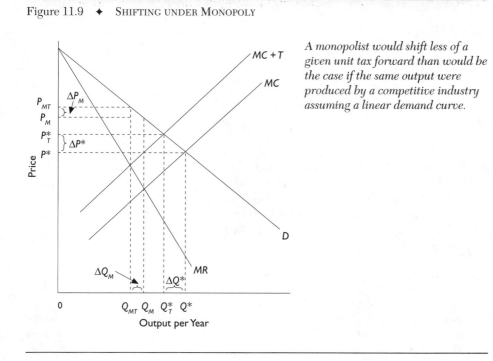

A monopolist would shift less of a given unit tax forward than would be the case if the same output were produced by a competitive industry assuming a linear demand curve.

imposed, output falls to Q_{MT}, and price rises to P_{MT}. The reduction in monopolistic output, ΔQ_M, due to the tax is less than the reduction in output, ΔQ^*, that would prevail for the same tax levied on a competitive industry. This is because the marginal revenue schedule is steeper than the demand schedule. The price rise to consumers, as a result of the tax, is less than that which would occur under perfect competition, because the reduction in quantity supplied as a result of the tax is less.[8] Therefore, in Figure 11.9, $\Delta P_M < \Delta P^*$. Less forward shifting occurs under monopoly than under perfect competition. This, however, is not really good news for consumers, because they pay a higher price for the commodity under monopoly in the first place! As can be seen in Figure 11.9, consumers still pay a higher price for the commodity in the taxed monopoly, relative to the taxed perfectly competitive industry ($P_{MT} > P_T^*$).

Under monopoly, the degree to which taxes are shifted in the long run also varies with the cost structure of the monopolistic firm. The greatest forward shifting is likely to occur under conditions of constant long-run average costs, because the marginal cost curve would be horizontal under those circumstances. In general, the greater the rate of increase of marginal costs with output for a monopolistic firm, the smaller is the portion of a unit or ad valorem tax shifted forward to buyers.

C H E C K P O I N T

1. Explain why a price-distorting tax will result in costs to citizens that exceed the sum of funds collected in tax revenue.
2. If you wanted to minimize the excess burden of taxation from price-distorting taxes, what kinds of goods or services would you tax?
3. Under what circumstances will a gasoline tax collected from the sellers be fully shifted forward to buyers?

GENERAL EQUILIBRIUM ANALYSIS OF THE EXCESS BURDEN AND INCIDENCE OF TAXES

In our discussion of the excess burden and incidence of taxes we have thus far examined only the impact of taxes on a single market. In reality, a system of taxes affects many markets and results in resource flows among many sectors of the economy. A general, or multimarket, analysis of excess burden and tax incidence helps us obtain a more realistic picture of the impact of taxes or resource use and provides insights to help reduce the efficiency loss from taxes.

---

[8]When both the demand and marginal cost curves are linear, the rise in consumer price under monopoly is precisely one-half of the rise that occurs under perfect competition. For proof of this statement, see Richard A. Musgrave, *The Theory of Public Finance* (New York: McGraw-Hill, 1959), 292.

An economy is composed of a complex of interrelated markets. This implies that the effect of a tax in any one market is not likely to be confined to that market alone. Instead, repercussions are likely in related markets, along with possible feedback effects in the market initially taxed.

For example, a tax on the consumption of electric power affects not only the price of electricity but also the demand for various electrical appliances and for natural gas for cooking and heating. These secondary shifts in demand affect the prices of these substitutable and complementary activities. This, in turn, might result in feedback effects on both the demand and the supply of electricity. Because electricity is used as an input in most productive processes, one also might expect that the goods that require proportionately more electricity than others for production likewise will rise in price, relative to those others. Tracing the full multimarket, or general equilibrium, effect on a tax on electricity is difficult because of the number of markets likely to be affected.

Minimizing the Excess Burden of Sales and Excise Taxes

Suppose tax authorities wish to minimize the excess burden associated with a system of sales and excise taxes. Surprisingly, they must tax various goods at differing rates, rather than at uniform rates, to accomplish this. To see why this is so, take two goods, say food and clothing. Assume that the demand for food is more inelastic than the demand for clothing and that the demand for each of these goods is independent of the price of the other. Accordingly, when the price of either good changes, the demand curve for the other does not shift.

Figure 11.10 shows the demand curves for food and clothing. Assume that income effects of price changes for these goods are negligible so that the resulting changes in quantities demanded reflect only the substitution effects caused by the taxes. The curves have been drawn under the presumption that, at any given price, the demand for food is more inelastic than the demand for clothing. Now suppose a flat-rate sales tax of t percent is levied on both of these goods. Prior to the tax, the price of food is P_F and the price of clothing is P_C. Assume that the supply of both of these goods is infinitely elastic in the long run, so that ultimately the tax raises the price of each of these goods by t percent.

Because the demand for food is more inelastic than the demand for clothing, the excess burden in the clothing market exceeds that in the food market. The excess burden in the food market is the triangular area AE_2E_1 in Figure 11.10A. The excess burden in the clothing market is the triangular area BE_2E_1 in Figure 11.10B. The excess burden is higher in the clothing market because the substitution effect of the tax is greater there than in the food market.

This analysis suggests a way to minimize the excess burden associated with any system of sales or excise taxes. The total excess burden associated with the sales tax could be reduced if the tax rate were raised in the food market and lowered in the clothing market. By adjusting the tax rates in the two markets until the marginal reduction in the excess burden in the clothing market is balanced by the marginal increase in the excess burden in the food market, the total excess burden can be minimized.

Figure 11.10 ✦ MULTIMARKET ANALYSIS OF EXCESS BURDEN

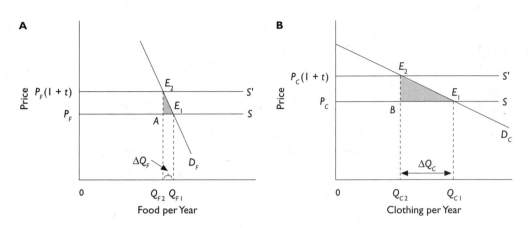

*A flat-rate sales tax of t percent levied on both food and clothing results in greater excess burden in the clothing market as shown in **B** than in the food market as shown in **A**. Total excess burden can be reduced by increasing the tax rate on food and lowering the tax rate on clothing until the marginal increase in the excess burden in the food market equals the marginal decrease in excess burden in the clothing market.*

The implication of this analysis is that efficiency loss can be minimized if, other things being equal, goods are taxed at rates that decrease with the elasticity of demand. The more inelastic the demand, the higher the tax rate necessary to ensure minimization of efficiency loss.[9] Such a tax rate structure will ensure that the percentage reduction in the quantity demanded due to the substitution effect of the tax-induced price increase is equal for each good.

An efficient system of sales and excise taxes is likely to face considerable political opposition if it is regarded as unfair. In fact, the demand for such necessities as food

---

[9]For any two goods, F, and C, the following condition minimizes the total excess burden:

$$t_F E_F = t_C E_C,$$

where t is the tax rate for each good (indicated by the subscript) and E is its price elasticity of demand. This is sometimes called *Ramsey's rule*, which states that the percentage reduction in the quantity demanded of each of the goods must be equal. To see this, note that t_F and t_C are the percentage changes in the prices of food and clothing, respectively. Therefore,

$$t_F \frac{(\Delta Q_F/Q_F)}{t_F} = t_C \frac{(\Delta Q_C/Q_C)}{t_C}.$$

Therefore, $\Delta Q_F/Q_F = \Delta Q_C/Q_C$. Given E_C and t_C, the lower E_F, the higher the tax rate on food necessary to achieve this condition. For a more advanced analysis, see Agnar Sandmo, "Optimal Taxation—An Introduction to the Literature," *Journal of Public Economics* 6 (July–August 1976): 37–54.

and housing is likely to be more inelastic than the demand for luxury goods. There-fore, a system of excise taxes that minimizes excess burden is likely to call for higher tax rates on the consumption of necessities. This will bear more heavily on the in-comes of the poor, relative to the rich.

Multimarket Analysis of Incidence

Some of the basic ideas of a multimarket analysis of tax incidence can be illustrated simply by expanding the analysis to deal with two markets. Assume, for example, that the economy produces only two goods, food and clothing, and that a tax is levied on the sale of clothing but not on food. The resource flows induced by taxation and con-sequent effects are illustrated in Figure 11.11.

The tax on clothing acts to decrease the supply of clothing, with a consequent in-crease in its market price from P^* to P_G and a reduction in quantity demanded from Q^* to Q', as shown in Figure 11.11A. The reduced production of clothing caused by the tax frees productive resources from clothing production for alternative use. If these resources are used to produce government-supplied services, they will be reemployed in the government sector. However, if government does not require the same resources directly freed by the tax, or if the tax revenues are used to finance transfers, the productive resources that are released would have to find employment in alternative industries.

The tax can cause the price of specialized inputs used in the production of the taxed good to fall. This will reduce the incomes of owners of these inputs, thereby forcing them to bear a portion of the incidence of the tax. This is because the reduc-tion in output in the taxed industry results in suppliers of input to that industry seek-ing work in other industries where their specialized skills are worth less.

Figure 11.11 ✦ MULTIMARKET ANALYSIS OF INCIDENCE

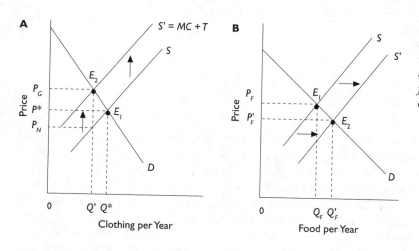

A tax on output in one market can affect prices in other markets. Here the tax-induced increase in the price of clothing causes inputs to flow into the food industry. This increases the supply of food and decreases its market price.

The tax on clothing shifts the supply curve from S to S', raises the price of clothing to P_G, as shown in Figure 11.11A, and releases inputs from clothing production. The flow of resources from clothing to food production results in a shift in the supply curve of food to S' and a decrease in the price of food from P_F to P'_F, as shown in Figure 11.11B.

The determination of the incidence of the tax is now more complex. Although the tax causes the price of clothing to increase, it indirectly causes the price of food to decrease. From the point of view of consumers, the increase in clothing prices is balanced to some extent by a corresponding decrease in the price of food. If, on average, the impact of the increase in the price of clothing is exactly offset by the decrease in the price of food, consumers are made no worse off by the tax. The tax is borne by owners of all specialized inputs in clothing production as a reduction in income. If, for example, machine operators who have special skills and who are freed to transfer to food production for employment receive lower wages now, they will be worse off as a result of the tax. Consumers who spend relatively more on clothing than on food also suffer a decrease in real income.

A single-market, or partial equilibrium, analysis often gives a good approximation of the incidence of the tax. If the resources that seek alternative employment as a result of tax-induced decreases in production in one market are absorbed in many markets, little effect on input and output prices in other markets is likely. This is because the amount of resources freed will be small, relative to the total supplies of those resources. If these inputs are not specialized, they can be reemployed in other industries, with no decrease in their prices or those on the outputs that they produce. Therefore, the extent to which the results of a multimarket analysis differ from a single-market analysis depends on the degree to which tax-induced resource flows are concentrated in particular markets and the extent to which displaced inputs have specialized uses in the taxed industry.

The situation is more complex still if the possibility of overall changes in the aggregate supplies of particular inputs, as a result of the tax, is considered. If workers or owners of capital decide to work or invest less, as a result of the lower returns available after taxation, further changes in input prices will occur.

TAXES, GOVERNMENT EXPENDITURES, AND THE DISTRIBUTION OF INCOME

Policymakers and citizens must have reasonably accurate information concerning the effect of government activity on the distribution of well-being among households in the community. Insofar as a household's well-being is correlated with its real income, changes in the distribution of welfare can be approximated by measuring changes in the distribution of disposable income. Predictions of the effect of proposed tax and expenditure policies on the distribution of income can permit more-informed collective choices on the extent and nature of government activities. Quantitative estimates of the extent and nature of government expenditures and tax policies help voters compute their true cost shares of collectively supplied services, relative to the net benefits that they receive from government activities.

The incidence of a specific government policy refers to the resulting change in the distribution of income available for private use attributable to that policy.[10] To determine the incidence of a policy, no other factors can be attributable to, say, other policies simultaneously affecting the distribution of income. This implies that other variables that affect income distribution (for example, other government policies) must be held fixed in order to obtain a meaningful measure of the incidence of any specific policy.

With that caution in mind, three concepts of incidence that relate to government taxes *and* expenditures can be distinguished:

1. Budget incidence
2. Expenditure incidence
3. Tax incidence

Budget and Expenditure Incidence

Budget incidence evaluates the effects of both government expenditure and tax policies on the distribution of income in the private sector. A comprehensive analysis of budget incidence in the United States would generate data relative to the influence of governments (federal, state, and local government activities) on the distribution of income. Alternatively, the incidence of a change in the size of the government budget could be evaluated. This would analyze the effects on the distribution of income of a particular increase in government expenditures, accompanied by increases in taxes.[11]

Expenditure incidence evaluates the effects of alternative government expenditure projects on the distribution of income. To be sure that only the expenditure project being evaluated is affecting the distribution of income, all other possible influences on the distribution of income must be held fixed. This implies that the total level of expenditure is held constant in real terms and that the particular project being evaluated is substituted for some other project or group of projects. At the same time, we must adjust for any change in the tax structure that alters the distribution of income. This *differential* approach to the incidence of expenditures allows the economist to generate data concerning the relative redistributive effects of alternative expenditure policies alone.[12] It allows policymakers and citizens to evaluate the relative redistributive effects of alternative expenditure policies. The determination of expenditure incidence remains difficult because of the inherent problems involved in imputing the collectively consumed benefits of government-provided goods and services to specific households and business firms.

---

[10]See Musgrave, *Theory of Public Finance,* 207–208.
[11]Musgrave calls this "balanced-budget incidence." See *Theory of Public Finance,* 214–215.
[12]See Musgrave, *Theory of Public Finance,* 212–225, for a more extensive discussion of differential incidence.

Differential Tax Incidence

Differential tax incidence is the resulting change in the distribution of income when one type of tax is substituted for some alternative tax, or set of taxes, yielding an equivalent amount of revenue in real terms, while both the mix and level of government expenditures are held constant. Because any given level and mix of government expenditures can be financed through alternative tax schemes, the concept of differential tax incidence enables one to determine the relative redistributive impact of alternative taxes and tax structures. An analysis of differential tax incidence attempts to delineate all direct and indirect effects of the substitution of one tax for another. This includes all secondary shifts in relative prices that result from tax shifting, as well as direct transfers of income.

However, the concept of differential incidence ignores the interdependence between the revenue and expenditure sides of the budget. Because alternative tax schemes, other things being equal, do having varying effects on the distribution of income in the private sector and on tax shares, the assumption of holding the level and mix of government expenditures constant is questionable. The reason is that changes in the distribution of income and tax shares are likely to change the demand pattern for public services. The willingness to vote approval on specific projects is, in part, a function of tax shares.

The Lorenz Curve

The effect of taxes on income shares can be partially tabulated by using Lorenz curves. A **Lorenz curve** gives information on the distribution of income by size brackets. A hypothetical Lorenz curve is plotted in Figure 11.12. The horizontal axis gives the percentage of households ranked in terms of their income, while the vertical axis measures the percentage of income. The line 0E is called the *line of equal distribution*. An economy whose income distribution is measured along line 0E has a perfectly uniform distribution of real income. To understand why this is so, consider the percentage of income going to the lowest 10 percent of households (the bottom decile) for an economy with a Lorenz curve of 0E. Because 0E is at a 45-degree angle to the horizontal axis, the lowest decile of households ranked in terms of income size has 10 percent of the nation's real income. Similarly, the lowest 90 percent of households has 90 percent of the nation's income. The top 10 percent of households ranked in terms of income (the top decile) also has 10 percent of the nation's income. Any decile rank chosen has 10 percent of the nation's total real income. Income would be equally distributed.

No nation has a Lorenz curve such as 0E. Significant degrees of income inequality exist. For example, the income distribution might be measured by the Lorenz curve 0xyE in Figure 11.12. Such an income distribution implies that the bottom decile of households ranked in terms of income has only 3 percent of the nation's real income, at point x, while the top decile of households has 40 percent of the nation's real income, at point y.

Now consider the effect of taxation on the distribution of income. After all changes in input and output prices and direct reductions of income have been deter-

Figure 11.12 ✦ A LORENZ CURVE

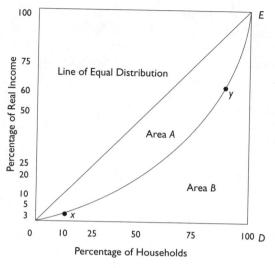

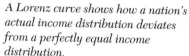

A Lorenz curve shows how a nation's actual income distribution deviates from a perfectly equal income distribution.

mined, along with changes in quantities purchased and sold by households, the new data can be tabulated by income size brackets and plotted in Figure 11.12 as a new Lorenz curve. This permits comparison of the new income distribution by size classes with the income distribution that existed before the policy change. However, insofar as households trade places within the income distribution, with no change in the degree of income inequality, the Lorenz curve does not reflect the change in the distribution.

Measuring Income Inequality: The Gini Coefficient

A summary index of the information contained in a Lorenz curve is a **Gini coefficient,** which measures the degree of inequality for any income distribution by calculating the ratio of the area between the Lorenz curve corresponding to that distribution and the 45-degree line to the total area under the 45-degree line. Thus, in Figure 11.12, call A the area between the 45-degree line and the Lorenz curve and call B the area under the Lorenz curve; then, the Gini coefficient, G, is

$$G = \text{Area } A/(\text{Area } A + \text{Area } B). \tag{11.9}$$

If the Gini coefficient were equal to zero, the Lorenz curve would be the 45-degree line. The closer the Gini coefficient is to zero, the more equal is the income distribution. Gini coefficients are often calculated for pretax and posttax income distributions. If the Gini coefficient is lower for the posttax distribution of income, then taxes have served the function of reducing income inequality. The Gini coefficient provides only a rough index of income inequality. It is of limited usefulness when changes in income distribution, induced by taxes or other policies, result in new Lorenz curves that intersect the initial Lorenz curve and when the ranking of households changes.[13] To the extent to which the Gini coefficient corresponding to posttax income is less than that corresponding to pretax income, taxes have served to decrease income inequality as measured by the Gini coefficient.

A study of the incidence of the overall 1980 tax structure (all federal, state, and local taxes) in the United States concluded that, except for those with very high incomes and very low incomes, the overall distribution of the tax burden is roughly proportional to income.[14] Joseph A. Pechman, in a major study done at the Brookings Institution, concluded that, based on 1980 effective tax rates, the Gini coefficient of the pretax income distribution was reduced by taxation by no more than 2.5 percent. Using the Gini coefficient as a rough index of income inequality, this implies that the overall combined effect of federal, state, and local taxes in the United States on the income distribution was negligible in that year. A similar study by the Congressional Budget Office for federal taxes alone concluded that federal taxes reduced the Gini coefficient by between 4 and 5 percent based on the tax law prevailing in 1988.[15] Federal taxes, taken by themselves, contribute more to reducing income inequality than do taxes levied by all levels of government in the United States.

Recent analysis of the effect of changes in the federal tax structure in 1990 and 1993 by the Congressional Budget Office indicate that reforms, particularly those enacted under the Clinton Administration, will make the U.S. tax system more progressive. Much of this change is accounted for in sharp reductions in average income tax rates for families with the lowest incomes in the United States. Increases in marginal income tax rates to 36 percent and 39.6 percent for the highest income groups enacted in 1993 will further increase the progressivity of the U.S. tax system.[16]

CHECKPOINT

1. Explain why minimizing the excess burden from a state sales tax would require that products with inelastic demand be taxed at higher rates than products with elastic demand.
2. Explain how a tax on one product such as gasoline can cause the price of other products to decline.
3. What is differential tax incidence? How can a Gini coefficient be used to determine whether a substitution of one tax for another results in a more equitable income distribution?

---

[13]More refined measures of the degree of progressiveness of taxes are possible. See Daniel B. Suits, "Measurement of Tax Progressivity," *American Economic Review* 67 (September 1977): 747–752.

[14]Joseph A. Pechman, *Who Paid the Taxes: 1966–1985?* (Washington, D.C.: The Brookings Institution, 1985).

[15]U.S. Congress, Congressional Budget Office, *The Changing Distribution of Federal Taxes: 1975–1990* (Washington, D.C.: Congress of the United States, October 1987), appendix C.

[16]See Congress of the United States, Congressional Budget Office, *The Economic and Budget Outlook: Fiscal Years 1995–1999* (Washington, D.C.: U.S. Government Printing Office, January 1994), pp 56–57.

Summary

Taxes can affect prices of outputs and inputs, causing losses in efficiency by preventing prices from accurately reflecting marginal social costs and benefits of goods and services. Price-distorting taxes induce individuals to take actions with lower social value than they would choose if no such tax existed. The excess burden of a tax is a measure of the tax-induced loss in efficiency in private use of resources due to the substitution effects of taxes.

The standard of comparison for measuring losses associated with price-distorting taxes is the lump-sum tax, which does not prevent prices from being equal to the marginal social cost and marginal social benefit of goods and services. Such a tax transfers resources from private use to government use without offering any opportunity or incentive to substitute one private activity for another. Lump-sum taxes result only in income or wealth reductions; they do not cause losses in the efficiency with which private resources are used.

Price-distorting taxes act as wedges in markets, making prices paid by buyers diverge from net prices received by sellers. This prevents competitive markets from automatically equating marginal social costs and marginal social benefits. The result is a loss in efficiency. Efficiency loss, or excess burden, depends on the tax rate, the expenditure on the taxed good, and its price elasticities of demand and supply. Excess burden varies quadratically with the tax rate. Excess burden is minimized when taxing activities for which substitution effects of price changes are close to zero.

The burden of paying a tax can be shifted from persons who are liable for the tax to other groups. This occurs when prices change as a result of a tax. The incidence of a tax measures the distribution of the burden of paying a tax among persons. In general, other things being equal, the more inelastic the demand for a taxed good or service, the greater is the portion of the tax paid by buyers of the item. Similarly, other things being equal, the more inelastic the supply of a taxed good or service, the greater is the portion of the tax paid by sellers.

A multimarket analysis of incidence considers the effect of tax-induced resource flows on the prices of inputs and outputs in markets other than those directly taxed. The determination of incidence in such cases is more complex. Input prices often fall and prices of goods produced with inputs released by taxation also fall.

Data on income shares by income class can be tabulated with a Lorenz curve, which plots the percentage of households ranked according to income against their share of income. A Gini coefficient, which summarizes information contained in a Lorenz curve, provides a rough index of income inequality. The smaller the Gini coefficient, the more equal the income distribution.

A number of empirical studies on the overall incidence of the tax structure have concluded that it is only mildly progressive. However, federal taxes remain progressive with respect to income despite recent changes in the tax rate structure. These studies, however, are based only on rough estimates of price elasticities and extent of intermarket effects. The extent to which retail sales taxes, payroll taxes, corporate income taxes, and property taxes are reflected in higher consumer prices and lower input returns is particularly controversial.

A Forward Look

The next chapter discusses budget deficits. In recent years, the federal government has made increasing use of borrowed funds to cover expenditures, which raises questions about the implications of growing government debt on resource use and the distribution of well-being between present and future generations.

Important Concepts

Lump-Sum Tax
Head Tax
Price-Distorting Tax
Individual and Total Excess Burden of Taxation
Unit Tax
Efficiency-Loss Ratio
Shifting of a Tax
Forward Shifting
Backward Shifting
Incidence of a Tax
Ad Valorem Tax
Budget Incidence
Expenditure Incidence
Differential Tax Incidence
Lorenz Curve
Gini Coefficient

Questions for Review

1. Why are most taxes likely to cause losses in efficiency? Be sure to relate your answer to the impact of taxes on prices.

2. Why should the excess burden of taxation be added to revenue collected from taxes in order to accurately measure the opportunity costs of government-supplied goods and services?

3. Explain in your own words why lump-sum taxes will not cause any losses in efficiency. Are lump-sum taxes feasible? Lump-sum taxes do not result in substitution effects, but they do affect prices. Is this a contradiction?

4. Show how a gasoline tax of 10 cents per gallon collected from sellers affects the market equilibrium for gasoline. Assume that the demand curve for gasoline is downward sloping and that the supply curve is upward sloping. Show the excess burden of the tax on your diagram. What is the incidence of the tax between buyers and sellers? How would your answer be affected if the tax were collected from buyers instead of sellers?

5. The price elasticity of demand for automobiles is -2 and the price elasticity of supply is 3. Expenditure on automobiles after imposing a sales tax of 2 percent is $5 billion. Calculate the excess burden of the tax, assuming that automobiles are sold in perfectly competitive markets. Assume that the price elasticities given are based on the substitution effect of the tax and that the difference between pretax and posttax prices of cars is very small.

6. Why would a national land tax be likely to have zero excess burden? Show the incidence of a tax on land between landlords and tenants. In answering this question, assume that the supply of land is perfectly inelastic.

7. Suppose that the efficiency-loss ratio of taxes on capital income is 30 percent. The capital income taxes currently collect $50 billion of revenue per year. What would be the gain in well-being if a lump-sum tax replaced the current taxes on capital income?

8. Under what circumstances does a single-market analysis of tax incidence give a good approximation of the multimarket incidence?

9. How would the differential tax incidence of replacing an income tax with a lump-sum tax be determined?

10. What is a Gini coefficient? How can this coefficient be used to determine the impact of taxes on income distribution?

Problems

1. The annual demand for liquor in a certain state is given by the following equation: $Q_D = 500,000 - 20,000P$, where P is the price per gallon and Q_D is quantity of gallons demanded per year. The supply of liquor is given by the equation $Q_S = 30,000P$. Solve for the equilibrium annual quantity and price of liquor.

   Suppose that a $1 per gallon tax is levied on the price of liquor received by sellers. Use both graphic and algebraic techniques to show the impact of the tax on market equilibrium. Calculate the excess burden of the tax, the amount of revenues collected, and the incidence of the tax between buyers and sellers.

2. Figure 11.11 shows that a tax on clothing can reduce the price of food. Suppose that after the tax on clothing consumption is imposed, another tax is levied on the consumption of food. For example, the consumption of both commodities could be subject to a tax of 5 percent. Show how the conclusions of the analysis in the text are modified when the same tax is present in both markets. Analyze the incidence of the tax. In your answer, assume that the tax revenue is returned in equal lump-sum transfers to all citizens.

3. The price elasticity of demand for wine is estimated to be -1 at all possible quantities. Currently 200 million gallons of wine are sold per year and the price averages $6 per bottle. Assuming that the price elasticity of supply of wine is 1 and the current tax rate is $1 per bottle, calculate the current excess burden of the tax on wine. Suppose the tax per bottle is increased to $2 per bottle. What will happen to the excess burden of the tax as a result of the tax increase? Under what circumstances can a doubling of the tax on wine actually improve resource use in the United States, despite the increase in the excess burden of the tax?

4. Suppose you had to design a system of taxation for a republic of the former Soviet Union that was transforming its economy into a modern Western-style mixed economy. What criteria would you consider to minimize the excess burden of the system of taxation? Why would a uniform system of sales taxes likely have a higher excess burden than a system of excise taxes in which tax rates varied among taxed products? What would be the possible distortions resulting from a tax system that only taxed consumption of goods and services and did not tax leisure activities? Why would a very efficient tax system be unlikely to gain broad political support in the republic?

Suggestions for Further Reading

Fullerton, Don and Rogers, Diane Lim. *Who Bears the Lifetime Tax Burden?* Washington, D.C.: The Brookings Institution, 1993. An innovative extension of incidence analysis that examines tax burdens over the lifetime of individuals. Much of the analysis in this book is quite technical.

Harberger, Arnold C. *Taxation and Welfare.* Boston: Little, Brown, & Co., 1974. A collection of classic articles by Harberger, developing techniques for measuring efficiency loss.

Miezkowski, Peter. "Tax Incidence Theory: The Effect of Taxes on the Distribution of Income." *Journal of Economic Literature* 7 (December 1969). A review of basic incidence theory.

Pechman, Joseph A. *Who Paid the Taxes: 1966–1985?* Washington, D.C.: The Brookings Institution, 1985. An analysis of tax incidence for all taxes in the United States.

Slemrod, Joel. "Optimal Taxation and Optimal Tax Systems," *Journal of Economic Perspectives* 4, 1 (Winter, 1990): 157–178. A readable discussion of theoretical and practical issues in designing tax systems based on normative criteria including efficiency and various concepts of horizontal and vertical equity.

Slemrod, Joel, ed. *Do Taxes Matter? The Impact of the Tax Reform Act of 1986.* Cambridge, MA: The MIT Press, 1990. A collection of essays on the economic effects of changes in tax laws in the United States on various markets.

Tresch, Richard W. *Public Finance: A Normative Theory.* Plano, TX: Business Publications, 1981. Chapter 15 contains a general equilibrium analysis of excess burden. Recommended for students with a good mathematical background.

U.S. Congress, Congressional Budget Office. *Federal Taxation of Tobacco, Alcoholic Beverages, and Motor Fuels,* Washington, D.C.: U.S. Government Printing Office, June 1990. An analysis of excise taxes in the United States including the economic effects of increasing excise taxes.

Appendix
11

THE EXCESS BURDEN OF
TAXATION: TECHNICAL
ANALYSIS

DERIVATION OF THE FORMULA FOR THE EXCESS BURDEN OF A UNIT TAX

It's easy to show that the excess burden of a unit tax varies with the square of the tax per unit, T. Begin with the formula for the area of the triangle representing the loss in well-being attributable to the excess burden of the tax:

$$W = \tfrac{1}{2}T\Delta Q, \tag{11A.1}$$

where ΔQ is the change in the sale of the good or service due only to the substitution effect of the tax-induced price increase. The unit tax, T, can be expressed as the difference between the gross price paid by buyers and the net price received by sellers:

$$T = P_G - P_N. \tag{11A.2}$$

The change in the gross price paid by buyers is

$$\Delta P_G = P_G - P^\circ, \tag{11A.3}$$

where P° is the pretax market equilibrium price.

The change in the net price received by sellers is

$$\Delta P_N = P_N - P^\circ. \tag{11A.4}$$

The change in price to buyers is positive whereas the change in the net price received by sellers is negative.

The price elasticities of demand and supply at any price and quantity, P, Q, are

$$E_D = \frac{\Delta Q/Q^\circ}{\Delta P_G/P^\circ} \tag{11A.5}$$

and

$$E_S = \frac{\Delta Q/Q^\circ}{\Delta P_N/P^\circ} \tag{11A.6}$$

where $Q°$ is the initial equilibrium quantity. When the elasticities are based on changes in quantities due only to substitution effects, they are called *compensated elasticities.* Substituting Equations 11A.3 and 11A.4 in 11A.5 and 11A.6 gives the following:

$$E_D = \frac{\Delta Q}{Q°} \cdot \frac{P°}{P_G - P°} \tag{11A.7}$$

and

$$E_S = \frac{\Delta Q}{Q°} \cdot \frac{P°}{P_N - P°} \tag{11A.8}$$

Solving for P_G and P_N,

$$P_G = \frac{\Delta Q P°}{Q° E_D} + P° \tag{11A.9}$$

and

$$P_N = \frac{\Delta Q P°}{Q° E_S} + P°. \tag{11A.10}$$

Substituting Equations 11A.9 and 11A.10 in 11A.2 yields

$$T = \frac{\Delta Q P°}{Q°} \cdot \frac{E_S - E_D}{E_S E_D}. \tag{11A.11}$$

Solving Equation 11A.11 for ΔQ gives

$$\Delta Q = T \frac{Q°}{P°} \cdot \frac{E_S E_D}{E_S - E_D}. \tag{11A.12}$$

Finally, substituting Equation 11A.12 in the expression for W gives

$$W = \frac{1}{2} T^2 \frac{Q°}{P°} \cdot \frac{E_S E_D}{E_S - E_D}. \tag{11A.13}$$

This is the formula used in the text for determining the loss in well-being from the excess burden of a unit tax. The price elasticity of demand, E_D, is a negative number; therefore, the value of W is negative, indicating a loss.

EXCESS BURDEN OF AN AD VALOREM TAX WHEN THE TAXED GOOD OR SERVICE IS PRODUCED UNDER CONDITIONS OF CONSTANT COSTS

If a good is produced under conditions of constant costs, its long-run supply curve will be infinitely elastic. Remember, if the difference between the pretax and posttax price is small, the excess burden of an ad valorem tax can be approximated by

$$W = \frac{1}{2}t^2(P \circ Q^\circ)\frac{E_S E_D}{E_S - E_D}, \tag{11A.14}$$

which can be written as

$$W = \frac{1}{2}t^2(P \circ Q^\circ)E_D\frac{E_S}{E_S - E_D}. \tag{11A.15}$$

The horizontal supply curve associated with constant costs implies an infinite elasticity of supply. As E_S approaches infinity, the value of the ratio $E_S/(E_S - E_D)$ approaches 1. The formula in Equation 11A.15 therefore reduces to

$$W = \frac{1}{2}t^2 P \circ Q^\circ E_D. \tag{11A.16}$$

Thus, under conditions of constant costs, calculation of the excess burden requires an estimate of the price elasticity of the taxed good and an estimate of current expenditures on the good. The more inelastic the demand for the good, the lower is the excess burden.

Suppose, in the long run, the supply of new housing is infinitely elastic. If the total annual revenue of the housing industry is currently $50 billion in new home sales, a tax of 2 percent of new home sales would result in an annual excess burden of $10 million per year in the long run, when the compensated price elasticity of demanded is equal to -1.

INDIVIDUAL LOSSES IN WELFARE UNDER CONDITIONS OF PERFECT COMPETITION

It is often useful to calculate the excess burden borne by certain groups in the economy. If the taxed output or input is traded under conditions of perfect competition, owners can sell as much as they like at the going market price. This implies that, from their point of view, the demand curve that they face is perfectly elastic at the going market price. In this case, the price elasticity of demand relevant for computing the excess burden is infinite. Substituting an infinite E_D in Equation 11A.14 for the excess burden of an ad valorem tax gives

$$W = \frac{1}{2}t^2(P \circ Q^\circ)E_S. \tag{11A.17}$$

For example, a formula like the one above could be used to calculate the excess burden associated with each marginal tax rate, t, on labor income for the personal income tax. The amount of income in each tax bracket would correspond to $P^\circ Q^\circ$ in the formula because labor income represents the product of wages and labor hours per year. An estimate of the price elasticity of supply of labor based on the substitution effects of tax-induced wage changes then would be required to calculate the excess burden for each tax bracket. The total excess burden then could be obtained by summing the excess burden associated with each tax bracket.

COMPENSATED DEMAND CURVES

The price elasticities of demand of taxed outputs used to calculate excess burden are based on the substitution effects of price changes. These are calculated from points on a compensated demand curve. A **compensated demand curve** of a good shows the relationship between the price and the quantity demanded of a good due only to substitution effects of price changes.

Figure 11A.1 shows that the compensated demand curve for a normal good can be derived from a regular demand curve. Consumption of a normal good increases as income increases and decreases as income decreases. Compensated demand curves do not include any of the effects of changes in well-being for consumers that result from price changes. Each time a price increases, consumers would have to be given a compensating increase in income to offset the decrease in well-being caused by the income effect of the price rise. Similarly, the consumer would have to be compensated by decreases in income each time prices fell to adjust for the increase in real income. The adjustments in income remove the income effects of price changes.

In Figure 11A.1, the current market price of gasoline is P_1. Suppose the price increases. If gasoline is a normal good, the income effect of the price increase will reduce its consumption. This is because the increase in price reduces consumers' real income. When income is reduced, consumers reduce the consumption of a normal good such as gasoline. If consumers were given a compensating increase in income to make them as well off as they were before the price increase, they would consume *more* than otherwise would be the case. It follows that removing the income effect of price increases would increase the consumption of gasoline. Therefore points on a

---

Figure 11A.1 ◆ Regular and Compensated Demand Curves for a Normal Good

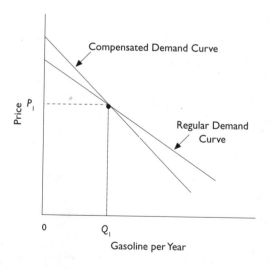

Compensated demand curves remove the income effects of price changes from demand responses. The compensated demand curve in the graph shows the substitution effects for all price changes above and below the initial price P_1. The compensated demand curve for a normal good is more inelastic than the regular demand curve at any given price above or below the initial price.

compensated demand curve reflecting *only* the substitution effects of price increaess would lie to the right of points on the regular demand curve for prices higher than P_1.

Similarly, price decreases below P_1 would make the consumer better off. The increase in real income would result in an income effect that would increase the consumption of a normal good such as gasoline. Removing the income effect by decreasing consumers' income would decrease the quantity demanded in response to the price decline. Points on a compensated demand curve below P_1 would lie to the left of points on the regular demand curve.

Points on compensated demand curves for normal goods tend to have lower price elasticity than points corresponding to the same price on regular demand curves. The difference between the compensated and regular demand curves depends on the size of the income effects of price changes. When these income effects are relatively small, using price elasticities based on the regular demand curve will give a good approximation of the excess burden of a tax.

Figure 11A.2 shows that a compensated demand curve can be used to determine the excess burden of a tax on gasoline when the income effect of the tax-induced increase in market price is not negligible. Assume that gasoline is a normal good. The

---

Figure 11A.2   ✦   USING A COMPENSATED DEMAND CURVE TO ISOLATE THE SUBSTITUTION EFFECT OF A TAX-INDUCED PRICE INCREASE

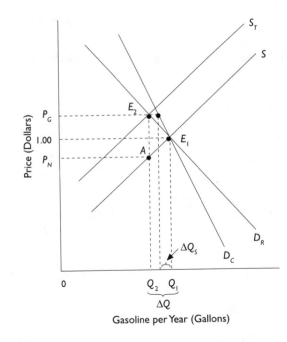

A tax on gasoline raises the market price from $1 per gallon to P_G. The corresponding reduction in quantity demanded, ΔQ, is the combined income and substitution effects of the tax-induced price increase. The compensated demand curve is used to show the substitution effect of the price increase, ΔQ_S. Using the actual reduction in quantity demanded overestimates the excess burden if the taxed item is a normal good.

supply curve of gasoline is labeled S on the graph. The regular, or market, demand curve for gasoline is labeled D_R. The initial market equilibrium corresponds to point E_1, at which the regular market demand curve and the market supply curve intersect. The equilibrium quantity sold per year is Q_1 and the equilibrium price is $1. The imposition of a unit tax on gasoline shifts the supply curve upward from S to S_T. The new market equilibrium corresponds to point E_2, at which the market price of gasoline increases to P_G, and the net price received by sellers corresponds to P_N. The equilibrium quantity of gasoline demanded per year declines to Q_2. The total decline in the annual consumption of gasoline of ΔQ gallons per year reflects the combined income and substitution effects of the tax-induced price increase.

The compensated demand curve, labeled D_C, is used to isolate the substitution effect of the tax-induced price increase. Along the compensated demand curve, quantity demanded declines by the amount ΔQ_S, in response to the tax-induced price increase. The excess burden then can be calculated from the formula $\frac{1}{2}T\Delta Q_S$. The substitution effect can be predicted by using a compensated price elasticity of demand calculated for points along a compensated demand curve. Measuring the excess burden as the area of the triangle AE_2E_1 *overestimates* the actual excess burden when the income effect of a tax-induced price increase is not negligible.

COMPENSATED SUPPLY CURVES

The price elasticities of supply used to calculate the excess burden of taxes on input services are based on price elasticities of supply that reflect only the substitution effects of changes in wages and other input prices. The **compensated supply curve** of an input is one that reflects only the substitution effects of input price changes. Compensated supply curves for input services can be derived by eliminating the income effects of input price changes on the supply decisions of sellers.

For example, a labor supply curve shows that labor hours supplied vary with wage changes. An increase in wages results in a substitution effect that not only encourages persons to work more but also causes an income effect. The income effect of an increase in wages increases the demand for normal goods. If leisure is a normal good, the income effect serves to reduce hours worked. Removing the income effect of a wage increase therefore increases the labor supply response of workers to wage increases.

Similarly, removing the income effect of wage decreases dampens the labor supply response of workers, because a wage decrease decreases income and therefore decreases the demand for leisure, assuming that it is a normal good. As a result, the income effect encourages workers to work more when wages decline. Removing the income effect of wage declines therefore results in less work than otherwise would be the case. Compensated labor supply curves are more elastic than regular labor supply curves, as shown in Figure 11A.3. In Chapter 13, compensated labor supply curves are used to determine the excess burden of taxes on labor income.

Figure 11A.3 ✦ A Compensated Supply Curve for an Input

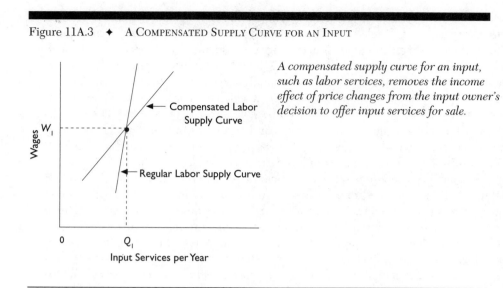

A *compensated supply curve for an input, such as labor services, removes the income effect of price changes from the input owner's decision to offer input services for sale.*

12

BUDGET DEFICITS AND
GOVERNMENT DEBT

LEARNING OBJECTIVES

After reading this chapter you should be able to

1. Discuss the magnitude of the federal government budget deficit and issues involved in measuring the deficit and its impact on interest rates, national saving, economic growth, and resource use.
2. Define the net federal debt and explain how growth of the debt is related to the federal budget deficit.
3. Describe the ownership pattern of the national debt and the distinction between external and internal debt, and the burden of the debt.
4. Examine economic issues relating to borrowing by state and local governments.

*E*ach year since 1970, the federal government has spent more than it has collected in receipts from taxes and other sources of revenue. In fiscal year 1993, the federal budget deficit was a whopping $254.9 billion dollars—an amount equal to 4 percent of GDP that year. Nearly one of every five dollars spent by the federal government in fiscal 1993 was borrowed!

As the federal government has run up deficits during the past 35 years, its debt has increased. Each year the federal government fails to balance its budget, its debt increases. As of 1993, the national debt was more than $3 trillion and growing as a percent of GDP. The fact is that borrowing has become a major means of financing federal government spending. Although politicians have ranted and raved about the deficit and passed legislation to control it, borrowing continues to be used as a major method of public finance. Borrowing to finance government spending postpones the burden of taxation to the future and requires that more of future tax revenue must be allocated to pay interest on government debt.

Congress passed its first deficit control legislation, the Balanced Budget and Emergency Deficit Control Act, in 1985. When it became clear that the goals of the 1985 act could not be met in 1987, the legislation, commonly called the Gramm-Rudman-Hollings Act was revised and the date at which the budget was supposed to be balanced was moved up several years. The revised goal was to have a balanced budget by fiscal year 1993. Then, in 1990 the budget deficit hit $221 billion, when its target level under the new legislation was supposed to be only $100 billion! It was becoming clear that no way existed for the budget to be balanced by 1993. So, Congress passed the Budget Enforcement Act of 1990, which completely modified the old Gramm-Rudman-Hollings Act and sought to balance the budget by sometime after 1995.

In 1993 it was Bill Clinton's turn to tackle the deficit. Clinton had run on a platform of deficit reduction. Through his leadership, the Congress (by a scant margin of one vote in the Senate) passed the Omnibus Budget Reconciliation Act of 1993, a major change in U.S. fiscal policy that increased tax rates, mainly for upper income Americans, and enacted spending cuts. However, the 1993 legislation was not designed to eliminate the federal budget deficit. Instead the new law had the more modest goal of reducing the rate of growth of the deficit. As a result of the new legislation the federal budget deficit is expected to be around $170 billion in 1996 but unless a major change occurs in federal budget policy during the interim, the deficit is expected to increase again to around $200 million by 1999. So, despite recent legislation, borrowing to finance federal outlays will remain with us through the rest of this century.

Why all the concern about the federal budget deficit and the national debt? What, if anything, is wrong with government borrowing as a means of financing its activities? This chapter investigates both the current and the future impact of government budget deficits and increased government debt on the well-being of citizens. We examine the possible impact of the federal budget deficit on interest rates, savings, private investment, and future living standards.

In recent years federal government budget deficits in the United States have not been incurred to stabilize the economy. In fact, in late 1990, when it was clear that the U.S. economy was drifting into a recession, Congress enacted new legislation designed to reduce the deficit—exactly the opposite action required to stabilize an economy that was contracting! Fiscal policy, the use of the government budget to stabilize the economy, has been dominated in recent years by long-term concerns about the impact of the deficit on national saving and future living standards. The deficits of the 1980s were structural in the sense that they represented basic imbalances between federal revenues and spending. These deficits would have persisted even if the economy were at full employment. For example, the U.S. economy was operating at close to full employment in 1988 when the unemployment rate was below 5.5 percent for most of the year. However, during that year the federal government incurred a deficit of $155 billion. In fiscal year 1993, the Congressional Budget Office estimated that if the economy were operating at full employment, the actual federal deficit would still be a whopping $215 billion, down only slightly from the actual $254 billion deficit that year.

This chapter also examines budget imbalances in state and local governments. The discussion concentrates on the implications of borrowing by nonfederal governments to finance capital expenditures.

THE FEDERAL BUDGET DEFICIT

As pointed out in Chapter 10, borrowing is an alternative to current taxation as a means of financing government expenditures. A **budget deficit** is the excess of government outlays over receipts taken in from taxes, fees, and charges levied by government authorities. Figure 12.1 plots federal government outlays and federal receipts from 1950 to 1993. As you can see from the graph, outlays have exceeded receipts in every year since 1970. The federal government has had to borrow to cover

Figure 12.1 ✦ FEDERAL BUDGET OUTLAYS, RECEIPTS, AND DEFICIT, 1950–1993[a]

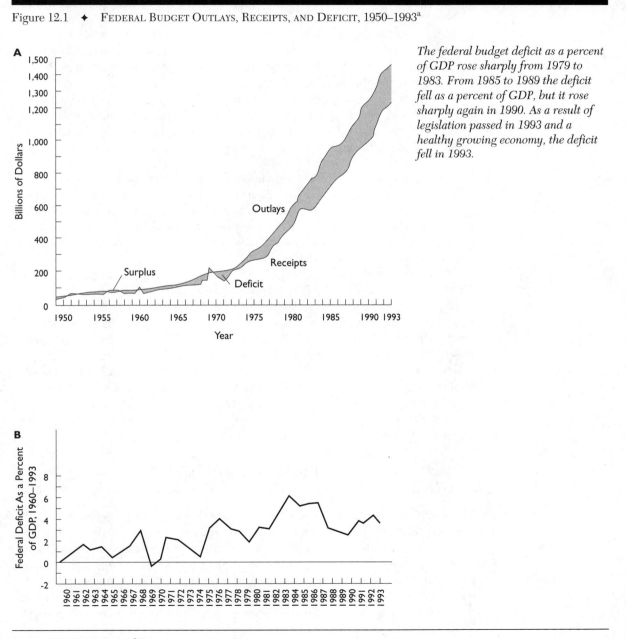

The federal budget deficit as a percent of GDP rose sharply from 1979 to 1983. From 1985 to 1989 the deficit fell as a percent of GDP, but it rose sharply again in 1990. As a result of legislation passed in 1993 and a healthy growing economy, the deficit fell in 1993.

Source: U.S. Department of Commerce

its deficit annually for the past 30 years. As the federal government has borrowed, its debt has grown and so have the portions of its annual expenditures that it has had to devote to paying interest on that debt. In 1993 the federal government allocated 14 percent of expenditures to paying interest on its debt.

From a public finance point of view, using borrowing to finance government expenditures implies lower current taxes for citizens in the year deficits are incurred but that greater portions of future tax revenue be used to pay interest on debt instead of being used to provide government services. If budget deficits persist for many years, current generations of taxpayers will shift the burden of taxation for government goods and services they enjoy to future generations of taxpayers. As you will soon see, the deficits also can reduce living standards of future generations by contributing to reduced industrial investment and lower economic growth.

Rather than looking at the dollar amount of the deficit, most economists prefer to measure it as a share of GDP. GDP is a measure of the aggregate income generated from domestic production of goods and services. When we view the deficit as a percentage of GDP, we get a picture of the burden of federal borrowing as a share of aggregate income of the nation.

We have noted that the federal budget deficit has increased as a percentage of GDP since 1970. As is also shown in Figure 12.1, the share of total income borrowed by the federal government peaked at 5.2 percent of GDP in 1983. Although the deficit declined as a percentage of GDP between 1983 and 1989, it began to rise as a share of GDP again in 1990. However, as a result of a growing economy and new legislation, the deficit declined in 1993.

Concern about growing budget deficits in the 1980s led to passage of the Gramm-Rudman-Hollings Act (GRH) by Congress in 1985. This legislation was an attempt to establish a framework to reduce the federal budget deficit through permanent cancellation of federal budget authority to spend funds (called a sequester of funds) when the federal deficit in a given year was projected to exceed certain preestablished levels. The Budget Enforcement Act of 1990 modified the GRH rules and sought to reduce the budget deficit significantly by 1995. The new rules place annual "caps" on defense, international, and domestic spending and require that Congress operate on a "pay-as-you-go" basis for new programs and tax cuts. This system requires that taxes be increased or other spending cut whenever new spending programs are approved or existing taxes are cut.

Measuring the Deficit: The High-Employment Deficit and the Real Deficit

The size of the federal budget deficit in any given year is influenced by the fluctuations in economic activity normally associated with the business cycle. Federal government expenditures, such as those for unemployment insurance and public assistance to the needy, increase when unemployment rates go up. Tax revenues automatically increase with increases in employment and GDP. Corporate income tax collections are particularly sensitive to fluctuations in economic activity. Personal income tax collections, based on a progressive rate structure, also fluctuate with the level of economic activity.

The advantage of the automatic changes in the deficit with the level of economic activity is that they help stabilize the economy. They do so by directly adding to the demand for goods and services when unemployment rates increase. Tax revenues decline more than proportionately with increases in unemployment, thereby maintaining disposable income. Similarly, unemployment insurance payments enable workers who are laid off to maintain their spending until they go back to work.

In any given year, the budget deficit (or surplus) reflects *both* the level of economic activity in that year and the structural imbalance between revenues and expenditures. It is possible to adjust for the influence of fluctuations in economic activity by computing the **high-employment deficit** (or **surplus**). This calculation estimates the budget deficit (or surplus) that would prevail at a certain designated level of unemployment in the economy. The standardized level of unemployment is usually set at between 5 and 6 percent. To estimate this deficit, receipts and expenditures are adjusted accordingly to reflect their levels if 94 to 95 percent of those in the labor force were actually employed. The benchmark level of unemployment is selected arbitrarily; some might argue that other levels should be used as the benchmark to calculate the deficit. In any event, after removing the impact of the deviations of economic activity from the benchmark high-employment level, any remaining deficit reflects a basic structural imbalance between government revenues and expenditures.

From 1960 to 1980, the high-employment budget deficit averaged less than 2 percent of GDP. In 1988 the economy was close enough to full employment so that the actual deficit could be viewed as the high-employment deficit. In that year, the deficit amounted to 2.9 percent of GDP. A positive high-employment deficit indicates that increases in the level of economic activity alone are not sufficient to eliminate the deficit. In 1993, an estimate of the high employment deficit by the Congressional Budget Office placed its value at 3.3 percent of GDP, indicating the deficit was not the result of the sluggish economy and the deficit was providing considerable spending power to support economic activity at a time when the U.S. economy was expanding. Clearly, the federal deficit has been used in the United States primarily as a means of financing government expenditures rather than a means to stabilize the economy. Let's now examine the economic effects of using deficits as a means of government finance.

Inflation, Interest Rate Fluctuations, and the Real Deficit and Real Net Federal Debt Change

Like most economic magnitudes, the federal government deficit can be adjusted for inflation. The **real deficit** is a measure of the change in the federal debt after adjustment for the effects of inflation and changing interest rates on the real market value of the outstanding net debt. Like all debtors, the federal government benefits from inflation because a rising price level causes the real value of its previously issued outstanding debt to decline. Fluctuating interest rate levels also affect the market value of outstanding debt in a given year. When interest rates rise, the market value of outstanding debt issued at lower interest rates tends to fall. Similarly, decreases in market interest rates tend to increase the market value of outstanding debt previously issued at higher interest rates. It follows that rising interest rates contribute to decreases in real debt while falling interest rates contribute to increases in real debt.

This decline in the real market value of the net federal debt can be viewed as an increase in revenue to the federal government. The inflation tax is the reduction in the value of the government debt caused by increased prices. Rising interest rates also place a tax on the holders of the debt by further decreasing its value. This represents the decrease in wealth of the holders of government debt resulting from inflation and rising interest rates. In 1980, 1981, 1983, 1984, and 1987, the adjusted (real) deficit was smaller than the official deficit. However, in 1982, 1985, and 1986, the real deficit was actually greater than the official deficit. In those years, falling interest rates contributed to an increase in the value of the outstanding net federal debt. In 1987, rising interest rates resulted in a sharp drop in the market value of outstanding federal debt, and this, combined with the effect of inflation on the net federal debt, resulted in an adjusted deficit of only $13 billion compared with the official deficit of $157.8 billion. In 1990, inflation and rising interest rates reduced the value of outstanding federal debt by a whopping $97.8 billion. The real deficit in 1990 was therefore only $122.7 billion, while the nominal deficit was $220.5 billion.[1]

The federal budget deficit also excludes or fails to measure properly costs of credit and insurance programs that provide implicit subsidies to specific industries. For example, federal deposit insurance subsidizes the banking industry. Critics of the treatment of such programs argue that the liabilities that are incurred as a result of these programs should be added to the budget as expenditures annually instead of when they are actually paid out, as would be the case when a bank fails under deposit insurance.

While adjustments, such as those for inflation, substantially change the size of the deficit in any given year, their combined effect does not change the fact that deficits absorb loanable funds that could have been used for other purposes. For example, the inflation adjustment reduces the size of the deficit. However, the inflation adjustment also implies that a portion of the real value of savings by U.S. households and businesses who hold government debt has been transferred to government. The decrease in the deficit that results from the effects of inflation and rising interest rates that accompany it comes at the expense of a reduction in the real value of accumulated savings of U.S. citizens!

Recent analysis by the Congressional Budget Office suggests that unadjusted *changes* in the deficit as a percent of GDP provide a reliable measure of the impact of the federal budget deficit on the performance of the economy.[2] In particular, the

---

[1]Robert Eisner and Paul J. Pieper, "A New View of the Federal Debt and Budget Deficits," *American Economic Review* 74 (March 1984): 11–29. The data cited are revisions of the results presented in the 1984 article based on revised GDP deflators and made available to the author by Professor Paul Pieper of the University of Illinois at Chicago. The 1990 data are from the 1992 *Economic Report of the President* (Washington, D.C.: U.S. Government Printing Office, 1992).

[2]See U.S. Congress, Congressional Budget Office, *The Federal Deficit: Does It Measure the Government's Effect on National Saving* (Washington, D.C., U.S. Government Printing Office, March 1990).

CBO concludes that changes in the unadjusted deficit *as a percent of GDP* provide a good indication of the burden of deficit finance on the public. An increase in the deficit implies an increase in the share of GDP that is borrowed by the federal government while a decrease in the deficit signals a decrease in the share of GDP that is borrowed by the federal government. The next step is to examine the impact of government borrowing on national saving and the current, and more importantly, future performance of the U.S. economy.

C H E C K P O I N T

1. From a public finance point of view, what are the implications of a government budget deficit?
2. What is the high-employment deficit?
3. What is the real deficit?

ECONOMIC EFFECTS OF THE FEDERAL DEFICIT

The Deficit and Political Equilibrium

The mix and quantity of government services and investment depends, in part, on the means used to finance such government expenditures. By borrowing, rather than using taxes, to finance government activities, politicians can influence the willingness of voters to vote for increased spending. In other words, the political equilibrium quantity of government spending can be affected when we use deficit as opposed to tax finance. Deficits can affect both resource allocation (by influencing the types of government spending) and the overall size of the government sector in the economy. They also can influence prices and interest rates thereby affecting the distribution on income.

By using deficit finance we can keep taxes lower than they otherwise would be and still enjoy a given quantity and mix of government services. However, deficit finance also can allow higher government spending either for transfers or for purchases of goods and services without raising taxes. In fact, the federal deficits of the 1970s and 1980s were in part used to finance investments in military technology. However, much of the growth in federal spending since the 1970s (as shown in Chapter 1) is accounted for by an unprecedented increase in transfers both in-kind and as income support mainly to the elderly.[3]

Because borrowing to finance deficits postpones the burden of taxation to the future, it makes sense to use deficits to finance government investments that will

---

[3]During the 1980s when federal deficits were increasing as a share of GDP, spending on the elderly continued to grow, and it now absorbs nearly one-half of noninterest domestic spending by the federal government. See Rudolph G. Penner, "Federal Government Growth: Leviathan or Protector of the Elderly?," *National Tax Journal*, 44, 1 (December 1991): 437–450.

provide a stream of future benefits. This is efficient because taxes will then be distributed among future generations who will share the benefits of such government investments as roads, structures, transportation and communication networks, and environmental protection. Traditionally, nations have relied heavily on borrowing to finance wars and investments in military technology and equipment under the presumption that the removal of a threat to national security will provide future benefits for which future taxpayers should pay.

However, the deficits of the 1970s and 1980s were not incurred in a period of war or a period of significant increased national investment in infrastructure. Instead, much of the growth of spending that, in effect, was financed by the deficit, was in the form of transfers of income and services (especially medical services) to the poor and the elderly. These federal expenditures mainly financed consumption as opposed to investment. The ratio of taxes to GDP remained quite stable during this period at around 20 percent of GDP while federal outlays increased to 25 percent of GDP. The growing deficits of the 1970s and 1980s could be viewed as the outcome of a political system that satisfied the demand for increased federal transfer programs (many of which benefited the elderly) while preventing federal average tax rates from increasing significantly. It is possible that this growth in transfers could not have been approved through the political system if it were financed by increased taxes (or cuts in other types of spending) rather than by borrowing. Of course, it is difficult to pin down exactly what the deficit financed during this period because borrowing is not earmarked to any specific purpose. For example, use of the deficit also made it easier for both the Carter and Reagan administrations to gain political approval for increased government purchases for programs of investment in military technology.

The Effect of the Deficit on Credit Markets

The economic effects of the federal budget deficit on the economy also depend on how it affects interest rates, national savings, and investment. The influence of the deficit on these economic variables is contingent on how the federal deficit influences the demand and supply of loanable funds in credit markets. A federal budget deficit adds to the national debt and, by doing so, increases the future interest costs to the federal government. Therefore, each year more and more tax revenues must be devoted to paying interest on the national debt instead of providing goods and services to citizens. Net interest paid by the federal government has increased from 6.8 percent of total expenditures in 1959 to 15 percent of expenditures in 1990. An annual deficit of $150 billion per year adds $12 billion in annual interest costs to the federal budget at 8 percent interest. In 1993 interest cost accounted for 14 percent of federal outlays.

The traditional view of the economic effects of federal government budget deficits hypothesizes that, other things being equal, the deficit contributes to higher interest rates. By doing so, the deficit can choke off private investment, thereby slowing the real rate of economic growth for the nation. Figure 12.2 shows that an increase in demand for loanable funds by the government to finance a deficit can increase market interest rates. The market demand for loanable funds is composed of the demand for credit by households, business firms, state and local governments,

Figure 12.2 ✦ Government Demand for Loanable Funds and the Market Rate of Interest

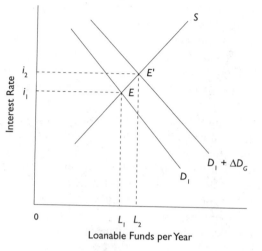

An increase in government demand for loanable funds to cover budget deficits shifts the demand curve from D_1 to $D_1 + \Delta D_G$. This increases the equilibrium market rate of interest from i_1 to i_2.

and the federal government. When the federal government increases the demand for funds, it can bid up interest rates because it borrows a significant amount of the total available funds per year. The initial equilibrium is at point E, where the interest rate is i_1 and the total quantity of funds borrowed is L_1.

As shown in Figure 12.2, an increase in government demand for funds shifts the market demand curve from D_1 to $D_1 + \Delta D_G$ and results in a new market equilibrium at E'. The market rate of interest increases to i_2, and the quantity of loanable funds supplied increases to L_2. The increase in the market rate of interest decreases the quantity of loanable funds demanded by business firms for investment. It also chokes off some borrowing by households to finance acquisition of such durable goods as automobiles and homes. At the same time, the higher interest rates encourage more saving, thereby decreasing private consumption in the current year.

Many, but not all, economists attribute the high real interest rates of the mid-1980s in the United States to the effect of the budget deficit on the demand for credit.[4] High interest rates therefore hurt consumers by making it more difficult to borrow funds to purchase homes and other durable goods. They harm workers by

---

[4]See Laurence H. Meyer, ed., *The Economic Consequences of Government Deficits* (Boston: Kluwer-Nijhoff Publishing, 1983). Some research, however, indicates little relation between government deficits and interest rates. One recent research study on the impact of federal borrowing on short-term interest rates found that increased borrowing had little effect on the market interest rates. See Gregory P. Hoelscher, "Federal Borrowing and Short-Term Interest Rates," *Southern Economic Journal* 50 (October 1983): 319–333.

decreasing the quantity of annual investment. This, in turn, decreases job opportunities. Reduced private investment also contributes to lagging worker productivity thereby resulting in lower wages than otherwise would be the case. Higher interest rates also increase the demand for U.S. dollars by foreigners who seek to invest dollars earned from foreign trade. This bids up the price of dollars compared with other currencies and makes U.S. goods less competitive in international markets.

The idea that the federal deficit can increase interest rates and choke off investment is not accepted by all economists. The classical economists of nineteenth century England believed that interest rates, current economic activity, and economic growth would be unaffected by the way the government financed its expenditures. David Ricardo, the famous English classical economist (1772–1832), argued that increased government borrowing can result in increased saving by forward-looking taxpayers. These taxpayers know that the government will have to raise taxes in the future to pay back what it borrowed and the interest on those funds. To prepare for the higher future tax burdens, Ricardo argued that they will increase their current saving by an amount exactly equal to the deficit. When the government runs a deficit, according to Ricardo, households will cut their consumption so they can save more and prepare for the higher future taxes they know will come.

If an increase in government borrowing to finance a deficit causes a sufficient increase in private saving to keep the level of interest rates in the economy fixed, **Ricardian equivalence** prevails. According to the idea of Ricardian equivalence, both tax finance and deficit finance have the same impact on current aggregate spending and future economic growth. If Ricardian equivalence prevails, an increase in government borrowing will be exactly offset by an equal reduction in consumption as households seek to save to finance higher future taxes. The result is no increase in aggregate current spending, no effect on interest rates, no crowding out of private investment, and therefore no reduction in future economic growth.[5] The idea of Ricardian equivalence has been advanced in recent years by the American economist Robert Barro of Harvard University.

It's easy to see why increased private saving as a result of deficit finance can offset the impact of increased demand for funds on interest rates as the government borrows more to finance its deficit. The graph in Figure 12.3 shows that the increase in government borrowing to cover the deficit increases the demand for loanable funds. However, as a direct result of this borrowing, the supply of savings increases from S to S' to provide funds for higher taxes anticipated in the future. The increase in the supply of loanable funds results in a new equilibrium at point E''. At that point, an additional ΔL dollars of loanable funds are made available per year to finance private investment. The equilibrium amount of loanable funds is now L_3 dollars per year. If these extra funds exactly equal the amount of funds required to finance the deficit, the interest rate under the equilibrium is i_1, the initial level.

Thus, this view concludes that government borrowing to cover deficits does not increase the market rate of interest. It causes no crowding out of private investment

---

[5]See John J. Seater, "Does Government Debt Matter? A Review," *Journal of Monetary Economics* 16 (July 1985): 121–131.

Figure 12.3 ✦ Ricardian Equivalence: Deficits Do Not Affect Interest Rates

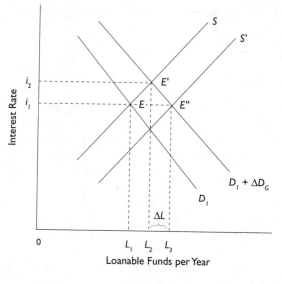

Under Ricardian equivalence, the increase in government borrowing to finance the deficit is exactly offset by an increase in annual private savings to pay the taxes necessary in the future to retire the debt. Consequently, the interest rate does not increase above its initial level i_1.

or of consumer borrowing for durable goods. The deficit does not matter according to this view.[6] This means that changes in the deficit will not affect aggregate demand, because changes in government borrowing will be offset by changes in private saving.

Empirical research on the impact of deficits on saving suggests that an increase in saving occurs as a result of budget deficits in the United States. However, the research also indicates that the increase in saving does not appear to offset exactly the increase in government borrowing, which implies that upward pressure on interest rates is likely as a result of government deficits.[7] Increased private saving caused by government deficits can lead to increased bequests, or intergenerational transfers, between citizens who are living now and their heirs. The increased saving by those who currently pay taxes, resulting from deficit-induced saving, allows them to increase their own voluntary private bequests to their children, beyond the amounts that would be possible if tax finance were used. These bequests help the future generation to pay the higher taxes that will be necessary to cover the interest payments

---

[6]Considerable empirical evidence supports this view. See Charles I. Plosser, "Government Financing Decisions and Asset Returns," *Journal of Monetary Economics* 9 (May 1982): 325–353; and John J. Seater and Roberto S. Mariano, "New Tests of the Life Cycles and Tax Discounting Hypotheses," *Journal of Monetary Economics* 15 (March 1985): 195–215.

[7]See Michael J. Boskin, "Consumption, Saving, and Fiscal Policy," *American Economic Review* 78, 2 (May 1988): 401–407.

on the debt in the future. Similarly, the reduced tax burden on the current generation, made possible by debt finance, decreases the likelihood that these taxpayers, in their old age, will need transfers from their children. The compensating intergenerational transfer therefore decreases the burden of the debt on the future generation.[8]

Deficit, National Saving, and Economic Growth

A nation's rate of economic growth, the expansion of its potential to produce goods and services, depends on investment. Investment requires a sacrifice of current consumption so that the resources used to produce goods for today can be reallocated to the production of capital goods. When we save more, we can allocate more resources to the development of new technology, the production of new machinery and to investment in people through education. The more we save today, the greater our future rate of growth of output. Conversely, the less we save, the smaller our future potential to produce expand.

National saving is the sum of personal saving by households, business saving, and saving by the government sector. The government sector contributes to an increase in national saving when it spends less than it taxes in. In other words, in order for government to help increase national saving, it would have to run a budget *surplus* instead of a deficit. When the government sector runs a deficit, it spends more than it takes in and therefore must borrow instead of save.

The net contribution of the government sector to national saving is the combined deficit or surplus of the federal government and all state and local governments. When the government sector runs a deficit, it contributes to a decline in national saving. In effect, a government deficit amounts to negative saving that absorbs loanable funds rather than making them available for investment.

Table 12.1 shows national saving and its components as a percent of aggregate income (using gross national product as a proxy), on average for the periods 1950–1979 and 1980–1991. National saving declined from an average of 16.3 percent of GNP between 1950 and 1979 to 14 percent of GNP over the 1980–1991 period. Business saving, which consists of capital consumption allowances and undistributed corporate profits, was actually higher in the 1980s than it had been in the past. Household savings declined substantially as a percent of GNP and amounted to only 3.7 percent of GNP on average over the 1980–1991 period. However, a major contributor to the reduction in our national savings rate has been the government sector, which was a net borrower. The negative saving of the government sector actually increased from an average of −0.4 percent of GNP from 1950 to 1979 to −2.5 percent of GNP. The negative savings rate of the government sector in the 1980s largely reflected federal deficits. During the same period state and local governments in the aggregate actually ran surpluses, therefore contributing to national saving.

Why worry about reduced savings? A reduced supply of savings can contribute to higher real interest rates and lower economic growth. If we save less we will devote

---

[8]See Robert J. Barro, "Public Debt and Taxes," in *Federal Tax Reform*, ed. Michael J. Boskin (San Francisco: Institute for Contemporary Studies, 1978).

Table 12.1 ✦ NATIONAL SAVING AS A PERCENT OF GNP

| | SAVING (AVERAGE PERCENT OF GNP FOR PERIOD) | |
SOURCE OF SAVINGS	1950–1979	1980–1991
Households	5.0	3.7
Businesses[a]	11.8	12.8
Government[b]	−0.4	−2.5
Gross National Saving	16.3	14.0

[a]Gross saving includes corporate retained earnings and capital consumption allowances to replace depreciated equipment and structures.
[b]Includes federal, state, and local governments.
Note: Figures may not add because of rounding.
Source: U.S. Department of Commerce.

less of our current production to investment, which is the driver of future economic growth. Lower economic growth causes a slowdown in the rate of improvement of living standards. U.S. savings rates have been much lower than those of other industrial nations in recent years. For example, while the U.S. national savings rate from 1975 to 1987 averaged 15 percent, Japan's saving rate exceeded 30 percent over the same period! One argument for reducing the deficit is therefore that a reduction in the national deficit, other things being equal, will decrease the negative contribution of the federal government to saving.

One recent estimate suggests that a reduction in the federal deficit equal to 1 percent of GDP could raise the standard of living, measured by output per person, by between 1 and 7 percent by the middle of the twenty-first century.[9] The federal deficits averaged 4.5 percent of net national product (which is gross national product less depreciation) in the 1980s. In the 1970s, the federal deficit averaged only 2 percent of net national product. The rising share of GDP absorbed by the government deficit reduces national saving and lowers future living standards, other things being equal.

By absorbing saving that could otherwise be used for private investment, the federal deficit therefore can slow economic growth and reduce the rate at which our standards of living improve.

The Incidence of Deficit Finance in the United States

What is the incidence of deficit finance? If, as many economists believe, deficit finance bids up real interest rates and contributes to both a reduction in national saving and a reduction in national investment, then deficit finance contributes to a slowdown in capital formation and economic growth. This, in turn, implies that the rate

---

[9]Congressional Budget Office, "The Federal Deficit."

of growth of income will be slower in the future so that future taxpayers (younger people) will have lower future incomes than otherwise would be possible. Unfortunately, these young people also will be subject to higher taxes and greater portions of their tax payments being used to finance interest costs of growing federal debt. Thus, deficit finance is likely to redistribute the burden of finance government outlays from the current generation to future generations of taxpayers. If, on average, these taxpayers have lower income than the current generation, in part because of the undesirable effects of taxes on economic growth, then this incidence could be regressive.

However, to get a full picture of the incidence of deficit finance we also need to look at possible offsetting effects. One possible effect is suggested by the hypothesis of Ricardian Equivalence. If the current generation of taxpayers realizes that deficit finance implies higher taxes for themselves and their descendants, they could increase their current saving. This increase in saving increases the supply of loanable funds in credit markets and could offset both the negative saving of the deficit itself and any possible crowding out of private investment.

It also is possible that deficit finance permits a change in political equilibrium so that more government spending is allocated to investment in infrastructure and other spending that will yield a stream of benefits to future generations. Under these circumstances, even if private investment is crowded out as a result of higher interest rates, future economic growth rates need not decline as long as the government investment is at least as productive as the private investment that it displaces.

Government deficits also can contribute to increased government purchases that keep the economy from having severe recessions and help keep it on a steady path of economic growth near its potential. If this is the case, the deficit can actually increase private investment by contributing to economic stability. A stable economy with few severe downturns not only encourages investment by domestic producers but also can encourage inflow of foreign saving and investment.

Unfortunately, the federal deficits in the 1970s and 1980s in the United States appear to have allowed growth in federal transfers (mainly to persons older than 65) that encouraged consumption rather than investment. Therefore, unless a significant increase in national saving has occurred as a result of the deficit (which does not seem to be the case), the incidence of deficit finance will be a decline in future living standards.

C H E C K P O I N T

1. How can a government budget deficit cause the level of interest rates to rise for an economy?
2. What is Ricardian equivalence, and what does it imply about the impact of the government budget deficit on the economy and the desirability of borrowing versus raising taxes to finance government expenditures?
3. What is national saving, and how does the government sector of the economy affect the national savings rate?

THE FEDERAL BUDGET DEFICIT AND INTERNATIONAL TRADE

When a government budget deficit contributes to higher interest rates it also can adversely affect a nation's balance of international trade. High real interest rates in the United States resulting from higher demand for loanable funds by the federal government to finance expenditures also increases the demand for U.S. dollars by foreigners. When interest rates are high relative to those elsewhere in the world, foreigners seek to acquire dollars to purchase U.S. government securities and other U.S. financial assets. The increased demand for the dollar, other things being equal, puts upward pressure on its exchange rate in terms of such foreign currencies as the German mark and the Japanese yen. As the price of the dollar rises in terms of foreign currency, U.S. exports become more expensive to foreigners paying in their own currency and the prices of imported goods to U.S. buyers in dollars fall. As a result of changes in the exchange rate, the quantity of imported products demanded increases while the quantity of our exports demanded abroad falls. This can spell trouble for the U.S. economy as decreased economic activity in export industries and reduced sales in industries that face still competition from imports reduce income to owners of inputs used in those industries and decrease job opportunities for workers.

In the early 1980s the growing deficits of the federal government contributed to high real interest rates and a higher real exchange rate for the dollar. As this occurred, the U.S. balance of international trade became negative and expenditures on imports outstripped expenditures on exports. The higher budget deficit contributed to a higher international trade deficit throughout the 1980s.

The budget deficit also adversely affects the international balance of trade through its influence on disposable income in the United States. Because deficit finance uses borrowing instead of taxes to finance a portion of government expenditures, households have higher incomes after taxes than they would if all expenditures were tax financed. Thus they have more income to spend on all products including imported products. The greater volume of import purchases made possible by the budget deficit therefore also adversely affects the U.S. balance of international trade.

Finally, in the long run, a budget deficit also can contribute to decreased competitiveness of U.S. industries in international markets. Because budget deficits absorb savings that could otherwise be used to finance private business investment, they can slow the advance of new technology and the development and acquisition of cost-reducing new capital. If this occurs, it means that average costs of production for U.S. businesses could become higher than those of competing foreign industries that do invest in cost-saving devices and keep up with advances in technology. Private investment is a crucial factor in the improvement in industrial productivity. To the extent to which the federal budget deficit crowds out private business investment and is not used to finance government investment, future competitiveness of U.S. industries in global markets will be impaired as will the potential for the U.S. economy to grow by creating more and better jobs that contribute to higher future living standards.

THE NATIONAL DEBT

As of early 1994, the gross public debt of the U.S. Treasury amounted to $4.5 trillion. The debt of state and local governments amounted to nearly $1 trillion at the end of fiscal year 1991. Borrowing has been a major source of government finance, despite the controversy that surrounds its use. By far, the major share of controversy concerns the federal debt, rather than the debt of state and local governments. This is not merely because the federal debt is larger than the debt of state and local governments but also because of the real economic differences in the use, funding, and ownership pattern of the securities that are issued by federal governments and by state and local governing bodies. The problem of the federal, or central, government use of debt is considered next, followed by a discussion the use of debt as a means of finance for state and local governments.

The Magnitude and Structure of Federal Debt in the United States

The **net federal debt** is that portion of the debt of the federal government held by the general public, excluding the holdings of U.S. government agencies, trust funds, and the Federal Reserve banks. As of early 1994, the net debt totaled about $33 trillion, representing 53.5 percent of GDP. Between 1950 and 1970, however, the net federal debt, when expressed as a percentage of GDP on a fiscal year basis, declined steadily, from about 75 percent to approximately 22 percent. From 1970 to 1980, the monetary amount of debt outstanding rose astronomically, but debt, as a percentage of GDP, remained more or less constant.

The net federal debt has increased from 27 percent of GDP in 1980 to 53.5 percent of GDP by 1993. Figure 12.4 charts the net federal debt in the United States

Figure 12.4   ✦   NET FEDERAL DEBT: AMOUNT OUTSTANDING

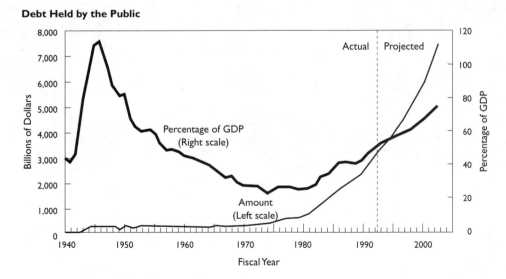

Although the total dollar value of the net federal debt has increased since 1950, net debt as a percentage of GDP has declined. Since 1980, however, the net debt has increased as a percentage of GDP and it is projected to rise in the future as a percentage of GDP.

Sources: Office of Management and Budget for 1940–1992; Congressional Budget Office projections, 1993–2003.

since 1950, both in monetary terms and as a percentage of GDP along with projection of the increase in the debt to 2003. As the chart shows, the monetary value of the net debt outstanding shot sharply upward in 1975. As a percentage of GDP, the net debt has increased much more slowly, but the net federal debt as a percentage of GDP has increased noticeably since 1980 as a result of the large budget deficits of the 1980s. Increased use of debt finance could have contributed to rising price levels, which, in turn, served to decrease the real value of the debt.

The total volume of the gross federal government debt outstanding at any point in time reflects the previous and current budget deficits and the accumulated interest burden on the securities issued to cover those deficits. To retire the public debt—that is, to allow existing issues of securities to be paid off at their maturity without replacing them with additional debt obligations of the federal government—would require that the federal government budget be operated at a surplus for a considerable number of years.

A budget surplus, if run at modest levels so as to permit the government to continue its functions, would have to be continued for many, many years to retire public debt. At the extreme, it would take about three full years of government spending, at its current level, to retire the debt in full. There is, however, little reason even to consider the retirement of the full amount of the debt outstanding; and there is, in fact, good reason for the government to continue to use borrowing as a means of finance. As a practical political matter, it is unlikely that any significant reduction in the gross debt outstanding could occur in a relatively short period (less than ten years) without significant reduction in the levels of services provided by the federal government. The main issues concern the size of the debt and the costs involved in borrowing as an alternative to current taxation. The influence of the public debt on inflation is another controversial issue.[10]

Ownership Pattern of the Federal Debt

To help evaluate the costs of the debt, it is useful to study the structure of the federal debt in terms of its ownership pattern. Table 12.2 presents data on the gross federal debt of the U.S. Treasury, by type of holder, as of the end of fiscal year 1992. As of that period, the total federal debt outstanding was $4 trillion, of which 17.6 percent was held by government agencies and trust funds and 7.4 percent by the Federal Reserve System. The remaining 75 percent was held by various financial institutions and private investors, and represents the net debt of the U.S. Treasury. The federal debt held by the Federal Reserve banks represents acquisitions of such securities as part of the Federal Reserve's open market activities. Such holdings represent an exchange of interest-bearing securities of the U.S. government for noninterest-bearing dollars. The Federal Reserve System purchases such securities in exchange for deposits in the various Federal Reserve banks, which become part of the commercial banking system's reserve base.

---

[10]See Ansel M. Sharp and Phyllis S. Flenniken, "Budget Deficits: A Major Cause of Inflation?" *Public Finance Quarterly* 6 (January 1978): 115–127.

Table 12.2 ✦ GROSS PUBLIC DEBT OF THE U.S. TREASURY BY HOLDER, END OF FISCAL YEAR, 1992

HOLDER	AMOUNT OF DEBT (BILLIONS OF DOLLARS)	PERCENTAGE OF TOTAL
U.S. Government Agencies and Trust Funds	707.7	17.6
Federal Reserve Banks	296.4	7.4
Private Investors	2,998.6	75.0
Total	4,002.7	100.0

Source: U.S. Office of Management and Budget.

Table 12.3 shows the ownership pattern of the net debt outstanding as of September 1993. Commercial banks in the United States held 9.8 percent of the debt at that time while 10.2 percent was held by individual citizens of the United States, 19.21 percent by state and local governments, and 18 percent by foreigners or in international accounts. The remainder was held mainly by various types of financial institutions.

The net debt is mainly owed to U.S. firms and citizens. The portion of a government's indebtedness owed to its own citizens is an **internal debt.** Repayment of internal debt represents a redistribution of purchasing power from certain groups of citizens who pay taxes and other citizens who, in the past, have been creditors of the federal government. When a central government borrows mainly from its citizens, the opportunity cost is forgone consumption and investment in this country rather than from foreign sources. Nearly one-fifth of the net debt outstanding as of the end of December 1990 represented funds, or **external debt,** borrowed from abroad. When

Table 12.3 ✦ NET PUBLIC DEBT OF THE U.S. TREASURY BY HOLDER (PERCENT DISTRIBUTION), SEPTEMBER 1993

HOLDER	PERCENTAGE OF TOTAL
Commercial Banks	9.8
Money Market Funds	2.9
Insurance Companies	6.7
Other Companies	6.5
State and Local Governments	19.2
Individuals	10.2
Foreign and International	18.0
Other Investors	26.7
	100.0

Source: U.S. Department of Treasury.

SOCIAL SECURITY AND THE DEFICIT

The Budget Enforcement Act of 1990 requires that the Social Security trust fund surpluses, which are expected to grow substantially in the years to come, be excluded from the official measures of the federal budget deficit. The idea behind this special treatment of Social Security is that the surpluses of the Social Security trust funds should add to national saving rather than help finance other government programs. The deficit reduction targets through fiscal year 1990 specified by the Budget Enforcement Act of 1990 therefore exclude the surpluses from the Social Security trust fund accounts.

The idea that Social Security should be treated differently from other programs masks the fact that the Social Security programs are exactly like any other government program. When outlays under the program exceed receipts, as they did for much of the 1970s and the 1980s, the balance on the trust fund declines and the deficit of the Social Security programs contributes to an increase in demand for loanable funds by the government, thereby absorbing savings that could be used for other purposes. As we approach the year 2000, the Social Security trust funds will grow because receipts from the payroll tax will exceed pension benefits paid. The surplus on the funds will, in effect, be loaned to the Treasury, as it is used to purchase special Treasury securities. These special government securities are interest-bearing, and the interest earned on the securities also will contribute to growth in the Social Security trust fund balance. A surplus on the trust fund accounts decreases net borrowing from the public by the federal government. By offsetting the deficit of other government programs, the Social Security trust fund surplus decreases the negative saving by the federal government. The resulting decline in borrowing by the federal government allows saving that otherwise would be absorbed to finance government spending instead to be made available for private investment that can help increase productivity in private industry.

Some critics of the way the Social Security trust fund is handled argue that the balance in the fund should be invested directly in private industry through purchase of industrial stocks and bonds. But, in effect, the balance in the trust fund increases the amount of saving that can be invested in industry simply by reducing net borrowing from the public on the part of the federal government so, really, no need exists to invest the surplus directly in private securities. As long as the Social Security trust fund surplus reduces negative saving by the government sector of the economy, the amount of funds available for private investment will be increased and real interest rates will be lower than they otherwise would be, thereby increasing the quantity of funds demanded for new investment.

The growth of the Social Security trust fund is projected to continue through the year 2025. Thereafter, special Treasury securities are going to be cashed in to pay pensions for retirees who will become a growing portion of the U.S. population. When the trust funds are drawn down, the U.S. Treasury will have to repay, with interest, the special government securities held by the trust funds as they are cashed in to pay pension and other Social Security benefits to retirees. Where will the funds come from to do this? The answer is from taxes levied on households and business at that time. Unless the U.S. real GDP grows faster than the 2 percent per year projected now, this will require sharp increases in taxes or still larger deficits will accrue as the trust funds stop contributing to a reduction in net government lending from the public.

The answer to keeping future tax rates low or to preventing a sharp reduction in other government-provided goods and services, as government outlays for Social Security pensions and other benefits grow in the future, is increased savings today. The higher savings will allow more of our current resources to be allocated to investments that will increase future productivity and income. The rationale for Congress treating the Social Security trust fund separately therefore is to make sure that its surplus is dedicated to an increase in national saving rather than to help finance other government programs without the need to increase taxes. However, the real issue is to reduce the deficit so that negative saving by government can be reduced and private investment increased so as to increase the future rate of economic growth. It makes no difference whether the Social Security trust fund surplus is treated on budget or off budget. The fact is that its surplus, by itself, does contribute to an increase in national saving!

external debt is repaid, resources necessarily flow out of the nation, with a consequent loss in productive opportunities. The external debt varies with interest rates in the United States, relative to those that can be earned on funds abroad. For example, in June of 1980, when interest rates were relatively higher in the United States compared with other nations, the proportion of the net debt held by foreigners was 22 percent.

Because the bulk of the U.S. debt is an internal debt, many argue that repayment will not involve export of economic resources to foreign nations. Those who hold this view further argue that only little concern is justified about the total volume of the debt and its interest charge because any refunding or payment of interest on the debt at maturity involves merely a redistribution of purchasing power among citizens.

However, the portion of debt actually held by foreigners has grown rapidly since 1970. It could grow even faster in the future if the U.S. government runs balance of trade deficits, which puts dollars into the hands of foreigners, and if interest rates increase significantly above those available on competing securities (both foreign and domestic). Conversion of the national debt into one that is increasingly more external can have serious consequences for future growth opportunities in the United States if taxes must be raised to pay foreigners for past loans to the federal government. Under such circumstances, paying off the debt would involve outflows of funds and real losses in productive opportunities, rather than mere redistributive effects.

BORROWING BY STATE AND LOCAL GOVERNMENTS

The ability of central, or federal, governments to print money as a last resort makes the risk of default on the securities of such governments virtually nil (unless the government is overthrown). However, federal debt does remain subject to the risk of reduced value due to inflation. On the other hand, state and local governments, because they cannot monetize their debt, conceivably can default on their debt obligations. As a result, from the point of view of investors, state (or provincial) and municipal securities are inherently more risky than federal government securities. The interest that state and local governments must pay on their various security issues depends not only on the maturity of such issues but also on the risks of default as well as the risks of inflation.

Typically, the debt issues of various state and local governments are evaluated by private bond-rating services, according to their riskiness based on past repayment history. If a state or local government defaults on repayment of a security issue, its bond rating would be unfavorably affected. This will result in higher risk premiums, causing the cost of borrowing to that particular government to rise. Any given state or local government borrows such a small amount in the markets for loanable funds, at any given time, that it cannot influence interest rates as can the federal government.

Characteristics of State and Local Government Debt

Because the debts of state and local governments are marketed nationally, the particular governing body that issues the securities has no control over who purchases them. Much of the holdings of the debt of any particular state or local government is likely to be in the external debt category; that is, it is held by persons not residing in the government jurisdiction. This implies that issuance of the debt allows importation of funds, but repayment necessarily will involve a significant drainage of purchasing power out of the government jurisdiction in question. Thus, undue reliance on debt finance can result in a significant redistribution of future income away from residents of the locality, as tax revenues are used to pay creditors who reside in other jurisdictions. This makes borrowing by state and local governments somewhat similar to private borrowing by individuals, unlike borrowing by the federal government. Whereas the federal debt is largely an internal debt, the debt of state and local governments is largely external.

State and Local Debt Management

State and local government authorities must concern themselves with minimizing the interest burden on their debt and with the risk of default. State and local governments issue two broad types of securities to cover their debt: general obligation bonds and revenue bonds.

General obligation bonds are backed by the taxing power of the government that issues the securities, whereas **revenue bonds** are backed by the promise of revenue to be earned on the facility being financed by the bonds. Revenue bonds, typically, are used to finance roads and bridges and other facilities that will generate revenue through tolls and other forms of user charges. Investors often consider general obligation bonds to be safer than revenue bonds; as a result, general obligation bonds often can be floated at interest rates lower than those on revenue bonds of similar maturity for the same government unit. Nevertheless, some inherent risk does exist for investors, in that even general obligation bonds are subject to default risk. This is because reductions in state or local economic activity could make it difficult for these government units to raise the tax revenues necessary to repay their debts.

Long-term debt financing by state and local governments can be justified on the basis of the benefit principle for financing capital projects. Because capital expenditures by state and local governments involve the construction of facilities (roads, public institutions, and other structures) that will provide a stream of public services to future citizens of the state or municipality, it is reasonable to finance such expenditures through debt. This postpones the burden of taxation to future taxpayers, making particular sense in a community where citizens are mobile. Financing capital expenditures through current taxation results in the taxation of current residents who often will not be residents of the taxing jurisdiction when the capital facilities are completed. Debt finance, for this reason, allows collective approval for projects that will benefit future citizens, even though those citizens are not present to vote at the time of approval. Spreading the cost over time induces current residents to consider voting affirmatively for projects that they would not support if they knew they were to be taxed for the full cost in one year. For this reason, many state and local governments have separate capital budgets that involve projects financed exclusively by public borrowing.

BURDEN OF THE DEBT

Debt financing implies the sale of a security that bears the promise to pay interest over a given number of years and to return the principal loaned at the end of the given time period. No compulsion is involved in the sale of such securities. Instead, governments compete with other borrowers in the market for loanable funds. The government pays the going market rate of interest, adjusted for risk and maturity characteristics of the obligation that it issues. Accordingly, the issuance of government debt is similar to the sale of services that have the regular characteristics of private goods. Governments sell securities of various types and maturities (for example, savings bonds or U.S. Treasury bills) that compete with various private securities, such as commercial-bank savings deposits, savings and loan shares, bank acceptances, and corporate bonds.

A great deal of controversy exists concerning the appropriateness of debt finance by the various levels of government in the United States. The onerous burden of the debt on future generations is often cited as a reason to reduce the debt. On the other hand, many argue that, because the public debt is largely held by citizens of this country rather than by foreigners, no burden exists because it is an internal debt. That is to say, because we owe the debt to ourselves, payment of interest and principal of the debt merely transfers income from taxpayers to debt holders. What is the *burden* of the debt, and what are the relative advantages of debt financing compared with tax financing?

Burden of the Debt and Income Redistribution

No general agreement exists among economists concerning a definition of the burden of the debt. The **burden of the debt** is the redistributive effect of debt financing. Consider the impact of debt financing in elementary terms. When governments obtain funds to finance public expenditures by issuing debt, no compulsion is involved, unlike tax financing. Instead, securities issued by government authorities are purchased voluntarily by individual citizens, financial institutions, and other private economic units.

The individuals who purchase such securities surrender present consumption opportunities for future consumption opportunities, or they substitute public debt for private securities in their portfolio. They make this voluntary sacrifice because the return that they expect to receive on their forgone consumption exceeds their subjective estimate of the cost of sacrificing current consumption opportunities. At the same time, debt financing makes it unnecessary to increase current taxes, thereby avoiding the need to force citizens to curtail current consumption and saving. Under debt financing, private investment is "choked off" only to the extent to which increased government borrowing causes, by increasing the demand for credit, the general level of interest rates to rise. Thus, compared with tax financing, debt financing allows the current generation more private consumption opportunities over its lifetime than could be enjoyed if taxes were used.

To pay interest on the debt and return the principal, the government usually increases taxes. If so, other things equal, taxpayers in the future undergo reductions in consumption or saving. The increased tax revenues necessary to pay interest on the debt redistribute income from the taxpayers to the holders of public debt. Because the bulk of the federal debt in the United States is owed to U.S. citizens, its retirement would not represent a drain of resources from the country; therefore, the effect of such retirement would be to redistribute income among citizens.

Impact of the Debt on Future Generations

Some economists argue that the burden of the debt cannot be transferred to future generations but must be borne by the present generation, because resources are withdrawn from the private sector at the time the debt is created. This definition of burden implies that debt creation merely involves forgone private consumption in the current period. It neglects the fact that this sacrifice of consumption is completely voluntary on the part of the private economic units and is compensated by greater opportunities for future consumption, as a result of interest payments on the government securities.[11]

Under the assumption that the future generation must be taxed to pay the interest burden on the debt, that generation must undergo a real reduction of income, without the compensation of increased future consumption. In this sense, the burden of the debt does fall on the future generation; it bears the brunt of compulsory taxes. The burden of the debt, therefore, is a reduction in welfare for future taxpayers who do not hold or inherit government securities that are paid off in the future.[12] Future generations will pay more in taxes to pay interest instead of receiving government goods and services in return for those taxes. Interest amounted to about 14 percent of GDP in the early 1990s, so 14 cents of each dollar taxpayers paid were used to pay interest to holders of the net federal debt rather than to provide such services as roads and education.

Future generations also will suffer a reduction in their living standards as a result of the federal debt if past deficits cause interest rates to rise and reduce private investment. A reduction in private investment implies that the capital stock of the nation will grow more slowly than it would have otherwise. The effect will be lower economic growth for the economy. Because workers in the private sector will have less capital to work with than they otherwise would have, the productivity and therefore their incomes also will be lower. This implies a growing national debt and a reduction in future living standards. This burden, however, can be offset if increased saving by the current generation of taxpayers results from the use of deficit financing. According to this view of government deficits, this is a likely outcome and will result in increased bequests to future taxpayers that offset the burden of the debt.

The burden of the debt can also be offset if the revenue obtained from the issuance of public debt is used to finance projects that yield future benefits. On the

---

[11]See James M. Buchanan, "The Italian Tradition in Fiscal Theory," in *Public Debt and Future Generations,* ed. James M. Ferguson (Chapel Hill: University of North Carolina Press, 1964), 48–49.

[12]The interpretation has been emphasized by James M. Buchanan in *Public Principles of Public Debt* (Homewood, IL: Richard D. Irwin, 1958).

basis of the benefit principle, it might be viewed, in fact, as efficient to transfer the burden of present expenditures to future generations if it can be demonstrated that particular expenditures will benefit them. For example, it is reasonable to postpone until the future the burden of taxes for financing war, because the benefits of a successfully completed (that is, won) war will accrue to those living in the country in the future.

Unfortunately, the federal deficits of the 1970s and 1980s were not accompanied by new government investment. Instead, they helped finance federal entitlement programs, including Social Security pensions, Medicare, and Medicaid. These programs have important social benefits but they finance mainly consumption expenditures.

Use of Borrowing to Finance Capital Expenditures of Nonfederal Governments

The transference of the burden of finance to the future has particular relevance for capital expenditures undertaken by state and local governments because the makeup of the population in these areas changes over time. Such changes are due not solely to the life cycle of individuals but also because individual citizens move in and out of the area. This implies that the population that receives the benefits of current capital expenditures (say, a new sewer system or a new school) might be, in the future, a completely different aggregation of people compared with those who currently live in the area.

Therefore, on the basis of the benefit principle, it is legitimate to finance projects that yield the bulk of their benefits in the future, and in a particular local area, through borrowing. The taxes levied to pay the interest and principal on the debt can coincide, more or less, with the benefits flowing from the project. Those actually receiving the benefits—the individuals of the future tax base—therefore also will bear the tax cost of financing the projects. The postponement of taxes as a result of debt issue is often referred to as "pay-as-you-use" finance. Citizens are taxed for capital expenditures at the time the expenditures yield benefits, and not at the time the capital expenditures are initiated. The principle underlying this method of finance is similar to that of financing an automobile or a home through a loan. Many local governments have special capital budgets that list expenditures to be financed by the issuance of public debt.

CHECKPOINT

1. What is the net federal debt, and how much of it is an external debt?
2. What is the possible future burden of the net federal debt?
3. Under what circumstances can borrowing by state and local governments contribute to improved resource allocation?

Should the Federal Government Run a Surplus as We Move Toward the Twenty-First Century?

National saving in the United States remains low by international standards. Little increase in private saving occurred either in the 1980s or so far in the 1990s to offset the negative effects of large federal deficits on the national savings rate. Many economists urge rapid elimination of the federal deficit as we approach the twenty-first century to make the funds it currently absorbs available for private investment. If the federal government were actually to start running a surplus, it would make a positive contribution to our national savings rate. A federal budget surplus would reduce the net federal debt and put downward pressure on interest rates. Unless a budget surplus causes private saving to decline (as would be the case if Ricardian equivalence held), a budget surplus would increase national saving.

A federal budget surplus can offset low household savings rates in the United States and therefore contribute to an increase in the availability of funds for private investment and lower interest rates. A compelling argument in favor of running a budget surplus is to help increase national saving to pay Social Security pensions in the twenty-first century. As the proportion of the population that is retired increases in the twenty-first century, additional tax revenue will be required to pay Social Security pensions. Unless the economy grows more rapidly than the 2 percent rate of income increase anticipated in the near future, higher tax rates will be needed to finance the pensions of future retirees. Increased investment made possible by increasing our savings through a budget surplus can help increase the future growth rate and make it possible to generate tax revenue without sharply increased tax rates after the year 2025.

Summary

In recent years, budget deficits have been common for the federal government in the United States. A deficit reflects an imbalance between expenditures and revenues. In any given year, the actual budget deficit reflects the impact of unemployment rates on revenues and expenditures. However, in recent years, a deficit would have prevailed even if the economy were at a high level of employment for which no more than 5 to 6 percent of the labor force is unemployed. The high-employment deficit is a structural imbalance that would prevail between expenditures and revenues even if the economy were at its high-employment level. Deficits increase the federal debt and also can contribute to higher market interest rates and increased inflation.

Borrowing to finance public expenditures postpones the tax burden to the future. The net federal debt (that held by the public, excluding government and Federal Reserve holdings), as a percentage of GDP, is currently in the range of 40 percent.

The federal debt is largely internal, in the sense that it is owed mainly to U.S. citizens and institutions. Repayment of the federal debt, therefore, does not imply a significant drain of either capital or productive opportunities out of the nation. Repayment of the debt represents mainly a redistribution of income within the nation, away from taxpayers and toward citizens who hold government securities.

Because state and local governments lack the power to create money, the securities of these governments are inherently more risky to investors than are those of the federal government. State and local debt holdings are likely to be more external to the issuing jurisdiction than are federal debt holdings, implying that repayment of such debt might withdraw significant amounts of resources to other jurisdictions.

The burden of the government debt can be defined as the decrease in well-being of citizens who are taxed to pay off the principal and interest on past debt. It can be argued that no burden is incurred until the debt is repaid, because purchasers of government securities lend money to the government voluntarily without compulsion. Presumably, they are compensated for any lost consumption or investment opportunities by the rate of interest that they receive. The burden of the debt on future generations can be offset if current taxpayers increase saving to pay taxes anticipated in the future as a result of the deficit.

A Forward Look

Part Four considers tax theory and tax policy in detail. Major forms and methods of taxation in the United States are analyzed and detailed. Before beginning Part Four, students should be certain that they have mastered the analysis in Part Three.

Important Concepts

Budget Deficit
High-Employment Deficit (or Surplus)
Real Deficit
Ricardian Equivalence
Net Federal Debt
Internal Debt
External Debt
General Obligation Bonds
Revenue Bonds
Burden of the Debt

Questions for Review

1. Explain why a budget deficit in a given year when the unemployment rate is 10 percent could be, in fact, a surplus in that year if the unemployment rate were 5 percent.
2. Why do some economists argue that budget deficits contribute to increased market rates of interest and reduced private investment?
3. Why has the real debt remained relatively constant in recent years, despite increased reliance on deficit financing by the federal government?
4. What is the significance of the distinction between internal debt and external debt?
5. Why is the actual net liability of the federal government much less than the gross public debt? How do increases in market rates of interest and increased inflation affect the burden of the debt?
6. In what sense does repayment of the federal debt constitute a redistribution of income among citizens?
7. How can deficit finance influence political equilibrium? Has deficit finance been associated with increased federal investment in the 1980s?

8. Why is repayment of state and local government debt more likely to drain purchasing power from citizens of state and local governments?
9. What are some of the advantages of financing capital expenditures with debt for governments with mobile populations?
10. In what sense does the use of debt financing by a national government impose a burden on the future generation? How does debt financing increase the "wealth" of the current generation compared with tax financing? Under what circumstances will the burden of the debt on future generations be offset?

Problems

1. The current market rate of interest is 8 percent. At that rate of interest, businesses borrow $500 billion per year for investment and consumers borrow $100 billion per year to finance purchases. The government is currently borrowing $100 billion per year to cover its budget deficit. Derive the market demand for loanable funds, and show how investors and consumers will be affected if the budget deficit increases to $200 billion per year. Show the impact on the market rate of interest, assuming that taxpayers do not anticipate any future tax increases. How would your conclusion differ if taxpayers fully anticipate future tax increases?
2. Suppose 90 percent of the net federal debt was acquired by foreign investors. How would this affect the burden of the debt for U.S. citizens?
3. The classical economists argued that budget deficits would not affect current spending. Suppose the federal government increases its purchases of goods and services by $100 billion this year. Classical economists, who believe in the idea of Ricardian equivalence, would argue that the increase in federal spending would have no effect on aggregate spending in the economy and no effect on private investment. Explain how a $100 billion increase in spending financed by a deficit can have no effect on the economy other than a reallocation of resources from private to government use.
4. Suppose the federal government not only balances its budget but also begins to run a budget surplus. Trace out the implications of a government budget surplus on the following:
   a. national saving
   b. interest rates
   c. private investment

d. economic growth

e. future living standards

When tracing out the effects of the budget surplus make sure that you list the assumptions you are making.

Suggestions for Further Reading

Barro, Robert J. "Public Debt and Taxes." In *Federal Tax Reform,* edited by Michael J. Boskin, 189–209. San Francisco: Institute for Contemporary Studies, 1978. A readable summary of some of Barro's ideas on debt versus taxes.

Buchanan, James M. *Public Principles of Public Debt.* Homewood, IL: Richard D. Irwin, 1958. An analysis of the burden of debt.

Schultze, Charles L. "Of Wolves, Termites, and Pussycats or, Why We Should Worry about the Budget Deficit," *The Brookings Review* (Summer 1989): 26–33. A good review of arguments on the pros and cons of reducing the federal deficit.

U.S. Congress, Congressional Budget Office. *The Federal Deficit: Does It Measure the Government's Effect on National Saving?* Washington, D.C.: U.S. Government Printing Office, March 1990. A discussion of issues relating to the economic effect of the deficit and the federal debt on national savings rates and economic growth.

Yellen, Janet L. "Symposium on the Budget Deficit." *Journal of Economic Perspectives* 3, 2 (Spring 1989): 17–21. This issue of the journal has a number of articles on the budget deficit. The article by Yellen summarizes the ideas of the articles in this issue.

Taxation:

Theory and

Structure

IV

The Theory of
Income Taxation

When you mention taxes to most people, what immediately comes to mind is "April 15." That's the date the federal income tax returns and income tax returns for most states in the nation become due. Taxes on personal income represent the dominant source of revenue for the federal government in the United States. Personal income taxes accounted for 40 percent of federal revenue in 1993. Since 1960, personal income taxes have become an increasingly important source of revenue for state governments. As of 1993, all but five states in the United States used a personal income tax levied on individual incomes, and income from personal income taxes accounted for 30 percent of state government revenue. The personal income tax has enjoyed strong political support in the United States.

Direct taxation of personal income is a relatively new phenomenon in the United States. Prior to 1913, the major source of revenue for the federal government was the customs duty, or tariffs. Although an income tax was utilized briefly from 1861 to 1872 on the national level, as an emergency measure during the Civil War, it did not become a permanent feature of the federal tax structure until 1913. An attempt in 1894, by President Grover Cleveland, to introduce the income tax on the national level failed when the U.S. Supreme Court declared the enacted law unconstitutional. In 1913, a constitutional amendment was adopted that empowered Congress to levy taxes on both personal and business incomes. The initial income tax passed under the new amendment exempted the first $3,000 of income from taxation for a single person and the first $4,000 for a married person. All income above this exemption, and up to $20,000, was taxed at the proportional rate of 1 percent, with surcharges ranging as high as 7 percent for higher levels of income. The highest tax rate was applied to taxable income in excess of $500,000. The newly enacted income tax provided a significant amount of revenue to finance military expenditures for World War I.

At the state level, experience with an income tax had been unfavorable prior to the early twentieth century. Although six states had experimented with income taxation in the nineteenth century, the tax proved both unpopular and difficult to administer. The first successful income tax on the state level was instituted by Wisconsin in 1911. The Wisconsin tax law featured improved administrative techniques that facilitated equitable collection of the tax. The income tax was soon adopted by other states.

The complexities of the tax code are not discussed in this chapter. Instead, the chapter defines income from an economic point of view and assumes that *all income, regardless of its source or use, is taxed at the same rate.* The consequences of a flat-rate, or proportional, income tax in labor markets and markets for investible funds are traced. It is assumed that taxes on personal income are the only taxes being utilized by government authorities and that a fixed, proportional rate of taxation is applied to income, with no exclusions, exemptions, or deductions allowed from the tax base.

COMPREHENSIVE INCOME: THE HAIG-SIMONS DEFINITION

Two preliminary steps are necessary before any comprehensive definition of income can be developed. First, the taxpaying unit must be selected. In the case of a personal income tax, that unit must be the individual. All individuals who earn income, regardless of age or the amount of income earned, will be subject to the tax. No separate tax on business income is necessary. All businesses are owned by individuals. Business income, therefore, in one form or another (profits, dividends, retained earnings), accrues to the person(s) who own the businesses. In the case of corporate income, a comprehensive personal income tax would require that all income of the corporation be allocated to shareholders in proportion to their ownership of shares.

The second step is to define the time period relevant for measuring personal income. The concept of income is meaningless unless a time period is specified. Income is a flow over time and will vary in amount with the time interval chosen. It makes no sense to say that an individual's income is $10,000, for this might mean $10,000 per hour, per day, per month, or per year. Income can even be defined over a person's lifetime. For tax purposes, the income of an individual is usually specified per year. A yearly accounting of income causes few problems in a system of income taxation that has a fixed, proportional rate, invariable over time.

In an economic sense, income is usually viewed as a measure of a person's power to purchase goods and services in a given year. As defined by Henry Simons, income is an indicator of "the exercise of control over the use of society's scarce resources."[1] Income can be spent, thereby converting purchasing power into consumption, or it can be stored for future use.

---

[1] Henry Simons, *Personal Income Taxation* (Chicago: University of Chicago Press, 1938), 49.

Income can be measured according to its sources or its uses. Sources of income, calculated from the beginning to the end of the accounting period, are earnings from the sale of productive services; transfers from either government or individuals; and increases in the value of assets owned by the individual. Uses of income include consumption, or purchase, of goods and services; taxes; donations; and saving. Increased holdings of assets over liabilities constitute saving. Positive saving in a given year stores income for future consumption. Saving represents an increase in a person's net worth. **Net worth** is the value of a person's assets held at any point in time less the value of a person's liabilities, or debts. A person's net worth, at any point in time, can be positive or negative.

In a given year, an individual might save negatively by borrowing funds or by liquidating some assets into cash and spending the cash on consumption items. In a given year, also, the dollar value of income received from sources must equal the dollar value of all uses of income.

Comprehensive income is the sum of a person's annual consumption expenditures and the increment in that person's net worth in a given year:

$$I = C + \Delta NW, \tag{13.1}$$

where I is annual income, C is annual consumption, and ΔNW is annual change in net worth. If a person saves more than is borrowed in a given year, the increment in net worth will be positive. It will be negative if the person draws on accumulated savings and spends the funds or if the person borrows more than is saved in a given year. Comprehensive income must be adjusted for inflation to accurately measure increases in potential purchasing power. As will be shown, inflation creates significant problems for administering an income tax. The concept of comprehensive income also is called the *Haig-Simons definition of income.*[2] Consumption includes all voluntary expenditures, including donations to charity and gifts.

Comprehensive income also can be defined in terms of its sources. Income is any payment or increment in a person's net worth that increases that person's ability to purchase or use goods and services in a given year. Table 13.1 shows three major sources of personal income: earnings from the sale of productive services, transfer payments received from government and private organizations or persons, and capital gains on existing assets currently held. **Capital gains** are increases in the value of assets over the accounting period.

Earnings include both income from labor and income from capital. Labor income is measured by wages and salaries from the sale of labor services; capital income represents the sum of interest and dividends and rents. Transfers are payments for which no good or service is received in return. Gifts are transfers, as are government payments to individuals such as cash assistance to the poor.

---

[2]See Simons, *Personal Income Taxation,* 49. Also see Robert Murray Haig, "The Concept of Income: Economic and Legal Aspects" in *The Federal Income Tax,* ed. Robert Murray Haig (New York: Columbia University Press, 1921), 7, reprinted in *Readings in the Economics of Taxation,* eds. Richard A. Musgrave and Carl S. Shoup, American Economic Association (Homewood, IL: Richard D. Irwin, 1959), 59.

Table 13.1 ✦ AN INCOME STATEMENT

SOURCES	USES
Earnings from Sale of Productive Services	Consumption
Transfer Payments Received	Taxes, Donations, and Gifts
Capital Gains (or Losses)	Savings (Increases in Net Worth)

$$\text{Sources} = \text{Uses}$$
$$\text{Earnings} + \text{Transfer Payments} + \text{Capital Gains} = \text{Consumption} + \text{Taxes, Gifts, and Donations} + \text{Saving}$$

Comprehensive income measures capital gains on assets as they accrue regardless of whether the asset is sold or exchanged; that is, it includes both realized capital gains and unrealized capital gains. *Realized capital gains* result when an asset is sold for cash or exchanged for another asset. *Unrealized capital gains* are increases in the value of assets in a given year that accrue on assets that are not sold for cash or exchanged for other assets. An example of an unrealized capital gain is the increase in the value of a corporate stock over a year that is not converted into cash by selling the stock or not exchanged for another asset. The logic behind including unrealized capital gains in income is that any increase in the value of assets, be it converted to cash or not, increases the individual's potential to purchase items in a given year. *Net capital gains* are capital gains minus capital losses. Comprehensive income deducts the transactions costs incurred in earning income. Thus, brokerage fees, costs of tools, uniforms, travel, and other costs of acquiring income would be the only legitimate deductions from the comprehensive tax base. The sources and uses of income are, therefore, as follows:

$$\text{Sources} = \text{Earnings} + \text{Transfers} + \text{Net Capital Gains} - \text{Cost of Acquiring Income,} \tag{13.2}$$

$$\text{Uses} = \text{Consumption} + \text{Gifts and Donations} + \text{Savings} - \text{Cost of Acquiring Income.} \tag{13.3}$$

Sources are always equal to uses. A comprehensive income tax is levied on all income, irrespective of its use or its source.[3] Table 13.1 summarizes the alternative ways of measuring comprehensive income. It also includes taxes as one of the uses of income. Of course, taxes represent compulsory payments that reduce a person's spendable income.

---

[3]For a more detailed analysis of the comprehensive base, see U.S. Department of the Treasury, *Blueprints for Basic Tax Reform* (Washington, D.C.: U.S. Government Printing Office, 1977), chap. 3.

Let's use a numerical example to illustrate how comprehensive income would be computed. Suppose that, in a given year, a person earns $20,000 from the sale of labor services and also earns $1,000 in interest from certificates of deposit, which represent funds loaned to a bank. The total annual earnings for this person therefore equal $21,000. The person also receives $2,000 as a gift from his parents that year to help with his expenses. He also was unemployed for one month during the year, during which time he received $800 in unemployment insurance payments from the government. Both the $2,000 gift and the $800 unemployment insurance payments would be regarded as transfers and therefore would be included in his comprehensive income. Total transfer income for the person, therefore, would be $2,800. In addition, the person earns capital gains of $1,500 and incurs $600 in capital losses from stock market transactions. His net realized capital gains therefore are $900 that year.

Suppose the value of the stock he owns, but does not sell, falls by $500. He therefore would incur unrealized capital losses of that amount on unsold stock. Over the same year, market appraisal indicates that the value of this person's home has increased by $2,000. The net unrealized capital gains therefore would be $2,000 − $500 = $1,500. Adding all the sources of the person's income indicates that his comprehensive income is $26,200. This example assumes that the costs of earning income have already been netted out of earnings and capital gains.

The uses of his annual income also must be $26,200. Suppose the person pays $2,500 in taxes and saves $2,500 of his income. Assuming that he does not give monetary gifts to other persons and that his donations to charity are also zero, his consumption this year will be $21,200.

Problems of Measurement

A means of measuring income, either from the sources side or the uses side, must be developed before any income tax can be implemented. Most systems of accounting use the sources side as the base for measurement. The Haig-Simons definition of income would require that both realized and unrealized capital gains be included in income; a mechanism would have to be developed to measure increments (and decrements) in the value of all capital assets held by individuals as these gains or losses accrue. Whatever system might be developed also has to adjust these gains for inflation, so that only real increases in the potential to consume would be included in income. Although measurement of unrealized gains might be relatively easy for assets that are traded frequently in secondary markets, such as stocks and bonds, administrative problems would make it difficult to measure such gains for all types of assets. For instance, devising an equitable system that could accurately measure annual gains and losses on such assets as real estate, antiques, jewelry, and livestock is probably impossible.

Another set of problems stems from adequately defining and delineating costs of earning income. Such expenses are analogous to the costs of running a business and might include such items as tools, work clothes, union dues, child care expense, and such legitimate travel expense as commuting costs to and from work. In other words, all those expenditures that are made neither for consumption nor for adding to net worth would be deductible, as expenses, from income.

Some tools that an individual uses in work also might be used for personal purposes and therefore would be considered consumption. The acquisition of skills in training programs or in continued education adds to the individual's human capital; thus, expenditures for such activities might be legitimately deducted from income, insofar as they will result in higher earnings that will be subject to taxation. However, education that produces human capital for home use is not legitimately deductible if the increased consumption enjoyment stemming from taking crafts courses and various "how-to-do-it" courses escapes taxation. Many arbitrary judgments would have to be made to decide which expenses are legitimate costs of earning income and which should be considered consumption or increases in net worth. One common method of avoiding these problems is to allow all taxpayers to take a lump-sum deduction, designed to cover basic expenses involved in commuting to work, buying work clothing, and so on.

As previously indicated, a comprehensive income tax would eliminate the need for a separate tax on corporate business income. In individual proprietorships and partnerships in the United States, business income is already declared as part of the owner's personal income. A comprehensive income tax would attribute all corporate income to shareholders, in proportion to their ownership of stock in the corporation, thereby eliminating the need for a separate corporate income tax.

Income-In-Kind

Income-in-kind is income in the form of goods and services rather than cash payments. One of the most serious problems involved in administering any type of income tax is the treatment of nonmonetary transactions. Difficult problems arise in measuring and tracing various forms of income-in-kind. Nonmarket transactions that increase consumption without increasing monetary earnings result in income-in-kind. For reasons of administrative feasibility, most tax codes make only feeble attempts to tax various forms of income-in-kind.

Income-in-kind often results from home production of goods and services. In this case, persons make things for themselves or provide themselves with services rather than purchasing those goods and services from others in markets. Individuals who build additions to their own homes, sew for their family, or provide such basic homemaking functions as cooking and cleaning produce valuable services that accrue to members of their households and that usually escape taxation. A comprehensive income tax base would include these services.

Similarly, individuals who own their own homes receive income-in-kind in the form of imputed rent, which represents a flow of housing services that the individuals, in effect, sell to themselves, insofar as they are both landlord and tenant. Failing to subject such income-in-kind to taxation acts as a subsidy to undertake such activities and results in distortions in resource allocation. As a matter of administrative practicality, however, the inclusion of all types of income-in-kind is infeasible. The ultimate line between what is or is not income therefore is likely to be drawn by arbitrary decisions. One type of income-in-kind that is fairly easy to tax is fringe benefits provided by employers for their employees. These include such compensation to employees as medical and life insurance, use of vehicles for personal purposes, and free meals. Recent tax reform proposals have advocated taxing noncash employee fringe benefits by estimating the market value of these benefits and including it in the employee's taxable income.

Nonpecuniary returns associated with various occupations are yet an additional aspect of the income-in-kind problem. *Nonpecuniary returns* represent satisfaction that individuals receive from their employment that is not reflected in their wages. For example, some occupations allow workers flexible hours and freedom from pressures. Wages in those occupations are likely to be lower than in occupations that require the same level of skills but more strict scheduling of worker time. Two occupations with the same required skills might be able to attract workers at differing wages, depending on the extent to which they offer nonpecuniary returns. The job with better nonpecuniary benefits will pay less, and the actual wage differential will reflect the value of the nonpecuniary returns.

To the extent to which nonpecuniary returns are not taxed, the attractiveness of jobs that provide such benefits increases, relative to other jobs. This affects occupational choice. Thus, when income-in-kind for various jobs escapes taxation, the tax system encourages individuals to enter those jobs, and it encourages employers to provide nonpecuniary benefits in lieu of taxable monetary benefits.[4]

C H E C K P O I N T

1. What is comprehensive income?
2. How would capital gains be treated under a comprehensive income tax?
3. What is income-in-kind? What are some of the difficulties involved in including income-in-kind in a measure of comprehensive income?

A GENERAL TAX ON COMPREHENSIVE INCOME

A general proportional tax on comprehensive income is a flat-rate on all income, regardless of its source or use.[5] The analysis in this chapter presumes that all earnings are either wages or interest and that the costs of earning income are zero. Because all income is taxed at the same rate, regardless of its source, the ratio of the price of labor to the price of capital is not distorted by the tax. Similarly, because taxes paid are independent of the uses to which income is put, the comprehensive income tax does not distort the relative prices of consumption of goods and services. The tax neither will distort choices in the income-producing activities in which individuals engage,

---

[4]For an analysis of in-kind compensation of employees (nontaxable fringe benefits), see Charles R. Clotfelter, "Equity, Efficiency, and the Tax Treatment of In-Kind Compensation," *National Tax Journal* 32 (March 1979): 51–60.

[5]If some initial amounts of income, say, $5,000 per person, were tax exempt, as is the case in many proposals for a flat-rate tax, the tax really would have a two-bracket progressive rate structure, with a zero marginal tax rate in the first bracket.

INTERNATIONAL VIEW

TREATMENT OF CAPITAL GAINS UNDER THE INCOME TAX

Although the Haig-Simons definition of comprehensive income suggests that both realized and unrealized capital gains are part of income, few nations actually tax capital gains. In the United States capital gains have been taxed in the past at preferential rates below that applied to ordinary income. However, the Tax Reform Act of 1986 started taxing realized capital gains as ordinary income. Then in 1991 Congress passed new legislation which still maintained that capital gains were ordinary income but put a ceiling of 28 percent on the rate at which they were taxed. No attempt has been made to tax unrealized capital gains in the United States.

Capital gains on real and financial assets are taxed in Australia, Canada, Sweden, and the United Kingdom. Canada increased the portion of capital gains subject to taxation as part of its tax reforms of the 1980s but capital gains still are not treated as ordinary income in Canada. None of the nations that tax capital gains adjust realized gains for inflation as is required under the Haig-Simons definition of income. Most other nations, including Japan and the European countries, tax capital gains only from the sale of real estate and exempt capital gains from the sale of securities from income taxation. Some nations are concerned that if they were to tax capital gains they would lose investment to other nations where the tax did not exist.

In the United States, certain types of capital gains still receive preferential treatment. For example, capital gains on inherited assets are not taxed, which provides an incentive for those who wish to leave bequests to hold their capital assets and not sell them during their lifetimes. Also in the United States, there is special treatment of capital gains on owner-occupied homes that effectively allow such gains in many cases to be realized tax free.

Because the greatest capital gains are usually earned on very risky investments, some economists justify exclusion or preferential treatment of capital gains on the grounds that it will encourage entrepreneurship and economic growth. However, little evidence suggests that capital gains taxation actually encourages the formation of new businesses. One study has documented the fact that much of the funding for the formation of new ventures in the United States comes from sources that would not be affected if capital gains tax rates were reduced. In recent years more than 75 percent of the funds invested by individuals and organizations in new ventures have not been subject to U.S. capital gains taxation. These investors include tax-exempt pension funds, foundations, and foreign investors whose home nations do not tax capital gains and who are not subject to U.S. income taxation on their realized capital gain.[*]

The bulk of realized capital gains in the United States come from appreciation of real estate assets. Only one-third of the reported realized capital gains in the United States are from appreciation of corporate stocks and only a small portion of the appreciation of corporate stock is from capital gains on start-up businesses.[†] Reducing capital gains tax rates in the United States therefore is likely to benefit the upper-income groups who realize most of the capital gains in the United States without appreciably encouraging new business ventures. Although a reduction in the capital gains tax does increase the return to capital, it remains unclear whether preferential tax treatment of capital gains in the United States can significantly increase economic growth in the nation. In any event, preferential tax treatment of capital gains is not the only way to use the tax system to encourage investment. For example, an investment tax credit is a way to subsidize investment directly through the tax system by giving firms a tax reduction equal to a certain percentage of the new capital they purchase each year.

[*]See James M. Poterba, "Capital Gains Tax Policy toward Entrepreneurship," *National Tax Journal* 42, 3 (September 1989): 375–389.
[†]Ibid.

nor will it distort the pattern of consumption of taxpayers in ways that prevent attainment of efficiency.

Although no loss in efficiency will occur in the way individuals spend their income or earn it, the tax *is* likely to distort the choices that are made concerning the allocation of time between work and leisure and between consumption and saving or productive investment. The flat-rate tax on comprehensive income can therefore prevent labor markets and investment markets from attaining efficiency.

TAXATION OF LABOR EARNINGS AND THE WORK-LEISURE CHOICE

By far, the major source of income in the United States today is wages. Income from the sale of labor services accounts for more than 75 percent of gross income in this nation. Labor income therefore is a dominant component of comprehensive income. Efficiency losses caused by taxation of labor income are of serious concern because of the importance of wages as a percentage of national income. This section analyzes the impact of the portion of a flat-rate comprehensive income tax that is levied on wages.

The impact of income taxation on the choice to work cannot be predicted unequivocally. The tax sets up both income and substitution effects; these work in opposite directions on workers' choices to work. Given preferences between work and income on the one hand and the market wage rate on the other, each worker is presumed to allocate time between work and leisure to maximize utility. The equilibrium allocation of time depends on individual preferences and the wage a worker can earn per hour.

A Graphic Analysis of Taxation of Labor Income

Figure 13.1 shows a typical worker's indifference curves for money income from work and leisure. In drawing the curves, it is assumed that leisure is a normal good for the worker. The indifference curves exhibit diminishing marginal rates of substitution of leisure for income. Twenty-four hours are available each day to allocate between gainful employment and all other activities for which the worker is not paid. Leisure is a catchall term for any activity other than work for an employer. You can think of leisure as nonmarket activity including home production activities such as cooking, cleaning, and engaging in do-it-yourself projects.

The line *HJ* represents the opportunities for the individual to trade leisure for money income through the sale of labor services to an employer. Nonlabor income is presumed to be zero in Figure 13.1. Therefore, if the worker chooses not to work at all, her income is zero in this simple model. This is illustrated at point *H* in the figure. At that point, the individual spends twenty-four hours per day in leisure activity and therefore would earn zero money income. For any other point along *HJ*, the individual's income can be expressed as

$$I = w(24 - L),\tag{13.4}$$

Figure 13.1 ✦ THE IMPACT OF A FLAT-RATE INCOME TAX ON THE WORK-LEISURE CHOICE

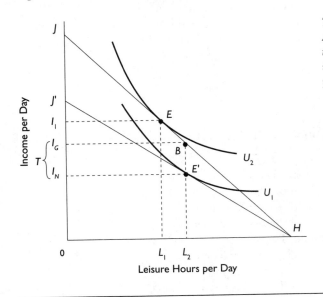

The income tax reduces the slope of the worker's wage line. As a result, the worker moves from point E to point E'. In this case, leisure per day increases. The tax therefore results in a decrease in hours worked per day, on average, over the year.

where L is the amount of hours of leisure per day and w is the wage per hour. The variable L is best thought of as the average amount of leisure per day over a year. The maximum income that the individual can earn in this case is $0J$ dollars per day. This is her income when she chooses to work twenty-four hours per day and therefore enjoys zero leisure hours per day.

Under the assumption of a diminishing marginal rate of substitution of leisure for income, neither the extreme J, no leisure, nor H, no work, is a likely choice. Instead, the worker is likely to maximize her utility at some intermediate point on the line HJ. In Figure 13.1, this occurs at point E, where the indifference curve U_2 is tangent to the wage line HJ. At that point, the slope of the indifference curve, $-MRS_{LI}$, is equal to the slope of the line HJ. But from Equation 13.4, the slope of HJ is simply $-w$, the rate of return from work effort. Because both slopes are negative, the equilibrium condition for the utility-maximizing allocation of time between work and leisure is

$$w = MRS_{LI}. \tag{13.5}$$

The introduction of a flat-rate tax on the worker's labor income of t percent reduces the return to work effort at all levels of work. Assuming no change in the gross, or market, wage paid by employers, the *net wage* received by workers after payment of the income tax is now

$$w_N = w_G(1 - t). \tag{13.6}$$

This rotates the line that depicts the market possibilities for transforming leisure into income through work effort from HJ down to HJ'. The equation for this line now becomes

$$I = w_G(1 - t)(24 - L). \tag{13.7}$$

The new equilibrium for the worker now occurs at point E'. The new equilibrium condition is

$$w_G(1 - t) = MRS_{LI}. \tag{13.8}$$

For the individual whose indifference curves are depicted in Figure 13.1, the proportional income tax has the following effects:

1. A reduction in utility from U_2 to U_1. (This ignores any benefits from government expenditures accruing to the individual.)
2. An increase in leisure hours per day, from L_1 to L_2. This worker therefore chooses to work fewer hours per day as a result of the tax on labor earnings.
3. A consequent reduction in actual labor earnings per day, from I_I to I_G, because of the reduction in hours worked. Because taxes are levied on I_G, net income available to spend falls to I_N.

The government collects $E'B = T$ dollars per day of this individual's income in taxes. This represents the differences between gross daily wages paid by employers, I_G, and net wages per day received by the worker, I_N, after payment of taxes. Net income after taxes is $I_N = I_G - T$. In this case, the tax has been detrimental to work effort. The individual reduces her hours worked per day by L_1L_2, as a result of the income tax.

For example, suppose w_G = \$5 per hour. If t = 0.2, the net wage declines as a result of the tax to \$4 per hour. If hours worked are $(H - L_1)$ = 8 hours, on average, over the year, suppose that the tax decreases average hours worked per day to $(H - L_2)$ = 7 hours. Gross daily labor income will fall from \$40 per day to \$35 per day after the tax. Net daily income will be \$28 per day. The total tax per day therefore will be \$7.

Income and Substitution Effects of a Tax on Labor Earnings

The impact of the tax on work effort of any worker depends on the income and substitution effects of the tax-induced reduction in the wages received by individual workers. The tax can be viewed as lowering the opportunity cost of an hour of leisure by reducing the wages that workers receive, from w_G to $w_G(1 - t)$. In effect, the tax lowers the implicit price of leisure by reducing the return from work effort, which is the opportunity cost of leisure.

The income tax results in a substitution effect that is unfavorable to work effort. The tax reduces the return from work effort, thereby making work less remunerative. This, in turn, makes leisure more attractive. The incentive is to substitute leisure for work effort because the per hour opportunity cost of leisure (the net hourly return from work effort) has fallen as a result of the introduction of the income tax. Thus, the substitution effect induced by the income tax tends to increase the consumption of leisure by the individual. This substitution effect represents a potential loss of output of goods and services due to the reduction in the incentive to work.

An income effect also results from the tax-induced decline in the net wage. The income effect tends to be favorable to work effort, provided that leisure is a normal good. The income tax reduces income at all levels of work. Even if the individual chooses to work the same number of hours as he did prior to the imposition of the tax, he earns less income, after taxes, than he did previously. The effective reduction in income results in a decrease in the consumption of all normal goods. Because leisure is likely to be a normal good for most people, the income effect results in a decrease in leisure consumption by the individual. If the worker reduces consumption of leisure per day, then it follows that hours devoted to work per day must increase. Thus, the income effect of taxation provides an incentive to increase work effort when leisure is a normal good. In a sense, the individual tends to work harder to maintain his previous income level.

The actual effect on individual work effort depends on the relative magnitudes of the income and substitution effects. If the substitution effect outweighs the income effect, the individual tends to consume more leisure and, consequently, works less as a result of the tax. This is evidently the case for the individual whose indifference curves are depicted in Figure 13.1. If, however, the individual's preferences are such that the income effect outweighs the substitution effect, the result of the tax-induced wage reduction is a decrease in the daily consumption of leisure and a consequent increase in work per day.

Graphic Analysis of Income and Substitution Effects of Tax-Induced Wage Decreases

Figure 13.2 shows how the substitution effect of a wage reduction caused by the income tax can be separated from the income effect. As a result of the tax, the worker's wage declines, thereby shifting the budget line from HI to HI'. The actual worker equilibrium shifts from the allocation of time corresponding to point E_1 to that corresponding to point E_2.

To isolate the substitution effect of the reduction in the wage, the worker would have to be given a compensating increment in average daily income to make her as well off as she was before the tax reduced the wage. Suppose the worker were given $BH = CI'$ dollars per day, as shown in Figure 13.2, after the tax is imposed on wages. This is a lump-sum daily payment that shifts the leisure-income line upward, parallel to itself, from $I'H$ to CB. Now, the worker has BH dollars per day of nonlabor income. This is exactly enough to return her to indifference curve U_2, which is the level of well-being that she enjoyed before the tax. If it were possible to make such a compensating variation in the worker's income, the resulting change in the allocation of time observed would represent the substitution effect. This is the change in the daily number of hours of leisure due only to the decrease in the net wage caused by the tax.

The worker would be in equilibrium at point E' if the income effect could be removed by such a compensating increase in income. The substitution effect is the increase in leisure per day from L_1 to L', labeled ΔL_S in Figure 13.2. The convexity of the indifference curves for income and leisure guarantees that the substitution effect will increase leisure hours per day. This is because the lower wage caused by the tax means that the slope of the line CB is less than the slope of the original leisure in-

Figure 13.2 ✦ Income and Substitution Effects of a Tax-Induced Wage Decline

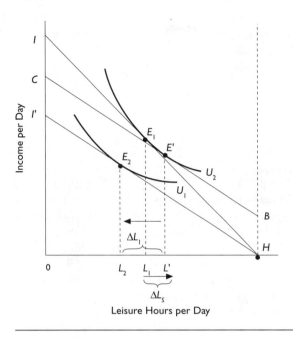

The substitution effect is separated from the income effect by giving the worker a compensating variation in income equal to an average of BH dollars per day over the year. In this case, the income tax results in an increase in work effort because the income effect, ΔL_I, outweighs the substitution effect, ΔL_S.

come line *IH*. The tangency at E' therefore must be to the right of the tangency, at E_1, as long as the marginal rate of substitution of leisure for income declines. It follows that the substitution effect of a tax-induced wage decrease always serves to decrease the number of hours worked per day (or per month or per year).

If the compensating increase in income were then taken away from the worker, the resulting change in the allocation of time between work and leisure would represent the income effect. Taking away *BH* dollars per day from the worker returns the worker to E_2. If leisure is a normal good, this will reduce the hours of leisure chosen per day. In Figure 13.2, the income effect is the reduction of leisure hours from L' to L_2 labeled ΔL_I. The income effect is opposite in direction to the substitution effect if leisure is a normal good. In this case, the income effect is actually stronger than the substitution effect. As a result, the wage reduction caused by the tax results in the worker whose indifference curves are drawn in Figure 13.2 choosing to work *more* hours per day. Compare this with the case of the worker whose indifference curves are drawn in Figure 13.1. In that graph, the substitution effect of the tax-induced wage decrease outweighs the income effect for that worker because she chooses to work fewer hours per day after the tax. Similarly, it is possible to envision a case in which the income and substitution effects are equal in magnitude and thus cancel one another. Under those circumstances, the observed labor supply would be perfectly inelastic.

LABOR MARKET ANALYSIS OF INCOME TAXATION

The impact of taxes on labor income, market wages, net wages, and efficiency depends on the responsiveness of workers to tax-induced wage declines. The analysis to follow considers two broad cases. The first case assumes that the market supply of labor is perfectly inelastic. The second case assumes the elasticity of supply of labor exceeds zero. In both cases, the demand for labor is presumed to be downward sloping.

Case 1: Perfectly Inelastic Labor Supply

The total excess burden of the comprehensive income tax on labor income depends on the substitution effect of the tax-induced net wage decline and the tax rate. All taxes, including lump-sum taxes, result in income effects that, other things being equal, make taxpayers worse off. Therefore, the tax-induced distortion in the work-leisure choice used to measure the excess burden of the tax must be based only on the change in work hours due to the substitution effect caused by the tax. Therefore, the labor supply response of workers must be adjusted to remove the income effect of the tax-induced wage change. A curve that shows how hours worked per day (or per year) vary with wages when the income effect of wage changes is removed is called a **compensated labor supply curve.** Such a curve reflects only the substitution effects of wage changes. (See the appendix to Chapter 11 for more detailed analysis of compensated supply curves.) Statistical techniques are used to remove the income effect from labor supply responses to estimate labor supply curves. Points on such supply curves can be used to measure the excess burden of a tax on labor income.

Even if the regular, or uncompensated, market supply curve of labor is perfectly inelastic, the excess burden of the tax will *not* be zero. In Figure 13.3A, the regular market supply curve of labor is assumed to be perfectly inelastic. The demand curve, D, is based on the gross wage, W_G, that employers must pay to attract any given number of labor hours per year. The impact of a tax on labor income is to reduce the wages received by workers, from W_G to $W_N = W_G(1 - t)$, for any amount of hours supplied. This is reflected by the gross wage curve, W_G, swiveling down to W_N. The extent of the reduction in wages at any given level of employment depends on the flat-rate tax rate, t. Workers respond to the net wage in deciding how many hours of work to supply per year. However, because the market supply of labor is perfectly inelastic, the tax-induced reduction in wages received by workers does not result in any reduction in the quantity of labor hours supplied. No change occurs in the initial market wage of W_G°. Net wages received by workers therefore fall by the full amount of the tax per hour of labor to $W_N = W_G^\circ(1 - t)$. Under these circumstances, the income tax is borne entirely by workers in the form of a reduction in wages.

Recall that the substitution effect of a wage decline always causes a worker to reduce hours worked per year. The perfectly inelastic supply curve of labor in Figure 13.3A therefore indicates that the substitution effect is exactly offset by an equal and opposite income effect, assuming that leisure is a normal good. Removing the income effect of the wage changes from the market supply curve results in the upward-sloping compensated labor supply curve, as shown in Figure 13.3B. The tax-induced

Figure 13.3 ✦ Impact of an Income Tax on Labor Markets and Efficiency When the Market Supply of Labor Is Perfectly Inelastic

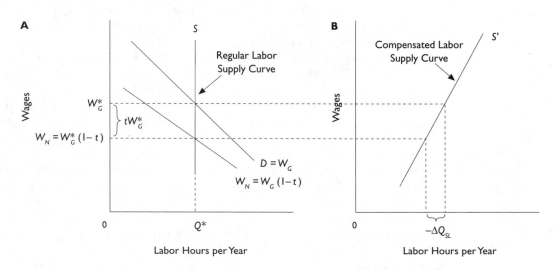

*An income tax on labor reduces wages by the full amount of the tax per hour when the supply of labor is perfectly inelastic as shown in **A**. However, the excess burden of the tax is not zero because the substitution effect of the tax reduces labor hours supplied per year. If a lump-sum were used, workers would work more hours per year. **B** shows that the compensated labor supply curve is upward sloping.*

decline in net wages received by workers is $tW_G^\ast$ when the market supply curve is perfectly inelastic. This decline in wages received therefore results in a substitution effect of $-\Delta Q_{SL}$ hours per year, as shown in Figure 13.3B. The excess burden of the tax equals $\frac{1}{2}(tW_G^\ast)\Delta Q_{SL}$. One study has concluded that the excess burden per dollar of taxes on labor income based on the tax rate structure prevailing in the United States in the mid-1970s would have been 8.1 cents, even if the market, or uncompensated, elasticity of supply of labor were zero.[6]

Also, when the supply of labor is perfectly inelastic, the incidence of taxes on labor will be borne entirely by workers. This is because the net wage falls by the full amount of the tax per labor hour.

Case 2: The Elasticity of Supply of Labor Exceeding Zero

Now suppose that the market supply curve of labor is upward sloping. When the income effect of the tax is believed to be small, the regular labor supply curve could be

---

[6]Charles L. Ballard, John B. Shoven, and John Whalley, "The Total Welfare Cost of the United States Tax System: A General Equilibrium Approach," *National Tax Journal* 38 (June 1985): 125–140.

used to approximate the excess burden of the tax. Otherwise, a compensated labor supply curve is necessary to estimate the substitution effect of the tax-induced wage decline.

In Figure 13.4, the pretax equilibrium is at point A. At that point, the wage is W_1 and Q_1 hours per year are supplied. The tax reduces the net wage for any number of hours worked per year from W_G to $W_G(1 - t)$. The new equilibrium is at point B, where the net wage is $W_N^* = W_G^*(1 - t)$. As a result of the tax, hours worked per year decline from Q_1 to Q_2. The gross, or market, wage increases from W_1 to W_G^*. Net wages received by workers decline to $W_N^* = W_G^*(1 - t)$. In this case, workers succeed in shifting a portion of the tax to employers. Wages do not decline by the full amount of the tax, tW_G^*, paid per hour. The increase in wages reduces the profits of employers or results in higher market prices of goods and services, as marginal costs of production increase. This results in some shifting of the tax burden to groups other than workers.

If the reduction in hours worked, ΔQ, were entirely attributable to the substitution effect, the triangular area BCA could be used to estimate the excess burden of the tax. If this is not the case, a compensated supply curve must be used. When leisure is a normal good, the compensated supply curve is more elastic at any wage level than the regular supply curve (see the appendix to Chapter 11). In Figure 13.4, the compensated supply curve is labeled S_C and the regular supply curve is labeled S_R. As shown on the graph, the reduction in net wages caused by the tax, ΔW, would result in

Figure 13.4 ✦ The Effect of Income Taxes on Labor Markets When the Supply of Labor Is Responsive

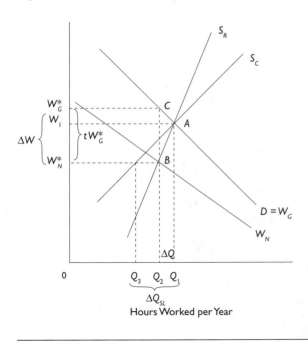

If the supply curve of labor is not perfectly inelastic, a tax on labor income increases market wages and decreases the quantity of labor hours supplied per year. If a regular supply curve, S_R, is used to estimate the excess burden of the tax, the burden will be underestimated. The compensated supply curve, S_C, must be used to estimate the substitution effect of the tax ΔQ_{SL}.

a reduction in hours worked equal to ΔQ_{SL} as hours worked per year decline to Q_3 when the income effect of the tax-induced wage change is removed. The change in hours worked due to the substitution effect, ΔQ_{SL} exceeds ΔQ, the uncompensated response. Using the area of the triangle BCA to measure the excess burden therefore, will underestimate the actual excess burden when income effects are not negligible.

When the supply of labor is not perfectly inelastic, workers can shift the tax to other groups. In addition, the excess burden of the tax will be greater than when the supply of labor is perfectly inelastic.

Empirical Evidence on Labor Supply

The excess burden of a tax on labor income depends on total labor income, the tax rate, and the willingness of workers to substitute leisure for work. The substitution effect depends on the elasticity of supply of labor along the compensated labor supply curve.

Empirical evidence on labor supply suggests that for males between the ages of 25 and 55 the income effect of wage changes is roughly equal to the substitution effect. The observed responsiveness of males in this age range to changes in tax rates is therefore quite low because the overall wage elasticity of labor supply with respect to the wage is close to zero. A zero overall elasticity of labor supply suggests that the incidence of a comprehensive income tax on labor income is borne by workers as a reduction in net wages.

However, some empirical research has suggested that the substitution effect of wage reductions caused by income taxes is fairly large but is offset by an equally large income effect.[7] This is consistent with low labor supply responses to changes in tax rates. Because the substitution effects of wage changes are of relevance in calculating the excess burden of the income tax, this implies that the income tax can result in fairly large losses of efficiency in labor markets, even though the overall wage elasticity of supply of labor is close to zero.

Using econometric techniques, it is possible to remove the income effect from estimated market labor supply elasticities to derive a compensated elasticity of supply that reflects only the substitution effect of tax-induced wage changes. Empirical evidence indicates that the efficiency-loss ratio of taxes on labor income in the United States in the 1970s was in the range of 5 to 30 cents of revenues collected. For example, one study concluded that in the tax system of the 1970s, the efficiency loss ratio for the average married male was 22 percent. This implies that taxes on married males in the 1970s in the United States caused distortions in resource use resulting in an excess burden of 22 cents for each dollar of revenue collected. More recent estimates based on the income tax laws prevailing in 1988, which had much lower marginal tax rates than those of the 1970s, suggests that the efficiency-loss ratio for income taxes in the United States had fallen to 13.5 percent. This suggests that a dollar of revenue raised by taxes on labor income in the United States in 1988 resulted in only 13.5 cents of excess

---

[7]See Jerry A. Hausman, "Labor Supply," in *How Taxes Affect Economic Behavior,* eds. Henry J. Aaron and Joseph J. Pechman (Washington, D.C.: The Brookings Institution, 1981).

THE INCIDENCE OF PAYROLL TAXES IN THE UNITED STATES

Most workers pay a payroll tax on their earnings of 7.65 percent of wages they earn in the United States. The taxes are deducted from their pay by their employers. Employers pay an additional 7.65 percent tax on the wages they pay. The taxes are levied on worker earnings up to a maximum amount, which was set at $57,600 in 1993 in most cases.° The total combined tax rate was therefore 15.3 percent for workers earning $57,600 or less in 1991. The payroll tax has been the fastest growing tax in the United States in recent years. Many workers with moderate earnings now pay more in payroll taxes than they do in federal income taxes! A worker earning $50,000 would have $3,825 withheld from his earnings to pay the tax and the worker's employer would pay an additional $3,825 so that the wages of a worker earning $50,000 would generate $7,650 in payroll taxes earmarked to pay Social Security benefits—mainly to retirees!

Although only half the total Social Security payroll tax is withheld from worker's wages there is good reason to believe that the incidence of the payroll tax falls entirely on workers because the supply of labor is close to perfectly inelastic in the United States! Actually it makes no difference whether the tax is collected from employees or employers. If the supply of labor is very inelastic, the bulk of the tax will be borne by workers no matter how its collection is split between the two groups. Most empirical evidence suggests that labor supply on average is very unresponsive to changes in tax rates in the United States.[†]

The graph below analyzes the impact of the U.S. payroll tax on labor markets, assuming a perfectly inelastic supply of labor.

THE PAYROLL TAX

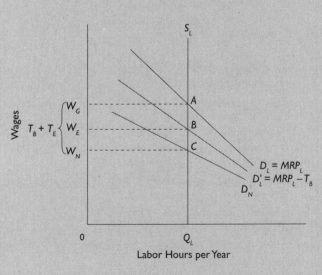

If the supply of labor is perfectly inelastic, a payroll tax collected from both employers and employees would be fully borne by workers as the hourly wage falls by the full amount of the tax per labor hour.

[°]Workers with earnings in excess of this limit, which is indexed with the rate of inflation, are subject to a 2.9 percent tax on their earnings without limit effective 1994.
[†]See Jerry A. Hausman and James M. Poterba, "Household Behavior and the Tax Reform Act of 1986, *Journal of Economic Perspectives* 1, 1 (Summer 1987), for a review of these studies.

The gross wage before the introduction of the payroll tax is w_G. Assuming a perfectly competitive labor market, this equilibrium wage is equal to the marginal revenue product of labor, MRP_L. Now assume that a payroll tax is levied on all wages. This tax will be split between employees and employers, so that each pays an equal amount per hour of labor.

The introduction of the payroll tax reduces the demand for labor from D_L to D'_L. This is because the employer's part of the tax is subtracted from MRP_L at any point. Employers therefore make their hiring decisions on the basis of MRP_L minus the tax T_B, per hour of work they must pay. A worker's contribution to a firm's revenues now is less at any point, because the employer's portion of the tax must be deducted from the revenues generated by workers as more are hired. The decrease in the demand for labor by employers caused by the tax decreases the equilibrium market wage received by employees from the initial level, w_G, to w_E, in the accompanying figure.

The portion of the tax paid by employees will be deducted from the market wage, w_E, that they receive. This reduces the net wage received by employees at all hours of work. The curve labeled D_N in the figure gives the net wage for workers. The net wage received by employees in equilibrium is $w_E - T_E$, where T_E is the workers' share of the tax per hour of work.

If the total labor hours employed per year were Q_L, the total tax deducted from workers' labor earnings would be $T_E Q_L$. This tax is represented by the area $w_E B C w_N$. But is this all the tax borne by workers? The answer is no, because the tax also has reduced the market wage received by employees from w_G to w_E. If the supply of labor were perfectly inelastic, the entire portion of the employer's tax would be shifted backward to

workers. The market wage received by employees falls by the full amount of the tax per hour of work paid by employers, T_B. The portion of the tax collected from employers is $T_B Q_L$ per year, represented by the area $w_G A B w_E$. That entire amount is the annual reduction in the payroll paid to workers due to the tax-induced reduction in the market wage from w_G to w_E. This result is independent of how the nominal collection of the payroll tax is split between the employer and the employee. If the entire tax were levied on the employer, the result would be exactly the same. In that case, the market demand would fall to D_N, and the gross market wage received by workers would decline to w_N.

The payroll tax also might have an effect on labor market behavior, due to some of the peculiarities of its application. In particular, the labor force participation of family members other than the major breadwinner can be affected. This is because, in many cases, spouses who work would have their wages reduced by the tax without any real expected benefits, inasmuch as most Social Security benefits already accrue to them from the package made available to the main breadwinner in the family. For example, a dependent spouse over retirement age is entitled to 50 percent of his or her retired spouse's Social Security pension when he or she reaches sixty-five.[†] This pension benefit is independent of whether the dependent spouse has paid Social Security taxes. The net benefit of paying taxes is reduced accordingly for dependent spouses who seek work. This, in turn, can affect their willingness to find work outside the home. This phenomenon might also provide incentives for workers to engage in work at home "off the books," either for themselves or for others, in order to avoid the payroll tax. This contributes to the development of the so-called underground economy.

[†] Some evidence indicates that high net payroll taxes in the United States discourage labor force participation of many married women. See Therese A. McCarty, "The Effect of Social Security on Married Women's Labor Force Participation," *National Tax Journal* 43, 1 (March 1990): 95–110.

burden. The reduction in excess burden is due entirely to lower tax rates because both the 1970s and 1988 estimates were based on the same labor supply elasticities.[8]

Estimates of the effect of income taxes on efficiency of use of labor remain controversial. The overall effect in labor markets requires estimates of compensated

[8] See Jerry A. Hausman and James M. Poterba, "Household Behavior and the Tax Reform Act of 1986," *Journal of Economic Perspectives* 1, 1 (Summer 1987).

labor supply elasticities of various demographic groups. For example, income taxes can affect household labor supply by influencing labor supply decisions of spouses. Some studies indicate that the income tax affects the labor supply decisions of spouses substantially and results in efficiency losses by decreasing their incentive to participate in the labor force.[9] Income taxes also can affect labor supply by influencing retirement decisions, intensity of work, willingness to acquire skills that increase labor income, and choice of occupation.

C H E C K P O I N T

1. What effects will a comprehensive income tax have on the incentive to work?
2. Why is it difficult to predict whether work effort will increase or decrease as a result of an income tax?
3. Why do many economists believe that the excess burden of the income tax in labor markets is low and that the tax on labor income is borne fully by workers?

TAXATION OF INTEREST INCOME AND ITS EFFECT ON SAVING

The taxation of interest income also results in both income and substitution effects. Taxation of interest income lowers the return to saving but can either increase or decrease the actual amount of saving observed. Considerable controversy surrounds the interest elasticity of supply of savings. Many economists believe that its value is close to zero. Others believe that this elasticity is greater in magnitude than the low wage elasticities of work previously discussed.[10]

The impact of a tax on interest income on choices can be understood with a simple intertemporal analysis of consumption in two periods. The allocation of a given

---

[9]Ibid., 108. Also see Robert K. Triest, "The Effect of Income Taxation on Labor Supply in the United States," *Journal of Human Resources,* 25, 3 (Summer 1990): 491–516. Also see Thomas MaCurdy, David Green, and Harry Paarsch, "Assessing Empirical Approach for Analyzing Taxes and Labor Supply." *Journal of Human Resources* 25, 3 (Summer 1990): 415–490.

[10]See Michael J. Boskin, "Taxation, Saving, and the Rate of Interest," *Journal of Political Economy* 86 (April 1978): S3–S28. Boskin's estimate of the interest elasticity of supply of saving is 0.4. Critics of Boskin's work argue that his methodology was flawed and that when properly estimated, changes in interest rates in the United States do not affect saving and investment. See Alan S. Blinder and Angus Deaton, "The Time Series Consumption Function Revisited," *Brookings Papers on Economic Activity* 2 (1985): 465–511. Research by Bernheim and Shoven suggests that rising real interest rates actually seem to *decrease* saving. See D. Bernheim and J. Shoven, "Pension Funding and Saving," NBER Working Paper 1622 (Cambridge, MA: National Bureau of Economic Research, May 1985). Also see Jonathan Skinner and Daniel Feenberg, "The Impact of the 1986 Tax Reform on Personal Saving," in Joel Slemrod, ed., *Do Taxes Matter: The Impact of the Tax Reform Act of 1986* (Cambridge, MA: The MIT Press, 1990).

amount of income over the two periods depends both on individual tastes and the interest rate that a saver can earn.

Graphic Analysis of Taxation of Interest Income

Figure 13.5 uses indifference curve analysis to analyze an individual's choice between consumption and saving. In effect, by saving, a person forgoes present consumption in exchange for more future consumption. The two variables in the analysis are consumption in the current period, C_1, and consumption in the second period, C_2. The individual's willingness to forgo present consumption for future consumption is, in part, a matter of taste.

The **marginal rate of time preference (MRTP)** is the slope of an indifference curve for present and future consumption multiplied by minus one. It is a measure of the willingness of savers to forgo current consumption in exchange for future consumption. A high marginal rate of time preference implies that the individual strongly prefers current consumption to future consumption (he is impatient). It is generally presumed that the marginal rate of time preference for most persons exceeds one. In other words, it would require more than a dollar of future consumption to compensate the person for giving up a dollar of present consumption out of current income and still be at the same level of utility.

The opportunity to transform present consumption into increased future consumption depends on the market rate of interest, r. If the individual's income is fixed

Figure 13.5 ✦ Income Taxation and Intertemporal Choice

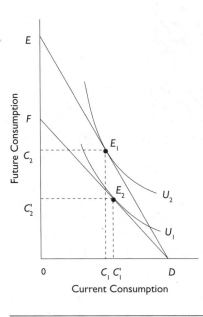

The income tax reduces the net interest earned by savers. This shifts the intertemporal budget line downward, from ED to FD. In this case, the substitution effect of the tax-induced decline in net interest received increases current consumption out of income and therefore reduces saving.

at I in the beginning of the current period and is zero in the second period, future consumption of current income will be equal to

$$C_2 = (1 + r)S, \tag{13.9}$$

where S is the amount of current income saved. For example, suppose the person's income is \$30,000, and he saves \$5,000 in year 1. He will be able to consume \$5,500 in year 2 if the interest rate is 10 percent.

S also can be expressed as the difference between income and current consumption:

$$S = I - C_1. \tag{13.10}$$

The equation of transformation line ED therefore is

$$C_2 = (1 + r)(I - C_1). \tag{13.11}$$

The slope of the line is $-(1 + r)$. The individual maximizes utility by allocating income between present and future consumption until the transformation line ED is tangent to an indifference curve. This occurs where the slope of the indifference curve, $-MRTP$, is equal to the slope of the transformation line, $-(1 + r)$:

$$MRTP = (1 + r). \tag{13.12}$$

The introduction of a tax on interest income reduces the net return obtained from saving. In this analysis it is assumed that the market rate of interest paid by borrowers, r, is unchanged when the tax is introduced. If the tax is levied at a rate, t, then the net yield after payment of the tax becomes $r(1 - t)$. This reduces the slope of the transformation line, and it swivels downward to FD, which, in turn, moves the individual to a new equilibrium in response to the lower return to savings. The new equilibrium is at point E_2, where the individual adjusts his allocation of income between present and future consumption to reduce his marginal rate of time preference so as to make it equal to the new lower return to saving:

$$MRTP = [1 + r(1 - t)]. \tag{13.13}$$

As shown in Figure 13.5, this results in an increase in current consumption, from C_1 to C_1', and a consequent reduction in saving. The actual impact on saving for any individual represents the combined income and substitution effects of the tax-induced reduction in the net interest rate. It is not possible to predict unequivocally the impact of the tax on savings.

The income effect of the reduction in the interest rate savers receive from r to $r(1 - t)$ provides incentive to reduce consumption of all normal goods in the current period and in the future. However, the tax reduces consumption of all goods in the second period, through the reduction in interest income. The only way that consumption can decline in the current period is for saving to increase. In effect, the income effect of the tax provides an incentive for the person to save more so as to make up for the reduction in second period consumption due to the tax-induced decline in interest income.

The substitution effect of the decrease in the net return to savings caused by the tax increases current consumption and therefore results in less saving. The decline in the interest rate raises the implicit price of future consumption by increasing the amount of current consumption that must be given up to obtain any dollar amount of future consumption. This provides incentives to save less.

The actual effect on saving is the combined effect of the opposing income and substitution effects forces and cannot be predicted by theory alone. Insofar as savers seek to save specific amounts, or "target" levels of saving, the income effect of the tax dominates, and savers actually may increase their rates of saving to offset the effect of the tax on their net returns.

MARKET ANALYSIS OF TAXATION ON INTEREST AND INVESTMENT INCOME

Excess Burden

Figure 13.6 shows the impact that a tax on interest income has on market saving and investment. The initial equilibrium is at point *A*, at an interest rate of r_1, which results in an efficient allocation of resources by equating the marginal social cost of saving with the marginal social benefit of investment. The introduction of the tax inserts a wedge between the interest received by savers and paid by investors and other

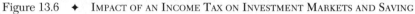

Figure 13.6 ◆ IMPACT OF AN INCOME TAX ON INVESTMENT MARKETS AND SAVING

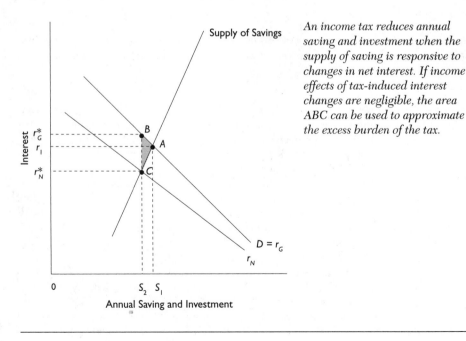

An income tax reduces annual saving and investment when the supply of saving is responsive to changes in net interest. If income effects of tax-induced interest changes are negligible, the area ABC can be used to approximate the excess burden of the tax.

borrowers, causing a loss in efficiency. Investment and saving fall from their initial equilibrium level, S_1, to a reduced level, S_2.

The tax lowers the return to saving at all levels, from r_G to $r_G(1 - t)$, thereby swiveling down the net interest at all levels, resulting in the curve r_N. The consequent reduction in the quantity of saving raises the market interest rate to r_G^* but leaves the net interest received by savers below its initial level, r_1. Net interest now equals $r_N^* = r_G^*(1 - t)$. To measure the excess burden of the tax, the reduction in savings due only to the substitution effect of the tax must be measured. This would require measuring the reduction in saving, S_1S_2, along a compensated supply curve of savings.

The excess burden of the tax is approximated by the area of the triangle *ABC* if income effects of a tax-induced interest rate changes are negligible.[11] The excess burden depends on the tax rate applied to interest income and on the interest elasticity of supply of savings. Quite a controversy has arisen over the interest elasticity of the supply of savings in the United States. Some research studies have indicated that the (uncompensated) interest elasticity of the supply of savings was about 0.4 in the late 1970s.[12] Under those circumstances, the excess burden of taxes on capital income in the United States would have been more than $50 billion, or more than 30 cents per dollar of revenue. Some economists, however, maintain that the actual interest elasticity is, in fact, much higher than 0.4 in this country.[13] Studies based on this higher elasticity indicate that the excess burden of the tax could be three times higher than estimates based on the 0.4 elasticity. However, still other studies provide evidence that the interest elasticity of supply of savings is quite low.[14] Thus, economists disagree on the actual value of the interest elasticity of supply of savings and therefore on the excess burden of taxes falling on capital income.

Incidence of Taxes on Interest Income

The value of the interest elasticity of supply of saving is also crucial to a determination of the degree of shifting of the tax on interest income. If the annual amount of saving

---

[11]Feldstein has argued that the excess burden of taxation of income from saving and investment is more appropriately thought of as a distortion in the timing of consumption over the life cycle, rather than as a decrease in saving. Even if the amount of saving is unaffected by a tax on interest income (because of perfectly inelastic supply), future consumption will fall as a result of the tax-induced decline in net interest. A decline in the interest rate, in effect, raises the "price" of future consumption by increasing the amount of present consumption that must be given up to get any dollar amount of future consumption. Using a methodology to calculate the efficiency loss in capital taxation in this way, Feldstein calculates the cost at 0.5 percent of national income when the amount of saving is unaffected by the tax. See Martin Feldstein, "The Welfare Cost of Capital Income Taxation," *Journal of Political Economy* 86, pt. 2 (April 1978): S29–S51.

[12]Boskin, "Taxation, Saving, and the Rate of Interest," S11–S28.

[13]Lawrence H. Summers, "Capital Taxation and Accumulation in a Life Cycle Growth Model," *American Economic Review* 71 (September 1981): 533–544.

[14]Irwin Friend and Joel Hasbrouck, "Savings and After-tax Rates of Return," *The Review of Economics and Statistics* 65 (November 1983): 537–543. See also, Blinder and Deaton, "The Time Series Consumption Function."

P U B L I C   P O L I C Y   P E R S P E C T I V E

THE SUPPLY-SIDE TAX CUTS OF THE 1980S

Instead of lowering tax revenue, can decreases in income tax rates increase tax revenue by causing the amount of work and investment to increase? This was the basic idea of the supply-side approach to economic policy that was put forth by the Reagan administration in the 1980s. Reagan put his ideas into force with a major tax decrease—the Economic Recovery Tax Act of 1981 (ERTA). This new law resulted in a 25 percent across-the-board reduction in tax rates. The top marginal tax rate applied to nonlabor income was reduced from 70 percent to 50 percent and was accompanied by a series of special tax breaks designed to encourage saving and investment.

The 1981 tax rate cuts *did not* increase tax revenues as the supply-siders maintained it would. However, in response to the declines in marginal tax rates, federal revenues did not decrease by as much as most non-supply-siders thought would be the case. This implies that workers and investors respond to tax rate cuts but not by enough to offset the negative effect of tax rate cuts on revenue collected.[*]

In general, declines in income tax rates will increase tax revenues only if income subject to tax is highly elastic with respect to the tax rate. The elasticity of the income tax base in the ratio of the percentage change in income subject to tax attributable to any given percentage change in the income tax base. When the income tax base is negative and elastic, a given percentage decline in tax rates results in a larger percent-age *increase* in income earned. In such cases the negative effect of the reduction in taxes rates (which was 25 percent) in 1981 is offset by the positive effect of increased work and investment that increases both labor and capital income subject to tax.

However, in one case that tax cut did increase revenue in the 1980s. Realization of capital gains is apparently quite elastic with respect to the tax base in the short run. When tax rates on realized capital gains were cut significantly in 1982, the amount of taxable capital gains realized in that year by taxpayers increased by a greater percentage than the percentage of decline in tax rates. Because the dates of capital gain realizations can be controlled and because accrued unrealized capital gains are not taxable, the reduction in the tax rates in 1982 released a tide of selling of assets to take advantage of the lower tax rates.[†] The very elastic capital tax gains base caused tax revenues from taxation of realized capital gains to increase despite the lower tax rates. However, this was a one-time effect. Other portions of the income tax base, namely labor and forms of capital income other than capital gains, were not elastic enough to result in increases in tax revenue.

The general consensus among economists is that both work effort and investment, which provides the bulk of income, are highly unresponsive to changes in tax rates. This would imply an inelastic income tax base. Apparently this was the case for the United States in the 1980s because the ERTA tax cuts did not increase income enough to cause revenue to increase in the United States.

[*]See Martin Feldstein, "Supply-Side Economics: Old Truths and New Claims," *American Economic Review* 76, 2 (May 1986): 26–30.
[†]See Lawrence B. Lindsey, "Capital Gains Rates, Realizations, and Revenues," in *The Effects of Taxation on Capital Accumulation*, ed. Martin S. Feldstein (Chicago: University of Chicago Press, 1987): 69–97.

is responsive to tax-induced declines in net interest payments, the tax can be shifted from savers to borrowers through an increase in the market rate of interest. In Figure 13.6, the market interest rate rises, from r_1 to r_G^*, as a result of the total reduction in the quantity of savings supplied because of the tax on interest. Higher interest offsets some of the tax burden on savers, but it increases production costs and results in some of the tax being shifted to consumers in the form of higher prices for goods and services. This means that part of the incidence of the tax is shifted to persons who are not savers.

Decreased investment also results in slower growth of the capital stock of a nation. Workers will have less capital to work with than would be the case if a lump-sum tax, which did not influence the interest rate, were used. Because a lower ratio of capital to labor decreases labor productivity, the implication is that in competitive labor markets, where the marginal product of labor is a crucial determinant of the wage, wages would be lower than if there were no tax on interest income. The tax on interest income, therefore, could be shifted, in part, to workers in the form of lower wages when market interest rates rise. Under these circumstances, removal of taxes on interest earnings in the United States would result in decreases in the market rate of interest and eventual increases in wages. Therefore, workers, as well as savers, would benefit from a reduction in the tax rate applied to interest income. Of course, the lower the reduction in actual savings as a result of taxes on interest income, the less the increase in the market rate of interest. At the extreme, if the interest elasticity of supply of savings were actually zero, the market rate of interest would be unaffected by the income tax. Under such circumstances, only savers would benefit from reduction in the tax on interest income. Only when the interest elasticity of supply of savings is zero will a tax on interest income be borne exclusively by savers. In other cases, the incidence of the tax will be shared by savers and others who do not save any of this income.

C H E C K P O I N T

1. Why is it difficult to predict the effect of a comprehensive income tax on saving?
2. Why is there a controversy about the excess burden of the income tax in investment markets?
3. How can the income tax decrease future living standards?

Summary

Taxes on personal income account for nearly one-half of federal government revenues in the United States. Income is viewed by many as an appropriate index of ability to pay taxes.

For tax purposes, income is usually measured as an annual flow of earnings. The economist's definition of income is, however, an annual accretion of purchasing power. This is known as comprehensive income and is measured as the sum of annual consumption and increased net worth. Consumption represents spent purchasing power, while increases in net worth represent purchasing power stored for future use. Sources of income include earnings from the sale of productive resources, transfer payments received, and net capital gains accrued. Uses of income include consumption of goods and services, taxes, and saving, or increases in net worth. Comprehensive income includes unrealized capital gains and allows deductions for the costs required to earn income.

Among the problems encountered in implementing a tax on comprehensive income are (1) measuring the value of income-in-kind and other nonmarket transactions, (2) measuring unrealized capital gains, and (3) determining what constitutes a cost of earning income. Under a comprehensive income tax, income of corporations would be allocated to individuals according to the proportion of their share in ownership of the corporation, with no separate corporate income tax.

A general tax on comprehensive income would tax all income at the same rate, regardless of its source or use. Although such a tax does not distort choices concerning sources of income or consumption expenditures, it will distort choices between work and leisure and between present and future consumption.

The tax on comprehensive income causes the wages, as seen by employers and employees, to diverge. This results in an efficiency loss in labor markets. The actual effect of the tax on hours worked depends on income and substitution effects; it cannot be predicted by theory alone. Empirical estimates of the excess burden of taxes on labor income range from 5 to 29 percent of revenue collected.

Taxation of interest income causes the interest rate paid by investors to diverge from that received by savers. The result is a loss in efficiency in markets for loanable funds used to finance investment and accumulation of assets. Most evidence appears to indicate that savings is quite unresponsive to changes in the market rate of interest. When interest rates change, income and substitution effects influence both current and future consumption making it difficult to predict the effect of the change in the interest rates on saving. Although some empirical studies have suggested that saving is somewhat responsive to change in interest rates, most economists believe that the effect, if any, is small—implying that taxation of interest income has little effect on savings rates in the United States.

A Forward Look

The following chapter continues the analysis of income taxation by considering the basic provisions of the personal income tax in the United States. In practice, income taxes do not tax all income, regardless of its source or use, at the same rate. This results in distortions in resource use that would not prevail under a comprehensive income tax. In Chapter 14, these additional distortions are discussed and proposals for tax reform are reviewed.

Important Concepts

Net Worth
Comprehensive Income
Capital Gains
Income-in-Kind
Compensated Labor Supply Curve
Marginal Rate of Time Preference (MRTP)

Questions for Review

1. What is comprehensive income, and how is it related to an individual's command over resources? Explain how income can be measured from either the sources or the uses side.
2. Why would a comprehensive income tax eliminate the need for a separate tax on corporate income?
3. Why is income-in-kind often excluded from income in implementing an income tax? What are some major forms of income-in-kind, and what are the economic consequences of excluding such items from taxation?
4. What distortions are introduced by a general tax on comprehensive income that taxes all income, regardless of its source or use?
5. What is the major source of income in the United States?
6. How does a proportional income tax introduce a wedge between the gross wage paid by employers and the net wage received by workers? Explain how this tax wedge results in efficiency losses in labor markets.
7. Why must the substitution effect be separated from the income effect of tax-induced wage reductions to measure the excess burden of a comprehensive tax on labor income? Draw a graph that shows how the excess burden of the tax can be measured. Explain why it is impossible to predict the effect of an income tax on labor hours worked using theory alone.
8. What is the consequence of a highly responsive supply of labor hours for the excess burden of an income tax on wages? Show that a low elasticity implies that workers bear most of the income tax on wages.
9. How does a tax on interest income influence a person's willingness to save? Can the impact of the tax on saving be unequivocally predicted from theory? Explain why or why not.
10. Under what circumstances will the supply of savings be unresponsive to changes in interest rates? Why does a perfectly inelastic supply of savings not imply zero excess burden from income taxes on interest income?

Problems

1. Mary has earnings of $50,000 this year. She also has been fortunate because the market value of the condominium she purchased this year for $100,000 has increased by 5 percent. Assuming that the rate of inflation is 3 percent, and that Mary has neither capital losses nor other earnings, and receives no transfers, calculate Mary's comprehensive income. If she were subject to a comprehensive income tax at a 20

percent flat rate, what would her tax liability be for the year?

2. An estimate of the efficiency-loss ratio of taxes on labor income is 15 percent. The efficiency-loss ratio of taxes on capital income is estimated to be 45 percent. Assuming that these estimates are accurate, calculate the change in well-being that would result from a $10 billion reduction in taxes on capital income, accompanied by a $10 billion increase in taxes on labor income.

3. Suppose that the current market rate of interest is 8 percent. John is subject to a 31 percent marginal tax rate on his interest income. What is John's equilibrium marginal rate of time preference? Suppose the marginal tax rate John is subject to decreases to 20 percent. Can you predict the effect of the decrease in marginal tax rates on John's current saving?

4. Suppose leisure is an inferior good for a worker. Set up this worker's indifference curves for money income and leisure, and derive the income and substitution effects of a tax-induced wage decline. Derive the compensated labor supply curve for this worker, and explain how it differs from the compensated supply curve of a worker for whom leisure is a normal good.

Suggestions for Further Reading

Aaron, Henry J., and Joseph A. Pechman, eds. *How Taxes Affect Economic Behavior.* Washington, D.C.: The Brookings Institution, 1981. A collection of research studies on the impact of income taxes on labor supply, investment in equipment, stock prices, saving, and other economic variables.

Bosworth, Barry and Gary Burtless. "Effects of Tax Reform on Labor Supply, Investment, and Saving." *Journal of Economic Perspectives*, 6, 1 (Winter 1992): 3–25. An analysis of the effects of tax reforms in the 1980s on resource use in the United States.

Bovenberg, A. Lans. "Tax Policy and National Saving in the United States, a Survey." *National Tax Journal* 62, 2 (June 1989): 123–138. A good analysis of the possible ways the U.S. tax system affects saving in the United States.

McClure, Charles E. Jr., and Zodrow, George R. "The Study and Practice of Income Tax Policy," in Quigley, John M. and Smolensky, Eugene, eds. *Modern Public Finance,* Cambridge, MA, Harvard University Press, 1994: 165–212. A review of theoretical issues and research on the economics of income taxation.

Pechman, J. A., ed. *Comprehensive Income Taxation.* Washington, D.C.: The Brookings Institution, 1977. A collection of essays on the concept of comprehensive income and its taxation.

U.S. Department of the Treasury. *Blueprints for Basic Tax Reform.* Washington, D.C.: U.S. Government Printing Office, 1977. An analysis of basic concepts of income taxation and analysis of possible reform of the income tax code to increase the comprehensiveness of the tax base and remove inequities.

14

TAXATION OF PERSONAL INCOME IN THE UNITED STATES

LEARNING OBJECTIVES

After reading this chapter you should be able to

1. Define adjusted gross income and taxable income, and describe how personal exemptions and various deductions influence the portion of a household's income actually subject to tax in the United States.

2. Discuss the tax rate structure of the U.S. personal income tax and the degree of progressivity of taxation.

3. Explain how tax preferences can distort choices and prevent efficiency from being attained in markets.

4. Analyze the possible effects of major tax preferences in the United States on decisions and resource use.

5. Discuss major issues relating to economic effects of income taxation in the United States.

*E*ven if you file the simplest of tax forms, you might be bewildered by the complexity of the U.S. income tax rules. The income tax in the United States is almost continually being reformed in the hopes of simplifying it. However, to the consternation of everyone involved—including the Internal Revenue Service, whose officials and agents must administer and enforce the tax laws—it seems to get ever more complex after each round of reform enacted by Congress. The Tax Reform Act of 1986 was supposed to be the definitive income tax overhaul of the twentieth century. This reform of the U.S. personal income tax sharply reduced tax rates and the number of tax brackets for the federal personal income tax while eliminating many of the deductions, exclusions, and exemptions from income that influence how much of a person's income is actually subject to tax. Then, in 1990, under pressure to raise revenue to cope with a growing federal deficit, the president and Congress tinkered with the income tax once more, changing both the tax rate structure and some of the rules that determine how much of a taxpayer's income is subject to tax. In 1993, to cope with the budget deficit, President Clinton proposed higher marginal tax rates on upper income groups and additional reforms of the income tax. Congress responded in that year with legislation that reversed the trend toward lower marginal tax rates. It is safe to say that still more changes in the U.S. income tax lie ahead as we approach the twenty-first century.

Because of the special provisions of the income tax, taxpayers can influence their annual tax bills by controlling the sources and the uses of their income. The tax code is a very complicated set of rules. Only a portion of the comprehensive Haig-Simons measure of income is actually subject to tax in the United States. Issues in tax policy and tax reform often relate to questions concerning the degree of progression of the tax rate structure and the impact of deductions, exemptions, and exclusions from the tax base on market efficiency and the distribution of the tax burden. Because of the complexity of the tax code, the income tax results in losses in efficiency as taxpayers consider the tax as well as the social benefits of their decisions. The income tax in the United States not only distorts choices regarding use of labor and capital, it also distorts choices regarding the sources and uses of income. In this chapter we examine the personal income tax in the United States based on laws prevailing in the early 1990s.

The Tax Base: Basic Rules for Calculating Taxable Income and Why Much of Income Is Untaxed

If you are like most American adults, you are required to file a federal (and state) income tax return by April 15 of each year. The amount of tax you pay depends on how much income you have received during the year from earnings and other sources subject to tax, the deductions and exemptions you are entitled to, and the tax rate to which you are subject.

Taxable income is the portion of income received by individuals that is subject to the personal income tax. In practice, taxable income is considerably less than the Haig-Simons definition of comprehensive income discussed in Chapter 13. This section shows how taxable income in the United States is calculated.

The first step in calculating taxable income is to list the basic sources of income subject to taxation. **Gross income** is all income received during the year from taxable sources. Included in gross income are wages and salaries, interest income from taxable sources, dividends, rental income, and profits from business activity. Also included in gross income, under rules prevailing in 1994, are realized capital gains from sale or exchange of securities and other property. Unemployment compensation received from government is subject to tax and upper income retired taxpayers are required to pay tax on part of their Social Security pensions. Among the miscellaneous income that is subject to tax under the provision of the U.S. income tax code are prizes and awards, royalties, a portion of private pension benefits, alimony, and net gambling gains. Even income illegally obtained by criminals is subject to tax in the United States when the authorities are successful in getting crooks to report their earnings! For example, a convicted embezzler is required by law to pay taxes on his embezzlements! Table 14.1 shows the components of gross income based on tax rules prevailing in 1994.

Once gross income has been computed, certain adjustments are permitted. **Adjusted gross income** is gross income minus any allowable adjustments. The adjustments to gross income include subtraction of reimbursed employee business ex-

Table 14.1 ✦ Calculating Taxable Income under the U.S. Personal Income Tax System (Based on Rules Prevailing in 1994)

Sources of Income Subject to Tax:
  Wages and Salaries
  Interest Income Received
  Dividends
  Rental Income
  Profits from Noncorporate Business Activity
  Taxable Pension Benefits
  Realized Capital Gains
  Unemployment Compensation and a Portion of Other Government Payments to Individuals
  Alimony Received
  Miscellaneous Income (e.g., Awards and Prizes)
Total Equals: Gross Income

Less Adjustments to Gross Income:
  Reimbursed Employee Business Expenses
  Contributions to Special Retirement Plans
  Penalties for Early Withdrawal of Savings
  Alimony Paid
Equals: Adjusted Gross Income

Less Exemptions and Deductions (Either Standard or Itemized)

Equals: Taxable Income

penses, contributions made by the individual to special retirement plans, penalties for early withdrawal of savings, and alimony paid.

Once adjusted gross income is computed, personal exemptions and deductions are subtracted from it to obtain taxable income. A **personal exemption** is a certain sum of money that a taxpayer is allowed to deduct from adjusted gross income that varies with the number of dependents claimed on the return. In 1994 most taxpayers were allowed a $2,450 personal exemption for themselves and each dependent. A personal exemption could not be claimed by a person who was claimed as a dependent on another taxpayer's return. For example, if you have a part-time job and your parents still claim you as a dependent on their income tax return, then you could *not* claim yourself as a dependent. Also, higher-income taxpayers were subject to a phase-out (reduction of the dollar amount) of their personal exemptions after their taxable income reached a certain level. Very high-income taxpayers lose their personal exemptions completely as a result of this phaseout rule. The dollar value of the personal exemption is adjusted each year for inflation to keep its real value constant.

The final step in calculating taxable income is to make additional deductions from adjusted gross income allowable under the law. Taxpayers can either take the **standard deduction,** which is a fixed dollar amount that is adjusted for inflation each year and varies with the filing status of the taxpayer, or they can itemize their deductions. The base standard deduction established in 1994 was $3,800 for a single taxpayer and $6,350 for a married couple filing a joint return.

Taxpayers also have the option to itemize specific allowable tax-deductible expenses *instead* of taking the standard deduction. **Itemized deductions** are expenses that can be legally deducted as an alternative to the standard deduction from adjusted gross income in figuring taxable income. Persons whose itemized deductions exceed the standard deduction to which they are entitled can obtain a lower taxable income by itemizing their deductions on a special form (Schedule A). As of 1994, limits were placed on itemized deductions of upper-income households. Married couples with more than $111,800 and single filers with more than $55,900 adjusted gross income usually could not deduct all the itemized deductions to which they normally would be entitled.

Between 1980 and 1985, taxable income in the United States averaged 46.3 percent of *personal income*, which is a measure of income available for persons to spend before personal taxes.[1] In 1990, after most of the provisions of the Tax Reform Act of 1986 went into effect, the ratio of taxable income to personal income increased to 49 percent.[2] This suggests that the U.S. income tax is far from comprehensive in that it allows a substantial portion of personal income received each year to escape taxation. The fact that individuals can control their taxable income and therefore the amount of tax they pay by controlling the sources and uses of their income results in distortions in economic choices.

The Tax Rate Structure

Once taxable income has been computed, the next step is to calculate tax liability. To do this taxpayers use a tax rate schedule that applies to them. Different tax rate schedules apply to different taxpayers, depending on their filing status. One tax rate schedule applies to single taxpayers, another to married taxpayers filing joint returns, a third to married taxpayers filing separate returns, and yet a fourth to taxpayers filing as head of household.

A **tax bracket** is a range of income subject to a given marginal tax rate. Before 1987 the tax schedule contained as many as sixteen different tax brackets, each with its own marginal tax rate. In 1980 the top marginal tax rate applied to nonlabor income in the highest tax bracket was 70 percent! As of 1994, the schedule contained only five tax brackets for taxpayers with taxable income and the highest marginal tax rate was 39.6 percent.

Figure 14.1 shows the way the marginal tax rates vary with taxable income under the tax rate schedule prevailing in 1994. Taxable income is taxed at a marginal rate of only 15 percent up to a certain level indicated as *A* on the graph. For example, point *A* corresponded to $22,750 of taxable income in 1994 for a single taxpayer and

---

[1] Internal Revenue Service, Statistics of Income, *SOI Bulletin* 8, 2 (Fall 1988): 134.

[2] Internal Revenue Service, *Statistics of Income, Industrial Income Tax Returns*, 1995 and U.S. Department of Commerce.

Figure 14.1   ✦   Satutory Marginal Tax Rates for the U.S. Personal Income Tax, 1994

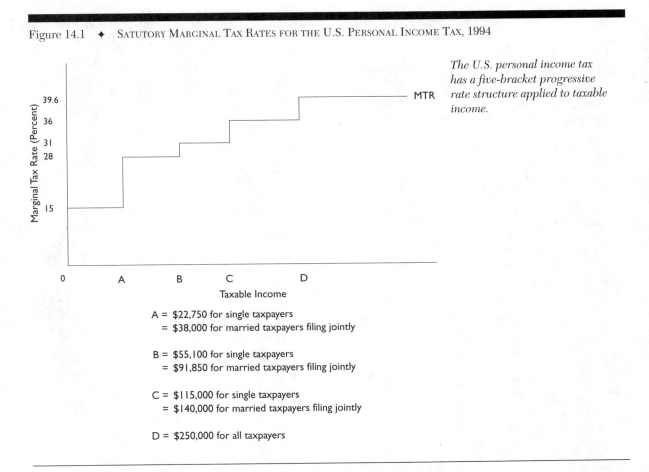

The U.S. personal income tax has a five-bracket progressive rate structure applied to taxable income.

A = $22,750 for single taxpayers
  = $38,000 for married taxpayers filing jointly

B = $55,100 for single taxpayers
  = $91,850 for married taxpayers filing jointly

C = $115,000 for single taxpayers
  = $140,000 for married taxpayers filing jointly

D = $250,000 for all taxpayers

$38,000 for married taxpayers filing jointly. If you were a single taxpayer with no dependents and your taxable income in 1994 was $10,000, you would have paid 15 percent of your taxable income, or $1,500, in taxes. As long as your taxable income was less than $22,750 your marginal tax rate would be 15 percent. If you earned more than $22,750 in 1994, you would have paid a 28 percent marginal tax rate on your taxable income in excess of $22,750, provided that your total taxable income was less than $55,100. If you earned more than $55,100 in taxable income in 1991, you would pay a 31 percent marginal tax rate on the excess over that amount. You can use the graph to see how your marginal tax rate would increase to 36 percent and then to 39.6 percent as your taxable income were to grow. Each year the taxable incomes corresponding to points A, B, C, and D in Figure 14.1 are adjusted for inflation.

Remember that taxable income is always less than gross income. If you claimed one personal exemption worth $2,450 on your tax return in 1994 and took the standard deduction of $3,800 and made no adjustments to your gross income, then if your gross income were $15,000, your taxable income would be: $15,000 − $6,250 = $8,750.

PUBLIC POLICY PERSPECTIVE

HOW PROGRESSIVE ARE FEDERAL INCOME TAXES? EFFECTIVE AVERAGE AND MARGINAL TAX RATES

Every one knows that the rate schedule for the federal income tax is progressive when viewed against *taxable* income. But, as you know from the analysis of income measurement, taxable income is much less comprehensive income because of exemptions, deductions, and exclusions from the tax base. How progressive is the federal income tax when tax burdens are calculated using a more comprehensive measure of gross income? Does the effect of other federal taxes diminish the progressivity of the personal income tax?

To answer these questions the Congressional Budget Office (CBO) has used a broad measure of family income calculated as the sum of wages, salaries, business income, rents, interest, dividends plus cash pension benefits.° It then divided families in the United States into five groups of equal number ranked according to their income. An estimate of taxes paid, based on the tax law prevailing in 1994, by each of these groups was then made and divided by the gross income of each group. The results show the estimated **average effective tax rate,** which are actual taxes as a percent of a measure of gross (rather than taxable) income for each group.

The first bar graph shown in A demonstrates that average effective income tax rates for the U.S. individual income tax do rise as gross income increases. The federal income tax therefore really does distribute the burden of taxation in a progressive manner. The lowest income group has a *negative effective tax rate* of about 5 percent of its income. In other words, on average, this group receives an amount equivalent to 5 percent of its earnings as a transfer from the federal government. Effective tax rates increase with income steadily and the effective income tax rate on the highest income group is about 15 percent.

What about the effect of other federal taxes on the distribution of income? For example, the federal government now relies on payroll taxes more heavily than the income tax and many families pay more in these social insurance taxes than they do income taxes. The payroll tax is essentially a tax on labor income. A more complete picture of income tax progressivity can be obtained if the impact of the federal income tax on income is combined with that of the payroll tax.

The CBO also has estimated the progressivity of federal taxes when payroll taxes are combined with the federal income tax and federal excise taxes. Their estimates indicate when all these taxes are taken into account effective tax rates in 1994 range from 5.1 percent for the 20 percent of the population with the lowest incomes to 27.7 percent for the portion of the population with the highest incomes. The bar graph B shows the average effective federal tax rates for 1994. Notice that low-income families pay significant amounts in both payroll and excise taxes to offset the positive effects of the EITC on their incomes. However, overall the federal tax structure appears to be quite progressive in 1994. In fact, the recent increases in marginal tax rates on the upper income groups has contributed to a marked increase in progressivity compared to the system existing in 1985.

Also shown in the graph C are **effective marginal tax rates** on earnings in 1994. This graph shows the combined effect of both personal income taxes and payroll taxes on the tax rate applied to an additional dollar of earnings as gross income increases. Notice how this tax rates schedule differs from the statutory rate schedule shown in Figure 14.1. First of all it is based on actual earnings rather than taxable income. Second it includes the effects of the payroll tax on earnings in addition to the statutory federal income tax rates. As you can see this actual schedule is a lot more complex than the statutory schedule. It's more like a roller coaster ride with both ups and downs. Marginal tax rates are negative for the lowest income groups who are eligible for the earned income tax credit. However, marginal

°This measure is less than comprehensive income because it excludes unrealized capital gains, employer contributions to pension funds, and in-kind income. In the estimates presented here, corporate income tax paid by households is assumed to vary with a family's capital income. Payroll taxes are included in family income. For details of the calculations, see U.S. Congressional Budget Office, *The Changing Distribution of Federal Taxes, 1975–1990* (Washington, D.C.: U.S. Congress, October 1987), chap. V, 42–48. See Congress of the United States, Congressional Budget Office, *The Economic and Budget Outlook: Fiscal Years 1995–1999* (Washington, D.C.: U.S. Government Printing Office, January 1994), 52–57 for estimates of progressivity of the U.S. income tax in 1994.

tax rates increase sharply for these groups as the earned income tax credit is phased out.

With the combined effects of both personal income taxes and social insurance taxes, taxpayers with the highest incomes are now subject to a whopping 43-percent marginal tax rate. In 1990 these groups were subject to a marginal tax rate of only 28 percent. So it is clear that the recent changes in tax law have impacted heavily on the upper income groups by increasing their marginal tax rate nearly 40 percent. However, surprisingly, the upper

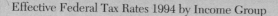

Effective Federal Tax Rates 1994 by Income Group

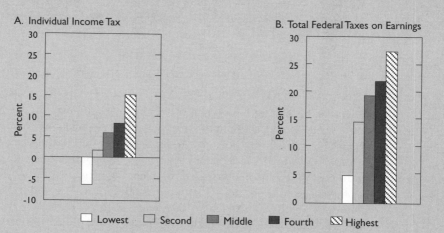

Source: Congressional Budget Office.
Note: Families are ranked by adjusted family income, with an equal number of people per quintile. Rates for 1994 are projected using the fully implemented rates for the earned income tax credit set in the Omnibus Budget Reconciliation Act of 1993.

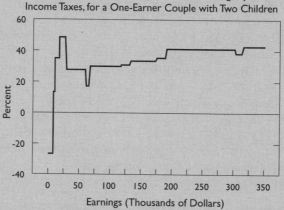

Source: Congressional Budget Office.
Note: All calculations use 1994 tax law except for the earned income tax credit, which is at 1996 levels. The estimates assume that all income is from self-employment and that the taxpayer has deductions equal to the greater of the standard deduction or 20 percent of earnings.

income groups are subject to a slightly lower marginal tax rate than a couple with two dependent children earning enough to begin to have their earned income tax credit phased out. These groups lose about 21 cents of their EITC payments for each dollar of earnings when their earnings increase above the $20,000 per year range. They also are subject to social insurance taxes that puts their effective marginal tax rate as high as 49 percent! The big difference for these lower income groups is that after a while, as their income increases, their marginal tax rates fall sharply. For the highest income groups no relief is available from the high marginal tax rates!

We can conclude that the federal income tax of 1994 by itself is quite progressive. The entire federal tax system, despite heavy reliance on payroll taxes, also is progressive with respect to income. However, marginal effective tax rates vary in a complex way that reflects the complexity of the federal tax code itself. These changes in marginal tax rates are likely to have complex effects on labor supply decisions of individuals.

Taxation of Low-Income Households

The income tax system has certain provisions that minimize the tax burden for low-income families and actually provide negative tax payments to some low-income workers! First of all, the personal exemptions and standard deduction imply that a substantial portion of the income of low-income taxpayers is nontaxable. For example, suppose a low-income family of four has gross income of $16,150 in 1994 and takes the standard deduction. That family therefore will be entitled to four personal exemptions, worth $2,450 each in 1994, and a standard deduction of $6,350 from income. The family deducts $9,800 in personal exemptions from its gross income, which when combined with the $6,350 standard deduction would result in $16,150 in deductions from gross income. The family's taxable income therefore would be zero!

In addition to benefiting from the personal exemptions and a standard deduction that are high proportions of a low income, those low-income taxpayers with dependent children and some workers without children also are eligible for a special payment from the government if they work. The **earned income tax credit** (EITC) is a payment from the Internal Revenue Service to workers with dependent children equal to a certain percentage of wage and salary income to those eligible. *In effect, the earned income tax credit is a tax refund to persons who do not owe any tax!* The credit therefore amounts to a negative tax, or a subsidy, to the working poor with dependent children. A certain maximum earned income tax credit per family applies, and the amount actually received depends on the families' actual earnings. The credit rises with wage and salary income at first and then is eventually phased out as income increases. The EITC provides income support to the working poor who are not eligible for federal income support through other programs and also supplements the income of part-time workers who are also receiving support from the AFDC and SSI programs (see Chapter 7 for a discussion of these programs and the details of EITC).

CHECKPOINT

1. How is taxable income derived from gross income under the U.S. income tax code?
2. Why can't the U.S. income tax be regarded as a *comprehensive* income tax?
3. Describe the rate structure of the U.S. federal income tax.

Tax Preferences

Still more complexity results from the federal income tax because individuals can, in part, control their taxable income by varying the sources and uses of their gross income. Let's now analyze how the rules and regulations of the income tax affect individual choices and the functioning of the economy.

Tax preferences are exclusions, exemptions, and deductions from the tax base. The tax preferences in the U.S. income tax code account for differences between taxable income and comprehensive income. Tax preferences can be thought of as subsidies—intentional or unintentional—to certain economic activities. Tax preferences are sometimes referred to as *tax loopholes,* but this term implies that they enter the tax code by accident, when, in fact, only a minority of the existing deductions and exemptions are present unintentionally. In any event, the existence of tax preferences changes the behavior of taxpayers, so that they can avoid or manage their tax burden by taking advantage of the special provisions. Since tax preferences reduce the size of the tax base, their elimination would increase the amount of revenue that a given tax rate structure can collect. Tax preferences also affect the distribution of the tax burden and therefore influence equity aspects of taxation.

Justification for Tax Preferences

Tax preferences are justified on various grounds: (1) administrative difficulty in taxing certain activities, (2) improving equity, and (3) encouraging private expenditures that generate external benefits. Whatever the justification, the existence of tax preferences has consequences both for the efficiency with which private resources are used and for the distribution of income.

Such exclusions from income as income-in-kind and unrealized capital gains represent tax preferences and often are allowed because of administrative difficulties in measuring their values. It would be difficult to develop a method of taxing all forms of income-in-kind in a consistent and equitable manner. Enforcement costs could be very high in administering a tax on these items, given the difficulties involved in measuring such items accurately. Similarly, it would be hard to measure unrealized capital gains or losses on such assets as owner-occupied homes that are infrequently sold.

Many exemptions and deductions from the tax base are justified in terms of equity considerations. For example, the basic personal exemption in the income tax varies with family size. It is based on the notion that it is equitable for families who have more children to pay less in taxes than families who have the same income but fewer children. Of course, in effect, this provides a subsidy for children. However, as currently administered, the personal exemption is phased out for upper income families. This means that the tax reduction resulting from the personal exemptions depends on actual taxable income as well as the number of dependents, and upper income groups receive no benefit no matter how many children they have. Similarly, deductions for medical expenses and casualty losses are based on the presumption that a loss in well-being occurs when either medical expenses or casualty losses, resulting from theft or disaster, over a certain percentage of income are not compensated with insurance reimbursement. Thus, individuals with high expenses of this type essentially are viewed as being less capable of paying taxes than are individuals who have the same income but no losses or medical expenses.

Finally, tax preferences are justified to encourage particular activities. For example, deductions from adjusted gross income for charitable donations constitute subsidies to charitable giving.[3] When these tax preferences serve to encourage expenditures that generate positive externalities, they act as proxies for corrective subsidies. As such, these tax preferences could serve to help achieve efficiency. When viewed as corrective subsidies, tax preferences must be evaluated in terms of their costs (revenues sacrificed), the extent to which they internalize externalities, and their impact on the distribution of both the tax burden and income.[4]

Excess Burden of Tax Preferences

Tax preferences can distort the relative prices of items and activities with values that can be excluded, exempted, or deducted from taxable income in ways that lead to efficiency losses in markets. The **marginal tax benefit** of an activity is the extra tax reduction that results when an individual engages in it. For example, when an individual is allowed to deduct the interest on a mortgage, then her decision to obtain a mortgage to buy a home depends not only on the marginal social benefit from doing so but also on the marginal tax benefit (a reduction in taxes) that results. The marginal tax benefit results in efficiency losses when it causes persons to make decisions that result in divergences between marginal social benefits and marginal social costs of activities. Unless marginal tax benefits are balanced by marginal external benefits, tax preferences decrease efficiency by encouraging more than the efficient amount of an activity to be undertaken.

Let's assume a perfectly competitive market and also that, as more of the activity is demanded, its market price remains unaffected. This assumption implies a perfectly elastic supply curve of the activity. This activity could be one that provides income from a certain source that is eligible for exclusion or exemption from taxable income. It also could be an activity, such as charitable donations or payment of interest on mortgages, that is tax deductible. The supply curve of the activity for the taxpayer is a horizontal line reflecting the marginal social cost of the activity, as shown in Figure 14.2. The efficient output, Q°, assuming no externalities corresponds to point A. At that point, the marginal social cost of the activity equals its marginal social benefit. The market price of the item is P_G.

Now assume that good X is an item for which annual personal expenditures can be deducted before computing personal income. This has the effect of decreasing the

---

[3]For an analysis of the impact of tax preferences on charitable giving, see Charles T. Clotfelter, "The Impact of the Tax Reform on Charitable Giving: A 1989 Perspective," in Joel Slemrod, ed., *Do Taxes Matter?* (Cambridge, MA: The MIT Press, 1990).

[4]Feldstein has argued that it might be desirable, in certain cases, to subsidize activities through tax preferences. See Martin Feldstein, "A Contribution to the Theory of Tax Expenditures: The Case of Charitable Giving," in *The Economics of Taxation*, eds. Henry J. Aaron and Michael J. Boskin (Washington, D.C.: The Brookings Institution, 1980), 99–122.

Figure 14.2 ✦ TAX PREFERENCE AND EFFICIENCY

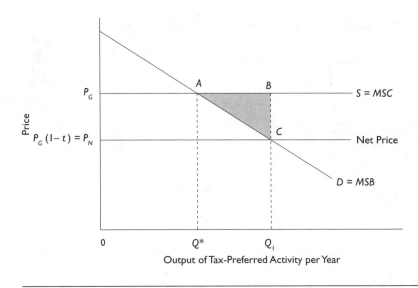

Tax preferences reduce the net prices of engaging in tax-preferred activities. The efficient output corresponds to the point at which MSC = MSB. The tax preference reduces the net price of purchasing or supplying tax-deductible or other tax-preferred activities. As a result, annual output increased from Q^* to Q_1. The loss in efficiency is represented by the shaded area ABC.

price of the preferred item to certain taxpayers according to their marginal tax rate, t. The effect is to lower the net price, as seen by those taxpayers, from P_G to:

$$P_N = P_G(1 - t)$$

The decrease in the price to P_N is only for those taxpayers eligible for the tax preference, and it varies with the marginal tax rate. In the case of tax preferences from deductions, taxpayers who do not itemize their deductions would still pay P_G, the gross price of the good. For example, assume that the tax-preferred activity is borrowing money to finance purchase of a home. Suppose a taxpayer who is subject to a marginal tax rate of 28 percent borrows money at 12 percent interest. If interest is tax deductible for this person, the net interest rate is $i_N = 12\%(1.0 - 0.28) = 8.64\%$.

By lowering net prices in this way, tax preferences increase the annual amount of the tax-preferred item or activity from Q^* to Q_1. There is an efficiency loss measured by the excess of the marginal social cost over the marginal social benefit of the good. For the taxpayer whose demand curve is illustrated in Figure 14.2, the social loss in net benefits due to the tax-induced increase in resources used in the annual amount of the tax-preferred activity is the area ABC.

Notice that the excess burden of a tax preference depends not only on the number of persons that qualify for it or take advantage of it but also on the marginal tax rate. Figure 14.3 shows the impact of marginal tax rates on tax preference activities. Suppose an upper income tax payer is subject to a 50-percent marginal tax rate. The price of engaging in the tax preferred activity is P_G. In the absence of any tax preference the individuals would choose Q^* units of the preferred activity. This the amount for which the marginal social cost of the activity equals its marginal social benefit. Under a 50-percent

Figure 14.3 ♦ Decrease in Excess Burden of Tax Preferences

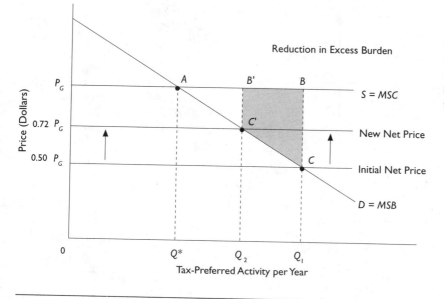

A decrease in the marginal tax rate results in a decrease in the excess burden from tax preferences. The area B'BCC' represents the gain in net social benefits as a result of the reduction in the marginal tax rate.

marginal tax rate, this person engages in Q_1 units of the tax-preferred activity per year. The excess burden of the tax preference is represented by the area of the triangle ABC. Assume that this person is now subject to a 28 percent marginal tax rate. The price of the tax-preferred activity is now $.72 P_G$. The increase in the net price in engaging in the activity decreases the annual amount from Q_1 to Q_2. The corresponding decrease in the excess burden is $B'BCC'$. For example, mortgage interest deductions, tax-free interest income from municipal bonds, and charitable contributions all will be worth less to taxpayers as a result of the decrease in marginal tax rates. In general, this would imply a decrease in the volume of activities that are still tax preferred.

We can conclude that the excess burden of existing tax preferences depends in part on the marginal tax rate paid by those who can engage in them. When marginal tax rates decline on average then the excess burden of existing tax preferences also will fall as the incentive to engage in them diminishes. Conversely, when marginal tax rates increase, as was the case in 1993 for upper income groups in the United States, the excess burden of tax preferences will go up as the incentive to engage in tax-preferred activities increases.

Tax Preferences Under the U.S. Income Tax System of the Mid-1990s

We can now examine major tax preferences in the tax code that account for differences between taxable income and a comprehensive measure of income and discuss their economic effects. Tax preferences can be divided into three major categories: exclusions from income, itemized deductions from income, and tax credits.

Exclusions from Income

1. Income-in-Kind and Imputed Housing Rental Income.   Much of income-in-kind, such as that stemming from do-it-yourself activities, is simply difficult to measure. These items typically are excluded from taxable income. It is unlikely that any consistent and equitable manner could be devised to measure and tax this form of income. Other types of income-in-kind, such as imputed rentals on housing, conceivably could be measured and taxed. For example, some European countries do tax the imputed rentals on owner-occupied homes, and data from the local property tax on housing values conceivably could be used to derive a consistent and reasonable equitable measure of imputed rent.[5]

Exemption of imputed rentals on owner-occupied homes gives considerable subsidy to home ownership in the United States. Some of this subsidy, however, might be offset by the impact of local property taxes on the cost of home ownership. Homeowners in owner-occupied homes essentially rent their homes to themselves. Because no market transaction takes place and no cash is exchanged, the housing services thus obtained escape taxation. However, the value of housing services they receive, less the costs of home ownership, is part of their comprehensive income. The exclusion of imputed rentals on owner-occupied homes is a subsidy to home ownership that encourages more than the efficient amount of resources to be allocated to the production of housing.

One estimate of the distortion in the choice between renting and owning homes, due to the exclusion of imputed rent and other preferential treatment of housing in the tax code, suggests that one-fourth of the U.S. growth in the proportion of home ownership from World War II through the 1970s is traceable to such preferential tax treatment.[6] In general, tax reform proposals have rarely suggested broadening the tax base by trying to tax nonmonetary rents, because it would be hard to accurately measure these rents. It is also likely that such a proposal would be politically unpopular with homeowners. If imputed rents were taxed and the mortgage interest deduction eliminated, De Leeuw and Ozanne estimate that the price of a typical home would fall by more than 14 percent.[7]

However, the reduction in marginal tax rates, particularly for upper income taxpayers since 1980 in the United States has reduced the value of the exclusion of imputed rentals significantly. These reductions in marginal tax rates make home

---

[5]See Paul E. Merz, "Foreign Income Tax Treatment of the Imputed Rental Value of Owner-Occupied Housing: Synopsis and Commentary," *National Tax Journal* 30 (December 1977): 435–439.

[6]Harvey S. Rosen and Kenneth T. Rosen, "Federal Taxes and Homeownership: Evidence from Times Series," *Journal of Political Economy* 88 (February 1980): 59–75.

[7]See Frank D. De Leeuw and Larry O. Ozanne, "Housing," in *How Taxes Affect Economic Behavior*, eds. Aaron and Pechman, 29.

ownership a much less attractive option to many taxpayers compared to what it was once. The reduced tax benefit of home ownership implies a reduced demand for homes, particularly expensive homes, that will put downward pressure on home prices.[8] The values of homes in many areas of the nation have in fact declined in the early 1990s, due in part to changes in the tax law. The 1993 increase in marginal tax rates to upper income groups could reverse this trend.

2. Fringe Benefits.   Workers are typically compensated in forms that supplement their wages and salaries and are excluded from current taxable income. For example, if you have a pension or retirement plan at your job, it is likely that your employer contributes to this plan. Although employer contribution to pension or retirement plans constitute part of the compensation of workers, and certainly adds to the employees' net worth, these contributions are excluded from current gross income under the current U.S. tax laws.

Similarly employer contributions for employees' insurance is another fringe benefit that is part of a worker's income that also is excluded from gross income. Group-term life insurance, health insurance, educational benefits, legal services, and child care provided by employers is really a form of income-in-kind that is excluded from income.

Self-employed workers also can defer taxation on pension contributions by deducting as an adjustment to gross income their contributions to special retirement plans they can set up under current law. Finally, the portion of their own payments for pension contributions and some insurance programs provided by workers also can be excluded from gross income under current law. However, retired workers receiving pensions do pay taxes on the portion of their pensions that was excluded from their income during their working years. The exclusion of pension contributions and other employer contributions from gross income of workers results in a loss of income tax revenue to the government amounting to $100 billion in 1993.

3. Transfers.   Most government transfers to individuals are excluded from gross income. Government transfers may be either in the form of government income support or social insurance payments to individuals. Private transfers also exist in the form of private charity or gifts. Under a comprehensive income tax, transfers represent taxable income for the recipient.

The U.S. federal tax code does not treat transfers consistently. Gifts and inheritances are excluded from the income of the recipient under the presumption that as income to the donor they already have been taxed. There are, however, separate from the income tax, gift and inheritance taxes that are discussed in Chapter 17. In most cases, a gift cannot be deducted from the income of the donor, unless it is a charitable contribution. According to the Haig-Simons definition, a gift qualifies as a use of income to the donor and therefore represents a form of consumption to the donor that

---

[8]See James M. Poterba, "Taxation and Housing Markets: Preliminary Evidence," in Joel Slemrod, ed., *Do Taxes Matter? The Impact of the Tax Reform Act of 1986* (Cambridge, MA: The MIT Press, 1990): 141–161.

would be included in income. Similarly, because a gift increases the donee's command over resources, it is technically part of his income as well. Although this subjects a gift to double taxation, it is a consistent way of treating the tax base, which is defined on an individual basis.[9] An exception to this rule is court-ordered alimony, which the tax code treats as taxable income to the recipient but constitutes an adjustment subtracted from the gross income of the person who pays them. However, child support payments are not included in the income of the recipient, nor are they deductible as an adjustment to income for the person paying them.

No attempt is made to tax such transfers-in-kind as food stamps, Medicare and Medicaid payments, and such other subsidies as public housing, even if these subsidies accrue to individuals whose annual income exceeds any basic tax-free allowance. Even if these items were to be included in the income of the recipients it is unlikely that they would be taxable because of the fact that personal exemptions and the standard deduction remove most persons in poverty from the tax rolls. Unemployment compensation is, however, now included in gross income and therefore fully taxable. Social Security retirement benefits are partially taxable for persons with incomes above certain levels. As much as 85 percent of the Social Security pensions of those with relatively high incomes can be subject to tax under rules prevailing in 1994.

4. Unrealized Capital Gains and the Controversy Over Tax Treatment of Realized Capital Gains. Perhaps the most controversial area in defining taxable income is the treatment of capital gains. *Only realized capital gains are included in taxable income.* A realized capital gain is one that is obtained when an asset is sold for cash or exchanged for another asset. In 1994, realized capital gains on most assets were taxed as ordinary income but were subject to a maximum tax rate of 28 percent. Prior to 1987, long-term realized capital gains were taxed at a lower rate than ordinary income; the maximum tax rate applied to net long-term capital gains on assets held for at least six months was 20 percent.

Net positive capital gains, adjusted by an index of the price level, do constitute an increase in a person's potential purchasing power. The federal income tax code currently does not adjust capital gains for inflation.[10] In this sense, much of the tax on capital gains is not levied on increased purchasing power.[11] Some economists have argued that preferential tax treatment of realized capital gains is justified in the United States to compensate for the fact that such gains are not indexed for the rate of inflation. Failure to adjust capital gains for inflation creates serious problems in tax equity and efficiency. This is considered later in this chapter.

---

[9]Gift and inheritance taxes do subject the donor or his estate to taxes. These are property transfer taxes, which are discussed in Chapter 17.

[10]For a discussion of issues involved in indexing capital gains for tax purposes, see U.S. Congress, Congressional Budget Office, *Indexing Capital Gains* (Washington, D.C.: U.S. Government Printing Office, August 1990).

[11]See Martin Feldstein and Joel Slemrod, "Inflation and the Excess Taxation of Capital Gains on Corporate Stock," *National Tax Journal* 31 (June 1978): 107–118.

Exclusion of unrealized capital gains from taxation makes those who have such gains better off. This is because they can defer the tax on any gains that they do not convert into cash. For example, if a person buys $5,000 worth of corporate stock and the value of that stock increases to $10,000 over the year, she will have earned $5,000 in capital gains. If all her capital gains, realized and unrealized, are subject to a tax of 28 percent, she would have a tax liability of $1,400 on the gain. If only *realized* gains are taxed, she can postpone the tax by holding on to the stock, and not converting it to cash. This makes her better off because she can earn interest, and possibly additional capital gains, on the $1,400 that she otherwise would have had to pay in taxes that year.

Under current rules, capital gains are not taxed at death. This means that unrealized capital gains can escape taxation completely if they are held until death. An investor therefore can leave more to his heirs by not cashing in his capital gains before he dies.

Some evidence indicates that exclusion of unrealized capital gains from taxation does discourage investors from selling assets on which they have accumulated gains. This is sometimes called the *lock-in effect*, resulting from the exclusion of unrealized capital gains from taxation. One study found that a reduction in actual capital gains tax rates would be likely to increase turnover of assets.[12] A number of studies have found that capital gains realizations are very sensitive to the tax rate applied to realized capital gains.[13]

Very liberal provisions exist for deferring long-term capital gains on owner-occupied housing, if the gains are reinvested in another house to be used as a principal residence. Under current rules, taxpayers completely escape taxation of capital gains on principal residences (up to a maximum of $125,000) if they continue to reinvest such gains in housing or otherwise defer converting such gains into cash until they attain the age of 55.

The controversy over tax treatment of capital gains continues with some arguing that exclusion of a portion of realized capital gains from taxation can increase the return to investment and encourage the start of new businesses. However, preferential treatment of capital gains also can encourage conversion of other forms of income into capital gains. For example, a lower tax applied to capital gains could encourage corporations to reduce payout of dividends. Instead, the corporations would take income normally used to finance dividends and use it as a means of increasing their acquisition of capital. This would provide shareholders with income in the form of capital gains, which then would be taxed at a lower rate than dividend income.

5. Interest on State and Local Bonds.   Exclusion of interest earned on state and local government bonds from taxable income represents a subsidy to these govern-

---

[12]Gerald E. Auten and Charles T. Clotfelter, "Permanent versus Transitory Tax Effects and the Realization of Capital Gains," *The Quarterly Journal of Economics* 97 (November 1982): 613–632.

[13]For a summary of these studies, see U.S. Congress, Congressional Budget Office, *How Capital Gains Tax Rates Affect Revenues: The Historical Evidence* (Washington, D.C.: The Congress of the United States, March 1988).

ments. This tax preference subsidizes state and local governments by allowing them to borrow money at lower rates than would be the case if purchasers of their bonds had to pay tax on their interest earnings. The attractiveness of such bonds to holders depends on their net yield (which, in turn, depends on the taxpayer's marginal tax rate) and the interest spread between municipal bonds and securities with similar risk and return attributes but a yield that is subject to taxation. For example, an investor who is in a 33-percent tax bracket and who can earn 14 percent on a fully taxable bond would require a yield of at least 9.32 percent on a municipal bond of equal riskiness to be induced to buy it. This is because his after-tax return on the taxable bond is 9.32 percent, which is equal to $14(1 - .33)$ percent. An investor in a 15-percent marginal tax bracket, however, would earn 11.90 percent after taxes on the 14 percent bond. This investor would not buy the municipal bond unless it returned at least 11.90 percent. The actual interest rate paid by local governments depends on the demand and supply of their bonds. However, the more bonds they must sell to investors in tax brackets below 33 percent to obtain their required funds, the higher the interest rate that state and local governments must pay to attract funds.

The subsidy to state and local governments is measured by the yield spread between the interest rate at which they can borrow and the rate at which they would have to borrow in the absence of the exclusion. This second rate can be approximated by the rate on taxable securities of similar maturity and risk. The cost of the subsidy to the federal government is measured by the loss in tax revenues from excluding the interest from taxable income.

Suppose state and local governments save, on average, about 20 percent on their interest rates, because they have to make their bonds attractive to taxpayers with marginal tax rates below 33 percent to raise enough funds. They might pay 8 percent instead of the 10 percent that corporations pay, on average. Suppose, however, the federal government loses, on average, 30 percent of the interest rate. This is because many investors with marginal tax rates in excess of 30 percent buy the bonds. The market interest rates for the bonds must be low enough to make them attractive to at least some investors in the lower tax brackets. For example, if $5 billion in interest is earned on tax-exempt bonds, the government would lose 30 percent of this amount, or $1.5 billion per year in revenues. The savings to state and local governments are only $1 billion, or 20 percent of the $5 billion interest costs. The subsidy costs more than it is worth. In other words, those who pay federal taxes would be better off, and local governments could be as well off, if the federal government made payments to local governments equal to the interest spread that prevails under exclusion, instead of excluding the interest from taxation.

6. Miscellaneous Exclusions and Adjustments. Scholarships and fellowships are excluded from income for degree candidates only. However, these sources of income are excluded only to the extent to which they do not exceed tuition and other course-related expenses. Amounts for room, board, and other incidental expenses are not excluded from gross income.

Saving for retirement in special accounts is an adjustment to income. Individuals with incomes below a certain level and others who are not active participants in an employer-maintained retirement plan can deduct limited amounts of saving from their gross income when computing adjusted gross income. Employees also can exclude some of their income from taxation by contributing to special retirement plans called 401(k) and 403(b) plans, which are permitted by these numbered sections of the Internal Revenue Code. Finally, self-employed persons can also deduct retirement contributions made to special "Keogh" and "SEP" plans as adjustments to their gross income.

Adjustments to income for retirement saving are designed as a subsidy to saving that allows amounts deposited in such accounts along with accrued earnings tax free status until withdrawn as retirement income after the worker reaches a certain age, usually 59½. Exclusions from and adjustments to gross income give taxpayers taking advantage of such provisions ample opportunity to "defer" taxable income. **Deferral of taxable income** means that income that is ordinarily taxable can be excluded or deducted from gross income in the current year but will eventually be taxed along with the accrued interest and capital gains. Deferral of tax liability makes taxpayers better off by allowing them to earn both interest and possible capital gains on the amount they would have paid in taxes.

The advantage of postponing tax liability can be enormous. For example, suppose you are self-employed and put $10,000 this year into a Keogh retirement plan. Also assume that you are in the 28 percent marginal tax bracket. This means that, of the $10,000 saved, $2,800 would have been paid in taxes. In effect, you would be saving $7,200 of your own income and $2,800 in taxes. Assume that you hold this money in an account that earns 10 percent annually for twenty years and that you remove the principal and accumulated interest from the account and pay the regular 28 percent tax on the sum after twenty years. When saving that was previously tax deferred is removed from an account, it is taxed as if it were current income.

As the $10,000 is held in the account, the interest income accrues *tax free*. After 20 years, assuming annual compounding, the $10,000 will be worth

$$\$10,000(1 \ + \ .10)^{20} \ = \ \$67,000.$$

The net income over the twenty-year period therefore would be $57,000. When the asset is cashed in, a tax liability of 28 percent of the net income *and* the $10,000 principal will be incurred of $0.28(\$67,000) \ = \ \$18,760$. The net income earned over the twenty-year period after taxes therefore would be $57,000 \ - \ \$18,760 \ = \ \$38,240$.

If, instead, the $10,000 saving was *not allowed to be deducted* from gross income, then, by saving, the taxpayer would not reduce his tax liability by $2,800 in the year the $10,000 is saved. Therefore after deduction of $2,800 of taxes due on the $10,000 of taxable income saved, the net saving will be only $7,200. Further, if the interest on the saving is treated as normal income, it will be taxed as it accrues because it will no longer be in a special tax-deferred account. The *after tax* interest rate will be

$$10(1 \ - \ .28)\% \ = \ 10(.72)\% \ = \ 7.2\%.$$

After twenty years the net saving of $7,200 will be worth:

$$\$7,200(1 \ + \ .072)^{20} \ = \ \$28,944.$$

The net income after taxes in twenty years therefore will be $28,944 minus $7,200, or $21,744. This is substantially less than the net income of $38,240 that can be obtained after taxes when saving is deductible as an adjustment to income and the interest accrues tax free until the funds are removed from the account. Tax deductibility of funds put into special savings accounts and deferral of taxes on interest and other earnings on those accounts therefore represents a substantial subsidy to saving.

Itemized Deductions from Adjusted Gross Income

Taxpayers have the option of itemizing deductions. When itemized deductions a taxpayer can claim exceed the standard deduction entitled to the taxpayer, then it pays to itemize. By increasing the standard deduction substantially, the Tax Reform Act of 1986 increased the threshold over which itemized deductions must pass to make it worthwhile. As a result, the number of taxpayers itemizing deductions has declined. Nonetheless, upper-income taxpayers still take advantage of itemization, and their choices are strongly influenced by the rules governing what is or is not deductible.

The major tax-deductible expenses are reviewed in this section. Remember that the benefit of a tax deduction varies with the taxpayer's marginal rate tax rate. If a person subject to a marginal tax rate of 31 percent obtains a mortgage of 10 percent and can deduct all interest payments, her *net interest* is only $10(1 - 0.31)\%$ or 6.9 percent, after the benefit of the tax deduction is considered. A person who is subject to a marginal tax rate of 15 percent and who can deduct interest payments would pay a net interest of $10(1 - 0.15)\%$ or 8.5 percent, on a loan at 10 percent after the tax deduction. Of course, one who does not itemize deductions does not enjoy any tax-induced price reduction on borrowed funds. Tax deductibility of an expense therefore provides a reduction in the net price of the associated activity available to those who itemize deductions according to the taxpayer's marginal tax bracket. Discussions of the major tax deductible expenses follow.

1. Medical Expenses. Unreimbursed medical expenses in excess of 7.5 percent of adjusted gross income are tax deductible. The floor in medical expense, before deductibility is allowed, can be viewed as consistent with the notion that a certain minimal amount of medical expense increases individual well-being and does not decrease the ability to pay taxes. The generalization that all medical expenses greater than the minimal amount decrease well-being and the ability to pay is somewhat broad. Elective cosmetic surgery and voluntary psychiatric treatment are examples of chosen medical expenditures that are likely to increase well-being.

The result of allowing individuals to deduct a portion of their medical expenses is that the federal government pays part of the medical bills of certain households. After an individual who itemizes deductions incurs medical expenses in excess of 7.5 percent of adjusted gross income, the federal government in effect pays a portion of any additional bills according to the taxpayer's marginal tax rate. For example, if the taxpayer is subject to a 31-percent marginal tax rate, then after incurring a certain amount of expense the federal government ends up paying nearly one-third of this person's out-of-pocket additional medical bills in excess of 7.5 percent of the taxpayer's adjusted gross income. This subsidizes medical services above the tax deductibility threshold. Taxpayers also can be induced to adjust the timing of some out-of-pocket medical expenses so that they are lumped in a single year and will exceed 7.5 percent of AGI.

2. *State and Local Income and Property Taxes.*   Certain taxes, including income and property taxes, paid to state and local governments are tax deductible. These deductions constitute indirect subsidies to those governments, encouraging them to adjust their tax structures to include more types of taxes that are deductible from adjusted gross income under the federal income tax. These subsidies occur because the deductions reduce the tax burden to taxpayers in states and localities, making it easier to gain collective approval on extensions of local public spending. The benefit of this provision varies from taxpayer to taxpayer according to the marginal tax bracket, but it might be offset by higher federal tax rates to compensate for the resulting loss in federal revenues. In addition, citizens in states or localities with above-average tax rates or income levels gain as a result of this provision, relative to citizens in other areas.

Some reform proposals have recommended the elimination of these tax deductions, which would cut the subsidies to state and local government expenditures. The argument is that services supplied by state and local governments provide benefits to citizens exactly as private goods do; therefore, they should be viewed analogously. Also, subsidies accrue more than proportionately to high-tax, urban states. In addition, high-income taxpayers subject to high marginal tax rates receive proportionately more of the benefits. Eliminating the deductibility of state and local taxes would make it more difficult for state and local governments to raise revenues. The Tax Reform Act of 1986 removed the deductibility of state and local sales taxes, but income and property taxes levied by state and local governments are still included in federal itemized deductions.

3. *Interest Payments.*   Certain interest payments made by households are tax-deductible. Interest on mortgages of a taxpayer's first and second home is deductible. No deduction, however, for such personal interest expense as car loans, credit cards, or other personal loans, including educational loans, is permitted.

Interest incurred to make financial investments, such as to buy stock on margin, is deductible but is limited to total investment income. *Interest on mortgages for first and second homes is deductible.* However, the total mortgage debt on which interest can be deducted is subject to some constraints. Interest on mortgage debt incurred to buy, build, or improve a person's main home after October 1987 in excess of $1 million of mortgage debt is not deductible. And mortgage interest on mortgage debt greater than $100,000 is not deductible if that debt was incurred on the main home for a purpose other than to buy, build, or improve a home. However, special deductibility limits are available for homeowners who refinance their mortgages and obtain line-of-credit mortgages.

The deduction of mortgage interest is based on an analogy between the business firm and the household, arguing that interest is a cost of production. The difference between household mortgage credit and business credit is important. Firms borrow to finance their productive operations; income from production is then subject to tax. Individuals who receive credit to finance homes obtain assets or consumer services that produce income-in-kind, which is not subject to taxation. Using a comprehensive definition of income, deduction of interest would be warranted as a cost of earning income only to the extent to which income-in-kind, stemming from expenditures made possible by borrowing, were taxed.

Another problem with the mortgage interest deduction stems from the fungibility of money. Money can be used for a multitude of purposes. By limiting interest deductions to mortgages, Congress hoped to discourage borrowing for consumer purchases like vacations, stereos, cars, and other consumer durables. However, when a person borrows to finance a home, it frees income to be used for other purchases. Some taxpayers now may choose to borrow more than they would have otherwise on their homes—or build or buy more expensive homes. The resulting increases in their cash balances enable them to buy more consumer items without incurring debt specifically for those purchases. The banks and financial institutions realized this quickly and developed "line of credit home equity loans" that enabled consumers who owned homes to use their homes as collateral for credit. The limits on deductibility of interest imposed by Congress are designed to limit the incentive to use mortgages in place of consumer credit.

Recent evidence of the impact of the limitations on deductibility of interest from adjusted gross income suggests that although the limits did reduce taxpayer reliance on personal borrowing, it was not effective in reducing overall borrowing. The wealthier taxpayers who owned homes and itemized deductions consolidated and reshuffled their personal debts into home mortgage loans leaving total credit extended unchanged.[14]

4. Charitable Contributions. As discussed previously, deductibility of charitable contributions, including those made in kind, constitutes a subsidy to private transfers to charitable and other nonprofit organizations, including educational institutions. A number of studies have provided evidence indicating that charitable giving is highly responsive to tax deductibility.[15] The tax deduction decreases the "price" of charitable giving by the giver's marginal tax rate. For example, a taxpayer subject to a marginal tax rate of 31 percent really gives only 69 cents each time she donates $1 to charity. The other 31 cents is represented by a reduction in tax revenues to the federal government. If charitable donations are elastic with respect to tax deductibility, the percentage increase in giving that results from the tax deduction exceeds the percentage reduction in taxes paid. This means that the 31 cents lost revenue to the Treasury from the tax deduction results in *more* than 31 cents worth of additional giving. For this reason the tax deduction for charitable contributions seems to be a very effective means of encouraging donations. This could even act to reduce government expenditures, if the private giving made it possible for the government to devote less of its resources to helping the poor than it would otherwise.

Research on the impact of reduced marginal tax rates since 1986 has provided evidence that the reductions in the marginal tax rates did result in a fall of charitable contribution by taxpayers for which the "price" of giving was increased.[16]

---

[14]See Jonathon Skinner and Daniel Feenberg, "Impact of the 1986 Tax Reform on Personal Saving," in Slemrod, ed., *Do Taxes Matter?*, 1990.

[15]See Charles T. Clotfelter and C. Eugene Steurle, "Charitable Contributions," in *How Taxes Affect Economic Behavior*, eds. Henry J. Aaron and Joseph A. Pechman, 403–446.

[16]See Charles T. Clotfelter, "Impact of Tax Reform on Charitable Giving: A 1989 Perspective," in Slemrod, ed., *Do Taxes Matter?*

5. *Miscellaneous Deductions.* Employees who incur unreimbursed business expenses including those for travel can deduct those expenses but only to the extent to which they exceed 2 percent of adjusted gross income. However, attendance at conventions or seminars is not deductible unless it is for trade or business purposes, and only 50 percent of meals and entertainment expenses are tax-deductible.

Minimum Tax on Preference Income: The Alternative Minimum Tax (AMT)

The existence of tax preferences in the tax code offers an opportunity for high-income taxpayers to shelter a substantial portion of their gross incomes from taxation. To reduce this incentive, an alternative minimum tax (AMT) is levied on taxpayers who make extensive use of tax preferences. The minimum tax on preference items is designed to increase taxes paid by persons who reduce their taxable income significantly by itemizing deductions and obtaining tax-free income. The details of the tax computation are complicated. In effect, the AMT is designed to include excluded income such as some interest earned on state and local bonds and various itemized deductions in taxable income. Taxpayers who have considerable tax preferences will find that their "alternative minimum taxable income," which is calculated by adding in tax preference items to regular income, is quite high. However, a certain portion of minimum taxable income is tax exempt. The amounts above this minimum are subject to a tax rate that ranged from 26 to 28 percent in 1994.

Tax Deductions Versus Tax Credits

Tax credits, instead of tax deductions, have been available for such activities and expenses as child care. The difference between a tax credit and a tax deduction is that credits are based on a certain percentage of the expense incurred, and this percentage is fixed for all taxpayers, regardless of their income and marginal tax rates and whether they itemize deductions. The value of tax deductions, on the other hand, varies with the taxpayer's marginal tax bracket in terms of the reduction in taxes that the deductions entail. They give more benefit, in monetary terms, to upper-income taxpayers, who are subject to higher marginal tax rates. Those who favor an increase in the progressivity of the federal tax rate structure generally favor tax credits over tax deductions. Another advantage of credits to lower income tax is that individuals get a tax reduction from engaging in the activity for which a credit is provided even if they do not itemize their deductions. Because most low-income taxpayers do not itemize, this is of considerable benefit to them.

Tax Expenditures

Tax preferences not only cause losses in efficiency but also result in reduction in revenue collection by decreasing the size of the tax base. **Tax expenditures** are losses in tax revenues attributable to tax preferences. The Office of Management and Budget is required to compute tax expenditures annually and submit them to Congress as part of the president's budget. Tax expenditures also are estimated by the Joint Committee on Taxation of the U.S. Congress, which publishes five-year projections of tax expenditures for use by the Congress. Tax expenditures provide a useful starting point for evaluating tax preferences in terms of the loss in tax revenues.

Elimination of tax preferences broadens the tax base and allows lower rates of taxation without reducing revenues collected. However, the elimination would increase the net price of engaging in tax-preferred activities and, therefore, reduce the levels of such activities. Taxable income, therefore, would not increase by the full amount of income on which tax expenditures are calculated. Elimination of certain tax preferences would cause persons to adjust their behavior to decrease tax-preferred activities and to increase the amount of activities that still receive preferential treatment for tax purposes. Therefore, it is likely that gains in revenue to the Treasury due to the elimination of tax preferences are overestimated. In effect, the Treasury in computing tax expenditures assumes that all activities are perfectly inelastic with respect to their tax-preferred treatment and that elimination of any one tax preference does not affect the value of any other tax preference.

Table 14.2 shows ten major tax preferences of the personal income tax and the projected revenue losses for fiscal year 1994. The two largest tax expenditure items in the tax code are exclusion of pension contributions and earnings and of employer contributions for medical insurance and health care from taxable income. Together these two tax preferences were projected to result in a loss of $133 billion in revenue for the Treasury in 1994. Deductibility of mortgage interest on owner-occupied

Table 14.2 ◆ TEN LARGEST TAX EXPENDITURES RESULTING FROM TAX PREFERENCES IN THE U.S. INDIVIDUAL INCOME TAX (BILLIONS OF DOLLARS)

ITEM	PROJECTED REVENUE LOSS FOR FISCAL YEAR 1994
Net Exclusion from Income of Pension Contributions and Earnings	70.4
Exclusion of Employer Contributions for Medical Insurance and Health Care	63.2
Deductibility of Mortgage Interest on Owner-Occupied Homes	48.1
Exclusion of Social Security Benefits	24.5
Deferral of Capital Gains on Home Sales and Exclusion of People 55 and Over Plus Exclusion of Capital Gains at Death	21.0
Deductibility of State and Local Income Taxes	27.2
Deductibility of Charitable Contributions	15.0
Exclusion of Interest on General Purpose State and Local Bonds	15.0
Deductibility of Real Estate Taxes	14.0
Exclusion of Untaxed Medicare Benefits	13.3

Source: U.S. Office of Management and Budget.

homes cost the Treasury $481 billion in 1994. Similarly, as the table shows, the Treasury forgoes billions of dollars of revenue from exclusion of Social Security benefits from taxation, deductibility of state and local income and property taxes, deductibility of charitable contributions, deferral of capital gains of home sales, and exclusion of capital gains at death.

CHECKPOINT

1. What are tax preferences? List the major types of tax preferences.
2. How do tax preferences cause losses in efficiency of resource use? How is the excess burden affected by marginal tax rates?
3. List three major tax preferences of the U.S. income tax code, and discuss who is subsidized and how the subsidy varies with the taxpayer's marginal tax rate.

ISSUES IN INCOME TAX POLICY

The income tax in the United States is perennially subject to reform. Some issues, such as the comprehensiveness of the tax base and the tax rate structure, are discussed in this and the previous chapter. In general, because the excess burden of the tax in labor and capital markets as well as the distortions caused by tax preferences depend on marginal tax rates, we can always reduce the excess burden of the tax by reducing marginal tax rates. However, reductions in marginal tax rates imply losses in revenue that are difficult to endure when the federal government is struggling to balance its budget as we approach the twenty-first century. To prevent losses in revenue, tax rate reductions can be balanced by base broadening through the elimination of tax preferences. However, the politics of income taxation often make it difficult to gain agreement on broad elimination of such time-honored deductions as deductibility of mortgage interest.

However, several issues that continually arise in U.S. income taxation are likely to become political issues as we approach the year 2000. In this section we look at a selection of these issues.

Inflation, Interest, and Capital Gains

Inflation can change income tax rates without an act of Congress! Inflation implies that nominal income increases faster than real income. **Bracket creep** is an increase in the effective rates of taxation of real taxable income when the tax rate schedules are based on nominal values of income rather than real values. Bracket creep was a serious problem in the late 1970s when inflation was very high. During that period inflation eroded the real value of personal exemptions, the standard deduction, and some itemized deductions. At the same time, bracket creep pushed taxpayers into higher tax brackets as their nominal income increased at a faster rate than their real income. Beginning in 1985, nominal income in tax brackets as well as personal exemptions and the standard deduction were indexed to the rate of inflation. Indexation of tax brackets, personal exemptions, and the standard deduction were also part of the provisions of the Tax Reform Act of 1986 to prevent inflation from increasing real tax burdens.

Although indexation of tax brackets can prevent bracket creep, inflation can still cause serious distortions in taxation of capital income. Inflation creates serious problems in accurately measuring interest income and capital gains. In the case of interest income, the problem is obvious. At 10 percent inflation, a yield on savings deposits of 5 percent implies that the saver is losing a net 5 percent of the value of savings. Although interest accrues at 5 percent at the end of the year, the value of the dollars in the account, including the interest accrued, is worth 10 percent less. However, the tax system taxes nominal interest as it accrues, with no adjustment for inflation. Savers who earn negative rates in real terms pay positive taxes on those negative returns. This, in turn, reduces the return to saving still further and is likely to result in a decline in annual saving.

Similar problems occur for interest deductions allowed in computing taxable income. The interest deductible is based on the nominal balance outstanding. However, during inflation, debtors benefit because their outstanding balances on any loans decrease in real terms. Put differently, they pay off their loans in dollars that are worth less than those they borrowed. Allowing an interest deduction on the basis of the nominal interest paid on the outstanding balance overstates the real value of that deduction and decreases the tax liability of debtors, relative to other taxpayers. To adjust for inflation, the deduction should be in terms of real interest paid.

Finally, the tax system taxes nominal capital gains without adjustment for inflation. This can create serious problems in capital mobility and incentives to make investments. The argument here is similar to the one made for other types of income. However, since capital gains are taxed only as they are realized, there are some additional problems that stem from the fact that taxpayers can postpone or avoid the tax by continuing to hold the asset. By holding the asset and avoiding annual payment of taxes on accrued gains, taxpayers can increase their net return over the life of the asset by earning gains both on the value of the asset and the value of the amount of tax that they would have paid on the gains had they been taxed on accrual.[17] As discussed previously, if a person holds an asset until death, his unrealized gain escapes taxation completely.

Taxation of the nominal gain on an asset means that the effective rate on the real gain is much higher than indicated by the rate schedule. This reduces the net return to capital and can adversely affect savings and capital accumulation. The gain itself is only taxable on realization. Because annually accrued gains escape taxation, the tendency is for the tax to "lock in" investors, as pointed out earlier in this chapter. This discourages shifts in investment portfolio composition in response to changing market conditions and impairs the efficiency in the operation of capital markets.

Martin Feldstein and Joel Slemrod have estimated that individuals paid more than $500 million extra tax on corporate stock capital gains as a result of inflation in 1973.

---

[17]For proof of this, see Shoven, "Inflation," in *Federal Tax Reform*, ed. Boskin, 177.

Their research also indicates that 40 percent of the capital gains taxes paid in 1973 would not have been due had the nominal gains been adjusted for inflation.[18] Other research by the same authors provides some evidence that the "lock-in effect" of the capital gains tax is, indeed, significant, and it does decrease capital mobility.[19] One research study on the effect of a significant reduction in the tax rate on capital gains realizations concluded that a tax cut on capital gains in 1982 increased realizations to such a degree that more revenue was collected by the Treasury despite the lower tax rates.[20]

More general analysis of the effect of expected inflation on the relative income from capital, compared to labor, concludes that inflation causes nominal capital income to grow more rapidly than labor income. The reason for this is that inflation increases both the return to investment (the nominal interest rate) and the value of capital assets. As these two separate effects compound, the rate of growth of nominal capital income exceeds that of wages when wages are adjusted for inflation. Thus, inflation biases the nominal income of capital, relative to the nominal income of labor, and therefore results in increased nominal rates of taxation on capital relative to labor.[21]

The Taxpaying Unit: Does the Tax System Discriminate Against Married Couples?

The tax rate structure applied to taxable income depends on the status of the taxpaying unit. Separate rate schedules apply to single, married couples filing jointly, married couples filing separately, and head-of-household taxpayers. In all cases, the schedules are defined according to the marginal tax rates that apply to various brackets of income. The standard deduction amount differs, depending on filing status.

The standard deduction for married couples is less than the sum for two single people. For example, in 1994 the standard deduction for a single taxpayer was $3,800. However, a married couple filing jointly was entitled to only a $6,350 standard deduction, which is $1,250 less than they would be entitled to if they were not married and each filed singly. A couple in the 28-percent bracket would have a tax bill that was $350 higher because of the $1,250 difference between the combined single and joint standard deduction.

Two single people who earn the same income and live together pay lower rates of taxation than a married couple, other things being equal, if each spouse earns the same income as each of the single persons. The joint rate schedule, in effect, provides benefits to taxpayers only to the extent to which the income of one of the spouses is significantly higher than the other's. This is the so-called income-splitting effect, which divides the income of both taxpayers equally between them in computing taxes

---

[18]Feldstein and Slemrod, "Inflation," 110–113.

[19]Joel Slemrod and Martin Feldstein, "The Lock-in Effect of the Capital Gains Tax: Some Time Series Evidence," *Tax Notes*, 7 (August 7, 1978).

[20]See Lawrence B. Lindsey, "Capital Gains Rates, Realizations, and Revenues," in Martin S. Feldstein, ed., *The Effects of Taxation on Capital Accumulation* (Chicago: University of Chicago Press, 1987), 69–97.

[21]For proof, see Peter A. Diamond, "Inflation and the Comprehensive Tax Base," *Journal of Public Economics* 4 (August 1975): 227–244.

I N T E R N A T I O N A L   V I E W

WORLD INCOME TAX REFORM IN THE 1980s

The 1980s very well could be described as the decade of world income tax reform. Following the lead of the United States' landmark Tax Reform Act of 1986, several nations have acted to reduce the excess burden of their tax system by broadening the income tax base and lowering marginal tax rates applied to personal income. Tax preferences have been eliminated, and their value to taxpayers has been cut because of declining tax rates.

The income tax reforms were of greatest significance in the United States, which relies more heavily on the income tax for revenue than do European nations (where payroll taxes and taxes on consumption are relatively more important). However, most industrial nations have taken steps to reduce marginal tax rates applied to income and have made up the loss in revenue from lower tax rates by eliminating tax preferences. The number of tax brackets also has been reduced in most nations.

Actually, the first round of income tax rate reductions began in 1979 when the United Kingdom reduced its personal income tax rates and financed the loss in revenue with an increase in other taxes. The United States reduced marginal tax rates and the number of tax brackets in 1981 and then further reduced the number of tax brackets and marginal tax rates in 1986. Then, in the 1980s, the U.K. enacted several other tax reforms that reduced personal income tax rates and eliminated many tax deductions and allowances. Sweden, Canada, Australia, New Zealand, Mexico, and Japan also reduced tax rates and the number of tax brackets and eliminated many income tax preferences in the 1980s.

The table shows changes in the number of tax brackets and the top marginal tax rates for the personal income tax for seven nations that have followed the lead of the United States in reforming their income tax systems in the 1980s.* As you can see, except for Canada where the top marginal rate was 29 percent in the late 1980s, most of the nations still have much higher marginal tax rates than those of the United States. The highest marginal income tax rates are in Sweden and Japan, both of which had top marginal tax rates of 50 percent in the late 1980s. Although Sweden had the highest tax rates, their tax reforms were expected to remove 90 percent of the taxpayers from the income tax rolls by 1991. In Sweden, only 10 percent of the population (those with the highest incomes) were subject to the personal income tax. In most cases the reduction in marginal tax rates were accompanied by removal of tax preferences.

*Based on John Whalley, "Foreign Responses to U.S. Tax Reform" in *Do Taxes Matter?*

CHANGES IN TAX BRACKETS, TOP MARGINAL TAX RATES IN THE 1980s†

Australia: Number of tax brackets reduced from 5 to 4. Top marginal tax rate reduced from 60 to 49 percent.

Canada: Number of tax brackets reduced from 10 to 3. Top marginal tax rate reduced from 34 to 29 percent.

Japan: Number of tax brackets reduced from 15 to 5. Top marginal tax rate reduced from 70 to 50 percent.

Mexico: Number of tax brackets reduced from 28 to 12. Top marginal tax rate reduced from 55 to 40 percent.

New Zealand: Number of tax brackets reduced from 5 to 2. Top marginal tax rate reduced from 60 to 43 percent.

Sweden: Number of tax brackets reduced from 11 to 4. Top marginal tax rate reduced from 80 to 50 percent.

United Kingdom: Number of tax brackets reduced from 13 to 2. Top marginal tax rate reduced from 80 to 40 percent.

†Based on Whalley, "Foreign Responses to U.S. Tax Reform," 288.

and pulls the income of the spouse who earns the higher income into a lower tax bracket under progressive taxation. If, for example, a husband with a dependent spouse earns $50,000 per year and his wife has no taxable income, $50,000 would be taxed as if the husband earned $25,000 per year and the wife earned $25,000, as well. This income splitting, which is built into the tax rate schedule for those who are married but filing jointly, lowers the marginal tax rate of the single-earner couple. As the incomes of the two spouses become equal, the benefit disappears. This is the so-called marriage tax, which has been present in the tax structure since 1969, when a reform designed to reduce the rate of taxation on single taxpayers resulted in this quirk: the rate for equal-income married taxpayers rose above the corresponding rate for two single taxpayers with the same income.

For example, suppose your taxable income was $50,000 in 1994. If you were single, your tax liability based on tax rates prevailing in 1994 would have been $11,042.50. If instead, you were married *and your spouse had no taxable income,* your tax liability would have been only $9,060. By marrying someone with no taxable income, you would save $1,982.50 in 1994 taxes over what you would pay as a single taxpayer. However, if you were to file a "married filing separately" return rather than a joint return after you married, your tax bill would be $11,704—an increase of $661.50 over the single rate. This is because the tax rate schedule for a married person filing separately has tax brackets that result in relatively higher tax rates applied to a given income compared to single taxpayers. In addition, by filing separately all the $50,000 is taxed as your income instead of being allocated half to you and half to your spouse. Naturally, assuming you are rational, you would choose to file jointly with your spouse after marrying.

The situation differs if you marry a person who earns the same taxable income as you. Two single persons earning $25,000 taxable income each per year in 1994 would have paid $4,042.50 each in taxes for a total tax of $8,085. If these two were to marry and file jointly, their tax bill would be $9,060, an increase of $975 over what they would have paid together on single returns. Reduction of the marginal tax rates and the degree of progression of the income tax rate structure have reduced the marriage tax somewhat for lower-income taxpayers. However, it is greater for upper-income taxpayers subject to higher marginal tax rates.

Summary

Taxable income is the portion of income received by individuals that is subject to the personal income tax. Taxable income is calculated as adjusted gross income less the sum of personal exemptions and the standard deduction or itemized deductions. The U.S. income tax rate structure is progressive. Average effective tax rates rise with income. Because of generous personal exemptions, standard deductions in relation to income, and the earned income credit, very low-income taxpayers pay zero or negative average tax rates in the United States under the personal income tax.

Tax preferences can be thought of as subsidies to certain activities, even though they are often introduced to achieve equity objectives and lower administrative costs of collecting taxes. Tax expenditures are losses in revenue attributable to tax preferences. In addition to revenue losses, tax preferences result in efficiency losses through their distorting effects on prices and incentives. Because of tax preferences, the personal income tax distorts the choice to engage in various activities in addition to distorting the work-leisure choice and savings decisions.

Although the tax brackets, standard deduction, and personal exemptions are indexed for inflation, problems remain in equity and efficiency that result when inflation increases nominal incomes. Inflation causes an increase in the rate of taxation of capital income relative to labor income; these distortions reduce the return to saving and investment.

A Forward Look

The next chapter discusses additional taxation of capital earnings under the corporate income tax. The corporate income tax has complex effects on the U.S. economy, affecting product prices, interest rates, and the return to investment in both corporate and noncorporate assets.

Important Concepts

Taxable Income
Gross Income
Adjusted Gross Income (AGI)
Personal Exemption
Standard Deduction
Tax Bracket
Earned Income Tax Credit
Itemized Deductions
Effective Tax Rates
Tax Preferences
Marginal Tax Benefit
Deferral of Taxable Income
Tax Expenditures
Bracket Creep

Questions for Review

1. What is gross income? Why is gross income less than the Haig-Simons comprehensive measure of income? How does taxable income differ from gross income?
2. What are the major types of income excluded from gross income? Why are certain items excluded from adjusted gross income, even though they qualify as income under the Haig-Simons definition?
3. How does the treatment of capital gains under the federal income tax compare with the way in which capital gains would be treated under a comprehensive income tax?
4. What are tax preferences? What are major justifications for tax preferences? What are the economic consequences of tax preferences?
5. What are tax expenditures? How can tax expenditures be used to evaluate the desirability of tax preferences? Why do tax expenditures overestimate the gains in revenue that would come about from eliminating tax preferences? Explain how tax preferences distort prices and cause losses in market efficiency.
6. What are the major tax deductions from adjusted gross income that are allowed in computing taxable income? What are the economic justifications and consequences of allowing such deductions?
7. The Tax Reform Act of 1986 sharply reduced marginal tax rates for most taxpayers. Explain why this is likely to reduce the excess burden of tax preferences.
8. What is bracket creep? How can indexation of tax brackets, the standard deduction, and the personal exemption eliminate bracket creep?
9. Why does inflation distort interest payments and receipts, thereby resulting in tax inequities?
10. Discuss the current tax treatment of capital gains under the personal income tax. Why do some economists argue that reduction in the rate of taxation of capital gains can actually increase tax revenue collected from such gains?

Problems

1. A taxpayer faces the following marginal tax rates for labor income:

AVERAGE DAILY LABOR (DOLLARS)	MTR (PERCENT)
0–20	0
20–40	20
40–80	30
80 and above	40

The taxpayer can earn $10 per hour. In the absence of any taxes, he would work an average of eight hours a day. Show how the tax affects his income-leisure budget line and analyze the possible effects on his equilibrium allocation of time to work and leisure, assuming that leisure is a normal good.

2. Suppose that the expected inflation rate is 4 percent this year and the nominal interest rate is 8 percent. Assuming that a taxpayer is subject to a 28-percent marginal tax rate, show how an increase in the rate of

inflation next year to 8 percent while the nominal interest rate rises to 10 percent affects taxation of nominal interest. How does inflation affect taxation of capital gains?

3. A single worker has gross income subject to tax of $40,000. She makes a $5,000 contribution to a special tax-deferred retirement plan offered by her employer. The worker claims one personal exemption for herself and has the following deductible payments: $1,000 in mortgage interest, $1,000 in state income tax, and $500 in property tax. Does it pay the worker to itemize deductions when filing her 1994 tax return? Using the 1994 tax rate schedule shown in Figure 14.1, calculate the worker's tax liability.

4. A worker lives in a state that has its own income tax. The worker is in the 31 percent federal tax bracket. In addition, he is subject to a 9 percent marginal tax rate for his state income tax. Assume that mortgage interest is deductible both on his federal and state income tax and that state income taxes are deductible on the federal income tax; also assume that he itemizes deductions. Calculate the effective marginal tax rate the taxpayer is subject to after considering the tax deductibility of state income tax payments on the fed-

eral return. Show how the state income tax effects the excess burden of the mortgage interest deduction for the worker. Assuming that the worker also pays a 7.65 percent Social Security tax on his labor earnings, calculate the marginal tax rate for his labor earnings.

Suggestions for Further Reading

Pechman, Joseph A. "The Future of the Income Tax." *American Economic Review* 80, 1 (March 1990). An analysis of issues relating to the incidence and excess burden of the federal income tax in the late 1980s.

Slemrod, Joel, ed. *Do Taxes Matter?: The Impact of the Tax Reform Act of 1986*. Cambridge, MA: The MIT Press, 1990. A collection of research on the impact of recent changes in the federal income tax on personal saving, housing markets, charitable giving, and economic decisions.

U.S. Department of the Treasury, Internal Revenue Service. *Your Federal Income Tax*. Published annually in November by the IRS, this booklet has just about everything you wanted to know but were afraid to ask about your income tax.

15

TAXATION OF
CORPORATE INCOME

L E A R N I N G   O B J E C T I V E S

After reading this chapter you should be able to

1. Discuss general issues involved in taxation of business income, including the treatment of normal profit and depreciation of capital.
2. Explain how corporate income would be treated under a comprehensive income tax.
3. Describe the possible economic consequences of separate taxation of corporate income.
4. Analyze both the short-run and long-run impacts of the corporate income tax on output, the allocation of investment, and efficiency of resource use.
5. Discuss the incidence of the corporate income tax, including its effect on product prices, the return to investment, and wages.

*I*f you were to operate your own business, the income that you would earn from its operations would be subject to taxation. As the sole owner of the business, you would be required to file a "Schedule C" as part of your personal income tax. After deduction of all the costs of operating your business, including the cost of materials, use of capital, and labor you hire, you would include the net profit as part of your personal income. The tax you paid on your business income would depend on the tax bracket you fell into after all your taxable income had been computed.

The income of sole proprietorships and partnerships is treated as personal income to the owners of businesses. Although sole proprietorships and partnerships account for about 80 percent of the business organizations in the United States, the bulk of business income (about 90 percent of the total) accrues to corporations in the United States. A **corporation** is a business that is legally established under state laws that grant it an identity separate from that of its owners. The law looks at the corporation *as if* it were a person! The corporation is a "legal fiction" that is granted the right to engage in litigation, to own property in its own name, and to incur debts. In the United States and in many other nations the corporation is treated as a person from the point of view of taxation. The profits of the corporation are subject to a corporate income tax in the United States.

The owners of a corporation are its shareholders, who acquire transferable stock in the corporation. The portion of their ownership can be measured by their relative share of the value of outstanding stock. For example, if a person has stocks worth $2,000 in a corporation for which the current market value of all stock outstanding is $200,000, she has a 1-percent ownership in that corporation. Stockholders are protected by the provision of *limited liability* for the debts of the corporation; that is, their liability for debts incurred by the corporation is limited to the amount of funds they have invested in the corporation.

Many argue that separate taxation of corporations obscures the fact that the tax ultimately must be borne by the corporation's shareholders, by other investors, by consumers, or by workers. The ultimate incidence of the corporate income tax among these groups depends on the impact of the tax on the prices of goods and services, the return to investment, and wages. The separate taxation of corporate income, therefore, is a subject of controversy.

This chapter discusses the issues involved in the taxation of corporations and business income in general. Some politicians believe that corporations should pay a larger share of taxes than they pay now. On the other hand, many have argued that the separate corporate income tax is unnecessary and that the tax should be abolished. Critics of the tax also argue that it causes large losses in efficiency by distorting the return to investment and by causing a reduction in investment throughout the economy.

In the modern global economy, taxation of corporations also can influence the location of multinational business organizations. If one nation taxes corporations at a higher rate than other nations, it might find that more corporations choose to locate their operations in foreign nations. The U.S. economy of the 1990s is part of a vast global economy in which tax rates influence not only domestic decisions but also foreign decisions regarding the location of international investment. In recent years concern has been growing about the impact of the corporate income tax on the international competitiveness of U.S. business and the incentives to invest in the United States.

THE TAX BASE: MEASURING BUSINESS INCOME

Annual business income is measured by subtracting all business costs from business receipts over a period of one year. To calculate business income, we would first add up the receipts the business takes in from sale of its products or services. Then we would add net capital gains on all business assets held during the year to business income. After gross income was calculated, we would deduct the costs of operating the business during the year. These costs would include labor costs, interest payments, payments for materials and services purchased from other firms, and a measure of the cost of capital equipment used during the year. After deducting all business costs we will have a measure of the profit of the business—its *net* taxable income.

As with the measurement of personal income, some discrepancies exist between the way corporate income is measured in practice and the comprehensive measure of income. From an economic point of view, both realized and unrealized capital gains should be included in the measure of the business's gross income. However, in the United States, when measuring business income, only realized capital gains are included in business income. Net realized capital gains (capital gains less an allowable portion of capital losses) are included in corporate income in the United States.

Another problem is the treatment of owner-supplied inputs. For example, in the case of a sole proprietorship operated by its owner, part of the cost of operation is the opportunity cost of the owner-operator's labor. Because the labor of the owner is not hired in the marketplace, neither payment for labor services nor deduction for that labor cost is ever recorded on the business's books. However, the owner-operator's labor is part of the opportunity cost of running the business and it should be deducted from gross income. The opportunity cost of this owner-supplied service is not deductible in practice when computing business income for taxable purposes in the United States. This implies that business income as measured in practice includes both the *normal profit*, which is the opportunity cost of owner-supplied inputs, and the *economic* profit, which is the surplus of revenues over the opportunity cost of all inputs used over the year.

Everyone who works for a corporation is an employee; no owner-supplied labor exists in corporations. However, the corporation's owners, its shareholders, do supply funds to the corporation and the opportunity cost of those funds net of any debt must be included in the costs of operating the corporation. The **equity** of a corporation is the difference between the value of its assets (including the cash that could be obtained if its equipment and real estate were sold) and the value of its outstanding debt. For example, if a corporation has equity of $1 million and shareholders on average could have earned 10-percent interest on that equity had they not invested it in the corporation, the opportunity cost of owner-supplied funds for the corporation would be $100,000. This sum must be deducted from corporate receipts to calculate economic profit of the corporation. However, this is not done in administering the corporate income tax in the United States. The corporate income tax is therefore a tax on the sum of both normal and economic profits.

Net corporate income either can be retained by a corporation to finance expenses including the acquisition of new capital or it can be paid out as personal income to the shareholders of the corporation. The portion of a corporation's profits paid out to its stockholders is called **dividends.** The portion kept by the corporation is **retained earnings.** Corporate profits therefore can be distributed to shareholders or can remain as undistributed corporate profits used for whatever purposes the corporation's managers see fit. The portion paid out as dividends is part of the taxable income of those who receive the payments.

Economic Depreciation: How the Cost of Capital is Distributed over a Number of Years When Computing Business Income

Some of the inputs purchased by a business, such as fuel, are used up in the process of production within a short period. However, capital inputs, such as equipment and structures, are long-lived. Vehicles can last four to ten years before they need to be replaced and structures can last for fifty years and longer. Because capital inputs are seldom consumed or used up completely in the year in which they are purchased, accountants usually distribute their purchase prices over a number of years by including a measure of the depreciation of the capital, rather than its total purchase price, in the annual costs of operating the business. Problems occur in defining the tax base treatment of the replacement cost of capital through depreciation. **Economic depreciation** measures the value of the durable physical capital used by firms in the productive process as that capital is "used up." Capital equipment is used up in the sense that it wears out and becomes obsolete over time as technology improves. Depreciation is sometimes referred to as a *capital consumption allowance*. Its inclusion in cost provides a means for the firm to accumulate a fund so as to recover its capital cost and replace such assets as machines and buildings when they wear out. Ideally, the rate at which an asset is depreciated for tax purposes should coincide with the actual useful economic life of the asset. In fact, however, depreciation rules are arbitrary, and the useful lives of assets, as defined by Internal Revenue Service guidelines, do not always coincide with the actual useful economic lives of the asset. This is of importance in defining the tax base and taxes due from the corporation, because the rate at which the firm is allowed to recover its initial capital cost affects the amount of taxes paid.

Accelerated Depreciation and Expensing

More rapid depreciation allowances give corporations a larger deduction in computing taxable income in early years of the asset's use. The consequent reduction in tax liability due to faster depreciation allows the corporation to earn more interest income than otherwise would be the case. **Accelerated depreciation** allows a firm to deduct more than the actual economic depreciation from its income each year. In effect, accelerated depreciation allows a firm to recover the costs of capital equipment more quickly than the equipment is actually used up.

The benefit of accelerated depreciation for tax purposes can be substantial to the corporation. For example, suppose a corporation acquires a machine that has a useful economic life of ten years. The purchase price of the machine is $100,000. At the extreme, the firm could be allowed to depreciate the machine fully in the year of its acquisition; that is, it could deduct the *full purchase price* of the machine from its taxable income in the year that the machine is acquired. Deduction of the full purchase price of an asset in the year of its acquisition is called **expensing a capital asset.**

Suppose a firm is subject to a marginal tax rate of 34 percent. By expensing the $100,000 machine, it reduces its tax liability by $34,000 in the year of purchase. Its after-tax income therefore is that much greater that year. If the firm can earn a return of 10 percent by investing this $34,000, it would be able to increase its future income by $3,400 per year as a result of expensing the machine. However, it forgoes the opportunity to deduct any depreciation on the machine in following years.

Deduction of the same fraction of the cost of an asset each year over its useful economic life is called **straight-line depreciation.** Under straight-line depreciation, the firm deducts only $10,000 from revenues in the year of purchase of the $100,000 machine lasting ten years. Assuming a marginal tax rate of 34 percent, the firm's tax liability is reduced by only $3,400 per year. The firm then is able to invest this $3,400 at 10 percent interest and earns only $340 per year.

In general, assuming a flat-rate tax, the firm's after-tax income in any given year is greater the more quickly it can depreciate its capital expenditures and the greater the proportion of the expenditures it can write off in earlier years of use.

In 1981, the Accelerated Cost Recovery System (ACRS) was established as part of the Economic Recovery Act of 1981 to govern depreciation allowances for business firms. The system, as first introduced, involved very rapid write-offs especially for equipment and vehicles that encouraged investment in these assets compared with investment in structures. The Tax Reform Act of 1986 substantially deaccelerated the recovery periods for most assets and sought to adjust depreciation rates to equalize the rate at which alternative assets are taxed.

Inflation, Depreciation, and the Cost of Capital

An additional problem in dealing with depreciation stems from the effect of inflation on the replacement costs of capital assets. Inflation increases the replacement cost of capital. However, depreciation is based on **historic cost,** or the acquisition price of the asset. There is no difference between historic cost and replacement cost when the price level is stable. However, during inflation, depreciation calculated on the basis of historic cost understates the replacement cost of capital and therefore overstates the profits of the firm. Similar problems occur for valuing the firm's inventory in computing its profits. If inventory is valued at its acquisition costs and inflation makes it more expensive to replace that inventory, then the profits of the firm would be overstated.

Inflation also benefits firms, insofar as it decreases the value of their debt outstanding. In effect they experience capital gains on their outstanding debt balances, and the real value of those balances declines with inflation. This is identical to advantages for individual taxpayers, as discussed in the previous chapter. Loans are paid off in dollars that are worth less than they were initially. The nominal interest deduction allowable to the corporation overstates the true interest cost.

Research on the effect of inflation on the corporate income tax has shown that the main effect on corporate profits stems from the understatement of depreciation and inventory costs. The researchers conclude that, in 1977, a year of rapidly rising prices, inflation increased the effective taxes paid by corporations by 50 percent.[1]

SEPARATE TAXATION OF CORPORATE INCOME: ISSUES AND PROBLEMS

Corporate Income as Personal Income Under a Comprehensive Income Tax

Why should a separate tax be levied on the income of corporations? Although from a legal point of view, a corporation is treated as though it were a person, this is not a sufficient economic reason to tax it as if it were a person. Some argue that a separate

---

[1]Martin Feldstein and Lawrence Summers, "Inflation and the Taxation of Capital Income in the Corporate Sector," *National Tax Journal* 32 (December 1979): 445–470.

corporate income tax is necessary to make corporations pay for the special privileges obtained from their corporate charters.

Under a comprehensive personal income tax, separate taxation of corporate income would not be needed. Total corporate income simply would be allocated to its shareholders on a pro rata basis, according to the percentage value of outstanding stock that they owned. For example, suppose the total taxable income of the XYZ corporation were $1 million this year and that an individual owned 1 percent of the stock of this corporation. At the end of the year, he would receive from the corporation a statement indicating that his share of corporate income this year is $10,000, or 1 percent of total corporate income. He then would be required to include $10,000 as part of his taxable income when he files his personal income tax for the year. Similarly, all the income of the corporation would be allocated to all its shareholders and would be taxed as personal income. It would make no difference if the corporation paid out its income to shareholders as dividends or retained its earnings to finance future expansion. No separate taxation of dividend income under the corporate income tax would be necessary. All income would be allocated to shareholders for tax purposes. The corporation would be treated like a partnership with the income share of each partner being allocated according to the ownership share.

A scheme for integrating the corporate income tax with the personal income would, however, create some practical problems. For example, if realized capital gains are taxable, then unless pro rata portions of income retained by corporations are deducted from realized capital gains such gains would be double-taxed. For example, suppose an individual purchased a share of stock for $100. She holds the stock for a year and then sells it for $150. However, during the year the corporation earns $30 per share, which she must declare as personal income. If of this $30 the corporation retained $20 to finance expansion, then $20 of the $50 capital gain this individual would realize by selling the stock represents her pro rata share of retained earnings that *she has already been taxed on.* Therefore, the capital gain should be adjusted downward by $20 to reflect the increase in the capital value per share that results from retained earnings. The correct taxable capital gain would be $30.

Undistributed Corporate Profits, Dividends, and Interest Cost

The personal income tax base in the United States is, in fact, far less than comprehensive income. Given the tax preferences in the income tax code, separate taxation of corporate income might be necessary. The main tax preference that supports this argument is the exclusion of all unrealized capital gains from the tax base.

Assume that, given current tax treatment of capital gains and the definition of taxable income, corporate income is not subject to a separate tax. Consider the impact of this on the behavior of corporations in allocating earnings between dividend payments to shareholders each year, and retained earnings for use within the corporation including investment. With no separate tax on the net income of the corporation, undistributed corporate profits would escape taxation under the personal income tax. Accordingly, the incentive for a corporation would be to plow its profits back into the business. In effect this provides income to owners of stock in the corporation in the form of potential capital gains in lieu of dividends and keeps a substantial portion of the income tax base free of taxation because unrealized capital gains are not taxed. This reduces revenues to the U.S. Treasury from that particular source and creates inequities.

The source of the incentive to retain earnings as undistributed corporate profits lies in the way taxable income is defined under the personal income tax code. Under a comprehensive income tax base, both realized and unrealized capital gains are taxable annually. If the tax base under the personal income tax were to correspond to comprehensive income, stockholders would be indifferent to the disposition of corporate profits, inasmuch as they are divided between dividends and retained earnings. Under the definition of taxable income used in the personal income tax code in the United States, managers of corporations could help stockholders avoid taxes by retaining earnings as undistributed corporate profits.

Undistributed corporate profits are a form of corporate savings used to finance expansion of operations without borrowing or issuing more stock. Insofar as these retained earnings increase the value, or net worth, of the firm, they provide income for stockholders in the form of capital gains. Unrealized capital gains are nontaxable. Stockholders' tax liability therefore can be reduced as more earnings are retained and less are paid out as dividends. Under the personal income tax, dividends are subject to full taxation. Thus, in the absence of either a separate corporate income tax or a method of allocating retained earnings as taxable income to shareholders, a significant amount of annual income would escape taxation.

However, this argument does not consider the important cost to shareholders when profits are retained. Under current law, when the corporation borrows funds to finance expansion, it can deduct the interest payments from its income. When undistributed profits are used to finance expansion, the firm incurs interest costs in terms of forgone interest on its retained earnings. These implicit interest costs, representing the opportunity cost of retained earnings, are *not* tax deductible. Thus, by retaining earnings instead of paying them out as dividends, the corporation's net taxable income, and therefore its annual tax bill, increases. Dividends cannot be deducted as a cost in figuring a corporation's taxable income under tax laws prevailing in 1994 but interest can be so deducted.

Double Taxation of Dividends

The current policy of separate taxation of total corporate income and of the portion of income paid out as dividends to individuals subjects a substantial portion of corporate income to double-taxation. The reason for this is that all corporate income is subject to taxation when it is earned, and that portion of profits paid out as dividends is then subject to taxation under the personal income tax, as part of the tax liability for shareholders who receive dividend income. Such double-taxation of corporate income paid out as dividends serves to increase the effective rate of taxation on corporate investment.

If the corporate income tax were to be integrated into the personal income tax, as has been suggested by those advocating a comprehensive income tax, no such double-taxation would exist.[2] Under comprehensive income taxation, corporate profits

---

[2]See U.S. Department of the Treasury, *Blueprints for Basic Tax Reform* (Washington, D.C.: U.S. Government Printing Office, 1977).

would be distributed to shareholders on a pro rata basis, according to their share of ownership in the corporation. This reduces the rate of taxation of corporate profits, due to the elimination of double-taxation of corporate income paid out as dividends. Owners of corporate stock would experience windfall gains in terms of an increase in the value of their corporate stock, but only if the value of previous excess taxation had been capitalized into reduced stock prices in the past. However, these gains, when realized, would be subject to taxation under the provisions of the personal income tax.

A Possible Bias Toward Debt Finance

In recent years some have been concerned that corporate finance has been biased in favor of debt finance because dividends cannot be deducted from a corporation's income but interest can. Leveraged buyouts (LBOs) in corporate takeovers usually involve heavy borrowing by those who acquire the corporation that leaves the corporation heavily in debt. This gives the corporation high interest costs, which are tax deductible. In effect, a corporation can always borrow to purchase its own shares on the market. By purchasing shares, it no longer has to pay dividends to households on those shares, and it in effect exchanges obligations to pay dividends for tax-deductible interest costs. Shareholders who sell their shares to the corporation then receive taxable income in the form of realized capital gains, but total after-tax corporate income is higher because deductible interest costs reduce taxable income.

The corporate income tax reduces the incentive to retain income that would otherwise prevail in a system in which unrealized capital gains are not taxed as personal income. In addition, because interest, but not dividends, is tax deductible, the tax provides incentive for debt finance. For this reason, many economists argue that the corporate income tax biases corporate finance away from equity and toward debt as a means of raising funds.

This can be seen with a simple example. Take two corporations each with $1 million in assets. Assume that the first is financed entirely with equity while the second is 50-percent debt financed and that both corporations earn $150,000 operating income. Assume that both corporations are subject to a 34 percent income tax.

Table 15.1 shows the balance sheet and income statement of the all-equity and 50 percent debt-financed (leveraged) corporations.[3] Assuming that the leveraged corporation pays 10 percent interest, it will have $50,000 in deductible interest. The all-equity corporation will have no interest to deduct. Taxable income therefore will be $150,000 for the all-equity corporation but only $100,000 for the leveraged corporation. The income tax paid at the 34 percent rate will be $51,000 for the all-equity corporation but only $34,000 for the leveraged one. By borrowing, a corporation re-

---

[3]This example follows a similar one appearing on page 54 of *Federal Income Tax Aspects of Corporate Tax Structures,* prepared by the staff of the Joint Committee on Taxation for hearings before the Senate Committee on Finance and the House Committee on Ways and Means, January 18, 1989.

Table 15.1 ✦ Effect of Debt Financing on Returns to Equity Investment

Item	All-Equity Corporation	50-Percent Debt-Financed Corporation
Beginning Balance Sheet:		
Total Assets	$1,000,000	$1,000,000
Debt	0	500,000
Shareholders' Equity	1,000,000	500,000
Income Statement:		
Operating Income	150,000	150,000
Interest Expense	0	50,000
Taxable Income	150,000	100,000
Income Tax	51,000	34,000
Income after Corporate Tax	99,000	66,000
Return on Equity[a]	9.9%	13.2%

[a]Return on equity is computed as income after corporate tax divided by beginning shareholders' equity.

duces its taxable income and therefore its tax. The income after corporation tax is consequently higher for the leveraged corporation in that it enjoys a 13.2 percent return on the initial shareholder equity of $500,000, while the all-equity corporation registers only a 9.9 percent return on initial shareholder equity of $1,000,000.

Replacement of Equity with Debt

Because of the tax disadvantage of financing activities with equity, the trend in recent years has been for corporations to replace equity with debt. In general when a corporation's ratio of debt to equity increases, the firm is said to become more leveraged. This has occurred through leveraged buyouts, leveraged employee stock ownership plans (ESOPs) in which the company borrows to provide stock for the plan, and outright exchanges of equity for debt and stock redemptions. Between 1983 and 1987 net corporation equity decreased by $313.3 billion while new corporate borrowing increased by $613.3 billion in the United States. By converting equity to debt, corporations swap nondeductible dividend payments for tax-deductible interest payments. In effect, this results in distribution of corporate operating income to creditors as interest instead of to shareholders as dividends.

To reduce the incentives for debt finance, recent proposals have advocated allowing at least limited tax deductibility of dividends paid before computing taxable income for a corporation. The bias against equity finance also could be reduced by limiting interest deductions. However, the latter option would increase overall financing costs for corporations while the former would reduce such costs.

TAX TREATMENT OF MULTINATIONAL CORPORATIONS

The world is becoming smaller year by year. Improvements in communication and increased international competition have changed the face of business. More large corporations are multinational operations with foreign subsidiaries throughout the world. The foreign subsidiaries are incorporated under the laws of a foreign nation and are legally separate from the parent corporation.

Let's look at some of the issues involved in taxation of multinational corporations. Of course, when a U.S. firm invests in a subsidiary on foreign soil it becomes liable for foreign corporate income taxation. Similarly a foreign firm with a subsidiary in the United States is subject to U.S. corporate income taxation on the income earned in the United States. There is, however, wide variation in corporate income tax rates and the rules for treating foreign source income in terms of domestic taxation. Usually foreign-source income is subject to tax by the parent corporation's home nation only if the foreign income is "repatriated" to the parent corporation through payment of dividends, interest, or

royalties. If the income is not repatriated, no domestic tax is due.

The United States and other nations such as Japan and the United Kingdom that tax on a worldwide basis do however allow a credit for taxes paid to foreign governments that is deducted from the repatriated foreign source income. This credit serves to prevent onerous double-tax burdens that would decrease the incentive to invest abroad. There is, however, a limit on the credit allowed for foreign taxes paid that is usually equal to the home country tax that would have been paid on the foreign income had it been earned as domestic income. This limit comes into effect when a corporation has a subsidiary in a nation for which the corporate income tax is higher than that of the parent's home nation. In the United States this limit to the foreign tax credit is designed to prevent foreign governments from levying very high taxes on U.S. subsidiaries that would increase foreign tax revenue at the expense of reducing U.S. tax revenue. The high taxes would not increase corporate tax liability of the U.S. corporation provided they were not greater than its total U.S. tax liability, but they would reduce federal tax collections by reducing the share of the repatriated foreign income that is subject to tax do-

THE TAX RATE STRUCTURE

The corporate income tax rate structure as of 1994 is progressive with three brackets, as shown in Table 15.2. The maximum marginal tax rate is 35 percent applied to taxable income more than $10 million per year. The benefits of lower marginal tax rates for income less than $75,000 per year are phased out for corporations with annual taxable incomes greater than $335,000. In effect, most large U.S. corporations pay a flat-rate statutory tax of at least 34 percent on their taxable income, because most profitable large corporations earn more than $335,000 pear year.

The tax base for the corporate income tax is notoriously unstable, and the taxes collected can fluctuate widely from year to year. The reason for this is that corporate profits are highly sensitive to swings in the business cycle. It is not unusual for large corporations to make hefty profits in one year, only to register sharp losses in the following year if, due to an existing recession, their sales are curtailed significantly.

mestically. Any excess credit can be carried forward to later years. In general, however, the limit to the foreign tax credit can act to discourage investment in high tax nations. A firm that has excess foreign tax credits is likely to be very sensitive to differences in tax rates among nations because it will not immediately get a credit for foreign taxes it pays. Under worldwide taxation therefore, corporate tax policies can affect industrial locations by encouraging firms to set up subsidiaries in relatively low tax nations. As of the late 1980s, Belgium, Ireland, Luxembourg, and Spain had relatively low taxes on investment income, while Denmark, France, Germany, Greece, Italy, the Netherlands, and Portugal had relatively high taxes. The system of worldwide taxation of income therefore in effect distorts the pattern of worldwide investment toward the low-tax nations because of the limits to the foreign tax credit.

Multinational corporations also have opportunities to control the tax allocation of total earnings between home and foreign operations. Naturally, a corporation can have higher after-tax income by shifting the source claimed for shares of income from high-tax nations to low-tax nations. The company can do this by charging off transfers of goods, services, and technical knowhow as costs to the parent corporation when those items are transferred for subsidiary use in a nation with lower corporate income taxes. The income from the low-tax nation is higher because of the transfer of goods or other resources but the cost of those resources is charged to the parent thereby reducing taxable income in the high-tax jurisdiction. To avoid this problem of manipulating the source of income, a system of "transfer pricing" is necessary to charge goods and technical knowhow received from the home against the income of the foreign subsidiary. This increases apparent domestic income while it decreases foreign source income. But how should the transfer price be established in the absence of any transaction? One way is to use the "arm's length" rule, which treats the home office and the foreign subsidiary as two independent firms and tries to impute a price for the transfer of goods, services, or technical knowhow based on what two independent firms would agree on to trade the input. Another way to allocate the cost of commonly used resources, such as technical knowhow, is to divide it between the parent and the subsidiary according to sales or assets of each of the companies.

Another problem in determining the allocation of income between parents and subsidiaries of a multinational firm involves treatment of borrowing. Multinational firms have incentives to borrow in the high-tax jurisdictions because they get a bigger tax deduction in those jurisdictions from their interest payments. This makes their income in the high-tax jurisdiction appear lower.

Effective Tax Rates

A measure of the *effective* corporate tax rate shows the tax rate paid by corporations on their *economic* profits. Effective tax rates for corporations differ from the statutory rates because real economic profits differ from taxable profits. The effect of inflation

Table 15.2 ✦ Corporate Income Tax Rate Structure, 1994

Taxable Income	Average Tax Rate at Beginning of Bracket	Marginal Tax Rate
Less than $50,000	0%	15%[a]
More than $50,000 but Less than $75,000	15	25[a]
More than $75,000 but Less than $10 Million	18	34
More than $10 Million[b]	34	34

[a]Not available for corporations with annual incomes greater than $335,000.
[b]Corporations with taxable income greater than $15 million annually are subject to an additional 3 percent tax on the excess greater than $15 million up to a maximum additional tax of $100,000.

on profits subject to tax—a decrease in the real value of depreciation allowances and a reduction in real interest rates—must be accounted for in calculating effective tax rates for corporations. In addition, dividends paid out by corporations are subject to double taxation as discussed above. Inflation increases the cost of capital to the firm, and its net impact is to increase the effective rate of taxation on real economic profits.

Estimates of the marginal effective tax rate on corporate income indicate that when the tax is based on a measure of real economic profits, the marginal effective tax rate exceeds the statutory marginal tax rate. Fullerton, Henderson, and Mackie estimate that the marginal effective tax rate on corporate income under provisions of the Tax Reform Act of 1986 is in the range of 40 percent.[4] Despite lowering the statutory tax rates, the Tax Reform Act of 1986 actually *increased* the effective marginal tax rate on corporate income. This is because in addition to lowering statutory marginal tax rates, the new law made depreciation rules less generous and eliminated the special investment tax credit. The reduction in depreciation allowances and removal of the investment tax credit acted to increase effective tax rates.

The effective marginal tax rate on corporate income is higher than that on business income earned in the noncorporate sector. The decreases in the marginal tax rates on personal income resulting from the Tax Reform Act of 1986 combined with the increased marginal effective tax rates on corporate income have been estimated to increase the taxation of corporate income relative to noncorporate business income. The differential between the corporate tax rate and the personal tax rate applying to noncorporate income was, however, narrowed by increases in top marginal tax rates for personal income enacted in 1993.

CHECKPOINT

1. How is corporate income measured? How can accelerated depreciation affect the taxable income of a corporation?
2. How could corporate income be taxed under a comprehensive personal income tax?
3. How can the corporation income tax, as administered in the United States, affect the choice between equity and debt finance?

SHORT-RUN IMPACT OF THE CORPORATE INCOME TAX

The corporate income tax is a discriminatory tax on the income of one particular form of business organization—the corporation. As such, it is expected to reduce the net return to investment in corporate businesses in the short run, unless corporations are capable of making immediate adjustments to shift the tax in some way. The most obvious way of shifting the tax in the short run is to adjust output in response to the tax,

---

[4]Don Fullerton, Yolanda K. Henderson, and James Mackie, "Investment Allocation and Growth under the Tax Reform Act of 1986," in Office of Tax Analysis, Department of the Treasury, *Compendium of Tax Research, 1987* (Washington, D.C.: U.S. Government Printing Office, 1987), 173–201.

so as to raise prices. This would shift the burden of taxation from owners of the corporation (the stockholders) to consumers of output produced by the corporation. The ultimate impact of the corporate income tax on efficiency, and on the distribution of income, depends on whether the tax depresses the return to corporate investment in the first place. Accordingly, the question of short-run shifting of the tax is of crucial importance in determining the ultimate incidence and excess burden of the tax.

Conflicting theories, and conflicting evidence, exist on the short-run impact of the tax on output prices and on the return to capital invested in the corporate sector of the economy. The effect of the tax on prices and other variables, which potentially can be influenced by managers of the corporation in the short run, determines whether the tax is borne by stockholders in the short run. The short-run impact of the tax on stockholder income, in turn, influences the long-run adjustments that can take place.[5]

Taxes on Economic Profits

Economic profits are a surplus in excess of the opportunity costs of running a business. Economic theory of the profit-maximizing firm suggests that a tax on economic profits cannot be shifted in the short run. A profit-maximizing firm adjusts output produced per year to equate marginal cost and marginal revenue. Figure 15.1 shows the profit-maximizing output of a perfectly competitive firm fortunate enough to be earning economic profits in the short run. The competitive firm's marginal revenue

---

[5]For a review of the theories and evidence, see J. Gregory Ballentine, *Equity, Efficiency, and the United States Corporation Income Tax* (Washington, D.C.: American Enterprise Institute, 1980), chap. 2.

Figure 15.1 ✦ A TAX ON ECONOMIC PROFITS

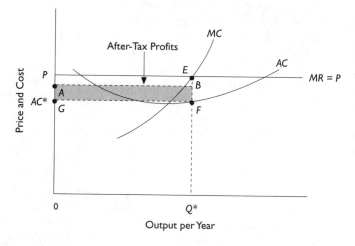

A tax on economic profits affects neither marginal revenue nor marginal cost—it merely takes a percentage of profits. A profit-maximizing firm has no incentive to change output. The output that maximizes total profits is the same output that maximizes profits after taxes. Because output does not change as a result of the tax, quantity supplied, and therefore price, is unaffected. The tax cannot be shifted. It is borne by owners of the firm in the short run.

schedule graphs as a horizontal line. Along that line, the price of the firm's output also is equal to its marginal revenue. The firm maximizes profits by producing the output Q^*, which corresponds to the point at which $MC = MR$. The average cost of producing Q^* units per year is AC^*. The area $PEFG$ represents the firm's annual economic profits. If the industry is competitive, these profits will fall to zero in the long run. This suggests that a tax on economic profits collects revenues only during the short-run period for which the firm earns economic profits.

A tax on economic profits affects neither marginal costs nor marginal revenues. It merely reduces the firm's profits. For example, suppose the firm is subject to an effective average tax rate of 40 percent. Therefore, the tax reduces the firm's profits to 60 percent of its pretax amount. In general, if a firm earns X in profits, a tax rate of t percent per year would reduce those profits to $X(1 - t)$. Profits after taxes are represented by the area $ABFG$ in Figure 15.1

Because the tax affects neither marginal revenues nor marginal costs, firms have no incentive to reduce output as a result of the tax. If the output Q^* maximizes total pretax profits, it also would maximize the 60 percent of pretax profits that remains after the firm pays the tax. Because the firm has no incentive to reduce output, the price of the product does not increase. The firms in the industry do not succeed in shifting the tax forward to buyers, because they cannot increase profits by reducing output in response to the tax. The short-run incidence of a tax on economic profits therefore is borne by the owners of the firm.

A Tax on the Sum of Economic and Normal Profits

As administered in the United States, the corporate income tax does not allow firms to deduct the opportunity cost of owner-supplied funds for investment. Remember, the value of assets, net of debt, is called the equity of a corporation. The opportunity cost of the equity is the normal profit. The corporate income tax therefore is levied on the sum or normal and economic profits. Does this affect the validity of the conclusion that the tax will not affect output and therefore will have no influence on the output price in the short run?

In the short run, the firm operates with a fixed amount of equity that it cannot control; thus, normal profits, which are a fixed percentage of this equity, are also fixed, and the firm cannot increase its normal profits by altering the output that it produces. Because these normal profits are a fixed cost in the short run, marginal costs, which change only when variable costs change, are not affected by taxation of normal profits. It follows that, even when the corporate income tax is levied on the sum of normal and economic profits, profit-maximizing firms have no incentive to adjust their output. The tax, therefore, can have no effect on consumer prices in the short run and must be borne by owners of the firm in the form of decreased returns on capital invested in the corporation.[6]

---

[6]This conclusion must be modified by the extent to which the tax, when introduced, is capitalized into lower stock values. Under those circumstances, portfolio adjustments by investors might bid up stock prices to offset some of the initial burden on corporate stockholders. See Martin Feldstein, "The Surprising Incidence of a Tax on Pure Rent: A New Answer to an Old Question," *Journal of Political Economy* 85 (April 1977): 349–360.

Alternative Theories and Empirical Evidence

The conclusion that the corporate income tax cannot be shifted in the short run depends on the assumption that firms are profit maximizers that operate in competitive markets. More complex models, which allow explicit consideration of some of the peculiarities of oligopolistic markets and nonprofit-maximizing behavior by firms, describe situations in which firms might act to reduce output in response to the tax. Such models argue that short-run shifting of the tax in the form of higher prices can occur.[7]

Empirical evidence on the short-run impact of the tax on prices is conflicting. Conclusions range from zero shifting to shifting in excess of 100 percent. Firms that use the tax as an excuse to raise prices by amounts that more than cover the total tax due are said to be shifting in excess of 100 percent.[8]

LONG-RUN IMPACT OF THE CORPORATE INCOME TAX

The ultimate impact of the corporate income tax depends on its long-run influence on choices. This is dependent, as stressed previously, on the impact the tax has in the short run on the return to capital invested in corporations. Assume, at first, that the tax is not shifted in the short run and is therefore borne by owners of capital in the corporate sector in the form of reduced capital income.

Long-Run Market Equilibrium

A model for analyzing the resource flows set up by the tax in the long run, under the assumption that it decreases the net return to capital in the corporate sector, was developed by Arnold Harberger in the early 1960s.[9] The model assumes that the economy

---

[7]See, for example, Sergio Bruno, "Corporation Income Tax, Oligopolistic Markets, and Immediate Tax Shifting: A Suggested Theoretical Approach," *Public Finance* 25 (1970): 363–378.

[8]Evidence on shifting in excess of 100 percent was found by Marion Krzyzaniak and Richard Musgrave, *The Shifting of the Corporation Income Tax* (Baltimore: Johns Hopkins University Press, 1963). Another study finding evidence of shifting in excess of 100 percent is Richard Dusansky, "The Short-Run Shifting of the Corporation Income Tax in the United States," *Oxford Economic Papers* 24 (November 1972): 357–371. A study by John Mikesell found evidence of shifting of about 58 percent by electric utilities. See John L. Mikesell, "The Corporation Income Tax and the Rate of Return in Privately Owned Electric Utilities," *Public Finance* 28 (1973): 291–300.

Gregg, Harberger, and Mieszkowski found no evidence of shifting. See John G. Gregg, Arnold C. Harberger, and Peter Mieszkowski, "Empirical Evidence on the Corporation Income Tax," *Journal of Political Economy* 75 (December 1967): 811–821.

A study by Oakland also found little or no evidence of shifting. See William Oakland, "Corporate Earnings and Tax Shifting in United States Manufacturing, 1930–1968," *Review of Economics and Statistics* 54 (August 1972): 235–244.

[9]Arnold C. Harberger, "The Incidence of the Corporation Income Tax," *Journal of Political Economy* 70 (June 1962): 215–240.

can be thought of as being divided into two sectors: the corporate sector and the non-corporate sector, with the noncorporate sector being composed of alternative investments not subject to the corporate income tax. This would include housing and other investments owned by noncorporate investors. The model assumes that the corporate income tax is the only tax being used. Perfect competition is presumed to prevail in all markets. Finally, the total supply of funds for investment each year, as well as the supply of other inputs, is assumed to be fixed.

The basic reasoning of Harberger's analysis can be presented with the aid of a simple supply-and-demand analysis of the impact of a newly introduced corporate income tax on the long-run equilibrium of a two-sector economy. This is shown in Figure 15.2. The total supply of loanable funds available for investment each year is assumed to be fixed. The curve labeled S in Figure 15.2A represents the supply of savings available to finance investments in any given year. The initial total demand for funds for investment D is in Figure 15.2A. The market for loanable funds is in equilibrium at point E. The corresponding equilibrium interest rate is i_1. The corresponding equilibrium amount of dollars invested per year is the sum of I_C, corporate investment, and I_N, noncorporate investment. The equilibrium return to investment in both the corporate and noncorporate sectors of the economy must equal the equilibrium interest rate. If that were not the case, the amount of annual investment would change, or investors would reallocate their funds between the two alternative investment sectors until the returns were equal (assuming zero transactions costs). Thus, a pretax capital market equilibrium exists when the marginal return to investment in each of the two sectors, r_1, is equal to the market rate of interest.

Figure 15.2 ✦ LONG-RUN IMPACT OF THE CORPORATE INCOME TAX

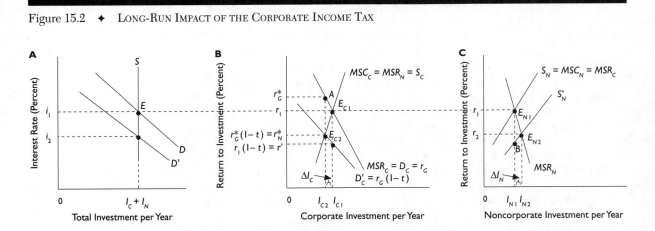

The corporate income tax causes a reduction in investment in the corporate sector shown in **B**. Assuming a perfectly inelastic supply of savings as shown in **A**, this implies an increase in the supply of investable funds in the noncorporate sector as illustrated in **C**. This lowers the return to these investments. In the long-run equilibrium, the net return in the corporate sector $r_N^* = r_2$, the return to noncorporate investment. The tax reduces the return to all investment.

Initially, before the introduction of the tax, the return to investment is r_1, no matter where the funds are invested. At that equilibrium, I_{C1} per year is invested in the corporate sector and I_{N1} per year invested in the noncorporate sector. This is illustrated in Figure 15.2B and Figure 15.2C. The demand for investment in the corporate sector reflects the marginal social return to investment in corporate projects, MSR_C. The supply of funds for investment in the corporate sector reflects the marginal social cost of funds used to finance that investment, MSC_C. This represents the opportunity costs of using funds to finance corporate investment *instead of* the alternative of noncorporate investment. The marginal social cost of investment in the corporate sector is the marginal social return that can be earned on noncorporate investment. If additional funds are allocated to corporate investment per year, fewer funds will be available for noncorporate investment each year. Because the marginal social return of noncorporate investment, MSR_N, increases as fewer funds are invested there, as shown in Figure 15.2B, the marginal social cost of making corporate investments increases as more are made.

The graphs in Figure 15.2B and Figure 15.2C are mutually dependent. The sum of the annual investments in each of the two sectors must equal the fixed supply of savings each year. Increases in corporate investment imply decreases in noncorporate investment and vice versa. The marginal social cost of investing in the noncorporate sector is the forgone return on investment in the corporate sector.

The initial equilibrium allocation of investment is efficient. At point E_{C1} in Figure 15.2B, the marginal social return to investment in the corporate sector equals its marginal social cost. The efficient amount of investment is I_{C1}. Similarly, investment of I_{N1} per year in the noncorporate sector, as shown in Figure 15.2C, is also efficient because the marginal social return to that investment equals its marginal social cost at point E_{N1}.

Introduction of a corporate income tax subjects the return to funds invested in the corporate sector to a discriminatory tax that is not present in the noncorporate sector. The tax has the effect of decreasing the net return earned by investing in the corporate sector at any level of investment. This decreases the demand for loanable funds for investment in the corporate sector from D_C to D'_C, as shown in Figure 15.2B. All points along D'_C reflect the net return to investment, after payment of taxes, in the corporate sector. This net return is the gross return less the tax. If the tax is t percent of the gross return, points on D'_C would equal $r_G(1 - t)$. For example, if the tax rate were 40 percent, the net return to any investment after taxes would be 60 percent of r_G.

Initially, in the short run, the investors would not be able to reduce the amount of capital employed in the corporate sector, and the return would fall by the full amount of the tax to r' where $r' = r_1(1 - t)$. Thus, the return to corporate investment now would be lower than the return to noncorporate investment, since $r' < r_1$.

In the long run, fewer funds each year would be allocated to corporate investment. Instead, investors would use their funds to finance the more lucrative returns that now could be earned in the noncorporate sector. Thus, in the long run, in response to the tax, the supply of funds to the noncorporate sector would increase. This increase in supply reflects the lower opportunity cost of making noncorporate investment. Investors now forgo the lower after-tax return, $r_G(1 - t)$, instead of r_G, for corporate investment when they use their funds to finance noncorporate investment.

As shown in Figure 15.2C, the increase in the supply of funds for investment in the noncorporate sector *decreases* the equilibrium return to investment in that sector to r_2, and the new market equilibrium at E_{N2} is attained. The process of reallocation of funds for investment would continue until the return in the noncorporate sector falls to a level equal to the net return, after taxes, that could be earned in the corporate sector. When this occurs, a new general equilibrium is reached. The new equilibrium in the corporate sector corresponds to E_{C2}. At that point, investment in the corporate sector falls to I_{C2} per year. The equilibrium gross return to investment at that point is r_G^*. The net return to corporate investment is $r_G^*(1 - t) = r_N^*$. The decrease in corporate investment, ΔI_C, must exactly equal the increase in noncorporate investment, ΔI_N because the annual supply of savings is fixed. The return now earned from noncorporate investment, r_2, must equal the net return from investment in the corporate sector:

$$r_2 = r_G^*(1 - t). \tag{15.1}$$

If this were not the case, additional reallocation of investment would occur until it was no longer possible to earn a higher return in one of the sectors.

The decrease in funds supplied to the corporate sector increases the gross return to capital there to r_G^*, but the after-tax net return is below the initial pretax return of r_1. The increased supply of funds to the noncorporate sector decreases the return there to r_2. The return to investment for the economy as a whole therefore declines, as the tax decreases the return to investment earned throughout the economy. It makes no difference where, or to what use, loanable funds are put; the tax lowers their return. Thus, the corporate income tax is effectively a tax on all savings and investment income. Table 15.3 summarizes the effect of the tax on the return to investment.

Excess Burden of the Corporate Income Tax

Assuming no taxes on investments in the noncorporate sector (or that the tax on corporate income exceeds that on the income of noncorporate business), the corporate income tax distorts the pattern of investment. Less than the efficient amount of investment is in the corporate sector. Also, as a result of the tax, more than the efficient amount of investment is in the noncorporate sector. This is illustrated in Figure 15.2.

Table 15.3 ✦ LONG-RUN IMPACT OF THE CORPORATE INCOME TAX

	NET RETURN TO CORPORATE INVESTMENT	RETURN TO NONCORPORATE INVESTMENT
Pretax Equilibrium	r_1	r_1
Short-Run Impact of a Tax[a]	r'	r_1
Long-Run Posttax Equilibrium[b]	$r_N^* = r_G^*(1 - t) = r_2$	r_2

[a]$r' < r_1$
[b]$r_2 < r_1$

As shown in Figure 15.2B, in the long-run equilibrium in the corporate sector, there is I_{C2} of investment per year. The marginal social return to that investment is r_G^*. This exceeds the marginal social cost of investment in that sector, which is equal to r_2, the return that can be earned in noncorporate investment. Similarly, as shown in Figure 15.2C, annual investment in the long run in the noncorporate sector is I_{N2}. This is more than the efficient amount of investment because the marginal social cost, r_G^*, the return that can be earned in the corporate sector, exceeds the marginal social return, r_2, that is earned on noncorporate investment.

The excess burden of misallocation of investment in the two sectors can be measured by either of the triangular areas: $AE_{C1}E_{C2}$ in Figure 15.2B or $BE_{N2}E_{N1}$ in Figure 15.2C. These two areas are equal because $\Delta I_C = \Delta I_N$ and because the difference ($r_G^* - r_2$) is the same in both graphs. The excess burden of the misallocation of investment between the two sectors as a result of the corporate income tax has been estimated to be about 12 percent of revenues collected from the tax.[10]

This efficiency loss could be further compounded if the supply of savings in the economy is responsive to the lower return to investment induced by the tax. If the supply of savings were moderately responsive to changes in the return to investment, the conclusions of Harberger's analysis would have to be modified somewhat. The total supply of savings in Figure 15.2 now would not be fixed. As a result, as shown in Figure 15.3, the reduction in the return to investment caused by the tax would de-

---

[10]John B. Shoven, "The Incidence and Efficiency Effect of Taxes on Income from Capital," *Journal of Political Economy* 84 (December 1976): 1261–1283.

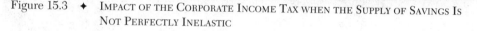

Figure 15.3 ✦ IMPACT OF THE CORPORATE INCOME TAX WHEN THE SUPPLY OF SAVINGS IS NOT PERFECTLY INELASTIC

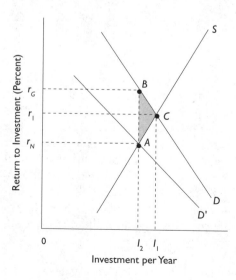

When the supply of savings is not perfectly inelastic, the corporate income tax results in a decline in annual investment, from I_1 to I_2. The gross return to investment increases, while the after-tax return declines. The excess burden of the tax is the area ABC when income effects are negligible.

PUBLIC POLICY PERSPECTIVE

A NEW WAY TO TAX CORPORATE INCOME— THE CORPORATE CASH FLOW TAX

A major criticism of the corporate income tax is that it distorts the pattern of investment between corporate and noncorporate uses and that it also reduces the return to capital in general, possibly reducing national investment. One way to avoid the distortions of the corporate income tax while still making corporations and their stockholders pay a fair share of taxes on corporate income is a *corporate cash flow tax*. This type of tax would tax the difference between a corporation's revenues and its expenditures on both current and capital inputs except that the cost of financial resources as measured by interest payments on debt would *not* be deductible. This simple tax eliminates the bias toward debt finance inherent in the current corporate income tax, which allows interest payments as tax-deductible but not dividends paid on stock.

Let's see how the corporate cash flow tax would work. In effect the tax would eliminate depreciation of capital acquired by corporations. Instead, all capital acquisitions would be *expensed*—deducted immediately as a cost of production. This, of course, would be a powerful tax incentive to encourage investment because the firms could recover part of the cost of their capital equipment as tax savings in the year they acquire the equipment rather than over a longer period. The revenue the government would forgo by not taxing a portion of the cost of capital inputs in the year they are acquired and in later years would be made up in part by the increase in the corporate tax base made possible by not deducting interest paid from corporate revenues. Many firms with heavy debt burdens would see their tax bills rise on average as all their interest from previous borrowings could no longer be deducted from revenue when computing taxable profits.°

The cash flow tax would not distort investment decisions in any way. This is because, by making an investment purchase, a corporation would be able to deduct the full cost. For example, if the corporation were subject to a 34-percent marginal tax rate, the net cost of the investment would be 66 percent of the dollar cost with the remaining 34 percent being borne by the government as a loss in current tax revenue. Then, as the investment began to yield income for the corporation, the government would collect 34 percent of the return

°For a complete analysis of this type of tax, see John Shoven, "Using the Corporate Cash Flow Tax to Integrate Corporate and Personal Taxes," in National Tax Association–Tax Institute of America, *1990 Proceedings of the Eighty-Third Annual Conference on Taxation* (Columbus, OH: National Tax Association–Tax Institute of America, 1991), 19–27. This section is based on Shoven's analysis. The examples apply mainly to nonfinancial corporations. Financial corporations, such as banks, that deal primarily in loans and securities, would have to be treated in a special way under a corporate cash flow tax.

crease savings and investment, from I_1 to I_2. An additional loss in efficiency would be caused by the reduction in the growth of the capital stock. This additional excess burden is the area *ABC* in Figure 15.3. The added excess burden would have to be included with the intersectoral distortions in resource allocation caused by the tax. Studies of the total excess burden induced by the corporate income tax conclude that it is quite high. A number of studies suggest that the excess burden of the combined distortion in the pattern of investment and reduction in total investment is between one-third and two-thirds of revenues collected.[11]

The preceding analysis presumes that the short-run impact of the tax is such as to decrease the return to capital invested in the corporate sector in the first place. If,

[11]See Ballentine, *Equity*, chap. 5, for a review of these studies. See, in particular, Shoven, "Incidence and Efficiency Effects."

on the investment. Because the investment is fully deductible as a cost and its return is subject to the same tax rate as the deduction, the incentive to invest is unaffected. The logic here is the same as that discussed in the text for the short-run impact of a tax on profits. The government, in effect, becomes a partner in the investment purchase, by sharing a fraction of the cost, and then recoups its reward of partnership with the same share of the return to the investment. In this case the volume of investment that maximizes the gross return to the corporation is exactly the same as the volume that maximizes 66 percent of the return when the full cost of the investment is deductible.[†]

Because a corporate cash flow tax will not impair investment decisions, it will not reduce corporate investment and will not distort the pattern of investment between corporation and noncorporate assets. Only *new* investment will be eligible for expensing under the tax so no windfall gain will accrue to corporate shareholders for investment undertaken in previous years.[‡] Another advantage of a cash flow tax is that inflation would no longer be a distortionary tax influence because no depreciation allowances would be eroding away with inflation, and interest payments would no longer be tax deductible.

The final remarkable fact about a corporate cash flow tax is that even though investment would be expensed, the Treasury need not necessarily suffer a reduction in tax revenue because of the shift from the existing corporate income tax. The Treasury would lose revenue from the introduction of expensing of new investments. However, it would gain revenue from discontinuing all old depreciation deductions on past investments and by disallowing all deductions for net interest paid by corporations. One study suggests that the dollar volume of corporate income subject to tax under a cash flow tax would have been greater in 1982 and 1986 than it was under the prevailing corporate income tax at that time.[§] This implies that the federal government could provide the economy with a strong growth stimulus by encouraging investment through the corporate cash flow tax while at the same time giving up but little revenue.

[†]For this to hold the government would have to allow an investment to be fully deductible, even if it results in negative net taxable income for the corporation such that firms with heavy investment in a given year could receive negative tax payments (subsidies) from the government. Measures also would have to be taken to make sure that only productive investment (as opposed to investment that is really consumption and does not yield future income) is eligible for expensing. See Shoven, 21.

[‡]There would, of course, be some transition problems in moving to a corporate cash flow tax and some issues regarding foreign investments and tax treatment of multinational corporations would also have to be resolved before the tax were introduced. See Shoven, 25–26, for a discussion of these issues.

[§]See Shoven, 24–25, for details of this calculation.

however, the tax is shifted forward to consumers in the form of higher prices, or if it is capitalized into lower stock prices, the long-run adjustment process described by the model would not take place.

INCIDENCE OF THE CORPORATE INCOME TAX

Impact on Output, Prices, and Wages

The tax-induced flow of investment caused by the corporate income tax can affect output prices and wages in the long run. Over time, the output produced by the corporate sector tends to fall relative to that produced by the noncorporate sector because of the reduction in investment in the corporate sector. Depending on the price elasticities of demand, these changes in the supply of goods result in an increase in the price of goods produced by the corporate sector and a decrease in the price of goods produced by the noncorporate sector. Households spending relatively large portions of their budgets on goods produced by the corporate sector experience a reduction in real income, relative to other households.

The tax also can affect the wages earned by labor in the two sectors of the economy. For example, if labor and capital are used in fixed proportions in the corporate sector, then it follows that when the reduction in investment reduces capital input in the corporate sector in the long run, a corresponding reduction in the amount of labor used in that sector would result. If the noncorporate sector does not employ capital and labor in the same ratio as the corporate sector, wages would have to change before the economy can return to a general equilibrium. The general level of wages in the economy might fall as a result of the tax. If the corporate sector is relatively more labor-intensive than the noncorporate sector, wages would fall in order to induce the noncorporate sector to absorb the labor flowing from the corporate sector. The extent of such changes in the prices of other inputs depends on the elasticities of substitution in production between capital and other factors, both in the corporate and noncorporate sectors. Thus, the corporate income tax also can affect the real income of those who own noncapital inputs.

Impact on Income Distribution

Arnold Harberger's general conclusion regarding the corporate income tax is that it is borne according to the ownership of capital. Although Harberger acknowledges that the long-run price effects of the tax are important, he presumes that individuals, on average, benefit as much by price decreases of noncorporate goods caused by the tax as they suffer from price increases for corporate goods caused by the decrease in investment in the corporate sector.

The implication of Harberger's conclusion for the evaluation of the incidence of the tax, from an equity point of view, is that its burden is distributed in a progressive manner with respect to income. This results because the distribution of the ownership of capital (wealth) in the United States is highly unequal and is concentrated in the hands of upper-income groups. If the model is correct, then the tax is paid by anyone who owns capital, including homes, human capital, consumer durables, as well as corporate stock and productive capital. The burden is spread throughout the economy according to the ownership of wealth. The inequality of the pattern of ownership of wealth ensures that the tax is progressive. It is more progressive than it would be if it were borne solely according to the ownership pattern of corporate stock, and it is certainly more progressive than it would be if it were shifted in the short run in the form of higher prices. In fact, considerable econometric analysis tends to support Harberger's conclusion.[12]

A portion of the burden of the tax on capital could be shifted to workers in the form of lower wages. If this were true, the progressivity of the tax would be decreased. The shifting of the tax to workers stems from the tax-induced decline in capital formation. This decreases the amount of capital per worker and, in turn, de-

---

[12]See Gregg, Harberger, and Mieszkowski, "Empirical Evidence," and Oakland, "Corporate Earnings."

creases worker productivity, relative to what it would be in the absence of the tax. The decline in worker productivity, now that each worker has less equipment, such as machines and tools, causes a decline in wages, which, in turn, decreases worker income. Thus, the workers bear a portion of the tax on capital. Owners recoup part of the tax, as the tax-induced decrease in quantity of funds supplied for investment raises the market return to investment (see Figure 15.3). Estimates by Feldstein indicate that as much as 29 percent of the burden of the corporate income tax may be shifted to labor in this way.[13] Other analysis indicates that as much as 80 percent of the burden of the tax may be shifted to labor.[14]

Thus, the incidence of the corporate income tax remains unresolved. The tax is most likely to be widely diffused in the economy. Conflicting studies indicate that the tax is shared, in a complex fashion, by consumers, capitalists, and workers.

---

[13]Martin Feldstein, "The Incidence of a Capital Income Tax in a Growing Economy with Variable Savings Rates," *Review of Economic Studies* 41 (October 1974): 505–513.

[14]J. Gregory Ballentine, "The Incidence of a Corporation Income Tax in a Growing Economy," *Journal of Political Economy* 86 (October 1978): 863–876.

CHECKPOINT

1. What effect does a tax on economic profits have on profit-maximizing a corporation's output decision in the short run?
2. Assuming that corporations maximize profits and investors maximize the return on their investments what are the long-run effects of a corporate income tax on resource use?
3. Why does Harberger's model imply that the incidence of the corporate income tax is borne according to the ownership of capital?

Summary

The corporate income tax is levied on profits of corporations and is a subject of great controversy. The actual burden of this tax appears to be diffused in a complex fashion among consumers, owners of capital, and workers.

Corporations cannot deduct the imputed interest associated with expansion financed by retained earnings. Neither can they deduct dividend payments as a cost. In consequence, many economists believe that the corporate income tax provides incentives for corporations to use debt as opposed to equity finance.

The tax base under the corporate income tax is the sum of normal and economic profits. Because the tax does not allow a deduction for the opportunity cost of capital invested in the firm, it biases financial decisions toward borrowing to finance capital expansion. The size of the tax base is influenced by allowable rules for depreciating assets. Although the Tax Reform Act of 1986 reduced the statutory marginal tax rates applied to corporate income, effective marginal tax rates have actually increased because depreciation rules have become less generous and the elimination of the investment tax credit has increased the taxable corporate income.

The major controversy concerning the incidence, and other economic effects, of the corporate income tax stems from its short-run impact. Some economists believe the tax to be shifted forward immediately to consumers in the form of higher prices; others argue that its initial impact is to reduce the return to holding corporate stock. If the return to investing in corporate business is reduced as a result of the tax, a series of resource flows would be induced, until a new long-run equilibrium is achieved, so that the after-tax return on corporate stock is once again equal to the return available on untaxed investment. Many believe that the net impact of this adjustment process would be such that the incidence of the tax would be borne by all investors, not only those who invest in the corporate sector. The tax also tends to cause losses in efficiency, insofar as its results in a distortion in the pattern of investment between the corporate and the noncorporate sector and also reduces capital formation. Reduced capital formation reduces wages, and, in this way, some of the tax could be shifted to workers.

A Forward Look

Increased concern about the responsiveness of investment and saving to taxes on capital income has led to renewed interest in consumption as a tax base. The following chapter discusses some of the pros and cons of taxing consumption and evaluates various forms of sales taxes. Included in an analysis of the value-added tax, which is used extensively by European nations and has been proposed as an addition to the tax structure in the United States.

Important Concepts

Corporation
Equity
Dividends
Retained Earnings
Economic Depreciation
Accelerated Depreciation
Expensing a Capital Asset
Straight-Line Depreciation
Historic Cost

Questions for Review

1. How is business income measured? How can the tax rules for calculating taxable business income affect incentives to invest?

2. What is the "equity" of a corporation? Assuming that a corporation has $5 million in equity and that shareholders forgo a return of 9 percent by keeping their equity in the corporation, calculate the corporation's normal profit.

3. Why would expensing of capital assets for tax purposes encourage investment in new capital?

4. Explain how corporate income could be taxed under a comprehensive income tax without recourse to a corporate income tax. How can separate taxation of corporate income be justified? Given the favorable treatment of capital gains under the current rules of the personal income tax, what would be some of the consequences of eliminating separate taxation of corporate income?

5. In what sense does the corporate income tax subject corporate profits to double taxation?

6. Why do economists argue that the tax definition of corporate profits overstates the true profits of corporations? How can this misdefinition of profit affect the financial structure of the corporation?

7. How can depreciation allowances affect the size of the tax base for the corporate income tax? How can accelerated depreciation reduce a corporation's tax burden? What problems are caused by inflation in accurately allowing depreciation to reflect the replacement cost of capital?

8. Why is the short-run impact of the corporate income tax on prices of corporate output so crucial in determining the final impact of the tax in the long run? Explain why a profit-maximizing corporation has no incentive to adjust its short-run output in response to a tax on its profits. Who would bear the short-run incidence of the tax if the firm does not produce more or less after the tax is imposed?

9. Explain why the corporate income tax causes resources to flow out of the corporate sector when the short-run effect of the tax is to reduce the after-tax return to capital invested in the corporate sector, relative to alternative investments not subject to the tax? What effect do these resource flows have on the return to capital, output prices, and the return to various factors of production?

10. Assuming a fixed aggregate supply of saving, how does the corporate income tax reduce efficiency according to the results of Harberger's model? How will further losses in efficiency result when the aggregate supply of saving is responsive to changes in its return? Assuming that the aggregate supply of saving is not fixed, how can the corporate income tax be shifted to workers in the long run?

Problems

1. A corporation has $7 million in equity. During the tax year it takes in $4 million in receipts and earns $2 million in capital gains from sale of a subsidiary. It incurs labor costs of $1 million, interest costs of $250,000,

material costs of $500,000, and pays rent for structures of $250,000. Calculate the corporation's total accounting profit and, assuming that the profit is fully taxable, calculate its tax liability using the tax rates in Table 15.2. Calculate the average tax rate of the corporation as a percent of its *economic* profit assuming that the opportunity cost of capital is 8 percent.

2. A corporation has $5 million in assets and $3 million in debt. During the year it takes in $750,000 in net revenue after deduction of all costs except for interest and incurs interest expenses of $300,000. The corporation pays an average tax rate of 33 percent on its profit.

   a. Calculate the percentage return on equity after taxes for the corporation.

   b. Calculate the percentage return on equity for the corporation if it had the same net revenue but no debt and therefore no interest expense for the year.

3. Suppose the corporate profits are subject to a 34-percent marginal tax rate but the profits of noncorporate investment are not taxed. The gross return to corporate investment is 10 percent. Calculate the net return to corporate and noncorporate investment in the long run, assuming that the total supply of savings is perfectly inelastic for the economy. How would your answer differ if the elasticity of supply of saving were 0.5?

4. Suppose the corporate income tax were eliminated and corporate income allocated to shareholders on a pro rata basis, according to their proportion of outstanding stock. How would such a change in tax policy affect the excess burden and incidence of the tax, assuming that all forms of investment income are included in a comprehensive income tax base?

Suggestions for Further Reading

Amerkhail, Valerie; Spooner, Gillian; and Sunley, Emil. "The Fall and Rise of the U.S. Corporate Tax Burden." *National Tax Journal* 41, 3 (September 1988): 273–284. This article examines how economic factors and changes in tax law have affected effective corporate tax rates since 1960.

Ballentine, J. Gregory. *Equity, Efficiency, and the United States Corporation Income Tax.* Washington, D.C.: American Enterprise Institute, 1980. A review of the literature on the incidence and allocative effects of the corporate income tax. Much of the analysis is non-technical and accessible to readers with only minimal background in economics.

Feldstein, Martin, and Summers, Lawrence. "Inflation and the Taxation of Capital Income in the Corporate Sector." *National Tax Journal* 32 (December 1979): 445–470. An analysis of the impact of inflation on capital income and the corresponding distortions in resource allocation.

Harberger, Arnold C. "The Incidence of the Corporation Income Tax." *Journal of Political Economy* 70 (June 1962): 215–240. Harberger's classic tax incidence analysis. This is a fine example of economic model building and application of economic theory to policy. This article has had considerable influence on economic thought. Requires a good background in economic theory.

Shoven, John. "Using the Corporate Cash Flow Tax to Integrate Corporate and Personal Taxes." In National Tax Association–Tax Institute of America, *1990 Proceedings of the Eighty-Third Annual Conference on Taxation.* Columbus, OH: National Tax Association–Tax Institute of America, 1991, 19–27. A novel proposal to change the way corporate income is taxed while at the same time encouraging investment.

U.S. Department of the Treasury. *Blueprints for Basic Tax Reform.* Washington, D.C.: U.S. Government Printing Office, 1977. A discussion of income tax reform, including an analysis of the possibility of integrating the corporate income tax with the personal income tax.

U.S. Department of the Treasury, Office of Tax Analysis. *Compendium of Tax Research.* Washington, D.C.: U.S. Government Printing Office, 1987. Chapters 5 and 6 examine the impact of the Tax Reform Act of 1986 on corporate tax rates.

16

TAXES ON CONSUMPTION
AND SALES

LEARNING OBJECTIVES

After reading this chapter you should be able to

1. Discuss the equity aspects of direct taxation of consumption through a tax that allows households to deduct savings from their income.
2. Determine the economic effects of a general direct tax on comprehensive consumption.
3. Analyze the consequences for labor and investment markets of substituting a comprehensive consumption tax for a

comprehensive income tax yielding the same amount of revenue.
4. Evaluate alternative types of sales taxes including retail sales taxes, excise taxes, turnover taxes, and the value-added tax.
5. Explain how the value-added tax is administered in Europe through the invoice method and the advantages and disadvantages of the tax.

You are probably used to paying a sales tax because most state and many local governments rely on it as a major source of revenue. Usually the sales tax is added on to retail purchase of goods by the retail seller at the time the product is sold to a final user. Sales taxes also are widely used in Europe, but it is not so obvious to buyers that they are paying the tax. If you have visited Europe recently, you might have been shocked by the high prices charged for goods and services. Many are surprised to learn that one reason for the high prices is that all European nations rely heavily on a type of national sales tax that is included in the prices of most goods *and* services, such as hotel room rentals and transportation services. The European sales tax, called the value-added tax, is seldom itemized by the retail seller, but is included in the price of most items. Such a tax, which is currently in use by 50 countries including Canada, has been proposed for the United States as a sort of national sales tax to help the federal government obtain more revenue to balance its budget.

One easy way to avoid sales taxes is not to consume. In fact one of the advantages of taxes on consumption is that they encourage people to save because interest is not subject to sales taxes as it accrues. Taxes on consumption can be used to encourage saving. Recently, because of concerns about the long-term effects of low national saving in the United States, some congressional leaders and economists have been advocating conversion of the income tax to a tax on consumption by allowing taxpayers to deduct their savings from their income before computing their tax. This new way to have a consumption-based tax would directly tax household consumption in the same way income is currently taxed.

In this chapter we examine the possibility of shifting to consumption rather than income-based direct taxation. We also look at the way governments tax consumption indirectly through retail sales taxes, excise taxes, and multistage sales taxes like the value-added tax used throughout Europe.

CONSUMPTION AS A TAX BASE

Consumption, or current expenditure, is an alternative to income as a tax base. The heavy reliance on income taxes at the federal level in the United States, however, reflects a commonly held notion that income is a superior index of the ability to pay. This notion also is reflected in economic analysis, inasmuch as taxes are evaluated in terms of their effects on the distribution of income. Incidence is almost always calculated with respect to an income base. In recent years, renewed interest by economists in the consumption base reflects a persistent belief by some economists that consumption is, in fact, a good (superior, some argue) index of the ability to pay. Also, concern is increasing about relatively high efficiency losses associated with taxation of income from saving and investment. Consumption taxes are more favorable to saving and investment incentives than income taxes.

A general tax on consumption is equivalent to an income tax that allows savings to be excluded from the tax base. Annual **comprehensive consumption** is annual comprehensive income minus annual savings. This chapter discusses the feasibility of a general tax on comprehensive consumption. The advantages and disadvantages of such a tax, compared with a comprehensive income tax, are analyzed.

The dominant form of taxation of consumption in the United States is the retail sales tax. Used mainly by state governments in this country, retail and other general sales taxes account for approximately one-third of aggregate state government revenues. Local governments also use the retail sales tax, but revenues collected from the tax supply an average of less than 5 percent of total local government revenues. The value-added tax commonly used in European nations is levied on both retail and wholesale transactions, with deductions allowable for taxes paid on intermediate transactions.

The federal government taxes consumption mainly through the use of excise taxes, which are selective sales taxes levied on particular items and often collected from manufacturers. Excise taxes have accounted for less than 4 percent of total federal government revenues in recent years. Excise taxes include those levied on cigarettes, gasoline, tires, telephone services, and alcoholic beverages. Excise taxes are also used by state governments, where they account for nearly 10 percent of total revenues. State excise taxes include those on motor fuels, tobacco products, alcoholic beverages, and various miscellaneous items. The federal government also uses customs duties as a means of taxing the consumption of imported goods.

DIRECT TAXATION OF CONSUMPTION: THE EXPENDITURE TAX

The notion of directly taxing consumption in a manner similar to the way income is taxed was recommended for consideration by studies published in the United States and Great Britain in the late 1970s.[1] The method of taxation would involve annual declaration of consumption expenditures, similar to annual declarations of income, by filing annual returns on which taxable consumption would be calculated and taxed according to an appropriate rate structure. This could allow progressive taxation of consumption in a fashion similar to the way progressive rates are applied to taxable income.

Taxable consumption would be calculated directly from data on income, simply by excluding that portion of income that is saved rather than spent. Although implementing such a general consumption tax poses serious problems, economists who propose its adoption argue that these problems are less serious than those that would be encountered in defining a truly comprehensive income base, because measuring annual changes in net worth would not be necessary.[2] In fact, in recent years, U.S. taxpayers have been allowed to exclude a limited amount of savings deposited in qualified retirement accounts from their adjusted gross income. These savings, and the interest and other earnings accumulated in the account, are not taxable until they are withdrawn. Funds withdrawn before the taxpayer has reached the age of 59-1/2 are subject to an additional penalty of 10 percent.

A comprehensive consumption tax, or as it is sometimes called, *an expenditure tax*, would work somewhat like an income tax that allows exclusion of retirement savings from the tax base. However, *all savings, without limit*, no matter for what purpose, would be excluded from income. No tax penalty would be incurred for withdrawing funds from savings accounts. When funds were withdrawn and spent, they would be taxed. In effect, such a tax allows persons to defer the tax on their savings: no tax is due on funds saved and interest earned on those funds as long as they remain in savings accounts. The tax is paid only when the funds are converted to cash and spent.

Consumption, Saving, and Economic Capacity

In 1955, Nicholas Kaldor argued that consumption is a better index of the ability to pay than income.[3] Kaldor's argument is based on the notion that personal satisfaction

---

[1]See U.S. Department of the Treasury, *Blueprints for Basic Tax Reform* (Washington, D.C.: U.S. Government Printing Office, 1979), and Institute for Fiscal Studies, *The Structure and Reform of Direct Taxation: Report of the Committee Chaired by Professor J. E. Meade* (London: George Allen and Unwin, 1978).

[2]See, for example, Peter Mieszkowski, "The Choice of the Tax Base: Consumption versus Income Taxation," in *Federal Tax Reform: Myths and Realities*, ed. Michael J. Boskin (San Francisco: Institute for Contemporary Studies, 1978), 27–54.

[3]See Nicholas Kaldor, *An Expenditure Tax* (London: Allen and Unwin, 1955), chap. 1. Kaldor's idea of an expenditure tax was put into practice briefly in a modified form in India and Ceylon. However, both nations eliminated the tax by 1966.

is obtained when goods and services are consumed. Consumption of goods and services uses up resources and prevents them from being used by others. Saving entails sacrifice and results in no increase in well-being during the current tax period.

The act of saving adds to a nation's capital stock and benefits all, insofar as it allows increased future consumption. Individuals obtain direct benefits from their saving only when they liquidate their assets into cash and increase consumption. The social benefit of saving, Kaldor argues, exceeds the private benefit of consumption, insofar as it adds to a nation's capital stock and improves productivity of resources.

A more modern version of Kaldor's argument is that ability to pay is more appropriately measured by a person's basic capacity to earn income. This implies that, on the basis of horizontal equity, two individuals with equal potential to earn income should pay the same amount of taxes over their lifetimes. Lifetime income depends on basic labor earnings plus a person's basic endowment of capital. To the extent that a person saves or defers consumption in other ways (such as increased time in school), she can increase her stock of physical or human capital. An increase in a person's stock of capital (wealth) implies increased capital income over her lifetime. Because an income tax includes capital income in the tax base, it tends to discriminate according to the way income is timed over a person's lifetime.

Two persons who begin life with the same endowments of physical and human capital, and therefore have the same economic capacity to pay taxes, would be taxed differently, according to the way in which they differ in their tendencies to defer consumption. Quite simply, the individual who prefers to save nothing would be taxed entirely on the basis of his labor income, whereas the individual who prefers to save would pay taxes both on labor earnings and income from accumulated capital. When economic capacity is defined in terms of basic endowments of skills and physical capital, an income tax taxes savers relatively more than those who immediately consume everything that they earn. A tax on consumption avoids discrimination against savers by exempting their savings and interest income from taxation until they are consumed.

Many also argue that income taxation results in double taxation of savings, in the sense that the saver is taxed on her income in the year that she accumulated her savings and then is taxed again when she earns interest on her savings. Under a flat-rate tax on comprehensive income, savers would pay higher taxes over their lifetimes than individuals who consume the bulk of their income when they earn it. This results from the taxation of interest. The discrimination against savers is more acute when interest earned is not adjusted for the rate of inflation.

An Illustration: Taxation of Income Versus Taxation of Consumption of "Equals"

An adult's *life cycle* can be considered to begin at age eighteen and end at death. Assume that, at age eighteen, two individuals enter the labor force and begin to earn a living. They have equal levels of skill and training, with no accumulated physical capital; therefore, they have equal economic capacity. Because these two workers are viewed as having an equal ability to pay taxes, the principle of horizontal equity suggests that they could pay equal taxes over their lifetimes. Assume that they both face the same wage rates and interest rates over their lifetimes. Neither worker ever receives transfers, such as gifts, bequests, or government assistance. The only way they can obtain capital income is to defer present consumption. If one worker is unwilling to do this, he will never save. He will never accumulate savings; therefore, he will never earn interest or any return on investment. On the other hand, the other worker has a high rate of saving in her early years but then draws from the accumulated capital and interest as she ages (leaving no bequests); she will earn interest income over her lifetime, in addition to her wage income. Under the income tax, the interest is taxable. The present value of taxes paid by the saver would exceed that paid by the nonsaver over the life cycle.

To see this, suppose that only two tax periods occur during the life cycle. Both workers earn annual labor income of $30,000 per year in each of the two periods. One worker, A, does not save any income, consuming his entire income in each of the two periods. The second worker, B, saves $5,000 of her $30,000 income in the first period. In the second period, she liquidates her savings and spends them. The market rate of interest is 10 percent. She therefore would have $5,500, in addition to her $30,000 income to spend in the second period.

Under a flat-rate tax of 20 percent on income, the discounted present value of income taxes for worker A, the nonsaver, would be

$$
\begin{aligned}
T_A &= \$6{,}000 + \$6{,}000/(1 + .1) \\
&= \$6{,}000 + \$5{,}455 = \$11{,}455,
\end{aligned}
\tag{16.1}
$$

where $6,000 is the 20 percent tax liability on labor income in each of the two years. Taxes in the second period are discounted at the market rate of interest at 10 percent.

Worker B, the saver, would pay *more* tax in the second period because of the $500 interest earnings. Total tax liability of this worker is $6,000 in the current period and $6,100 in the second period. The discounted present value of income taxes for worker B would be

$$
\begin{aligned}
T_B &= \$6{,}000 + \$6{,}100/(1 + .1) \\
&= \$6{,}000 + \$5{,}545 = \$11{,}545.
\end{aligned}
\tag{16.2}
$$

The discounted present value of income taxes over the two-period lifetime is $90 higher under the income tax for the saver compared with the nonsaver. In general, if interest income is taxed as it is accrued, the income tax, other things being equal, would force savers to pay more taxes than nonsavers.

If, on the other hand, the tax base were consumption, the present value of taxes paid by the two workers over their lifetimes would be equal and independent of the pattern of consumption and saving. Although, because of the interest earned, the worker who saves more will consume more than her forgone consumption in later years, the tax would treat them equally. The additional tax paid on interest income when it is consumed compensates for the deferral of the tax on savings. This holds, regardless of the pattern of consumption, over the life cycle. Thus, the consumption tax treats these two workers equally, according to the equality of their economic capacity.

To see this, suppose both workers were subject to a tax of 20 percent on consumption. As before, assume that the life cycle consists of two periods and that B saves \$5,000 of income in the first period so that she can consume more in the second period. The market rate of interest is 10 percent. A's tax liability is 20 percent of his \$30,000 income in both periods. Because this person saves nothing, the consumption tax is equivalent to an income tax of 20 percent for him. The present value of his tax liability therefore is the same as it was under the income tax, as computed in Equation 16.1. This amount is \$11,455. For nonsavers, a tax on consumption is equivalent to a tax on income!

The tax liability for the saver, however, is quite different under the consumption tax. In the first period, she would pay 20 percent of the \$25,000 that she consumes. Her tax liability would be only \$5,000 in the first period. Because, in the second period, she liquidates and spends her savings, her total consumption in the second period would be \$30,000 from her income plus \$5,500 from her redeemed savings and interest. The total tax due in the second period therefore is .2(\$35,500) = \$7,100. The present value of her tax liability under the consumption tax is

$$
\begin{aligned}
T'_B &= \$5,000 + \$7,100/(1 + .1) \\
&= \$5,000 + \$6,455 = \$11,455.
\end{aligned}
\tag{16.3}
$$

This is the same amount as the discounted present value of taxes paid by the nonsaver!

In effect, when a consumption tax is used, both the saver and the nonsaver are taxed only according to their labor income. Under the consumption tax, savers do not pay any tax on interest income as it accrues in their accounts, as they would under an income tax. Interest is taxed under an income tax as it accrues, reducing the net interest rate received by savers to $r_N = (1 - t)r_G$, where r_G is the gross interest earned and t is the income tax rate.

The consumption tax therefore is equivalent to a flat-rate tax on labor income alone. Interest income is not taxed as it is earned. When taxpayers spend accumulated savings and accumulated interest in future periods, the extra tax due merely represents interest on the tax that has been deferred through saving. The market rate of interest is not distorted in any way by the consumption tax.

To understand this, examine the tax paid on savings that are liquidated and spent in future periods. In effect, under a consumption tax, those who save merely *postpone* their tax liability to the future. The amount that they would have paid in taxes, had they not saved, can be thought of as a loan from the government. For example, under the consumption tax, the saver in the preceding example would save \$1,000 in current taxes by deferring \$5,000 of first-period consumption to the second period. When the savings were spent in the second period, the taxpayer repaid the government the \$1,000 in deferred taxes *plus* 10 percent interest on the deferred \$1,000 tax. The total tax liability in the second period therefore would be \$7,100.

In general, if the interest rate is r and the tax rate is t, at the end of one year, C_1 dollars saved would be worth $(1 + r)C_1$. The tax paid would be $t[(1 + r)C_1]$ when the accumulated interest and savings are spent at the end of one year. If the C_1 dollars had been spent immediately, the tax would have been tC_1. The extra tax paid after a year of saving therefore would be $t[(1 + r)C_1] - tC_1 = r[tC_1]$, which represents interest on the tax deferred for one year.

A COMPREHENSIVE CONSUMPTION TAX BASE

A comprehensive base for taxing consumption can be derived from the comprehensive income tax base. Comprehensive income is defined as the sum of annual consumption and increased net worth. The comprehensive consumption tax base merely excludes any increases in net worth from the tax base.

Some of the advantages of the consumption tax could help solve some of the difficult measurement problems involved in administering the income tax. Only current expenditures are taxed under the consumption tax. Measuring either realized or unrealized capital gains is unnecessary. The tax administrators would not tax these until they are converted into cash and spent. Only at that point are capital gains taxable.

Inflation is no problem under the consumption tax because only current expenditures are taxed. For example, under the comprehensive income tax, taxation of capital gain would require that it be indexed for the rate of inflation. A capital gain on an asset held for many years includes the effect of inflation. However, when the gain is liquidated at any point in time, the cash obtained is also used to buy goods at the current inflated values. Therefore, adjusting the purchasing power of the gain under a consumption tax is no longer necessary—it is done automatically by current prices!

Anything that increases the net worth of the taxpayer would be excluded from the tax base. This would include all forms of saving in accounts at financial institutions and such acquisitions of income-producing physical assets as land, business inventories, and claims against income-producing assets (stocks and bonds).

Implementation of a Tax on Consumption

In treating consumption-in-kind from consumer durables, problems develop in implementing the tax base that are similar to those encountered in defining income-in-kind.[4] For example, the consumption of housing services flowing to occupants of owner-occupied dwellings would have to be included in the tax base if it were to be truly comprehensive. This means that an annual implicit rental must be computed to owner-occupied homes and included in the owner's taxable consumption. Similarly, all consumer durables would have to have consumption flows imputed to their use. In developing a consistent and equitable way of doing this, administrative problems could very well result in those items being excluded from the tax base, as many income-in-kind items are excluded from taxable income.

---

[4]For a discussion of some of these problems, see Advisory Commission on Intergovernmental Relations, *The Expenditure Tax: Concept, Administration, and Possible Applications* (Washington, D.C.: U.S. Government Printing Office, 1974), chap. 3.

Alternatively, consumer durables could be taxed at purchase by applying the appropriate tax rate to their purchase price. This, in effect, would levy a tax on the purchaser equal to a certain percentage of the discounted, present value of future service flows that stem from the asset over its useful life. For such high-priced assets as homes, this creates a liquidity problem for buyers. The problem could be solved by allowing the taxpayer to spread the tax payments over time, in the form of annual installments; thus, in effect, the government would lend purchasers the funds to pay the taxes on houses by allowing their amortization over time.[5]

Transfers would be included in the tax base to the extent to which they were consumed. Contributions to retirement funds, including Social Security taxes, would be treated as saving and therefore excluded from taxation. Bequests at death would have to be treated as a form of final consumption at death and taxed accordingly.[6] This would prevent individuals from avoiding taxes permanently by transferring accumulated wealth at death.

An interesting difference between an income tax and an expenditure tax lies in the treatment of borrowed funds. Loans, under the consumption tax, are taxed when they are spent. Under an income tax, loans are never added to the taxpayer's income, but interest payments on the loan are deductible from taxable income. The consumption tax includes the loan proceeds in the tax base, as they are spent, and allows the interest to be deducted from consumption as the loan is paid off.

The Cash-Flow Tax

A modified form of a general consumption tax is the **cash-flow tax.**[7] Under such a tax, savers would be permitted, in computing their tax liability each year, to deduct from their income those funds deposited in "qualified accounts." Such a mechanism for deferring tax burden until funds are withdrawn from special accounts already exists as part of the federal income tax code. Currently, such deductions are allowable only for special accounts—Keogh plans and IRAs—for those eligible. As discussed, the current system limits the amounts that can be deposited in these funds and imposes penalties for early withdrawal. The cash-flow tax simply would extend such treatment to a broad array of qualified accounts and allow taxpayers to withdraw and spend funds from these accounts whenever they wished, at which time they would incur a tax liability, but not a penalty.

The proposed cash-flow tax would allow taxpayers, in computing tax liability, to deduct from adjusted gross income all savings deposited in qualified accounts. When such funds and accumulated interest are withdrawn from these accounts, and therefore converted into a cash flow, they would be taxed. Taxpayers could further defer

---

[5]See Miezkowski, "Choice of the Tax Base," 41–51, for a discussion of some implementation problems.

[6]Alternatively, bequests could be treated as transfers and, when spent, included in the tax base of heirs. If never liquidated, the perpetual saving never would be taxed.

[7]See U.S. Treasury, *Blueprints for Basic Tax Reform*, 113–143.

tax liability on withdrawals from existing accounts simply by redepositing the withdrawals into qualified accounts.

Under the cash-flow tax, deposits in checking accounts would not be considered qualified, because funds in checking accounts are demand deposits intended to meet transactions demand for cash, rather than to provide savings. However, the cash-flow tax would not tax interest earned on checking and other nonqualified accounts. To implement the tax, important decisions would have to be made concerning which accounts would be qualified for the deduction.

Also, under the cash-flow tax, loans would be added to adjusted gross income as they are received but would be deducted from income as they are repaid. Purchases of durable assets by consumers would not be considered a form of saving, and such purchases would be subject to a tax.

The administrative mechanism already exists to implement some form of expenditure tax similar to the cash-flow tax model proposed by the U.S. Treasury study. However, important decisions would have to be made concerning the types of saving that would be deductible from income for the purpose of defining taxable consumption, so as to avoid distortions in behavior. One difficult problem that would have to be resolved is the consistent and equitable treatment of saving in the form of investment in human, as opposed to physical, capital.

Some difficult transition problems could be posed in moving from an income-based to a consumption-based tax. For example, the elderly who consume all of their current income and draw down previously accumulated savings to live on could be hard hit by the shift to the consumption tax. This is because the elderly tend to consume more than their current income as they dissave.[8] The elderly would have paid income taxes on their capital income during their working years and would then have to pay the consumption tax when they liquidated their saving. Special rules to avoid double-taxing the elderly would have to be developed to avoid hitting them hard with a consumption tax.

C H E C K P O I N T

1. What is comprehensive consumption?
2. How would an expenditure tax work?
3. In what sense can a comprehensive consumption tax be regarded as achieving the goal of horizontal equity?

A GENERAL TAX ON COMPREHENSIVE CONSUMPTION

The advantages and disadvantages of a general tax on comprehensive consumption can be highlighted by comparing the tax with a general tax on comprehensive income.

---

[8]For a discussion of some of the transition problems, see M. Kevin McGee, "Alternative Transitions to a Consumption Tax," *National Tax Journal* 42, 2 (June 1989), 155–166.

Assume that both taxes raise the same amount of revenue and finance the same mix of government services. Assume, as well, that both taxes are levied at a proportional rate. The consumption tax generally is more favorable to savers and is most likely to result in no efficiency loss in the allocation of resources between current and future consumption. These benefits, in turn, must be balanced by the possibility of reduced efficiency in labor markets and correspondingly higher tax burdens borne by workers.

Substituting a Flat-Rate Consumption Tax for an Equal-Yield Flat-Rate Income Tax

Consider, first, the efficiency effects of substituting a flat-rate comprehensive consumption tax for a flat-rate comprehensive income tax. If both taxes are to raise the same amount of revenue, and if saving in any given year is positive, then the tax rate under the consumption tax would have to be higher than the tax rate under an equal-yield income tax. This is simply because the tax base is smaller under a consumption tax than it would be under an income tax. Because comprehensive income is the sum of consumption and increased net worth in any year, the exclusion of increases in net worth (saving) from the tax base requires an increase in tax rates, if both taxes are to raise the same amount of revenue.[9]

If, for example, savings are 20 percent of income after the consumption tax is introduced, and income does not increase in response to the substitution of the consumption tax for the income tax, then the consumption tax rate would have to be 25 percent higher than the income tax rate to raise the same revenue. This is because, with a savings rate equal to 20 percent, income is equal to 125 percent of consumption. The consumption tax taxes only 80 percent of the income base. Therefore,

$$\text{Tax Revenue } = t_I I = t_C(.8)I$$
$$1.25 t_I = t_C, \tag{16.4}$$

where t_I is the income tax rate, t_C is the consumption tax rate, and I is income.

Impact on Savings and Excess Burden in Investment Markets

The higher tax rate required under the consumption tax to raise the same revenue as the income tax is of no consequence for the impact of the tax on the capital market because interest income is not taxable under a consumption tax. When interest is spent, the only extra tax liability incurred by savers represents repayment of interest on deferred taxes to the government during the period the interest was being earned. The interest rate itself is not affected by the tax. Therefore, no excess burden is introduced in choices between current and future consumption as a result of the introduction of the tax.

---

[9]It is possible that lower tax rates on capital income might increase GDP and therefore increase consumption over and above what it would be under the income tax. If this were the case, the tax rate would not have to increase as much as it would if GDP did not increase.

If the taxes replace a preexisting income tax, then any excess burden existing because of tax-induced distortion in interest rates is eliminated. This is because the income tax taxes interest as it accrues and therefore results in a loss in efficiency as individuals reallocate resources between current and future use. The removal of the tax influence on the rate of interest restores efficiency in the capital market, as the consumption tax is substituted for the income tax. This is illustrated in Figure 16.1.

Under the income tax, the net return to savings falls short of the gross return. The substitution of the flat-rate consumption tax for the income tax removes the wedge between the gross interest rate and the net interest rate. Efficiency in the market for loanable funds is restored, and the gain in well-being is approximated by the area of triangle FGE. The market rate of interest declines from r^*_G to r^*. As a result of the substitution of the consumption tax for the income tax, annual investment increases by ΔQ_I.

IMPACT ON EFFICIENCY IN LABOR MARKETS

The gains from achieving efficiency in the market for loanable funds must be balanced with the possibility of additional losses in labor markets. This is because the higher tax rate required for the consumption tax further decreases the return to work effort and induces further efficiency losses in the labor market resulting from distortion in the work-leisure choice. If, for example, the tax rate under the consumption

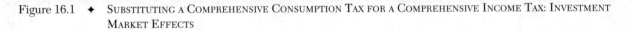

Figure 16.1   ✦   SUBSTITUTING A COMPREHENSIVE CONSUMPTION TAX FOR A COMPREHENSIVE INCOME TAX: INVESTMENT
MARKET EFFECTS

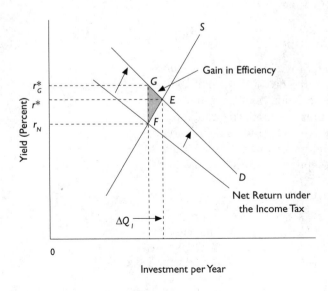

Substituting a comprehensive consumption tax for an income tax removes the tax wedge between the gross and net returns to investment. The result is a gain in efficiency in investment markets, approximated by the area FGE. Market interest rates decline to r°, and annual investment increases up to the efficient amount.

tax must be 125 percent of the tax rate under the income tax in order to raise the same amount of revenue, workers would pay 25 percent more taxes on their wages under the consumption tax.

In Figure 16.2, the efficient allocation corresponds to point B, where wages are w_o and the quantity of labor hours is L_1. Under the income tax at rate t_I, the effective wage received by workers falls to $w_G(1 - t_I)$ at all hours of work, resulting in equilibrium at point C, where the gross wage is w_{G1} and the net wage received by workers is w_{N1}. Labor hours fall from L_1 to L_2. The loss in efficiency is measured by the triangle ABC if the reduction in labor hours reflects the substitution effect caused by the income tax.

Substitution of the consumption tax for the income tax increases the effective tax on wages and further shifts down wages received at all hours of work to $w_G(1 - t_C)$. This results in a further decline in net wages at the new equilibrium C' because t_C exceeds t_I, and a further increase in gross wages paid, as labor hours decline again, to L_3. The loss in efficiency now is measured by the excess burden $A'BC'$ assuming that the reduction in hours worked does not include the income effect of the tax.

The substitution of the consumption tax for the income tax increases the excess burden by the area $A'ACC'$. Recall that the excess burden increases with the square of the tax rate. The increased excess burden therefore is more than proportionate to the increase in the tax rate (see Chapter 11).

The gain in efficiency introduced by a consumption tax, as a result of removal of the excess burden in the capital market, must be compared with the added loss in efficiency in the labor market due to the higher rate of taxation made necessary by the

Figure 16.2 ✦ Substituting an Equal-Yield Comprehensive Consumption Tax for an Income Tax: Labor Market Effects

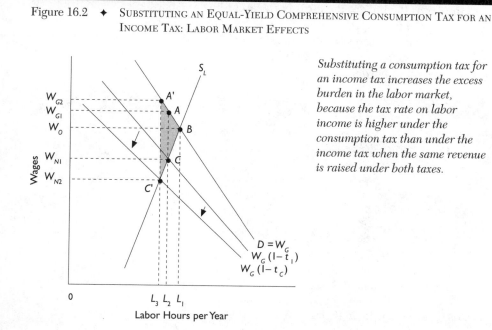

Substituting a consumption tax for an income tax increases the excess burden in the labor market, because the tax rate on labor income is higher under the consumption tax than under the income tax when the same revenue is raised under both taxes.

exclusion of savings from taxation. Even if the supply of labor hours is quite unresponsive to the wage, the added excess burden due to the higher tax on labor income could be substantial. This is because labor income accounts for more than three-quarters of all income earned in the United States; therefore, even small percentage increases in the excess burden in labor markets could involve large losses in well-being due to the large amount of earnings and therefore dollars involved. However, if the excess burden per dollar of revenue raised by consumption taxes is lower than that per dollar of revenue raised by the income tax, as some estimates suggest, the net gain from substituting the consumption tax for the income tax would be positive.

Given reasonable estimates of the elasticities of supply of savings and labor, some research has estimated that a consumption tax would have a smaller excess burden than an equal-yield income tax. For example, one research study concluded that the efficiency gain from moving from an income tax to a consumption tax could be as much as 3 percent of gross domestic product per year.[10]

Incidence of a Consumption Tax

Because capital income is excluded from taxation under the consumption tax, the tax would be borne according to labor earnings. The portion borne by labor income could be shifted to consumers if workers adjusted the quantity of hours of work supplied in response to the tax. Under the assumption of a relatively inelastic supply of labor, the portion of the tax that could be shifted to others would be small.

Assuming a relatively inelastic labor supply, as is shown in Figure 16.2, gross wages rise only slightly, relative to what they would be in the absence of the tax. Thus, in Figure 16.2, under the consumption tax, wages rise from a pretax level of w_o to w_{G2}.

Insofar as the bulk of the tax is borne according to labor income, and capital income escapes taxation, the consumption tax is likely to be more regressive, with respect to income, than an equal-yield income tax. However, if an expenditure tax were used, the rate structure of the tax could be modified to achieve a collectively chosen distribution of tax burden.

CHECKPOINT

1. Explain why the tax rate for a comprehensive consumption tax designed to replace an equal-yield comprehensive income tax would have to be higher than the income tax rate.
2. Why would replacement of a comprehensive income tax with a comprehensive consumption tax result in a gain in efficiency in investment markets?
3. Why would replacement of a comprehensive income tax with a comprehensive consumption tax result in a loss in efficiency in labor markets?

---

[10]See Don Fullerton, John B. Shoven, and John Whalley, "Replacing the U.S. Income Tax with a Progressive Consumption Tax: A Sequenced General Equilibrium Approach," *Journal of Public Economics* 20 (February 1983): 3–23.

SALES TAXES

In practice, few sales taxes are implemented in such a way as to conform to a comprehensive consumption tax base. This is attributable to both administrative problems and political constraints. For example, many retail sales taxes are levied only on the consumption of tangible goods. The consumption of professional services (medical, legal, educational) and such personal services as haircuts, entertainment, and transportation are usually exempt from the tax.

Perhaps the most conspicuous exemption is housing services. In addition, many states that levy retail sales taxes exempt the consumption of certain basic goods regarded as necessities from taxation in order to achieve a more equitable distribution of the tax burden. The consumption of food and grocery items was exempted in 27 states in 1990. Medicine and drugs also are often exempt from taxation. Finally, many consumption taxes are levied on the purchase of capital goods. For example, most retail sales taxes in the United States are levied on the purchases of automobiles and other consumer durables. When these durable goods that are subject to consumption taxes are purchased by business firms, they increase the marginal costs of production and are reflected in higher retail prices, which then are used as the base to apply the consumption tax all over again. This results in pyramiding taxes on taxes and a consequence higher tax rate to be borne by consumers.

Retail Sales Taxes

A **retail sales tax** usually is an ad valorem levy of a fixed percentage on the dollar value of retail purchases made by consumers. A true retail sales tax is levied only on consumption at its final stage and is collected from business establishments that make retail sales. The tax usually is added on to the retail price of goods and services. Thus, retailers merely act as intermediaries between consumers and the government in collecting the tax. However, as the previous discussion has indicated, in many instances, the tax exempts personal services and basic food items from the tax base. Furthermore, the tax sometimes is applied to purchases by business firms that intend to use them for further production, such as office furniture, automobiles, fuel, and other equipment. Therefore, in practice the retail sales tax cannot be considered either a general tax or one that is levied solely on final consumption.

As it is implemented in the United States, the retail sales tax is a state and local fiscal instrument, rather than a national one. Its merits therefore must be discussed as a locally administered tax within the framework of the federal system. Sales taxes are utilized as a major source of revenue in state governments. In addition, many local governments use retail sales taxes as revenue sources. Sales taxes were first enacted on the state level in the 1930s in response to the need for a more stable revenue source in the face of falling incomes and property values. The first local sales tax was enacted by the city of New York in 1934. Currently, many local governments utilize retail sales as a tax base. Most state and local retail sales taxes are collected from retailers; therefore, much of the administrative cost of the tax is borne by retail firms. Some states compensate retailers for bearing the administrative costs.[11]

A possible effect of local sales taxation is a loss of retail trade to neighboring jurisdictions where the sales tax is either absent or applied at a lower rate. The migration of retail sales to another taxing jurisdiction can have the effect of reducing employment, business profits in the taxing jurisdiction, or both. This, in turn, could decrease the actual amount of taxes collected. Only partial shifting to consumers of the retail sales tax would occur if the tax caused sales to migrate. This means that retail prices would not rise by the full amount of the tax. The tax would decrease the net incomes of local sellers. If the consumption tax base were elastic with respect to the rate of taxation, then increases in the rate of sales taxation would result in less, not more, revenue collected.

In some cases, a local tax can be levied on items purchased in neighboring jurisdictions but used in the taxing jurisdiction. This is accomplished through *use taxes*. For example, for an automobile purchased outside the taxing jurisdiction, the state or locality levying the tax can require the tax to be paid before the automobile can be registered in that area. Use taxes are difficult to enforce for consumption goods that are not required to be registered. Empirical evidence has indicated that sales tax-rate differentials among neighboring taxing jurisdictions (for example, the central city and the suburbs) do have significant effects on per capita retail sales distribution among the taxing jurisdictions.[12]

Many state governments have been under pressure to raise more revenue. To do so, several state governments have raised their sales tax rate. In 1991, 28 states had basic sales tax rates of 5 percent or more and in many cases local sales taxes were piggybacked on to the state sales tax rate. In 1989, the state of Connecticut had the highest sales tax rate at 8 percent. In many large cities that have a local sales tax, the total rate paid by consumers is close to 10 percent.

Also, more revenue can be raised from sales taxes by broadening the sales tax base instead of raising tax rates. For example, in states where food is exempt from the tax, additional revenue can be obtained by taxing food. Taxation of services such as rentals of housing and other products, cable television services, and lawn care also would generate more revenue and several states tax these services. In 1987, the state of Florida expanded its retail sales tax base to include services to consumers and some services sold to businesses. The new taxes were very unpopular and were repealed shortly after their introduction.

Because the retail sales tax is a state and local tax in the United States, ample opportunity exists to avoid the tax. One way of avoiding the tax is to purchase items in one state for delivery to a residence in another state. This can be accomplished either by visiting the state or through a mail order. Typically, the transaction is viewed as an

---

[11]For a complete discussion of sales tax administration, see John F. Due and John L. Mikesell, "State Sales Tax Structures and Operations in the Last Decade—A Sample Study," *National Tax Journal* 32 (March 1980): 21–43.

[12]John L. Mikesell, "Central Cities and Sales-Tax Differentials," *National Tax Journal* 23 (June 1970): 213.

out-of-state sale if the buyer has a residence in another state and if the seller does not operate in the state in which the buyer resides. No sales tax is levied on the sale by the originating state and in most cases the buyer can avoid paying the tax to the state in which he resides. Some states have passed laws that make local residents liable for sales tax on out-of-state mail order purchases, but these taxes have proved difficult to collect.

Excise Taxes

Excise taxes are selective taxes levied on certain types of consumption activities. As such, they distort choices among goods and services and result in efficiency losses to the economy. These stem from the tax wedge inserted between relative prices, as perceived by consumers and producers and explained in Chapter 11.

Some excise taxes are designed to raise revenue, while others are intended to discourage particular consumption activities. Excise taxes on tires, for example, are primarily designed to raise revenue, while taxes on liquor consumption, although they do raise considerable revenue, also are intended to discourage liquor consumption. A special "gas guzzler excise tax" has been in place for several years in order to discourage purchase of cars with poor fuel economy. For example, a car that got less than 12.5 miles per gallon in 1993 was subject to a unit excise tax of a whopping $7,700! Some types of tariffs are designed to discourage consumption of foreign merchandise. A *tariff* lowers the net price received by foreign suppliers but raises the price paid for goods to consumers. In effect, a tariff redistributes income from the domestic consumers and foreign suppliers of the merchandise toward the owners and workers of the protected domestic industries. At the same time, it increases revenues of the federal government.

Both federal and state governments tax liquor and cigarette consumption. Federal excise taxes also are levied on gasoline, telephone service, and tires. In many cases, the consumption activities singled out for taxation are alleged to generate negative externalities or can be considered luxury goods or services.

Prior to 1913, the federal government relied extensively on customs duties as a revenue source. Today, tariffs represent less than 1 percent of revenues collected by the federal government. The rates applied to many items are high and are clearly designed to discourage importation of foreign merchandise, rather than to raise revenue. In a sense, tariffs that are successful revenue instruments cannot fulfill their function as protective devices for domestic industries, simply because the high revenue capability implies that they are ineffective in discouraging domestic consumption of foreign merchandise.

The incidence of a tariff depends on the income elasticity of the protected merchandise. When the tariff succeeds in inducing consumers to substitute domestic merchandise for cheaper foreign goods, the effect is to redistribute income from consumers toward the high-cost producers of domestic goods. When the protected commodities are consumed largely by high-income households and produced by low-income workers, the resulting redistribution of income can be progressive. However, a net efficiency loss to the economy results from the indirect subsidization of the relatively inefficient domestic producers.

PUBLIC POLICY PERSPECTIVE

ORIGINS, DESTINATIONS, AND ISSUES IN COLLECTING SALES TAXES

In 1967, the U.S. Supreme Court ruled, in the case of *National Bellas Hess v. Illinois Department of Revenue,* that on the basis of the interstate commerce clause in the U.S. Constitution states could not require mail order firms located in other states to collect their state sales taxes if the firm does not maintain business sales facilities in the state where the purchaser resides. Since that decision, the mail order business has grown substantially and state governments hard-pressed for revenue have continued to pursue taxing out-of-state purchases. A number of states have passed legislation requiring residents to declare their out-of-state purchases and pay state sales tax on them, even though that sales tax is not collected by the seller. For example, the state of North Carolina requires its residents to file a special form with their state income tax to pay state sales taxes on out-of-state purchases. However these use taxes on out-of-state purchases have proved to be very difficult to collect.

The possibility of avoiding sales taxes has been a boon to mail order sales in the United States. Here's the way the current system works. As long as a seller that mails catalogues or similar information to residents in a state does not maintain a business presence in that state through offices or retail sales outlets, it is not required to collect sales tax on orders shipped to that state. If you order a jacket from L.L. Bean in Maine and L.L. Bean has no sales outlets in your state, then you do not pay the sales tax for either the state of Maine or your state. On the other hand, if Eddie Bauer has a retail store in your city and you place a mail order for a similar jacket with this firm, Eddie Bauer will then have to collect the sales tax on the shipment. You also can avoid the sales tax in many cases if you make a purchase while visiting another state and then have the purchase shipped to your home in another state. Under those circumstances you pay neither the sales tax of the state in which you buy the item nor the sales tax levied by your home state.

Sales taxes in the United States are based on the *destination principle,* which argues that taxes on consumption can be levied only at the point at which the item is consumed. This principle implies that a purchase by a resident of the state of North Carolina either from a New York mail order firm or from a New York seller made while visiting New York and shipped to

---

When the tariff is ineffective in reducing the consumption of foreign goods, it reduces the real income of consumers of these goods and increases government revenue without affecting the domestic production of the protected goods. The overall incidence of the tariff, in this case, depends on the income class of consumers of the good upon which the duty is levied and on the disposition of the additional federal revenue.

Incidence of Sales and Excise Taxes

A common criticism of retail sales and excise taxes is that they are regressive with respect to income. This is based on the notion that annual consumption expenditures, as a percentage of annual income, are higher for low-income taxpayers, relative to high-income taxpayers, and that the tax is shifted forward, so that it is borne according to purchases. The alleged regressiveness of these taxes has been challenged by research that suggests that the tax might not be reflected in higher prices in the first place.[13]

---

[13]See Edgar K. Browning, "The Burden of Taxation," *Journal of Political Economy* 86 (August 1978): 649–671.

North Carolina, is not taxable by New York State because the destination of the good for consumption would be North Carolina. It's up to North Carolina to levy a use tax on the consumption if it can feasibly track it down. This destination principle provides a loophole in sales tax administration that costs state governments $1.5 billion in lost revenue in 1985, according to one estimate. Naturally, firms that specialize in mail order sales are not eager to collect sales taxes for out-of-state governments. This issue was still smoldering between the states and mail order firms in the early 1990s, and new legal action can be expected to try to change the law so that mail order sales taxes can be collected from large out-of-state sellers.

Some sales taxes are based on the *origin principle.* Under those circumstances, a tax would be levied by states on the production of all items, no matter where they are consumed. If retail sales taxes were based on the origin principle you would pay out-of-state sales taxes on your purchases. This would mean that if you ordered an item from L.L. Bean in Maine, you would pay the sales tax prevailing in Maine.

The value-added tax, which is a common form of sales tax used by nations of the European Community, are collected from sellers irrespective of the destination of consumption. However, the *General Agreement on Tariffs and Trade (GATT),* an international organization of nations recently renamed the "World Trade Organization" that sets rules for international trade, allows rebates of origin-type sales taxes. So a Mercedes produced in Germany and subject to the German value-added tax can have the tax rebated to the manufacturer when the car is exported to the United States. This rebate lowers the price of the Mercedes to U.S. buyers and makes the car more competitive in U.S. markets. The GATT rules also allow imposition of origin taxes on imports, that is, a U.S. aircraft exported to Germany would be subject to German value-added taxes. This imposition of the tax makes U.S. aircraft more costly and therefore less competitive in German markets. Because European nations use more origin-based sales taxes than we do to tax corporate businesses, this could put us at a competitive disadvantage in European markets. The corporate income tax in the United States puts upward pressure on the price of corporate products, but it is a direct tax that cannot be rebated on exports or imposed on imports according to GATT rules.

However, the common belief that the tax is regressive has led many states to exempt specific consumption items from the tax bases. For example, in the United States in 1990, all states except New Hampshire, Delaware, Montana, Oregon, and Alaska used retail sales taxes. In 1990, twenty-seven of the states that used the tax exempted food purchases from taxation, in an attempt to decrease the tax burden on low-income groups, which spend a relatively high proportion of income on food.

Research by Pechman on the incidence of retail sales and excise taxes in the United States concluded that they were regressive with respect to income. The research showed that the rates paid declined steadily from about 9 percent of income for the lowest-income groups to a little more than 3 percent for the highest-income groups.[14] Recent changes in the federal income tax code have removed the tax deductibility of state sales taxes. This change will act to diminish the regressivity of sales taxes by increasing the effective tax paid by upper-income groups who itemize their

---

[14]Joseph A. Pechman, *Who Paid the Taxes: 1966–1985?* (Washington, D.C.: The Brookings Institution, 1985).

income tax deductions. Recent analysis of the short-lived Florida sales tax on some household and business services concluded that the incidence of the tax on services in Florida was regressive.[15] The national effects of sales taxes are likely to be similar to those of a national consumption tax. The tax would be borne according to labor income.

TURNOVER TAXES

Turnover taxes are multistage sales taxes that are levied, at some fixed rate, on transactions at all levels of production. The effective tax rate on various goods and services therefore is conditioned by the number of stages of production. The turnover tax has been used in Germany, and other European countries, as a major revenue source. Germany, however, replaced its turnover tax with a value-added tax in 1968. The turnover tax provides an incentive to vertical integration among firms, so as to reduce the number of production stages and interfirm transactions and, consequently, reduce the tax liability. The tax usually is reflected in higher final consumption prices. However, the rates of taxation vary with the number of stages of production. The distributive effects of the tax therefore depend on consumer preferences for, and among, goods and services that entail a number of stages in their production.

The turnover tax is an extremely productive levy, producing high, stable yields at very low rates. The relatively low rate employed at any level of transaction is believed to discourage tax evasion. The reason for the high yield is the sheer number of transactions taxed, plus the pyramiding of tax rates on tax rates for multistage production, considerably increasing the final effective rate of taxation. The pyramiding occurs when firms apply percentage markups to purchase prices to include the tax.

The turnover tax, as used in Germany, was criticized by some as being regressive. However, empirical studies have shown that the tax actually was somewhat progressive.[16] This is because the effective rates on many food items were lower than those on clothing and other manufactured goods. Any changes in production techniques that alter the number of processing stages could influence the final effective tax rates. It is administratively difficult to grant specific exemptions under turnover taxation, relative to retail sales taxation. The turnover tax is not a truly general tax, because it applies discriminatory rates to alternative goods and services that are dependent on the number of productive stages.

VALUE-ADDED TAXES

The **value-added tax** (VAT) is a general tax on consumption levied on the value added to intermediate products by businesses at each stage of production. As of 1994

---

[15]See John J. Siegfried and Paul A. Smith, "The Distributional Effects of a Sales Tax on Services," *National Tax Journal* 44, 1 (March 1991): 41–54.

[16]See John F. Due, *Sales Taxation* (Urbana: University of Illinois Press, 1957), 59.

various forms of the value-added tax were in use in more than fifty nations of the world including Canada, Japan, and all nations of the European Union (EU). The tax was first adopted in 1954 by the French National Government. When a nation is admitted to the EU, it is required to introduce the VAT as a condition of membership. The value-added tax also is used in several Latin American nations. In the United States, a type of value-added tax was used by the state of Michigan between 1953 and 1967 and was readopted in 1975 as a "single business tax."

The value-added tax, though not currently used by the federal government, has been seriously considered in the past. The tax has been considered both as a full or a partial substitute for the existing corporate income tax and also as a new source of revenue.

The Meaning of Value Added

The value-added tax is simply a multistage sales tax that exempts the purchase of intermediate goods and services from the tax base. *Value added* is the difference between sales proceeds and purchases of intermediate goods and services over a certain period. For example, the value added for a grocery store in a given month is the difference between the total sales receipts that month and the total invoices for goods and services from its suppliers. Suppose the store had total sales receipts of $150,000 that month. If it purchased $75,000 of groceries from its suppliers and $10,000 of goods and services from other firms, its value added would be $65,000 that month.

Total transactions less intermediate transactions (that is, purchases made from firms by other firms) is equal to the sum of wages, interest, rent, and other input payments in the nation, summing up to the gross national product. This may be expressed as the following identity:

$$
\begin{aligned}
\text{Value Added} &= \text{Total Transactions} - \text{Intermediate Transactions} \\
&= \text{Final Sales} = \text{GDP} \\
&= \text{Wages} + \text{Interest} + \text{Profits} + \text{Rents} + \text{Depreciation,}
\end{aligned}
\tag{16.5}
$$

where intermediate transactions represent purchases by firms of goods and services to be further processed in production. For example, the purchase of steel by an automobile manufacturer is an intermediate purchase, because the steel is to be further processed and converted into automobile frames and other parts of automobiles that then will be incorporated into the value of the final product when it is sold. In measuring gross national product, such intermediate sales are netted out to avoid double-counting the steel both as an input and as part of the automobile. Similarly, seed and fertilizer purchases are intermediate purchases for farmers because both items will be further processed into agricultural produce, which will reflect, in part, the cost of the seed and fertilizer to the farmer.

Netting out the dollar value of intermediate transactions from all transactions leaves the dollar value of final sales. Because final sales must cover the producers' costs, with profit left over as a residual, it follows that such final sales represent the dollar value of all domestic wages, interest, rents, depreciation, and profits. This is the definition of *gross domestic product (GDP)*. It therefore becomes clear that the sum of value added by all business firms at each stage of production is merely another way of defining GDP. A general tax on value added therefore would be equivalent to a tax on national product.

Different types of value-added taxes customarily are classified according to the manner in which they apply to a firm's purchase of capital goods. One approach is to allow no deduction from the tax base, either for a firm's initial outlays on capital goods or for amortized deductions on such outlays. This is known as a *product-type* value-added tax. A second alternative, known as an *income-type* tax, allows no deduction for the costs of capital equipment in the year of purchase but permits a deduction for annual depreciation over the life of the equipment. A third alternative, known as a *consumption-type* tax, allows the full cost of capital to be deducted in the year of purchase. In short, the base for the consumption-type tax is the same as that for a general tax on comprehensive consumption, while that for the income-type tax is the same as for a proportional income tax.

The consumption-type tax is used in most nations. Therefore, as it is commonly administered, the tax base for the VAT is equivalent to that of any general consumption tax. One study of the tax system in the United States has suggested that if a consumption-type value-added tax were to be substituted for all taxes currently used, considerable reduction in the excess burden could result. Based on the system of taxation prevailing in the late 1970s, the study concluded that the excess burden per dollar of revenue could be reduced from about 24 cents to 13 cents if the consumption-type VAT were substituted for existing taxes.[17]

A more recent study estimated that compared with an income tax surcharge raising $150 billion additional revenue in the United States, a VAT raising the same revenue would add about 0.4 percentage points to the U.S. annual savings rate in the long run by lowering the cost of capital. In the long run this would add a 5-percent increment to the nation's capital stock and would allow income to grow by about 0.8 percent more per year over the long run. However, the cost of administering and complying with a new and complex VAT like that used in Europe would run from $5 billion to $8 billion per year and these administrative costs would offset much of the benefits of improved efficiency in capital markets and would absorb much of the extra income generated by faster growth.[18] The consumption-type VAT would lower costs of production in capital-intensive industries (including agriculture) but raise costs of production in labor-intensive industries.

Administration of the VAT

Administration of a value-added tax does not require firms to calculate value added. The most common means of administering the tax is the invoice method developed in

---

[17]This is based on an uncompensated elasticity of supply of labor of 0.15 and an uncompensated elasticity of supply of savings of 0.4. See Charles L. Ballard, John B. Shoven, and John Whalley, "The Total Welfare Cost of the United States Tax System: A General Equilibrium Approach," *National Tax Journal* 38 (June 1985): 125–140.

[18]Congress of the United States, Congressional Budget Office, *Effects of Adopting a Value-Added Tax*, Washington, D.C.: U.S. Government Printing Office, February, 1992.

CURRENT USE OF THE VAT IN EUROPEAN NATIONS AND PROSPECTS FOR ITS USE IN THE UNITED STATES

The VAT currently accounts for more than 20 percent of revenue in most member nations of the European Union (EU). Most nations that use the tax employ the consumption-type VAT. However, the VAT actually used by these nations can in no way be considered a general tax on consumption. It is common for the tax to include exemptions, and attempts are made to achieve various income redistribution goals through the VAT by taxing certain goods at rates higher and lower than the basic rate to adjust the tax in accordance with commonly held notions of the ability to pay.

The average basic rate used by European nations in administering the VAT has been about 15 percent. Some countries apply lower rates to particular transactions and higher rates to others. In addition, many transactions are exempt from the tax and therefore are taxed effectively at a zero rate. The tax rates of various classes of goods in the nations of the European Union are now being harmonized so they are the same in all member nations.

This high rate is usually applied to luxury goods, such as jewelry, furs, cashmere items, and certain hobby equipment (photographic goods and sporting equipment, for example). The lower rates are usually applied to food, clothing, books, and other such items. The tax, as used in European nations, does not share the bias of exempting personal services from taxation that is inherent in the retail sales tax as used by state governments in the United States.

In many nations using the VAT, the tax is applied to entertainment services, transportation services, legal and other professional services, telephone service and other public utility services, some real estate services, and certain financial transactions. It is common to tax food items at a reduced rate. Books and newspapers have been exempt from the tax in the United Kingdom but are subject to taxation in most other nations. Except in France, used equipment, including used cars, have been subject to the VAT. Medicines, housing services, hospital services, security transactions, insurance transactions, postal service, and some public utility services also are commonly exempt from the tax.

The net effect of such exemptions, and the application of reduced rates of taxation, is to change the VAT from a general consumption tax to a selective consumption tax, which is likely to distort choices among various consumption alternatives and distort the basic work-leisure choice.[*] The selective tax rates apparently are successful in relieving the regressive effects of the tax on income distribution. Estimates of the distribution of tax burden from the tax in France and Italy indicate that the incidence of the value-added tax in those countries has been roughly proportional with respect to income.[†] Judicious taxation of goods complementary with leisure also could reduce the excess burden in the labor market by discouraging leisure activities. For example, high taxes on sporting equipment, hobby equipment, second homes, and vacation-related activities could offset some of the excess burden that results from the distortion in the work-leisure choice.

Concern about the impact of income taxes on saving and investment makes the consumption-type value-added tax on attractive alternative to income taxes for many economists.

[*]For a discussion of the use of the tax in European nations, see Henry J. Aaron, ed., *The Value-Added Tax: Lessons from Europe* (Washington, D.C.: The Brookings Institution, 1981).
[†]Ibid., 8–9.

France and used in European Union nations to collect the tax. Under the invoice method, all transactions are taxed at a fixed proportional rate, regardless of whether they are final or intermediate transactions. Taxpayers then are allowed to deduct the taxes paid on intermediate purchases from the taxes collected from their sales in determining their tax liability. This is called the *invoice method* because payment of the tax merely requires firms to maintain invoices on sales and purchases for each tax payment period (usually monthly or quarterly). Tax liability is determined simply by applying the fixed rate of taxation to total sales invoices and then deducting the amount of VAT paid previously on intermediate purchases as indicated on purchase invoices, where the tax is usually separately itemized.

This method results in taxation of value added without the need to actually calculate value added:

$$
\begin{aligned}
\text{Tax Liability} &= \text{Tax Payable on Sales} - \text{Tax Paid on Intermediate Purchases} \\
&= [(t)(\text{Sales})] - [(t)(\text{Purchases})] \\
&= (t)(\text{Total Sales} - \text{Total Intermediate Purchases}) \\
&= (t)(\text{Value Added}),
\end{aligned}
\tag{16.6}
$$

where t is the rate of taxation.

In effect, the tax is charged to purchasers at each stage of production. At the final stage of production, consumers purchase goods with the value-added tax included in the price; and because consumers have no intermediate transactions to offset the tax liability, they end up paying the entire amount of the tax, with no tax offset. Only producers can offset their tax liability to the extent to which they purchase intermediate goods and services.

Firms that make capital purchases are allowed an additional tax credit for taxes paid on capital goods. So the tax liability of a firm that makes capital purchases in a given tax period would be

$$
\begin{aligned}
\text{Tax Liability} &= [(t)(\text{Total Sales} - \text{Total Intermediate Purchases})] \\
&\quad - [(t)(\text{Capital Purchases})] \\
&= (t)(\text{Total Sales} - \text{Total Purchases} \\
&\quad - \text{Capital Purchases}) \\
&= (t)(\text{Value added} - \text{Investment}).
\end{aligned}
\tag{16.7}
$$

In most nations that use the value-added tax, it is customary not to itemize the tax on the final transaction. However, it would be simple to itemize the tax to consumers by simply tacking it on to the sale, as is done for the retail sales tax in the United States. Because of this practice of not itemizing the tax at the retail level, in many European nations, the VAT is often accused of being a hidden tax, which is likely to result in fiscal illusion on the part of consumers, who pay the final tax. This need not be the case because the VAT easily can be made visible by collecting it from consumers at the fixed rate t on final sales.

Also, the invoice method embodies a sort of built-in antievasion mechanism. If any firm fails to pay its tax liability at some stage of production, it then becomes the tax liability of the producer in the following stage of production. This is not to say that tax evasion is impossible. In some nations that use the tax, it has been evaded by arrangements between firms and consumers to engage in transactions without issuing invoices. Without an invoice, no record of the transaction exist, and the tax becomes difficult to collect. Problems of tax evasion have been most acute for small firms and professional services, such as those of physicians, lawyers, and insurance salespersons, where the costs of enforcement are high. Compliance has been fairly good for larger firms.

The value-added tax is typically rebated on export sales. This makes goods of nations that use the tax more competitive in international markets when they are exported to nations, such as the United States, where there is no national sales tax. Imported products are subject to the VAT, which increases their prices to domestic consumers. Many nations allow rebate of the tax on such services such as hotels and tourist purchases of items for export. For example, Canada allows foreign tourists to receive an instant rebate of their VAT taxes on non-food purchase of goods and services while in Canada at the border by presenting their receipts for hotels and non-food purchases for export.

One criticism of the VAT is that its costs of administration and compliance are relatively high compared with other taxes. If it were introduced as a new tax in the United States, setup costs such as new tax forms and computer programs would add to both administrative and compliance costs for the government and businesses. The CBO estimates that administrative and compliance costs for a new VAT could be as much as $8 billion per year. Costs of administering the VAT in Europe range from 0.4 to 1 percent of revenue collected. In general, it is more costly to administer a complex VAT that taxes different types of goods at different rates than it is to administer a general VAT that taxes all goods at the same rate. Nations that have recently adopted the tax—such as Japan, Canada, and New Zealand—have chosen to tax all transactions at the same rate as a way of minimizing the costs of collecting the tax. For example, the national General Sales Tax (GST) in Canada taxes all transactions, except groceries (all of which are exempt) at 7 percent. It is also more costly for small firms to comply with the tax than it is for large firms and it is typical to exempt small businesses from the tax.

CHECKPOINT

1. Is the retail sales tax, as used by state and local governments in the United States, a general tax on consumption?
2. What are the issues involved in determining the incidence efficiency loss effects of retail sales taxes?
3. What is a value-added tax?

Summary

A consumption tax is equivalent to an income tax that excludes saving from the tax base. A consumption tax, in effect, exempts interest income from taxation. Many argue that consumption is a better index of the ability to pay than income. These arguments are based on the notion that well-being in any given year depends on a person's consumption. Those who save sacrifice present satisfaction for increased satisfaction in the future. Income taxes discriminate against those who defer consumption, because interest obtained from saving is taxable. Because interest is simply the payment for deferred consumption, savers pay

higher taxes, relative to individuals who do not save, even if lifetime labor income is the same for both the saver and the nonsaver. This argument implies that lifetime consumption, including bequests, is a better index of economic capacity than income to ensure equal treatment of savers and nonsavers. The consumption tax does not affect the interest rate because interest is nontaxable. It is therefore equivalent to a tax on labor income.

A general tax on comprehensive consumption is called an expenditure tax. It would be administered like an income tax. Individuals would compute annual consumption by excluding additions to net worth from their income. Progressive rates of taxation could be applied to consumption, so as to adjust the burden of taxation with notions of equity.

A general tax on comprehensive consumption does not result in any losses in the efficiency with which choices regarding saving and investment are made, because the tax does not affect the interest rate. Compared with an equal-yield tax on comprehensive income, the consumption tax would reduce excess burden in capital markets to zero. However, because a consumption tax excludes saving, higher rates on labor income would be necessary to raise the same revenue as an income tax. This would result in added efficiency loss in labor markets as the wage is further reduced by a consumption tax rate that exceeds that of an equal-yield income tax. A consumption tax is likely to be borne according to labor income, with little shifting in the form of higher prices or reduced interest.

Retail sales taxes are used extensively by state governments in the United States. Retail sales taxes exempt many consumption items and, in some cases, tax capital outlays. They are not general taxes and are likely to distort the pattern of consumption, as is the case for excise taxes.

Other forms of sales taxes include turnover taxes and value-added taxes. The value-added tax is extensively used in Western Europe. Most nations use a variant of the tax that exempts investment purchases and saving from taxation.

A Forward Look

The following chapter concludes the analysis of taxes on alternative economic bases with a discussion of taxes on wealth. The advantages and disadvantages of taxes on wealth are highlighted. The economic effects of a general tax on wealth are compared with those of general taxes on income and consumption. This is followed by a discussion of the local property tax in the United States.

Important Concepts

Comprehensive Consumption
Cash-Flow Tax
Retail Sales Tax
Excise Taxes
Turnover Taxes
Value-Added Tax (VAT)

Questions for Review

1. How could the current personal income tax be modified so that it becomes a consumption tax? What are the advantages of taxing consumption in this way?

2. Explain why many economists argue that an income tax penalizes savers but a consumption tax would not. In what sense can consumption be regarded as a better index of the ability to pay taxes than income?

3. Show how, under an income tax, the present value of the amount of tax paid over a person's lifetime will vary with the difference in saving for two individuals who begin the life cycle at age eighteen and have equal economic capacity. Why is the tax paid independent of the timing of income under a consumption tax?

4. An income tax that taxes only labor income would be equivalent to a consumption tax. Do you agree?

5. How would loans be treated under a general tax on comprehensive consumption? What are some of the problems encountered in defining the tax base?

6. Why must the tax rate on a general tax on consumption exceed that of a general tax on income if the two are to raise the same revenue?

7. Why will substitution of an equal-yield general consumption tax for a general income tax reduce efficiency losses in capital markets but increase efficiency losses in labor markets? Why is the consumption tax likely to be regressive with respect to income?

8. How do retail sales taxes, as used in most states, tax a base that is smaller than a comprehensive consumption base? What are the consequences of excluding certain items from the consumption base?

9. What is a value-added tax? How can it be administered without any need for a firm to calculate value added? Why is a general consumption-type VAT equivalent to a tax on comprehensive consumption?

10. Explain why the invoice method of collecting the value-added tax does not require firms to compute value added. How does the invoice method act to discourage tax evasion?

Problems

1. Suppose two workers earn labor incomes of $20,000 per year in each of three tax accounting periods. One worker saves 20 percent of her labor earnings in each of the first two periods and spends all her savings and accumulated interest in the final period. The other worker never saves any of her labor earnings. The market rate of interest is 10 percent.

    Calculate the discounted present value of taxes paid over the three periods for each of the workers under a 15-percent comprehensive income tax. What would be the discounted present value of taxes paid for each worker under a 15-percent comprehensive consumption tax? Comment on the equity and efficiency aspects of each of the two taxes.

2. Your state has a retail sales tax of 10 percent but it exempts food, prescription drugs, and all services including housing services, repair services, and consumption of electricity and other public utility services. Use supply-and-demand analysis to explain how the prices of untaxed consumption items can be affected by the retail sales tax even though they are not subject to taxation. How can changes in the prices of nontaxed items affect the incidence of the retail sales tax?

3. Suppose legislation were passed that abolished all state and local sales taxes and replaced then with one uniform sales tax on all consumption including consumption of services. The federal government would collect the tax and then return the revenue collected to the state governments. Discuss the economic effects of such a national sales tax on work effort and saving as well as the changes in behavior that would result from moving to a national as opposed to state and local sales tax base.

4. A furniture manufacturer sells $500,000 worth of tables, chairs, and other items in a given year. The manufacturer earns a profit of $100,000 that year. His purchase invoices indicate that he bought $200,000 worth of lumber, varnish, nails, and other materials during the year. His labor costs were $150,000, and he purchased $50,000 of new equipment that year. Calculate his tax liability under a 15-percent consumption-type value-added tax.

Suggestions for Further Reading

Aaron, Henry J., ed. *The Value-Added Tax: Lessons from Europe.* Washington, D.C.: The Brookings Institution, 1981. A collection of articles on the use of the value-added tax in European nations and the prospects for use in the United States.

Aaron, Henry J., Harvey Galper, and Joseph A. Pechman, eds. *Uneasy Compromise: Problems of a Hybrid Income-Consumption Tax.* Washington, D.C.: The Brookings Institution, 1988. A collection of essays on issues involved in tax systems that seek to provide incentives to save and to invest.

Advisory Commission for Intergovernmental Relations. *The Expenditure Tax: Concept, Administration, and Possible Application.* Washington, D.C.: U.S. Government Printing Office, 1974. A clearly written exposition of the expenditure tax and the feasibility of introducing such a tax.

Congress of the United States. Congressional Budget Office. *Effects of Adopting a Value-Added Tax.* Washington, D.C.: U.S. Government Printing Office, February, 1992. An analysis of the economic effects of introducing a VAT in the United States as a way of raising an additional $150 billion of revenue annually.

Due, John F. *Sales Taxation.* Urbana: University of Illinois Press, 1957. A classic analysis of the retail sales tax and other forms of sales taxation.

Kaldor, Nicholas. *An Expenditure Tax.* London: Allen and Unwin, 1955. An analysis of the expenditure tax. Chapter 1 contains Kaldor's arguments in favor of consumption as a superior index of the ability to pay.

Mieszkowski, Peter. "The Choice of the Tax Base: Consumption versus Income Taxation." In *Federal Tax Reform: Myths and Realities,* edited by Michael J. Boskin, 27–53. San Francisco: Institute for Contemporary Studies, 1978. A discussion of the difference between income and consumption bases, the advantages of a tax on comprehensive consumption, and some of the problems involved in implementing such a tax.

U.S. Department of the Treasury. *Blueprints for Basic Tax Reform.* Washington, D.C.: U.S. Government Printing Office, 1977. Contains the outline of a cash-flow tax and discusses some of the implementation problems and economic effects of introducing such a tax into the tax structure in the United States.

17

Taxes on Wealth,
Property, and Estates

LEARNING OBJECTIVES

After reading this chapter you should be able to

1. Discuss the issues involved in implementing a general tax on a comprehensive wealth tax base, including problems involved in the assessment of property value.

2. Show how a comprehensive wealth tax is related to a comprehensive income and how the tax can be viewed as falling on accumulated saving.

3. Analyze the incidence and effect on resource use of a general tax on comprehensive wealth and the economic effects of property taxation in the United States.

4. Discuss estate, inheritance, and gift taxes.

*I*f you were to own your own home, you would have to pay property taxes on it. In the United States most real estate is taxed by local governments. Land and structures on the land used for housing, commercial trade, or for agriculture and manufacturing are taxed at varying rates depending on the city, town, or county in which they are located. Property taxes are used to finance local government services and schooling.

In the United States more than 80,000 local government jurisdictions use the local property tax. The tax is levied primarily on one form of wealth, real estate, and the variety of tax rates numbers in the thousands. Naturally, because the property tax is a local tax, it can influence the location of investment. For example, suppose you were to receive a job offer in New York after you graduated from college and wanted to buy a home in the New York metropolitan area. You could choose among thousands of communities in three neighboring states (New York, New Jersey, and Connecticut) where you could live and commute to your job in the city. In each town you would pay a property tax on your home and get a bundle of government services such as schools, trash collection, and police and fire protection in return for the taxes you pay. Where you locate your home will depend in part on the tax rates in the various towns in the metropolitan area and the services you get in return for those taxes at these various locations.

The impact of the property tax in the United States is complex and strongly influences both investment and locational decisions. In this chapter we trace out the economic impact of taxes on wealth and property. First we look at the economic effects of a general wealth tax on all forms of wealth. We then trace out the economic effects of a national tax that is levied primarily on real estate. Once we understand the effects of national taxes on property, we can then trace out the complicated effects of the system of local property taxation as used in the United States. Finally, we also examine taxes on transfers of wealth through estate, gift, and inheritance taxes.

A COMPREHENSIVE WEALTH TAX BASE

Wealth is the value of accumulated savings and investments in a nation. Persons can acquire wealth through saving or, if they are lucky enough, from gifts or inheritances from their parents or other relatives or friends. A person who never saves any income and receives no gifts and inheritances never will accumulate wealth. To obtain wealth, persons must refrain from consuming all their income in a given year. A comprehensive wealth tax base would include all wealth in the economy.

The wealth tax has a long history of utilization by governing authorities.[1] A general property tax was used in England during the medieval period to finance the Crusades. Such taxes were levied on rents and movable property. Evidence also exists that the tax was utilized in ancient Rome. In the colonial period of the United States, wealth taxes were utilized by many of the colonial governments. Although colonies initially relied on poll taxes to finance their modest requirements for public expenditures, they switched to taxes on real and personal property as differences in wealth developed among the Colonists.

Many economists have observed that the utilization of wealth as the base for taxation appears to run a cyclical course. This "property-tax cycle" is correlated with the economic development of a society.[2] The tax first appears as a per unit levy on land alone. As income and wealth differentials become more pronounced during economic development, it becomes a proportional tax on the holding of all wealth—land, other real assets, and personal property. Finally, as the society reaches economic maturity and wealth takes on new and heterogenous forms, the general property tax becomes difficult to administer effectively; essentially, it becomes a tax on real estate. **Real estate,** or **real property,** is land and structures.

The bulk of the revenue currently raised by property taxes in the United States comes from taxes on real estate. The property tax is mainly used by local governments in the United States.

Many argue that it is necessary to tax wealth, in addition to income and consumption, in order to achieve an equitable tax structure. Quite often, individual households with relatively low incomes have substantial holdings of wealth in the form of real assets. In the case of homes and other consumer durables that yield nonmonetary

---

[1]For a good discussion of the historical development of property taxation, see Arthur D. Lynn, Jr., "Property-Tax Development: Selected Historical Perspectives," in *Property Taxation: U.S.A.,* ed. Richard W. Lindholm (Madison: University of Wisconsin Press, 1967), 7–19.
[2]Ibid., 16.

returns, households might escape taxation completely under an income tax because of problems associated with measuring imputed rent and service flows.

Measuring Wealth

Wealth can be measured by determining the net value of financial assets, capital assets, and land owned by citizens of a nation. The value of these assets represents the value of accumulated savings in a nation. It follows that a tax on wealth can be viewed as equivalent to a tax on the return earned in any given year on all savings and investments.

Administering a wealth tax is complicated by the fact that wealth is a stock, rather than a flow like income and consumption. A **stock** is a variable with a value defined at a particular point in time. To administer a wealth tax, the value of taxable assets must be determined at a particular point in time. It is often difficult to determine the value of assets that are infrequently traded on markets. Moreover, the value of assets can change quite rapidly. Without frequent reevaluation of the taxable asset values, serious inequities are likely to result.

To determine the base for wealth, all forms of property owned by taxpayers must be listed and values must be assessed. In listing property, care must be taken to avoid double-counting assets. Assessing the value of wealth that is not often sold on the market is one of the most difficult aspects of property taxation.

Of the two approaches to listing the wealth of taxpayers, the first considers only the net assets of households, while the second considers the net assets of both persons and corporations. Both methods yield the same results. The first approach merely takes into account the fact that corporations are ultimately owned by persons, and the net assets of such corporations are reflected in the value of outstanding corporate stock.

Using the first approach, total wealth is considered to have the following three components:

1. All *real property* (that is, land and improvements thereon) owned by households.
2. All *tangible personal property* owned by households. This includes all movable assets, such as cars, furniture, clothing, and jewelry.
3. All *intangible personal property* owned by households. This includes stocks, bonds, cash, and other "paper" assets that reflect claims on assets owned by corporations and governments.

Furthermore, all debt incurred by households and firms (for example, mortgages and loans) has to be subtracted from the tax base to obtain a measure of net wealth and to avoid double counting assets. This is because such debt represents paper claims against such assets as homes owned by households and is already included in the tax base. A fourth possible form of wealth that might be included in the tax base is human capital. This includes special skills persons are endowed with or acquire through educational investments. However, it is difficult to assess the value of human capital.

The second approach includes the assets of corporations but excludes intangible property that represents claims on the assets of such corporations. Thus, this approach does not tax outstanding corporate stock, for to do so involves double taxation of corporate assets. In addition, this approach deducts from the tax base all debt incurred by the private sector to obtain a measure of net wealth.

Of course, problems are encountered in implementing a general property tax in an economically mature society. This stems, in part, from the complexities of listing all forms of property, particularly tangible personal property and intangible property. Many forms of movable personal property, such as jewelry, are easy to conceal, and this encourages tax evasion. Taxes on personal property often place a disproportionate share of the burden on honest taxpayers, who list all their movable personal assets, even though they realize that the costs of checking the validity of their listings are so prohibitive as to prevent governments from enforcing honest listings. Except for movable personal property that must be registered with local governments, such as automobiles, taxes on this form of wealth prove both easy to evade and difficult to enforce. The same holds true for intangible personal property. For unregistered securities, concealment is relatively easy and, again, enforcement of tax laws can prove costly to governing authorities.

The administrative problems encountered in taxing both tangible and intangible personal property have led to a wealth tax that falls mainly on real estate and exempts other forms of wealth. This is in accordance with the property-tax cycle previously discussed. Taxes on real estate are difficult to evade, because it is virtually impossible to conceal such assets. Real estate is registered with local authorities, and the structures on land are open to view by all. The problem now becomes one of determining which real estate is taxable and then assessing the value of such real estate.

In the United States, all localities exclude from the tax base most property owned by religious and charitable institutions. This is largely real estate owned by churches and educational institutions. In addition, constitutional law prohibits local governments from levying taxes on real estate owned by the federal government. However, the federal government often makes payments in lieu of taxes to localities in which it owns property. State government property is usually exempt from local property taxes, but some state governments make payments to local governments in lieu of property taxes.

ASSESSMENT OF PROPERTY VALUE

After all property subject to taxation has been listed, it is necessary to estimate, or assess, the value of the property before the tax can be implemented. **Assessment** is the valuation of taxable wealth by government authorities. Assessment practices are often criticized as being too subjective. In fact, for infrequently traded assets, assessment is often more of an art than a science. Ideally, the assessed value of an asset should reflect its current value.

In a general property tax, assessors estimate the value of both real estate and movable personal property. If assessment is to be reasonably accurate and fair, the asset value of property should closely approximate the market value. Typically, the property tax is levied as a percentage of assessed valuation.

The assessor's task is relatively easy for intangible personal property. Well organized markets exist for trading stocks, bonds, mortgages, and other paper assets; and prices are available on a daily basis. Similarly, good markets exist for trading automobiles. But, markets for the most prevalent form of taxable wealth, real estate, are not as well organized. The assessor often approximates the value of such assets on a subjective basis.

One method that the economist might suggest to assess the value of real estate is to attempt to determine the capitalized value of such assets. This entails estimating both the net annual rent flowing from the land and structures thereon in monetary terms and the probable life of the structure. Once estimates of these two parameters are made, it is a simple matter to compute the present value of the real estate using a discount rate that reflects the opportunity cost of capital. However, it can be difficult to estimate rentals for nonincome-producing property and vacant lots.

Often, the assessor projects rents into the future, based on expected future development in the area. Assessors typically keep records of recent sales of property within an area. They also must be acquainted with growth trends in the area to predict possible changes in property values over time. Property must be reassessed periodically to reflect changing market values. In a particular community with a given supply and demand of real estate, values of structures are likely to vary with such factors as location, age of structure, quality of construction, size of structure, and appearance.

A Comprehensive Wealth Tax

A **comprehensive wealth tax** is one that would be levied on all forms of capital and land at a flat rate. Because capital and land represent assets that yield flows of productive services over time, a general wealth tax can be thought of as being levied on the discounted present value of those land and capital services over time. Comprehensive wealth, W, therefore is

$$W = \Sigma \frac{R_i}{(1 + r)^i}, \tag{17.1}$$

where R_i is the annual dollar return to savings and investments and r is the market rate of interest. If the tax rate under the wealth tax is t_W, annual revenue from the tax would be $t_W W$. Exactly the same annual tax revenue could be obtained from an annual tax on the return to savings. Because R_i is the annual dollar return to saving, the annual revenue from a savings tax levied at a rate t_S would be $t_S R_i$. The effective tax on savings under a wealth tax can be computed by setting $t_W W$ equal to $t_S R_i$. Thus, the effective tax on the annual return to accumulated savings associated with a comprehensive wealth tax at rate t_W is

$$t_s = \frac{t_W W}{R_i}. \tag{17.2}$$

The wealth tax directly reduces the return to savings or to holding land and accumulating capital; therefore, it has the effect of reducing interest income from accumulated savings, no matter what the form of the savings, such as land, capital equipment, or financial assets. In effect, it is a tax on interest and rental income. If a person earns an annual dollar return of R_G on accumulated savings in any given year, the net return earned after taxes would be $R_N = R_G - t_W W$.

For example, suppose total wealth in a nation amounts to $100 trillion. A flat-rate wealth tax of 1 percent would yield a total of $1 trillion annual revenue. If the dollar return to invested capital is $10 trillion per year, which amounts to 10 percent of assets, the property tax revenue of $1 trillion is equivalent to a 10-percent annual tax on the return to accumulated savings.

Most of the problems of administering a general wealth tax stem from the fact that capital is a stock rather than a flow. This leads to difficulty in developing fair and accurate mechanisms to assess and reassess the value of the tax base. As previously discussed, one of the most difficult problems encountered would be the treatment of human capital. If a tax on wealth excluded human capital, strong incentives would exist to invest in this form of wealth, as opposed to physical forms of wealth. Despite the constraints imposed by the administrative problems involved, it is worthwhile discussing the hypothetical effects of a general wealth tax as the basis for dealing with the economic effects of specific wealth taxes, such as those levied mainly on real property.

Because substitutes in production exist for capital, it is reasonable to assume that the demand for capital is somewhat elastic. The economic effects of a general wealth tax therefore depend on the elasticity of supply of all forms of saving for the purpose of accumulating assets. First, consider a closed economy (no opportunities exist for exporting capital) in which taxpayers are unwilling to substitute consumption for saving in response to changes in the return to saving. Under such circumstances, the elasticity of supply of savings would be zero.

Impact of a Comprehensive Wealth Tax When the Supply of Savings is Perfectly Inelastic

The effect of a proportional tax on all forms of wealth on the market for investable funds is shown in Figure 17.1. Assuming a perfectly inelastic supply of savings, the impact of the tax is to reduce the return to savings by the full amount of the tax. The curve labeled D gives the gross percentage return, r_G, earned on investments before payment of the tax. The net return is the annual return minus the annual wealth tax as a percentage of the dollar return to savings, $t_S = t_W W/R_i$. For example, a 1-percent annual comprehensive wealth tax is equivalent to a 10-percent tax on the return to savings and investments when the equilibrium gross return is 10 percent. The wealth tax therefore reduces the percentage return to savings, from r_G to $r_N = r_G - t_W W/R_i$.

The impact of the tax is to reduce the annual return to savings and investments from r_G° to r_N°. Because the supply of saving is perfectly inelastic in this case, the return falls by the full percentage equivalent of the ratio of annual wealth tax payments to the dollar annual return to savings, $t_W W/R_i$. The incidence of the tax is likely to be progressive, because it would be paid in accordance with the ownership of wealth. In most nations, the distribution of capital is heavily concentrated in the

Figure 17.1 ✦ IMPACT OF A GENERAL WEALTH TAX WHEN THE SUPPLY OF SAVINGS IS PERFECTLY INELASTIC

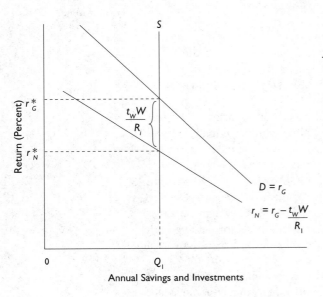

If the supply of savings is perfectly inelastic, a general wealth tax reduces the annual return to savings by the full amount of the tax as a percentage of the dollar annual return to savings, $t_W W/R$. Although the annual savings are unchanged, the tax does result in an excess burden because it causes a substitution effect that is offset by an equal and opposite income effect.

hands of middle- and upper-income groups. This implies that these groups would pay higher wealth taxes in relation to their income than would lower-income groups.

The excess burden of the tax is not likely to be zero, even if the supply of savings is perfectly inelastic. This is because a perfectly inelastic supply curve of savings is consistent with behavior for which the income effects of interest changes are offset by equal substitution effects. As shown in Chapter 13, a decrease in the return to saving results in a substitution effect that tends to decrease saving but an income effect that tends to increase saving. When the two effects exactly offset each other, the aggregate supply of saving is perfectly inelastic. However, because the tax does result in a substitution effect that decreases saving, it would result in a reduction in saving, compared with that which would prevail under a lump-sum tax. This is because the lump-sum tax could raise the same revenue as the wealth tax but would generate *only* income effects.[3]

Impact of the Tax When the Supply of Savings is Responsive

When the supply of savings is not perfectly elastic, either because the economy is open so that capital can be exported or because savers are willing to substitute consumption for saving, the tax would result in an increase in the gross return to savings and investments. In addition, further losses in efficiency would occur in investment markets as annual savings and investments decline.

---

[3]The point is illustrated in Chapter 13 for the case of a perfectly inelastic labor supply curve.

This is illustrated in Figure 17.2. As before, the tax shifts the investment demand curve downward, from $D = r_G$ to $r_N = r_G - t_W W/R_i$. Because the supply of savings is presumed not to be perfectly inelastic, the quantity of funds supplied for investment falls from Q_1 to Q_2. The gross return to investment rises from r_G^* to r_{G1}^*, but the net return to investment falls to r_{N1}. The fall in the return to capital, in this case, is less than the annual wealth tax expressed as a percentage of annual savings. The increase in the market rate of interest caused by the tax shifts the burden to those other than savers. Higher interest rates increase costs of production and could result in increases in the price of goods and services, which shifts the tax to consumers. Also, the annual reduction in investment caused by the tax eventually would reduce the capital-labor ratio in production, thereby lowering worker productivity in the long run. This would result, in the long run, in shifting the burden of taxation to workers in the form of lower wages.

Finally, the substitution effect of the tax-induced decline in the net return to savings is larger than when the supply of savings is perfectly inelastic. As a result, when the supply of savings is responsive to changes in its return, the excess burden of the tax is correspondingly greater. For a complete analysis of the implications of tax-induced reductions in the return to savings and investments, see Chapter 13.

It follows that when the elasticity of supply of saving exceeds zero, owners of capital succeed in transferring part of the burden of the tax to others, as the cost of capital, as an input, rises. The incidence of the tax, in this case, is more difficult to determine,

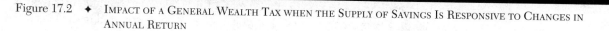

Figure 17.2 ✦ Impact of a General Wealth Tax when the Supply of Savings Is Responsive to Changes in Annual Return

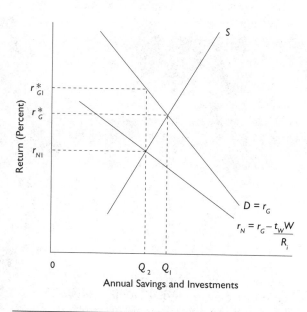

When the supply of savings is responsive to changes in the net return, a general wealth tax reduces the annual amount of saving and investment and increases the annual gross return to investment.

Annual Savings and Investments

because the tax reduces both the return to capital and the income of workers. The tax, in this case, reduces annual investment. As a result, it adversely affects the rate of economic growth.

If, as many economists contend, the supply of savings is responsive to changes in interest, the wealth tax would be detrimental to the incentive to save. Compared with equal-yield income and consumption taxes, it would result in greater distortion in investment markets, because the tax rate on savings would be higher, inasmuch as all revenue would be raised from taxes on capital income. On the other hand, a general wealth tax has no effect on the return to work effort. A person who never saves will never accumulate assets, and the tax is avoided. The tax is independent of labor earnings; the wage is not reduced. The amount of tax that a person pays over a lifetime depends on how that person allocates wage income, over time, so as to accumulate assets, and on the capital assets acquired through transfers, such as bequests. Thus, when compared with equal-yield taxes on income and consumption, the wealth tax does not distort the work-leisure choice.

In practice, a wealth tax is not likely to be completely general because of administrative difficulties encountered in measuring and assessing all forms of wealth. In particular, it is reasonable to assume that human capital escapes taxation, even under a comprehensive wealth tax. If this is, in fact, the case, then the wealth tax induces a reallocation of investment choices toward human capital and away from other assets, resulting in still further efficiency loss.

If the supply of savings is moderately responsive to its return, the incidence of the general wealth tax would be borne largely according to a person's holdings of capital, with some shifting to labor as wages decline in the long run, in response to decreased productivity attributable to lower capital-labor ratios. Given that the bulk of the tax is borne according to ownership of capital, which is heavily concentrated in the hands of upper-income groups, it is likely to be progressive with respect to income.

CHECKPOINT

1. What is wealth?
2. List the major components of wealth, and discuss some of the difficulties involved in assessment of the wealth tax base.
3. Explain why a general wealth tax would be equivalent to a tax on savings, and discuss the possible economic effects of a general wealth tax on resource use and income distribution.

SELECTIVE PROPERTY TAXES

A general tax on wealth is likely to prove administratively infeasible. Most property taxes are selective taxes, in the sense that they are levied on only certain forms of wealth. Taxes on real assets (land and improvements thereon) account for approximately 80 percent of all revenue collected from property tax levies in the United

INTERNATIONAL VIEW

WEALTH TAXES AND INVESTMENT INCENTIVES IN AN OPEN ECONOMY

In recent years a dramatic increase has occurred in the world mobility of capital. As a result, investors looking for opportunities to build new plants and equipment or to invest in the stocks of a company now have a worldwide perspective. The United States, which has been a capital exporting nation for much of the twentieth century, has come to rely more and more on foreign saving and investment in this country to make up for an anemic domestic savings rate that is not sufficient to meet the domestic demand for loanable funds that finances both private investment and the government budget deficit.

As a result of the international demands for capital and the increased mobility of funds in world markets, concern is growing that any tax that reduces the return to capital can have adverse affects on a nation's rate of investment and therefore future economic growth by reducing capital formation. Even if the domestic supply of savings is perfectly inelastic, the total supply of sav-

ings could be responsive to changes in its return when the economy is open. Increased openness of the U.S. economy therefore implies that it is more likely that taxes that fall on savings can cause an excess burden in capital markets. The United States has to worry about relatively high taxes on capital, including the impact of our system of local property taxes, having an effect on the incentives of both U.S. and foreign investors to save in the United States.

In recent years, net foreign savings inflows have increased substantially in the United States. The table shows national saving, investment, and the net foreign saving inflow in the United States for the periods 1950–1979 and 1980–1991. As you can see, domestic saving has fallen on average between these two periods while the net inflow of foreign saving has increased substantially. In discussing the economic impact of increased taxation of capital income, including a general wealth tax, the impact of the tax on the flows of net flow of foreign saving must be considered to determine the efficiency and distributive effects of the tax.

U.S. GROSS PRIVATE DOMESTIC INVESTMENT, GROSS NATIONAL SAVING, AND NET FOREIGN SAVING INFLOW (AVERAGE PERCENT OF GDP FOR EACH PERIOD)

PERIOD	1950–1979	1980–1991
Gross Private Domestic Investment Equals	16.0	15.5
Gross National Saving Plus	16.3	14.0
Net Foreign Saving Inflow	−0.3	1.5

Source: Department of Commerce, Bureau of Economic Analysis.

States. About two-thirds of the taxes collected on real property in the United States comes from nonfarm, residential real estate.[4]

As a tax on real estate, the property tax provides an incentive to substitute alternative inputs for real property. In addition, in states where personal property is not

---

[4]U.S. Bureau of the Census, *Census of Governments*, vol. 2, *Taxable Property Values and Assessment/Sale Price Ratios* (Washington, D.C.: U.S. Government Printing Office, 1982), xiii.

taxed, or is taxed at lower rates than real property, the tax, other things being equal, can affect choices between the consumption of real property and that of consumer durables by making the latter relatively more attractive. Therefore, it is possible that the property tax discourages the production and consumption of housing. For example, in 1981, 52.8 percent of the tax base was represented by the assessed value of single-family homes.[5]

The property tax, as it is utilized in the United States, also is likely to induce some locational adjustments because it is a local levy, and rates of taxation differ among communities. The property tax can be a factor in determining the location of an industry. Real-property-intensive industries, other things being equal, tend to locate in areas where the property tax is relatively low. However, to include all factors in a firm's location decision, the benefits financed by property taxation in alternative location sites also must be considered. Communities with low property tax rates might lack essential public services or have lower-quality public services to be utilized by industry.

A National Tax on Real Property

In effect, a selective wealth tax, such as that which mainly affects property held in the form of real estate, can be viewed as a discriminatory tax on the investment income from taxed assets. To abstract from the complications ensuing from local variations in tax rates, assume that all real estate is taxed nationally at the same rate. The long-run impact of such a tax can be analyzed with the aid of a model similar to that developed by Harberger for analyzing the incidence of the corporate income tax (see Chapter 15).[6] Assume first that a national tax on real estate exists, with all real estate subject to the same proportional rate of taxation, irrespective of its location. Suppose, as well, that the aggregate supply of saving is perfectly inelastic and that owners of real estate do not raise rents to cover the tax. It is easy to demonstrate that, in the long run, such a tax would be borne by the owners of all forms of capital.

The tax would disturb the initial capital market equilibrium by reducing the return to real estate investment, relative to alternative forms of holding assets. In the long run, investment funds would be reallocated away from real estate and toward investments in alternative assets, where the return is not subject to taxation. This would reduce the quantity of annual savings supplied to real estate investments, thereby raising the net return to holding real estate. Likewise, the tax would increase the supply of savings funds for alternative investments, thereby depressing their return.

Investable funds would continue to flow among the various sectors until the return on real estate, net of taxation, once again is equal to the return available on alternative investments. Therefore, the end result would be a reduction in the net return to investment in *all* forms of capital. Thus, in the long run, the incidence of the tax on real estate would be similar to that of a general wealth tax. It would be borne

---

[5]Ibid.

[6]Arnold C. Harberger, "The Incidence of the Corporation Income Tax," *Journal of Political Economy* 70 (June 1962): 215–240.

by those who supply funds to create capital. The analysis is exactly the same as that employed in Chapter 15 for the corporate income tax.

If the aggregate supply of savings were not perfectly inelastic, the effect of the national real estate tax would be more complex. In this case, the tax also would induce a flight of savings out of the country, so that the burden of taxation could be avoided, or reduce the rate of saving, as individuals substitute consumption for saving to avoid the tax. The quantity of investment funds supplied would diminish, and the market rate of interest would rise, resulting in a tendency for prices of consumer goods and services to rise along with the increased cost of capital. Over the long run, the reduction in investment would result in a shifting of part of the burden of taxation to labor, as already described for a general wealth tax.

A Local Property Tax on Real Estate

Now, consider the case that reflects most accurately the actual use of the property tax in the United States: a locally administered tax on real estate, with tax rates collectively chosen by citizens of each local governing authority. Given the diversity that exists among local governments, considerable variation exists among the rates of taxation from jurisdiction to jurisdiction. In this case, movements of investment funds caused by the tax would be still more complex. In addition to the investment flows resulting from a national property tax discussed previously, there also would be movement of investment among political jurisdictions due to differentials in rates of taxation among jurisdictions. Other things being equal, those local governments where property tax rates are higher than the national average can expect a reduction in local investment; those for which the rates of taxation are below the national average can expect an increase in investment.

The average rate of property taxation reflects the portion of the property tax that is common to all jurisdictions; therefore, it cannot be avoided by changing the jurisdiction in which investments are made. That portion of the tax lowers the return to capital in all uses, similar to the way a national property tax would lower the return to capital. **Property tax rate differentials** are differences above or below the national average rate of property taxation. The tax rate differentials above or below the average rate of taxation among jurisdictions can be avoided, however, by reallocation of investment from high-to low-tax jurisdictions. These differentials can be shifted to noncapital input owners.

In states with positive tax differentials where property taxes exceed the national average, a reduction in annual investment would result. Investment would be reallocated to low-tax jurisdictions. As this process of tax-induced reallocation of investment would continue, the stock of capital eventually would decline in high-tax areas but increase in low-tax jurisdictions. This, in turn, would result in shifting the tax burden to owners of other inputs. For example, a reduction in building and construction in the high-tax areas eventually would reduce the ratios of capital to land and capital to labor. This would result in decreases in the productivity of labor and land at those locations. If labor did not migrate out as investment declines, local wages would decline. Land, of course, is an immobile input. Reductions in the capital-land ratio caused by high property taxes therefore would definitely reduce land rents.

Conversely, land rents would rise in low-tax jurisdictions that benefit from the reallocation of investment.

Some of the burden of the property tax rate differentials therefore is transferred to workers and local landlords through input price changes caused by capital migration. These changes in local input prices, in turn, can affect the prices of locally produced goods and services. This portion of the tax is similar to an excise tax in its effect on prices. The impact of the tax differentials on prices therefore is sometimes referred to as an *excise-tax effect.*[7]

Many locally produced services, most notably housing services, are sold in local markets, where they need not directly compete with similar services produced in other parts of the nation. Therefore, other things being equal, communities with positive property tax differentials—their rates of taxation are higher than those of other jurisdictions—can expect to lose resources, as developers invest in real estate located in jurisdictions where property taxes are lower. In such areas, this reduction in the supply of capital to real estate investments would make housing and other locally sold services scarcer. The price of those services would be raised, and some of the burden of the positive property tax differential would be transferred to consumers of such services as housing. Renters therefore might suffer reductions in real income, as housing costs rise when the tax is shifted. However, housing costs would fall in areas where increased investment takes place as a result of negative property tax differentials.

A Recapitulation

The impact of the local property tax, as used in the United States, is of a twofold nature. First, the average tax that is common to all jurisdictions serves to reduce the return to all capital assets (including land), as a result of the long-run market reequilibrium process and the investment flows thereby induced. This portion of the tax is borne by owners of capital.

Second, the tax differentials among communities induce regional investment movement. These differentials tend to be positively associated with regional income, implying that the shifting of the tax, in ways that reduce real income of owners of noncapital inputs, is most likely to occur in regions where average income is greater than the national median.[8] In other regions with lower income, the capital inflows induced by the tax increase real income.

From the point of view of particular localities, increases in property tax rates are likely to be shifted in ways that result in either increased prices of locally produced goods or decreased income to owners of land and labor in the community, depending on the extent of reduced investment caused by any increase in tax rates.[9]

---

[7]See Peter M. Mieszkowski, "The Property Tax: An Excise Tax or a Profits Tax?" *Journal of Public Economics* 1 (April 1972): 73–96, and Henry J. Aaron, *Who Pays the Property Tax?* (Washington, D.C.: The Brookings Institution, 1975).

[8]Ibid., 45–49.

[9]See Charles E. McClure, Jr., "The 'New View' of the Property Tax: A Caveat," *National Tax Journal* 30 (March 1977): 69–75.

Tax Capitalization

Tax capitalization is a decrease in the value of a taxed asset equal to the discounted present value of future tax liability of its owners. Property tax differentials among taxing jurisdictions can be capitalized into lower property values. The tax differentials result from variance in the property tax rates among communities and among various classes of property. Recall that the portion of the property tax rate common to all taxing jurisdictions causes a decrease in the return to capital in all uses. Tax capitalization is a discount in the price of a taxed asset that adjusts the annual market return of the asset to a level that is competitive with other assets not subject to the tax. Capitalization can be full or partial. The extent to which the burden of a tax is capitalized into lower asset values depends on the degree to which owners of the taxed asset can adjust the amounts available in response to the tax.

The process of tax capitalization can be illustrated algebraically. The present value of any capital asset depends on (1) the annual dollar return earned by holding the asset, (2) the life span of the asset, and (3) the rate of discount for the economy. The rate of discount represents the opportunity cost of holding any one particular form of wealth; it roughly can be considered the average market return to investment in the economy. Thus, the value of any capital asset that yields an annual return of Y dollars each year can be expressed as follows:

$$V = \sum_{i=0}^{n} \frac{Y}{(1 + r)^i},$$

(17.3)

where V is the market value of the asset, n is the number of years that the asset will last, and r is the rate of discount. If it is assumed that the asset has an infinite life, then $n = $ infinity and equation 17.3 reduces to

$$V = \frac{Y}{r}.$$

(17.4)

This is because the value of the ratio $1/(1 + r)^i$ gets smaller and smaller as i, the life of the asset, increases. As i approaches infinity, the sum represented by Equation 17.3 approaches a limit, represented by Equation 17.4.

For example, Equation 17.4 can be used to calculate the value of a parcel of land that will last indefinitely. If the annual rent expected on the parcel is $10,000 per year and the market rate of interest is 10 percent, then the value of the parcel is $10,000/0.10 = $100,000. If an asset that yields $10,000 per year in rent had less than infinite life, its value would be somewhat less.

Suppose that a parcel of land is subject to a property tax rate that is t percent greater than the national average. The t percent property tax rate differential is likely to be fully capitalized. The tax at rate t reduces the annual rent earned on the land by the amount tV_t, where V_t is the market value of the parcel after the tax is imposed. The posttax annual dollar return on the asset therefore is $Y - tV_t$. The new market value of the asset can be expressed as follows:

$$V_t = \frac{Y_t}{r} = \frac{Y - tV_t}{r},$$

(17.5)

where Y_t is the posttax return. Solving for V_t, Equation 17.5 can be reduced to

$$V_t = \frac{Y}{r + t}. \tag{17.6}$$

Equation 17.6 is the formula for full capitalization of a tax on an asset of infinite life. The expression for the effect of the tax on the market value of an asset of less than infinite life can be easily derived, but it is somewhat more complicated than Equation 17.6. In effect, full tax capitalization puts the entire burden of taxation on current property holders who are selling the assets. For assets that yield the same annual return, the magnitude of reduction in price therefore varies directly with the anticipated life span of the asset.

For example, suppose a wealth tax of 5 percent is levied on one specific asset of infinite life having a pretax return of $10,000 per year. If the rate of discount is 5 percent, the pretax market value of that asset is $10,000/0.05 = $200,000, from Equation 17.4. By substituting in Equation 17.6, the effect of full capitalization of the tax on market value of the asset can easily be determined. The new value of the asset is $10,000/(0.05 + 0.05), or only $100,000. Thus full capitalization of the tax reduces the value of the asset subject to taxation by a factor of 50 percent! If the asset has a shorter life span, the reduction in market value, accordingly, is less.

Also, the annual property tax bill in the preceding example would be (.05)($100,000) = $5,000. The $100,000 decline in the market value of the asset equals the discounted present value of future tax liability of its owners. This is $5,000/.05 = $100,000. The seller of the asset therefore must sell it at a capital discount equal to the present value of all future taxes, assuming that other assets are not subject to the tax.

CAPITALIZATION AND THE ELASTICITY OF SUPPLY OF TAXED ASSETS

Full capitalization occurs only if the owners of the taxed asset cannot adjust the quantity supplied in response to the decrease in the annual return to holding it caused by the tax. This is clearly the case for land which, in the aggregate, is in perfectly inelastic supply. Because landholders cannot make land any scarcer in response to the tax, the market rents do not increase, and the landlords bear the full tax burden. However, other taxed assets, such as structures, equipment, and vehicles, are likely to have elastic supply curves in the long run. A reduction in investment in these forms of taxable wealth in the long run is likely to make these assets scarcer and therefore increase their market rents. A tax-induced increase in market rents will prevent full capitalization of property tax differentials.

When market rents of taxed assets rise in response to the tax, part of the annual burden of the tax is shifted to users of these assets by their owners. This is illustrated in Figure 17.3. Suppose the current rent per square foot of housing per year is $100. Assume that all housing structures last indefinitely, so that Equation 17.4 can be used

Figure 17.3 ✦ IMPACT OF A PROPERTY TAX ON HOUSING RENTS

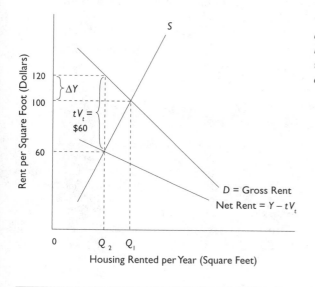

The decrease in the quantity of housing supplied per year after the property tax is imposed results in an increase in housing rents from $100 per year to $120 per year. The net rents received by building owners do not fall by the full amount of the annual property tax per square foot

to compute their values. If the market rate of interest is 10 percent, then the pretax value per square foot of housing is $100/.10 = $1,000. Now, suppose that housing is subject to a differential property tax rate of 10 percent. If the tax were to be fully capitalized, the market value of each square foot of housing would be reduced to $100/.2 = $500, based on Equation 17.6 for full capitalization.

Suppose, however, in the long run, the decrease in the net return to housing caused by the tax reduces the annual quantity supplied from Q_1 to Q_2, as shown in Figure 17.3. This raises the annual market rent from $100 per square foot to $120 per square foot in the long run. The $20 increase in rent offsets some of the burden of the annual property tax to owners of housing. Call ΔY the increase in market rent caused by the tax-induced decrease in the quantity of housing supplied. The value of each square foot of housing now is

$$V_t = \frac{Y + \Delta Y}{r + t} = \$120/.2 = \$600. \tag{17.7}$$

The tax-induced increase in market rents offsets some of the tax capitalization. The market value of each square foot of housing falls by only $400 instead of $500. It follows that whenever the property tax can be shifted to tenants in the form of an increase in rents, only partial shifting takes place. Then, net rent per square foot received by building owners falls to $60. This equals the market rent of $120 less the tax of 10 percent of the new $600 value of each square foot.

Only differentials in the rate of taxation among local governments, or among classes of property within a local jurisdiction, can result in tax capitalization effects.

Because the portion of the property tax common to all jurisdictions results in a decline in the return to investment (including investment in land) everywhere in the economy, it has the effect of lowering the rate of discount itself and therefore has no effect on the relative prices of capital assets.

With a few exceptions, empirical research has indicated a marked capitalization of tax differentials among communities. Several studies also have shown that capitalization results from discriminatory taxation among various types of real estate within a given jurisdiction.[10]

C H E C K P O I N T

1. Why would a national tax on real estate reduce the return to all forms of investment (not only real estate)?
2. Explain how the system of local taxation of property in the United States causes resource flows across regions that can affect both land prices and the price of housing at various locations.
3. What is tax capitalization? Explain why a national property tax on *all* forms of wealth could not be capitalized. Under what circumstances is a property tax fully capitalized?

PROPERTY TAXATION IN THE UNITED STATES

The administration of the property tax in the United States varies from state to state and from locality to locality. A good part of the dissatisfaction with the tax, often expressed by individual citizens, stems from assessment practices and the method of payment of the tax, rather than from any intrinsic deficiency in the tax itself.

The actual tax base varies greatly from state to state. Several states attempt to levy the tax on all forms of physical property, including personal property and intangible financial assets representing claims against corporations located outside of the state. Other states limit the taxable base to real estate. About two-thirds of the taxes collected are from those levied on single-family, nonfarm homes.

Assessment Practices and Effective Tax Rates

A peculiar phenomenon in the administration of the property tax is the practice of fractional assessment of property. Fractional assessment exists when real property is

---

[10]See Wallace E. Oates, "The Effects of Property Taxes and Local Public Spending on Property Values: An Empirical Study of Tax Capitalization and the Tiebout Hypothesis," *Journal of Political Economy* 77 (November–December, 1969): 957–971; Larry L. Orr, "The Incidence of Differential Property Taxes on Urban Housing," *National Tax Journal* 21 (September 1968): 253–262; Albert M. Church, "Capitalization of the Effective Property Tax Rate on Single Family Residences," *National Tax Journal* 27 (March 1974): 113–122; and David N. Hyman and E. C. Pasour, Jr., "Real Property Taxes, Local Public Services, and Residential Property Values," *Southern Economic Journal* 29 (April 1973): 601–611.

P U B L I C   P O L I C Y   P E R S P E C T I V E

CAPITALIZATION OF PROPERTY TAX RATE DIFFERENTIALS

A number of studies have provided empirical confirmation and measurement of tax capitalization in the United States. For example, one study analyzed the impact of Proposition 13 on housing prices in northern California. Proposition 13, approved by California voters in 1978, placed a ceiling on effective property rates applied to real property under local property taxation in that state. In effect, the passage of this proposition resulted in a massive reduction in local property tax rates in that state. Furthermore, the tax rate ceilings resulted in a substantial reduction in the tax rate differentials among taxing jurisdictions in the state. At the same time, the state government used its own tax revenues to maintain the level of local public services among taxing jurisdictions. The reduction in tax rate differentials resulting from the passage of Proposition 13 was expected to increase property values of homes in jurisdictions that had positive tax differentials prior to 1978.

Research by Kenneth T. Rosen has isolated the impact of the reduction in property tax differentials on housing prices in northern California.[*] His research indicates that the reduction in property tax differentials in the San Francisco Bay area were partially capitalized in the year following passage of Proposition 13. Each $1 reduction in positive property tax differentials in a high-tax jurisdiction increased home values in that jurisdiction by about $7. Nothing changed in the quality or level of government services to these local communities because the state government intervened to fi-nance these services at the pretax reduction levels. Therefore, the observed increase in property values could be attributed entirely to the reduction in relative property tax bills. Other factors influencing property values were adjusted for in conducting the statistical analysis of property values.

Another study investigated the impact of interjurisdictional differences in property tax rates applied to commercial property on the value of office buildings in the Boston metropolitan area. Research by William Wheaton supports the hypothesis that the bulk of property taxes on commercial property is borne by owners of buildings and is therefore capitalized into lower property values.[†] Wheaton argues that this is because the demand for office space in a particular area is quite elastic. Decreases in the local annual quantity of office space in response to positive property tax differentials in an area therefore do not result in significant increases in market rents per square foot of office space. Wheaton's research confirms that positive property tax rate differentials are not associated with positive differentials in office leasing rates in the Boston metropolitan area. This provides support for the hypothesis that the incidence of property taxes on commercial property is borne by landlords and investors. Because office leasing rates do not rise substantially, only a small percentage of the tax can be shifted to consumers or workers. This research also suggests that jurisdictions where property tax rates are greater than the average of all jurisdictions in a region can expect to suffer a reduction in growth as the quantity of square feet of commercial property demanded per year declines.

[*]Kenneth T. Rosen, "The Impact of Proposition 13 on House Prices in Northern California: A Test of the Interjurisdictional Capitalization Hypothesis," *Journal of Political Economy* 90 (February 1982): 191–200.
[†]William C. Wheaton, "The Incidence of Interjurisdictional Differences in Commercial Property Taxes," *National Tax Journal* 37 (December 1984): 515–527.

assessed at only a fraction of its market value. Much of the observed fractional assessment results from infrequent assessment of property in periods of rising property values. However, some fractional assessment is the result of state law.

Under fractional assessment, the property tax rate overstates the real rate of taxation. For example, if the property tax rate is nominally 3 percent but the assessment ratio is only 33.3 percent of true market value, then the effective rate of taxation would be merely 1 percent.

Table 17.1 shows effective property rates in selected cities, ranked according to their level of taxation in 1991 along with the nominal tax rates and assessment levels. In cases where the assessment level is less than 100 percent, the nominal tax rate overstates the effective rate of taxation. As you can see effective tax rates vary considerably from a high of 4.4 percent in Detroit, Michigan, to a low of 0.37 percent in Honolulu, Hawaii.

Evidence indicates that assessment ratios decline with increases in home values. Expensive properties therefore are taxed at lower effective tax rates than less expensive properties. Apparently, this practice is widespread. It could have the effect of increasing the property tax burden on low-income groups that rent or own relatively inexpensive homes.[11]

Incidence of the Property Tax in the United States

Considerable controversy exists concerning the incidence of the property tax in the United States. One point of view is that the tax is regressive with respect to income because a major portion of the tax is equivalent to a tax on the consumption of housing. However, reasonable doubt exists. In fact, economic theory suggests that the burden of the local property tax is likely to be progressive with respect to income.

Studies indicating that the property tax is regressive are based on a number of assumptions regarding the shifting of the tax, even though these have not been empirically verified.[12] The studies assume that the bulk of the burden of the local property tax falls on housing. Inasmuch as housing expenditures tend to decline as a percentage of income as income rises, the effect of a major portion of the tax would appear to be regressive with respect to income. Netzer, for example, has argued that the local property tax can be viewed as analogous to a sales tax on housing.[13] Given this view of the tax and the belief that much of the tax falling on business property is reflected in higher prices, the conclusion has been that the tax is regressive with respect to income.

This view of the tax conflicts with theoretical analysis of the impact of the local property tax in the United States.[14] As discussed, much of the local property tax is reflected in a lower return to all uses of capital. Because the distribution of ownership of capital is concentrated in the hands of upper-income groups, the incidence of this portion of the tax probably is progressive with respect to income.

The local property tax also causes regional reallocation away from jurisdictions where property taxes exceed the national average and toward low-tax jurisdictions.

---

[11]See David E. Black, "Property Tax Incidence: The Excise Tax Effect and Assessment Practices," *National Tax Journal* 30 (December 1977): 429–434.

[12]See, for example, Dick Netzer, *Economics of the Property Tax* (Washington, D.C.: The Brookings Institution, 1966).

[13]See Dick Netzer, *Economics and Urban Problems*, 2d ed. (New York: Basic Books, 1974), 249.

[14]See Mason Gaffney, "The Property Tax Is a Progressive Tax," in National Tax Association, *Proceedings of the 64th Annual Conference on Taxation*, 1971 (National Tax Association, 1972).

Table 17.1 ✦ Residential Property Tax Rates in Selected Cities: 1991

City	Effective Tax Rate per $100		Assessment Level (Percent)	Nominal Rate per $100	City	Effective Tax Rate per $100		Assessment Level (Percent)	Nominal Rate per $100
	Rank	Rate				Rank	Rate		
Detroit, MI	1	4.40	49.4	8.92	Burlington, VT	27	1.44	60.7	2.37
Milwaukee, WI	2	3.75	96.7	3.88	Billings, MT	28	1.43	3.9	37.14
Newark, NJ	3	3.14	15.8	19.96	Columbia, SC	29	1.43	4.0	35.64
Des Moines, IA	4	2.66	65.8	4.04	Minneapolis, MN	30	1.39	12.1	11.50
Philadelphia, PA	5	2.64	32.0	8.26	Charlotte, NC	31	1.20	99.6	1.21
Portland, OR	6	2.64	100.0	2.64	Kansas City, MO	32	1.15	19.0	6.03
Manchester, NH	7	2.59	100.0	2.59	Virginia Beach, VA	33	1.09	100.0	1.09
Providence, RI	8	2.55	100.0	2.55	Salt Lake City, UT	34	1.08	60.0	1.80
Bridgeport, CT	9	2.49	39.4	6.33	Seattle, WA	35	1.05	95.5	1.10
Baltimore, MD	10	2.46	40.0	6.16	Oklahoma City, OK	36	1.04	11.0	9.45
Sioux Falls, IA	11	2.36	84.9	2.78	Albuquerque, NM	37	1.04	33.3	3.11
Omaha, NE	12	2.31	88.1	2.63	Las Vegas, NV	38	1.02	35.0	2.92
Jacksonville, FL	13	2.15	100.0	2.15	Denver, CO	39	0.97	14.3	6.73
Chicago, IL	14	2.05	16.0	9.96	Little Rock, AR	40	0.95	18.7	5.08
Houston, TX	15	2.00	100.0	2.00	Louisville, KY	41	0.95	92.0	1.03
Columbus, OH	16	2.00	35.0	5.70	Wilmington, DE	42	0.94	57.7	1.63
Boise City, ID	17	1.92	96.9	1.98	Washington, DC	43	0.91	94.7	0.96
Fargo, ND	18	1.78	4.5	39.59	Boston, MA	44	0.89	100.0	0.89
Wichita, KS	19	1.76	12.0	14.66	New York City, NY	45	0.87	8.0	10.89
Indianapolis, IN	20	1.75	15.0	11.65	Cheyenne, WY	46	0.72	9.5	7.59
Atlanta, GA	21	1.74	30.0	5.81	Birmingham, AL	47	0.70	10.0	6.95
Anchorage, AK	22	1.74	96.0	1.81	Charleston, WV	48	0.65	37.4	1.73
Portland, ME	23	1.74	46.4	3.75	Los Angeles, CA	49	0.63	61.2	1.03
New Orleans, LA	24	1.61	10.0	16.12	Memphis, TN	50	0.54	25.0	2.15
Phoenix, AZ	25	1.47	10.0	14.74	Honolulu, HI	51	0.37	100.0	0.37
Jackson, MS	26	1.47	10.0	14.73					

Source: Government of the District of Columbia, Department of Finance and Revenue, Tax Rates and Tax Burdens in the District of Columbia: A Nationwide Comparison, annual.

The jurisdictions with positive property tax rate differentials above the national average suffer a reduction in annual investment. In the long run, these regions therefore lose capital to regions with negative property tax rate differentials below the national average. The ratio of capital to land in the high-tax jurisdictions therefore declines in the long run. This decline in the capital-land ratio lowers land rents and therefore reduces the income of landowners in the high-tax jurisdictions. On the other hand, land rents in the low-tax jurisdictions *increase* because the capital-land ratio increases in those areas. Similarly, if labor is relatively immobile, the decline in capital in high-tax jurisdictions also can contribute to lower wages in those jurisdictions over the long run as the ratio of capital to labor declines. Conversely, wages increase in low-tax jurisdictions in response to increases in capital investment in those areas.

The evidence seems to indicate that the regions with positive property tax rate differentials are those with citizens who have income, on average, greater than the national median income. This suggests that the regions where land rents and wages are likely to fall are those in which citizens have income greater than the national median. The rent and wage declines in these areas are offset by increases in land rents and wages in areas where the property tax rates are less than the national average (negative property tax rate differentials exist). These jurisdictions are likely to be located in the poorer regions of the nation. The earnings of workers and landlords decline in the upper-income regions of the nation, relative to the poorer regions, as a result of the tax-induced shifts in investment. This implies that the burden of the property tax rate differentials is likely to be progressively distributed with respect to income.

The question of who bears the burden of the property tax remains controversial. The tax differentials are significant in that they range from less than 20 percent of the median rate to more than five times the average tax rate. Thus, the effect on prices of inputs other than capital is likely to be significant, because much of the tax is in the form of a differential. As with the case of corporate income tax, the incidence of the local property tax remains unresolved. Considerable disagreement remains concerning who bears the tax; it is probably shared by consumers in general, owners of capital, workers, and landlords.

Tax Preferences

Despite increased reason to believe that the burden of the property tax is progressively distributed with respect to income, many states have granted, in recent years, special property tax relief to certain groups. Among the most common group to be singled out for such special property tax relief is the elderly. All states now have some form of property tax relief for the elderly.

Many often argue that the elderly find it difficult to pay property taxes because their income is much lower at retirement than it had been in the past; and, insofar as they live in homes with heavy property tax liability, they would be forced to sell those homes to pay the tax. However, in computing the eligibility of the elderly for special property tax relief, no state attempts to include the imputed value of rent accruing to the taxpayers in granting such relief.

In many cases, individuals with low money income are living in homes that are considered to be expensive at current market prices and that are owned without any mortgage debt. The real problem concerning their difficulty in meeting property tax bills is one of cash flow, rather than poverty. The problem could be alleviated by allowing the state to borrow money against the value of the property in question to obtain the tax due. Then, at the death of the taxpayers, the property would be sold, with the amount pledged against taxes given to the local governments and the remainder given to the heirs of the taxpayers. In the absence of such an arrangement, any subsidy received by elderly taxpayers eventually ends up as a benefit to their heirs, who might not be in low-income groups.

In the United States, more than thirty states currently grant special property tax exemptions to the elderly or the poor. Still others make use of a *circuit-breaker* approach, in the form of state income tax credits, to offset some of the burden of local property taxes. The details of these various tax relief packages vary from state to state.[15] All these packages suffer from the problem of inadequately measuring income.

Because they do not consider the value of income-in-kind in the form of housing services that accrue to taxpayers who live in owner-occupied housing, these packages often aid persons who are not poor and, likewise, they subsidize their heirs, who eventually inherit such real property.

LAND TAXES

A common criticism against the property tax, as administered in the United States, is that it decreases incentives for land development and redevelopment, particularly in high-tax areas. For this reason, strong support is often voiced to substitute a tax falling on land alone for the existing tax on real estate. Those who support this idea argue that it would have no excess burden and would have progressive redistributive effects. Because, in effect, the supply of land is perfectly inelastic, a tax on land results in no substitution effects. A land tax is equivalent to a lump-sum tax. That is to say, a national tax on land alone, with no exclusions, does not affect the quantity of land supplied to any particular area, because landowners cannot control the amount of land. Therefore, the tax induces no change in behavior to affect the quantity of land on the market. The rent earned on the land is a pure economic surplus that can be taxed without any effect on quantity supplied. The land tax reduces rents earned on the land by the full amount of the tax, and land prices fall to reflect the future tax burden.[16] As shown in Figure

---

[15]See Advisory Commission on Intergovernmental Relations, *Property Tax Circuit Breakers: Current Status and Policy Issues* (Washington, D.C.: U.S. Government Printing Office, 1975).

[16]Feldstein challenges the conclusion that a tax on land is fully borne by landlords. He argues that the decrease in the price of land, initially caused by the tax, results in a portfolio disequilibrium for investors. The decreased value of land increases demand for land by investors who seek to balance risk associated with holding various assets. The portfolio reallocation raises the price of land and thereby shifts part of the burden of the tax to others. The conclusion of zero excess burden remains the same. See Martin Feldstein, "The Surprising Incidence of a Tax on Pure Rent: A New Answer to an Old Question," *Journal of Political Economy* 85 (April 1977): 349–360.

Figure 17.4 ✦ IMPACT OF A LAND TAX

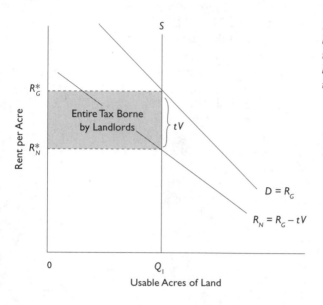

Because the supply of usable acres is fixed at Q_1, a tax on land results in no change in quantity available. The entire tax is borne by landlords as net rents received per acre fall by tV, where V is the market value of an acre and t is the tax rate.

17.4, a tax on land reduces gross rents received by landlords from R_G^* to R_N^*, where R_N is the gross rent less the annual property tax per acre, tV.

Taxes on land alone have a long history of advocacy in the United States. Perhaps the most important name associated with land taxation is that of Henry George (1839–1897).[17] George's ideas have led to an almost fanatical advocacy of the "single-tax doctrine," under which all taxes except those levied on land would be rescinded.[18] The tax on land then would be such as to appropriate all rents from landlords. George correctly reasoned that rent was a pure economic surplus and that its full taxation would not alter the quantity of land supplied.

George further believed that such high rates of land taxation would encourage investment in the land in the form of structures of various sorts, thereby accelerating economic development. Although the utilization of the land tax as a single tax today would scarcely yield enough revenue to finance state and local public expenditures, to say nothing of federal expenditures, many economists believe it would be an improvement over current taxation of real estate (both land and structures) because it would result in a more efficient land use pattern. To separate the value of land from the value of structures thereon, however, may be administratively difficult.

---

[17]For a discussion of George's ideas, see Reid R. Hansen, "Henry George: Economics or Theology?" in Lindholm, *Property Taxation*, 65–76.

[18]George qualified his "single-tax doctrine" to allow for taxes on liquor, gambling, and bequests, as well. See Ibid., 68.

A land tax would not cause any substitution effects and therefore would have no excess burden. Land developers would be forced to develop parcels to offset the burden of the tax; the incentive would be to use land in the most efficient manner because the development of land would not directly affect the tax bill, insofar as the land value can be taken to be independent of the value of structures on the land.

The historical tendency in most nations is for the value of land to decline as a percentage of gross national product as the economy grows. A land tax therefore can yield only relatively small amounts of revenue, even at very high tax rates.[19]

Special Treatment of Agricultural Land

Another form of fiscal relief adopted in many states in recent years is the special treatment for land used in agriculture. Such treatment consists of special provisions that commonly permit assessment of agricultural land to be based on the value of that land in agricultural use, rather than on its market value. In effect, this provides benefits only for owners of farmland near urban areas, where differentials exist between the value of land in agricultural use and the value of land in urban use. In such areas, urban growth pushes the value of farmland above its value in agriculture. The objective of such special provisions for farmers is to slow down the process of urban development by subsidizing farmers so that they remain in agriculture, despite the temptation to sell their land to urban developers for prices that exceed the discounted present value of that land in current agricultural use. Many often argue that such subsidization also would benefit urban residents by preserving open space near the city and improving urban environmental quality. Further, many assert that such provisions provide benefits to poor farmers, who otherwise might not remain in farming.

In many cases, however, the farmer finds that the best alternative, in terms of maximizing income, is still to sell the land to urban developers, despite the subsidy that would be received by remaining in agriculture. Even though many states require that farmers who sell their land to developers must pay back taxes equal to the subsidies that they received when holding their land in agricultural use, many farmers still decide to sell.

C H E C K P O I N T

1. What is fractional assessment?
2. What issues must be resolved to uncover the actual incidence of the system of local property taxes used in the United States?
3. Why will a tax on land be fully capitalized and result in zero excess burden?

PROPERTY TRANSFER TAXES

Property transfer taxes include estate, inheritance, and gift taxes. These taxes are levied on transfers of wealth among citizens. Property transfer taxes represent a feasible

---

[19]For an estimate of the revenue that might be obtained by taxing all rents, see Ibid., 70.

method of taxing accumulations of wealth that normally escape other forms of taxation. When wealth is tranferred at time of death, the government supervises the administration of the bequest. Because reasonably accurate data exist on the accumulation of wealth, it is relatively easy for the government to levy taxes on wealth accumulations transferred from one generation to another.

Estate, Inheritance, and Gift Taxes

Estate and inheritance taxes are sometimes referred to as *death duties*. They are levied, essentially, as excise taxes on the rights to transfer property at time of death. The federal government levies taxes on property transfers before death, as well, in the form of gift taxation. Federal death taxes are levied on inheritances and therefore represent the tax liabilities of the heirs.

Federal estate taxes account for about 1 percent of total federal revenue. Although levied according to a fairly progressive rate scale, the tax allows many exemptions. It allows, for example, a generous basic exemption, plus other specific deductions and exemptions, and taxes the remainder according to a progressive rate structure. Included among the specific deductions from the tax base are legal and funeral expenses, debts, and charitable contributions. In addition, estates may be left to the surviving spouse, exempt of all taxes. When the surviving spouse dies, the remainder of the estate presumably is bequeathed to the remaining heirs. As of 1994, the maximum nominal federal estate tax rate was 55 percent of taxable estates in excess of $3 million.

In the absence of a federal gift tax, all estate taxes could be avoided by transferring property prior to death. The federal gift tax prevents such avoidance to some degree. Gift taxes are levied on the individual who makes the gift. Since 1977, the rates and exemptions that apply to gifts have been the same as those existing under the estate tax for a combined base of gifts and estates.

Most states levy taxes on inheritances. These taxes are the liabilities of the beneficiaries of the estate. Many often argue that this is a more equitable property transfer tax because the effective tax rates can be correlated with the ability of the heirs to pay. Furthermore, higher exemptions and lower effective tax rates are generally allowed to closer relatives of the deceased.

Property transfer taxes can be avoided by establishing trusts that are not subject to estate taxation until dissolved. Wealthy individuals make extensive use of this provision. In addition, bequests to charitable foundations are deductible, without limit, from the tax base.

Economic Effects

Estate and gift taxes represent levies on accumulated wealth. They therefore can be viewed as taxes on accumulated savings that reduce the return to savings when that wealth is transferred. Some people argue that it is a good idea to tax gifts and estates as transfers to the heirs because they are not taxed as income to the recipients. Remember, the U.S. tax code flatly declares that gifts and other transfers are *not* income despite the fact that they would be included in income under the Haig-Simons definition. You also can argue that a gift or inheritance will have an income effect that is unfavorable to the work effort of its recipient. An estate (or inheritance) tax along with a gift tax could therefore have the desirable social effect of reducing the undesirable income effect to the recipient of the transfer by reducing the amount of the net transfer.

However, high estate and inheritance taxes could adversely affect the work incentives of prospective donors. For example, if you wanted to leave a large fortune to your children, you might think twice about it if you knew that half of everything you worked hard for would be taxed away at your death rather than transferred to your chosen heirs. The tax therefore has a substitution effect that is unfavorable to the work effort of prospective donors. However, the estate tax also has an income effect on the work incentive of prospective donors. If you stubbornly wanted to leave $1 million to your children, you might work *harder* because of the estate tax so that you could accumulate that amount *after taxes* to bequeath to your heirs! Because estate taxes have both income and substitution effects on the incentives of donors, we really can't predict the effect that the tax would have on their incentives to work and save.

However, estate taxes also can have an effect on the way that a donor transfers wealth to heirs. The estate, gift, and inheritance taxes are levied only on transfers of financial wealth and physical capital such as real estate. A prospective donor could avoid the tax by investing heavily in his or her children's education rather than by accumulating savings in taxable form that would be subject to the tax when transferred. Thus, very high property transfer taxes could encourage overinvestment in human capital.

Wealth transfer taxes are levied on the wealth itself, rather than as income of the recipient of the transfer. Separate taxation of wealth transfers would be less desirable if a comprehensive income tax were used. Under a comprehensive income tax, any transfer received would be treated as income to the recipient, and it would be taxed accordingly. Under progressive taxation, treatment of the transfer as income could have the effect of taxing large transfers heavily—to the extent that they would push the recipient into high tax brackets. The effective tax rates on accumulated capital probably would be much higher than is currently the case with estate and gift taxes, which tax the transfer as wealth, rather than as income to the recipients. Thus, the tax on the transfer is lower than would be the case if it were treated as capital income to the recipient.

Estimates of effective tax rates on wealth transfers in the United States indicate that generous deductions result in very low rates of taxation, relative to the statutory rates. Although a number of conceptual problems are posed in calculating these tax rates, one estimate indicates that, in 1979, the positive tax rates on taxable estates ranged from 1.7 percent for estates between $175,000 and $250,000 to 18.5 percent on estates between $5 million and $10 million. Estates in excess of $10 million were taxed at about 15 percent. In the same year, the statutory average tax rates on estates ranged from 5.0 percent to 65.3 percent for taxable estates. Thus, tax preferences apparently reduce the tax rates on estates to well below the statutory levels.[20]

---

[20]Harry L. Gutman, "Effective Federal Tax Rates on Transfers of Wealth," *National Tax Journal* 32 (September 1979): 391–404.

Although many argue that, generally, an estate tax is necessary to reduce inequality of income, recent analysis suggests that it can actually increase income inequality if saving is responsive to the tax rates for the estate tax. This is because the tax, insofar as it reduces capital accumulation, reduces capital-labor ratios in the long run, thereby reducing labor productivity and income. Under certain circumstances, this has the effect of increasing the share of income going to capital in the long run.[21]

---

[21]Joseph E. Stiglitz, "Notes on Estate Taxes, Redistribution, and the Concept of Balanced Growth Path Incidence," *Journal of Political Economy* 86, pt. 2 (April 1978): S137–S150.

Summary

General wealth taxes are levied on all forms of wealth, while selective property taxes are levied only on certain forms of wealth. Most of the revenue collected through property taxation in the United States comes from the real estate tax.

Determining the value of wealth that is infrequently traded is one of the most difficult aspects of property taxation. A comprehensive wealth tax is difficult to administer because of problems involved in measuring all forms of wealth, especially human wealth. The estimation of the value of an asset is called assessment. Accurate assessment closely approximates the market value of an asset. Property must be reassessed periodically to reflect changing market values.

Compared with equal-yield general taxes levied on the alternative economic bases of income and consumption, a general wealth tax is more detrimental to saving incentive but less detrimental to work incentive. If the supply of savings is perfectly inelastic, a general wealth tax is borne by owners of capital. The tax can be shifted only when the quantity of savings supplied is responsive to changes in its return.

The process through which the prices of taxed assets fall in value, relative to untaxed assets, is called tax capitalization. In tax capitalization, the full burden of future tax payments is concentrated on owners of taxed wealth at the time the tax is initially levied. If the property tax results in decreases in real estate investment so that rent is raised, the depressing effect that the tax has on asset prices may be offset.

The property tax in the United States tends to reduce the return to capital in all uses. The positive property tax differentials among communities are reflected in lower land rents and lower wages in areas where investment declines. Tax-induced reduction in investment in new housing and in local goods and services also can contribute to higher prices for housing and other goods and services. Although considerable controversy concerns the incidence of the property tax, many economists now believe that its effects on the distribution of income are progressive.

A Forward Look

The property tax is the main source of tax financing for local governments. Part Five considers questions of public finance and government expenditures within the context of a federal system. The advantages and disadvantages of decentralized government, compared with those of centralized government, are extensively examined in Chapter 18. Intergovernmental fiscal relations and local fiscal problems also are discussed in the chapter that follows.

Important Concepts

Wealth
Real Estate or Real Property
Stock
Assessment
Comprehensive Wealth Tax
Property Tax Rate Differentials
Tax Capitalization

Questions for Review

1. Explain why a comprehensive wealth tax is equivalent to a tax on the annual return to savings. If the annual return to holding wealth is 10 percent calculate the tax rate on annual savings and investments associated with a 1-percent wealth tax.

2. How is the tax base defined for a comprehensive wealth tax? What are some of the problems associated with measuring wealth? Why would inclusion of the assets of corporations and outstanding corporate stock double-count the wealth of corporations?

3. Who bears the incidence of a general wealth tax when the interest elasticity of supply of savings is zero? Why is the incidence most likely to be progressive?

4. How can a general wealth tax be shifted to workers and consumers when the aggregate supply of saving is not perfectly inelastic? What effect does the tax have on the work-leisure choice? What are the consequences of excluding human capital from the tax base?

5. Why is a national tax on real estate likely to be at least partially borne by owners of all forms of capital, regardless of the use to which that capital is put?

6. How can property tax differentials be shifted to others who do not own capital? Why is the average property tax rate likely to be borne by owners of all forms of capital?

7. Suppose the discount rate is 10 percent. Calculate the tax capitalization resulting from a property tax rate differential of 5 percent above the national average for an asset with a $5,000 annual income before taxation, assuming that the tax is fully capitalized and that the asset has an infinite life.

8. Under what circumstances will a property tax be only partially capitalized?

9. Suppose that property in state X is assessed at 60 percent of its market value and that the nominal property tax rate is 4 percent. Calculate the effective tax rate.

10. Why is the property tax often asserted to be regressive with respect to income in the United States? Do you agree with this view?

Problems

1. The annual return to savings is currently $100 billion per year in a certain nation. The estimated value of wealth in the nation is $1 trillion. Calculate the percentage gross return to savings. Assuming that the supply of saving is perfectly inelastic, calculate the impact of a 1 percent tax on wealth on the gross and net percentage return to savings. How would your answer differ if the interest elasticity of supply of savings were positive rather than zero?

2. Suppose you were appointed economic advisor to a less-developed nation in Africa. The nation seeks to encourage capital formation and wants to increase the rate of saving of its own residents and encourage foreigners to invest in their nation. What role would you assign to property taxes in this nation to achieve its objectives?

3. A parcel of land is expected to yield annual rents equal to $10,000 per year forever. If the market rate of interest is 10 percent, calculate the market price of the parcel. Suppose you purchase the parcel of land. After your purchase, a 5-percent property tax on the land is imposed. Calculate the impact of the tax on the market value of the land parcel. Can you avoid the tax by selling the land?

4. Suppose, as a result of the imposition of a 5-percent local property tax, the rent on a parcel of property increases from $12,000 to $12,500 per year. Assuming that the current rate of discount is 8 percent and that the property will last forever, calculate the value of the property before and after the imposition of the tax. How much of the tax is capitalized and how much of it is shifted to others rather than absorbed by the owner of the property at the time the tax is imposed?

Suggestions for Further Reading

Aaron, Henry J. *Who Pays the Property Tax?* Washington, D.C.: The Brookings Institution, 1975. An analysis of the incidence of the property tax.

Lindholm, Richard W., ed. *Property Taxation: U.S.A.* Madison: University of Wisconsin Press, 1967. A collection of papers on the history and administration of, and problems in, using property taxes.

Mieszkowski, Peter M. "The Property Tax: An Excise Tax or a Profits Tax?" *Journal of Public Economics* 1 (April 1972): 73–96. A provocative and influential analysis of the impact of the property tax as used in the United States.

State and Local Government Finance

V

18 FISCAL FEDERALISM AND STATE AND LOCAL GOVERNMENT FINANCE

FISCAL FEDERALISM AND STATE AND LOCAL GOVERNMENT FINANCE

LEARNING OBJECTIVES

After reading this chapter you should be able to

1. Define the concept of fiscal federalism, and discuss issues relating to the supply of public goods in a multilevel system of government.
2. Use the Tiebout model of supply for local public goods in a system of decentralized governments to analyze the relationship between local government finance and location decisions.
3. Explain the consequences of interjurisdictional externalities.
4. Describe how the elasticity of local tax bases acts as a constraint on state and local government tax policy.
5. Discuss variation in fiscal capacity among state and local governments, intergovernmental grants, the impact of grants on resource allocation, and current fiscal problems of state and local governments in the United States.

Most of you rely on state and local governments to provide road maintenance, criminal justice, police and fire protection, and primary and secondary education. State and local governments also are active in the provision of health care to the needy and the subsidization of higher education. As the federal government in the United States struggled to deal with a cumbersome and growing deficit in the 1980s and early 1990s, it shifted more responsibilities for supplying public services to state and local governments. These governments will be getting less financial help from the federal government than they have in the past. The federal government financed 25 percent of state and local spending in the late 1970s. However, by 1990 it was financing only 17 percent of state and local budgets. The trend to reduce federal aid to state and local governments is likely to continue. County governments, which are mainly responsible for social services and health services to the poor in their community, are likely to be under particular stress as federally mandated spending by state and local governments for health and social services increases.

As we approach the year 2000, state and local governments will be competing for tax bases in an era of slower growth. At the same time they will be under pressure to provide health services under the Medicaid program to an aging population while also meeting the educational demands of a growing school age population. Much of the burden of coping with problems of crime and AIDS also will be borne by state and local governments.

In this final chapter we examine some of the issues involved in state and local government finance in a federal system. We discuss theoretical issues relating to the division of responsibility for supplying public goods among various levels of government. We also examine such practical issues as the problems of local government in raising revenues and the implications of reduced federal aid to state an local governments.

FISCAL FEDERALISM

The United States has a **federal system of government** characterized by numerous levels of government, each with its own powers to provide services and raise revenue. The levels of government can be divided into three broad categories: federal, or central; state; and local. The various local governments range from large counties and cities with populations in the millions to small towns and special districts with less than 1,000 citizens.

A multilevel governing system raises some interesting and important questions. What is the most efficient allocation of responsibilities among alternative levels of government? In general, the more decentralized the government, the greater is the opportunity for expressing the desire for various kinds of government services and for obtaining the means to finance those services. However, diversity can be accompanied by fragmented or noncoordinated collective decision making among jurisdictions. In addition, government provision of services on a small scale often results in higher average costs because all economies of scale cannot be realized.

Fiscal federalism is the division of taxing and expenditure functions among levels of government. Economic theory offers some insights into the consequences of alternative arrangements for supplying public goods and services and for financing them among the various levels of government. In general, collective choices by citizens will probably result in the central government's undertaking of those functions most likely to have benefits that are collectively consumed on the national level. Accordingly, in most nations, the supply and finance of armed forces is observed as a central government function. All citizens, regardless of their location, collectively benefit from national defense and other public services that have the characteristics of pure public goods. They can reasonably be expected to agree to a national public choice arrangement for determining the level of such services and a system of finance in which all citizens pay a share for such services, independent of the region or locality in which they reside.

Many government-supplied services require central coordination and can be costly or impossible to provide in a decentralized way by local governments. It is almost inconceivable to expect a local or state government to undertake its own economic stabilization program. Such programs would be doomed to failure by virtue of the simple fact that the economic base for state and local governments is heavily dependent on those in other regions of the nation. Any attempt by state and local governments to alleviate inflation and unemployment within their own borders, either by adjusting aggregate demand through fiscal policy or monetary demand through restrictions on credit, will do little to solve these problems because much of the spending by local citizens will be for goods and services produced in other states. Increased demand that results from a tax reduction in one state is likely to provide increased income in all states, because citizens spend only a fraction of their income on locally produced goods.

No one state can control its own inflation and unemployment rates because these are tied to events in national markets that cannot in any way be controlled by the economic policies of the state or the locality. Monetary and fiscal policies can be more effectively implemented by a national government.

Similarly, attempts by local or state governments to engage in social programs that significantly redistribute income among their citizens are likely to result in resource flows that limit the effectiveness of such programs. Although, in fact, state and local governments do redistribute income among citizens with some degree of success, these programs are likely to entail efficiency losses higher than those that would be encountered if the central government undertook the same level of redistribution. This is because it is easier to avoid state and local taxes than federal taxes and because the availability of transfers at one location, as opposed to others, is likely to induce in-migration of eligible recipients. As a result, the costs to finance a given amount of redistribution per recipient probably will be higher than anticipated, as the tax base declines due to out-migration of local resources and as the number of eligible recipients rises due to in-migration.

A national income redistribution program would be less wasteful because it would not encourage migration of eligible recipients in response to differential transfer payments among jurisdictions. The taxes necessary to finance collectively agreed-upon transfers would be impossible to avoid by changing location of personal residence within the nation. Opportunities for a centralized governing authority to redistribute income are less limited than those for local governments, principally because the mobility of resources between nations is much less than mobility among areas within a nation.[1]

The Supply of Local Public Goods in a Federal System

Local public goods are public goods with benefits that are nonrival only for that portion of the national population who live within a certain geographical area. Such

---

[1] A strong case for centralized supply of stabilization and redistributive programs is made by Oates. See Wallace E. Oates, *Fiscal Federalism* (New York: Harcourt Brace Jovanovich, 1972), chap. 1. However, some basis does exist for a limited role by noncentral governments in supplying these two services. For an analysis of the desirability of local government participation in stabilization and redistribution programs, see Albert Breton and Anthony Scott, *The Economic Constitution of Federal States* (Toronto: University of Toronto Press, 1978).

goods and services are likely to be most effectively produced by local governing units. Local governments are likely to be formed almost exclusively for producing such goods and services and financing them by taxes that are paid entirely by local residents. Among the services that are likely to result in locally consumed collective benefits are police and fire protection, public sanitation and refuse collection, traffic control and roads, water and sewer services, and educational services. Similarly, services that are typically financed by state governments result in collectively consumed benefits on a somewhat larger scale, such as state road networks, bridges, a share of educational programs, highway patrols, and certain social services.

The main advantage of local and regional supply and finance of government-provided services is that it allows the system of governments to accommodate a wide array of tastes and demands for their services, in accordance with local variations in demand patterns and cost conditions. Each local governing unit, with its own political institutions, can articulate the demands for government-supplied services within its own collective choice process. This adds great flexibility to the political process and allows citizens the option of locating their residences with at least some consideration of the kinds and types of government-provided services offered at alternative locations. In fact, citizens with similar tastes in certain public services tend to congregate together and form local governments.

Thus, communities whose citizens have strong preferences for recreation can choose to tax themselves to pay for parks and other public recreational facilities. Other communities, whose citizens are relatively more interested in the arts, can choose collectively to have few public parks and, instead, use significant amounts of their resources for public concerts, art exhibits, and libraries. In a sense, the political process is most efficient when individuals of relatively similar preferences congregate in local communities, where they can best satisfy their preferences for public services. Under these conditions, both transactions costs and external costs of political action are likely to be low.

CENTRALIZED VERSUS DECENTRALIZED GOVERNMENT

National Versus Local Political Equilibriums

Under centralized government, collective choices on government-provided services are made nationally. Central provision of these services tends to result in uniformity of the quality and quantity of public goods across all regions of a nation. The resulting collective choices represent national political equilibriums. Under centralized provision of government-supplied services, all citizens vote on the quantity and kinds of services to be supplied at all locations. If such choices are made under majority rule, the resulting equilibrium is likely to reflect the preferences of the median national voter (see Chapter 5).

A national consensus on the amount of public goods with truly national collective benefits is necessary because those goods, when provided, are consumed by all residents, independent of the location of their residence. With local public goods (those with geographically constrained collective benefits), a national consensus on the amount to provide makes less sense, because when these goods are produced, they are consumed by only a subset of the population. For such goods, decentralized decision making provides the advantage of taking into account variations in preferences for those goods among residents of specific communities. Allowing local public choice of the amount of these goods provides more flexibility and improves efficiency because government output then can respond to variations in tastes.

Under decentralized collective choices made by majority rule, the political equilibrium reflects the median most-preferred outcome of local voters. The quantity and kinds of government-provided services preferred by these voters can vary considerably across regions and might be very different from the median most-preferred outcome of all national voters on similar issues.

The means of financing government-provided services can vary with local desires when government is decentralized. Communities with strong interests in encouraging certain types of development, such as housing or new industry, can adapt their tax structures to provide incentives to achieve those goals. Similarly, insofar as notions of fairness in taxation vary across jurisdictions, a decentralized system of government can adjust its tax structure to attain those objectives.

However, as will be made clear presently, the tax and expenditure decisions in one governing jurisdiction are not independent of those in other jurisdictions. Within a system of decentralized government, citizens can be viewed as "shopping" for places to reside. Their locational decisions, in part, are influenced by the menu of services and the associated taxes at alternative local government jurisdictions. By the same token, local governments can find their goals upset by reactions to their local political decisions. For example, a local jurisdiction that tries to tax the rich heavily while excusing the poor from taxes might find that its population mix changes over time as the rich leave, or choose not to reside there, while the poor flock in.

An Example

At the extreme, imagine a group of individuals who have similar tastes and who live together in a local community, each one of whom places a zero benefit on tennis courts. In such a community, under decentralized, local collective decision making, an election to consider government provision of such a good would receive no votes. In fact, it would be unlikely that any resident would even propose that such an issue be put up for vote, because a locally provided tennis court would benefit no one in town. If, however, the number of tennis courts per town were decided in a national election, with given tax shares under majority rule, the outcome would be the national median most-preferred number of tennis courts per town.

If the preferred number of tennis courts per town in other communities is greater than zero, the resultant equilibrium is likely to be some positive number of tennis courts. This means that residents in the town where no one wants tennis courts, even at zero price, would be forced to submit to construction of tennis courts in their town and to pay taxes to finance those tennis courts. Such an outcome is not efficient, and welfare can be improved by allowing each town to decide locally whether collectively to provide and finance such services. This assumes that tennis courts are local public goods and that no one living in other communities would be harmed or benefited in any way by the choice of a particular community to forgo tennis courts.

For certain government-provided services that have the characteristics of pure national public goods, uniformity across all regions is inevitable; and centralized provision of uniform amounts of such services in all locations are efficient, relative to local government attempts to supply diverse services. The opportunities for local diversity in national defense, economic stabilization, and income redistribution programs are nil, or at best, limited, as discussed previously.

Advantages of a Federal System of Government

The central problem of fiscal federalism is to understand the process by which various government functions are paired with various levels of government. This, in turn, requires an investigation of the linkage between the geographical portion of the population that makes collective choices on various public goods, the legal boundaries of political jurisdictions, and the range of external benefits for various government-supplied services. Likewise, given the size of government and the variation in tastes among citizens and regions, the variation in costs of producing government services also must be studied. In a normative sense, the problem of fiscal federalism is to find the efficient pairing of responsibility for deciding how much of, and what kinds of, government-provided goods and services to produce with geographically defined subsets of the population.

C H E C K P O I N T

1. What resource allocation issues are relevant to fiscal federalism?
2. What are local public goods?
3. What are the advantages of a federal system of government?

CITIZEN MOBILITY AND DECENTRALIZED GOVERNMENT

A **political jurisdiction** is a defined geographical area within which individuals make collective choices on government functions and government-provided services. Each political jurisdiction has a governing authority and its own political institutions. In a federal system of government, political jurisdictions are both centralized and decentralized. This provides both a national, or central, government as well as "lower" levels of government. Each citizen is within the jurisdiction of the central government. Lower levels of government represent subsets of the population, defined in terms of geographic boundaries. Only citizens of local political jurisdictions can participate in public choices that affect the provision of government-supplied services in that jurisdiction. Also, taxes to finance locally provided government services are paid mainly by residents of the political jurisdiction.

INTERNATIONAL VIEW

THE MODERN GLOBAL ECONOMY AND ITS CHALLENGES TO FEDERALISM

Federalism is on the move as we approach the twenty-first century. It is, however, moving in different directions. In the former Soviet Union, amid economic and political chaos, federalism has disintegrated as the republics that composed the former Union of Soviet Socialist Republics established themselves as sovereign political entities. Meanwhile in Europe, 1992 was a landmark year as the nations of the European Union pushed federalism beyond their national borders by agreeing to establish uniform regulations and harmonize their tax systems to establish an integrated economic community. "Europe 1992" eliminated trade barriers among the member states of the community. The reforms expanded the role of federalism by establishing a governmental authority that crosses borders of the European states. Border and customs controls between member nations of the European Union will be eliminated. Eventually a single currency for most members of the European Union will be created, and such currencies as French francs and Italian lira will become artifacts of the past.

The changes in Europe and the rest of the world will imply challenges for U.S. federalism. The European Union will become a formidable economic competitor. And the nations of Eastern Europe and the former Soviet Union also will become inviting places for foreign investment and job growth if they can achieve political and economic stability. The increased international competition for business and jobs will put pressures on American federalism to deliver better quality public services. Infrastructure and education have increasingly become the responsibility of state and local governments in the United States.° Adequate government inputs into private production and the highly educated and skilled labor force required to compete effectively in the modern global economy will require more resources allocated to traditional state and local government functions. To keep their economies healthy and ensure adequate economic growth, state governments will have to attract more industry. However, in the 1990s the 50 states not only will be competing among themselves for new industries and more jobs, they also will be competing with the European Union, the Pacific Rim, and indeed, the whole world! The challenge to the federal system is to provide government services that compete effectively with those offered at other locations in the world.

Because tax competition among states often limits their ability to raise revenue to finance infrastructure and education, some economists advocate an increasingly active federal role in the provision of these public services. One possibility to keep local control over these services is the use of national taxes with revenues dedicated to education and infrastructure and return these revenues to the states on the basis of a predetermined formula. The federal government will have to cope with both getting its deficit under control and making sure that key public services necessary to attract industry, currently a responsibility of state governments, can be financed in a period of increased fiscal stress for state governments.

°For a discussion of some of these issues, see Robert P. Strauss, "Fiscal Federalism and the Changing Global Economy," *National Tax Journal* 43, 3 (September 1990): 315–320.

The Tiebout Model

Some useful insights into government expenditures within such a decentralized system of local jurisdictions are obtained from a model developed by Charles M. Tiebout.[2] Tiebout points out that the level and mix of local expenditures and taxes are

---

[2]Charles M. Tiebout, "A Pure Theory of Local Expenditures," *Journal of Political Economy* 64 (October 1956): 416–424.

likely to exhibit wide variations among local political jurisdictions. Therefore, many citizens will choose to live in communities where the government budget best satisfies their own preferences for public services, provided they are not restricted in their mobility among communities. Thus, government expenditure and revenue patterns tend to be set on the local level; and the mobile citizen maximizes personal well-being by choosing to live in some particular political jurisdiction.

The Tiebout model assumes that all citizens are fully mobile among communities and possess full knowledge of the government budgets in alternative political jurisdictions. Many communities offer similar employment opportunities to citizens. An optimum community size is defined as that which corresponds to minimum unit costs of government services. Communities larger than the optimal size try to discourage new residents, while communities smaller than the optimal size attempt to attract new residents.

Under this set of restrictive assumptions, a quasi-market equilibrium is attained when all residents are located in the community that best satisfies their political preferences, subject to the constraint that all communities are providing government services at minimum unit costs. The constraint implies that some citizens might have to be content with a second-choice community. If all communities can supply government services at constant costs, implying no economies or diseconomies of scale, then equilibrium will be completely analogous to a market equilibrium. This is because, in the extreme case, an iconoclast can establish a one-person community that provides all the government services that he requires, and infinite number of communities are available to satisfy every citizen's preferences. In this situation, competition among communities would result in an efficient solution, similar to that produced by a perfectly competitive market economy.

Applicability of the Tiebout Model

Although the Tiebout model's basic assumptions are extremely restrictive, it does offer insights into some of the unique problems of government expenditure analysis within a decentralized context. Citizens are not completely mobile among communities, and often they possess only imperfect knowledge of local government budgets. Although there are a large number of communities within the federal system, they differ in their employment opportunities and in geographical and climatic conditions. That is to say, many factors other than political preferences for government expenditure are likely to affect the locational choices of citizens. The Tiebout model is relevant, though, because, at least at the margin, some households do respond to differences among government budgets in alternative communities.

In particular, the model appears to be useful in partially explaining the exodus of households from the central city to surrounding suburban communities that has occurred in the United States since the end of World War II. Clearly, mobility of households is not perfect. But, within a constrained geographic area, a citizen can change her place of residence to one in a neighboring political jurisdiction while maintaining her employment in her old political jurisdiction. The proliferation of private automobiles in the postwar era, and generally improved roads, made such moves relatively easy.

In part, citizens are motivated to move to smaller political jurisdictions in the suburbs of central cities because of lower tax rates and better quality government-provided services, such as schools, relative to those prevailing in the central cities. This is in accord with the basic tenets of the Tiebout hypothesis. Thus, the model is useful in explaining movements within a constrained geographical area constituting one relatively large labor market. It is not very useful in explaining moves across larger geographical areas, such as interstate, because of the impediments to mobility and the variety of other factors that influence locational choices.

INTERJURISDICTIONAL EXTERNALITIES AND LOCATIONAL CHOICES

Interjurisdictional externalities are costs or benefits of local government goods and services to residents who live in other political jurisdictions. These interjurisdictional externalities create problems for efficient operation of a federal system of governments because they result in benefits or costs that spill across the geographic boundaries of political jurisdictions. Interjurisdictional externalities also complicate the Tiebout model, because they cause residents of local communities to make decisions based on inadequate data. The Tiebout approach implies that local taxes are analogous to prices for local government services. Citizens who desire high quality and quantity of government services gravitate to those communities with relatively higher tax rates. The model suggests that citizens shop for a set of local government services in much the same manner as they shop for automobiles. Their choices of communities as residence sites depend on tax rates, local government services financed by revenues, and relative preferences for government and private expenditures. If, however, all government services are not financed through taxes on local bases, the alternative community tax rates do not accurately reflect the costs of those services and cannot be considered the full prices for such services. Furthermore, when local jurisdictions receive state or federal aid, the prices paid by residents are subsidized by higher levels of government.

The deduction of state and local taxes from the federal income tax base is an example of a cost spillover than enables local communities to finance their government services through a reduction in federal income tax collections. Thus, where there are spillover costs and benefits of local government activities, the competition among local governments is less likely to achieve efficiency.

A Recapitulation

In summary, the ability of households to express their preferences for alternative local government budgets by "voting on their feet" provides a partial explanation of residential choices in a constrained metropolitan area that comprises a relatively large labor market. The Tiebout model suggests that citizens choose their residence among communities solely on the basis of their demand for local public goods. The Tiebout equilibrium is efficient because, given personal demands for public services, no single voter can be made better off by moving to another political jurisdiction. The model implies that citizens of similar tastes congregate together in communities based on their preferences for local public goods.

Impediments to mobility on the regional and national levels, due chiefly to restrictions in employment opportunities, make the conclusions of the Tiebout model questionable, if applied to regional residential choices.

Local taxes are not likely to be an accurate measure of the prices for local government services because of the existence of spillover costs and benefits. All these factors result in an equilibrium residential-choice pattern that is not efficient. At any point in time, some persons are dissatisfied with their current political jurisdiction but, for one reason or another, are not able to move. Other residents can move either into or out of a community in response to tax rates that do not represent the true marginal costs of local government services.

THE THEORY OF TAXATION WITHIN A DECENTRALIZED SYSTEM

The Local Tax Base

The ability of tax bases to migrate partially from one taxing jurisdiction to another creates problems that constrain the revenue-raising capabilities of local governing units. The possibility of induced locational effects of local taxation is well recognized by local governing authorities.[3] Such recognition might account, in part, for local reliance on property taxation in the United States. Real property is relatively immobile compared with the other tax bases. It is impossible to relocate land from one community to another, and shifts in the supply of structures on the land generally occur only in the long run. However, this does not suggest that local property tax policy can have no effect on the value of the property tax base. Unrestrained property taxation can result in reduced economic development of a locality and, consequently, reduced value of its real property tax base.

However, the local government-supplied goods and services financed with local taxes also can have an effect on property values in a community. If a community uses its property taxes to finance high-quality schools, the demand for property in that jurisdiction could be increased. The increase in the demand for real property increases its price in the jurisdiction. This increase in price could more than offset the reduction in price due to positive differentials in property tax rates.

Elasticity of the Local Tax Base

The **elasticity of the tax base,** E_T, is the ratio of the percentage change in the tax base attributable to any given percentage change in the tax rate applied to that base:

$$E_T = \frac{\Delta B/B}{\Delta t/t} = \frac{t\Delta B}{B\Delta t},$$

(18.1)

---

[3]See Advisory Commission on Intergovernmental Relations (ACIR), *Interstate Tax Competition* (Washington, D.C.: U.S. Government Printing Office, March 1981).

where B is the tax base in dollars, and t is the percentage rate of taxation. Tax revenue is equal to tB. For example, if the tax base is \$10 million of labor income per year and the tax rate is 20 percent, tax revenue is $(.2)($10 million)$, which is \$2 million per year.

The elasticity of the tax base is usually negative. Two opposing influences are exerted on the revenues collected when tax rates are changed. An increase in tax rates causes a favorable effect on revenues, stemming from the increase in the rates themselves. On the other hand, an offsetting effect decreases revenues, resulting from the decrease in the size of the tax base induced by the rate increases. Which effect dominates depends on the magnitude of the elasticity of the tax base with respect to the tax rate.

The three possibilities are that the tax base may be elastic ($E_T < -1$), of unitary elasticity ($E_T = -1$), or inelastic ($E_T > -1$). If it is elastic, any given percentage increase in the tax rate is offset by a larger percentage decrease in the size of the tax base. Under such circumstances, an increase in tax rates will reduce tax revenues collected because the change in revenues collected is the combined effect of the percentage increase in tax rates and the percentage decrease in the size of the tax base. When the tax base is elastic, the percentage decrease in the size of the base exceeds the percentage increase in tax rates, causing a fall in revenues.

By similar reasoning, if the elasticity of the tax base, with respect to the tax rate, is unitary, any given percentage change in tax rates will be exactly offset by an equal and opposite percentage change in the tax base, causing total revenues collected to remain constant. Only in those circumstances for which the elasticity of the tax base, with respect to the tax rate, is greater than -1 (that is, close to zero) can an increase in the rate of taxation increase revenues collected. The relation among elasticity of the tax base, tax rates, and revenues collected is summarized in Table 18.1.

Tax bases are very elastic when individuals can engage in the taxed activity in alternative political jurisdictions, where the tax is not present or exists at lower rates. This is of particular concern to state and local governments. If, for example, one state increases its income tax rates significantly above the rates in neighboring states, some workers, and employers, will relocate to neighboring states where the income tax rates are lower. At the extreme, if the tax-rate differential becomes very high, the high-tax state might find tax revenues actually decreasing in response to high tax

Table 18.1 ✦ Tax Base Elasticity, Tax Rates, and Revenues (Assuming a Negative Relationship between the Tax Base and Tax Rates)

Values of E_T	Changes in T (Tax Rates)	Changes in Revenues (TB)
$E_T > -1$ (Inelastic)	An increase in t A decrease in t	Revenues increase Revenues decrease
$E_T = -1$ (Unit Elastic)	Either an increase or decrease in t	No change in Revenues
$E_T < -1$ (Elastic)	An increase in t A decrease in t	Revenues decrease Revenues increase

rates. Local taxing authorities therefore are concerned with the elasticity of the local tax base with respect to the rate of taxation. So long as resources are mobile among political jurisdictions, the knowledge of elasticities is crucial to the implementation of effective local tax and expenditure policies. If the local tax base is elastic with respect to the rate of taxation, then increases in the rates of taxation result in a reduction, rather than an increase, in tax revenue collected. An increase in the rate of taxation applied to any base results in an increase in revenue collections from that base if, and only if, the tax base is inelastic with respect to the rate of taxation.

Among the factors that determine the elasticity of the tax base are the degree of mobility of taxed resources, the rates of taxation applied to similar tax bases in surrounding communities, the public services supplied by surrounding communities, and the initial amount of revenues collected from that base compared with, for example, local income. In addition, the services financed through the increase in tax rates affect locational choices by households and business firms, which, in turn, affect the value of the local tax base. If individual economic units feel that extra taxation exceeds the benefits that they obtain from increased public expenditure, they will consider relocation, other things being equal.

Because of mobility of resources and the presence of alternative tax jurisdictions that provide similar public services, taxes that might be neutral when imposed on the national level can have distorting effects when imposed on the local level. For example, a lump-sum tax has zero excess burden on the national level but is likely to induce locational effects when imposed on the local level, if households are mobile and alternative communities exist. Individuals who wish to avoid the local lump-sum tax can simply move to another community where the tax is not used. If the adult population (the tax base under the lump-sum tax) of the locality is elastic with respect to the rate of taxation, any increase in the tax results in a decrease in revenue.

Taxes that account for only very small percentages of taxpayers' income are likely to have tax bases that are inelastic with respect to the rate of taxation. For example, an increase of 10 percent in the rate of taxation applied to a tax base that currently yields revenue equal to less than 1 percent of local income results in less resource transfers among communities than does an equivalent increase applied to a tax base that currently yields 15 percent of local income. In general, the greater the degree of uniformity among local tax and expenditure policies, the less elastic is the local tax base. Within local taxing jurisdictions in the federal system, no tax base is completely inelastic. Injudicious taxation of any given base eventually erodes that base, as resources are reallocated among jurisdictions to avoid the burden of local taxation.[4] Because tax rates are often changed in discrete rather than continuous variations,

---

[4]Elasticities of supplies of inputs to particular areas are much higher than their national levels. Research estimates indicate that those elasticities vary from 20 to 100. See Timothy W. McGuire and Leonard A. Rapping, "The Role of Market Variables and Key Bargains in the Manufacturing Wage Determination Process," *Journal of Political Economy* 76 (September–October 1968): 1015–1036, and "The Supply of Labor and Manufacturing Wage Determination in the United States: An Empirical Estimation," *International Economic Review* 11 (June 1970): 258–268.

threshold levels of taxation come into play, beyond which any sharp increases induce economic decision-making units to relocate their economic activities. The tax base also is likely to become more elastic over time, as it often takes time for citizens to make the adjustments required to avoid taxes.

Tax Competition and Tax Exporting

The elasticity of tax bases often results in competition among communities for residents and business firms whose economic activities increase the value of local tax bases. Such competition often acts as a constraint on the sizes of local public budgets. Local tax jurisdictions hesitate to increase tax rates for fear of putting themselves at competitive disadvantages, relative to other jurisdictions, as sites for the conduct of various kinds of economic activities. The expenditure sides of local budgets also are considered factors in the location decisions of economic units. Jurisdictions that are reluctant to raise taxes might lack public services that attract citizens as residents.

The willingness of local residents to support higher taxes also can depend on the extent to which local jurisdictions succeed in exporting their taxes to residents of other political jurisdictions. Thus, a $1 increase in taxes might be valued at less than $1 by local taxpayers, if they know that part of the increase in taxes will be paid by residents of other political jurisdictions.

Tax exporting is common in many resort communities, where environmental attributes make them unique and popular with tourists. Taxes on hotel accommodations are likely to be paid exclusively by tourists and other nonresidents, but they might be used to finance locally produced public services. To the extent to which cities also must provide public services to these nonresidents, it can be argued that those taxes finance police departments and sanitation services that are necessarily bigger to meet the demands for services by these nonresidents, particularly during peak-season periods.

In a sense, the deductibility of state and local income taxes from federal income taxes is a form of tax exporting. It allows state and local governments to shift a portion of their taxes to the national level in the form of reduced federal income tax collections.

C H E C K P O I N T

1. What are the assumptions and major conclusions of the Tiebout model of decentralized government?
2. What are interjurisdictional externalities?
3. Why are local tax bases more elastic than national tax bases?

VARIATION IN FISCAL CAPACITY

Fiscal capacity is a measure of the ability of a jurisdiction to finance government-provided services. The fiscal capacities of local governing units are likely to vary with the values of local tax bases and with the ability to "export" taxes. Taxing jurisdictions

P U B L I C   P O L I C Y   P E R S P E C T I V E

INTERSTATE TAX EXPORTATION IN THE UNITED STATES

Many state governments in the United States do succeed, to varying degrees, in exporting their tax burden to residents of other states. Both winners and losers emerge in the tax-exporting game. Some states are net exporters of their tax burden, while other states, in effect, are net importers of the tax burdens of other states.

Tax exportation arises in a variety of ways. State taxes can reduce the income of out-of-state input owners who employ their inputs in the state's taxing jurisdiction. Tax exporting also can occur if state taxes raise the price of goods and services purchased by out-of-state individuals. Nonresidents who buy these goods pay part of the taxes that are shifted forward to consumers.

Finally, the deductibility of state and local income and property taxes from taxable income under the federal personal income tax also can result in tax exportation. This is because deductibility reduces the federal income tax liability of state residents. The resulting loss in federal revenue implies that federal tax rates must be higher than they otherwise would be or that the federal budget deficit is greater than otherwise would be the case. In addition, if state taxes reduce the income of input owners in the state, federal tax revenue will also fall. This implies that high-tax states with high-income residents who itemize deductions indirectly shift the burden of their taxes to residents of other states through a consequent reduction in federal tax collections.

Recent research on state corporate income taxes and business property taxes indicates that states with a large proportion of capital input owned predominantly by out-of-state individuals will tend to be net exporters of these taxes. The state of New York is a major exporter

of both these taxes. Florida is a state whose residents are net importers of business and corporate taxes levied in other states.[*]

In 1980, estimates by Morgan and Mutti indicate, Alaska succeeded in exporting more than 60 percent of its total business and personal taxes. In addition to Florida, states whose residents pay major portions of taxes raised in other states included Delaware, Washington, and Alabama. Business taxes appear to be more easily exported to residents of other states than are personal taxes.

Another recent research study on tax exporting concentrated on local taxes designed to fall on out-of-state visitors. These include hotel occupancy taxes and taxes on entertainment activities. Analysis of the incidence of a hotel room occupancy tax in Hawaii indicated that a substantial portion of the tax is exported to residents of other states (and nations).[†] The researchers estimate that the price elasticity of demand for hotel rooms is about −1, while the price elasticity of supply is about 2. This implies that about two-thirds of the hotel room tax is reflected in higher prices for a room. The remainder of the tax is borne by owners of the hotels. They also estimate about 45 percent of the hotel rooms in Hawaii are owned by nonresidents. This implies that almost half of the remaining one-third of the tax is also borne by out-of-state individuals. A tax on hotel rooms, particularly if many of the hotels are owned by out-of-state investors, therefore is a good means of exporting taxes.

Taxes on nonlodging expenditures by tourists are less likely to be exported, because a large portion of these expenditures is by residents. According to the researchers, general sales taxes, taxes on amusements, and taxes on food and alcoholic beverages, although likely to be shifted to consumers, are less likely to be exported than hotel room taxes.

[*]William E. Morgan and John H. Mutti, "The Exportation of State and Local Taxes in Multilateral Framework: The Case of Business Type Taxes," *National Tax Journal* 38 (June 1985): 191–208.
[†]Edwin Fujii, Mohammed Khaled, and James Mak, "The Exportability of Hotel Occupancy and Other Tourist Taxes," *National Tax Journal* 38 (June 1985): 169–177.

with relatively low tax bases in dollar terms find it more difficult to raise tax revenues than do wealthier, high-income jurisdictions. Insofar as the demands for local public services do not increase with fiscal capacities, low tax-base communities are likely to encounter difficulties in supplying acceptable minimum levels and qualities of public services. Given the tax revenue required, the lower the average income in a community, the higher the tax rates.

For example, consider the fiscal consequences of different per capita income levels among states. If each state supplies the same per capita amount of public services at the same cost to its citizens, and finances all these expenditures by income taxes that fall solely on residents in the state, then it follows that the proportionate per capita tax burdens as a percentage of income are greater in those states with lower incomes. Alternatively, if tax rates are the same in all states, and all public expenditures are financed by state taxes, then those states with lower per capita income supply less and lower-quality public services.

Measures of Fiscal Capacity

Among the commonly used measures of fiscal capacity for state and local governments are per capita income; per capita retail sales; and assessed valuation per capita, or per pupil, for school districts. All these measure the value of the tax base per person in the political jurisdiction. Because local governments rely heavily on property taxes, the measure most relevant for this level of government would be *assessed valuation per capita*. When the property tax base is used mainly to finance schooling services, *assessed valuation per pupil* might be a better measure of the capacity to finance government-supplied services. These measures are imperfect in that they do not consider the extent to which a jurisdiction exports tax burdens to residents of other jurisdictions, and vice versa.

In addition to measuring fiscal capacity, it is useful, on occasion, to measure the extent to which subnational governments provide services to their residents. A common measure of this is *per capita expenditure*. However, per capita expenditure is only imperfectly correlated with actual per capita services because of unit cost variations.

It is also useful to measure the extent to which the fiscal capacity of a state compares with that of other states. Usually, this is done by dividing measures of the fiscal capacity, such as per capita income, of that state or locality by the national average of that measure. Similarly, per capita expenditure could be divided by the national average for other nonfederal governments. States and localities with fiscal capacity less than the national average, and per capita expenditure less than the national average, would be candidates for fiscal equalization grants by the central government.

Revenue Effort

Revenue effort is the ratio of tax collections from all sources in a taxing jurisdiction, as a percentage of personal income in that jurisdiction, to the national average of that ratio for all jurisdictions. As a measure of the extent to which a local government is tapping its tax base, revenue effort has a number of serious shortcomings. It does not consider the fact that jurisdictions with low levels of personal income require high revenue effort to maintain the same level of per capita public expenditure financed in jurisdictions that have high levels of personal income. Differences in revenue effort also can be explained by different costs and demands among the taxing jurisdictions. In general, areas with higher population densities and greater percentages of their populations living in cities require greater levels of local government expenditure.

Differences in revenue effort also reflect differences in collective choices among communities for the allocation of resources between public and private uses.

A value for revenue effort that is greater than 100 percent for a given type of taxing jurisdiction implies that the jurisdiction is raising a greater amount of revenue than the national average per dollar of personal income. This, in turn, can imply a number of things. First, citizens in this taxing jurisdiction might have strong demands for local government-supplied services compared with other communities. Second, it might be that the community has a lower level of per capita income relative to other communities and therefore requires greater revenue effort to maintain the national average of per capita government expenditure. Finally, it could be that this community, because of either geographic or demographic characteristics, requires more per capita expenditure than the national average to meet the basic demands for government-provided services by its populace.

The chief shortcoming of the revenue-effort measure is the fact that it ignores the expenditure side of the budget. The extent to which citizens in a community wish to tax themselves depends on the collective choices made concerning the allocation of resources between government and private uses. Revenue-effort statistics therefore must be used in conjunction with data on per capita expenditure and per capita tax base values to provide useful information on the need for fiscal equalization of the capacity to finance goods and services.

INTERGOVERNMENTAL FISCAL RELATIONS

Variation in fiscal capacity among states and local governments provides a basis in intergovernmental aid to ensure minimum levels of certain public services in all regions of a nation. Intergovernmental aid is also a way to help achieve a more efficient allocation of resources in the government sector by internalizing interjurisdictional externalities. In fiscal year 1989, federal aid was a major source of revenue to state and local government, accounting for 16 percent of revenue. Local governments also rely heavily on grants from state governments to finance their expenditures. Grants are intergovernmental transfers of purchasing power that can be used to help achieve a wide variety of social objectives.

Grants differ mainly in terms of the restrictions that are placed on the use of funds by recipient governments. Some grants are transfers with literally no strings attached. Other grants merely require that the recipient government spend the funds in a broad general area, such as education or transportation. The most restrictive types of grants are those that the recipient government must spend on a particular service or project. A review of the various types of grants currently in use is an appropriate way to start the analysis of intergovernmental fiscal relations.

Types of Grants

A **categorical grant-in-aid** is a transfer of funds from a higher level of government to a lower level, with specified conditions attached to the expenditure of the funds.

Many categorical grants from the federal to state and local governments are for payments to individuals for income support or health care. The Medicaid program is a categorical grant to states to provide health services to low-income persons and is the largest federal grant-in-aid program. Federal highway grants are categorical grants to states to help fund roads and bridges. Some federal grants contain the requirement that recipient jurisdictions match each dollar of federal aid with a certain amount of locally raised revenue. These are known as **matching grants.** General **unconditional grants** differ from categorical grants in that revenues are shared among governments, with no strings attached to the use of the funds.

Federal aid to encourage expenditure on particular projects is used as an inducement to state and local governments to pursue activities in general accord with national goals. Perhaps the most famous example of an early categorical grant-in-aid program is the nineteenth century Morrill Act, which established the so-called land-grant colleges in the states. Essentially, this program granted both land and funds to states that agreed to establish colleges of various kinds. In effect, this served to internalize some of the interjurisdictional benefits associated with higher education by subsidizing state expenditure for public colleges.

Federal Grants

Since 1970 federal categorical grants that provide transfers to individuals have increased enormously. The bulk of these grants has been to state and local governments to fund federally mandated entitlements to individuals under such programs as Medicaid and cash transfer programs that provide public assistance to the poor including AFDC and SSI (see Chapter 7). An estimated 66 percent of total federal grants of $220 billion to state and local governments in 1994 was for entitlement programs that are essentially grants to individuals rather than grants to governments.

Table 18.2 shows that federal grants-in-aid to state and local governments grew rapidly in the 1970s and then slowed down considerably in the 1980s. Federal grants are expected to grow more quickly in the 1990s, both as a share of federal revenue and as a share of GDP, than they did in the 1980s mainly because of the projected growth in grants to individuals through entitlement programs. In 1991 half of all federal grants to state and local governments were accounted for by public welfare payments. Table 18.3 shows grants by category in 1991.

The major functions for which federal transfers are made directly to local governments include education, housing and community redevelopment, waste treatment facilities, and airport construction. Again, these are areas of expenditure likely to have spillover effects. If categorical grants are to be efficient tools for internalizing externalities, then they must be allocated according to a system that accurately evaluates spillovers and their ranges. To internalize externalities, a grant must reduce the net cost to local citizens of the activity that generates the externality to citizens of other local governments. In addition, if opportunities exist for communities to engage in bargaining to internalize externalities, then categorical grants are unnecessary and their use could result in inefficiencies.

States also make grants to their own local governmental subdivisions. As in federal aid, the bulk of such funds appears to be designed to internalize externalities caused

Table 18.2   ✦   FEDERAL GRANTS-IN-AID SUMMARY: FISCAL YEARS 1970 TO 1994

YEAR	TOTAL GRANTS (BIL. DOL.)	AVERAGE ANNUAL PERCENT CHANGE[a]	GRANTS TO INDIVIDUALS		GRANTS AS PERCENT OF—		
			TOTAL (BIL. DOL.)	PERCENT OF TOTAL GRANTS	STATE-LOCAL GOVT. OUTLAYS[b]	FEDERAL OUTLAYS	GROSS DOMESTIC PRODUCT
1970	24.0	17.2	8.6	35.8	19.0	12.3	2.4
1975	49.8	15.7	16.4	33.0	22.6	15.0	3.1
1980	91.5	10.4	31.9	34.9	25.8	15.5	3.3
1985	105.9	8.5	48.1	45.4	20.9	11.2	2.6
1988	115.3	6.4	61.0	52.9	18.2	10.8	2.4
1989	121.8	5.6	65.9	54.1	17.3	10.7	2.3
1990	136.9	12.2	78.6	57.5	17.9	10.9	2.5
1991	152.0	12.1	89.9	59.2	20.5	11.5	2.7
1992, estimate	182.2	19.9	114.6	62.9	(NA)	12.3	3.1
1993, projection	199.1	9.3	128.8	64.7	(NA)	13.1	3.2
1994, projection	220.1	10.5	145.5	66.1	(NA)	14.9	3.3

NA Not available.   [a]Average annual percent change from prior year shown.   [b]Outlays as defined in the national income and product accounts.
Source: Advisory Commission on Intergovernmental Relations, Washington, DC, *Significant Features of Fiscal Federalism,* 1992 Edition, vol. II, based on *Budget of the United States Government,* FY 93, table 12.1.

by inappropriate sizes of the collective decision making units. The major local functions subsidized by state-aid programs are education, public welfare, and highways.

When spillovers exist, the tendency is for either overspending or underspending, depending on whether costs or benefits are spilling over and on the extent of spillovers among communities. When the spillovers lead to an undersupply of public services, matching categorical grants-in-aid are reasonable tools to use to subsidize government activities that generate external benefits. The existence of a categorical grant program for a particular function induces an increase in local expenditure. However, in most functions that generate external benefits, all the benefits are not appropriable by the communities that are responsible for supply decisions. Educational expenditure, for example, tends to spill out because some of the recipients of education relocate to other areas after they finish their schooling. On the other hand, many recipients of educational services do remain in the community in which they are educated. Thus, efficiency considerations imply that some matching of funds is desirable.

Ideally, the federal share of costs for a program is equal to the percentage of net benefits spilling out from a particular local area. The local share is based on an estimate of the benefits retained by the community. Although this is desirable, in principle, accurate computations of spillouts virtually are impossible because of problems

Table 18.3   ◆   Federal Aid to State and Local Governments, By Category, 1991

Category	Amount (Millions of Dollars)
Public Welfare	72,661
Education	25,195
Highways	14,561
Housing and Community development	10,233
Health and Hospitals	6,504
Other	24,943
Total	154,097

Source: U.S. Bureau of the Census, *Government Finances, 1991.*

in quantifying and evaluating collectively consumed goods. However, some reasoned estimates of appropriate matching formulas are useful and are likely to improve resource allocations.

Unrestricted Grants and Fungibility

For the purpose of studying intergovernmental relations, it is useful to discuss unrestricted and restricted intergovernmental grants separately. Unrestricted grants include what often are referred to as **general revenue sharing.** The United States had a general revenue sharing program that was terminated in 1986. Restricted grants are those available only for a specific purpose, and they must be spent on that purpose. Restricted grants have auditing requirements that limit the way the funds, once granted, can be spent. **Block grants,** a principal type of unrestricted grant, have only minimal restrictions on the uses to which the funds can be put and rarely require matching funds raised locally.

The distinction between restricted and unrestricted grants is somewhat artificial because of the **fungibility** of money, which means that money can be used for more than one purpose. A grant, with or without restrictions on the use of funds, frees local tax monies that otherwise would be spent on government-provided services. The receipt of the grant could allow tax reductions that benefit citizens of recipient communities. If taxes are reduced as a result of the grant, citizens can increase their consumption of private goods and services beyond the amounts that would be possible if they had to finance all government-supplied goods and services through locally raised tax revenue. In other words, the funds might end up being used for any purpose, even though they were intended for a specific use. However, matching grants tend to stimulate government spending to a greater degree than nonmatching grants. A grant increases net resources flowing to a local or state government only to the extent to which the grant increases the net funds available for both government and private spending in that community, over and above the federal, or central, government taxes paid by the local citizens in that community to finance the grant program expenditures in all localities.

THE THEORY OF GRANTS

Grants and other forms of intergovernmental fiscal assistance are essentially gifts, or subsidies, from one level of government to another level. Usually, the recipient government is on a level lower than that of the donor government. These subsidies can be expected to affect the political equilibrium, with consequent changes in the observed expenditure and tax policies collectively agreed upon by citizens who live in the recipient political jurisdiction. The process by which such grants change behavior patterns in recipient jurisdictions must be understood in order to predict whether the grant will accomplish the result for which it is intended.

Matching grants, under various categorical grant programs, are more likely to stimulate citizens of recipient governments to agree collectively to expanded production of public goods than are equal-dollar-amount general-purpose grants. The latter grants neither require matching funds raised from local taxes nor restrict the purpose for which the grant funds must be spent. The basic reason for the more stimulative effect attributed to matching grants is the fact that such grants reduce the marginal and average cost of the public good to citizens of the recipient government. This sets up both income and substitution effects that influence citizens' collective choices. A nonmatching grant, such as that used for revenue sharing or general fiscal assistance, results only in income effects and is less effective in increasing the willingness of citizens to support increased local public spending.

Suppose the distribution of taxes among citizens per unit of a public good, such as a road, is given. For example, say each citizen pays $1 per mile of new road surfaces supplied per year. A matching grant for public goods will be available only if citizens allocate local tax revenue to the project. For example, if the grant requires a 50-percent matching of revenue, matching funds will be made available if local authorities allocate from their own revenue 50 cents per citizen per mile of new roads. In effect, *in terms of local taxes,* the matching grant reduces the marginal cost of each mile of road from $1 to 50 cents per citizen. This 50-percent reduction in the tax per mile of road per citizen results in a substitution effect, leading individual citizens to support more government spending on roads.

The income effect of the grant depends on the income elasticity of the demand for public goods. Depending on the individual tastes of citizens, the income elasticity can be positive or negative. The impact of the income effect of any grant on the political equilibrium therefore is difficult to predict. The income effect is likely to have the effect of increasing consumption of both private goods and public goods, as its effect on the political equilibrium might be to induce citizens to support local tax reductions.

General-purpose or categorical grants, without matching requirements, result *only* in income effects. No substitution effect is caused because such grants do not reduce the tax per unit of government-provided goods to individual citizens. Therefore, it is conceivable that, under certain circumstances, general-purpose grants can decrease the amount of government-supplied goods and services produced by the recipient community if enough citizens in the community view these goods and services as inferior (negative income elasticity of demand). This is less likely to be the result with matching grants because substitution effects always will occur to counter any income effects acting to decrease the consumption of the public good.

MATCHING VERSUS GENERAL-PURPOSE GRANTS: AN APPLICATION OF THE THEORY OF COLLECTIVE CHOICE UNDER MAJORITY RULE

Consider the case of two equal grants that finance a single public good. Assume that the grants are equal in amount but that one grant has a matching requirement while the other is simply a direct transfer to the recipient government. Assuming that collective choices are made by simple majority rule in the recipient jurisdiction, Bradford and Oates have shown that the matching grant will result in a political equilibrium at a higher level of production for the public good.[5]

The Initial Political Equilibrium

Suppose that collective choices in the recipient government are made under simple majority rule and that taxes per unit of the public good are given for each voter. If, as illustrated in Figure 18.1, the marginal tax per unit of the public good of each voter is

---

[5]David F. Bradford and Wallace E. Oates, "Towards a Predictive Theory of Intergovernmental Grants," *American Economic Review* 61 (May 1971): 440–449. The analysis presented here follows Bradford and Oates.

Figure 18.1 ◆ POLITICAL EQUILIBRIUM: A MATCHING GRANT VERSUS A NONMATCHING GRANT OF EQUAL VALUE

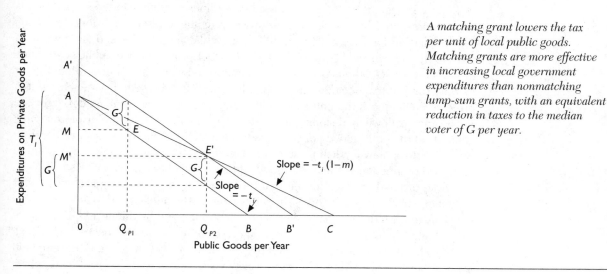

A matching grant lowers the tax per unit of local public goods. Matching grants are more effective in increasing local government expenditures than nonmatching lump-sum grants, with an equivalent reduction in taxes to the median voter of G per year.

t_i, then the initial budget line for each voter would have slope $-t_i$. This slope gives the expenditure on private goods per year that must be given up by each citizen to finance each extra unit of the public good, such as miles of new roads, per year. In actuality, the marginal tax per unit of the public good, t_i, varies from voter to voter.

In Figure 18.1, the indifference curves of the voter whose budget line is illustrated are omitted to avoid cluttering the diagram. Assume, however, that the indifference curves have the standard shapes and that, given the voter's tax per unit of the public good and his preferences, the voter has his most-preferred mix of expenditure on private goods per year and units of public goods per year represented by point E. At that point, he consumes Q_{P1} units of the public good, gives up AM of his income in taxes, and retains OM of his income for expenditure on private goods. Assume that the voter whose equilibrium is illustrated in Figure 18.1 is the median voter. It follows that his individual optimum will correspond to the political equilibrium, provided that all voters have single-peaked preferences (see Chapter 5).

Other voters whose most-preferred mixes of expenditure on private goods and public goods do not correspond to the median will end up consuming either more or less than their most-preferred amount of the public good, after the political equilibrium is reached.

Impact of a Matching Grant on the Political Equilibrium

Suppose, now, that a matching grant is made available to citizens in the local jurisdiction. The effect of the grant is to reduce the tax rate per unit of the public good for each voter. If the donor government's proportionate share of increased costs associated with more public goods is m, then each voter's tax share would fall by m times his original tax share. The tax share of each voter now is $t_i(1 - m)$. For example, if $m = .5$, the tax per unit of the public good would fall by 50 percent for each citizen. This would rotate the voter budget line from AB to AC as the introduction of the matching grants reduces tax rates per unit of the public good for all voters by the same fraction, m. Suppose, again, that the voter whose budget lines are illustrated in Figure 18.1 is the median voter. This voter's most-preferred outcome would move from E to say, E'. This implies an increase in the output of the public good to Q_{P2} and an increase in taxes to the voter from AM to AM'. The full cost of producing the public good, however, is $AM' + G$, where G is the voter's imputed dollar share of government grant to the community. Because the voter illustrated is the median voter, his most-preferred outcome is the political equilibrium. As long as the demand curve for the public good is downward sloping for each voter, all voters would prefer more annual amounts of the public good per year under the matching arrangement. It is therefore certain that the new median peak, or most-preferred outcome, would correspond to increased production of the public good and correspond to a point such as E'.

Bradford and Oates point out that the impact of the grant is equivalent to a tax reduction equal to the fraction of the tax per unit of the public good to individual voters. This result indicates that the effect of the grant could be duplicated, in terms of the political equilibrium it generates, by a tax credit to all voters equal to the fraction, m, of each voter's share of the total budget spent on the public good. For example, if the median voter is told that he will receive a cash payment in terms of a tax rebate each year equal to a fraction, m, of the amount actually paid in taxes, his most-preferred amount of the public good would be Q_{P2}. He would pay $T_i = (AM' + G)$ in taxes but would receive G as a rebate equal to mT_i. His net taxes therefore would be AM'.

This is a very interesting and useful result. It suggests that nothing is uniquely special about matching grants to governments. Insofar as these grants upset the political equilibrium in recipient governments, they do so by altering the tax shares to citizens. Provided that the grant itself does not change the basic political institutions of the recipient government, its effects are equivalent to a reduction in taxes to individual taxpayers, and the impact of the grant can be duplicated by simply giving local taxpayers tax credits against their local tax bills.

This model of grants assumes that the bureaucrats and politicians respond to the desires of the median voter. Some models suggest that the mechanism involved in government grants is such that the normal political process can be bypassed by bureaucrats who spend the funds. These models presume that the bureaucrats who receive the grant funds will spend the money according to their own goals without voters ever being given the opportunity to express their desires. The bypassing of the normal political process by local bureaucrats is called the **flypaper effect**.[6] The funds seem to stick to the hands of the local politicians and get spent before voters can be polled. In fact, some evidence shows that the tendency to spend grant money on government programs is higher than the tendency to spend private income on such programs.[7]

Impact of a Nonmatching General-Purpose Grant on the Political Equilibrium

Now, consider the effect of a nonmatching lump-sum or general-purpose grant, with no strings attached, made available to a local government. Essentially, this is a gift to citizens in that political jurisdiction and can be thought of, again, as a reduction in local taxes to individual citizens. To compare the effect of the general-purpose grant with the matching grant, suppose that the individual's imputed share of the general-purpose grant is G, equal to the matching grant at the political equilibrium of Q_{P2} units of the public good, as illustrated in Figure 18.1 and discussed previously. Such a grant can be illustrated as a parallel shift upward of the budget line by G to $A'B'$. For each voter, the aggregate grant to the government is equivalent to a subsidy, G, equal to the imputed share of what the voter would receive under the matching grant. The

---

[6]See Edward M. Gramlich, "Intergovernmental Grants: A Review of the Empirical Literature," in *The Political Economy of Fiscal Federalism*, ed. Wallace E. Oates (Lexington, MA: Lexington Books, 1977).

[7]See Martin C. McGuire, "A Method for Estimating the Effect of a Subsidy on the Receiver's Resource Constraint: With an Application to the U.S. Local Governments 1964–1971," *Journal of Public Economics* 10 (August 1978): 25–44. McGuire found that the tendency to convert grant funds to general fungible resources available for all uses rises with time, suggesting that, in the long run, the median preference model might prevail.

grant, because it has no strings attached, could allow voters to continue consuming Q_{P1} units of the public good and pocket the grant as a net increase in income to each taxpayer equivalent to AA'. However, this extreme result would occur only in the unlikely case that the income elasticity of the demand for public goods was zero for all voters. More likely, the grant will have the effect of increasing the production of public goods and allowing some reduction in tax rates to local citizens, so as to enable them to consume more private goods and public goods.

The new political equilibrium will be that corresponding to the most-preferred outcome of the median voter. As long as the income elasticity of demand for public goods is positive for at least some voters, an increased output of public goods is implied. This same political equilibrium could be generated by a federal income tax reduction for all citizens in the recipient government, proportionate to local citizens' local tax share in the total cost of the public good. In other words, the political outcome that results from a gift to the local government could have been achieved by a set of gifts to individual voters in that community. General-purpose grants therefore can be thought of as implicit subsidies that increase the income of residents of local jurisdictions and induce them to spend such increases in income on both public goods and private goods.

The impact of the general-purpose grant on the output of the public good will be less than is the case under the equivalent matching grant. The basic reason for this, as discussed, is that the matching grant will result in both income and substitution effects that influence the behavior of others, while the general-purpose grant therefore always will result in a political equilibrium to the left of point E' in Figure 18.1. The median voter therefore is likely to be in equilibrium under the lump-sum grant at a point to the left of E', implying that he consumes relatively less of the public good and retains more of the grant for other purposes through reduced local tax payments.[8]

Matching Grants and Efficiency

Categorical grants with matching requirements can be used to internalize interjurisdictional externalities and thereby promote efficiency. To see this, suppose that pollution control by local governments provides benefits not only to the citizens of the local jurisdiction but to *all* citizens. Suppose that the local political equilibrium results in the level of pollution control that corresponds to the point at which the sum of the marginal benefits of local residents equals the marginal social cost of abatement. If a positive interjurisdictional externality exists, less than the efficient amount of annual pollution abatement will be supplied by this local government, even though $\Sigma MB = MSC$ for local residents.

In Figure 18.2, a local government must spend \$10 to remove each pound of a certain pollutant from waste water. The current political equilibrium at point E corresponds to the point at which the sum of benefits to local citizens of the jurisdiction, ΣMB_L, equals the marginal social cost of pollution abatement, MSC, where MSC is assumed to be constant. At that point, 100,000 pounds of the pollutant are removed

---

[8]See Bradford and Oates, "Towards a Predictive Theory," for a more complete proof.

Figure 18.2 ✦ MATCHING GRANT

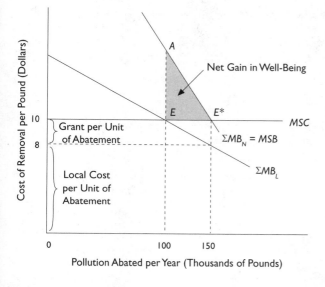

A matching grant can internalize interjurisdictional externalities. The grant allows a net gain in well-being.

each year at a cost to local taxpayers of $1 million per year. However, at point E, the marginal social benefit of pollution abatement exceeds its marginal social cost. This is because local pollution abatement results in positive interjurisdictional externalities to residents of other areas.

The efficient level of pollution abatement for this jurisdiction corresponds to point E^*, at which the sum of the *national* marginal benefits equals the marginal social cost of abatement. The sum of the national marginal benefits, ΣMB_N, is the marginal social benefit of pollution control, *MSB*. The efficient level of local abatement corresponds to 150,000 pounds per year.

A matching grant for pollution control can get the local residents to choose the efficient level of abatement. Local residents will demand 150,000 pounds of abatement per year if the price per pound is reduced from $10 to $8. This can be accomplished through a 20-percent matching grant. The federal government would agree to pay 20 percent, or $2 per pound, of pollution abatement. The local government would pay the remaining 80 percent of the costs. At a net price of $8 per pound, local citizens agree to provide 150,000 pounds of local pollution abatement. The total cost of this annual abatement is $1.5 million. Local taxpayers, however, pay only $1.2 million. The remaining $300,000 per year is paid and financed by the federal government.

The net increase in well-being to all citizens made possible by the matching grant is represented by the triangular area EAE^*. If the matching grant is provided to *all* localities, the increment in well-being would be equal to the gain in net benefits made possible by the improvement in efficiency in the pollution abatement decisions of *all* local jurisdictions.

CHECKPOINT

1. What is fiscal capacity and how well is it measured by revenue effort?
2. What types of grants are used by higher levels of government to aid lower levels of government?
3. What are the advantages of matching grants?

Summary

A federal system of government allows both centralized and decentralized collective choices. The more decentralized the government, the greater the opportunity to supply diverse levels and kinds of government-provided services. Fiscal federalism is the division of taxing and spending functions among levels of government. Central government most efficiently supplies those services most closely resembling pure public goods that benefit all citizens, regardless of their location. However, many public goods have only regional or local benefits, and these are possible to supply in a decentralized fashion, through local government and local political institutions.

Stabilization and income redistribution are two functions that have national collective benefits and are most effectively supplied by central government. The advantage of decentralized supply of government-supplied services, when feasible, is that it allows accommodation of a diversity of demands for such services within a nation. When individuals of similar tastes for government-provided services live together within a political jurisdiction, political externalities are minimized.

Pairing government-supplied services with political jurisdictions is a central problem of fiscal federalism. As the size of a political jurisdiction increases, so does the number of taxpayers; this decreases the per capita cost per unit of government output. This advantage is balanced against increased congestion costs when the size of the jurisdiction is expanded.

Citizen mobility allows individuals of similar tastes to congregate for the purpose of supplying government-provided services and sharing the costs of such services. This decreases political externalities within such jurisdictions. The Tiebout model examines the consequences of mobility in a decentralized system of government and concludes that mobility improves efficiency. In the Tiebout model, citizens are assumed to "shop" for local jurisdictions in which to reside, in much the same way that they shop for any consumer good.

Interjurisdictional externalities are caused by improper size of political jurisdictions. Such benefit or cost spillovers provide bases for government consolidation or federal subsidies to internalize the external effects. Local tax bases generally are more elastic than national tax bases, simply because individuals can easily avoid local taxes by changing the location of their economic activities.

Fiscal capacity is used as a basis of support for federal grants to equalize the capacity to finance basic public services among communities. Per capita expenditures are often used as an index of variations in government-supplied services among jurisdictions. Revenue effort is a crude index of the extent to which a jurisdiction is taxing its residents, relative to a national average.

Grants and other forms of intergovernmental fiscal assistance represent gifts, or subsidies, to recipient governments. As such, they disturb the political equilibrium in those governments and can influence the mix between public and private spending in the recipient jurisdiction. In general, matching grants are more likely to induce local governing authorities to increase public spending than are general-purpose grants.

Important Concepts

Federal System of Government
Fiscal Federalism
Local Public Goods
Political Jurisdiction
Interjurisdictional Externalities
Elasticity of the Tax Base

Fiscal Capacity
Revenue Effort
Categorical Grant-in-Aid
Matching Grants
Unconditional Grants
General Revenue Sharing
Block Grants
Fungibility
Flypaper Effect

Questions for Review

1. What are the advantages and disadvantages of decentralized government? Why can a federal system of government take advantage of both centralized and decentralized collective decision making?

2. Which public services are most likely to be efficiently provided by central government? What are the basic characteristics of such services?

3. Why are local governments likely to be limited to a greater degree than the central government in the extent to which they can engage in redistribution and stabilization programs?

4. Explain why the equilibrium quantities of government services supplied by a central government under majority rule, with all citizens voting, will differ from local political equilibriums for the amount of such goods when local elections are also decided by majority rule.

5. How many political jurisdictions do you reside in? List the government-provided services that you obtain from each of your jurisdictions. What kinds of taxes are levied in each jurisdiction to pay for those services?

6. Why does citizen mobility increase the desirability of decentralized decision making in relation to efficiency? What does Tiebout mean by "voting on your feet"? How does the Tiebout model explain residential location patterns?

7. What are interjurisdictional externalities? What problems does their existence create for a federal system?

8. How does the fungibility of money limit the value of the distinction between restricted and unrestricted grants?

9. Explain how a matching grant results in both income and substitution effects that affect the willingness of citizens to support increased local government spending. Why do nonmatching grants result only in income effects?

10. Why are matching grants likely to be more effective in increasing local government spending than are equal-dollar nonmatching grants? Explain how matching grants can help achieve efficiency by internalizing interjurisdictional externalities.

Problems

1. The average cost of employing each police officer per year is $30,000 for a small town. The current population of the town is 1,000. Calculate the per-capita cost per police officer. Explain why increased congestion costs associated with increased population can result in increased per-capita taxes, even though the per-capita cost per police officer declines with population.

2. Municipal zoning laws often are used as a means of controlling the population and income levels of citizens in a political jurisdiction. How can zoning laws that require homes to be built on a minimum lot size of one acre per residence affect the size and income level of a community? Why would a high-income community pass laws outlawing mobile homes and requiring minimum construction standards for homes?

3. The elasticity of the property tax base for the town of Elderberry is estimated to be -2. Assuming that this estimate is correct, what effect would a 10-percent increase in the property tax have on property value and tax revenue for Elderberry? Explain what economic factors could cause the results that you calculated?

4. All voters in a city pay an equal marginal tax rate of $10 per mile of roads paved per year. The federal government has a matching-grant program of road paving, in which 75 percent of the cost of road paving is paid. Show how the matching grant affects the budget constraint for a typical voter. In equilibrium, the community receives $1 million per year for road paving under the matching-grant program. Prove that the matching grant will be more effective in increasing road paving than a $1 million annual lump-sum grant.

Suggestions for Further Reading

Advisory Commission on Intergovernmental Relations. *Significant Features of Fiscal Federalism.* Published annually by the ACIR in two volumes with data on state and local government finance and analysis of trends in fiscal federalism.

Aronson, J. Richard, and Hilley, John L. *Financing State and Local Governments.* 4th ed. Washington, D.C.: The Brookings Institution, 1986. A textbook on general issues in state and local finance.

Break, George. *Financing Government in a Federal System.* Washington, D.C.: The Brookings Institution, 1980. Chapter 4 discusses urban fiscal systems and models of urban fiscal problems.

Conlan, Timothy. *New Federalism: Intergovernmental Reform from Nixon to Reagan.* Washington, D.C.: The Brookings Institution, 1988. Analysis of recent political and economic trends in U.S. federalism. Chapters 2 and 8 discuss block grants.

Fisher, Ronald C. *State and Local Public Finance.* Glenview, IL: Scott Foresman and Company, 1988. A textbook emphasizing issues in state and local government finance.

Gold, Steven D., ed. *The Unfinished Agenda for State Tax Reform.* Denver: National Conference of State Legislatures, November 1988. A collection of essays on recent state tax reforms and other issues relating to state government finance.

Hirsch, Werner Z. *The Economics of State and Local Government.* New York: McGraw-Hill, 1970. A comprehensive analysis of all aspects of state and local government expenditure and finance.

Oates, Wallace E. *Fiscal Federalism.* New York: Harcourt Brace Jovanovich, 1972. An analysis of public finance in a federal system. Discusses the question of optimal jurisdiction size and optimal division of responsibility among levels of government. Includes empirical analysis.

Oates, Wallace E., ed. *The Political Economy of Fiscal Federalism.* Lexington, MA: Lexington Books, 1977. Articles on various aspects of federalism and local government finance.

Oates, Wallace E. "Federalism and Government Finance" in John M. Quigley and Eugene Smolensky. *Modern Public Finance.* Cambridge, Mass.: Harvard University Press, 1994, pp. 126–164. An analysis of issues in local government finance including discussion of how tax exporting can lead to inefficient levels of spending by state and local governments and how such distortions justify federal grants.

GLOSSARY

Ability-to-Pay Principle
Maintains that taxes should be distributed according to the capacity of taxpayers to pay them.

Accelerated Depreciation
Deduction of more than the actual economic depreciation of a business asset each year to determine taxable income.

Ad Valorem Taxes
Taxes levied as a percentage of the price of a good or service.

Adjusted Gross Income
Gross income minus adjustments allowable by the Internal Revenue Service; includes various forms of miscellaneous income, such as contest earnings and most realized capital gains; excludes most transfer payments and interest on municipal bonds; adjustments include employee business expenses and contributions to individual retirement plans.

Aid to Families with Dependent Children (AFDC)
A major program of cash assistance to poor families with children in the United States in which one parent is absent or one parent is disabled or unemployed.

Arrow's Impossibility Theorem
States that it is impossible for public choices to meet a set of conditions for rationality when some voters have multiple-peaked preferences.

Assessment
Valuation of taxable wealth by government authorities.

Asset-Substitution Effect
The reduction in savings that results because the promise of a Social Security pension creates an asset to workers that substitutes for private saving for retirement.

Average Indexed Monthly Earnings (AIME)
A worker's average monthly earnings for which payroll taxes were paid; used as a basis for calculating a worker's Social Security pension in the United States.

Average Tax Rate (ATR)
Total dollar amount of taxes collected divided by the dollar value of the taxable base.

Backward Shifting
Transfer of the payment of a tax from buyers who are liable for its payment to sellers through a decrease in the market price of the taxed good.

Bequest Effect
The increase in the incentive to leave bequests to children that results from Social Security pensions.

Benefit Principle
Argues that the means of financing government-supplied goods and services should be linked to the benefits that citizens receive from government-provided services.

Block Grants
Intergovernmental grants that have minimal restrictions on the uses to which the funds can be put and rarely require matching funds raised from local revenues.

Bracket Creep
Increase in the effective rates of taxation on real taxable income when the tax rate schedules are based on nominal values of income not adjusted for inflation.

Budget Deficit
Excess of government expenditures over revenues raised by taxes, fees, and charges levied by government authorities.

Budget Incidence
Effect of both government expenditure and tax policies on the distribution of income in the private sector.

Burden of the Debt
Effect of government debt on the distribution of well-being of citizens.

Bureaucracy
Group of agencies in charge of implementing collective choices made through political institutions.

Capital Gains
Increases in the value of assets over a given accounting period.

Capitation Payments
Fixed amounts per patient per year received by health care providers in managed care facilities.

Cash-Flow Tax
Tax that would allow savers, in computing their tax liability each year, to deduct from their income those funds deposited in "qualified accounts."

Categorical Grant-in-Aid
Transfer of funds from a higher level of government to a lower level, with specified conditions attached to the expenditure of the funds.

Coase Theorem
States that governments, by merely establishing the rights to use resources, can internalize externalities when transaction costs of bargaining are zero.

Coinsurance
The portion of an insured expenditure that must be paid by the buyer rather than the insurance company.

Command-and-Control Regulation
A system of rules established by government authorities that requires all emitters of wastes to meet strict standards and requires the use of specific pollution control devices.

Compensation Criteria
Criteria used to recommend change in resource use if the value of the gains to gainers in dollar terms exceed the dollar value of the losses to losers.

Compensated Labor Supply Curve
Curve that shows how hours worked per day (or per year) vary with wages when the income effect of wage changes is removed.

Comprehensive Consumption
Annual comprehensive income minus annual savings.

Comprehensive Income
Sum of a person's annual consumption expenditures and the increment in that person's net worth in a given year.

Comprehensive Wealth Tax
One that would be levied on all forms of capital and land at a flat rate.

Congestible Public Goods
Those for which crowding or congestion reduces the benefits to existing consumers when more consumers are accommodated.

Corporation
A business that is legally established under state laws that grant it an identity separate from its owners.

Corrective Subsidy
Subsidy designed to adjust marginal private benefit in such a way as to internalize a positive externality.

Corrective Tax
Tax designed to adjust the marginal private cost of a good or service in such a way as to internalize a negative externality.

Cost-Benefit Analysis
Practical technique for determining the relative merits of alternative government projects over time.

Cost-Effectiveness Analysis
Technique for seeking the minimum-cost combination of government programs to achieve a given objective.

Deadweight Loss of a Subsidy
The extra benefit a recipient could enjoy from the dollar amount of a price-distorting subsidy if it were received in a lump-sum cash amount instead.

Debt Finance
Use of borrowed funds to finance government expenditures.

Deductibles
The amount of health expenditures a person with health insurance must incur before the insurance company begins paying benefits.

Deferral of Taxable Income
Income that is ordinarily taxable can be excluded or deducted from gross income in the current year but will eventually be taxed along with the accrued interest and capital gains.

Differential Tax Incidence
Resulting change in the distribution of income when one type of tax is substituted for some alternative tax, or set of taxes, yielding an equivalent amount of revenue in real terms, while both the mix and level of government expenditures are held constant.

Dividends
Direct payments by a corporation to its shareholders.

Donations
Voluntary contributions to government (or other organizations) from individuals or organizations.

Earmarked Taxes
Special taxes designed to finance specific government-supplied services.

Earned Income Tax Credit
Payment to workers by the federal government equal to a certain percentage of wage and salary income up to a certain maximum amount per year to those eligible.

Earnings Test
A requirement that reduces Social Security pensions benefits for retirees younger than seventy by $1 for each $3 of earnings greater than a certain amount each year.

Economic Depreciation
Measures the value of the durable physical capital used by firms in the productive process per year as that capital is "used up."

Effective Tax Rates
Actual taxes paid, divided by the taxable base.

Efficiency Criterion
Benchmark criterion for resource use that is satisfied when resources are used over any given period of time in such a way as to make it impossible to increase the well-being of any one person without reducing the well-being of any other person.

Efficiency-Loss Ratio
Ratio of the excess burden of a tax to the tax revenue collected each year by that tax.

Effluent Fees
Charges for the right to dump effluent, designed to internalize the negative externality associated with pollution.

Elasticity of the Tax Base
Ratio of the percentage change in the tax base attributable to any given percentage change in the tax rate applied to that base.

Entitlement Programs
Government programs requiring payments to all those persons meeting eligibility requirements established by law.

Equity
Judgment about the fairness of an outcome.

Equity (of a Corporation)
The difference between the values of assets and debts.

Excess Burden of a Subsidy
The difference between the cost of the subsidy to taxpayers and the gain in net benefits to recipients.

Excise Tax
Tax on the manufacture or sale of a particular good or service.

Expenditure Income
Effects of government expenditures on the distribution of income.

Expensing a Capital Asset
Deduction from gross income of the full purchase price of an asset in the year of its acquisition.

External Debt
Portion of a government's indebtedness owed to foreigners.

Externalities
Costs or benefits of market transactions not reflected in prices.

Federal System of Government
Numerous levels of government, each with its own powers to provide services and raise revenues.

Fiscal Capacity
Measure of the ability of a jurisdiction to finance government services.

Fiscal Federalism
Division of taxing and expenditure functions among levels of government.

Fixed Allotment Subsidies
Those that give eligible recipients the right to consume certain amounts of goods and services over a period.

Flat-Rate Tax
Tax with a proportional rate structure.

Flypaper Effect
Bypassing of the normal political process by local bureaucrats in spending federal grants.

Food Stamp Program
A federally financed food subsidy program for the poor that gives food coupons that can be redeemed for food and related items at retail outlets.

Forward Shifting
Transfer of payment of a tax from sellers who are liable for its payment to buyers, as a result of an increase in the price of the taxed good.

Free Rider
Problem that exists when people seek to enjoy the benefits of a public good without contributing anything to the cost of financing the amount made available.

Fully Funded Pension System
One in which benefits are paid out of a fund built up from contributions by, or on behalf of, members in a retirement system.

Fungibility
Property of money that allows it to be used for more than one purpose.

General Obligation Bonds
Bonds backed by the taxing power of the government that issues the securities.

General Revenue Sharing
No-strings-attached grant program that transfers funds from the federal government to state and local governments.

General Tax
One that taxes all of the components of the economic base, with no exclusions, exemptions, or deductions from the tax base.

General Theory of Second Best
States that, when two opposing factors contribute to efficiency losses, they can offset one another's distortions.

Gini Coefficient
Measures the degree of inequality for any income distribution by calculating the ratio of the area between the Lorenz curve corresponding to that distribution and the 45-degree line to the total area under the 45-degree line.

Government Goods and Services
Items provided by governments such as roads, schooling, and fire protection that are not usually sold in markets.

Government-Induced Inflation
General increase in prices caused by expansion of the money supply to pay for government-supplied goods and services.

Government Purchases
Those that require productive resources (land, labor, and capital) to be diverted from private use by individuals and corporations so they can be used by the government.

Government Transfer Payments
Government expenditures that redistribute purchasing power among citizens.

Governments
Organizations formed to exercise authority over the actions of persons who live together in a society and to provide and finance essential services.

Gross Income
All income received during the year from all taxable sources.

Gross Replacement Rate
A worker's monthly pension benefit as a percent of gross monthly earnings in the year prior to retirement.

Head Tax
Example of a lump-sum tax that would require all adults to pay an equal amount each year to governing authorities.

Historic Cost
Acquisition price of the asset.

High-Employment Deficit (or Surplus)
Budget deficit (or surplus) that would prevail at a certain designated level of unemployment in the economy.

Health Maintenance Organization (HMO)
An integrated delivery and finance system for health care.

Horizontal Equity
Condition that is achieved when individuals of the same economic capacity (measured, for example, by income) by the same amount of taxes per year (or over their lifetimes).

Housing Assistance Programs
Programs administered by governments that provide subsidized housing to low-income families.

Implicit Logrolling
Occurs when political interests succeed in pairing, on the same ballot or the same bill, two (or more) issues of strong interest to divergent groups.

Incidence of a Tax
Distribution of the burden of paying a tax.

Income-in-Kind
Income in the form of goods and services rather than cash payments.

Individual Excess Burden of Taxation
Loss in well-being to an individual taxpayer when a given sum of taxes is paid with a price-distorting tax instead of a lump-sum tax.

Induced-Retirement Effect
The increase in savings that results because the promise of a Social Security pension increases the period of retirement for which a worker will need assets to live from.

In-kind Benefits
Noncash transfers that increase the quantities of certain goods and services consumed by recipients.

Interjurisdictional Externalities
Spillover benefits or costs, to residents of other political jurisdictions who do not participate in the collective choice determining the level of that good to be produced and do not pay taxes to share in the finance of the good.

Internal Debt
Portion of a government's indebtedness owed to its own citizens.

Internalization of an Externality
Occurs when the marginal private benefit or cost of goods and services is adjusted so that the users consider the actual marginal social benefit or cost of their decisions.

Itemized Deductions
Expenses that can be legally deducted from adjusted gross income as an alternative to the standard deduction in figuring taxable income.

Lindahl Equilibrium
Exists when the voluntary contribution per unit of the public good of each member of the community equals his or her marginal benefit of the public good at the efficient level of output.

Lindahl Prices
Equilibrium contributions per unit of the public good that equal the marginal benefit received by each consumer.

Local Public Goods
Public goods with benefits that are nonrival for a geographical subset of national population.

Logrolling
Trading of votes on issues of great interest to voters.

Long-term Care Services
Medical, support, and rehabilitative services for patients who have functional limitations or chronic health problems and need daily assistance with the normal activities of living.

Lorenz Curve
Curve that gives information on the distribution of income by size brackets.

Lump-Sum Tax
Fixed sum that a person would pay as a tax each year, independent of that person's income, consumption of goods and services, or wealth.

Marginal Conditions for Efficient Resource Allocation
Conditions that are satisfied when resources are allocated to the production of each good over each period so that $MSB = MSC$.

Marginal External Benefit
Benefit of additional output accruing to parties other than buyers or sellers.

Marginal External Cost
Extra cost to third parties other than buyers or sellers of a good resulting from production of another unit of a good or service.

Marginal Net Benefit
Difference between the marginal social benefit and the marginal social cost of a good or service.

Marginal Private Benefit
Marginal benefit that consumers base their decisions on.

Marginal Private Cost
Marginal cost that producers base their decisions on.

Marginal Rate of Time Preference (MRTP)
Measure of the willingness of savers to forgo one dollar of current consumption in exchange for future consumption.

Marginal Social Benefit
Extra benefit obtained by making one more unit of a good available over any given time period.

Marginal Social Cost
Minimum amount of money that is required to compensate the owners of inputs used in producing a good for making an extra unit of it available.

Marginal Tax Benefit
Extra tax reduction that results when an individual engages in that activity.

Marginal Tax Rate (MTR)
Additional tax collected, expressed as a percentage of additional dollar values of the tax base as the tax base increases.

Matching Grants
Federal grants that contain the requirement that recipient jurisdictions match each dollar of federal aid with a certain amount of locally raised revenue.

Means Test
A requirement that establishes income or asset levels below which households become eligible for public assistance through government transfers.

Medicaid
A program that provides health insurance to the poor in the United

States, financed by federal and state taxes and administered by the states.

Medicare
The U.S. programs of health insurance for the elderly.

Median Voter
One whose most-preferred outcome is the median of the most-preferred outcomes of all those voting.

Median Voter Rule
Political equilibrium is the median most-preferred outcome of all voters when collective choices are made under majority rule and all voters have single-peaked preferences.

Mission (of a Government Agency)
Measurable output of a government agency.

Mixed Economy
One in which government supplies a considerable amount of goods and services and significantly regulates private economic activity.

Moral Hazard of Health Insurance
The increase in the incentives to consume and supply health care services that results from the reduction in price to consumers when third parties pay the bulk of medical expenses.

Most-Preferred Political Outcome
Quantity of the government-supplied good corresponding to the point at which the person's tax share is equal to his or her marginal benefit of the good.

Multiple-Peaked Preferences
Imply that persons who move away from their most-preferred alternative become worse off at first *but eventually become better off as the movement continues in the same direction.*

Negative Externalities
Costs of market transactions not reflected in prices.

Negative Income Tax (NIT)
A cash assistance program that would provide a minimum income guarantee for all persons through a cash subsidy that would be phased out with earnings.

Net Federal Debt
That portion of the debt of the federal government held by the general public, excluding the holdings of the United States government agencies, trust funds, and the Federal Reserve banks.

Net Replacement Rate
A worker's monthly pensions benefit as a percent of net income after taxes in the year prior to retirement.

Net Worth
Difference in the value of assets held at any point in time and the value of liabilities, or debts.

Nonexclusion
Property of a pure public good that exists when it is infeasible to price units of a good in a way that prevents those who do not pay from enjoying its benefits.

Nonmarket Rationing
Rationing of goods and services by any means other than pricing.

Nonrival in Consumption
Property of a pure public good that allows a given quantity of the good to be consumed by an entire population.

Normative Economics
Evaluates alternative policies and actions only on the basis of the underlying value judgments.

Old-Age, Survivors, and Disability Insurance (OASDI)
The U.S. system of Social Security pensions.

Pay-as-You-Go Pension System
A pension system that finances benefits for retired workers in a given

year entirely by contributions or taxes paid by currently employed workers.

Personal Exemption
Certain amount of taxable income that is exempt from taxation.

Physical Infrastructure
A nation's transportation and environmental capital including its schools, power and communication networks, health care system, and water supply and treatment facilities.

Political Equilibrium
Agreement on the level of production of one or more public goods, given the specified rule for making the collective choice and the distribution of tax shares among individuals.

Political Institutions
Rules and generally accepted procedures that evolve in a community for making collective choices.

Political Parties
Organizations of individuals with similar ideas on the role of government and other issues.

Political Externalities
Losses in well-being that occur when voters do not obtain their most-preferred outcomes, given their tax shares.

Political Jurisdiction
Defined geographical area within which individuals make collective choices on government functions and government-provided services.

Political Transactions Costs
Measures of the value of time, effort, and other resources expended to reach and enforce a collective agreement.

Pollution Abatement
Reduction in pollution that results from reduced emissions.

Pollution Rights
Transferable permits to emit a certain amount of particular wastes into the atmosphere or water per year.

Positive Economics
Scientific approach to analysis that establishes cause and effect relationships among economic variables.

Positive Externalities
Benefits of market transactions not reflected in prices.

Poverty Threshold
The level of income below which a household is classified as poor.

Price-Distorting Subsidies
Subsidies that result in losses in efficiency because their effect on prices induce substitution of subsidized products for others.

Price-Distorting Tax
One that causes the net price received by sellers of a good or service to diverge from the gross price paid by buyers.

Price-Excludable Public Goods
Those with benefits that can be priced.

Private Goods
Items such as food and clothing that are usually rival in consumption and are made available for sale in markets because persons easily can be excluded from benefits if they do not pay.

Program
Combination of government activities producing a distinguishable output.

Program Budgeting
System of managing government expenditures by attempting to compare the program proposals of all government agencies authorized to achieve similar objectives.

Progressive Tax Rate Structure
One for which the average tax rate eventually increases as the value of the tax base increases.

Property Tax Rate Differentials
Differences greater than or less than the national average rate of property taxation.

Proportional Tax Rate Structure
One for which the average tax rate, expressed as a percentage of the value of the tax base, does not vary with the value of the tax base.

Prospective Payment System
Used by Medicare to give hospitals a fixed payment per patient for the expected costs of treating specific illnesses.

Public Choices
Those made through political interaction of many persons according to established rules.

Public Finance
Field of economics that studies government activities and the alternative means of financing government expenditures.

Public Goods
Goods with benefits that are shared by large groups of consumers and are nonrival and nonexclusive.

Pure Private Good
Good that provides benefit *only* to the person who acquires it and not to anyone else after producers receive compensation for the full opportunity costs of production.

Pure Public Good
Good that is both nonrival in consumption for an entire population of consumers and has nonexclusionary benefits.

Rational Ignorance
Voter ignorance of either the benefits or costs of government activity stemming from the positive cost of attaining information.

Real Deficit
Measure of the change in the net federal debt after adjustment for the effects of inflation and changing interest rates on the real market value of the outstanding net debt.

Real Estate or Real Property
Land and structures.

Regressive Tax Rate Structure
One for which the average tax eventually declines as the value of the tax base increases.

Retail Sales Tax
Ad valorem levy of a fixed percentage on the dollar value of retail purchases made by consumers.

Retained Earnings
Corporate earnings retained by the corporation to finance expenses.

Revenue Bonds
Bonds backed by the promise of revenue to be earned on the facility being financed by the bonds.

Revenue Effort
Ratio of tax collections from all sources in a taxing jurisdiction, as a percentage of personal income in that jurisdiction, to the national average of that ratio for all jurisdictions.

Ricardian Equivalence
A situation that prevails when an increase in government borrowing to finance a deficit causes a sufficient increase in private saving to keep interest rates fixed.

Risk Aversion
The preference to incur a certain modest cost for insurance than risk high costs as a result of an unforeseen prospect.

Selective Tax
One that taxes only certain portions of the tax base, or allows exemptions and deductions from the general tax base.

Shifting of a Tax
Transfer of the burden of paying a tax from those who are legally liable for it to others.

Simple Majority Rule
Rule under which a proposal is approved if it receives more than half the votes cast in an election.

Single-Peaked Preferences
Imply that individuals behave as if a unique most-preferred outcome is available, and that the individuals are always made worse off when they move away from that outcome.

Small-Number Externalities
Externalities involving few enough parties so that the transaction costs of bargaining to internalize the externalities are negligible.

Social Opportunity Cost of Funds
Percentage rate of return that savers and investors forgo to give up either consumption or investment to finance a government project.

Social Rate of Discount
Percentage rate of return representing the opportunity cost of displaced private expenditure when a government project is undertaken.

Social Security and Insurance Programs
Government-provided pensions, disability payments, unemployment compensation and health benefits that insure individuals against interruption or loss of earning power.

Special-Interest Groups
Lobbies that seek to increase government expenditures that benefit their constituents.

Standard Deduction
Fixed dollar amount that can be deducted from adjusted gross income in computing taxable income that is adjusted for inflation each year and varies with the filing status of the taxpayer.

Status Test (for Public Assistance)
A requirement that establishes eligibility for public assistance based on such criteria as limited work capacity, need, age, or disability condition.

Stock
Variable with a value defined at a particular point in time.

Straight-Line Depreciation
Deduction of the same fraction of the cost of an asset each year over its useful economic life.

Supplement Security Income (SSI)
A federally funded and operated program that provides cash transfers to the aged, the blind, and the disabled who pass a means test.

Tax Avoidance
Change in behavior to reduce tax liability as taxpayers respond to the changes in prices caused by taxes.

Tax Base
Item or economic activity upon which a tax is levied.

Tax Bracket
Range of income subject to a given marginal tax rate.

Tax Capitalization
Decrease in the value of a taxed asset that reflects the discounted present value of future tax liability of its owners.

Tax Evasion
Noncompliance with the tax laws by failing to pay taxes that are due.

Tax Expenditures
Losses in tax revenues attributable to tax preferences.

Tax Preferences
Exclusions, exemptions, and deductions from the tax base.

Tax Rate Structure
Describes the relationship between the tax collected over a given accounting period and the tax base.

Tax Shares
Preannounced shares of the unit costs of a public good to be provided by government assigned to citizens voting in election.

Taxable Income
Portion of income earned by individuals that is subject to the personal income tax.

Taxes
Compulsory payments associated with certain activities.

Tax-Financed Pension System
A pension system with payments that are financed by taxes on the working population.

Third-Party Payments
Payments made directly to providers of services by persons other than those consuming those services. Health insurers are third-party payers for insurees consuming health services.

Total Excess Burden of Taxation
Loss in net benefits from resource use that results when a price-distorting tax causes inefficient allocation of resources in markets.

Total Social Benefit
Amount of satisfaction provided to consumers by any given quantity of an economic good available over a certain time period.

Total Social Cost
Value of all resources necessary to make a given amount of an economic good available over a given time period.

Transactions Costs
Value of the time, effort, and cash outlay involved in locating someone to trade with, negotiating terms of trade, drawing contracts, and assuming risks associated with the contracts.

Turnover Taxes
Multistage sales taxes that are levied, at some fixed rate, on transactions at all levels of production.

Unconditional Grants
Sharing revenues among governments, with no strings attached to the use of the funds.

Unemployment Insurance
A program administered by the states in the United States that provides income support for those temporarily out of work.

Unit Tax
Levy of a fixed amount per unit of a good exchanged in a market.

User Charges
Prices determined through political rather than market interaction.

Utility-Possibility Curve
Curve that illustrates the trade-off between improvements in efficiency.

Value-Added Tax (VAT)
Multistage sales tax that exempts the purchase of intermediate goods and services from the tax base.

Vertical Equity
Criterion that is achieved when individuals of differing economic ability pay annual tax bills that differ according to some collectively chosen notion of fairness.

Wage Rate Subsidies (WRS)
A government wage supplement to market wages designed to improve work incentives that provides transfers to the working poor that are phased out as wages or earnings increase.

Wealth
Value of accumulated savings and investments in a nation.

Name Index

SUBJECT INDEX